CASEBOOK ON

TORTS

Fourth Edition

Richard Kidner MA, BCL

Professor of Law, University of Wales, Aberystwyth

BLACKSTONE
PRESS LIMITED

First published in Great Britain 1990 by Blackstone Press Limited,
9-15 Aldine Street, London W12 8AW. Telephone 081–740 1173

© Richard Kidner, 1990

First edition, 1990
Second edition, 1992
Third edition, 1994
Fourth edition, 1996

ISBN: 1 85431 536 6

British Library Cataloguing in Publication Data
A CIP catalogue record for this book is available from the British Library

Typeset by Style Photosetting Ltd, Mayfield, East Sussex
Printed by Livesey Ltd, Shrewsbury, Shropshire

CONTENTS

ACKNOWLEDGMENTS

The publishers and author would like to thank the following for permission to reproduce extracts from the publications listed below:

The Incorporated Council of Law Reporting for England and Wales — The Law Reports, The Weekly Law Reports and the Industrial Cases Reports
Butterworths — The All England Law Reports and the New Law Journal
The Estates Gazette Ltd — The Estates Gazette Law Reports
The Law Book Company Ltd — The Commonwealth Law Reports
Canada Law Book Inc. — The Dominion Law Reports, reproduced with the permission of Canada Law Book Inc., 240 Edward St, Aurora, Ontario, Canada L4G 3S9
New Zealand Council of Law Reporting — New Zealand Law Reports
Supreme Court of Canada — Canada Supreme Court Reports, reproduced with permission of the Minister of Supply and Services.

PREFACE

This book has been written mainly for use by undergraduates or those taking professional courses in law, and is intentionally fairly traditional in character. The object is to provide, within a small compass and at a relatively low cost, those cases which students will commonly be referred to in their courses. It is not intended that the book should constitute a complete course in itself, for it ought to be used in conjunction with a text book. Furthermore, it is not intended to supplant the role of the lecturer or tutor, so while I have given a number of subsidiary examples of the application of the principal cases, I have refrained from extensive comment, believing that to be more the role of the teacher in conjunction with the student.

The law of tort is almost entirely based on case law, and a thorough knowledge of the leading cases is essential to understanding it. In addition, it is useful to know about other cases which apply those leading cases in order to understand their application, to illustrate the limits of liability, and to appreciate distinctions. Also the cases provide a useful peg upon which to hang one's knowledge, and they can give an instant insight into the proper analysis of a problem.

The selection has been based on what I regard as the standard cases, and the extracts attempt to provide the essence of the reasoning and the decision. If the extract is too short it is inadequate, but if it is too long it may not be read at all, and I hope I have found the right balance. Statutory materials have been included where they are necessary to understanding the subject.

In a book of this size some subjects have regrettably had to be omitted, and these include employer's liability, proof of negligence, and the 'industrial' torts such as inducing breach of contract, but I hope that what has been covered represents what is commonly included in a tort course.

For this fourth edition a number of substantial changes have been made. In particular, the chapter on the creation of new duties of care has been merged with the main chapter on duties of care, and the order of treatment has been re-arranged. There have been a number of important changes to tort in recent years and a number of new cases have been added, notably *Marc Rich* v *Bishop Rock Marine*, *X* v *Bedfordshire C.C.*, *Page* v *Smith*, *White* v *Jones* and *Henderson* v *Merrett Syndicates*. Also included are recent cases developing the law of defamation, together with parts of the Defamation Bill 1996. To make room for this new material and to keep the book to a reasonable length some old favourites have had to go, such as *Home Office* v *Dorset Yacht Co*. Indeed, it is remarkable how many cases that only recently appeared so revolutionary now look jaded. The law of tort has become remarkably sophisticated very quickly and one can see that more fundamental developments are on the way.

The order in which the topics are treated is not regarded as significant, as each lecturer will have his own preference, but I have grouped the trespass actions at the beginning because this provides analytical training in an area which students generally find easier. I have also split up the treatment of negligence so that the basic issues are dealt with first (duty, breach and remoteness) so that students can understand the structure of negligence, and this is followed by treatment of the more sophisticated duty issues, such as economic loss.

Finally, I must thank Mrs Christine Davies for typing the manuscript so willingly and efficiently.

This book contains materials available to me up to the beginning of June 1996.

Richard Kidner

TABLE OF CASES

Page numbers relating to extracts from cases reproduced or relating to references in the notes are printed in bold type. The case name is also printed in bold type.

TABLE OF STATUTES

Statutes from which extracts are given in the text, appear in bold type. The page at which the statute is printed is shown in bold type.

1 TRESPASS TO THE PERSON

Trespass is an ancient set of wrongs which mainly deals with the direct, and usually intentional, invasion of a plaintiff's interest in either his person, his land or his goods. The law of trespass today reveals much of its origins in the criminal law, and to some extent this is borne out by the fact that its function is more often deterrent than compensatory. For example, an action will lie in trespass, but not in negligence, even if the plaintiff has suffered no damage, and this shows its usefulness in protecting civil rights. It is the right itself which is protected, and not just the freedom from resulting damage, and much of the law of trespass is the basis of our civil liberties today.

This chapter covers the wrongs of assault, battery and false imprisonment (which are strictly trespass actions), and the analogous tort of intentional infliction of emotional distress, together with various defences. The principal use today of these torts relates not so much to the recovery of compensation but rather to the establishment of a right, or a recognition that the defendant acted unlawfully. For example, trespass to the person or false imprisonment will often be used to establish whether an arrest was lawful, but the special conditions applying to such cases, such as the powers of the police will not be dealt with here. The point to note is that as these torts are actionable without proof of damage (or actionable *per se*), they can be used to protect civil rights, and also will protect a person's dignity, even if no physical injury has occurred (for example the taking of finger prints).

Also, in a number of cases which amount to trespass to the person it will not be necessary to bring an action, for where a criminal offence has been committed the courts have power under the Powers of Criminal Courts Act 1973, s. 35 (as amended) to make a compensation order. (And note that under the Offences Against the Person Act 1861 a conviction for battery or assault will be a bar to further civil proceedings.)

Section 1: trespass and negligence

While the technical distinction between trespass and negligence (or actions on the case) has no procedural effect today, there are still theoretical differences between the two subjects which have not yet been resolved, and probably never will be. The cases in this section indicate that where a practical issue has arisen stemming from that theoretical problem, the issue has been resolved by making trespass subject to the same rules as negligence, as in the examples given here of burden of proof and time limits for bringing an action. The theoretical problem concerns the issue of negligent invasions of the plaintiff's interest, and while this was historically a trespass, there is a tendency today to say that in such cases only the tort of negligence, and not trespass, should be applied.

Letang v *Cooper*
Court of Appeal [1965] 1 QB 232; [1964] 2 All ER 929; [1964] 3 WLR 573

Doreen Letang was sunbathing in the grounds of the Ponsmere Hotel at Perranporth in Cornwall when the defendant negligently drove over her legs with his Jaguar. The writ was issued more than three years later, and under the Law Reform (Limitation of Actions) Act 1954 a writ should have been issued within three years of the accident if it related to personal injuries and the claim was for 'negligence, nuisance or breach of duty'. The plaintiff admitted that an action in negligence was time barred, but claimed that she could sue for trespass to the person on the grounds that this did not come within the phrase 'breach of duty'. In the High Court this claim succeeded. Held: allowing the appeal, that the action was time barred and the defendant was not liable.

LORD DENNING MR: The argument, as it was developed before us, became a direct invitation to this court to go back to the old forms of action and to decide this case by reference to them. The statute bars an action on the case, it is said, after three years, whereas trespass to the person is not barred for six years. The argument was supported by reference to text-writers, such as *Salmond on Torts,* 13th ed. (1961), p. 790. I must say that if we are, at this distance of time, to revive the distinction between trespass and case, we should get into the most utter confusion. The old common lawyers tied themselves in knots over it, and we should do the same. Let me tell you some of their contortions. Under the old law, whenever one man injured another by the direct and immediate application of force, the plaintiff could sue the defendant in trespass to the person, without alleging negligence . . ., whereas if the injury was only consequential, he had to sue in case. You will remember the illustration given by Fortescue J in *Reynolds* v *Clarke* (1725) 93 ER 747: 'If a man throws a log into the highway, and in that act it hits me, I may maintain trespass because it is an immediate wrong; but if as it lies there I tumble over it, and receive an injury, I must bring an action upon the case; because it is only prejudicial in consequence.' Nowadays, if a man carelessly throws a piece of wood from a house into a roadway, then whether it hits the plaintiff or he tumbles over it the next moment, the action would not be trespass or case, but simply negligence. . . .
    I must decline, therefore, to go back to the old forms of action in order to construe this statute. I know that in the last century Maitland said 'the forms of action we have buried, but they still rule us from their graves' (see Maitland, *Forms of Action* (1909), p. 296), but we have in this century shaken off their trammels. These forms of action have served their day. They did at one time form a guide to substantive rights; but they do so no longer. Lord Atkin, in *United Australia Ltd* v *Barclays Bank Ltd* [1941] AC 1, told us what to do about them: 'When these ghosts of the past stand in the path of justice

clanking their mediaeval chains the proper course for the judge is to pass through them undeterred'.

The truth is that the distinction between trespass and case is obsolete. We have a different sub-division altogether. Instead of dividing actions for personal injuries into trespass (direct damage) or case (consequential damage), we divide the causes of action now according as the defendant did the injury intentionally or unintentionally. If one man intentionally applies force directly to another, the plaintiff has a cause of action in assault and battery, or, if you so please to describe it, in trespass to the person. 'The least touching of another in anger is a battery', per Holt CJ in Cole v Turner (1704) 87 ER 907. If he does not inflict injury intentionally, but only unintentionally, the plaintiff has no cause of action today in trespass. His only cause of action is in negligence, and then only on proof of want of reasonable care. If the plaintiff cannot prove want of reasonable care, he may have no cause of action at all. Thus, it is not enough nowadays for the plaintiff to plead that 'the defendant shot the plaintiff'. He must also allege that he did it intentionally or negligently. If intentional, it is the tort of assault and battery. If negligent and causing damage, it is the tort of negligence.

The modern law on this subject was well expounded by Diplock J in Fowler v Lanning [1959] 1 QB 426, with which I fully agree. But I would go this one step further: when the injury is not inflicted intentionally, but negligently, I would say that the only cause of action is negligence and not trespass. If it were trespass, it would be actionable without proof of damage; and that is not the law today.

In my judgment, therefore, the only cause of action in the present case, where the injury was unintentional, is negligence and is barred by reason of the express provision of the statute. . . .

I come, therefore, to the clear conclusion that the plaintiff's cause of action here is barred by the Statute of Limitations. Her only cause of action here, in my judgment, where the damage was unintentional, was negligence and not trespass to the person. It is therefore barred by the word 'negligence' in the statute.

Notes

1. It should not be assumed that Lord Denning's views on the distinction between trespass and negligence are necessarily accepted, and it may well be that the traditional distinction as referred to by Fortescue J in *Reynolds* v *Clarke* (above) between direct and indirect acts is still valid. It is unlikely that this theoretical problem will ever need to be resolved. However, in *Wilson* v *Pringle* [1987] QB 237, Croom-Johnson LJ did say that 'It has long been the law that claims arising out of an unintentional trespass must be made in negligence'. For all practical purposes, therefore, it can be said that trespass deals with direct intentional acts, and negligence with careless or indirect acts.

2. In *Fowler* v *Lanning* [1959] 1 QB 426, the plaintiff merely alleged in his statement of claim that 'on Nov. 19 1957, at Vineyard Farm, Corfe Castle in the County of Dorset the defendant shot the plaintiff'. Neither intention nor negligence was alleged, but the plaintiff claimed that the statement of claim did allege a good cause of action on the grounds that in trespass the burden of disproving negligence was on the defendant. Diplock J rejected this argument, saying that 'trespass to the person does not lie if the injury to the plaintiff, although the direct consequence of the act of the defendant, was caused unintentionally and without negligence on the defendant's part' and that the onus of proving negligence lay on the plaintiff.

3. In *Letang* v *Cooper*, Lord Denning also said that he thought that the words 'breach of duty' in the Limitation Act covered any tort, including trespass, but in *Stubbings* v *Webb* [1993] 1 All ER 322 the House of Lords said that this was not so. Lord Griffiths said that 'breach of duty' did not cover deliberate assaults and that accordingly an action for rape, for example, is one in trespass to the person and the limitation period is six years.

Section 2:   battery and assault

In common usage the word 'assault' is used to mean actual contact, but it is probably useful to keep the terms battery and assault separate. Battery occurs where there is contact with the person of another, and assault is used to cover cases where the plaintiff apprehends contact.

Wilson v *Pringle*
Court of Appeal [1987] QB 237; [1986] 2 All ER 440; [1986] 3 WLR 1

Both Peter Wilson (the plaintiff) and Ian Pringle (the defendant) were aged 13 and attended Great Wyrley High School, Walsall. It was agreed that while in a corridor the plaintiff was carrying a hand grip type of bag, holding it over his shoulder with his right hand. The defendant admitted that as an act of ordinary horseplay he pulled the bag off the plaintiff's shoulder, and this caused the plaintiff to fall and injure his hip. The plaintiff applied for summary judgment on the ground that this admission amounted to a clear case of battery to which there was no defence. The trial judge accepted this view. Held: allowing the appeal, that the admitted facts did not automatically amount to a battery, and the defendant was given leave to defend the action.

CROOM-JOHNSON LJ: The first distinction between the two causes of action where there is personal injury is the element of contact between the plaintiff and defendant: that is, a touching of some sort. In the action for negligence the physical contact (where it takes place at all) is normally though by no means always unintended. In the action for trespass, to constitute a battery, it is deliberate. Even so it is not every intended contact which is tortious. Apart from special justifications (such as acting in self-defence) there are many examples in everyday life where an intended contact or touch is not actionable as a trespass. These are not necessarily those (such as shaking hands) where consent is actual or to be implied. They may amount to one of the instances had in mind in *Tuberville* v *Savage*, 1 Mod. 3 which take place in innocence. A modern instance is the batsman walking up the pavilion steps at Lord's after making a century. He receives hearty slaps of congratulation on his back. He may not want them. Some of them may be too heavy for comfort. No one seeks his permission, or can assume he would give it if it were asked. But would an action for trespass to the person lie?

Another ingredient in the tort of trespasss to the person is that of hostility. The references to anger sufficing to turn a touch into a battery (*Cole* v *Turner*, (1704) 87 ER 907) and the lack of an intention to assault which prevents a gesture from being an assault are instances of this. If there is hostile intent, that will by itself be cogent evidence of hostility. But the hostility may be demonstrated in other ways.

The defendant in the present case has sought to add to the list of necessary ingredients. He has submitted that before trespass to the person will lie it is not only the touching that must be deliberate but the infliction of injury. The plaintiff's counsel, on the other hand, contends that it is not the injury to the person which must be intentional, but the act of touching or battery which precedes it: as he put it, what must be intentional is the application of force and not the injury. . . .

In our view, the submission made by counsel for the plaintiff is correct. It is the act and not the injury which must be intentional. An intention to injure is not essential to an action for trespass to the person. It is the mere trespass by itself which is the offence. . . .

What, then, turns a friendly touching (which is not actionable) into an unfriendly one (which is)? We have been referred to two criminal cases. *Reg* v *Sutton (Terrence)* [1977] 1 WLR 182 was decided in the Court of Appeal (Criminal Division). It was a case concerning alleged indecent assault on boys who consented in fact although in law they were too young to do so. They were asked to pose for photographs. The only touching of the boys by the appellant was to get them to stand in poses. It was touching on the hands, arms, legs or torso but only for the purpose of indicating how he wanted them to pose; it was not hostile or threatening. The court which was presided over by Lord Widgery CJ held these were therefore not assaults.

A more recent authority is *Collins* v *Wilcock* [1984] 1 WLR 1172. The case was not cited to the judge. It had not been reported at the time of the hearing of the Order 14 appeal. The facts were that a woman police officer, suspecting that a woman was soliciting contrary to the Street Offences Act 1959, tried to question her. The woman walked away, and was followed by the police officer. The officer took hold of her arm in order to restrain her. The woman scratched the officer's arm. She was arrested, charged with assaulting a police officer in the execution of her duty, and convicted. On appeal by case stated, the appeal was allowed, on the ground that the officer had gone beyond the scope of her duty in detaining the woman in circumstances short of arresting her. The officer had accordingly committed a battery.

The judgment of the Divisional Court was given by Robert Goff LJ. It is necessary to give a long quotation to do full justice to it. He said, at pp. 1177-1178:

The law draws a distinction, in terms more easily understood by philologists than by ordinary citizens, between an assault and a battery. An assault is an act which causes another person to apprehend the infliction of immediate, unlawful, force on his person; a battery is the actual infliction of unlawful force on another person. Both assault and battery are forms of trespass to the person. Another form of trespass to the person is false imprisonment, which is the unlawful imposition of constraint upon another's freedom of movement from a particular place. The requisite mental element is of no relevance in the present case.

We are here concerned primarily with battery. The fundamental principle, plain and incontestable, is that every person's body is inviolate. It has long been established that any touching of another person, however slight, may amount to a battery. So Holt CJ held in *Cole* v *Turner* (1704) 87 ER 907 that 'the least touching of another in anger is a battery.' The breadth of the principle reflects the fundamental nature of the interest so protected. As Blackstone wrote in his *Commentaries*, 17th ed. (1830), vol. 3, p. 120: 'the law cannot draw the line between different degrees of violence, and therefore totally prohibits the first and lowest stage of it; every man's person being sacred, and no other having a right to meddle with it, in any the slightest manner.' The effect is that everybody is protected not only against physical injury but against any form of physical molestation.

But so widely drawn a principle must inevitably be subject to exceptions. For example, children may be subjected to reasonable punishment; people may be subjected to the lawful exercise of the power of arrest; and reasonable force may be used in self-defence or for the prevention of crime. But, apart from these special instances where the control or constraint is lawful, a broader exception has been created to allow for the exigencies of everyday life. Generally speaking, consent is a defence to battery; and most of the physical contacts of ordinary life are not actionable because they are impliedly consented to by all who move in society and so expose themselves to the risk of bodily contact. So nobody can complain of the jostling which is inevitable from his presence in, for example, a supermarket, an underground station or a busy street; not can a person who attends a party complain if his hand is seized in friendship, or even if his back is, within reason, slapped: see *Tuberville v Savage* (1669) 86 ER 684. Although such cases are regarded as examples of implied consent, it is more common nowadays to treat them as falling within a general exception embracing all physical contact which is generally acceptable in the ordinary conduct of daily life. We observe that, although in the past it has sometimes been stated that a battery is only committed where the action is 'angry, revengeful, rude, or insolent' (see *Hawkins, Pleas of the Crown*, 8th ed. (1824), vol. 1, c. 15, section 2), we think that nowadays it is more realistic, and indeed more accurate, to state the broad underlying principle, subject to the broad exception.

Among such forms of conduct, long held to be acceptable, is touching a person for the purpose of engaging his attention, though of course using no greater degree of physical contact than is reasonably necessary in the circumstances for that purpose. . . .

It still remains to indicate what is to be proved by a plaintiff who brings an action for battery. Robert Goff LJ's judgment is illustrative of the considerations which underlie such an action, but it is not practicable to define a battery as 'physical contact which is not generally acceptable in the ordinary conduct of daily life'.

In our view, the authorities lead one to the conclusion that in a battery there must be an intentional touching or contact in one form or another of the plaintiff by the defendant. That touching must be proved to be a hostile touching. That still leaves unanswered the question 'when is a touching to be called hostile? Hostility cannot be equated with ill-will or malevolence. It cannot be governed by the obvious intention shown in acts like punching, stabbing or shooting. It cannot be solely governed by an expressed intention, although that may be strong evidence. But the element of hostility, in the sense in which it is now to be considered, must be a question of fact for the tribunal of fact. It may be imported from the circumstances. Take the example of the police officer in *Collins v Wilcock* [1984] 1 WLR 1172. She touched the woman deliberately, but without an intention to do more than restrain her temporarily. Nevertheless, she was acting unlawfully and in that way was acting with hostility. She was acting contrary to the woman's legal right not to be physically restrained. We see no more difficulty in establishing what she intended by means of questions and answer, or by inference from the surrounding circumstances, than there is in establishing whether an apparently playful blow was struck in anger. The rules of law governing the legality of arrest may require strict application to the facts of appropriate cases, but in the ordinary give and take of everyday life the tribunal of fact should find no difficulty in answering the question 'was this, or was it not, a battery?' Where the immediate act of touching does not itself demonstrate hostility, the plaintiff should plead the facts which are said to do so.

Although we are all entitled to protection from physical molestation, we live in a crowded world in which people must be considered as taking on themselves some risk of injury (where it occurs) from the acts of others which are not in themselves unlawful.

If negligence cannot be proved, it may be that an injured plaintiff who is also unable to prove a battery, will be without redress.

Notes

1. In *Re F* [1990] 2 AC 1, at p. 73, Lord Goff said that he doubted whether it is correct to say that the touching must be hostile. He added that 'the suggested qualification is difficult to reconcile with the principle that any touching of another's body is, in the absence of lawful excuse, capable of amounting to a battery and a trespass'.

2. As in the criminal law, there must be both an act and intention. In *Fagan v Metropolitan Police* [1969] 1 QB 439 (a criminal case) Vincent Fagan unwittingly parked his car on a policeman's foot. Despite requests, he refused to move the car until some minutes later. It was held that he was rightly convicted as his actions could not be regarded as a mere omission. James J said Fagan remained in the car so that his body, through the medium of the car, was in contact with the policeman's foot. He switched off the ignition and maintained the car on the foot. Do you agree or do you prefer the dissenting view of Bridge J that he should have been acquitted because he actually did nothing?

3. An 'assault' occurs where the plaintiff apprehends imminent physical contact; but if the defendant is actually unable to deliver the blow, there is no assault (at least if the plaintiff should have realised that the attack was impossible). In *Thomas v NUM* [1986] Ch 20, pickets were jeering working miners who were being taken into a colliery by buses. It was held that there was no assault as the plaintiffs were in buses and the pickets were being held back by police. See also *Stephens v Myers* (1830) 172 ER 735.

4. Traditionally words have not by themselves amounted to an assault, but they may qualify an otherwise innocent act so as to make it intimidatory, or qualify an intimidatory act so as to make it innocent. In *Read v Coker* (1853) 138 ER 1437, the defendant's workmen gathered around the plaintiff, rolling up their sleeves and threatening to break the plaintiff's neck if he did not leave. The words characterised the otherwise innocent act as one threatening imminent contact. On the other hand, in *Tuberville v Savage* (1669) 86 ER 684, Tuberville put his hand on his sword and said 'If it were not assize time, I would not take such language from you.' In effect he was saying that he would not strike as the judges were in town, and this rendered the act innocent. However in *R v Ireland*, *The Times*, 22 May 1996 it was held that words, or even silence, which cause psychiatric damage may amount to the crime of assault occasioning actual bodily harm, i.e. in civil terms, a battery. Psychiatric damage means such things as palpitations, anxiety and inability to sleep but does not include fear, distress or panic (see *R v Chan-Fook* [1994] 1 WLR 689).

Questions

1. Is 'hostile' an appropriate word to use, especially in a civil case? Can you think of another word or phrase which expresses the point more clearly?

2. Is it an assault to point an unloaded gun at someone?

Section 3:   the intentional infliction of emotional distress

This principle, which generally relates to the intentional infliction of harm, is not strictly a trespass action but is analogous to it. Although it has not been much used, it nevertheless has considerable potential in cases of the intentional invasion of interests which are not otherwise protected. Privacy may be an example.

Wilkinson v *Downton*
Queen's Bench Division [1897] 2 QB 57; 66 LJQB 493; 76 LT 495

> The plaintiff's husband had gone to the races for the day, and the defendant came to her house and as a practical joke falsely told her that her husband had had an accident and was lying with both his legs broken at The Elms public house at Leytonstone. The plaintiff went to fetch her husband and later became ill from nervous shock. Held: the defendant was liable.

WRIGHT J: The defendant has, as I assume for the moment, wilfully done an act calculated to cause physical harm to the plaintiff — that is to say, to infringe her legal right to personal safety, and has in fact thereby caused physical harm to her. That proposition without more appears to me to state a good cause of action, there being no justification alleged for the act. This wilful injuria is in law malicious, although no malicious purpose to cause the harm which was caused nor any motive of spite is imputed to the defendant.

It remains to consider whether the assumptions involved in the proposition are made out. One question is whether the defendant's act was so plainly calculated to produce some effect of the kind which was produced that an intention to produce it ought to be imputed to the defendant, regard being had to the fact that the effect was produced on a person proved to be in an ordinary state of health and mind. I think that it was. It is difficult to imagine that such a statement, made suddenly and with apparent serious-ness, could fail to produce grave effects under the circumstances upon any but an exceptionally indifferent person, and therefore an intention to produce such an effect must be imputed, and it is no answer in law to say that more harm was done than was anticipated, for that is commonly the case with all wrongs. The other question is whether the effect was, to use the ordinary phrase, too remote to be in law regarded as a consequence for which the defendant is answerable. Apart from authority, I should give the same answer and on the same ground as the last question, and say that it was not too remote. . . .

Notes
1.   The Victorian judges used the word 'calculated' in an objective sense, so that when Wright J refers to an act calculated to do harm he does not mean that the defendant did the act intending the harm, but rather that he did an act, the natural consequence of which was the harm. The issue is sometimes said to be whether the defendant has engaged in extreme or outrageous conduct. For a detailed discussion see Handford, '*Wilkinson* v *Downton* and Acts Calculated to Cause Physical Harm' (1985) 16 Univ. Western Australia LR 31.

2. For an action to succeed it must be established that there was actual damage or that the acts were calculated to cause harm, and where this is possible the principle in *Wilkinson* v *Downton* can be used to restrain harassment. In **Burnett v George** [1992] 1 FLR 525 the plaintiff was subjected to harassment by unwelcome telephone calls and although the *Wilkinson* v *Downton* principle was thought to be applicable, the plaintiff was unsuccessful because she was unable to show impairment to her health. This view was endorsed in **Khorasandjian v Bush** [1993] 3 All ER 669 where in another case of harassment by telephone calls the plaintiff succeeded because of the obvious risk that the cumulative effect of continued and unrestrained telephone calls would cause physical or psychiatric illness. (An injunction as also granted on wider grounds without any need to prove damage on the basis of private nuisance for which see chapter 21.)

3. A possible application of the principle could be offensive invasions of privacy. In **Robbins v CBC** (1958) 12 DLR 2d 35, the plaintiff had criticised a television programme called Tabloid, and challenged the producer to read the letter on the air. He did so, but also invited viewers to telephone or write to the plaintiff in order to cheer him up. The plaintiff's address was flashed on the screen and he received a large number of abusive calls. The defendants were held liable under the Quebec Civil Code. Would this be a suitable application of *Wilkinson* v *Downton* if damage could be proved?

4. The common law does not recognise a right of privacy by itself (see *Kaye* v *Robertson* [1991] FSR 62 where journalists on the Sunday Sport entered the plaintiff's hospital room and interviewed him and took photographs although he was in no state to consent: he finally succeeded on grounds of malicious falsehood). However, in July 1993 the Lord Chancellor's Department in a consultation paper proposed a statutory tort for the protection of privacy in the following terms:

(a) A natural person shall have a cause of action, in tort or delict, in respect of conduct which constitutes an infringement of his privacy, causing him substantial distress, provided such distress would also have been suffered by a person of ordinary sensibilities in the circumstances of the complainant.

(b) A natural person's privacy shall be taken to include matters appertaining to his health, personal communications, and family and personal relationships, and a right to be free from harassment and molestation.

(c) The following defences, at least, shall be available in such proceedings: consent, lawful authority, absolute or qualified privilege, and a public interest defence.

Questions

1. Need the statement be false? Is there a duty to break bad news gently? If a person truthfully tells a mother that her child has been killed and describes the circumstances in lurid detail, could he be liable?

2. Need the statement or the act be 'aimed at' the plaintiff? In *Wilkinson* v *Downton,* if the husband's mother had heard the story, could the defendant have been liable to her?

Section 4:   false imprisonment

This tort protects a person in his interest in freedom from restraint, and is another example of trespass protecting important civil rights. The significance of *Bird* v *Jones,* below, is that the tort only protects a person against restraint and does not give a right to absolute choice in one's freedom of movement. That is a freedom or liberty and not a right.

Bird v *Jones*
Court of Queen's Bench (1845) 7 QB 742; 15 LJQB 82; 115 ER 668

In August 1843 the Hammersmith Bridge Company cordoned off part of their bridge, placed seats on it, and charged spectators for viewing a regatta. The plaintiff objected to this and forced his way into the enclosure, where he was stopped by two policemen. He was prevented from proceeding across the bridge, but was allowed to go back the way he came. He refused, and in the course of proceedings for his arrest the question arose whether he had been imprisoned on the bridge. Held: this was not an 'imprisonment' and the defendant was not liable for the subsequent arrest.

COLERIDGE J: And I am of opinion that there was no imprisonment. To call it so appears to me to confound partial obstruction and disturbance with total obstruction and detention. A prison may have its boundary large or narrow, visible and tangible, or, though real, still in the conception only; it may itself be moveable or fixed: but a boundary it must have; and that boundary the party imprisoned must be prevented from passing; he must be prevented from leaving that place, within the ambit of which the party imprisoning would confine him, except by prison-breach. Some confusion seems to me to arise from confounding imprisonment of the body with mere loss of freedom: it is one part of the definition of freedom to be able to go whither-soever one pleases; but imprisonment is something more than the mere loss of this power; it includes the notion of restraint within some limits defined by a will or power exterior to our own. . . .

LORD DENMAN (*dissenting*): I had no idea that any person in these times supposed any particular boundary to be necessary to constitute imprisonment, or that the restraint of a man's person from doing what he desires ceases to be an imprisonment because he may find some means of escape.
  It is said that the party here was at liberty to go in another direction. I am not sure that in fact he was, because the same unlawful power which prevented him from taking one course might, in case of acquiescence, have refused him any other. But this liberty to do something else does not appear to me to affect the question of imprisonment. As long as I am prevented from doing what I have a right to do, of what importance is it that I am permitted to do something else? How does the imposition of an unlawful condition shew that I am not restrained? If I am locked in a room, am I not imprisoned because I might effect my escape through a window, or because I might find an exit dangerous or inconvenient to myself, as by wading through water or by taking a route so circuitous that my necessary affairs would suffer by delay?
  It appears to me that this is a total deprivation of liberty with reference to the purpose for which he lawfully wished to employ his liberty: and, being effected by force, it is not the mere obstruction of a way, but a restraint of the person. The case cited as occurring

before Lord Chief Justice Tindal, as I understand it, is much in point. He held it an imprisonment where the defendant stopped the plaintiff on his road till he had read a libel to him. Yet he did not prevent his escaping in another direction.

Note
Whether a person is restrained is a matter of fact, and there need not be actual physical restraint. For example, an arrest, even if executed by merely touching the plaintiff, is a restraint, as it would be if a person has the physical capacity to leave but it is unreasonable to expect him to do so because, for example, he has no clothes on or he is imprisoned in a first floor room with an open window.

Robinson v *Balmain New Ferry*
Privy Council [1910] AC 295; 79 LJPC 84; 84 TLR 143

The defendants operated a ferry from Sydney to Balmain. On the Sydney side there were some turnstiles. A person travelling from Sydney to Balmain paid on the Sydney side (i.e. on entry), as did a person who travelled from Balmain to Sydney (i.e. he paid *after* using the ferry: the system was similar to that used on the Liverpool-Birkenhead ferry). By the turnstiles was a notice saying 'A fare of one penny must be paid on entering or leaving the wharf. No exception will be made to this rule, whether the passenger has travelled by the ferry or not.' The plaintiff entered on the Sydney side and paid one penny. Finding that no ferry was due to cross for 20 minutes, he decided to leave the wharf, whereupon he was asked to pay a further penny. He refused and for a short time was prevented from leaving. Held: dismissing the appeal, that the defendants were not liable for false imprisonment.

LORD LOREBURN LC: The plaintiff paid a penny on entering the wharf to stay there till the boat should start and then be taken by the boat to the other side. The defendants were admittedly always ready and willing to carry out their part of this contract. Then the plaintiff changed his mind and wished to go back. The rules as to the exit from the wharf by the turnstile required a penny for any person who went through. This the plaintiff refused to pay, and he was by force prevented from going through the turnstile. He then claimed damages for assault and false imprisonment.

There was no complaint, at all events there was no question left to the jury by the plaintiff's request, of any excessive violence, and in the circumstances admitted it is clear to their Lordships that there was no false imprisonment at all. The plaintiff was merely called upon to leave the wharf in the way in which he contracted to leave it. There is no law requiring the defendants to make the exit from their premises gratuitous to people who come there upon a definite contract which involves their leaving the wharf by another way; and the defendants were entitled to resist a forcible passage through their turnstile.

The question whether the notice which was affixed to these premises was brought home to the knowledge of the plaintiff is immaterial, because the notice itself is immaterial.

When the plaintiff entered the defendants' premises there was nothing agreed as to the terms on which he might go back, because neither party contemplated his going back. When he desired to do so the defendants were entitled to impose a reasonable condition before allowing him to pass through their turnstile from a place to which he had gone of his own free will. The payment of a penny was a quite fair condition, and if he did not choose to comply with it the defendants were not bound to let him through. He could proceed on the journey he had contracted for.

Herd v Weardale Steel, Coal and Coke Co.
House of Lords [1915] AC 67; 30 TLR 620; 84 LJKB 121

The plaintiff miners entered the Thornley Colliery owned by the defendants at 9.30 a.m. on 30 May 1911. In the ordinary course of events their shift would have ended at 4.00 p.m. During the morning they believed the work they were being asked to do was unsafe and in breach of an agreement with the employers, and at about 11.00 a.m. they asked to be taken to the surface. The employers refused, and they were not given permission to use the cages to return to the surface until 1.30 p.m. The employers sued the miners in the County Court for breach of contract and were awarded five shillings. The plaintiffs replied with an action for false imprisonment. Held: dismissing the appeal, that the defendants were not liable.

VISCOUNT HALDANE LC: My Lords, by the law of this country no man can be restrained of his liberty without authority in law. That is a proposition the maintenance of which is of great importance; but at the same time it is a proposition which must be read in relation to other propositions which are equally important. If a man chooses to go into a dangerous place at the bottom of a quarry or the bottom of a mine; from which by the nature of physical circumstances he cannot escape, it does not follow from the proposition I have enunciated about liberty that he can compel the owner to bring him up out of it. The owner may or may not be under a duty arising from circumstances, on broad grounds the neglect of which may possibly involve him in a criminal charge or a civil liability. It is unnecessary to discuss the conditions and circumstances which might bring about such a result, because they have, in the view I take, nothing to do with false imprisonment.

My Lords, there is another proposition which has to be borne in mind, and that is the application of the maxim volenti non fit injuria. If a man gets into an express train and the doors are locked pending its arrival at its destination, he is not entitled, merely because the train has been stopped by signal, to call for the doors to be opened to let him out. He has entered the train on the terms that he is to be conveyed to a certain station without the opportunity of getting out before that, and he must abide by the terms on which he has entered the train. So when a man goes down a mine, from which access to the surface does not exist in the absence of special facilities given on the part of the owner of the mine, he is only entitled to the use of these facilities (subject possibly to the exceptional circumstances to which I have alluded) on the terms on which he has entered. I think it results from what was laid down by the Judicial Committee of the Privy Council in *Robinson v Balmain New Ferry Co.*, [1910] AC 295 that that is so. There there was a pier, and by the regulations a penny was to be paid by those who entered and a penny on getting out. The manager of the exit gate refused to allow a man who had gone in, having paid his penny, but having changed his mind about embarking on a steamer, and wishing to return, to come out without paying his penny. It was held that that was not false imprisonment; volenti non fit injuria. The man had gone in upon the pier knowing that those were the terms and conditions as to exit, and it was not false imprisonment to hold him to conditions which he had accepted. So, my Lords, it is not false imprisonment to hold a man to the conditions he has accepted when he goes down a mine.

Note
The above two cases have caused a lot of controversy, and varying reasons have been given for the decisions. Although in *Robinson* the Privy Council thought the notice irrelevant, surely one answer is that the plaintiff was free to leave on the terms by which he had agreed to enter (either on the ferry, or by leaving the wharf on payment of one penny). In *Herd*, again it could be said that the contract was crucial, and this is one of many areas where the difficult question of the effect of a contract on duties in tort is raised. For a general discussion of the two cases see Tan, 'A misconceived issue in the law of tort' (1981) 44 MLR 166, where it is argued that the issue is one of consent and that in both cases the plaintiffs were entitled to withdraw their consent to being held where they were and should have won their cases.

Murray v Ministry of Defence
House of Lords [1988] 1 WLR 692; [1988] 2 All ER 521

The plaintiff was suspected of being involved in the collection of money for the purchase of arms for the IRA. Corporal Davies and five other soldiers went to her house at 7.00 a.m. The plaintiff opened the door and Corporal Davies and three others entered. The rest of the family were gathered in one room, and the plaintiff, accompanied by Corporal Davies, went upstairs to get dressed. When they returned downstairs at about 7.30a.m., Corporal Davies said 'As a member of Her Majesty's forces, I arrest you.' In an action for false imprisonment the plaintiff alleged that she had been detained unlawfully from 7.00 a.m. until 7.30 a.m., and although the court was sure that the plaintiff did realise that she was being restrained during that time, the House of Lords nevertheless discussed whether a person can be 'imprisoned' without being aware of the fact. Held: dismissing the appeal, that the defendants were not liable as it was reasonable under the Northern Ireland (Emergency Provisions) Act 1978 to delay formal words of arrest until the premises had been searched. However, it was also indicated that a person can be restrained without being aware of it.

LORD GRIFFITHS: Although on the facts of this case I am sure that the plaintiff was aware of the restraint on her liberty from 7.00 a.m., I cannot agree with the Court of Appeal that it is an essential element of the tort of false imprisonment that the victim should be aware of the fact of denial of liberty. The Court of Appeal relied upon *Herring v Boyle* (1834) for this proposition which they preferred to the view of Atkin LJ to the opposite effect in *Meering v Grahame-White Aviation Co. Ltd*, 122 LT 44. *Herring v Boyle* is an extraordinary decision of the Court of Exchequer: a mother went to fetch her 10-year-old son from school on 24 December 1833 to take him home for the Christmas holidays. The headmaster refused to allow her to take her son home because she had not paid the last term's fees, and he kept the boy at school over the holidays. An action for false imprisonment brought on behalf of the boy failed. In giving judgment Bolland B said, at p. 381:

as far as we know, the boy may have been willing to stay; he does not appear to have been cognisant of any restraint, and there was no evidence of any act whatsoever done by the defendant in his presence. I think that we cannot construe the refusal to the mother in the boy's absence, and without his being cognisant of any restraint, to be an imprisonment of him against his will; . . .

I suppose it is possible that there are schoolboys who prefer to stay at school rather than go home for the holidays but it is not an inference that I would draw, and I cannot believe that on the same facts the case would be similarly decided today. In *Meering* v *Grahame-White Aviation Co. Ltd,* the plaintiff's employers, who suspected him of theft, sent two of the works police to bring him in for questioning at the company's offices. He was taken to a waiting-room where he said that if he was not told why he was there he would leave. He was told he was wanted for the purpose of making inquiries about things that had been stolen and he was wanted to give evidence; he then agreed to stay. Unknown to the plaintiff, the works police had been instructed not to let him leave the waiting-room until the Metropolitan Police arrived. The works police therefore remained outside the waiting-room and would not have allowed the plaintiff to leave until he was handed over to the Metropolitan Police, who subsequently arrested him. The question for the Court of Appeal was whether on this evidence the plaintiff was falsely imprisoned during the hour he was in the waiting-room or whether there could be no 'imprisonment' sufficient to found a civil action unless the plaintiff was aware of the restraint on his liberty. Atkin LJ said, at pp. 53-54;

It appears to me that a person could be imprisoned without his knowing it. I think a person can be imprisoned while he is asleep, while he is in a state of drunkenness, while he is unconscious, and while he is a lunatic. Those are cases where it seems to me that the person might properly complain if he were imprisoned, though the imprisonment began and ceased while he was in that state. Of course, the damages might be diminished and would be affected by the question whether he was conscious of it or not. So a man might in fact, to my mind, be imprisoned by having the key of a door turned against him so that he is imprisoned in a room in fact although he does not know that the key has been turned. It may be that he is being detained in that room by persons who are anxious to make him believe that he is not in fact being imprisoned, and at the same time his captors outside that room may be boasting to persons that he is imprisoned, and it seems to me that if we were to take this case as an instance supposing it could be proved that Prudence had said while the plaintiff was waiting: 'I have got him detained there waiting for the detective to come in and take him to prison' — it appears to me that that would be evidence of imprisonment. It is quite unnecessary to go on to show that in fact the man knew that he was imprisoned. If a man can be imprisoned by having the key turned upon him without his knowledge, so he can be imprisoned if, instead of a lock and key or bolts and bars, he is prevented from, in fact, exercising his liberty by guards and warders or policemen. They serve the same purpose. Therefore it appears to me to be a question of fact. It is true that in all cases of imprisonment so far as the law of civil liability is concerned that 'stone walls do not a prison make,' in the sense that they are not the only form of imprisonment, but any restraint within defined bounds which is a restraint in fact may be an imprisonment.

I agree with this passage. In the first place it is not difficult to envisage cases in which harm may result from unlawful imprisonment even though the victim is unaware of it. Dean William L. Prosser gave two examples in his article in the Columbia Law Review, vol. 55 (June 1955), p. 847 ('False Imprisonment: Consciousness of Confinement'), in which he attacked section 42 of the *Restatement of Torts* which at that time stated the rule that 'there is no liability for intentionally confining another unless the person physically restrained knows of the confinement.' Dean Prosser wrote, at p. 849:

> Let us consider several illustrations. A locks B, a child two days old, in the vault of a bank. B is, of course, unconscious of the confinement, but the bank vault cannot be opened for two days. In the meantime, B suffers from hunger and thirst, and his health is seriously impaired; or it may be that he even dies. Is this no tort? Or suppose that A abducts B, a wealthy lunatic, and holds him for ransom for a week. B is unaware of his confinement, but vaguely understands that he is in unfamiliar surroundings, and that something is wrong. He undergoes mental suffering affecting his health. At the end of the week, he is discovered by the police and released without ever having known that he has been imprisoned. Has he no action against B? . . . If a child of two is kidnapped, confined, and deprived of the care of its mother for a month, is the kidnapping and the confinement in itself so minor a matter as to call for no redress in tort at all?

The *Restatement of Torts* has now been changed and requires that the person confined 'is conscious of the confinement or is harmed by it' (*Restatement of the Law, Second, Torts 2d.* (1965), section 35, p. 52).

If a person is unaware that he has been falsely imprisoned and has suffered no harm, he can normally expect to recover no more than nominal damages, and it is tempting to redefine the tort in the terms of the present rule in the American *Restatement of Torts*. On reflection, however, I would not do so. The law attaches supreme importance to the liberty of the individual and if he suffers a wrongful interference with that liberty it should remain actionable even without proof of special damage.

Questions
1.   Need the defendant know that if he does the act, imprisonment will follow? If a room has two doors and a person locks one door, believing the other door to be unlocked when in fact it is locked, is he liable?
2.   If a person locks the door to a room in which there is a man of 20 years old, knowing that there is an open window six feet above the ground, is he liable for imprisoning him if the man has fragile bones and dares not jump?

Section 5:   selected defences to trespass to the person

A: Consent

As we have seen from *Wilson* v *Pringle* (above), consent is not strictly a 'defence' to trespass to the person, but rather a denial that any tort was committed in the first place. This is so because if a trespass is defined as an offensive contact, a touching cannot be offensive to a person who has consented to it. Consent may be express or implied, so that, for example, a rugby player consents to contacts within the rules during a game. A particular problem concerns express consents, as in surgical operations, where the suggestion is that if the consent is to what is done, that absolves the defendant in trespass, whereas if the allegation is that the plaintiff did not fully consent because he was unaware or not fully informed of the consequences of the act, that is a matter for the tort of negligence.

Chatterton v *Gerson*
Queen's Bench Division [1981] QB 432; [1980] 3 WLR 1003;
[1981] 1 All ER 257

During an operation for a hernia the plaintiff's ileo-inguinal nerve was trapped and this caused her great pain. The defendant was a specialist in chronic intractable pain and he injected the plaintiff. This was unsuccessful in blocking the pain, but did render her right leg numb. She claimed in trespass on the ground that her consent to the injection was invalid as she had not been informed of the potential consequences, and in negligence on the ground that the defendant owed her a duty to warn her of the risks. Held: the defendant was not liable in either trespass or negligence.

BRISTOW J: It is clear law that in any context in which consent of the injured party is a defence to what would otherwise be a crime or a civil wrong, the consent must be real. Where for example a woman's consent to sexual intercourse is obtained by fraud, her apparent consent is no defence to a charge of rape. It is not difficult to state the principle or to appreciate its good sense. As so often, the problem lies in its application.

In my judgment what the court has to do in each case is to look at all the circumstances and say 'Was there a real consent?' I think justice requires that in order to vitiate the reality of consent there must be a greater failure of communication between doctor and patient that that involved in a breach of duty if the claim is based on negligence. When the claim is based on negligence the plaintiff must prove not only the breach of duty to inform, but that had the duty not been broken she would not have chosen to have the operation. Where the claim is based on trespass to the person, once it is shown that the consent is unreal, then what the plaintiff would have decided if she had been given the information which would have prevented vitiation of the reality of her consent is irrelevant.

In my judgment once the patient is informed in broad terms of the nature of the procedure which is intended, and gives her consent, that consent is real, and the cause of the action on which to base a claim for failure to go into risks and implications is negligence, not trespass. Of course if information is withheld in bad faith, the consent will be vitiated by fraud. Of course if by some accident, as in a case in the 1940's in the Salford Hundred Court where a boy was admitted to hospital for tonsilectomy and due to administrative error was circumcised instead, trespass would be the appropriate cause of action against the doctor, though he was as much the victim of the error as the boy. But in my judgment it would be very much against the interests of justice if actions which are really based on a failure by the doctor to perform his duty adequately to inform were pleaded in trespass.

In this case in my judgment even taking the plaintiff's evidence at its face value she was under no illusion as to the general nature of what an intrathecal injection of phenol solution nerve block would be, and in the case of each injection her consent was not unreal. I should add that getting the patient to sign a pro forma expressing consent to undergo the operation 'the effect and nature of which have been explained to me,' as was done here in each case, should be a valuable reminder to everyone of the need for explanation and consent. But it would be no defence to an action based on trespass to the person if no explanation had in fact been given. The consent would have been expressed in form only, not in reality.

Re T
Court of Appeal [1993] Fam 95; [1992] 3 WLR 782; [1992] 4 All ER 649

Miss T was involved in a road accident when she was 34 weeks pregnant. She was admitted to hospital and it was decided that she should have a Caesarean section in the course of which there might need to be a blood transfusion. Miss T was brought up by her mother who was a Jehovah's Witness although Miss T herself was not a member. Jehovah's Witnesses would refuse a blood transfusion. Before the operation Miss T was alone with her mother for some time and then said that she did not want a blood transfusion. She later signed a form refusing consent to a blood transfusion although the contents of the form were not explained to her. The operation was carried out but Miss T's condition deteriorated and her father sought a declaration from the court that a blood transfusion would be lawful. The judge at first instance granted the declaration and the transfusion was given. Held: dismissing the appeal, that it was correct to grant the declaration.

LORD DONALDSON MR:

The role of consent
The law requires that an adult patient who is mentally and physically capable of exercising a choice *must* consent if medical treatment of him is to be lawful, although the consent need not be in writing and may sometimes be inferred from the patient's conduct in the context of the surrounding circumstances. Treating him without his consent or despite a refusal of consent will constitute the civil wrong of trespass to the person and may constitute a crime. If, however, the patient has made no choice and, when the need for treatment arises, is in no position to make one — for example, the classic emergency situation with an unconscious patient — the practitioner can lawfully treat the patient in accordance with his clinical judgment of what is in the patient's best interest.

There seems to be a view in the medical profession that in such emergency circumstances the next of kin should be asked to consent on behalf of the patient and that, if possible, treatment should be postponed until that consent has been obtained. This is a misconception because the next of kin has no legal right either to consent or to refuse consent. This is not to say that it is an undesirable practice if the interests of the patient will not be adversely affected by any consequential delay. I say this because contact with the next of kin may reveal that the patient has made an anticipatory choice which, if clearly established and applicable in the circumstances — two major 'ifs' — would bind the practitioner. Consultation with the next of kin has a further advantage in that it may reveal information as to the personal circumstances of the patient and as to the choice which the patient might have made, if he or she had been in a position to make it. Neither the personal circumstances of the patient nor a speculative answer to the question 'What would the patient have chosen?' can bind the practitioner in his choice of whether or not to treat or how to treat or justify him in acting contrary to a clearly established anticipatory refusal to accept treatment but they are factors to be taken into account by him in forming a clinical judgment as to what is in the best interests of the patient. For example, if he learnt that the patient was a Jehovah's Witness, but had no evidence of a refusal to accept blood transfusions, he would avoid or postpone any blood transfusion so long as possible.
. . .

The conflict of principle

This situation gives rise to a conflict between two interests, that of the patient and that of the society in which he lives. The patient's interest consists of his right to self-determination — his right to live his own life how he wishes, even if it will damage his health or lead to his premature death. Society's interest is in upholding the concept that all human life is sacred and that it should be preserved if at all possible. It is well established that in the ultimate the right of the individual is paramount. But this merely shifts the problem where the conflict occurs and calls for a very careful examination of whether, and if so the way in which, the individual is exercising that right. In case of doubt, that doubt falls to be resolved in favour of the preservation of life for if the individual is to override the public interest, he must do so in clear terms.

Capacity to decide

The right to decide one's own fate presupposes a capacity to do so. Every adult is presumed to have that capacity, but it is a presumption which can be rebutted. This is not a question of the degree of intelligence or education of the adult concerned. However a small minority of the population lack the necessary mental capacity due to mental illness or retarded development: see, for example, *In re F (Mental Patient: Sterilisation)* [1990] 2 AC 1. This is a permanent or at least a long-term state. Others who would normally have that capacity may be deprived of it or have it reduced by reason of temporary factors, such as unconsciousness or confusion or other effects of shock, severe fatigue, pain or drugs being used in their treatment.

Doctors faced with a refusal of consent have to give very careful and detailed consideration to the patient's capacity to decide at the time when the decision was made. It may not be the simple case of the patient having no capacity because, for example, at that time he had hallucinations. It may be the more difficult case of a temporarily reduced capacity at the time when his decision was made. What matters is that the doctors should consider whether at that time he had a capacity which was commensurate with the gravity of the decision which he purported to make. The more serious the decision, the greater the capacity required. If the patient had the requisite capacity, they are bound by his decision. If not, they are free to treat him in what they believe to be his best interests.

This problem is more likely to arise at a time when the patient is unconscious and cannot be consulted. If he can be consulted, this should be done, but again full account has to be taken of his then capacity to make up his own mind.

As I pointed out at the beginning of this judgment, the patient's right of choice exists whether the reasons for making that choice are rational, irrational, unknown or even non-existent. That his choice is contrary to what is to be expected of the vast majority of adults is only relevant if there are other reasons for doubting his capacity to decide. The nature of his choice or the terms in which it is expressed may then tip the balance.

The vitiating effect of outside influence

A special problem may arise if at the time the decision is made the patient has been subjected to the influence of some third party. This is by no means to say that the patient is not entitled to receive and indeed invite advice and assistance from others in reaching a decision, particularly from members of the family. But the doctors have to consider whether the decision is really that of the patient. It is wholly acceptable that the patient should have been persuaded by others of the merits of such a decision and have decided accordingly. It matters not how strong the persuasion was, so long as it did not overbear the independence of the patient's decision. The real question in each such case is 'Does the patient really mean what he says or is he merely saying it for a quiet life, to satisfy someone else or because the advice and persuasion to which he has been subjected is such that he can no longer think and decide for himself?' In other words 'Is it a decision expressed in form only, not in reality?'

When considering the effect of outside influences, two aspects can be of crucial importance. First, the strength of the will of the patient. One who is very tired, in pain or depressed will be much less able to resist having his will overborne than one who is rested, free from pain and cheerful. Second, the relationship of the 'persuader' to the patient may be of crucial importance. The influence of parents on their children or of one spouse on the other can be, but is by no means necessarily, much stronger than would be the case in other relationships. Persuasion based upon religious belief can also be much more compelling and the fact that arguments based upon religious beliefs are being deployed by someone in a very close relationship with the patient will give them added force and should alert the doctors to the possibility — no more — that the patient's capacity or will to decide has been overborne. In other words the patient may not mean what he says.

The scope and basis of the patient's decision
If the doctors consider that the patient had the capacity to decide and has exercised his right to do so, they still have to consider what was the true scope and basis of that decision. If at the time the issue arises the patient still has capacity to decide, they can not only explore the scope of his decision with the patient, but can seek to persuade him to alter that decision. However, this problem will usually arise at that time when this *cannot* be done. In such circumstances what the doctors cannot do is to conclude that if the patient still had had the necessary capacity in the changed situation he would have reversed his decision. This would be simply to deny his right of decision. What they *can* do is to consider whether at the time the decision was made it was intended by the patient to apply in the changed situation. It may well have been so intended, as it was in the Canadian case of *Malette* v *Shulman* (1990) 67 DLR (4th) 321 where the Jehovah's Witness carried a card stating in unequivocal terms that she did not wish blood to be administered to her in any circumstances. But it may not have been so intended. It may have been of more limited scope, for example, 'I refuse to have a blood transfusion, so long as there is an effective alternative.' Or again it may have been based upon an assumption: for example, 'As there is an effective alternative, I refuse to have a blood transfusion.' If the factual situation falls outside the scope of the refusal or if the assumption upon which it is based is falsified, the refusal ceases to be effective. The doctors are then faced with a situation in which the patient has made no decision and, he by then being unable to decide for himself, they have both the right and the duty to treat him in accordance with what in the exercise of their clinical judgment they consider to be his best interests.

Refusal forms
I was surprised to find that hospitals appear to have standard forms of refusal to accept a blood transfusion and was dismayed at the layout of the form used in this case. It is clear that such forms are designed primarily to protect the hospital from legal action. They will be wholly ineffective for this purpose if the patient is incapable of understanding them, they are not explained to him and there is no good evidence (apart from the patient's signature) that he had that understanding and fully appreciated the significance of signing it. With this in mind it is for consideration whether such forms should not be redesigned to separate the disclaimer of liability on the part of the hospital from what really matters, namely the declaration by the patient of his decision with a full appreciation of the possible consequences, the latter being expressed in the simplest possible terms and emphasised by a different and larger type face, by underlining, the employment of coloured print or otherwise.

Informed refusal

As Ward J put it in his judgment, English law does not accept the transatlantic concept of 'informed consent' and it follows that it would reject any concept of 'informed refusal.' What is required is that the patient knew in broad terms the nature and effect of the procedure to which consent (or refusal) was given. There is indeed a duty on the part of doctors to give the patient appropriately full information as to the nature of the treatment proposed, the likely risks (including any special risks attaching to the treatment being administered by particular persons), but a failure to perform this duty sounds in negligence and does not, as such, vitiate a consent or refusal. On the other hand, misinforming a patient, whether or not innocently, and the withholding of information which is expressly or impliedly sought by the patient may well vitiate either a consent or a refusal.

The role of the courts

If in a potentially life threatening situation or one in which irreparable damage to the patient's health is to be anticipated, doctors or hospital authorities are faced with a refusal by an adult patient to accept essential treatment and they have real doubts as to the validity of that refusal, they should in the public interest, not to mention that of their patient, at once seek a declaration from the courts as to whether the proposed treatment would or would not be lawful. This step should not be left to the patient's family, who will probably not know of the facility and may be inhibited by questions of expense. Such cases will be rare, but when they do arise, as was the case with Miss T, the courts can and will provide immediate assistance.

Summary

1.   Prima facie every adult has the right and capacity to decide whether or not he will accept medical treatment, even if a refusal may risk permanent injury to his health or even lead to premature death. Furthermore, it matters not whether the reasons for the refusal were rational or irrational, unknown or even non-existent. This is so notwithstanding the very strong public interest in preserving the life and health of all citizens. However the presumption of capacity to decide, which stems from the fact that the patient is an adult, is rebuttable.

2.   An adult patient may be deprived of his capacity to decide either by long term mental incapacity or retarded development or by temporary factors such as unconsciousness or confusion or the effects of fatigue, shock, pain or drugs.

3.   If an adult patient did not have the capacity to decide at the time of the purported refusal and still does not have that capacity, it is the duty of the doctors to treat him in whatever way they consider, in the exercise of their clinical judgment, to be in his best interests.

4.   Doctors faced with a refusal of consent have to give very careful and detailed consideration to what was the patient's capacity to decide at the time when the decision was made. It may not be a case of capacity or no capacity. It may be a case of reduced capacity. What matters is whether at that time the patient's capacity was reduced below the level needed in the case of a refusal of that importance, for refusals can vary in importance. Some may involve a risk to life or of irreparable damage to health. Others may not.

5.   In some cases doctors will not only have to consider the capacity of the patient to refuse treatment, but also whether the refusal has been vitiated because it resulted not from the patient's will, but from the will of others. It matters not that those others sought, however strongly, to persuade the patient to refuse, so long as in the end the refusal represented the patient's independent decision. If, however, his will was overborne, the refusal will not have represented a true decision. In this context the

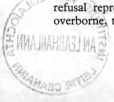

relationship of the persuader to the patient — for example, spouse, parents or religious adviser — will be important, because some relationships more readily lend themselves to overbearing the patient's independent will than do others.

6.   In all cases doctors will need to consider what is the true scope and basis of the refusal. Was it intended to apply in the circumstances which have arisen? Was it based upon assumptions which in the event have not been realised? A refusal is only effective within its true scope and is vitiated if it is based upon false assumptions.

7.   Forms of refusal should be redesigned to bring the consequences of a refusal forcibly to the attention of patients.

8.   In cases of doubt as to the effect of a purported refusal of treatment, where failure to treat threatens the patient's life or threatens irreparable damage to his health, doctors and health authorities should not hesitate to apply to the courts for assistance.

Notes

1.   As to medical operations on those who are unable to consent see *Re F* [1990] 2 AC 1 (below).

2.   On the issue of overriding an express choice when that choice may endanger the life of a viable foetus see *Re S* [1992] 4 All ER 671, noted after *Re F* (below).

3.   If a person touches another (who has consented to being touched) with a metal bar, but fails to disclose that it is charged with electricity, is he liable in trespass? Would it make any difference if he represents that the bar is not 'live'? If the matter is one of negligence the question will arise whether the defendant was under any obligation to inform the plaintiff. Compare the facts of *Hegarty v Shine* (1878) 14 Cox CC 145, where the defendant was sued for battery after he had sexual intercourse with his mistress without informing her that he had a venereal disease. The defendant was not liable: Ball C said 'We are not dealing with deceit as to the nature of the act done, such as occurred in the case cited in argument, of the innocent girl who was induced to believe that a surgical operation was being performed.'

4.   *Duress.* Duress can vitiate consent to trespass, but it may be limited to threats of violent or unlawful acts. In *Latter v Braddell* (1880) 50 LJQB 166 and 448, the defendants suspected that their maid, the plaintiff, was pregnant, and asked a male doctor to examine her. The plaintiff protested but reluctantly submitted to the examination. In holding there was no liability Lindley J said, 'The plaintiff had entirely in her own power physically to comply or not to comply with her mistress's orders . . .'. Should economic duress, such as this, vitiate consent? (In *Universe Tankships of Monrovia v ITF* [1981] ICR 129, shipowners were entitled to recover payments they had made to a seamen's union welfare fund in order to have the blacking of their ship lifted, on the grounds that the payments had been made under economic duress.)

B: Necessity

In re F (Mental Patient: Sterilisation)
House of Lords [1990] 2 AC 1; [1989] 2 WLR 1025; [1989] 2 All ER 545

F was a woman aged 36 who suffered from serious mental disability, having the mental capacity of a child aged four or five. She formed a relationship with a male patient at the same hospital and standard methods of contraception were thought to be unsuitable. The doctor advised that she be sterilised, and her mother applied to the court for a declaration that the operation would not be unlawful. There was no statutory power to order the operation and the question therefore was whether the operation would amount to a trespass to the person. Held: dismissing the appeal, that the operation would be lawful.

LORD GOFF: Upon what principle can medical treatment be justified when given without consent? We are searching for a principle upon which, in limited circumstances, recognition may be given to a need, in the interests of the patient, that treatment should be given to him in circumstances where he is (temporarily or permanently) disabled from consenting to it. It is this criterion of a need which points to the principle of necessity as providing justification.

That there exists in the common law a principle of necessity which may justify action which would otherwise be unlawful is not in doubt. But historically the principle has been seen to be restricted to two groups of cases, which have been called cases of public necessity and cases of private necessity. The former occurred when a man interfered with another man's property in the public interest — for example (in the days before we could dial 999 for the fire brigade) the destruction of another man's house to prevent the spread of a catastrophic fire, as indeed occurred in the Great Fire of London in 1666. The latter cases occurred when a man interfered with another's property to save his own person or property from imminent danger — for example, when he entered upon his neighbour's land without his consent, in order to prevent the spread of fire onto his own land.

There is, however, a third group of cases, which is also properly described as founded upon the principle of necessity and which is more pertinent to the resolution of the problem in the present case. These cases are concerned with action taken as a matter of necessity to assist another person without his consent. To give a simple example, a man who seizes another and forcibly drags him from the path of an oncoming vehicle, thereby saving him from injury or even death, commits no wrong. But there are many emanations of this principle, to be found scattered through the books. These are concerned not only with the preservation of the life or health of the assisted person, but also with the preservation of his property (sometimes an animal, sometimes an ordinary chattel) and even with certain conduct on his behalf in the administration of his affairs. Where there is a pre-existing relationship between the parties, the intervenor is usually said to act as an agent of necessity on behalf of the principal in whose interest he acts, and his action can often, with not too much artificiality, be referred to the pre-existing relationship between them. Whether the intervenor may be entitled either to reimbursement or to remuneration raises separate questions which are not relevant in the present case.

We are concerned here with action taken to preserve the life, health or well-being of another who is unable to consent to it. Such action is sometimes said to be justified as arising from an emergency; in *Prosser and Keeton, Handbook on Torts*, 5th ed. (1984), p. 117, the action is said to be privileged by the emergency. Doubtless, in the case of a person of sound mind, there will ordinarily have to be an emergency before such action taken without consent can be lawful; for otherwise there would be an opportunity to communicate with the assisted person and to seek his consent. But this is not always so; and indeed the historical origins of the principle of necessity do not point to emergency as such as providing the criterion of lawful intervention without consent. . . . But when a person is rendered incapable of communication either permanently or over a considerable period of time (through illness or accident or mental disorder), it would be an unusual use of language to describe the case as one of 'permanent emergency' — if indeed such a state of affairs can properly be said to exist. In truth, the relevance of an emergency is that it may give rise to a necessity to act in the interests of the assisted person, without first obtaining his consent. Emergency is however not the criterion or even a pre-requisite; it is simply a frequent origin of the necessity which impels intervention. The principle is one of necessity, not of emergency.

. . . But from [the cases there] can be derived the basic requirements, applicable in these cases of necessity, that, to fall within the principle, not only (1) must there be a necessity to act when it is not practicable to communicate with the assisted person, but also (2) the action taken must be such as a reasonable person would in all circumstances take, acting in the best interests of the assisted person.

On this statement of principle, I wish to observe that officious intervention cannot be justified by the principle of necessity. So intervention cannot be justified when another more appropriate person is available and willing to act; nor can it be justified when it is contrary to the known wishes of the assisted person, to the extent that he is capable of rationally forming such a wish. On the second limb of the principle, the introduction of the standard of a reasonable man should not in the present context be regarded as materially different from that of Sir Montague Smith's 'wise and prudent man', because a reasonable man would, in the time available to him, proceed with wisdom and prudence before taking action in relation to another man's person or property without his consent. I shall have more to say on this point later. Subject to that, I hesitate at present to indulge in any greater refinement of the principle, being well aware of many problems which may arise in its application — problems which it is not necessary, for present purposes, to examine. But as a general rule, if the above criteria are fulfilled, interference with the assisted person's person or property (as the case may be) will not be unlawful. Take the example of a railway accident, in which injured passengers are trapped in the wreckage. It is this principle which may render lawful the actions of other citizens — railway staff, passengers or outsiders — who rush to give aid and comfort to the victims: the surgeon who amputates the limb of an unconscious passenger to free him from the wreckage; the ambulance man who conveys him to hospital; the doctors and nurses who treat him and care for him while he is still unconscious. Take the example of an elderly person who suffers a stroke which renders him incapable of speech or movement. It is by virtue of this principle that the doctor who treats him, the nurse who cares for him, even the relative or friend or neighbour who comes in to look after him, will commit no wrong when he or she touches his body.

The two examples I have given illustrate, in the one case, an emergency, and in the other, a permanent or semi-permanent state of affairs. Another example of the latter kind is that of a mentally disordered person who is disabled from giving consent. I can see no good reason why the principle of necessity should not be applicable in his case as it is in the case of the victim of a stroke. Furthermore, in the case of a mentally disordered person, as in the case of a stroke victim, the permanent state of affairs calls for a wider range of care than may be requisite in an emergency which arises from accidental injury. When the state of affairs is permanent, or semi-permanent, action properly taken to preserve the life, health or well-being of the assisted person may well transcend such measures as surgical operation or substantial medical treatment and may extend to include such humdrum matters as routine medical or dental treatment, even simple care such as dressing and undressing and putting to bed.

The distinction I have drawn between cases of emergency, and cases where the state of affairs is (more or less) permanent, is relevant in another respect. We are here concerned with medical treatment, and I limit myself to cases of that kind. Where, for example, a surgeon performs an operation without his consent on a patient temporarily rendered unconscious in an accident, he should do no more than is reasonably required, in the best interests of the patient, before he recovers consciousness. I can see no practical difficulty arising from this requirement, which derives from the fact that the patient is expected before long to regain consciousness and can then be consulted about longer term measures. The point has however arisen in a more acute form where a surgeon, in the course of an operation, discovers some other condition which, in his opinion, requires operative treatment for which he has not received the patient's consent. In what circumstances he should operate forthwith, and in what circumstances he should postpone the further treatment until he has received the patient's consent, is a difficult matter which has troubled the Canadian Courts (see *Marshall* v *Curry* (1933) 3 DLR 260, and *Murray* v *McMurchy* (1949) 2 DLR 442), but which it is not necessary for your Lordships to consider in the present case.

But where the state of affairs is permanent or semi-permanent, as may be so in the case of a mentally disordered person, there is no point in waiting to obtain the patient's consent. The need to care for him is obvious; and the doctor must then act in the best interests of his patient, just as if he had received his patient's consent so to do. . . .

Note

In **Re S** [1992] 4 All ER 671, S refused on religious grounds to undergo a Caesarean operation. The doctors were clear that her unborn child could not survive without the operation and on an application by the health authority, Sir Stephen Brown (who had only 20 minutes to decide) granted a declaration that the operation would be lawful despite S's refusal. (In the event S survived but the child did not). In *Re F* Lord Goff said that in relation to necessity it must not be practicable to communicate with the assisted person. If *Re S* is a case on necessity, does it go against this requirement? If it does, is it a justified extension of the principle of necessity? For a discussion see Stern, Court-ordered Caesarean section — in whose interests? (1993) 56 MLR 238.

Could it be argued that in *Re S* the decision was taken in order to protect the interests of the foetus? The difficulty with this argument is that it was held in *Paton* v *Trustees of BPAS* [1979] QB 276 that a foetus had no independent rights. Baker P said 'The foetus cannot . . . have any right of its own until it is born and has a separate existence from its mother.' Does *Re S* go against this view? If the foetus does have an independent right could this be enforced against the mother? See *Re F* [1988] 2 All ER 193, where it was held that a foetus could not be made a ward of court.

Question

A is brought to hospital unconscious, and he is carrying a card which states that he does not want any surgical procedure performed on him. Can the principle of necessity overrule this previously expressed refusal of consent?

In *Airedale NHS Trust* v *Bland* [1993] 1 All ER 821 Lord Keith said at p. 860 that instructions given anticipating such an event would be effective, but could it not be argued that a person when confronted with the reality of his situation might have changed his mind? On this point see the views of Lord Donaldson in *Re T* (above).

C: *Provocation and contributory negligence*
Lane v Holloway
Court of Appeal [1968] 1 QB 379; [1967] 3 WLR 1003; [1967] 3 All ER 129

Relations were strained between the plaintiff, Mr Lane, who was a retired gardener aged 64, and his neighbour, Mr Holloway (aged 23), a café proprietor in Dorchester. One night Mr Lane came back from the pub and was talking to a Mrs Brake. Mrs Holloway called out 'You bloody lot'. Lane replied 'Shut up, you monkey faced tart'. Mr Holloway sprang up and said 'What did you say to my wife?' Lane replied 'I want to see you on your own', and he later threw a light punch at Mr Holloway, whereupon the younger man punched him in the eye. The wound needed 19 stitches. Held: allowing the appeal, that the defendant was liable and no deduction from damages should be made for Mr Lane's provocation.

LORD DENNING MR: It is said that the judge ought not to have reduced the damages. The judge had cases before him, both in this country and New Zealand and Canada, where it was held that provocation could be used to reduce the damages. But most of these cases were considered by the High Court of Australia in 1962 in *Fontin* v *Katapodis*, (1962) 108 CLR 177. The plaintiff struck the defendant with a weapon, a wooden T-square. It broke on his shoulder. There was not much trouble from that. But then the defendant picked up a sharp piece of glass with which he was working and threw it at the plaintiff, causing him severe injury. The judge reduced the damages from £2,850 to £2,000 by reason of the provocation. But the High Court of Australia, including the Chief Justice, Sir Owen Dixon, held that provocation could be used to wipe out the element of exemplary or aggravated damages but could not be used to reduce the actual figure of pecuniary compensation. So they increased the damages to the full £2,850.

I think that the Australian High Court should be our guide. The defendant has done a civil wrong and should pay compensation for the physical damage done by it. Provocation by the plaintiff can properly be used to take away any element of aggravation. But not to reduce the real damages. . . .

SALMON LJ: To say in circumstances such as those that ex turpi causa non oritur actio is a defence seems to me to be quite absurd. Academically of course one can see the argument, but one must look at it, I think, from a practical point of view. To say that this old gentleman was engaged jointly with the defendant in a criminal venture is a step which, like the judge, I feel wholly unable to take.

The defence of volenti non fit injuria seems to me to be equally difficult. It is inconceivable that the old man, full of beer as he was, was voluntarily taking the risk of having an injury of this kind inflicted upon him. I think the judge was quite right in rejecting the defence of volenti non fit injuria. . . .

There are many cases from the Commonwealth Law Reports in which the question has been considered as to whether or not the fact that the plaintiff behaved badly can diminish damages which are awarded as compensation for physical injury. Some of these decisions are conflicting. For my part I entirely accept what was said in the High Court of Australia in *Fontin* v *Katapodis*, (1962) 108 CLR 177. It was an exceptionally strong court consisting of Sir Owen Dixon CJ, McTiernan and Owen JJ. The case seems to me, for all practical purposes, indistinguishable from the present and it states in the plainest terms what, as I have already said, I should have been prepared to hold without any authority, namely, that on principle, when considering what damages a plaintiff is entitled to as compensation for physical injury, the fact that the plaintiff may have behaved badly is irrelevant. I think it is important to remember this. Some of the older English authorities and some of the Commonwealth cases appear to fall into the error, which until recently had by no means been eliminated, of thinking that damages for tort were partly to punish the defendant. We now know, certainly since *Rookes* v *Barnard* [1964] AC 1129, that they are nothing of the kind, that they are purely compensatory — with the exception, of course, of exemplary damages. And in the present case there was no question of exemplary damages being claimed or awarded.

The judge, however, was persuaded that he could take the plaintiff's conduct into account, and he obviously did so, and discounted a great deal on this account. To my mind, even if he was entitled to discount anything, which, in my view, he was not, he discounted much too much.

Mr O'Brien relied also upon contributory negligence to reduce the damages. At first he relied on a wider ground under the Law Reform (Contributory Negligence) Act, 1945, but in the end I think he restricted his argument under this Act to contributory negligence. As Winn LJ pointed out in the course of the argument, if the plaintiff on the facts of this case can be said to have been negligent, then before the statute what he did would have afforded the defendant a complete defence to the action — a somewhat surprising proposition. To my mind it is impossible to hold that what this old man did, however rude or silly or cantankerous, amounted to contributory negligence.

Notes

1.   This case is *not* about self defence, but about provocation.

2.   *Contributory negligence.* Following *Lane* v *Holloway* it was suggested that if a person genuinely shows a lack of regard for his own safety (which on the facts was not so in *Lane* v *Holloway*), damages might be reduced for contributory negligence. Nevertheless, in the state of Victoria in *Horkin* v *North Melbourne Football Club* [1983] VR 153, Brooking J held that, on historical and public policy grounds, contributory negligence is not a defence in trespass. One of the functions of trespass is to repress wrongful behaviour and to preserve public order. However, in **Barnes v Nayer**, *The Times*, 19 December 1986, it was said that contributory negligence would be allowed as a defence. The defendant alleged that he and his family were subjected to constant abuse by their neighbours, and that on one occasion, after threats to his son, the defendant killed the deceased with a machete. The Court of Appeal held that contributory negligence is available as a defence to trespass to the person but it did not apply to the facts of this case. See also Hudson, 'Contributory negligence as a defence to battery' (1984) 4 LS 332, and also Childs, 'Pause for thought: contributory negligence and intentional trespass to the person', (1993) 44 NILQ 334.

2 TRESPASS TO LAND

Trespass to land protects a person in possession of land against direct invasion of his property. (If the invasion is indirect, that is a matter for the law of nuisance.)

The fact that any invasion of land, however minute and whether it causes damage or not, is a trespass, indicates that the primary function of this tort is to protect rights in property, rather than simply to provide compensation. It is here that the question of remedies is important, as *Anchor Brewhouse* (below) indicates.

Gregory v Piper
Court of King's Bench (1820) 9 B & C 591; 109 ER 220

The plaintiff occupied the Rising Sun in Newmarket, and he owned the wall which separated his yard from that of the defendant. In the course of a dispute about a right of way, the defendant ordered his employee, Stubbings, to dump rubbish so as to block the way but not to touch the wall. The rubbish was loose and as it dried out some of it rolled or settled against the wall. Held: the defendant was liable.

PARKE J: I think that the defendant is liable in this form of action. If a single stone had been put against the wall it would have been sufficient. Independently of Stubbings's evidence there was sufficient evidence to satisfy the jury that the rubbish was placed there by the defendant, for he expressed his determination not to remove it. It does not rest there. Stubbings says he was desired not to let the rubbish touch the wall. But it appeared to be of a loose kind, and it was therefore probable that some of it naturally might run against the wall. Stubbings said that some of it of course would go against the wall. Now the defendant must be taken to have contemplated all the probable consequences of the act which he had ordered to be done, and one of these probable consequences was, that the rubbish would touch the plaintiff's wall. If that was so, then the laying the rubbish against the wall was as much the defendant's act as if it had been done by his express command. The defendant, therefore, was the person who caused the act to be done, and for the necessary or natural consequence of his own act he is responsible as a trespasser.

Note
Compare *Esso Petroleum* v *Southport Corporation* [1956] AC 218, where it was doubted, without deciding, whether it would be trespass to discharge oil at sea which was then washed onto the foreshore. The oil was 'committed to the action of wind and wave, with no certainty . . . how, when or under what conditions it might come to shore'.

Basely v Clarkson
Court of Common Pleas (1682) 3 Lev 37; 83 ER 565

Difference *inter* trespass involuntary, and *per* mistake

Trespass for breaking his closs called the *balk* and the *hade,* and cutting his grass, and carrying it away. The defendant disclaims any title in the lands of the plaintiff, but says that he hath a *balk* and *hade* adjoining to the balk and hade of the plaintiff, and in mowing his own land he involuntarily and by mistake mowed down some grass growing upon the balk and hade of the plaintiff, intending only to mow the grass upon his own *balk* and *hade,* and carried the *grass, &c. quæ est eadem, &C. Et quod ante emanationem brevis* he tendered to the plaintiff 2s. in satisfaction, and that 2s. was a sufficient amends. Upon this the plaintiff demurred, and had judgement; for it appears the fact was voluntary, and his intention and knowledge are not traversable; they cannot be known.

League Against Cruel Sports v Scott
Queen's Bench Division [1986] 1 QB 240; [1985] 3 WLR 400; [1985] 2 All ER 489

The plaintiffs owned various areas of unfenced moorland around Exmoor for the purpose of establishing a sanctuary for deer. Accordingly they did not allow hunting on their land. The defendants were joint masters of the Devon and Somerset staghounds, and it was shown that on a number of occasions hounds belonging to the hunt had entered the plaintiffs' property, and the plaintiffs alleged trespass by the defendants, their servants or agents. No material damage was caused. Held: the defendants were liable. Damages were awarded and in respect of one property an injunction was granted.

PARK J: In my judgment the law as I take it to be may be stated thus: where a master of staghounds takes out a pack of hounds and deliberately sets them in pursuit of a stag or hind, knowing that there is a real risk that in the pursuit hounds may enter or cross prohibited land, the master will be liable for trespass if he intended to cause hounds to enter such land, or if by his failure to exercise proper control over them he caused them to enter such land.

In the present case, on each of the occasions on which the league alleges trespass by hounds the master (or on some occasions the masters) had taken out the pack and set hounds in pursuit of a stag or hind. On each occasion the master or masters knew that there was a real risk that one or more hounds might enter league land; on each occasion one or more hounds did, in fact, enter league land. The question is, therefore, whether on any, and if so which, of those occasions the trespass was caused either by the master intending that hounds should enter or by his failure to exercise proper control over them.

This is, in each case, a question of fact. The master's intention, or the intention of those servants or agents or followers of the hunt for whose conduct he is responsible, has to be inferred from his or their conduct in all the circumstances of the case. For example, whether he or they stood by and allowed hounds which were plainly about to enter prohibited land to do so, or allowed hounds which were plainly on the land to remain there; or whether, by making appropriate sounds vocally or on the horn, he encouraged hounds to go on to or to remain on such land.

Further, if it is virtually impossible, whatever precautions are taken, to prevent hounds from entering league land, such as Pitleigh for example, yet the master knowing that to be the case, nevertheless persists in hunting in its vicinity, with the result that hounds frequently trespass on the land, then the inference might well be drawn that his indifference to the risk of trespass amounted to an intention that hounds should trespass on the land.

The master's negligence, or the negligence of those servants or agents or followers of the hunt for whose conduct he is responsible, has also to be judged in the light of all the circumstances in which the trespass in question occurred.

It involves consideration of such questions as the stage in the chase at which it ought reasonably to have been foreseen that there was a risk that hounds might trespass on league land and what precautions, if any, were taken by the master at that stage to prevent trespass by heading off the hounds.

Bernstein v Skyviews and General Ltd
Queen's Bench Division [1978] QB 479; [1977] 3 WLR 136;
[1977] 2 All ER 962

The defendants flew above Lord Bernstein's country house and took a photograph of it, which they then offered to sell to him. The plaintiff claimed damages for trespass by invasion of his air space. Held: the defendants were not liable.

GRIFFITHS J: I turn now to the law. The plaintiff claims that as owner of the land he is also owner of the air space above the land, or at least has the right to exclude any entry into the air space above his land. He relies upon the old Latin maxim, cujus est solum ejus est usque ad coelum et ad inferos, a colourful phrase often upon the lips of lawyers since it was first coined by Accursius in Bologna in the 13th century. There are a number of cases in which the maxim has been used by English judges, but an examination of those cases shows that they have all been concerned with structures attached to the adjoining land, such as overhanging buildings, signs or telegraph wires, and for their solution it has not been necessary for the judge to cast his eyes towards the heavens; he has been concerned with the rights of the owner in the air space immediately adjacent to the surface of the land. . . .

I can find no support in authority for the view that a landowner's rights in the air space above his property extend to an unlimited height. In *Wandsworth Board of Works v United Telephone Co. Ltd*, 13 QBD 904 Bowen LJ described the maxim, usque ad coelum, as a fanciful phrase, to which I would add that if applied literally it is a fanciful notion leading to the absurdity of a trespass at common law being committed by a satellite every time it passes over a suburban garden. The academic writers speak with one voice in rejecting the uncritical and literal application of the maxim . . . I accept their collective approach as correct. The problem is to balance the rights of an owner to enjoy the use of his land against the rights of the general public to take advantage of all that science now offers in the use of air space. This balance is in my judgment best struck in our present society by restricting the rights of an owner in the air space above his land to such height as is necessary for the ordinary use and enjoyment of his land and the structures upon it, and declaring that above that height he has no greater rights in the air space than any other member of the public.

Applying this test to the facts of this case, I find that the defendants' aircraft did not infringe any rights in the plaintiff's air space, and thus no trespass was committed. It was on any view of the evidence flying many hundreds of feet above the ground and it is not suggested that by its mere presence in the air space it caused any interference with any use to which the plaintiff put or might wish to put his land. The plaintiff's complaint is not that the aircraft interfered with the use of his land but that a photograph was taken from it. There is, however, no law against taking a photograph, and the mere taking of a photograph cannot turn an act which is not a trespass into the plaintiff's air space into one that is a trespass.

My finding that no trespass at common law has been established is sufficient to determine this case in the defendants' favour. I should, however, deal with a further defence under the Civil Aviation Act 1949, section 40(1) of which provides:

> No action shall lie in respect of trespass or in respect of nuisance, by reason only of the flight of an aircraft over any property at a height above the ground, which, having regard to wind, weather and all the circumstances of the case is reasonable, or the ordinary incidents of such flight so long as the provisions of Part II and this Part of this Act and any Order in Council or order made under Part II or this Part of this Act are duly complied with.

It is agreed that all the statutory provisions have been complied with by the defendants, nor is there any suggestion that the aircraft was not flying at a reasonable height; but it is submitted by the plaintiff that the protection given by the subsection is limited to a bare right of passage over land analogous to the limited right of a member of the public to pass over the surface of a highway, and my attention has been drawn to a passage in *Shawcross & Beaumont on Air Law*, 3rd ed. (1966), p. 561 in which the editors express this view. I see nothing in the language of the section to invite such a restricted reading which would withdraw from its protection many very beneficial activities carried on from aircraft. For example, we heard during this case that Granada Television, a company of which Lord Bernstein is chairman, made a series of educational films called 'The Land' for educational purposes. To make the films helicopters flew far and wide over the country and photographed the land below in all its various aspects. Of course they had not obtained the permission of every occupier whose land they photographed — it would have been an impossible task. According to the plaintiff's contention that innocent activity would not be protected even if the helicopters were flying at a reasonable height and complying with all statutory requirements, for they would not be mere birds of passage but making use of the air space for the purpose of aerial photography or survey. As I read the section its protection extends to all flights provided they are at a reasonable height and comply with the statutory requirements. And I adopt this construction the more readily because subsection (2) imposes upon the owner of the aircraft a strict liability to pay damages for any material loss or damage that may be caused by his aircraft.

It is, however, to be observed that the protection given is limited by the words 'by reason only of the flight,' so although an owner can found no action in trespass or nuisance if he relies solely upon the flight of the aircraft above his property as founding his cause of action, the section will not preclude him from bringing an action if he can point to some activity carried on by or from the aircraft that can properly be considered a trespass or nuisance, or some other tort. For example, the section would give no protection against the deliberate emission of vast quantities of smoke that polluted the atmosphere and seriously interfered with the plaintiff's use and enjoyment of his property; such behaviour remains an actionable nuisance. Nor would I wish this judgment to be understood as deciding that in no circumstances could a successful action be brought against an aerial photographer to restrain his activities. The present action is not founded in nuisance for no court would regard the taking of a single photograph as an actionable nuisance. But if the circumstances were such that a plaintiff was subjected to the harassment of constant surveillance of his house from the air, accompanied by the photographing of his every activity, I am far from saying that the court would not regard such a monstrous invasion of his privacy as an actionable nuisance for which they would give relief. However, that question does not fall for decision in this case and will be decided if and when it arises.

On the facts of this case even if contrary to my view the defendants' aircraft committed a trespass at common law in flying over the plaintiff's land, the plaintiff is prevented from bringing any action in respect of that trespass by the terms of section 40(1) of the Civil Aviation Act 1949.

Notes
1. The Civil Aviation Act 1949, s. 40(1) has been replaced by the Civil Aviation Act 1982, s. 75(1) which is in similar terms. The statute also imposes strict liability upon the owner of an aircraft for any material damage caused by any article, animal or person falling from an aircraft in flight.
2. For invasion of air space by structures on neighbouring land, see *Anchor Brewhouse* v *Berkley House* (below).

Anchor Brewhouse Developments Ltd v *Berkley House Ltd*
Chancery Division [1987] 2 EGLR 172

The defendants were developing a site in London and were using a tower crane in the construction work. The jib of the tower crane swung over the plaintiff's property, and this was held to be a trespass to the plaintiff's airspace. Another factor in the case was whether the plaintiffs were limited to a remedy in damages or whether they could obtain an injunction, and, if so, whether that injunction could be temporarily suspended to allow the defendants to complete their building. Held: it was a trespass to the airspace and an injunction was granted.

SCOTT J: In my view, it would be an incorrect use of authority to extract Griffiths J's approach [in *Bernstein* v *Skyviews*] to the difficult question of overflying aircraft and to seek to apply that approach to the invasion of air space in general. Griffiths J was dealing with an argument that the incursion by an aircraft into the air space above the plaintiff's land represented trespass. He was not prepared to accept that that was necessarily so. But he accepted in the first passage I cited that adjoining owners had no right to erect structures projecting over their neighbours' land. His dictum about balancing the owners' rights against the rights of the general public was not, in my opinion, intended to limit the complaints to trespass that might in that event be made by neighbours. Mr Moss argued that, in view of the *Bernstein* case, the critical question was whether the invasion of air space interfered with the ordinary use and enjoyment of the land. The owner of the land is entitled to complain of trespass if the invasion is at a level above the land that does so interfere. Otherwise the invasion should, said Mr Moss, be rejected as trespass. I am not satisfied that represents a permissible application of Griffiths J's approach in the *Bernstein* case nor that it would be workable in practice.

What is complained of in the present case is infringement of air space by a structure positioned upon a neighbour's land. The defendant has erected tower cranes on its land. Attached to each tower crane is a boom which swings over the plaintiffs' land. The booms invade the air space over the plaintiffs' land. Each boom is part of the structure on the defendant's land. The tort of trespass represents an interference with possession or with the right to possession. A landowner is entitled, as an attribute of his ownership of the land, to place structures on his land and thereby to reduce into actual possession the air space above his land. If an adjoining owner places a structure on his (the adjoining owner's) land that overhangs his neighbour's land, he thereby takes into his possession air space to which his neighbour is entitled. That, in my judgment, is trespass. It does not depend upon any balancing of rights.

The difficulties posed by overflying aircraft or balloons, bullets or missiles seem to me to be wholly separate from the problem which arises where there is invasion of air space by a structure placed or standing upon the land of a neighbour. One of the characteristics of the common law of trespass is, or ought to be, certainty. The extent of proprietary rights enjoyed by landowners ought to be clear. It may be that, where aircraft or overflying missiles are concerned, certainty cannot be achieved. I do not wish to dissent at all from Griffiths J's approach to that problem in the *Bernstein* case. But certainty is capable of being achieved where invasion of air space by tower cranes, advertising signs and other structures are concerned. In my judgment, if somebody erects on his own land a structure, part of which invades the air space above the land of another, the invasion is trespass. . . .

That brings me to Mr Moss' second point. He submitted that if the trial were now, the plaintiffs would not succeed in obtaining a permanent injunction. So, he submitted, they should not get an interlocutory injunction either.

Mr Martin has submitted that if I am satisfied, as I am, that the oversailing booms of the cranes are committing trespass and if it is the case, as it is, that the trespass is threatened to be continued by the defendant, the plaintiffs are entitled to an injunction as of course. An injunction is a discretionary remedy, but it is well settled that the discretion must be exercised in accordance with judicial precedent and principle and there is authority for Mr Martin's submission that a trespass threatened to be continued will be restrained by injunction as of course.

In *Woollerton and Wilson* v *Costain* [1970] 1 WLR 411 Stamp J said at p. 413:

> It is the plaintiffs' case that the absence of any damage caused by the trespass, either present or apprehended, is no reason for refusing the injunction for which they ask. It is their further contention that since the tort of trespass is admitted and is threatened to be continued there is no good reason for refusing interlocutory relief on the ground of balance of convenience. In my judgment both these submission are well founded.
>
> It is in my judgment well established that it is no answer to a claim for an injunction to restrain a trespass that the trespass does no harm to the plaintiff. Indeed, the very fact that no harm is done is a reason for rather than against the granting of an injunction: for if there is no damage done the damage recovered in the action will be nominal and if the injunction is refused the result will be no more nor less than a licence to continue the tort of trespass in return for a nominal payment. . . .

Mr Moss pointed out, and it is common ground, that there is a flaw in that exposition of the law [in *Woollerton and Wilson* v *Costain*]. The learned judge proceeded on the footing that nominal damages only could be recovered for the trespass. He was not referred by counsel to the line of authority enabling damages to be awarded to represent the sum that on a 'willing grantor/grantee' basis the plaintiff might have charged the defendant for a licence to commit the trespass. Mr Moss fastened on that error in order to submit that Stamp J's conclusion that an injunction should be granted to restrain the trespass was unsound. I do not agree. Stamp J based himself upon firm early authority in the form of the decision of Lord Selborne in *Goodson* v *Richardson* [(1874) 9 Ch App 221] and of Sir George Jessel in *Eardley* v *Granville* [(1876) 3 Ch D 826]. Both these authorities justify the grant of injunctive relief to restrain trespass notwithstanding that the damage to the plaintiff may be trivial only. Lord Selborne and Sir George Jessel adopted a robust Victorian approach which might, perhaps, find less sympathy now. The ownership of property entitled the owner to license or refuse to license the use of it by others. If he is asked to license the use of by others, he can charge whatever he chooses for the licence. The law will recognise and protect the monopoly that his ownership carries with it. That is the philosophy, as I read the two cases, underlying the judgments of Lord Selborne and of Sir George Jessel. The grant of the injunction by Stamp J was in accordance with the principle expressed in these two cases. It did not depend on the nominal damages point. It is to be noted that, having found that an injunction ought to be granted, Stamp J then proceeded to suspend the operation of it for the only period for which it could have been of any use. Some reservation as to the correctness of that suspension was subsequently expressed by the Court of Appeal in *Charrington* v *Simons & Co. Ltd* [1971] 1 WLR 598.

In *John Trenberth Ltd* v *National Westminster Bank Ltd* (1979) 39 P&CR 104 Walton J expressed the clear view that the suspension was wrong. . . .

What has troubled me about the plaintiffs' claim to an injunction is not any of the special circumstances relied on by Mr Moss but simply that it seems sensible that the defendant's building construction should be done by means of tower cranes. The injunctions which I feel obliged to grant in order to reflect the plaintiffs' proprietary rights will put the defendant in a position in which it must come to terms with the plaintiffs if it is going to continue to use its tower cranes.

It would in many respects be convenient if the court had power, in order to enable property developments to be expeditiously and economically completed, to allow, on proper commercial terms, some use to be made by the developers of the land of neighbours. But the court has no such power and ought not, in my view, to claim it indirectly by the withholding of injunctions in cases like the present. Some statutes have granted the court analogous powers: see eg the Medicines Act 1968, the Patents Act 1949, the Mines (Working Facilities and Support) Act 1966. There is a sense in which the grant of an injunction against trespass enables a landowner to behave like a dog in a manger. I am not suggesting that these plaintiffs are so behaving, but the conclusion that, even if they are, they are none the less entitled to their injunction sticks a little in my gullet. It would be possible for the law to be that the court should not grant an injunction to restrain a trifling trespass if it were shown to be reasonable and sensible that the trespass be allowed to continue for a limited period upon payment of substantial and proper damages. But I do not think it is open to me to proceed on that footing. There is too much authority in the way. The authorities establish, in my view, that the plaintiffs are entitled as of course to injunctions to restrain continuing trespass.

For these reasons, reached with some regret, I grant the injunctions as asked.

Notes

1. The problem of whether to award damages or to grant an injunction also arises in nuisance, where again the preferred view is that a plaintiff whose

interest is being invaded is generally entitled to an injunction. See for example *Kennaway* v *Thompson* [1981] QB 88. As Scott J admitted in *Anchor Brewhouse*, the effect is to dramatically alter the bargaining power of the plaintiff who may be tempted to charge an exorbitant sum for permission to use the airspace. In *LJP Investments* v *Howard Chia Investments* (1991) 24 NSWLR 499, where for complicated reasons it was necessary to measure damages for trespass to airspace by scaffolding, Hodgson J held that where the space used has peculiar value for a defendant then damages should reflect that value rather than the general market value. Damages should reflect the price which the plaintiff and defendant would reasonably have negotiated having regard to the plaintiff's position and the defendant's wish to develop the site and the judge said that one relevant factor in this would be the extra cost which the defendant would incur if he were not able to gain access to the plaintiff's air space.

Note also the Access to Neighbouring Land Act 1992 where a court may make an order allowing access but only where the entry is for the purpose of preservation and not for improvement or building a new structure.

2.   In *Jaggard* v *Sawyer* [1995] 2 All ER 189, the Court of Appeal approved the dictum in *Shelfer* v *City of London Electric Lighting* [1895] 1 Ch 287 that an injunction may be refused where: (1) the injury to the plaintiff's legal rights is small; (2) it is one which is capable of being estimated in money; (3) it can be adequately compensated by a small money payment; and (4) it would be oppressive to the defendant to grant an injunction. In deciding whether it would be oppressive in relation to a permanent invasion of land (e.g. by erecting a building on the plaintiff's land) the court would take into account whether the defendant knew he was committing a trespass and completed the work in the hope of presenting a court with a fait accompli.

3.   *Recovery of possession.*   Order 113 of the Rules of the Supreme Court provides an expeditious remedy when land is being occupied by trespassers. Apart from speed, the main advantage is that an order can be obtained against trespassers without knowing their names.

4.   *Criminal trespass.*   Trespass is not generally a crime, but several statutes make it so in particular circumstances. For example, the Criminal Law Act 1977, s. 6 makes it a crime (except for a displaced residential occupier) to use force to enter premises, and the Criminal Justice and Public Order Act 1994, s. 61 deals with the case of two or more persons entering land with a view to residing there, and causing damage or using abusive language or bringing six or more vehicles onto the land. Section 68 establishes an offence of aggravated trespass in relation to a person who trespasses on land in the open air and obstructs or disrupts a lawful activity on that or adjoining land. It is also a crime to trespass on specific kinds of land such as railways (Regulation of Railways Act 1868, s. 23), or airports (Civil Aviation Act 1982, s. 39)..

Questions
1.   If a person enters a shop and begins filming staff and customers, is he liable for trespass? (See *Lincoln Hunt Australia* v *Willesee* (1986) 4 NSWLR 457 and *TV3* v *BSA* [1995] 2 NZLR 720 at 733.)

2.   If a person is driven by another in a car onto the plaintiff's land when at the entrance there is a notice saying 'Private: no entry', is he liable for trespass? If so, when?

Burton v *Winters*
Court of Appeal [1993] 1 WLR 1077; [1993] 3 All ER 847

The defendant built a garage which encroached by $4\frac{1}{2}$ inches onto the plaintiff's land. Having failed to obtain an injunction to have the garage removed the plaintiff built a counter wall on the defendant's land which she refused to remove and was sentenced to 12 months' imprisonment for contempt. She later damaged the garage and was sentenced to two years' imprisonment. On appeal from that order one issue was whether she was entitled to use 'self help' (or exercise a right of abatement) in order to put an end to the trespass by the defendant's garage. Held: the plaintiff had no right of self help and was limited to damages; the sentence of two years was justified.

LLOYD LJ: There is a common law right of self-redress for trespass by encroachment, which was already regarded as an ancient remedy in the time of Bracton. It is similar to the common law right of abatement in the case of nuisance. But at an early stage of our history the right of abatement was supplemented by the assize of nuisance or 'quod permittat prosternere'. The action lay to have the nuisance abated by the defendants and to recover damages: see *Baten's Case* (1610) 9 Co Rep 536. If the plaintiff abated the nuisance himself, he lost his right to recover damages.

With the coming of equity, the common law action for abatement was supplanted by the mandatory injunction. But the remedy by way of self-help was still available . . .

Ever since the assize of nuisance became available, the courts have confined the remedy by way of self-redress to simple cases such as an overhanging branch, or an encroaching root, which would not justify the expense of legal proceedings, and urgent cases which require an immediate remedy. Thus, it was Bracton's view that where there is resort to self-redress, the remedy should be taken without delay. In *Blackstone's Commentaries on the Laws of England*, Book III, chapter 1, we find:

> And the reason why the law allows this private and summary method of doing one's self justice, is because injuries of this kind, which obstruct or annoy such things as are of daily convenience and use, require an immediate remedy; and cannot wait for the slow progress of the ordinary forms of justice.

The modern textbooks, both here and in other common law jurisdictions, follow the same line: see *Salmond & Heuston on Torts*, 20th ed. (1992) p. 485; *Clerk & Lindsell on Torts*, 16th ed. (1989), p. 36; *Fleming, The Law of Torts*, 7th ed. (1987), p. 415 and *Prosser & Keeton, The Law of Torts*, 4th ed. (1971), p. 641. In *Prosser & Keeton* we find:

> Consequently the privilege [of abatement] must be exercised within a reasonable time after knowledge of the nuisance is acquired or should have been acquired by the person entitled to abate; if there has been sufficient delay to allow resort to legal process, the reason for the privilege fails, and the privilege with it.

The authority cited for this proposition is *Moffett* v *Brewer* (1848) Iowa 1 Greene 348, 350, where Greene J said:

This summary method of redressing a grievance, by the act of an injured party, should be regarded with great jealousy, and authorised only in cases of particular emergency, requiring a more speedy remedy than can be had by the ordinary proceedings at law.

Applying this stream of authority to the facts of the present case, it is obvious that it is now far too late for the plaintiff to have her remedy by way of abatement. The garage wall was built in 1975. Not only was there ample time for the plaintiff to 'wait for the slow progress of the ordinary forms of justice;' she actually did so.

But it is not only a question of delay. There is modern House of Lords authority for the proposition that the law does not favour the remedy of abatement: see *Lagan Navigation Co.* v *Lambeg Bleaching, Dyeing and Finishing Co. Ltd* [1927] AC 226, 244, *per* Lord Atkinson.

In my opinion, this never was an appropriate case for self-redress, even if the plaintiff had acted promptly. There was no emergency. There were difficult questions of law and fact to be considered and the remedy by way of self-redress, if it had resulted in the demolition of the garage wall, would have been out of all proportion to the damage suffered by the plaintiff.

But, even if there had ever been a right of self-redress, it ceased when Judge Main refused to grant a mandatory injunction. We are now in a position to answer the question left open by Chitty J in *Lane* v *Capsey* [1891] 3 Ch 411. Self-redress is a summary remedy, which is justified only in clear and simple cases, or in an emergency. Where a plaintiff has applied for a mandatory injunction and failed, the sole justification for a summary remedy has gone. The court has decided the very point in issue. This is so whether the complaint lies in trespass or nuisance. In the present case, the court has decided that the plaintiff is not entitled to have the wall on her side of the boundary removed. It follows that she has no right to remove it herself.

Note

Similar problems arise in relation to trespass to goods, especially in regard to wheel clamping. In *Lloyd* v *DPP* [1992] 1 All ER 982 (a criminal case) the defendant parked his car in a private car park (and so was trespassing) and the car was clamped. He refused to pay the £25 fee and removed his car by cutting two padlocks. He was found guilty of criminal damage. It was said that self help involving the use of force was only available where there was no reasonable alternative, and here the alternative was to pay the fee and sue in the civil courts. But was the use of a wheel clamp by the landowner a reasonable alternative to suing for trespass to land? However, it has now been held that the trespasser has no civil action for the clamping as he is deemed to have consented to the risk that his car might be clamped, such consent being limited to a reasonable release fee which in this case was £40. (See *Arthur* v *Anker* [1996] 2 WLR 602). On the other hand in Scotland it has been held that wheel clamping and demanding a removal fee amounted to extortion and theft: see *Black* v *Carmichael*, 1992 SLT 897.

3 WRONGFUL INTERFERENCE WITH GOODS

The wrongs in this chapter protect a person's interest in the integrity of his goods, and here there is a connection with both commercial law and contract. For example, many cases which deal with the passing of title in commercial law raise that issue by way of an action for conversion.

Although statute collects the various torts under the generic title 'wrongful interference with goods', in fact the substantive rules of trespass to goods and conversion are hardly affected. Trespass to goods deals with any direct interference with a person's possession, whereas conversion deals with more serious invasions of property rights, so as, in effect, to deprive the plaintiff of the benefits of ownership.

TORTS (INTERFERENCE WITH GOODS) ACT 1977

1. Definition of 'wrongful interference with goods'
In this Act 'wrongful interference', or 'wrongful interference with goods', means—
   (a)   conversion of goods (also called trover),
   (b)   trespass to goods,
   (c)   negligence so far as it results in damage to goods or to an interest in goods,
   (d)   subject to section 2, any other tort so far as it results in damage to goods or to an interest in goods,
and references in this Act (however worded) to proceedings for wrongful interference or to a claim or right to claim for wrongful interference shall include references to proceedings by virtue of Part I of the Consumer Protection Act 1987 (product liability) in respect of any damages to goods or to an interest in goods or, as the case may be, to a claim or right to claim by virtue of that Part in respect of any such damage.

2. Abolition of detinue
   (1)   Detinue is abolished.
   (2)   An action lies in conversion for loss or destruction of goods which a bailee has allowed to happen in breach of his duty to his bailor (that is to say it lies in a case which

is not otherwise conversion, but would have been detinue before detinue was abolished).

3. Form of judgment where goods are detained

(1)   In proceedings for wrongful interference against a person who is in possession or in control of the goods relief may be given in accordance with this section, so far as appropriate.

(2)   The relief is—

(a)   an order for delivery of the goods, and for payment of any consequential damages, or

(b)   an order for delivery of the goods, but giving the defendant the alternative of paying damages by reference to the value of the goods, together in either alternative with payment of any consequential damages, or

(c)   damages.

(3)   Subject to rules of court—

(a)   relief shall be given under only one of paragraphs (a), (b) and (c) of subsection (2),

(b)   relief under paragraph (a) of subsection (2) is at the discretion of the court, and the claimant may choose between the others.

(4)   If it is shown to the satisfaction of the court that an order under subsection (2)(a) has not been complied with, the court may—

(a)   revoke the order, or the relevant part of it, and

(b)   make an order for payment of damages by reference to the value of the goods.

(5)   Where an order is made under subsection (2)(b) the defendant may satisfy the order by returning the goods at any time before execution of judgment, but without prejudice to liability to pay any consequential damages.

(6)   An order for delivery of the goods under subsection (2)(a) or (b) may impose such conditions as may be determined by the court, or pursuant to rules of court, and in particular, where damages by reference to the value of the goods would not be the whole of the value of the goods, may require an allowance to be made by the claimant to reflect the difference.

For example, a bailor's action against the bailee may be one in which the measure of damages is not the full value of the goods, and then the court may order delivery of the goods, but require the bailor to pay the bailee a sum reflecting the difference.

(7)   Where under subsection (1) or subsection (2) of section 6 an allowance is to be made in respect of an improvement of the goods, and an order is made under subsection (2)(a) or (b), the court may assess the allowance to be made in respect of the improvement, and by the order require, as a condition for delivery of the goods, that allowance to be made by the claimant.

5. Extinction of title on satisfaction of claim for damages

(1)   Where damages for wrongful interference are, or would fall to be, assessed on the footing that the claimant is being compensated—

(a)   for the whole of his interest in the goods, or

(b)   for the whole of his interest in the goods subject to a reduction for contributory negligence,

payment of the assessed damages (under all heads), or as the case may be settlement of a claim for damages for the wrong (under all heads), extinguishes the claimant's title to that interest.

6. Allowance for improvement of the goods

(1)   If in proceedings for wrongful interference against a person (the 'improver') who has improved the goods, it is shown that the improver acted in the mistaken but honest

belief that he had a good title to them, an allowance shall be made for the extent to which, at the time as at which the goods fall to be valued in assessing damages, the value of the goods is attributable to the improvement.

(2)   If, in proceedings for wrongful interference against a person ('the purchaser') who has purported to purchase the goods—
(a)   from the improver, or
(b)   where after such a purported sale the goods passed by a further purported sale on one or more occasions, on any such occasion,
it is shown that the purchaser acted in good faith, an allowance shall be made on the principle set out in subsection (1).

For example, where a person in good faith buys a stolen car from the improver and is sued in conversion by the true owner the damages may be reduced to reflect the improvement, but if the person who bought the stolen car from the improver sues the improver for failure of consideration, and the improver acted in good faith, subsection (3) below will ordinarily make a comparable reduction in the damages he recovers from the improver.

(3)   If in a case within subsection (2) the person purporting to sell the goods acted in good faith, then in proceedings by the purchaser for recovery of the purchase price because of failure of consideration, or in any other proceedings founded on that failure of consideration, an allowance shall, where appropriate, be made on the principle set out in subsection (1).

(4)   This section applies, with the necessary modifications, to a purported bailment or other disposition of goods as it applies to a purported sale of goods.

8.   Competing rights to the goods

(1)   The defendant in an action for wrongful interference shall be entitled to show, in accordance with rules of court, that a third party has a better right than the plaintiff as respects all or any part of the interest claimed by the plaintiff, or in right of which he sues, and any rule of law (sometimes called jus tertii) to the contrary is abolished.

(2)   Rules of court relating to proceedings for wrongful interference may—
(a)   require the plaintiff to give particulars of his title,
(b)   require the plaintiff to identify any person who, to his knowledge, has or claims any interest in the goods,
(c)   authorise the defendant to apply for directions as to whether any person should be joined with a view to establishing whether he has a better right than the plaintiff, or has a claim as a result of which the defendant might be doubly liable,
(d)   where a party fails to appear on an application within paragraph (c), or to comply with any direction given by the court on such an application, authorise the court to deprive him of any right of action against the defendant for the wrong either unconditionally, or subject to such terms or conditions as may be specified.

11.   Minor amendments

(1)   Contributory negligence is no defence in proceedings founded on conversion, or on intentional trespass to goods.

(2)   Receipt of goods by way of pledge is conversion if the delivery of the goods is conversion.

(3)   Denial of title is not of itself conversion.

Note

Despite the terms of s. 11, contributory negligence may be pleaded in certain circumstances by a bank which collects payment of a cheque: Banking Act 1979, s. 47.

Section 1:   trespass to goods and conversion

Fouldes v *Willoughby*
Court of Exchequer (1841) 8 M & W 540; 157 ER 1153

The defendant operated a steam boat ferry from Birkenhead to Liverpool, and in October 1840 the plaintiff came on board with two horses. It was said that the plaintiff behaved improperly, and in order to induce him to go ashore the defendant took hold of his two horses and led them ashore and let them loose on the road. The plaintiff sued for conversion of the horses. Held: the defendant was not liable for conversion.

LORD ABINGER CB: It is a proposition familiar to all lawyers, that a simple asportation of a chattel, without any intention of making any further use of it, although it may be a sufficient foundation for an action of trespass, is not sufficient to establish a conversion. I had thought that the matter had been fully discussed, and this distinction established, by the numerous cases which have occurred on this subject; but, according to the argument put forward by the plaintiff's counsel today, a bare asportavit is a sufficient foundation to support an action of trover. I entirely dissent from this argument; and therefore I think that the learned Judge was wrong, in telling the jury that the simple fact of putting these horses on shore by the defendant, amounted to a conversion of them to his own use. In my opinion, he should have added to his direction, that it was for them to consider what was the intention of the defendant in so doing. If the object, and whether rightly or wrongfully entertained is immaterial, simply was to induce the plaintiff to go on shore himself, and the defendant, in furtherance of that object, did the act in question, it was not exercising over the horses any right inconsistent with, or adverse to, the rights which the plaintiff had in them. . . . In order to constitute a conversion, it is necessary either that the party taking the goods should intend some use to be made of them, by himself or by those for whom he acts, or that, owing to his act, the goods are destroyed or consumed, to the prejudice of the lawful owner. As an instance of the latter branch of this definition, suppose, in the present case, the defendant had thrown the horses into the water, whereby they were drowned, that would have amounted to an actual conversion; or as in the case cited in the course of the argument, of a person throwing a piece of paper into the water for, in these cases, the chattel is changed in quality, or destroyed altogether. But it has never yet been held, that the single act of removal of a chattel, independent of any claim over it, either in favour of the party himself or any one else, amounts to a conversion of the chattel. In the present case, therefore, the simple removal of these horses by the defendant, for a purpose wholly unconnected with any the least denial of the right of the plaintiff to the possession and enjoyment of them, is no conversion of the horses, and consequently the rule for a new trial ought to be made absolute. . . .

Note
After the horses were left on the road, they were found to be in the stables of an hotel kept by the defendant's brother. The plaintiff refused to pay for their keep and they were sold at auction. Presumably it was accepted that their presence at the brother's hotel was mere coincidence, because if it had been the intention of the defendant to exercise any rights of ownership over the horses that would have been conversion. The point is that the defendant was saying the opposite.

He was saying simply 'get these horses and yourself off my ship'. He never intended to exercise any rights over them. Whether he would have been liable for trespass to goods depends on whether his holding of the horses was justified, and presumably as master of the ship it was.

Section 2:   conversion

Conversion is hard to define, but may generally be regarded as an interference with goods which is seriously inconsistent with the plaintiff's rights over the goods. In other words, have the goods been essentially lost to the plaintiff? Title to goods is often resolved by an action for conversion, and this may involve complicated questions of commercial law. For example if A's car is bought fraudulently by B who sells it to C, A may sue C in conversion, and the outcome will depend on rules of commercial law as to whether A passed title to B. However, such questions belong more appropriately in courses on commercial law and are not dealt with here. The object of this section is only to give examples of the basic rules of the tort of conversion, which may be committed in a variety of ways, some of which are discussed below.

A: Withholding possession

Perry v British Railways Board
Chancery Division [1980] ICR 743; [1980] 1 WLR 13; [1980] 2 All ER 579

In 1980 there was a strike by steelworkers which was supported by members of the National Union of Railwaymen. The plaintiffs were steel stockholders who owned 500 tons of steel which was lying in British Rail depots. For fear of exacerbating industrial relations, British Rail, while admitting that the steel belonged to the plaintiffs, refused to give it up. Held: the defendants were liable for conversion.

MEGARRY V-C: The main thrust of Mr Gidley Scott's contentions was that as a mere refusal in response to a demand was not itself a conversion, though it could be evidence of a conversion (see *Clerk & Lindsell on Torts*, p. 678), and the defendants had at no stage denied the plaintiffs' title to the steel, or attempted to deal with it in any way inconsistent with the plaintiffs' rights, there had been no conversion within the true meaning of that term. There was no conversion, he said, if the reason for the refusal to release the goods was a genuine or reasonable fear, unless this meant that the owner could never have his goods. He accepted that there could be a conversion if the threat induced a withholding of the goods for a long period, measured in months or years, but not if it was merely a matter of days or weeks; and he said that the present case fell into this latter category, though he could not be persuaded to prophesy when the strike of steel workers would end. This contention was based to some extent, I think, on words of Bramwell B in *Hiort v Bott* (1874) LR 9 Ex 86, 89. The judge there said that a good description of what constituted a conversion was 'where a man does an unauthorized act which deprives another of his property permanently or for an indefinite time'; and I think that Mr Gidley Scott interpreted 'indefinite time' as meaning a period which was not only uncertain in length but also of substantial duration.

There seems to me to be considerable force in the observation in *Clerk & Lindsell on Torts*, p. 682 that 'It is perhaps impossible to frame a definition which will cover every conceivable case.' What I have to consider here is a case in which the defendants are in effect saying to the plaintiffs: 'We admit that the steel is yours and that you are entitled to possession of it. Yet because we fear that industrial action may be taken against us if we permit you to remove it, we have refused to allow you to collect it for some weeks now, despite your demands, and we will continue to refuse to allow you to collect it until our fears have been removed.' Looking at the matter as one of principle, I would conclude that this is a clear case of conversion. The defendants are denying the plaintiffs most of the rights of ownership, including the right to possession, for a period which clearly is indefinite. It may be short, or it may be long; but it is plainly uncertain. I do not think that a period which will not end until the defendants reach the conclusion that their fears no longer justify the withholding of the steel can very well be called 'definite.' There is a detention of the steel which is consciously adverse to the plaintiffs' rights, and this seems to me to be of the essence of at least one form of conversion. A denial of possession to the plaintiffs does not cease to be a denial by being accompanied by a statement that the plaintiffs are entitled to the possession that is being denied to them.

It seems to me that this view is consistent with the authorities put before me, and also with some others. The cause of action in conversion was stated in the Common Law Procedure Act 1852, as follows: 'That the defendant converted to his own use, or wrongfully deprived the plaintiff of the use and possession of the plaintiff's goods.' I do not see how it could be said that the defendants are not at the moment wrongfully depriving the plaintiffs of the use and possession of the plaintiffs' goods, unless the defendants' fear of industrial action could be said to prevent their refusal to release the steel from being wrongful. . . .

My conclusion is accordingly that this contention of the defendants fails. For the defendants to withhold the steel from the plaintiffs is a wrongful interference with goods within the Act of 1977 unless the reason for the withholding provides a justification. I cannot see that it does. This is no brief withholding made merely in order that the defendants may verify the plaintiffs' title to the steel, or for some other purpose to confirm that the delivery of the steel would be proper. This is a withholding despite the plain right of the plaintiffs to the ownership and possession of the steel, on the ground that the defendants fear unpleasant consequences if they do not deny the plaintiffs what they are entitled to.

Note

Following the order some of the steel was loaded onto British Rail lorries and taken to the plaintiffs' premises. However, the steel was never delivered as there was not only a picket of steelworkers but also members of the Transport and General Workers Union said that they would not unload the steel, which in the event was returned to the British Rail depots.

B: Wrongful disposition

Hollins v Fowler
House of Lords (1875) LR 7 HL 757; 44 LJQB 169; 33 LT 73

Fowler & Co., the plaintiffs, sold 13 bales of cotton to H. K. Bayley for a shilling a pound. Bayley never paid Fowler, but sold the cotton to the defendants Hollins & Co., for 11d. per pound, and they sold it on to Micholls & Co. who spun it into yarn. Thus, due to the fraud of Bayley the value of the cotton had been abstracted, and the question was which of two innocent parties (the person who sold the cotton to the rogue or the person who bought it from him) should bear the loss. Held: dismissing the appeal, that the defendants (the buyers) were liable for conversion.

LORD CHELMSFORD: The question upon the facts is whether the Defendants were guilty of a conversion. There can be no doubt that the property and legal right of possession of the cotton remained in the Plaintiffs; and *Bayley,* who had fraudulently obtained possession of it, could not give a title to any one to whom he transferred the possession, however ignorant the transferee might be of the means by which *Bayley* acquired it. A great deal of argument was directed to the question, What amounts in law to a conversion? I agree with what was said by Mr Justice *Brett* in the Court of Exchequer Chamber in this case: 'That in all cases where we have to apply legal principles to facts there are found many cases about which there can be no doubt, some being clear for the Plaintiff and some clear for the Defendant; and that the difficulties arise in doubtful cases on the border line between the two.' But to my mind the proposition which fits this case is, that any person who, however innocently, obtains possession of the goods of a person who has been fraudulently deprived of them, and disposes of them, whether for his own benefit or that of any other person, is guilty of a conversion.

LORD O'HAGAN: The result of your Lordships' consideration of this case will, I fear, inflict hardship upon the Defendants. They are innocent of any actual wrongdoing, but those with whom they are in conflict are as innocent as they, and we can only regard the liability attached to them by the law, without being affected in our judgment by its unpleasant consequences. They appear to me to have been guilty of a conversion in dealing with the Plaintiffs' property, and disposing of it to other persons, without any right or authority to do so. Confessedly, that property never passed from the Plaintiffs. *Bayley's* fraud vitiated the sale to him, and he could not convey to the Defendants what in no way belonged to himself. They paid for it, and sampled it, and then disposed of it to Mr *Micholls,* whom they reasonably expected to make the purchase, but who had not made it, and was not bound to make it, when the void sale was effected with *Bayley,* and the Defendants got possession of the Plaintiffs' cotton. They had it conveyed to the railway station and forwarded to the purchaser in *Stockport,* who paid for it and made yarn of it. It seems to me that this state of facts entitles the Plaintiffs to recover in an action of trover, which rests on a right of property, wrongfully interfered with, at the peril of the person interfering with it, and whether the interference be for his own use or that of anybody else.

Notes

1. In *Bishopsgate Motor Finance Corp.* v *Transport Brakes Ltd* [1949] 1 KB 332, Denning LJ said:

> In the development of our law, two principles have striven for mastery. The first is for the protection of property; no one can give a better title than he himself possesses. The second is for the protection of commercial transactions: the person who takes in good faith and for value without notice should get a better title. The first principle has held sway for a long time, but it has been modified by the common law itself and by statute so as to meet the needs of our times.

2. A striking example of the fact that an honest belief that you are entitled to deal with the goods is no defence is provided by **Wilson v New Brighton**

Panelbeaters [1989] 1 NZLR 74, where one Walters telephoned the defendants, a towing company, and fraudulently asked them to collect a car from a house and take it to Worcester Street, Christchurch. Walters claimed that he had bought the car, but this was not so and the car belonged to the plaintiff. The towing company was not negligent but was held liable in conversion for delivering the car to Walters. Equally, an innocent auctioneer can be liable for selling the plaintiff's goods: *Union Transport Finance v British Car Auctions* [1978] 2 All ER 385.

3. There have been a number of exceptions to the principle enunciated in *Hollins v Fowler* and these more properly belong to a course on commercial law. See, for example, Sale of Goods Act 1979, ss. 24 and 25 (sale by a buyer in possession with the consent of the seller, and sale by a seller in possession with the consent of the buyer). Also see Hire Purchase Act 1964, s.27 (see Consumer Credit Act 1974, Sch. 4), which allows a person who sells a car in breach of a hire purchase agreement to give a good title to a private purchaser who acquires the car in good faith.

Question
In *Hollins v Fowler*, how did the rogue get away with the fraud? Who could have prevented it, and who should take the risk? A sells a car to a rogue, B, and accepts a cheque in payment which turns out to be worthless. B sells the car to C. How could the loss have been prevented? Who will bear the loss under the present law, and should it be changed?

C: *Wrongful use*

Penfolds Wines v Elliott
High Court of Australia (1946–47) 74 CLR 204

The plaintiffs were wine merchants who distributed wine in bottles marked 'This bottle is the property of Penfolds Wines Ltd.' The defendant ran an hotel and was in the habit of filling bottles for customers from a barrel of wine. The defendant's brother brought in two Penfolds bottles which the defendant filled with other wine. Held: dismissing the appeal, that the defendant was not liable for either trespass to goods or conversion.

DIXON J: . . . Conversion appears to me to be equally out of the question. . . . The essence of conversion is a dealing with a chattel in a manner repugnant to the immediate right of possession of the person who has the property or special property in the chattel. It may take the form of a disposal of the goods by way of sale, or pledge or other intended transfer of an interest followed by delivery, of the destruction or change of the nature or character of the thing, as for example, pouring water into wine or cutting the seals from a deed, or of an appropriation evidenced by refusal to deliver or other denial of title. But damage to the chattel is not conversion, nor is use, nor is a transfer of possession otherwise than for the purpose of affecting the immediate right to possession, nor is it always conversion to lose the goods beyond hope of recovery. An intent to do that which would deprive 'the true owner' of his immediate right to possession or impair it may be said to form the essential ground of the tort. There is nothing in the course followed by the respondent in supplying wine to his customers who brought bottles to receive it involving any deprival or impairment of property in the bottles, that is of the immediate right to possession. The re-delivery of the bottles to the persons who left them could not amount to a conversion: see per *Bigham* J in *Union Credit Bank Ltd* v *Mersey Docks and Harbour Board*, (1899) 2 QB 205. The re-delivery could not amount to a conversion because, though involving a transfer of possession, its purpose was not to confer any right over the property in the bottles, but merely to return or restore them to the person who had left them there to be filled. Indeed if they had been withheld from that person, he could have complained, at least theoretically, of an actionable wrong, that is unless it were done as a result of the intervention of the true owners and upon their demand.

To fill the bottles with wine at the request of the person who brought them could not in itself be a conversion. It was not a use of the bottles involving any exercise of dominion over them, however transitory. There was, of course, no asportation and the older cases to the effect that an asportation of chattels for the use of the person taking them, or of a third person, may amount to a conversion can have no application. In any event, an intention cannot be imputed to the respondent of taking to himself the property in the bottles or of depriving the appellants thereof or of asserting any title therein or of denying that of the appellants. It was not an act derogating from the proprietary right of the appellant. There was no user on the footing that the respondent was owner or that the appellants had no title, in short no act of ownership. The essential elements of liability in trover are lacking.

Question
If I receive a milk bottle from the milkman which is labelled 'property of Happy Cow Dairies', and I fill it with paraffin and place it in my garage, have I committed a conversion? What if a week later, as I had intended all the time, I wash it out and put it on the doorstep?

D: Finders: finder v occupier

Parker v British Airways
[1982] QB 1004; [1982] 2 WLR 50; [1982] 1 All ER 834

The defendants operated an 'executive' lounge at Heathrow Airport to which only holders of first class tickets or members of the Executive Club were admitted. While in this lounge the plaintiff found on the floor a gold bracelet which he handed to an official of the airline together with his name and address. When the true owner could not be found the defendants sold the bracelet for £850, but refused to pay the proceeds to the plaintiff. Held: dismissing the appeal, that the defendants were liable for conversion.

DONALDSON LJ: One of the great merits of the common law is that it is usually sufficiently flexible to take account of the changing needs of a continually changing society. Accordingly, Mr Desch rightly directed our attention to the need to have common law rules which will facilitate rather than hinder the ascertainment of the true owner of a lost chattel and a reunion between the two. In his submission the law should confer rights upon the occupier of the land where a lost chattel was found which were superior to those of the finder, since the loser is more likely to make inquiries at the place of loss. I see the force of this submission. However, I think that it is also true that if this were the rule and finders had no prospect of any reward, they would be tempted to pass by without taking any action or to become concealed keepers of articles which they found. Furthermore, if a finder is under a duty to take reasonable steps to reunite the true owner with his lost property, this will usually involve an obligation to inform the occupier of the land of the fact that the article has been found and where it is to be kept.

In a dispute of this nature there are two quite separate problems. The first is to determine the general principles or rules of law which are applicable. The second, which is often the more troublesome, is to apply those principles or rules to the factual situation. I propose to confront those two problems separately.

Rights and obligations of the finder

1.   The finder of a chattel acquires no rights over it unless (a) it has been abandoned or lost and (b) he takes it into his care and control.

2.   The finder of a chattel acquires very limited rights over it if he takes it into his care and control with dishonest intent or in the course of trespassing.

3.   Subject to the foregoing and to point 4 below, a finder of a chattel, whilst not acquiring any absolute property or ownership in the chattel, acquires a right to keep it against all but the true owner or those in a position to claim through the true owner or one who can assert a prior right to keep the chattel which was subsisting at the time when the finder took the chattel into his care and control.

4.   Unless otherwise agreed, any servant or agent who finds a chattel in the course of his employment or agency and not wholly incidentally or collaterally thereto and who takes it into his care and control does so on behalf of his employer or principal who acquires a finder's right to the exclusion of those of the actual finder.

5.   A person having a finder's rights has an obligation to take such measures as in all the circumstances are reasonable to acquaint the true owner of the finding and present whereabouts of the chattel and to care for it meanwhile.

Rights and liabilities of an occupier

1.   An occupier of land has rights superior to those of a finder over chattels in or attached to that land and an occupier of a building has similar rights in respect of chattels attached to that building, whether in either case the occupier is aware of the presence of the chattel.

2.   An occupier of a building has rights superior to those of a finder over chattels upon or in, but not attached to, that building if, but only if, before the chattel is found, he has manifested an intention to exercise control over the building and the things which may be upon it or in it.

3.   An occupier who manifests an intention to exercise control over a building and the things which may be upon or in it so as to acquire rights superior to those of a finder is under an obligation to take such measures as in all the circumstances are reasonable to ensure that lost chattels are found and, upon their being found, whether by him or by a third party, to acquaint the true owner of the finding and to care for the chattels meanwhile. The manifestation of intention may be express or implied from the circumstances including, in particular, the circumstance that the occupier manifestly accepts or is obliged by law to accept liability for chattels lost upon his 'premises,' e.g., an innkeeper or carrier's liability.

4.   An 'occupier' of a chattel, e.g., a ship, motor car, caravan or aircraft, is to be treated as if he were the occupier of a building for the purposes of the foregoing rules.

Application to the instant case

The plaintiff was not a trespasser in the executive lounge and, in taking the bracelet into his care and control, he was acting with obvious honesty. Prima facie, therefore, he had a full finder's rights and obligations. He in fact discharged those obligations by handing the bracelet to an official of the defendants' although he could equally have done so by handing the bracelet to the police or in other ways such as informing the police of the find and himself caring for the bracelet.

The plaintiff's prima facie entitlement to a finder's rights was not displaced in favour of an employer or principal. There is no evidence that he was in the executive lounge in the course of any employment or agency and, if he was, the finding of the bracelet was quite clearly collateral thereto. The position would have been otherwise in the case of most or perhaps all the defendants' employees.

The defendants, for their part, cannot assert any title to the bracelet based upon the rights of an occupier over chattels attached to a building. The bracelet was lying loose on the floor. Their claim must, on my view of the law, be based upon a manifest intention to exercise control over the lounge and all things which might be in it. The evidence is that they claimed the right to decide who should and who should not be permitted to enter and use the lounge, but their control was in general exercised upon the basis of classes or categories of user and the availability of the lounge in the light of the need to clean and maintain it. I do not doubt that they also claimed the right to exclude individual undesirables, such as drunks, and specific types of chattels such as guns and bombs. But this control has no real relevance to a manifest intention to assert custody and control over lost articles. There was no evidence that they searched for such articles regularly or at all.

Evidence was given of staff instructions which govern the action to be taken by employees of the defendants if they found lost articles or lost chattels were handed to them. But these instructions were not published to users of the lounge and in any event I think that they were intended to do no more than instruct the staff on how they were to act in the course of their employment.

It was suggested in argument that in some circumstances the intention of the occupier to assert control over articles lost on his premises speaks for itself. I think that this is right. If a bank manager saw fit to show me round a vault containing safe deposits and I found a gold bracelet on the floor, I should have no doubt that the bank had a better title than I, and the reason is the manifest intention to exercise a very high degree of control. At the other extreme is the park to which the public has unrestricted access during daylight hours. During those hours there is no manifest intention to exercise any such control. In between these extremes are the forecourts of petrol filling stations, unfenced front gardens of private houses, the public parts of shops and supermarkets as part of an almost infinite variety of land, premises and circumstances.

This lounge is in the middle band and in my judgment, on the evidence available, there was no sufficient manifestation of any intention to exercise control over lost property before it was found such as would give the defendants a right superior to that of the plaintiff or indeed any right over the bracelet. As the true owner has never come forward, it is a case of 'finders keepers.'

Notes
1. *Articles attached to or under land.* **Waverley Borough Council v Fletcher** [1995] 4 All ER 756 has re-affirmed the well-known principle that where an article is attached to land or is under the soil, the occupier has the better title, and this is so even if the land is public open space. In that case the respondent used a metal detector to find a valuable mediaeval gold brooch some 9 inches under the soil, and it was held that even though it was a public park the local authority, as occupier, had the better title.
2. *Owner v Finder.* Where the dispute is between the true owner and the finder, the true owner will always win. The only problem is usually to

determine whether in fact the claimant is the true owner or whether, for example, he has abandoned the goods. For example, in **Moffat v Kazana** [1969] 2 QB 152 the plaintiff had owned a house in which he had hidden (in the chimney) a biscuit tin containing £1,987 in £1 notes. When he sold the house the plaintiff failed to take the tin with him and it was later discovered by the defendants. It was held that the conveyance of the house did not transfer title to the biscuit tin and therefore the plaintiff was still the true owner.

If a golf ball is lost has it been abandoned? Is it conversion for (a) a trespasser, or (b) another golfer to pick up and keep a lost ball? If so, against whom? See *Hibbert* v *McKiernan* [1948] 2 KB 142.

3.   *Finder* v *stranger.*   Title is relative and therefore the winner will be the person who can establish the earlier possession. Thus, in a dispute between a finder and a person who subsequently obtains possession, the finder will win. (But note that under the Torts Act 1977, s. 8 a defendant can now say, 'it may not be mine, but it's not yours either'.) See **Armory v Delamirie** (1721) 93 ER 664, where the plaintiff was a chimney sweep's boy who found a jewel: he showed it to the defendant who was a goldsmith's apprentice. The apprentice refused to return the jewel and he was liable for conversion. Pratt CJ said 'The finder of a jewel, though he does not by such finding acquire an absolute property or ownership, yet he has such a property as will enable him to keep it against all but the rightful owner, and consequently may maintain trover.'

4.   *Treasure trove.*   The basic rule is that where a person hid gold or silver with the intention of returning to reclaim it, the treasure belongs to the Crown if the original depositor is unknown. On the protection of antiquities, see Palmer, 'Treasure Trove and the Protection of Antiquities' (1981) 44 MLR 178 and the Ancient Monuments and Archaeological Areas Act 1979, s. 42, which prohibits the use of metal detectors in a protected place. The Treasure Bill 1996 proposes the abolition of treasure trove and its replacement by a new system whereby treasure is: (a) any object (other than a coin) which is at least 300 years old and has a gold or silver content of at least 5 per cent; (b) one of at least two coins in the same find at least 300 years old and with a silver or gold content of at least 5 per cent; (c) one of at least 10 coins in the same find at least 300 years old; (d) any object at least 200 years old of a class designated by the Secretary of State as being of outstanding historical, archaeological or cultural importance.

The decision whether an object is treasure is made by a coroner and, if it is, it vests (subject to any prior rights) in the Crown. A reward is payable to the finder, the occupier or any other person with an interest in the land.

4 NEGLIGENCE: THE BASIC PRINCIPLES OF DUTY OF CARE

The arrangement of this and subsequent chapters
Negligence is a large and amorphous subject, and all parts of the law on it are interlocking. It is often difficult to understand one part without having studied the whole, and therefore in arranging the material I have decided to set out the basic principles first, leaving the more sophisticated developments until later. Accordingly the next three chapters on duty, standard of care, causation and remoteness of damage aim to explain the basic negligence action, principally in relation to an action for personal injuries or property damage where the concepts are easiest to understand. More difficult duty problems, such as liability for statements or for pure economic loss, will be dealt with later.

Duty is but one element in the tort of negligence, for it must be shown that not only was the defendant under a duty towards the plaintiff to be careful, but also that he failed to achieve the required standard of care and that that failure caused the damage, and finally that the damage was not too remote a consequence of the act.

Duty is about relationships, and it must be shown that the particular defendant stood in the required relationship to the plaintiff such that he came under an obligation to use care towards him. This relationship is sometimes referred to as 'proximity'. In cases of personal injury or damage to property the necessary relationship is established if the defendant ought to have foreseen damage to the plaintiff whereas in other cases a closer relationship may be required. Thus, duty means 'proximity' in the legal sense (this has nothing to do with geographical proximity), and proximity means the level of closeness of relationship required for the particular kind of damage. Thus, a closer relationship than mere foresight will be required for some kinds of damage, such as damage caused by statements (this will be dealt with later). Foresight of damage is a necessary ingredient in all cases of negligence and finally there is a policy element which is expressed by the view that it must be just and reasonable to impose a duty in that class of case.

Accordingly, in order to establish a duty of care it must be shown that:
 (a)   some damage was foreseeable to a foreseeable plaintiff;
 (b)   there is a sufficiently close relationship between the parties to establish
a duty in that class of case (proximity); and
 (c)   that it is just and reasonable to impose a duty.
 Duty of care is one of the ways in which risks can be allocated in society, i.e.
should potential plaintiffs or potential defendants bear the risk of injury
occurring? This will have both social and economic implications, and hence the
technical criteria of duty or the other concepts in negligence should not be
taken too literally. They are merely mechanical devices for performing and
expressing something deeper, that is a decision or an understanding about how
risks should be allocated. This point was well expressed by McDonald J in
Nova Mink v *Trans Canada Airlines* [1951] 2 DLR 241 when he said:

> When upon analysis of the circumstances and application of the appropriate
> formula, a court holds that the defendant was under a duty of care, the court
> is stating as a conclusion of law what is really a conclusion of policy as to
> responsibility for conduct involving unreasonable risk. It is saying that such
> circumstances presented such an appreciable risk of harm to others as to
> entitle them to protection against unreasonable conduct by the actor. It is
> declaring also that a cause of action can exist in other situations of the same
> type, and *pro tanto* is moving in the direction of establishing further categories
> of human relationships entailing recognised duties of care. . . . Accordingly
> there is always a large element of judicial policy and social expediency
> involved in the determination of the duty problem, however it may be
> obscured by the use of the traditional formulae. . . .

This chapter explains these formulae, but one must always bear in mind the
purpose they fulfil.

Section 1: proximity

Donoghue v *Stevenson*
House of Lords [1932] AC 562; 1932 SC 31; 147 LJ 281

At about 8.50 p.m. on 26 August 1928, Mrs May Donoghue (whose maiden
name was Mc'Alister) went to a cafe owned by Francis Minchella, known as
the Wellmeadow Cafe, in Wellmeadow Road, Paisley. A friend of hers
(probably a female friend) bought a bottle of ginger beer and an ice cream.
The bottle was made of opaque glass. Minchella poured part of the contents
into a tumbler containing the ice cream. Mrs Donoghue drank some of this
and the friend then poured the remainder of the ginger beer into the glass. It
was said that a decomposed snail floated out of the bottle and the pursuer
claimed that she suffered shock and gastro-enteritis, and asked for £500
damages from the manufacturer of the ginger beer, David Stevenson of

Paisley. The pursuer claimed that a manufacturer of products was liable in negligence to a person injured by the product, but the defendant claimed that there could be no liability as there was no contract between himself and the pursuer. Held: on the point of law involved, that such a defendant could be liable to such a plaintiff in negligence.

LORD ATKIN: We are solely concerned with the question whether, as a matter of law in the circumstances alleged, the defender owed any duty to the pursuer to take care.

It is remarkable how difficult it is to find in the English authorities statements of general application defining the relations between parties that give rise to the duty. The Courts are concerned with the particular relations which come before them in actual litigation, and it is sufficient to say whether the duty exists in those circumstances. The result is that the Courts have been engaged upon an elaborate classification of duties as they exist in respect of property, whether real or personal, with further divisions as to ownership, occupation or control, and distinctions based on the particular relations of the one side or the other, whether manufacturer, salesman or landlord, customer, tenant, stranger, and so on. In this way it can be ascertained at any time whether the law recognizes a duty, but only where the case can be referred to some particular species which has been examined and classified. And yet the duty which is common to all the cases where liability is established must logically be based upon some element common to the cases where it is found to exist. To seek a complete logical definition of the general principle is probably to go beyond the function of the judge, for the more general the definition the more likely it is to omit essentials or to introduce non-essentials. The attempt was made by Brett MR in *Heaven* v *Pender* (1883) 11 QBD 503, 509, in a definition to which I will later refer. As framed, it was demonstrably too wide, though it appears to me, if properly limited, to be capable of affording a valuable practical guide.

At present I content myself with pointing out that in English law there must be, and is, some general conception of relations giving rise to a duty of care, of which the particular cases found in the books are but instances. The liability for negligence, whether you style it such or treat it as in other systems as a species of 'culpa,' is no doubt based upon a general public sentiment of moral wrongdoing for which the offender must pay. But acts or omissions which any moral code would censure cannot in a practical world be treated so as to give a right to every person injured by them to demand relief. In this way rules of law arise which limit the range of complainants and the extent of their remedy. The rule that you are to love your neighbour becomes in law, you must not injure your neighbour; and the lawyer's question, Who is my neighbour? receives a restricted reply. You must take reasonable care to avoid acts or omissions which you can reasonably foresee would be likely to injure your neighbour. Who, then, in law is my neighbour? The answer seems to be — persons who are so closely and directly affected by my act that I ought reasonably to have them in contemplation as being so affected when I am directing my mind to the acts or omissions which are called in question. This appears to me to be the doctrine of *Heaven* v *Pender*, as laid down by Lord Esher (then Brett MR) when it is limited by the notion of proximity introduced by Lord Esher himself and A. L. Smith LJ in *Le Lievre* v *Gould* [1893] 1 QB 491. Lord Esher says: 'That case established that, under certain circumstances, one man may owe a duty to another, even though there is no contract between them. If one man is near to another, or is near to the property of another, a duty lies upon him not to do that which may cause a personal injury to that other, or may injure his property.' So A. L. Smith LJ: 'The decision of *Heaven* v *Pender* 11 QBD 503, 509 was founded upon the principle, that a duty to take due care did arise when the person or property of one was in such proximity to the person or property of another that, if due care was not taken, damage might be done by the one to the other.' I think that this sufficiently states the truth if proximity be not confined to mere physical proximity, but be used, as I think it was intended, to extend to such close and direct relations that the act complained of directly affects a person whom the person alleged to be bound to take care would know would be directly affected by his careless act. . . .

. . . I venture to say that in the branch of the law which deals with civil wrongs, dependent in England at any rate entirely upon the application by judges of general principles also formulated by judges, it is of particular importance to guard against the danger of stating propositions of law in wider terms than is necessary, lest essential factors be omitted in the wider survey and the inherent adaptability of English law be unduly restricted. For this reason it is very necessary in considering reported cases in the law of torts that the actual decision alone should carry authority, proper weight, of course, being given to the dicta of the judges. . . .

LORD MACMILLAN: It humbly appears to me that the diversity of view which is exhibited in such cases as *George* v *Skivington* LR 5 Ex 1 on the one hand and *Blacker* v *Lake & Elliot, Ld* 106 LT 533, on the other hand — to take two extreme instances — is explained by the fact that in the discussion of the topic which now engages your Lordships' attention two rival principles of the law find a meeting place where each has contended for supremacy. On the one hand, there is the well established principle that no one other than a party to a contract can complain of a breach of that contract. On the other hand, there is the equally well established doctrine that negligence apart from contract gives a right of action to the party injured by that negligence — and here I use the term negligence, of course, in its technical legal sense, implying a duty owed and neglected. The fact that there is a contractual relationship between the parties which may give rise to an action for breach of contract, does not exclude the co-existence of a right of action founded on negligence as between the same parties, independently of the contract, though arising out of the relationship in fact brought about by the contract. Of this the best illustration is the right of the injured railway passenger to sue the railway company either for breach of the contract of safe carriage or for negligence in carrying him. And there is no reason why the same set of facts should not give one person a right of action in contract and another person a right of action in tort. . . .

Where, as in cases like the present, so much depends upon the avenue of approach to the question, it is very easy to take the wrong turning. If you begin with the sale by the manufacturer to the retail dealer, then the consumer who purchases from the retailer is at once seen to be a stranger to the contract between the retailer and the manufacturer and so disentitled to sue upon it. There is no contractual relation between the manufacturer and the consumer; and thus the plaintiff, if he is to succeed, is driven to try to bring himself within one or other of the exceptional cases where the strictness of the rule that none but a party to a contract can found on a breach of that contract has been mitigated in the public interest, as it has been in the case of a person who issues a chattel which is inherently dangerous or which he knows to be in a dangerous condition. If, on the other hand, you disregard the fact that the circumstances of the case at one stage include the existence of a contract of sale between the manufacturer and the retailer, and approach the question by asking whether there is evidence of carelessness on the part of the manufacturer, and whether he owed a duty to be careful in a question with the party who has been injured in consequence of his want of care, the circumstance that the injured party was not a party to the incidental contract of sale becomes irrelevant, and his title to sue the manufacturer is unaffected by that circumstance . . .

. . . Having regard to the inconclusive state of the authorities in the Courts below and to the fact that the important question involved is now before your Lordships for the first time, I think it desirable to consider the matter from the point of view of the principles applicable to this branch of law which are admittedly common to both English and Scottish jurisprudence.

The law takes no cognizance of carelessness in the abstract. It concerns itself with carelessness only where there is a duty to take care and where failure in that duty has caused damage. In such circumstances carelessness assumes the legal quality of negligence and entails the consequences in law of negligence. What, then, are the circumstances which give rise to this duty to take care? In the daily contacts of social and business life human beings are thrown into, or place themselves in, an infinite variety of relations with their fellows; and the law can refer only to the standards of the reasonable man in order to determine whether any particular relation gives rise to a duty to take care as between those who stand in that relation to each other. The grounds of action may be as various and manifold as human errancy; and the conception of legal responsibility may develop in adaptation to altering social conditions and standards. The criterion of judgment must adjust and adapt itself to the changing circumstances of life. The categories of negligence are never closed. The cardinal principle of liability is that the party complained of should owe to the party complaining a duty to take care, and that the party complaining should be able to prove that he has suffered damage in consequence of a breach of that duty. Where there is room for diversity of view, it is in determining what circumstances will establish such a relationship between the parties as to give rise, on the one side, to a duty to take care, and on the other side to a right to have care taken.

Note

The ruling of the House of Lords was on a point of law only, on the assumption that the facts alleged were true. The trial of the actual action was set down for 10 January 1932, but by then Stevenson had died and the case was settled for £200. For the family history of Mrs Donoghue and other interesting points about the case, see Rodger, 'Mrs Donoghue and Alfenus Varus' [1988] CLP 1 and W. McBryde, '*Donoghue* v *Stevenson*: the story of the snail in the bottle case' in *Obligations in Context*, A. Gamble (ed.) (1990). See also Heuston, '*Donoghue* v *Stevenson* in retrospect' (1957) 20 MLR 1.

Anns v Merton London Borough Council
House of Lords [1978] AC 728; [1977] 2 All ER 492; [1977] 2 WLR 1024

The case concerned the potential liability of a local authority towards a lessee of a building for failure to ensure that the building complied with deposited plans, particularly in relation to the depth of the foundations. The actual decision has been overruled in *Murphy* v *Brentwood District Council* [1991] 1 AC 398 (see p. 57) and the dictum has also been disapproved, but is reproduced here for ease of reference.

LORD WILBERFORCE: Through the trilogy of cases in this House — *Donoghue* v *Stevenson* [1932] AC 562, *Hedley Byrne & Co. Ltd* v *Heller & Partners Ltd* [1964] AC 465, and *Dorset Yacht Co. Ltd* v *Home Office* [1970] AC 1004, the position has now been reached that in order to establish that a duty of care arises in a particular situation, it is

not necessary to bring the facts of that situation within those of previous situations in
which a duty of care has been held to exist. Rather the question has to be approached in
two stages. First one has to ask whether, as between the alleged wrongdoer and the
person who has suffered damage there is a sufficient relationship of proximity or
neighbourhood such that, in the reasonable contemplation of the former, carelessness
on his part may be likely to cause damage to the latter — in which case a prima facie duty
of care arises. Secondly, if the first question is answered affirmatively, it is necessary to
consider whether there are any considerations which ought to negative, or to reduce or
limit the scope of the duty or the class of person to whom it is owed or the damages to
which a breach of it may give rise . . . .

Note
This dictum is no longer followed but is included for reference purposes. For
discussion of the retreat from the *Anns* principle see Kidner, 'Resiling from the
Anns principle: the variable nature of proximity in negligence' (1987) 7 LS 319.

Caparo v Dickman
House of Lords [1990] 2 AC 605; [1990] 1 All ER 568

This case concerned the liability of auditors for negligent misstatement, and
the substantive issues are dealt with in Chapter 10. The extracts below deal
with general issues as to duty of care.

LORD BRIDGE: . . . since the *Anns* case a series of decisions of the Privy Council and
of your Lordships' House, notably in judgments and speeches delivered by Lord Keith
of Kinkel, have emphasised the inability of any single general principle to provide a
practical test which can be applied to every situation to determine whether a duty of care
is owed and, if so what is its scope: see *Governors of Peabody Donation Fund* v *Sir Lindsay
Parkinson & Co. Ltd* [1985] AC 210, 239F–241C, *Yuen Kun Yeu* v *Attorney-General of
Hong Kong* [1988] AC 175, 190E–194F; *Rowling* v *Takaro Properties Ltd* [1988] AC 473,
501D–G; *Hill* v *Chief Constable of West Yorkshire* [1989] AC 53, 60B–D. What emerges
is that, in addition to the foreseeability of damage, necessary ingredients in any situation
giving rise to a duty of care are that there should exist between the party owing the duty
and the party to whom it is owed a relationship characterised by the law as one of
'proximity' or 'neighbourhood' and that the situation should be one in which the court
considers it fair, just and reasonable that the law should impose a duty of a given scope
upon the one party for the benefit of the other. But it is implicit in the passages referred
to that the concepts of proximity and fairness embodied in these additional ingredients
are not susceptible of any such precise definition as would be necessary to give them
utility as practical tests, but amount in effect to little more than convenient labels to
attach to the features of different specific situations which, on a detailed examination of
all the circumstances, the law recognises pragmatically as giving rise to a duty of care of
a given scope. Whilst recognising, of course, the importance of the underlying general
principles common to the whole field of negligence, I think the law has now moved in
the direction of attaching greater significance to the more traditional categorisation of
distinct and recognisable situations as guides to the existence, the scope and the limits
of the varied duties of care which the law imposes. We must now, I think, recognise the
wisdom of the words of Brennan J in the High Court of Australia in *Sutherland Shire
Council* v *Heyman* (1985) 60 ALR 1, 43–44, where he said:

It is preferable, in my view, that the law should develop novel categories of negligence incrementally and by analogy with established categories, rather than by a massive extension of a prima facie duty of care restrained only by indefinable 'considerations which ought to negative, or to reduce or limit the cope of the duty or the class of person to whom it is owed.'

One of the most important distinctions always to be observed lies in the law's essentially different approach to the different kinds of damage which one party may have suffered in consequence of the acts or omissions of another. It is one thing to owe a duty of care to avoid causing injury to the person or property of others. It is quite another to avoid causing others to suffer purely economic loss. . . .

LORD ROSKILL: . . . I agree with your Lordships that it has now to be accepted that there is no simple formula or touchstone to which recourse can be had in order to provide in every case a ready answer to the questions whether, given certain facts, the law will or will not impose liability for negligence or in cases where such liability can be shown to exist, determine the extent of that liability. Phrases such as 'foreseeability,' 'proximity,' 'neighbourhood,' 'just and reasonable,' 'fairness,' 'voluntary acceptance of risk,' or 'voluntary assumption of responsibility' will be found used from time to time in the different cases. But, as your Lordships have said, such phrases are not precise definitions. At best they are but labels or phrases descriptive of the very different factual situations which can exist in particular cases and which must be carefully examined in each case before it can be pragmatically determined whether a duty of care exists and, if so, what is the scope and extent of that duty. If this conclusion involves a return to the traditional categorisation of cases as pointing to the existence and scope of any duty of care, as my noble and learned friend Lord Bridge of Harwich, suggests, I think this is infinitely preferable to recourse to somewhat wide generalisations which leave their practical application matters of difficulty and uncertainty. This conclusion finds strong support from the judgment of Brennan J in *Sutherland Shire Council* v *Heyman*, 60 ALR 1, 43–44 in the High Court of Australia in the passage cited by my noble and learned friends.

LORD OLIVER: . . . Thus the postulate of a simple duty to avoid any harm that is, with hindsight, reasonably capable of being foreseen becomes untenable without the imposition of some intelligible limits to keep the law of negligence within the bounds of common sense and practicality. Those limits have been found by the requirement of what has been called a 'relationship of proximity' between plaintiff and defendant and by the imposition of a further requirement that the attachment of liability for harm which has occurred be 'just and reasonable.' But although the cases in which the courts have imposed or withheld liability are capable of an approximate categorisation, one looks in vain for some common denominator by which the existence of the essential relationship can be tested. Indeed it is difficult to resist a conclusion that what have been treated as three separate requirements are, at least in most cases, in fact merely facets of the same thing, for in some cases the degree of foreseeability is such that it is from that alone that the requisite proximity can be deduced, whilst in others the absence of that essential relationship can most rationally be attributed simply to the court's view that it would not be fair and reasonable to hold the defendant responsible. 'Proximity' is, no doubt, a convenient expression so long as it is realised that it is no more than a label which embraces not a definable concept but merely a description of circumstances from which, pragmatically, the courts conclude that a duty of care exists.

There are, of course, cases where, in any ordinary meaning of the words, a relationship of proximity (in the literal sense of 'closeness') exists but where the law, whilst recognising the fact of the relationship, nevertheless denies a remedy to the injured party on the ground of public policy. *Rondel* v *Worsley* [1969] 1 AC 191 was such a case, as was *Hill* v *Chief Constable of West Yorkshire* [1989] AC 53, so far as concerns the alternative ground of that decision. But such cases do nothing to assist in the identification of those features from which the law will deduce the essential relationship on which liability depends and, for my part, I think that it has to be recognised that to search for any single formula which will serve as a general test of liability is to pursue a will-o'-the-wisp. The fact is that once one discards, as it is now clear that one must, the concept of foreseeability of harm as the single exclusive test — even a prima facie test — of the existence of the duty of care, the attempt to state some general principle which will determine liability in an infinite variety of circumstances serves not to clarify the law but merely to bedevil its development in a way which corresponds with practicality and common sense. In *Sutherland Shire Council* v *Heyman*, 60 ALR 1, 43–44, Brennan J in the course of a penetrating analysis, observed:

> Of course, if foreseeability of injury to another were the exhaustive criterion of a prima facie duty to act to prevent the occurrence of that injury, it would be essential to introduce some kind of restrictive qualification — perhaps a qualification of the kind stated in the second stage of the general proposition in *Anns* [1978] AC 728. I am unable to accept that approach. It is preferable, in my view, that the law should develop novel categories of negligence incrementally and by analogy with established categories, rather than by a massive extension of a prima facie duty of care restrained only by indefinable 'considerations which ought to negative, or to reduce or limit the scope of the duty or the class of person to whom it is owed.'

Perhaps, therefore, the most that can be attempted is a broad categorisation of the decided cases according to the type of situation in which liability has been established in the past in order to found an argument by analogy. Thus, for instance, cases can be classified according to whether what is complained of is the failure to prevent the infliction of damage by the act of the third party (such as *Dorset Yacht Co. Ltd* v *Home Office* [1970] AC 1004, *P. Perl (Exporters) Ltd* v *Camden London Borough Council* [1984] QB 342, *Smith* v *Littlewoods Organisation Ltd* [1987] AC 241 and, indeed, *Anns* v *Merton London Borough Council* [1978] AC 728 itself), in failure to perform properly a statutory duty claimed to have been imposed for the protection of the plaintiff either as a member of a class or as a member of the public (such as the *Anns* case, *Ministry of Housing and Local Government* v *Sharp* [1970] 2 QB 223, *Yuen Kun Yeu* v *Attorney-General of Hong Kong* [1988] AC 175) or in the making by the defendant of some statement or advice which has been communicated, directly or indirectly, to the plaintiff and upon which he has relied. Such categories are not, of course, exhaustive. Sometimes they overlap as in the *Anns* case, and there are cases which do not readily fit into easily definable categories (such as *Ross* v *Caunters* [1980] Ch 297). Nevertheless, it is, I think, permissible to regard negligent statements or advice as a separate category displaying common features from which it is possible to find at least guidelines by which a test for the existence of the relationship which is essential to ground liability can be deduced.

Note

The essential point of this case is that all cases of negligence need the requisite level of 'proximity' between the parties: i.e. a sufficient level of relationship. In cases of personal injury or damage to property this requirement will be satisfied by foreseeability, but in other cases, such as nervous shock (Chapter 9) or economic loss (Chapter 11) closer relationships between the parties will be necessary to establish liability.

Murphy v *Brentwood*
House of Lords [1991] 1 AC 398; [1990] 3 WLR 414; [1990] 2 All ER 908

This case involved a local authority negligently approving a design for a concrete raft foundation for a house, which subsequently caused defects in the house. The substantive issues are dealt with in Chapter 13 and the extracts below deal only with general issues relating to the duty of care.

LORD OLIVER: . . . The critical question, as was pointed out in the analysis of Brennan J in his judgment in *Council of the Shire of Sutherland* v *Heyman*, 157 CLR 424, is not the nature of the damage in itself, whether physical or pecuniary, but whether the scope of the duty of care in the circumstances of the case is such as to embrace damage of the kind which the plaintiff claims to have sustained: see *Caparo Industries Plc* v *Dickman* [1990] 2 AC 605. The essential question which has to be asked in every case, given that damage which is the essential ingredient of the action has occurred, is whether the relationship between the plaintiff and the defendant is such — or, to use the favoured expression, whether it is of sufficient 'proximity' — that it imposes upon the latter a duty to take care to avoid or prevent that loss which has in fact been sustained. That the requisite degree of proximity may be established in circumstances in which the plaintiff's injury results from his reliance upon a statement or advice upon which he was entitled to rely and upon which it was contemplated that he would be likely to rely is clear from *Hedley Byrne* and subsequent cases, but *Anns* [1978] AC 728 was not such a case and neither is the instant case. It is not, however, necessarily to be assumed that the reliance cases form the only possible category of cases in which a duty to take reasonable care to avoid or prevent pecuniary loss can arise. *Morrison Steamship Co. Ltd* v *Greystoke Castle (Cargo Owners)*, for instance, clearly was not a reliance case. Nor indeed was *Ross* v *Caunters* [1980] Ch 297 so far as the disappointed beneficiary was concerned. Another example may be *Ministry of Housing and Local Government* v *Sharp* [1980] 2 QB 223, although this may, on analysis, properly be categorised as a reliance case.

Nor is it self-evident logically where the line is to be drawn. Where, for instance, the defendant's careless conduct results in the interruption of the electricity supply to business premises adjoining the highway, it is not easy to discern the logic in holding that a sufficient relationship of proximity exists between him and a factory owner who has suffered loss because material in the course of manufacture is rendered useless but that none exists between him and the owner of, for instance, an adjoining restaurant who suffers the loss of profit on the meals which he is unable to prepare and sell. In both cases the real loss is pecuniary. The solution to such borderline cases has so far been achieved pragmatically (see *Spartan Steel & Alloys Ltd* v *Martin & Co. (Contractors) Ltd* [1973] QB 27) not by the application of logic but by the perceived necessity as a matter of policy to place some limits — perhaps arbitrary limits — to what would otherwise be an endless, cumulative causative chain bounded only by theoretical foreseeability.

I frankly doubt whether, in searching for such limits, the categorisation of the damage as 'material,' 'physical,' 'pecuniary' or 'economic' provides a particularly useful contribution. Where it does, I think, serve a useful purpose is in identifying those cases in which it is necessary to search for and find something more than the mere reasonable foreseeability of damage which has occurred as providing the degree of 'proximity' necessary to support the action. In his classical exposition in *Donoghue* v *Stevenson* [1932] AC 562, 580–581, Lord Atkin was expressing himself in the context of the infliction of direct physical injury resulting from a carelessly created latent defect in a manufactured product. In his analysis of the duty in those circumstances he clearly, equated 'proximity' with the reasonable foresight of damage. In the straightforward case of the direct infliction of physical injury by the act of the plaintiff there is, indeed, no need to look beyond the foreseeability by the defendant of the result in order to establish that he is in a 'proximate' relationship with the plaintiff. But, as was pointed out by Lord Diplock in *Dorset Yacht Co. Ltd v Home Office* [1970] AC 1004, 1060, Lord Atkin's test, though a useful guide to characteristics which will be found to exist in conduct and relationships giving rise to a legal duty of care, is manifestly false if misused as a universal; and Lord Reid, in the course of his speech in the same case, recognised that the statement of principle enshrined in that test necessarily required qualification in cases where the only loss caused by the defendant's conduct was economic. The infliction of physical injury to the person or property of another universally requires to be justified. The causing of economic loss does not. If it is to be categorised as wrongful it is necessary to find some factor beyond the mere occurrence of the loss and the fact that its occurrence could be foreseen. Thus the categorisation of damage as economic serves at least the useful purpose of indicating that something more is required and it is one of the unfortunate features of *Anns* that it resulted initially in this essential distinction being lost sight of.

Section 2:   the unforeseeable plaintiff

Duty of care operates on two levels. There is the question of whether, in the class of case in issue, there is a legal duty or not (for example whether there is a duty not to make careless statements). This might be regarded as the 'House of Lords' level of the issue. There is also the question which arises in every case of negligence of whether this particular defendant owes a duty to this particular plaintiff — the unforeseeable plaintiff problem. That is, it is known that the law puts the defendant under a general obligation to take care in the particular situation, but the question is whether there is a sufficient relationship between the particular defendant and the particular plaintiff for that defendant to owe a duty to that plaintiff. The problem usually arises where the defendant is known to be or could be liable to A for his loss, but the question is whether he is also liable to B for his loss. Although this is called the unforeseeable plaintiff problem the same issue arises where the degree of proximity required is closer than that of mere foreseeability. Thus, the question really is whether this plaintiff is sufficiently proximate to this defendant, and perhaps this section should more properly be entitled 'the non-proximate plaintiff'.

Bourhill v *Young*
House of Lords [1943] AC 92; 1942 SC 78; [1942] 2 All ER 396

Mrs Euphemia Bourhill was an Edinburgh fishwife who was travelling on a tram along Colinton Road, Edinburgh. She got off the tram and picked up her fish basket from the far side. John Young was a motorcyclist who passed the tram on the near side, and some 50 feet further on crashed into a car and was killed. John Young was negligent in that he was travelling too fast. After John Young's body had been removed Mrs Young approached the site and saw the blood on the road. She alleged that she suffered 'nervous shock' as a result of the accident and gave birth to a stillborn child about a month later.

Assuming John Young would have been liable to the owner of the car into which he crashed, could he also be liable to Mrs Bourhill? The case is relevant for two points: (1) whether the plaintiff was a foreseeable plaintiff; and (2) the extent to which psychological damage is recoverable. This latter point is discussed later. Held: dismissing the appeal, that no duty was owed to the plaintiff.

LORD RUSSELL: A man is not liable for negligence in the air. The liability only arises 'where there is a duty to take care and where failure in that duty has caused damage': see per Lord Macmillan in *Donoghue* v *Stevenson*. In my opinion, such a duty only arises towards those individuals of whom it may be reasonably anticipated that they will be affected by the act which constitutes the alleged breach.

Can it be said that John Young could reasonably have anticipated that a person, situated as was the appellant, would be affected by his proceeding towards Colinton at the speed at which he was travelling? I think not. His road was clear of pedestrians. The appellant was not within his vision, but was standing behind the solid barrier of the tramcar. His speed in no way endangered her. In these circumstances I am unable to see how he could reasonably anticipate that, if he came into collision with a vehicle coming across the tramcar into Glenlockhart Road, the resultant noise would cause physical injury by shock to a person standing behind the tramcar. In my opinion, he owed no duty to the appellant, and was, therefore, not guilty of any negligence in relation to her . . . .

LORD WRIGHT: My Lords, that damage by mental shock may give a cause of action is now well established and it not disputed in this case, but as Phillimore J pointed out in his admirable judgment in *Dulieu* v *White & Sons* [1901] 2 KB 669, the real difficulty in questions of this kind is to decide whether there has been a wrongful act or breach of duty on the part of the defendant vis-à-vis the plaintiff. That being the prior question, if it is answered against the plaintiff the the matter is concluded. I shall, therefore, consider that issue in the first place.

This general concept of reasonable foresight as the criterion of negligence or breach of duty (strict or otherwise) may be criticized as too vague, but negligence is a fluid principle, which has to be applied to the most diverse conditions and problems of human life. It is a concrete, not an abstract, idea. It has to be fitted to the facts of the particular case. Willes J defined it as absence of care according to the circumstances: *Vaughan* v *Taff Vale Ry Co.* (1860) 157 ER 1351. It is also always relative to the individual affected. This raises a serious additional difficulty in the cases where it has to be determined, not merely whether the act itself is negligent against someone, but whether it is negligent vis-à-vis the plaintiff. This is a crucial point in cases of nervous shock. Thus, in the present case John Young was certainly negligent in an issue between himself and the owner of the car which he ran into, but it is another question whether he was negligent vis-à-vis the appellant. In such cases terms like 'derivative' and 'original' and 'primary' and 'secondary' have been applied to define and distinguish the type of the negligence. If, however, the appellant has a cause of action it is because of a wrong to herself. She cannot build on a wrong to someone else. Her interest, which was in her own bodily security was of a different order from the interest of the owner of the car. That this is so is also illustrated by cases such as have been called in the United States 'rescue' or 'search' cases. This type has been recently examined and explained in the Court of Appeal in *Haynes* v *Harwood* [1935] 1 KB 146, where the plaintiff, a police constable, was injured in stopping runaway horses in a crowded street in which were many children. His act was due to his mental reaction, whether instinctive or deliberate, to the spectacle of others' peril. Maugham L J in the court of Appeal approved the language used by the trial judge, Finlay J ([1934] 2 KB 240, 247), when he held that to leave the horses unattended was a breach of duty not only to any person injured by being run over (in fact, no one was so injured), but also to the constable. Finlay J's words were: 'It seems to me that if horses run away it must be quite obviously contemplated that people are likely to be knocked down. It must also, I think, be contemplated that persons will attempt to stop the horses and try to prevent injury to life or limb.'. . . This again shows how the ambit of the persons affected by negligence or misconduct may extend beyond persons who are actually subject to physical impact. . . . There is no dispute about the facts. Upon these facts, can it be said that a duty is made out, and breach of that duty, so that the damage which is found is recoverable? I think not. The appellant was completely outside the range of the collision. She merely heard a noise, which upset her, without her having any definite idea at all. As she said: 'I just got into a pack of nerves and I did not know whether I was going to get it or not.' She saw nothing of the actual accident, or, indeed, any marks of blood until later. I cannot accept that John Young could reasonably have foreseen, or, more correctly, the reasonable hypothetical observer could reasonably have foreseen, the likelihood that anyone placed as the appellant was, could be affected in the manner in which she was. In my opinion, John Young was guilty of no breach of duty to the appellant, and was not in law responsible for the hurt she sustained. I may add that the issue of duty or no duty is, indeed, a question for the court, but it depends on the view taken of the facts. In the present case both courts below have taken the view that the appellant has, on the facts of the case, no redress, and I agree with their view. . . .

LORD PORTER: In the case of a civil action there is no such thing as negligence in the abstract. There must be neglect of the use of care towards a person towards whom the defendant owes the duty of observing care, and I am content to take the statement of Lord Atkin in *Donoghue* v *Stevenson* [1932] AC 562, 580, as indicating the extent of the duty. 'You must take,' he said, 'reasonable care to avoid acts or omissions which you can reasonably foresee would be likely to injure your neighbour. Who, then, in law is my neighbour? The answer seems to be — persons who are so closely and directly affected by my act that I ought reasonably to have them in contemplation as being so affected when I am directing my mind to the acts or omissions which are called in question.' Is the result of this view that all persons in or near the street down which the negligent driver is progressing are potential victims of his negligence? Though from their position it is quite impossible that any injury should happen to them and though they have no relatives or even friends who might be endangered, is a duty of care to them owed and broken because they might have been but were not in a spot exposed to the errant driving of the peccant car? I cannot think so. The duty is not to the world at large. It must be tested by asking with reference to each several complainant: Was a duty owed to him or her? If no one of them was in such a position that direct physical injury could reasonably be anticipated to them or their relations or friends normally I think no duty would be owed, and if, in addition, no shock was reasonably to be anticipated to them as a result of the defender's negligence, the defender might, indeed, be guilty of actionable negligence to others but not of negligence towards them. In the present case the appellant was never herself in any bodily danger nor reasonably in fear of danger either for herself or others. She was merely a person who, as a result of the action, was emotionally disturbed and rendered physically ill by that emotional disturbance. The question whether emotional disturbance or shock, which a defender ought reasonably to have anticipated as likely to follow from his reckless driving, can ever form the basis of a claim is not in issue. . . .

Notes
1.   A good example of the unforeseeable plaintiff rule is *Palsgraf* v *Long Island Railroad Co.* (1928) 248 NY 339. The plaintiff, Helen Palsgraf, was waiting on a platform for a train to Rockaway Beach. Another train stopped and two men ran to get it, and a guard pushed one of them from behind to help him in. In doing so he dislodged a parcel, which turned out to contain fireworks. The fireworks exploded when they fell, and this was alleged to have upset some scales some distance away which fell upon the plaintiff. It is unlikely that this fantastic scenario actually occurred, but, even assuming the facts to be true, it was said that while a duty may have been owed to the two men in the train, no duty was owed to the plaintiff. Cardozo CJ quoted *Pollock on Torts*, saying 'Proof of negligence in the air so to speak will not do.' He pointed out that a plaintiff must have an original and primary duty owed to her, and not one simply derived from a wrong to someone else, and that the orbit of the danger as disclosed to the eye of reasonable vigilance is the orbit of the duty. 'Negligence, like risk, is thus a term of relation.' In other words, the fact that a duty was owed by the guard to the men he was pushing onto the train, did not necessarily mean that a duty was owed to Mrs Palsgraf. She was outside the orbit of the risk, and therefore was an unforeseeable plaintiff.

For a full discussion of *Palsgraf*, see Prosser, 'Palsgraf Revisited', in Prosser, *Selected Topics on the Law of Torts* or 52 Mich LR 1.
2.   In *Marx* v *Attorney General* [1974] 1 NZLR 164, an attempt was made to extend the ambit of duty beyond the individual likely to be injured so as to include his family, but the rule that actions must not be derivative was upheld. In that case the defendants, New Zealand Railways, had injured the plaintiff causing him brain damage, and this caused him to become hyper-sexual. As a result of this condition he injured his wife, but it was held that she could not sue, for she was an unforeseeable plaintiff and her action was derivative.

For commentary upon this case see Binchy, (1975) 38 MLR 468, where it is argued that the wife's action was not derivative, but rather she was in the same position as a person who was injured by an inanimate object which had been rendered dangerous by the defendant. A conclusion similar to *Marx* is implicit in *Meah* v *McCreamer (No. 2)* [1986] 1 All ER 943, where it was said that where a car driver caused a person to suffer a personality change, as a result of which he raped two women, the rape victims would not be able to sue the driver.

Question
X, a surgeon, negligently removes Y's only kidney. Who, apart from Y, would be a foreseeable plaintiff? See *Urbanski* v *Patel* (1978) 84 DLR 3d 650.

Videan v *British Transport Commission*
Court of Appeal [1963] 2 QB 640; [1963] 2 All ER 860; [1963] 2 WLR 347

North Tawton is a small railway station on the edge of Dartmoor on the ex-London South Western Railway line to Plymouth. On 26 July 1959 the stationmaster, Dennis Videan, was going to take his family to Exeter when it was realised that his son Richard, aged 2, was missing. He was seen sitting on the railway line, and at the same time a motorised trolley, driven by one Souness, was approaching. Souness did not see the child until very late, and in an effort to save his son, Dennis Videan threw himself in front of the trolley and was killed. Richard was saved, but injured. The court held that as Richard was a trespasser he was unforeseeable and therefore could not sue. In an action by Mr Videan's widow it was held, allowing her appeal, that a duty was owed to her husband.

LORD DENNING MR: I turn now to the widow's claim in respect of the death of her husband. In order to establish it, the widow must prove that Souness owed a duty of care to the stationmaster, that he broke that duty, and that, in consequence of the breach, the stationmaster was killed. Mr Fox-Andrews says that the widow can prove none of these things. All depends, he says, on the test of foreseeability; and, applying that test, he puts the following dilemma: If Souness could not reasonably be expected to foresee the presence of the child, he could not reasonably be expected to foresee the presence of the father. He could not foresee that a trespasser would be on the line. So how could he be expected to foresee that anyone would be attempting to rescue him? Mr Fox-Andrews points out that, in all the rescue cases that have hitherto come before the courts, such as *Haynes* v *Harwood & Son* [1935] 1 KB 146, and *Baker* v *T. E. Hopkins & Sons Ltd* [1954] 1 WLR 966, the conduct of the defendant was a wrong to the victim or the potential victim. How can he be liable to the rescuer when he is not liable to the rescued?

I cannot accept this view. The right of the rescuer is an independent right and is not derived from that of the victim. The victim may have been guilty of contributory negligence — or his right may be excluded by contractual stipulation — but still the rescuer can sue. So also the victim may, as here, be a trespasser and excluded on that ground, but still the rescuer can sue. Foreseeability is necessary, but not foreseeability of the particular emergency that arose. Suffice it that he ought reasonably to foresee that, if he did not take care, some emergency or other might arise, and that someone or other might be impelled to expose himself to danger in order to effect a rescue. Such is the case here. Souness ought to have anticipated that some emergency or other might arise. His trolley was not like an express train which is heralded by signals and whistles and shouts of 'Keep clear.' His trolley came silently and swiftly upon the unsuspecting quietude of a country station. He should have realised that someone or other might be put in peril if he came too fast or did not keep a proper look-out: and if anyone was put in peril, then someone would come to the rescue. As it happened, it was the stationmaster trying to rescue his child; but it would be the same if it had been a passer-by. Whoever comes to the rescue, the law should see that he does not suffer for it. It seems to me that, if a person by his fault creates a situation of peril, he must answer for it to any person who attempts to rescue the person who is in danger. He owes a duty to such a person above all others. The rescuer may act instinctively out of humanity or deliberately out of courage. But whichever it is, so long as it is not wanton interference, if the rescuer is killed or injured in the attempt, he can recover damages from the one whose fault has been the cause of it. . . .

PEARSON LJ: I now come to the appeal of the widow, who claims damages for the death of her husband caused, as she contends, by the negligence of Souness acting as the servant of the defendant Commission. It is clear from the evidence and the judge's findings that Souness in his approach to the station was acting negligently in relation to anyone to whom he owed a duty of care, and that the conduct of Souness in this respect caused the accident. The only disputable question is whether Souness owed any relevant duty of care to the deceased. The Commission's argument, evidently accepted by the judge, has been that the position of the rescuer could not be any better than the position of the person rescued, and that, as the infant plaintiff's trespass was unforeseeable, so the act of his father in trying to rescue him was unforeseeable, and therefore both the infant plaintiff and his father were outside the zone of reasonable contemplation and the scope of duty. That would no doubt have been a formidable argument if the deceased had been only a father rescuing his son. But the deceased was the stationmaster, having a general responsibility for dealing with any emergency that might arise at the station. It was foreseeable by Souness that if he drove his vehicle carelessly into the station he might imperil the stationmaster, as the stationmaster might well have some proper occasion for going on the track in the performance of his duties. For this purpose it is not necessary that the particular accident which happened should have been foreseeable. It is enough that it was foreseeable that some situation requiring the stationmaster to go on the line might arise, and if any such situation did arise, a careless approach to the station by Souness with his vehicle would be dangerous to the stationmaster. On that ground I hold that Souness's careless approach to the station was a breach of a duty owing by him to the deceased as stationmaster, and it caused the accident, and consequently the Commission is liable to the widow and her appeal should be allowed.

Question

Harman LJ in *Videan* said 'Whether if the rescuer had been a member of the public there would have been liability, I leave out of account.' What would have been the result in such a case according to (a) Lord Denning and (b) Pearson LJ?

Note

'Danger invites rescue' (per Cardozo CJ in *Wagner* v *International Rly Co.* (1921) 232 NY 176). Hence, it is not unforeseeable that when a person puts another (or himself) in a position of peril, someone will attempt a rescue. In **Haynes v Harwood** [1935] 1 KB 146, a horse van was negligently left unattended and the horses bolted. The plaintiff was a policeman who was injured when attempting to stop the runaway horses. The defendant was liable and could not argue that the plaintiff was unforeseeable.

Why did not this case automatically resolve the problem in *Videan?*

Section 3: policy factors — 'fair and reasonable'

McLoughlin v *O'Brian*
House of Lords [1983] AC 410; [1982] 2 All ER 298; [1982] 2 WLR 982

The issue concerned the extent of liability for causing nervous shock, and in particular whether a defendant who caused a car accident could be liable to the mother of the victims when she saw her children (and her husband) in hospital shortly after the accident. Held: that there could be liability.

LORD EDMUND-DAVIES: My Lords, in the present case two totally different points arising from the speeches of two of your Lordships call for further attention. Both relate to the Court of Appeal's invoking public policy. Unless I have completely misunderstood my noble and learned friend, Lord Bridge of Harwich, he doubts that any regard should have been had to such a consideration and seemingly considers that the Court of Appeal went wrong in paying any attention to it. The sole test of liability, I read him as saying, is the reasonable foreseeability of injury to the plaintiff through nervous shock resulting from the defendants' conceded default. And, such foreseeability having been established to their unanimous satisfaction, it followed that in law no other course was open to the Court of Appeal than to allow this appeal. I have respectfully to say that I cannot accept this approach. It is true that no decision was cited to your Lordships in which the contrary has been held, but that is not to say that reasonable foreseeability is the *only* test of the validity of a claim brought in negligence. If it is surmounted, the defendant would probably be hard put to escape liability.

Lord Wright found it difficult to conceive that any new head of public policy could be discovered (*Fender* v *St John-Mildmay* [1938] AC 1, 41), and, were Lord Halsbury LC sound in denying that any court could invent a new head of policy (*Jansen* v *Driefontein Consolidated Mines Ltd* [1902] AC 484, 491), I should have been in the happy position of accepting the standpoint adopted by my noble and learned friend, Lord Bridge of Harwich. But, as I shall later indicate, the more recent view which has found favour in your Lordships' House is that public policy is not immutable. Accordingly, whilst I would have strongly preferred indicating with clarity where the limit of liability should be drawn in such cases as the present, in my judgment the possibility of a wholly new type of policy being raised renders the attainment of such finality unfortunately unattainable.

As I think, all we can say is that any invocation of public policy calls for the closest scrutiny, and the defendant might well fail to discharge the burden of making it good, as, indeed, happened in *Rondel* v *Worsley* [1969] 1 AC 191. But that is not to say that success for the defendant would be unthinkable, for, in the words of MacDonald J in *Nova Mink Ltd* v *Trans-Canada Airlines* [1951] 2 DLR 241, 256: 'there is always a large element of judicial policy and social expediency involved in the determination of the duty-problem, however it may be obscured by the use of traditional formulae.'

I accordingly hold, as Griffiths LJ [1981] QB 599, 618, did, that 'The test of foreseeability is not a universal touchstone to determine the extent of liability for the consequences of wrongdoing.' Authority for that proposition is both ample in quantity and exalted in status. . . .

I finally turn to consider the following passage in the speech of my noble and learned friend, Lord Scarman:

> Policy considerations will have to be weighed: but the objective of the judges is the formulation of principle. And, if principle inexorably requires a decision which entails a degree of policy risk, the court's function is to adjudicate according to principle, leaving policy curtailment to the judgment of Parliament. . . . If principle leads to results which are thought to be socially unacceptable, Parliament can legislate to draw a line or map out a new path.

And at a later stage my noble and learned friend adds: 'Why then should not the courts draw the line, as the Court of Appeal manfully tried to do in this case? Simply, because the policy issue as to where to draw the line is not justiciable.'

My understanding of these words is that my noble and learned friend shares (though for a different reason) the conclusion of my noble and learned friend, Lord Bridge of Harwich, that, in adverting to public policy, the Court of Appeal here embarked upon a sleeveless errand, for public policy has no relevance to liability at law. In my judgment, the proposition that 'the policy issue . . . is not justiciable' is as novel as it is startling. So novel is it in relation to this appeal that it was never mentioned during the hearing before your Lordships. And it is startling because in my respectful judgment it runs counter to well-established and wholly acceptable law.

I restrict myself to recent decisions of your Lordships' House. In *Rondel* v *Worsley* [1969] 1 AC 191, their Lordships unanimously held that public policy required that a barrister should be immune from an action for negligence in respect of his conduct and management of a case in court and the work preliminary thereto, Lord Reid saying, at p. 228:

> Is it in the public interest that barristers and advocates should be protected against such actions? Like so many questions which raise the public interest, a decision one way will cause hardships to individuals while a decision the other way will involve disadvantage to the public interest. . . . So the issue appears to me to be whether the abolition of the rule would probably be attended by such disadvantage to the public interest as to make its retention clearly justifiable.

My Lords, in accordance with such a line of authorities, I hold that public policy issues *are* 'justiciable.' Their invocation calls for close scrutiny, and the conclusion may be that its nature and existence have not been established with the clarity and cogency required before recognition can be granted to any legal doctrine, and before any litigant can properly be deprived of what would otherwise be his manifest legal rights. Or the conclusion may be that adoption of the public policy relied upon would involve the introduction of new legal principles so fundamental that they are best left to the legislature: see, for example, *Launchbury* v *Morgans* [1973] AC 127, and especially *per* Lord Pearson, at p. 142G. And 'public policy is not immutable' *per* Lord Reid in *Rondel* v *Worsley* [1969] 1 AC 191, 227. Indeed, Winfield, 'Public Policy in the English Common Law' (1928) 42 Harvard LR 76, described it as '*necessarily* variable,' (p. 93) and wisely added, at pp. 95, 96, 97:

> This variability . . . is a stone in the edifice of the doctrine, and not a missile to be flung at it. Public policy would be almost useless without it. The march of civilization and the difficulty of ascertaining public policy at any given time make it essential . . . How is public policy evidenced? If it is so variable, if it depends on the welfare of the community at any given time, how are the courts to ascertain it? Some judges have thought this difficulty so great, that they have urged that it would be solved much better by the legislature and have considered it to be the main reason why the courts should leave public policy alone . . . . This admonition is a wise one and judges are not likely to forget it. But the better view seems to be that the difficulty of discovering what public policy is at any given moment certainly does not absolve the bench from the duty of doing so. The judges are bound to take notice of it and of the changes which it undergoes, and it is immaterial that the question may be one of ethics rather than of law.

In the present case the Court of Appeal did just that, and in my judgment they were right in doing so. But they concluded that public policy required them to dismiss what they clearly regarded as an otherwise irrefragable claim. In so concluding, I respectfully hold that they were wrong, and I would accordingly allow the appeal.

LORD SCARMAN: The appeal raises directly a question as to the balance in our law between the functions of judge and legislature. The common law, which in a constitutional context includes judicially developed equity, covers everything which is not covered by statute. It knows no gaps: there can be no 'casus omissus.' The function of the court is to decide the case before it, even though the decision may require the extension or adaptation of a principle or in some cases the creation of new law to meet the justice of the case. But, whatever the court decides to do, it starts from a baseline of existing principle and seeks a solution consistent with or analogous to a principle or principles already recognised.

The distinguishing feature of the common law is this judicial development and formation of principle. Policy considerations will have to be weighed: but the objective of the judges is the formulation of principle. And, if principle inexorably requires a decision which entails a degree of policy risk, the court's function is to adjudicate according to principle, leaving policy curtailment to the judgment of Parliament. Here lies the true role of the two law-making institutions in our constitution. By concentrating on principle the judges can keep the common law alive, flexible and consistent, and can keep the legal system clear of policy problems which neither they, nor the forensic process which it is their duty to operate, are equipped to resolve. If principle leads to results which are thought to be socially unacceptable, Parliament can legislate to draw a line or map out a new path.

The real risk to the common law is not its movement to cover new situations and new knowledge but lest it should stand still, halted by a conservative judicial approach. If that should happen, and since the 1966 practice direction of the House [*Practice Statement: Judicial Precedent* [1966] 1 WLR 1234] it has become less likely, there would be a danger of the law becoming irrelevant to the consideration, and inept in its treatment, of modern social problems. Justice would be defeated. The common law has, however, avoided this catastrophe by the flexibility given it by generations of judges. Flexibility carries with it, of course, certain risks, notably a degree of uncertainty in the law and the 'floodgates' risk which so impressed the Court of Appeal in the present case.

The importance to be attached to certainty and the size of the 'floodgates' risk vary from one branch of the law to another. What is required of the law in its approach to a commercial transaction will be very different from the approach appropriate to problems of tortious liability for personal injuries. In some branches of the law, notably that now under consideration, the search for certainty can obstruct the law's pursuit of justice, and can become the enemy of the good. . . .

Why then should not the courts draw the line, as the Court of Appeal manfully tried to do in this case? Simply, because the policy issue as to where to draw the line is not justiciable. The problem is one of social, economic, and financial policy. The considerations relevant to a decision are not such as to be capable of being handled within the limits of the forensic process.

My Lords, I would allow the appeal for the reasons developed by my noble and learned friend, Lord Bridge of Harwich, while putting on record my view that there is here a case for legislation.

Note

For a discussion of the role of principle and policy as discussed by Lords Scarman and Edmund-Davies, see Weaver, 'Is a general theory of adjudication possible?—the example of the principle/policy distinction' (1985) 48 MLR 613.

Hill v Chief Constable of West Yorkshire
House of Lords [1989] AC 53; [1988] 2 All ER 238; [1985] 2 WLR 1049

Between 1975 and 1980 Peter Sutcliffe committed 13 murders and 8 attempted murders in the West Yorkshire area. The mother of the last victim,

Jacqueline Hill, sued the police on behalf of the estate of her daughter for alleged negligence in failing to catch Sutcliffe earlier than they did. Held: no duty was owed as there was insufficient proximity but the House also held that the action was barred on grounds of public policy.

LORD KEITH: . . . there is another reason why an action for damages in negligence should not lie against the police in circumstances such as those of the present case, and that is public policy. In *Yuen Kun Yeu* v *Attorney-General of Hong Kong* [1988] AC 175, 193, I expressed the view that the category of cases where the second stage of Lord Wilberforce's two stage test in *Anns* v *Merton London Borough Council* [1978] AC 728, 751–752 might fall to be applied was a limited one, one example of that category being *Rondel* v *Worsley* [1969] 1 AC 191. Application of that second stage is, however, capable of constituting a separate and independent ground for holding that the existence of liability in negligence should not be entertained. Potential existence of such liability may in many instances be in the general public interest, as tending towards the observance of a higher standard of care in the carrying on of various different types of activity. I do not, however, consider that this can be said of police activities. The general sense of public duty which motivates police forces is unlikely to be appreciably reinforced by the imposition of such liability so far as concerns their function in the investigation and suppression of crime. From time to time they make mistakes in the exercise of that function, but it is not to be doubted that they apply their best endeavours to the performance of it. In some instances the imposition of liability may lead to the exercise of a function being carried on in a detrimentally defensive frame of mind. The possibility of this happening in relation to the investigative operations of the police cannot be excluded. Further it would be reasonable to expect that if potential liability were to be imposed it would be not uncommon for actions to be raised against police forces on the ground that they had failed to catch some criminal as soon as they might have done, with the result that he went on to commit further crimes. While some such actions might involve allegations of a simple and straightforward type of failure — for example that a police officer negligently tripped and fell while pursuing a burglar — others would be likely to enter deeply into the general nature of a police investigation, as indeed the present action would seek to do. The manner of conduct of such an investigation must necessarily involve a variety of decisions to be made on matters of policy and discretion, for example as to which particular line of inquiry is most advantageously to be pursued and what is the most advantageous way to deploy the available resources. Many such decisions would not be regarded by the courts as appropriate to be called in question, yet elaborate investigation of the facts might be necessary to ascertain whether or not this was so. A great deal of police time, trouble and expense might be expected to have to be put into the preparation of the defence to the action and the attendance of witnesses at the trial. The result would be a significant diversion of police manpower and attention from their most important function, that of the suppression of crime. Closed investigations would require to be reopened and retraversed, not with the object of bringing any criminal to justice but to ascertain whether or not they had been competently conducted. I therefore consider that Glidewell LJ, in his judgment in the Court of Appeal [1988] QB 60, 76 in the present case, was right to take the view that the police were immune from an action of this kind on grounds similar to those which in *Rondel* v *Worsley* [1969] 1 AC 191 were held to render a barrister immune from actions for negligence in his conduct of proceedings in court.

Notes

1.   For recent cases against the police which also failed on grounds of public policy see *Alexandrou* v *Oxford* [1993] 4 All ER 328 and *Osman* v *Ferguson*

[1993] 4 All ER 344 and compare *Home Office* v *Dorset Yacht* [1970] AC 1004. Similar arguments apply in relation to fire services: see *John Munroe Acrylics* v *London Fire and Civil Defence Authority, The Times*, 22 May 1996. In *Elguzouli-Daf* v *Commissioner of Police* [1995] 1 All ER 833, the plaintiff had been held in custody for 85 days before the Crown Prosecution Service dropped the charges. It was held that the CPS owed no duty to the plaintiff, as such a duty would lead prosecutors to take a defensive attitude and the welfare of the community amounted to sufficient policy reason to preclude a duty. (But see *Welsh* v *Chief Constable of Merseyside* [1993] 1 All ER 692 where it was said that the CPS had *voluntarily* assumed a responsibility to the plaintiff — the CPS had told the plaintiff that certain offences would be taken into consideration in another case and would not be charged separately. They were taken into consideration in the other case but the magistrates were not told of this and the plaintiff was arrested for failing to answer to bail.)

2.   A further ground of public policy is that there will be no duty of care if the plaintiff has an adequate alternative remedy: for example in *Jones* v *Department of Employment* [1988] 1 All ER 725 the plaintiff was denied unemployment benefit but subsequently successfully appealed to the Social Security Appeal Tribunal. It was held that he could not sue the original adjudicating officer for negligently denying him benefit and causing him distress as he was limited to his statutory right of appeal.

3.   In *Rondel* v *Worsley* [1969] 1 AC 191 it was said that a barrister was immune from liability for his conduct of a case in court because potential liability might deflect him from his duty to the court. In *Home Office* v *Dorset Yacht* [1970] AC 1004 it was said that potential liability would not deflect borstal officers from their duty to rehabilitate offenders. Is there a distinction between the two situations? Should professionals be allowed to claim that they might be persuaded not to do their professional duty? Is there a potential conflict of duty?

Marc Rich v Bishop Rock Marine (The Nicholas H)
House of Lords [1996] 1 AC 211; [1995] 3 WLR 227; [1995] 3 All ER 307; [1995] 2 Lloyds Rep 299

The *Nicholas H* was on a voyage from Chile to Italy when cracks developed in her hull and she put into San Juan in Puerto Rico. A Mr Ducat was employed by NKK, a classification society, whose role is to certify ships as fit for sea for the purposes of insurance. Such societies are independent non-profit making organisations. Initially, Mr Ducat recommended permanent repairs but the shipowners objected and he was finally persuaded to allow temporary repairs. After the ship put to sea the temporary welds cracked and the ship sank with total loss of the cargo. The contract between the shipowners and the cargo owners incorporated the Hague Rules, an international convention which limited the liability of the shipowners. The claim by the cargo owners against the shipowners was settled for the amount of the limited liability ($500,000), and the cargo owners then sued NKK for the remainder of their loss ($5.7 million) on the assumption that Mr Ducat was negligent in allowing temporary repairs. Held: dismissing the appeal, that NKK was not liable.

LORD STEYN: . . . The dealings between shipowners and cargo owners are based on a contractual structure, the Hague Rules, and tonnage limitation, on which the insurance of international trade depends: Dr Malcolm Clarke, 'Misdelivery and Time Bars' [1990] LMCLQ 314. Underlying it is the system of double or overlapping insurance of cargo. Cargo owners take out direct insurance in respect of the cargo. Shipowners take out liability risks insurance in respect of breaches of their duties of care in respect of the cargo. The insurance system is structured on the basis that the potential liability of shipowners to cargo owners is limited under the Hague Rules and by virtue of tonnage limitation provisions. And insurance premiums payable by owners obviously reflect such limitations on the shipowners' exposure.

If a duty of care by classification societies to cargo owners is recognised in this case, it must have a substantial impact on international trade. In his article Mr Cane described the likely effect of imposing such duty of care as follows [1994] LMCLQ 363, 375:

> Societies would be forced to buy appropriate liability insurance unless they could bargain with shipowners for an indemnity. To the extent that societies were successful in securing indemnities from shipowners in respect of loss suffered by cargo owners, the limitation of the liability of shipowners to cargo owners under the Hague-Visby Rules would effectively be destroyed. Shipowners would need to increase their insurance cover in respect of losses suffered by cargo owners; but at the same time, cargo owners would still need to insure against losses above the Hague-Visby recovery limit which did not result from actionable negligence on the part of a classification society. At least if classification societies are immune from non-contractual liability, they can confidently go without insurance in respect of third-party losses, leaving third parties to insure themselves in respect of losses for which they could not recover from shipowners.

Counsel for the cargo owners challenged this analysis. On instructions he said that classification societies already carry liability risks insurance. That is no doubt right since classification societies do not have a blanket immunity from all tortious liability. On the other hand, if a duty of care is held to exist in this case, the potential exposure of classification societies to claims by cargo owners will be large. That greater exposure is likely to lead to an increase in the cost to classification societies of obtaining appropriate liability risks insurance. Given their role in maritime trade classification societies are likely to seek to pass on the higher cost to owners. Moreover, it is readily predictable that classification societies will require owners to give appropriate indemnities. Ultimately, shipowners will pay.

The result of a recognition of a duty of care in this case will be to enable cargo owners, or rather their insurers, to disturb the balance created by the Hague Rules and Hague-Visby Rules as well as by tonnage limitation provisions, by enabling cargo owners to recover in tort against a peripheral party to the prejudice of the protection of shipowners under the existing system. For these reasons I would hold that the international trade system tends to militate against the recognition of the claim in tort put forward by the cargo owners against the classification society.

. . .

The position and role of NKK
The fact that a defendant acts for the collective welfare is a matter to be taken into consideration when considering whether it is fair, just and reasonable to impose a duty of care: *Hill* v *Chief Constable of West Yorkshire* [1989] AC 53; *Elguzouli-Daf* v

Commissioner of Police of the Metropolis [1995] 2 WLR 173. Even if such a body has no general immunity from liability in tort, the question may arise whether it owes a duty of care to aggrieved persons, and, if so, in what classes of case, e.g. only in cases involving the direct infliction of physical harm or on a wider basis.

In *W Angliss and Co. (Australia) Proprietary Ltd v Peninsular and Oriental Steam Navigation Co.* [1927] 2 KB 456, 462, Wright J (later to become Lord Wright) — a great judge with special expertise in maritime law and practice — described classification societies, such as Lloyd's, as occupying 'a public and quasi-judicial position.' There is a refrain of this idea to be found in Singh & Colinvaux, (British Shipping Laws), (1967), vol. 13, pp. 167–169, paras 391–394, where the editors describe a classification society as an impartial critic and arbiter (as opposed to arbitrator). These observations are helpful but not definitive. Nowadays one would not describe classification societies as carrying on quasi-judicial functions. But it is still the case that (apart from their statutory duties) they act in the public interest. The reality is simply that NKK — and I am deliberately reverting to the evidence about NKK — is an independent and non-profit-making entity, created and operating for the sole purpose of promoting the collective welfare, namely the safety of lives and ships at sea. In common with other classification societies NKK fulfils a role which in its absence would have to be fulfilled by states. And the question is whether NKK, and other classification societies, would be able to carry out their functions as efficiently if they become the ready alternative target of cargo owners, who already have contractual claims against shipowners. In my judgment there must be some apprehension that the classification societies would adopt, to the detriment of their traditional role, a more defensive position.

Policy factors
Counsel for the cargo owners argued that a decision that a duty of care existed in this case would not involve wide ranging exposure for NKK and other classification societies to claims in tort. That is an unrealistic position. If a duty is recognised in this case there is no reason why it should not extend to annual surveys, docking surveys, intermediate surveys, special surveys, boiler surveys, and so forth. And the scale of NKK's potential liability is shown by the fact that NKK conducted an average of 14,500 surveys per year over the last five years.

At present the system of settling cargo claims against shipowners is a relatively simple one. The claims are settled between the two sets of insurers. If the claims are not settled, they are resolved in arbitration or court proceedings. If a duty is held to exist in this case as between the classification society and cargo owners, classification societies would become potential defendants in many cases. An extra layer of insurance would become involved. The settlement process would inevitably become more complicated and expensive. Arbitration proceedings and court proceedings would often involve an additional party. And often similar issues would have to be canvassed in separate proceedings since the classification societies would not be bound by arbitration clauses in the contracts of carriage. If such a duty is recognised, there is a risk that classification societies might be unwilling from time to time to survey the very vessels which most urgently require independent examination. It will also divert men and resources from the prime function of classification societies, namely to save life and ships at sea. These factors are, by themselves, far from decisive. But in an overall assessment of the case they merit consideration.

Is the imposition of a duty of care fair, just and reasonable?
Like Mann LJ in the Court of Appeal [1994] 1 WLR 1071, 1085H, I am willing to assume (without deciding) that there was a sufficient degree of proximity in this case to fulfil that requirement for the existence of a duty of care. The critical question is therefore whether it would be fair, just and reasonable to impose such a duty. For my

part I am satisfied that the factors and arguments advanced on behalf of cargo owners are decisively outweighed by the cumulative effect, if a duty is recognised, of the matters discussed in paragraphs [above] i.e. the outflanking of the bargain between shipowners and cargo owners; the negative effect on the public role of NKK; and the other considerations of policy. By way of summary, I look at the matter from the point of view of the three parties concerned. I conclude that the recognition of a duty would be unfair, unjust and unreasonable as against the shipowners who would ultimately have to bear the cost of holding classification societies liable, such consequence being at variance with the bargain between shipowners and cargo owners based on an internationally agreed contractual structure. It would also be unfair, unjust and unreasonable towards classification societies, notably because they act for the collective welfare and unlike shipowners they would not have the benefit of any limitation provisions. Looking at the matter from the point of view of cargo owners, the existing system provides them with the protection of the Hague Rules or Hague-Visby Rules. But that protection is limited under such Rules and by tonnage limitation provisions. Under the existing system any shortfall is readily insurable. In my judgment the lesser injustice is done by not recognising a duty of care. It follows that I would reject the primary way in which counsel for the cargo owners put his case.

Notes

1.   Lord Steyn assumes (without deciding) that there was sufficient proximity and decides the case on the basis of policy considerations. In the Court of Appeal it had been questioned whether 'proximity' and the fair and reasonable test are really separate issues, but the judgment above shows that they should be dealt with separately.

2.   There was a vigorous dissent by Lord Lloyd. He argued (1) that the existence of the Hague Rules in the contract between the shipowners and the cargo owners was irrelevant as it would be nonsense if NKK were liable if the rules were not incorporated but not liable if they were. Further, the Hague Rules are purely a matter between shipowners and cargo owners and have nothing to do with the potential liability of third parties. (2) There was no evidence that, if liable, classification societies would pass on the cost to shipowners. (3) The fact that classification societies are charitable non-profit making organisations was irrelevant. He pointed out that hospitals are charitable non-profit making organisations but are often held liable in tort.

3.   For a comment on the decision in the Court of Appeal (where NKK was also held not liable) see Cane, 'The liability of classification societies' [1984] LMCLR 363. He concludes that 'if we view the law of tort as a mechanism for allocating responsibility for losses on the basis of judgements of personal morality in the absence of agreement between the litigating parties as to how those losses should be borne, the decision rests on shaky foundations. But in terms of promoting economic efficiency in the international markets in ship classifications and carriage of goods by sea, there are good arguments in favour of the Court of Appeal decision.'

Questions

1.   Is it essential to the 'waste of resources' argument and the 'defensive attitude' point that the organisation should carry out a *public* role?

2.   If the ship repairer had been negligent would he have been liable? If so, how would that differ from the case of the ship surveyor?

5   BREACH OF DUTY: THE STANDARD OF CARE

Once it has been established that there is a sufficient relationship between the parties to establish a duty, the question then arises whether the defendant has been in breach of this duty. This involves a number of issues, many of which are obscured by resort to the judgment of the reasonable man. That fictitious being is no more than the 'anthropomorphic conception of justice', and justice is a complicated concept. The reasonable man may give the impression of certainty where there is none, for whether it is reasonable to take a certain risk involves questions of economic and social policy which are rarely expressed in the law reports. For example, how strong a sea wall should be involves balancing considerations of cost and safety; where a known risk is undertaken for good reasons (as in a police chase) who should bear the risk?

It is important to note, however, that we cannot be protected by the law against all risks: we must put up with the 'vicissitudes of life' and can only expect to be compensated for damage caused by unreasonable activities. The issue of the standard of care can be put in two ways: On the one hand we can ask whether the defendant created an unreasonable risk, and on the other we can ask what level of safety a potential plaintiff is entitled to expect. These are two sides of the same coin and will usually, but not always, lead to the same result. However, we also know that damage is going to occur as a result of human activity, and who should bear the risk of that damage is an important matter of social policy. To a great extent that question is answered by the fact that we have a fault rather than a no-fault system of compensation, but even within the fault system, how losses are distributed is to some extent governed by our understanding of what risks are unreasonable.

Section 1:   the reasonable man — the level of reasonable risk

The standard which the law requires a person to attain must be objectively determined. A person will be regarded as negligent if he fails to act according to that standard, even if it is more difficult for him as an individual to do so than for others. The reason is that we are all entitled to expect a certain level of protection from the acts of others. So the concept of the 'reasonable man' does two things: it judges whether the defendant was careless, but also defines the level of safety a plaintiff is entitled to expect. This is a social and not a moral judgment.

Glasgow Corporation v Muir
House of Lords [1943] AC 448; [1943] 2 All ER 44; 169 LT 53

The Corporation owned the old mansion in King's Park, Glasgow, in which there were tea rooms managed by Mrs Alexander. A picnic party of 30-40 people from the Milton Street Free Church asked her if they could take shelter in the old mansion and eat their tea there. Mrs Alexander agreed, and a tea urn weighing 100lbs was carried in by George McDonald and a boy called Taylor. As they entered the tea rooms George McDonald inexplicably dropped his side of the urn and six children were scalded by hot tea. The corridor was five feet wide, narrowing to three feet three inches, and a number of children were in there buying sweets. The plaintiffs alleged that the manageress was negligent in allowing the urn to be carried into the tea rooms. Held: allowing the appeal, that the manageress was not negligent.

LORD MACMILLAN: My Lords, the degree of care for the safety of others which the law requires human beings to observe in the conduct of their affairs varies according to the circumstances. There is no absolute standard, but it may be said generally that the degree of care required varies directly with the risk involved. Those who engage in operations inherently dangerous must take precautions which are not required of persons engaged in the ordinary routine of daily life. It is, no doubt, true that in every act which an individual performs there is present a potentiality of injury to others. All things are possible, and, indeed, it has become proverbial that the unexpected always happens, but, while the precept alterum non laedere requires us to abstain from intentionally injuring others, it does not impose liability for every injury which our conduct may occasion. In Scotland, at any rate, it has never been a maxim of the law that a man acts at his peril. Legal liability is limited to those consequences of our acts which a reasonable man of ordinary intelligence and experience so acting would have in contemplation. 'The duty to take care,' as I essayed to formulate it in Bourhill v Young ([1943] AC 92, 104), 'is the duty to avoid doing or omitting to do anything the doing or omitting to do which may have as its reasonable and probable consequence injury to others, and the duty is owed to those to whom injury may reasonably and probably be anticipated if the duty is not observed.' This, in my opinion, expresses the law of Scotland and I apprehend that it is also the law of England. The standard of foresight of the reasonable man is, in one sense, an impersonal test. It eliminates the personal equation and is independent of the idiosyncrasies of the particular person whose conduct is in question. Some persons are by nature unduly timorous and imagine every path beset with lions. Others, of more robust temperament, fail to foresee or nonchalantly disregard even the most obvious dangers. The reasonable man is presumed to be free both from over-apprehension and from over-confidence, but there is a sense in which the standard of care of the reasonable man involves in its application a subjective element. It is still left to the judge to decide what, in the circumstances of the particular case, the reasonable man would have had in contemplation, and what, accordingly, the party sought to be made liable ought to have foreseen. Here there is room for diversity of view, as, indeed, is well illustrated in the present case. What to one judge may seem far-fetched may seem to another both natural and probable.

With these considerations in mind I turn to the facts of the occurrence on which your Lordships have to adjudicate. . . . The question, as I see it, is whether Mrs Alexander, when she was asked to allow a tea urn to be brought into the premises under her charge, ought to have had in mind that it would require to be carried through a narrow passage in which there were a number of children and that there would be a risk of the contents of the urn being spilt and scalding some of the children. If, as a reasonable person, she ought to have had these considerations in mind, was it her duty to require that she should be informed of the arrival of the urn, and, before allowing it to be carried through the narrow passage, to clear all the children out of it in case they might be splashed with scalding water? . . .

In my opinion, Mrs Alexander had no reason to anticipate that such an event would happen as a consequence of granting permission for a tea urn to be carried through the passage way where the children were congregated, and, consequently, there was no duty incumbent on her to take precautions against the occurrence of such an event. I think that she was entitled to assume that the urn would be in charge of responsible persons (as it was) who would have regard for the safety of the children in the passage (as they did have regard), and that the urn would be carried with ordinary care, in which case its transit would occasion no danger to bystanders. The pursuers have left quite unexplained the actual cause of the accident. The immediate cause was not the carrying of the urn through the passage, but McDonald's losing grip of his handle. How he came to do so is entirely a matter of speculation. He may have stumbled or he may have suffered a temporary muscular failure. We do not know, and the pursuers have not chosen to enlighten us by calling McDonald as a witness. Yet it is argued that Mrs Alexander ought to have foreseen the possibility, nay, the reasonable probability of an occurrence the nature of which is unascertained. Suppose that McDonald let go his handle through carelessness. Was Mrs Alexander bound to foresee this as reasonably probable and to take precautions against the possible consequences? I do not think so. . . .

Note

The reasonable man has been described as 'the man on the Clapham omnibus' and as the man who mows his lawn in his shirtsleeves. A. P. Herbert in *Uncommon Law* described him as follows:

> All solid virtues are his, save only that peculiar quality by which the affection of other men is won. . . . Devoid in short of any human weakness, with not one single saving vice, *sans* prejudice, procrastination, ill nature, avarice, and absence of mind, as careful for his own safety as he is for that of others, this excellent but odious character stands like a monument in our Courts of Justice, vainly appealing to his fellow citizens to order their lives after his own example.

Bolton v Stone
House of Lords [1951] AC 850; [1951] 1 All ER 1078

The plaintiff, Miss Stone, was struck by a cricket ball hit out of a cricket ground at Cheetham Hill, Manchester. The ground was surrounded by a fence whose top, due to the slope of the ground, was 17 feet above the level of the pitch. The fence was 78 yards from the striker, and the plaintiff, when hit, was 100 yards away. One member of the club said that he thought that about six balls had been hit out of the ground in 28 years, none causing any injury. Held: allowing the appeal, that the club was not negligent.

LORD REID: Counsel for the respondent in this case had to put his case so high as to say that, at least as soon as one ball had been driven into the road in the ordinary course of a match, the appellants could and should have realized that that might happen again and that, if it did, someone might be injured; and that that was enough to put on the appellants a duty to take steps to prevent such an occurrence. If the true test is foreseeability alone I think that must be so. Once a ball has been driven on to a road without there being anything extraordinary to account for the fact, there is clearly a risk that another will follow, and if it does there is clearly a chance, small though it may be, that someone may be injured. On the theory that it is foreseeability alone that matters it would be irrelevant to consider how often a ball might be expected to land in the road and it would not matter whether the road was the busiest street, or the quietest country lane; the only difference between these cases is in the degree of risk.

It would take a good deal to make me believe that the law has departed so far from the standards which guide ordinary careful people in ordinary life. In the crowded conditions of modern life even the most careful person cannot avoid creating some risks and accepting others. What a man must not do, and what I think a careful man tries not to do, is to create a risk which is substantial. . . . In my judgment the test to be applied here is whether the risk of damage to a person on the road was so small that a reasonable man in the position of the appellants, considering the matter from the point of view of safety, would have thought it right to refrain from taking steps to prevent the danger.

In considering that matter I think that it would be right to take into account not only how remote is the chance that a person might be struck but also how serious the consequences are likely to be if a person is struck; but I do not think that it would be right to take into account the difficulty of remedial measures. If cricket cannot be played on a ground without creating a substantial risk, then it should not be played there at all. I think that this is in substance the test which Oliver J applied in this case. He considered whether the appellants' ground was large enough to be safe for all practical purposes and held that it was. This is a question not of law but of fact and degree. It is not an easy question and it is one on which opinions may well differ. I can only say that having given the whole matter repeated and anxious consideration I find myself unable to decide this question in favour of the respondent. But I think that this case is not far from the borderline. If this appeal is allowed, that does not in my judgment mean that in every case where cricket has been played on a ground for a number of years without accident or complaint those who organize matches there are safe to go on in reliance on past immunity. I would have reached a different conclusion if I had thought that the risk there had been other than extremely small, because I do not think that a reasonable man considering the matter from the point of view of safety would or should disregard any risk unless it is extremely small. . . .

LORD RADCLIFFE: My Lords, I agree that this appeal must be allowed. I agree with regret, because I have much sympathy with the decision that commended itself to the majority of the members of the Court of Appeal. I can see nothing unfair in the appellants being required to compensate the respondent for the serious injury that she has received as a result of the sport that they have organized on their cricket ground at Cheetham Hill. But the law of negligence is concerned less with what is fair than with what is culpable, and I cannot persuade myself that the appellants have been guilty of any culpable act or omission in this case.

I think that the case is in some respects a peculiar one, not easily related to the general rules that govern liability for negligence. If the test whether there has been a breach of duty were to depend merely on the answer to the question whether this accident was a reasonably foreseeable risk, I think that there would have been a breach of duty, for that such an accident might take place some time or other might very reasonably have been present to the minds of the appellants. It was quite foreseeable, and there would have been nothing unreasonable in allowing the imagination to dwell on the possibility of its occurring. But there was only a remote, perhaps I ought to say only a very remote, chance of the accident taking place at any particular time, for, if it was to happen, not only had a ball to carry the fence round the ground but it had also to coincide in its arrival with the presence of some person on what does not look like a crowded thoroughfare and actually to strike that person in some way that would cause sensible injury.

Those being the facts, a breach of duty has taken place if they show the appellants guilty of a failure to take reasonable care to prevent the accident. One may phrase it as 'reasonable care' or 'ordinary care' or 'proper care' — all these phrases are to be found in decisions of authority — but the fact remains that, unless there has been something which a reasonable man would blame as falling beneath the standard of conduct that he would set for himself and require of his neighbour, there has been no breach of legal duty. And here, I think, the respondent's case breaks down. It seems to me that a reasonable man, taking account of the chances against an accident happening, would not have felt himself called upon either to abandon the use of the ground for cricket or to increase the height of his surrounding fences. He would have done what the appellants did: in other words, he would have done nothing. Whether, if the unlikely event of an accident did occur and his play turn to another's hurt, he would have thought it equally proper to offer no more consolation to his victim than the reflection that a social being is not immune from social risks, I do not say, for I do not think that that is a consideration which is relevant to legal liability.

Question

Does the nature of the activity matter? Is cricket 'a good thing'? X is in the habit of holding all night parties. The guests habitually throw bottles into the garden. One night at 3.00 a.m., Y throws a bottle out of the window, which strikes Z, standing 20 yards away in the road. Only twice before have bottles reached the road. Is X liable for holding the party?

Blyth v *Proprietors of the Birmingham Waterworks*
Court of Exchequer (1856) 11 Ex 781; 156 ER 1047

The defendant had laid a water main 18 inches deep, and in the main was a 'fire plug'. This was a neck in the main stopped by a wooden plug, which when released allowed water to flow up a cast iron tube to street level. On 24 February 1855 water escaped from the main and forced its way through the ground into the plaintiff's house, the cast iron tube above the plug being stopped up with ice. It seemed that on 15 January 1855 there was a severe frost, and this may have caused the wooden plug to be dislodged by the expansion of water. Held: the defendants were not negligent.

ALDERSON, B: I am of opinion that there was no evidence to be left to the jury. The case turns upon the question, whether the facts proved shew that the defendants were guilty of negligence. Negligence is the omission to do something which a reasonable man, guided upon those considerations which ordinarily regulate the conduct of human affairs, would do, or doing something which a prudent and reasonable man would not do. The defendants might have been liable for negligence, if, unintentionally, they omitted to do that which a reasonable person would have done, or did that which a person taking reasonable precautions would not have done. A reasonable man would act with reference to the average circumstances of the temperature in ordinary years. The defendants had provided against such frosts as experience would have led men, acting prudently, to provide against; and they are not guilty of negligence, because their precautions proved insufficient against the effects of the extreme severity of the frost of 1855, which penetrated to a greater depth than any which ordinarily occurs south of the polar regions. Such a state of circumstances constitutes a contingency against which no reasonable man can provide. The result was an accident, for which the defendants cannot be held liable.

Notes
1.   This case introduces a very important problem. If the mains had been a foot lower they might have escaped the effects of the frost, but that would have been more expensive. Hence, the 'standard of care' involves difficult economic issues: how much should be paid for safety? At what level of cost is a potential defendant entitled to say that the proposed safety measure is too expensive? In *US* v *Carroll Towing* (1947) 159 F 2d 169, Judge Learned Hand said that if the probability of the damage occurring is called P, the extent of the potential damage (i.e. the liability) is called L and the cost of preventing the damage (i.e. the burden) is called B, then liability depends on whether B is less than L multiplied by P: i.e. whether $B < PL$. This may be a useful guide in some cases but is really too simplistic as other values may be relevant. For example, could the formula be used on its own to justify the possibility of cancer being contracted by workers in a chemical factory?
2.   The particular issue in *Blyth* has now been determined by statute: under the Water Industry Act 1991, s. 209 a water undertaker is strictly liable for the escape of water from any pipe which is vested in it.

Section 2:   the skill of the defendant

People have varying degrees of skill, but the test of liability must be objective. Nevertheless, the degree of skill which a potential plaintiff is entitled to expect from a potential defendant will not necessarily be that of the ordinary man, but rather the skill of the reasonable example of that kind of person. Thus doctors must conform to the level of skill of the reasonable doctor and not that of the man on the Clapham omnibus.

A: The safety we are entitled to expect

Wells v *Cooper*
[1958] 2 QB 265; [1958] 2 All ER 527; [1958] 3 WLR 1128

The plaintiff, Albert Wells, was delivering fish to the defendant's house. As he was leaving he pulled the back door to close it and the door handle came away in his hand, and he lost his balance and fell. The door needed quite a strong pull as a draught excluder was fitted to the bottom of it and there was quite a strong wind blowing against the door. The handle had been put on by the defendant himself a few months earlier, and consisted of a lever type handle fixed by a base plate which was held to the door by four $\frac{3}{4}$ inch screws. The defendant had some experience as an amateur carpenter. Held, allowing the appeal, that the defendant was not liable for using $\frac{3}{4}$ inch screws.

JENKINS LJ: As above related, the defendant did the work himself. We do not think the mere fact that he did it himself instead of employing a professional carpenter to do it constituted a breach of his duty of care. No doubt some kinds of work involve such highly specialized skill and knowledge, and create such serious dangers if not properly done, that an ordinary occupier owing a duty of care to others in regard to the safety of premises would fail in that duty if he undertook such work himself instead of employing experts to do it for him. See *Haseldine* v *C. A. Daw & Son Ltd, per* Scott LJ, [1941] 2 KB 343. But the work here in question was not of that order. It was a trifling domestic replacement well within the competence of a householder accustomed to doing small carpentering jobs about his home, and of a kind which must be done every day by hundreds of householders up and down the country.

Accordingly, we think that the defendant did nothing unreasonable in undertaking the work himself. But it behoved him, if he was to discharge his duty of care to persons such as the plaintiff, to do the work with reasonable care and skill, and we think the degree of care and skill required of him must be measured not by reference to the degree of competence in such matters which he personally happened to possess, but by reference to the degree of care and skill which a reasonably competent carpenter might be expected to apply to the work in question. Otherwise, the extent of the protection that an invitee could claim in relation to work done by the invitor himself would vary according to the capacity of the invitor, who could free himself from liability merely by showing that he had done the best of which he was capable, however good, bad or indifferent that best might be.

Accordingly, we think the standard of care and skill to be demanded of the defendant in order to discharge his duty of care to the plaintiff in the fixing of the new handle in the present case must be the degree of care and skill to be expected of a reasonably competent carpenter doing the work in question. This does not mean that the degree of care and skill required is to be measured by reference to the contractual obligations as to the quality of his work assumed by a professional carpenter working for reward, which would, in our view, set the standard too high. The question is simply what steps would a reasonably competent carpenter wishing to fix a handle such as this securely to a door such as this have taken with a view to achieving that object.

In fact the only complaint made by the plaintiff in regard to the way in which the defendant fixed the new handle is that three-quarter inch screws were inadequate and that one inch screws should have been used. The question may, therefore, be stated more narrowly as being whether a reasonably competent carpenter fixing this handle would have appreciated that three-quarter inch screws such as those used by the defendant would not be adequate to fix it securely and would accordingly have used one inch screws instead. . . .

In relation to a trifling and perfectly simple operation such as the fixing of the new handle we think that the defendant's experience of domestic carpentry is sufficient to justify his inclusion in the category of reasonably competent carpenters. The matter then stands thus. The defendant, a reasonably competent carpenter, used three-quarter inch screws, believing them to be adequate for the purpose of fixing the handle. There is no doubt that he was doing his best to make the handle secure and believed that he had done so. Accordingly, he must be taken to have discharged his duty of reasonable care, unless the belief that three-quarter inch screws would be adequate was one which no reasonably competent carpenter could reasonably entertain, or, in other words, an obvious blunder which should at once have been apparent to him as a reasonably competent carpenter. The evidence adduced on the plaintiff's side failed, in the judge's view, to make that out. He saw and heard the witnesses, and had demonstrated to him the strength of attachment provided by three-quarter inch screws. We see no sufficient reason for differing from his conclusion. Indeed, the fact that the handle remained secure during the period of four or five months between the time it was fixed and the date of the accident, although no doubt in constant use throughout that period, makes it very difficult to accept the view that the inadequacy of the three-quarter inch screws should have been obvious to the defendant at the time when he decided to use them.

Question
In order to decide whether the use of $\frac{3}{4}$ inch screws was negligent, who should you ask — the reasonable man, the reasonable householder, the reasonable handyman, or the reasonable carpenter? What question should you ask him? (Incidentally, at first instance the judge, Stable J, ignored the evidence of two expert witnesses to the effect that a reasonably competent carpenter would have thought $\frac{3}{4}$ inch screws to be inadequate.)

B: The underskilled

Nettleship v Weston
[1971] 2 QB 691; [1971] 3 All ER 581; [1971] RTR 425

The plaintiff, Eric Nettleship, was teaching a friend of his, Lavinia Weston, to drive. She negligently hit a lamp post and the plaintiff suffered a broken knee cap. Held: allowing the appeal, that the defendant was liable. (Note: the extracts below deal only with the issue of standard of care. The case also raised the issue whether the plaintiff consented to the risk of injury, and it was held that he did not.)

LORD DENNING MR:

The Responsibility of the Learner Driver towards Persons on or near the Highway
Mrs Weston is clearly liable for the damage to the lamp post. In the civil law if a driver goes off the road on to the pavement and injures a pedestrian, or damages property, he is prima facie liable. Likewise if he goes on to the wrong side of the road. It is no answer for him to say: 'I was a learner driver under instruction. I was doing my best and could not help it.' The civil law permits no such excuse. It requires of him the same standard of care as of any other driver. 'It eliminates the personal equation and is independent of the idiosyncrasies of the particular person whose conduct is in question': see *Glasgow Corporation* v *Muir* [1943] AC 448, 457 by Lord Macmillan. The learner driver may be doing his best, but his incompetent best is not good enough. He must drive in as good a manner as a driver of skill, experience and care, who is sound in mind and limb, who makes no errors of judgment, has good eyesight and hearing, and is free from any infirmity: see *Richley (Henderson)* v *Faull, Richley, Third Party* [1965] 1 WLR 1454 and *Watson* v *Thomas S. Whitney & Co. Ltd* [1966] 1 WLR 57.

The high standard thus imposed by the judges is, I believe, largely the result of the policy of the Road Traffic Acts. Parliament requires every driver to be insured against third party risks. The reason is so that a person injured by a motor car should not be left to bear the loss on his own, but should be compensated out of the insurance fund. The fund is better able to bear it than he can. But the injured person is only able to recover if the driver is liable in law. So the judges see to it that he is liable, unless he can prove care and skill of a high standard: see *The Merchant Prince* [1982] P 179 and *Henderson* v *Henry E. Jenkins & Sons* [1970] AC 282. Thus we are, in this branch of the law, moving away from the concept: 'No liability without fault.' We are beginning to apply the test: 'On whom should the risk fall?' Morally the learner driver is not at fault; but legally she is liable to be because she is insured and the risk should fall on her.

The responsibility of the Learner Driver towards Passengers in the Car
Mrs Weston took her son with her in the car. We do not know his age. He may have been 21 and have known that his mother was learning to drive. He was not injured. But if he had been injured, would he have had a cause of action?

I take it to be clear that if a driver has a passenger in the car he owes a duty of care to him. But what is the standard of care required of the driver? Is it a lower standard than he or she owes towards a pedestrian on the pavement? I should have thought not. But, suppose that the driver has never driven a car before, or has taken too much to drink or has poor eyesight or hearing: and, furthermore, that the passenger *knows* it and yet accepts a lift from him. Does that make any difference? Dixon J thought it did. In *The Insurance Commissioner* v *Joyce* (1948) 77 CLR 39, 56, he said:

> If a man accepts a lift from a car driver whom he *knows* to have lost a limb or an eye or to be deaf, he cannot complain if he does not exhibit the skill and competence of a driver who suffers from no defect. . . . If he knowingly accepts the voluntary services of a driver affected by drink, he cannot complain of improper driving caused by his condition, because it involved no breach of duty.

That view of Dixon J seems to have been followed in South Australia: see *Walker* v *Turton-Sainsbury* [1952] SASR 159; but in the Supreme Court of Canada Rand J did not agree with it: see *Car and General Insurance Co.* v *Seymour and Maloney* (1956) 2 DLR (2d) 369, 375.

We have all the greatest respect for Sir Owen Dixon, but for once I cannot agree with him. The driver owes a duty of care to every passenger in the car, just as he does to every pedestrian on the road: and he must attain the same standard of care in respect of each. If the driver were to be excused according to the knowledge of the passenger, it would result in endless confusion and injustice. One of the passengers may know that the learner driver is a mere novice. Another passenger may believe him to be entirely competent. One of the passengers may believe the driver to have had only two drinks. Another passenger may know that he has had a dozen. Is the one passenger to recover and the other not? Rather than embark on such inquiries, the law holds that the driver must attain the same standard of care for passengers as for pedestrians. The knowledge of the passenger may go to show that he was guilty of contributory negligence in ever accepting the lift — and thus reduce his damages — but it does not take away the duty of care, nor does it diminish the standard of care which the law requires of the driver: see *Dann* v *Hamilton* [1939] 1 KB 509 and *Slater* v *Clay Cross Co. Ltd* [1956] 2 QB 264, 270.

I would only add this: If the knowledge of the passenger were held to take away the duty of care, it would mean that we would once again be applying the maxim: 'Scienti non fit injuria.' That maxim was decisively rejected by the House of Lords in cases between employer and workmen; see *Smith* v *Baker & Sons* [1891] AC 325; and by Parliament in cases between occupier and visitor: see section 2 (4) of the Occupiers' Liability Act 1957, overruling *London Graving Dock Co. Ltd* v *Horton* [1951] AC 737. We should not allow it to be introduced today in motor car cases even though it was backed by Sir Owen Dixon. But that was in 1948. He might think differently today.

The Responsibility of a Learner Driver towards his Instructor
The special factor in this case is that Mr Nettleship was not a mere passenger in the car. He was an instructor teaching Mrs Weston to drive.

Seeing that the law lays down, for all drivers of motor cars, a standard of care to which all must conform, I think that even a learner driver, so long as he is the sole driver, must attain the same standard towards all passengers in the car, including an instructor. But the instructor may be debarred from claiming for a reason peculiar to himself. He may be debarred because he has voluntarily agreed to waive any claim for any injury that may befall him. Otherwise he is not debarred. He may, of course, be guilty of contributory negligence and have his damages reduced on that account. He may, for instance, have let the learner take control too soon, he may not have been quick enough to correct his errors, or he may have participated in the negligent act himself: see *Stapley* v *Gypsum Mines Ltd* [1953] AC 663. But, apart from contributory negligence, he is not excluded unless it be that he has voluntarily agreed to incur the risk. . . .

MEGAW LJ: . . . The important question of principle which arises is whether, because of Mr Nettleship's knowledge that Mrs Weston was not an experienced driver, the standard of care which was owed to him by her was lower than would otherwise have been the case.

In *The Insurance Commissioner* v *Joyce* (1948) CLR 39, 56-60, Dixon J stated persuasively the view that there is, or may be, a 'particular relation' between the driver of a vehicle and his passenger resulting in a variation of the standard of duty owed by the driver. He said, at p.56:

> The case of a passenger in a car differs from that of a pedestrian not in the kind or degree of danger which may come from any want of care or skill in driving but in the fact that the former has come into a more particular relation with the driver of the car. It is because that relation may vary that the standard of duty or of care is not necessarily the same in every case. . . . the gratuitous passenger may expect prima facie the same care and skill on the part of the driver as is ordinarily demanded in the management of a car. Unusual conditions may exist which are apparent to him or of which he may be informed and they may affect the application of the standard of care that is due. If a man accepts a lift from a car driver whom he knows to have lost a limb or an eye or to be deaf, he cannot complain if he does not exhibit the skill and competence of a driver who suffers from no defect.

He summarised the same principle in these words, at p.59:

> It appears to me that the circumstances in which the defendant accepts the plaintiff as a passenger and in which the plaintiff accepts the accommodation in the conveyance should determine the measure of duty. . . .

Theoretically, the principle as thus expounded is attractive. But, with very great respect, I venture to think that the theoretical attraction should yield to practical considerations.

As I see it, if this doctrine of varying standards were to be accepted as part of the law on these facts, it could not logically be confined to the duty of care owed by learner drivers. There is no reason in logic why it should not operate in a much wider sphere. The disadvantages of the resulting unpredictability, uncertainty and, indeed, impossibility of arriving at fair and consistent decisions outweigh the advantages. The certainty of a general standard is preferable to the vagaries of a fluctuating standard. . . .

Again, when one considers the requisite standard of care of the learner driver, if this doctrine were to apply, would not logic irresistibly demand that there should be something more than a mere, single, conventional, standard applicable to anyone who falls into the category of learner driver: that is, of anyone who has not yet qualified for (or perhaps obtained) a full licence? That standard itself would necessarily vary over a wide range, not merely with the actual progress of the learner, but also with the passenger's knowledge of that progress: or, rather, if the passenger has in fact over-estimated the driver's progress, it would vary with the passenger's reasonable assessment of that progress at the relevant time. The relevant time would not necessarily be the moment of the accident.

The question, what is the relevant time, would itself have to be resolved by reference to some principle. The instructor's reasonable assessment of the skill and competence of the driver (and also the driver's assessment of the instructor's skill and competence) might alter drastically between the start of the first lesson and the start of a later lesson, or even in the course of one particular spell of driving. I suppose the principle would have to be that the relevant time is the last moment when the plaintiff (whether instructor or driver) could reasonably have refused to continue as passenger or driver in the light of his then knowledge. The factor in itself would introduce yet another element of difficulty, uncertainty and, I believe, serious anomaly.

I, for my part, with all respect, do not think that our legal process could successfully or satisfactorily cope with the task of fairly assessing or applying to the facts of a particular case such varying standards, depending on such complex and elusive factors, including the assessment by the court, not merely of a particular person's actual skill or experience, but also of another person's knowledge or assessment of that skill or experience at a particular moment of time.

Notes
1. In *Philips* v *Whiteley Ltd* [1938] 1 All ER 566, the plaintiff had her ears pierced by a jeweller and subsequently suffered an infection. It was decided that the infection was probably not due to the ear piercing, but, even if it was, the jeweller would not have been liable as he had taken all reasonable precautions that a jeweller would take and could not be expected to conform to the standards of a surgeon. Is this view consistent with *Nettleship* v *Weston*? What level of care was Mrs Philips entitled to?

In *Wilsher* v *Essex Area Health Authority* [1987] QB 730, at p. 750, it was argued that a junior inexperienced doctor owed a lower duty of care: Mustill LJ rejected this, saying:

this notion of a duty tailored to the actor, rather than to the act which he elects to perform, has no place in the law of tort. . . . To my mind it would be a false step to subordinate the legitimate expectation of the patient that he will receive from each person concerned with his care a degree of skill appropriate to the task which he undertakes to an understandable wish to minimise the psychological and financial pressures on hard pressed young doctors.

(The case was reversed on appeal on a different point: [1988] AC 1074.)

2. In *Cook* v *Cook* (1986) 162 CLR 376, the High Court of Australia refused to follow *Nettleship* v *Weston*, preferring the views of Dixon J in *Insurance Commissioner* v *Joyce* (mentioned in *Nettleship*). The court said that the standard of care should be derived from the relationship between the parties, so that where the plaintiff knows of an incapacity of the defendant the standard will be lower. In this case the plaintiff encouraged the defendant to drive even though she knew that the defendant did not have even a provisional driving licence, and it was held that the appropriate standard was that of the inexperienced driver. Are such problems better dealt with by the defence of contributory negligence? See Kidner, 'The variable standard of care, contributory negligence and *volenti*' (1991) 11 LS 1.

C: Special skills

Bolam v Friern Hospital Management Committee
Queen's Bench Division [1957] 1 WLR 582; [1957] 2 All ER 118

The plaintiff suffered a fracture of the pelvis while he was undergoing electro-convulsive therapy. The issue was whether the doctor was negligent in failing to give a relaxant drug before the treatment, or in failing to provide means of restraint during it. Evidence was given of the practices of various doctors in this regard, and the extracts below deal with the appropriate test to be applied in assessing the conduct of the defendant. Held: the defendants were not liable.

MCNAIR J, *addressing the jury:* Before I turn to that, I must tell you what in law we mean by 'negligence.' In the ordinary case which does not involve any special skill, negligence in law means a failure to do some act which a reasonable man in the circumstances would do, or the doing of some act which a reasonable man in the circumstances would not do; and if that failure or the doing of that act results in injury, then there is a cause of action. How do you test whether this act or failure is negligent? In an ordinary case it is generally said you judge it by the action of the man in the street. He is the ordinary man. In one case it has been said you judge it by the conduct of the man on the top of a Clapham omnibus. He is the ordinary man. But where you get a situation which involves the use of some special skill or competence, then the test as to whether there has been negligence or not is not the test of the man on the top of a Clapham omnibus, because he has not got this special skill. The test is the standard of the ordinary skilled man exercising and professing to have that special skill. A man need not possess the highest expert skill; it is well established law that it is sufficient if he exercises the ordinary skill of an ordinary competent man exercising that particular art. I do not think that I quarrel much with any of the submissons in law which have been put before you by counsel. Mr Fox-Andrews put it in this way, that in the case of a medical man, negligence means failure to act in accordance with the standards of reasonably competent medical men at the time. That is a perfectly accurate statement, as long as it is remembered that there may be one or more perfectly proper standards; and if he conforms with one of those proper standards, then he is not negligent. Mr Fox-Andrews also was quite right, in my judgment, in saying that a mere personal belief that a particular technique is best is no defence unless that belief is based on reasonable grounds. That again is unexceptionable. But the emphasis which is laid by the defence is on this aspect of negligence, that the real question you have to make up your minds about on each of the three major topics is whether the defendants, in acting in the way they did, were acting in accordance with a practice of competent respected professional opinion. Mr Stirling submitted that if you are satisfied that they were acting in accordance with a practice of a competent body of professional opinion, then it would be wrong for you to hold that negligence was established. In a recent Scottish case, *Hunter* v *Hanley*, 1955 SLT 213, Lord President Clyde [at p. 217] said:

> In the realm of diagnosis and treatment there is ample scope for genuine difference of opinion and one man clearly is not negligent merely because his conclusion differs from that of other professional men, nor because he has displayed less skill or knowledge than others would have shown. The true test for establishing negligence in diagnosis or treatment on the part of a doctor is whether he has been proved to be guilty of such failure as no doctor of ordinary skill would be guilty of, if acting with ordinary care.

If that statement of the true test is qualified by the words 'in all the circumstances,' Mr Fox-Andrews would not seek to say that that expression of opinion does not accord with the English law. It is just a question of expression. I myself would prefer to put it this way, that he is not guilty of negligence if he has acted in accordance with a practice accepted as proper by a responsible body of medical men skilled in that particular art. I do not think there is much difference in sense. It is just a different way of expressing the same thought. Putting it the other way round, a man is not negligent, if he is acting in accordance with such a practice, merely because there is a body of opinion who would take a contrary view. At the same time, that does not mean that a medical man can obstinately and pig-headedly carry on with some old technique if it has been proved to be contrary to what is really substantially the whole of informed medical opinion. Otherwise you might get men today saying: 'I do not believe in anaesthetics. I do not believe in antiseptics. I am going to continue to do my surgery in the way it was done in the eighteenth century.' That clearly would be wrong.

Before I get to the details of the case, it is right to say this, that it is not essential for you to decide which of two practices is the better practice, as long as you accept that what the defendants did was in accordance with a practice accepted by responsible persons; if the result of the evidence is that you are satisfied that this practice is better than the practice spoken of on the other side, then it is really a stronger case. Finally, bear this in mind, that you are now considering whether it was negligent for certain action to be taken in August, 1954, not in February, 1957; and in one of the well-known cases on this topic it has been said you must not look with 1957 spectacles at what happened in 1954.

Note
This case has been approved by the House of Lords in *Sidaway* v *Bethlem Royal Hospital* [1985] AC 871 and in *Whitehouse* v *Jordan* [1981] 1 WLR 246. In the latter case Lord Denning, in the Court of Appeal, attempted to argue that there was a difference between error of judgment and negligence, saying 'When I give a judgment and it is afterwards reversed by the House of Lords, is it to be said that I was negligent?'. He duly was reversed by the House of Lords, Lord Edmund Davies saying that the phrase 'error of judgment' was wholly ambiguous, 'for while some such errors may be completely consistent with the

due exercise of professional skill, other acts or omissions in the course of exercising clinical judgment may be so glaringly below proper standards as to make a finding of negligence inevitable.'

Question
If the issue is to be tested by the standards of the relevant profession, does that mean that the profession is able to judge itself? What control does the law have?

Sidaway v *Governors of the Bethlem Royal Hospital*
House of Lords [1985] AC 871; [1985] 2 WLR 480; [1985] 1 All ER 643

Mrs Sidaway suffered persistent pain in her right arm and shoulder and a surgeon employed by the defendants recommended an operation to her spine to which Mrs Sidaway consented. The operation involved a risk, put at less than 1 per cent, of damage to the spine and Mrs Sidaway was not informed of this risk. The operation was properly conducted but unfortunately the risk materialised and the plaintiff became severely disabled. She sued the defendants on the ground that the surgeon had failed to inform her of the risk. Held: dismissing the appeal, that the defendants were not liable.

LORD BRIDGE: . . . The important question which this appeal raises is whether the law imposes any, and if so what, different criterion as the measure of the medical man's duty of care to his patient when giving advice with respect to a proposed course of treatment. It is clearly right to recognise that a conscious adult patient of sound mind is entitled to decide for himself whether or not he will submit to a particular course of treatment proposed by the doctor, most significantly surgical treatment under general anaesthesia. This entitlement is the foundation of the doctrine of 'informed consent' which has led in certain American jurisdictions to decisions, and in the Supreme Court of Canada, to dicta, on which the appellant relies, which would oust the *Bolam* test and substitute an 'objective' test of a doctor's duty to advise the patient of the advantages and disadvantages of undergoing the treatment proposed and more particularly to advise the patient of the risks involved.
   There are, it appears to me, at least theoretically, two extreme positions which could be taken. It could be argued that, if the patient's consent is to be fully informed, the doctor must specifically warn him of *all* risks involved in the treatment offered, unless he has some sound clinical reason not to do so. Logically, this would seem to be the extreme to which a truly objective criterion of the doctor's duty would lead. Yet this position finds no support from any authority, to which we have been referred, in any jurisdiction. It seems to be generally accepted that there is no need to warn of the risks inherent in all surgery under general anaesthesia. This is variously explained on the ground that the patient may be expected to be aware of such risks or that they are relatively remote. If the law is to impose on the medical profession a duty to warn of risks to secure 'informed consent' independently of accepted medical opinion of what is appropriate, neither of these explanations for confining the duty to special as opposed to general risks seems to me wholly convincing.
   At the other extreme it could be argued that, once the doctor has decided what treatment is, on balance of advantages and disadvantages, in the patient's best interest, he should not alarm the patient by volunteering a warning of any risk involved, however grave and substantial, unless specifically asked by the patient. I cannot believe that

contemporary medical opinion would support this view, which would effectively exclude the patient's right to decide in the very type of case where it is most important that he should be in a position to exercise that right and, perhaps even more significantly, to seek a second opinion as to whether he should submit himself to the significant risk which has been drawn to his attention. I should perhaps add at this point, although the issue does not strictly arise in this appeal, that, when questioned specifically by a patient of apparently sound mind about risks involved in a particular treatment proposed, the doctor's duty must, in my opinion, be to answer both truthfully and as fully as the questioner requires.

The decision mainly relied on to establish a criterion of the doctor's duty to disclose the risks inherent in a proposed treatment which is prescribed by the law and can be applied independently of any medical opinion or practice is that of the District of Columbia Circuit Court of Appeals in *Canterbury* v *Spence*, 464 F. 2d 772. The judgment of the Court (Wright, Leventhal and Robinson JJ), delivered by Robinson J, expounds the view that an objective criterion of what is a sufficient disclosure of risk is necessary to ensure that the patient is enabled to make an intelligent decision and cannot be left to be determined by the doctors. He said, at p. 784:

Respect for the patient's right of self-determination on particular therapy demands a standard set by law for physicians rather than one which physicians may or may not impose upon themselves.

In an attempt to define the objective crtierion it is said, at p. 787, that 'the issue on non-disclosure must be approached from the viewpoint of the reasonableness of the physician's divulgence in terms of what he knows or should know to be the patient's informational needs'. A risk is required to be disclosed 'when a reasonable person, in what the physician knows or should know to be the patient's position, would be likely to attach significance to the risk or cluster or risks in deciding whether or not to forgo the proposed therapy': 464 F. 2d 772, 787. The judgment adds, at p. 788 'Whenever non-disclosure of particular risk information is open to debate by reasonable-minded men, the issue is for the finer of facts.'

I recognise the logical force of the *Canterbury* doctrine, proceeding from the premise that the patient's right to make his own decision must at all costs be safeguarded against the kind of medical paternalism which assumes that 'doctor knows best'. But, with all respect, I regard the doctrine as quite impractical in application for three principal reasons. First, it gives insufficient weight to the realities of the doctor/patient relationship. A very wide variety of factors must enter into a doctor's clinical judgment not only as to what treatment is appropriate for a particular patient, but also as to how best to communicate to the patient the significant factors necessary to enable the patient to make an informed decision whether to undergo the treatment. The doctor cannot set out to educate the patient to his own standard of medical knowledge of all the relevant factors involved. He may take the view, certainly with some patients, that the very fact of his volunteering, without being asked, information of some remote risk involved in the treatment proposed, even though he describes it as remote, may lead to that risk assuming an undue significance in the patient's calculations. Secondly, it would seem to me quite unrealistic in any medical negligence action to confine the expert medical evidence to an explanation of the primary medical factors involved and to deny the court the benefit of evidence of medical opinion and practice on the particular issue of disclosure which is under consideration. Thirdly, the objective test which *Canterbury* propounds seems to me to be so imprecise as to be almost meaningless. If it is to be left to individual judges to decide for themselves what 'a reasonable person in the patient's position' would consider a risk of sufficient significance that he should be told about it, the outcome of litigation in this field is likely to be quite unpredictable.

Having rejected the *Canterbury* doctrine as a solution to the problem of safeguarding the patient's right to decide whether he will undergo a particular treatment advised by his doctor, the question remains whether that right is sufficiently safeguarded by the application of the *Bolam* test without qualification to the determination of the question what risks inherent in a proposed treatment should be disclosed. The case against a simple application of the *Bolam* test is cogently stated by Laskin CJC, giving the judgment of the Supreme Court of Canada in *Reibl* v *Hughes*, 114 DLR (3d) 1, 13:

> To allow expert medical evidence to determine what risks are material and, hence, should be disclosed and, correlatively, what risks are not material is to hand over to the medical profession the entire question of the scope of the duty of disclosure, including the question whether there has been a breach of that duty. Expert medical evidence is, of course, relevant to findings as to the risks that reside in or are a result of recommended surgery or other treatment. It will also have a bearing on their materiality but this is not a question that is to be concluded on the basis of the expert medical evidence alone. The issue under consideration is a different issue from that involved where the question is whether the doctor carried out his professional activities by applicable professional standards. What is under consideration here is the patient's right to know what risks are involved in undergoing or forgoing certain surgery or other treatment.

I fully appreciate the force of this reasoning, but can only accept it subject to the important qualification that a decision what degree of disclosure of risks is best calculated to assist a particular patient to make a rational choice as to whether or not to undergo a particular treatment must primarily be a matter of clinical judgment. It would follow from this that the issue whether non-disclosure in a particular case should be condemned as a breach of the doctor's duty of care is an issue to be decided primarily on the basis of expert medical evidence, applying the *Bolam* test. But I do not see that this approach involves the necessity 'to hand over to the medical profession the entire question of the scope of the duty of disclosure, including the question whether there has been a breach of that duty'. Of course, if there is a conflict of evidence as to whether a responsible body of medical opinion approves of non-disclosure in a particular case, the judge will have to resolve that conflict. But even in a case where, as here, no expert witness in the relevant medical field condemns the non-disclosure as being in conflict with accepted and responsible medical practice, I am of opinion that the judge might in certain circumstances come to the conclusion that disclosure of a particular risk was so obviously necessary to an informed choice on the part of the patient that no reasonably prudent medical man would fail to make it. The kind of case I have in mind would be an operation involving a substantial risk of grave adverse consequences, as, for example, the ten per cent risk of a stroke from the operation which was the subject of the Canadian case of *Reibl* v *Hughes*, 114 DLR (3d) 1. In such a case, in the absence of some cogent clinical reason why the patient should not be informed, a doctor, recognising and respecting his patient's right of decision, could hardly fail to appreciate the necessity for an appropriate warning.

In the instant case I can see no reasonable ground on which the judge could properly reject the conclusion to which the unchallenged medical evidence led in the application of the *Bolam* test. The trial judge's assessment of the risk at one to two per cent covered both nerve root and spinal cord damage and covered a spectrum of possible ill effects 'ranging from the mild to the catastrophic'. In so far as it is possible and appropriate to measure such risks in percentage terms — some of the expert medical witnesses called expressed a marked and understandable reluctance to do so — the risk of damage to the spinal cord of such severity as the appellant in fact suffered was, it would appear, certainly less than one per cent. But there is no yardstick either in the judge's findings or in the evidence to measure what fraction of one per cent that risk represented. In these circumstances, the appellant's expert witness's agreement that the non-disclosure complained of accorded with a practice accepted as proper by a responsible body of neuro-surgical opinion afforded the respondents a complete defence to the appellant's claim.

Note

This case established that the *Bolam* test applied as much to the question of whether a patient should be informed of the risk as it does to diagnosis and treatment, and it rejects the doctrine of informed consent. However, in *Rogers* v *Whitaker* (1992) 175 CLR 479 the High Court of Australia has declined to follow *Sidaway* and has followed the Supreme Court of Canada in *Reibl* v *Hughes* (1980) 114 DSLR 3d 1. In *Rogers* the court said (at p. 490) that 'the law should recognise that a doctor has a duty to warn a patient of a material risk inherent in the proposed treatment; a risk is material if, in the circumstances of the particular case, a reasonable person in the patient's position, if warned of the risk, would be likely to attach significance to it or if the medical practitioner is or should reasonably be aware that the particular patient, if warned of the risk, would be likely to attach significant to it.' (It was noted that there is an exception to this principle where it can be shown that the information would harm an unusually nervous, volatile or disturbed patient.)

If the *Bolam* test applies why should a doctor not disclose what a reasonable patient would want to know?

D: Children

McHale v Watson
High Court of Australia (1965-66) 115 CLR 199; 38 ALJR 266

The defendant, Barry Watson, aged 12, threw a piece of welding rod (like thick wire), which had been sharpened at one end, at a wooden post. It glanced off the post and struck the plaintiff, Susan McHale, in the eye. Held: dismissing the appeal, that the defendant was not liable.

KITTO J: In so far as 'proper' is an apt word to use in this connexion it connotes nothing but conformity with an objective standard of care, namely the care reasonably to be expected in the like circumstances from the normal person exercising reasonable foresight and consideration for the safety of others. Thus a defendant does not escape liability by proving that he is abnormal in some respect which reduces his capacity for foresight or prudence.

The principle is of course applicable to a child. The standard of care being objective, it is no answer for him, any more than it is for an adult, to say that the harm he caused was due to his being abnormally slow-witted, quick-tempered, absent-minded or inexperienced. But it does not follow that he cannot rely in his defence upon a limitation upon the capacity for foresight or prudence, not as being personal to himself, but as being characteristic of humanity at his state of development and in that sense normal.

By doing so he appeals to a standard of ordinariness, to an objective and not a subjective standard. In regard to the things which pertain to foresight and prudence — experience, understanding of causes and effects, balance of judgment, thoughtfulness — it is absurd, indeed it is a misuse of language, to speak of normality in relation to persons of all ages taken together. In those things normality is, for children, something different from what normality is for adults; the very concept of normality is a concept of rising levels until 'years of discretion' are attained. The law does not arbitrarily fix upon any particular age for this purpose, and tribunals of fact may well give effect to different views as to the age at which normal adult foresight and prudence are reasonably to be expected in relation to particular sets of circumstances. But up to that stage the normal capacity to exercise those two qualities necessarily means the capacity which is normal for a child of the relevant age; and it seems to me that it would be contrary to the fundamental principle that a person is liable for harm that he causes by falling short of an objective criterion of 'propriety' in his conduct — propriety, that is to say, as determined by a comparison with the standard of care reasonably to be expected in the circumstances from the normal person — to hold that where a child's liability is in question the normal person to be considered is someone other than a child of corresponding age....

MENZIES J, *dissenting:* I have found no English or Australian authority to support the statements in the United States and Canadian authorities to which I have referred and, in my opinion, what is there stated to be the law conflicts with the fundamental principle of the law of negligence, viz. that the standard of care fixed by the law to determine actionable negligence is an objective standard — that is, the care to be expected of an ordinary reasonable man. This, except in special categories, is the standard to be applied to any person capable of negligence in the absence of some consensual modification — express, implied or, perhaps, imputed. . . .

It may, of course, be objected that the adoption of a hard-and-fast rule to be applied to all cases will sometimes produce what appears to be some hardship but, if so, it should also be recalled that hard cases make bad law. It is, moreover, necessary to observe that the law of negligence is primarily concerned with the circumstances under which a person who suffers damage may recover compensation, and there is no necessary connexion between legal liability to make compensation and moral culpability. Another objection to a standard rule is that it may appear ridiculous in determining liability to judge immaturity by maturity or, as it was put in argument, to put an old head upon young shoulders. Again the answer to such a criticism is that it was not without good reason that the law has adopted a general standard to determine liability for negligence and the application of a general standard to anyone who is himself either above or below the standard may produce a result that is open to criticism as ridiculous when judged by an irrelevant philosophy. Were the law to require from every person the exercise of all the skill of which he is capable to avoid harm to others, it would be a different law from the established law of negligence and it would be based upon a philosophy different from that underlying the present law. Whether or not it would be a better law is outside any question here relevant, but an attempt to use the results which would follow from the application of such a law, to test the reasonableness of what I understand the present law to require, appears to me to be misconceived.

My conclusion is, therefore, that as the duty of care which the respondent owed to the appellant was to take such care as an ordinary reasonable man would have taken in the circumstances, the appeal should succeed.

Questions
1.   Was the law rightly applied to the facts in this case? What if the defendant had been using an air rifle?

2. Should the standard of care be looked at from the point of view of the defendant or the plaintiff? In other words, is it a question of asking whether the defendant acted carelessly or of asking whether the plaintiff was entitled to expect a greater degree of safety?

Note

In **Ryan v Hickson** (1974) 55 DLR 3d 196, a 12-year old boy was held liable for carelessly driving a snowmobile over rough terrain so as to throw his 9-year old passenger into the path of a following snowmobile. One reason for holding him liable was that if children engage in adult activities, they must live up to the adult standard of care. Further, the defendant's father was also held liable for failing to exercise adequate supervision or to provide adequate instruction.

E: The insane

Buckley v Smith Transport
Ontario Court of Appeal [1946] OR 798; [1946] 4 DLR 721

The plaintiff, Buckley, was driving a tram along Queen Street in Toronto, when he was run into by a lorry driven by one Taylor, an employee of the defendants. Taylor was suffering from syphilis of the brain and was under the delusion that he was under remote control from head office. (He was earlier heard to say 'It must be under electric control and the beam must be on . . .'.) Held: allowing the appeal, that Taylor was not liable in negligence.

ROACH JA: The fact that he was suffering from that particular delusion does not conclude the question of liability.

In *Slattery v Haley,* [1923] 3 DLR 156 at p. 160, 52 OLR 95 at p. 99, Middleton J whose judgment was later sustained by this Court, said: 'I think that it may now be regarded as settled law that to create liability for an act which is not wilful and intentional but merely negligent it must be shewn to have been the conscious act of the defendant's volition. He must have done that which he ought not to have done, or omitted that which he ought to have done, as a conscious being.'

He continues in the next paragraph, as follows:

When a tort is committed by a lunatic, he is unquestionably liable in many circumstances, but under other circumstances the lunacy may shew that the essential *mens rea* is absent; but, when 'the lunacy of the defendant is of so extreme a type as to preclude any genuine intention to do the act complained of, there is no voluntary act at all, and therefore no liability;' Salmond, 5th ed., pp. 74 and 75.

Although that latter statement is only *obiter* in that case, it is supported by English decisions and texts to which that learned Judge refers, and I subscribe to it. In my opinion the question of liability must in every case depend upon the degree of insanity.

Supposing a man who was labouring under the insane delusion that his wife was unfaithful to him, but who was otherwise mentally normal, due to the manner in which he operated a motor vehicle on the highway injured some other person on the highway, no one would suggest that he would not be liable in damages simply because of the fact that he had that one particular insane delusion. Then, add to that one delusion the further delusion that his next-door neighbour was conspiring against him to burn down his house, would he still be liable? I entertain no doubt that he might be liable. He might still be a man who, to use the language of Cockburn CJ in *Banks v Goodfellow, supra,* would be 'in all other respects rational, and capable of transacting the ordinary affairs and fulfilling the duties and obligations incidental to the various relations of life'. In particular, notwithstanding those delusions, he might still understand and appreciate the duty which rested upon him to take care. That surely must be the test in all cases where negligence is the basis of the action. If that understanding and appreciation exists in the mind of the individual, and delusions do not otherwise interfere with his ability to take care, he is liable for the breach of that duty. It is always a question of fact to be determined on the evidence, and the burden of proving that a person was without that apprecation and understanding and or ability is always on those who allege it. Therefore, the question here, to my mind, is not limited to the bare inquiry whether or not Taylor at the time of the collision was labouring under this particular delusion, but whether or not he understood and appreciated the duty upon him to take care, and whether he was disabled, as a result of any delusion, from discharging that duty.

The delusion or delusions may manifest the fact that due to mental disease the individual's mind has become so deteriorated or dilapidated or disorganized that he has neither the ability to understand the duty nor the power to discharge it. If I have correctly stated the law, as I think I have, then the question is: What was the extent of Taylor's insanity? Did he understand the duty to take care, and was he, by reason of mental disease, unable to discharge that duty?

Question
Is being struck by a syphilitic truck driver one of the risks of life one must be expected to put up with?

Notes
1.   The judge in *Buckley* also held that as Taylor was not liable, his employers could not be vicariously liable. This does not necessarily follow.
2.   In *Morris* v *Marsden* [1952] 1 All ER 925 the defendant was a schizophrenic who attacked the plaintiff. Stable J held him liable, saying that a person suffering from mental disease will be liable in intentional torts such as battery if he knew the nature and quality of his act even if he did not know it was wrong. See also *White* v *White* [1950] P 39, per Denning LJ.
3.   Automatism has been accepted as a defence to negligence. In *Roberts* v *Ramsbottom* [1980] 1 WLR 823, Neill J said:

> The driver will be able to escape liability if his actions at the relevant time were wholly beyond his control. But if he retained some control, albeit imperfect control, and his driving, judged objectively was below the required standard, he remains liable. His position is the same as a driver who is old or infirm.

(In the case itself the driver was held liable as his consciousness was merely impaired, and anyway he ought to have been aware that he was unfit to drive.)

Section 3:   other relevant factors in the standard of care owed

Whether a defendant is in breach of duty requires a decision whether a reasonable man would foresee the danger and regard the risk as unreasonable.

This can be a complicated and difficult question, and some of the factors which may be relevant in making such a judgment are outlined below.

Thompson v Smith Shiprepairers Ltd
Queen's Bench Division [1984] QB 405; [1984] 2 WLR 522;
[1984] 1 All ER 881

The plaintiffs worked in the defendants' shipbuilding yard and were subjected to excessive noise in their work, as a result of which they suffered impaired hearing. They had been employed since 1944 or earlier. The defendants knew of the excessive noise, but this was generally regarded as an inescapable feature of shipyard work and the industry did not take the problem seriously. There was no common practice of providing ear protection, and it was not until the early 1960s that effective protection was available, and in 1963 the Ministry of Labour published a pamphlet 'Noise and the Worker' on the dangers of noise for workers. The plaintiffs were not given ear protection until the 1970s. Held: the defendants were liable for the extent by which the hearing problems of the plaintiffs had been exacerbated after 1963. There was no breach before 1963 because of common practice in the industry not to provide protection, and lack of social awareness of the dangers of noise.

MUSTILL J: The plaintiffs allege that the defendants were negligent in the following respects — (i) in failing to recognise the existence of high levels of noise in their shipyards, and the fact that such noise created a risk of irreversible damage to hearing; (ii) in failing to provide any or sufficient ear protection devices, or to give the necessary advice and encouragement for the wearing of such devices as were provided; (iii) in failing to investigate and take advice upon the noise levels in their yards; (iv) in failing to reduce the noise created by work in their yards; (v) in failing to organise the layout and timing of the work so as to minimise the effect of noise. In the first instance I will concentrate on items (i) and (ii), since these are by far the most substantial.

There was general agreement that the principles to be applied when weighing-up allegations of this kind are correctly set out in the following passage from the judgment of Swanwick J in *Stokes v Guest, Keen and Nettlefold (Bolts and Nuts) Ltd* [1968] 1 WLR 1776, 1783:

> From these authorities I deduce the principles, that the overall test is still the conduct of the reasonable and prudent employer, taking positive thought for the safety of his workers in the light of what he knows or ought to know; where there is a recognised and general practice which has been followed for a substantial period in similar circumstances without mishap, he is entitled to follow it, unless in the light of common sense or newer knowledge it is clearly bad; but, where there is developing knowledge, he must keep reasonably abreast of it and not be too slow to apply it; and where he has in fact greater than average knowledge of the risks, he may be thereby obliged to take more than the average or standard precautions. He must weigh up the risk in terms of the likelihood of injury occurring and the potential consequences if it does; and he must balance against this the probable effectiveness of the precautions that can be taken to meet it and the expense and inconvenience they involve. If he is found to have fallen below the standard to be properly expected of a reasonable and prudent employer in these respects, he is negligent.

I shall direct myself in accordance with this succinct and helpful statement of the law, and will make only one additional comment. In the passage just cited, Swanwick J drew a distinction between a recognised practice followed without mishap, and one which in the light of common sense or increased knowledge is clearly bad. The distinction is indeed valid and sufficient for many cases. The two categories are not, however, exhaustive; as the present actions demonstrate. The practice of leaving employees unprotected against excessive noise had never been followed 'without mishap.' Yet even the plaintiffs have not suggested that it was 'clearly bad,' in the sense of creating a potential liability in negligence, at any time before the mid-1930s. Between the two extremes is a type of risk which is regarded at any given time (although not necessarily later) as an inescapable feature of the industry. The employer is not liable for the consequences of such risks, although subsequent changes in social awareness, or improvements in knowledge and technology, may transfer the risk into the category of those against which the employer can and should take care. It is unnecessary, and perhaps impossible, to give a comprehensive formula for identifying the line between the acceptable and the unacceptable. Nevertheless, the line does exist, and was clearly recognised in *Morris* v *West Hartlepool Steam Navigation Co. Ltd* [1956] AC 552. The speeches in that case show, not that one employer is exonerated simply by proving that other employers are just as negligent, but that the standard of what is negligent is influenced, although not decisively, by the practice in the industry as a whole. In my judgment, this principle applies not only where the breach of duty is said to consist of a failure to take precautions known to be available as a means of combating a known danger, but also where the omission involves an absence of initiative in seeking out knowledge of facts which are not in themselves obvious. The employer must keep up to date, but the court must be slow to blame him for not ploughing a lone furrow.

Notes
1. In times of fierce competition, when costs must be kept down, there is little incentive to spend money on safety. Mustill J said that there was general apathy about the problems of noise, and it was not until government advice became available that he felt that the employers should have taken action. Does this suggest that the common law is not an effective tool for promoting safety?
2. In *Thompson* the employers were liable for hearing loss caused since 1963, but in *Baxter* v *Harland and Wolff* [1990] IRLR 516, the Northern Ireland Court of Appeal took the period back to 1952 on the ground that the employers should have thought about the issue of noise and sought advice even before the Ministry of Labour's pamphlet of 1963. MacDermott LJ cited *McCafferty* v *Metropolitan Police Receiver* [1977] 2 All ER 756, where it was said that the duty was to take reasonable care to protect the plaintiff from dangers to safety or health of which the employer knew or ought to have known, and the employer must take steps to keep himself informed of developments and increased knowledge in the sphere in which he operates.

Latimer v *AEC Ltd*
Court of Appeal [1952] 2 QB 701; [1952] 1 TLR 1349; [1952] 1 All ER 1302

The defendants owned a factory, and in the floor was cut a channel or conduit in which there flowed an oily cooling agent known as mystic. One day there was a heavy rainstorm and the factory was flooded: the oil rose out of the channel and mixed with the water, and when the flood subsided the whole floor was covered with a thin film of the oily mixture. The defendants put sawdust down on most, but not all, of the floor. The plaintiff slipped and fell on an untreated part of the floor. It was argued that the defendants should have closed the factory. Held: allowing the appeal, that the defendants were not liable as they had acted as a reasonable employer would have acted.

DENNING LJ: . . . it seems to me that [Pilcher J] has fallen into error by assuming it would be sufficient to constitute negligence that there was a foreseeable risk which the defendants could have avoided by some measure or other, however extreme. That is not the law. It is always necessary to consider what measures the defendant ought to have taken, and to say whether they could reasonably be expected of him. In a converse case, for example, a brave man tries to stop a runaway horse. It is a known risk and a serious risk, but no one would suggest that he could reasonably be expected to stand idly by. It is not negligence on his part to run the risk. So here the employers knew that the floor was slippery and that there was some risk in letting the men work on it; but, still, they could not reasonably be expected to shut down the whole works and send all the men home. In every case of foreseeable risk, it is a matter of balancing the risk against the measures necessary to eliminate it. It is only negligence if, on balance, the defendant did something which he ought not to have done, or omitted to do something which he ought to have done. In this case, in the circumstances of this torrential flood, it is quite clear the defendants did everything they could reasonably be expected to do. It would be quite unreasonable, it seems to me, to expect them to send all the men home. I agree, therefore, that there was no negligence at common law.

Question
Why should the employers be entitled to make the employees bear the risk of injury? The court assumes there were only two choices open to the employers, but surely there were three:

(a)   to close the factory,
(b)   to keep it open, without compensation for any injury,
(c)   to keep it open, agreeing to pay compensation to anyone who slipped.

Which choice would a reasonable employer have made?

Notes
1.   A risk of greater damage than normal may increase the obligations of a potential defendant. In **Paris v Stepney Borough Council** [1951] AC 367 the plaintiff was a one-eyed garage hand who was struck in his only eye by a splinter from a bolt. He was not wearing goggles. The House of Lords, by a majority, held that although the disability did not increase the risk of injury, it did increase the risk of the injury being more serious (i.e. becoming blind rather than one-eyed), and therefore the employers should have supplied him with goggles, even though they need not have done so for a two-eyed man.
2.   An increased risk of injury to particular individuals may also be relevant; for example, if children are likely to be present, special precautions may be

necessary. In *Haley* v *London Electricity Board* [1965] AC 778 the defendants had dug a trench along a pavement, and as a barrier had placed a punner hammer across it with one end resting on the ground and the other about two feet above it. The plaintiff was blind and his stick failed to touch the barrier, and he fell and was rendered deaf. The House of Lords held that the presence of blind persons was foreseeable, and the increased likelihood of injury to them obliged the defendants to take precautions which would not be necessary in the case of sighted persons.

Watt v *Hertfordshire C.C.*
Court of Appeal [1954] 1 WLR 835; [1954] 2 All ER 368

An accident occurred and a woman was trapped under a heavy lorry about 200-300 yards from a fire station. The fire station had a heavy jack for lifting, but the vehicle (an Austin) which was equipped to carry it was elsewhere, and the jack was loaded onto a Fordson lorry which had no means of securing the jack. On the way to the accident the lorry had to brake suddenly and the jack moved forward, injuring the plaintiff's ankle. Held: dismissing the appeal, that the defendants were not negligent in sending out the jack unsecured.

SINGLETON LJ: Would the reasonably careful head of the station have done anything other than that which the sub-officer did? I think not. Can it be said, then, that there is a duty on the employers here to have a vehicle built and fitted to carry this jack at all times, or if they have not, not to use the jack for a short journey of 200 or 300 yards? I do not think that that will do.

Asquith LJ, in *Daborn* v *Bath Tramways Motor Co. Ltd*, said, [1946] 2 All ER 333, 336:

> In determining whether a party is negligent, the standard of reasonable care is that which is reasonably to be demanded in the circumstances. A relevant circumstance to take into account may be the importance of the end to be served by behaving in this way or in that. As has often been pointed out, if all the trains in this country were restricted to a speed of five miles an hour, there would be fewer accidents, but our national life would be intolerably slowed down. The purpose to be served, if sufficiently important, justifies the assumption of abnormal risk.

> The purpose to be served in this case was the saving of life. The men were prepared to take that risk. They were not, in my view, called on to take any risk other than that which normally might be encountered in this service. I agree with Barry J that on the whole of the evidence it would not be right to find that the employers were guilty of any failure of the duty which they owed to their workmen. In my opinion the appeal should be dismissed.

DENNING LJ: It is well settled that in measuring due care you must balance the risk against the measures necessary to eliminate the risk. To that proposition there ought to be added this: you must balance the risk against the end to be achieved. If this accident had occurred in a commercial enterprise without any emergency there could be no doubt that the servant would succeed. But the commercial end to make profit is very different from the human end to save life or limb. The saving of life or limb justifies taking considerable risk, and I am glad to say that there have never been wanting in this country men of courage ready to take those risks, notably in the fire service.

In this case the risk involved in sending out the lorry was not so great as to prohibit the attempt to save life. I quite agree that fire engines, ambulances and doctors' cars should not shoot past the traffic lights when they show a red light. That is because the risk is too great to warrant the incurring of the danger. It is always a question of balancing the risk against the end. I agree that this appeal should be dismissed.

Wooldridge v *Sumner*
Court of Appeal [1963] 2 QB 43; [1962] 2 WLR 616; [1962] 2 All ER 978

The plaintiff, Edmund Wooldridge, was a photographer who was attending the National Horse Show at White City. The perimeter of the arena was marked by a line of tubs with shrubs in them, and the plaintiff was standing just behind these. The defendant owned a horse called 'Work of Art' which was ridden by Ronald Holladay. The judge found that in attempting to take a corner the horse was going too fast, and it plunged through the line of tubs, injuring the plaintiff. Held: allowing the appeal, that the defendant was not liable as, in the heat of the moment, Mr Holladay had merely made an error of judgment and was not negligent.

DIPLOCK LJ: To treat Lord Atkin's statement 'You must take reasonable care to avoid acts or omissions which you can reasonably foresee would be likely to injure your neighbour', [1932] AC 562, 580, as a complete exposition of the law of negligence is to mistake aphorism for exegesis. It does not purport to define what is reasonable care and was directed to identifying the persons to whom the duty to take reasonable care is owed. What is reasonable care in a particular circumstance is a jury question and where, as in a case like this, there is no direct guidance or hindrance from authority it may be answered by inquiring whether the ordinary reasonable man would say that in all the circumstances the defendant's conduct was blameworthy.

The matter has to be looked at from the point of view of the reasonable spectator as well as the reasonable participant; not because of the maxim volenti non fit injuria, but because what a reasonable spectator would expect a participant to do without regarding it as blameworthy is as relevant to what is reasonable care as what a reasonable participant would think was blameworthy conduct in himself. The same idea was expressed by Scrutton LJ in *Hall* v *Brooklands* [1933] 1 KB 205, 214: 'What is reasonable care would depend upon the perils which might be reasonably expected to occur, *and the extent to which the ordinary spectator might be expected to appreciate and take the risk of such perils.*'

A reasonable spectator attending voluntarily to witness any game or competition knows and presumably desires that a reasonable participant will concentrate his attention upon winning, and if the game or competition is a fast-moving one, will have to exercise his judgment and attempt to exert his skill in what, in the analogous context of contributory negligence, is sometimes called 'the agony of the moment.' If the participant does so concentrate his attention and consequently does exercise his judgment and attempt to exert his skill in circumstances of this kind which are inherent in the game or competition in which he is taking part, the question whether any mistake he makes amounts to a breach of duty to take reasonable care must take account of those circumstances.

The law of negligence has always recognised that the standard of care which a reasonable man will exercise depends upon the conditions under which the decision to avoid the act or omission relied upon as negligence has to be taken. The case of the workman engaged on repetitive work in the noise and bustle of the factory is a familiar example. More apposite for present purposes are the collision cases, where a decision has to be made upon the spur of the moment. 'A's negligence makes collision so threatening that though by the appropriate measure B could avoid it, B has not really time to think and by mistake takes the wrong measure. B is not to be held guilty of any negligence and A wholly fails.' (*Admiralty Commissioners* v *S.S. Volute,* [1922] 1 AC 129, 136) A fails not because of his own negligence; there never has been any contributory negligence rule in Admiralty. He fails because B has exercised such care as is reasonable in circumstances in which he has not really time to think. No doubt if he has got into those circumstances as a result of a breach of duty of care which he owes to A, A can succeed upon this antecedent negligence; but a participant in a game or competition gets into the circumstances in which he has no time or very little time to think by his decision to take part in the game or competition at all. It cannot be suggested that the participant, at any rate if he has some modicum of skill, is, by the mere act of participating, in breach of his duty of care to a spectator who is present for the very purpose of watching him do so. If, therefore, in the course of the game or competition, at a moment when he really has not time to think, a participant by mistake takes a wrong measure, he is not, in my view, to be held guilty of any negligence.

Furthermore, the duty which he owes is a duty of care, not a duty of skill. Save where a consensual relationship exists between a plaintiff and a defendant by which the defendant impliedly warrants his skill, a man owes no duty to his neighbour to exercise any special skill beyond that which an ordinary reasonable man would acquire before indulging in the activity in which he is engaged at the relevant time. It may well be that a participant in a game or competition would be guilty of negligence to a spectator if he took part in it when he knew or ought to have known that his lack of skill was such that even if he exerted it to the utmost he was likely to cause injury to a spectator watching him. No question of this arises in the present case. It was common ground that Mr Holladay was an exceptionally skilful and experienced horseman.

The practical result of this analysis of the application of the common law of negligence to participant and spectator would, I think, be expressed by the common man in some such terms as these: 'A person attending a game or competition takes the risk of any damage caused to him by any act of a participant done in the course of and for the purposes of the game or competition notwithstanding that such act may involve an error of judgment or a lapse of skill, unless the participants' conduct is such as to evince a reckless disregard of the spectator's safety.'

Question
A horse show is being held in a local field. A takes a corner too fast and the horse ploughs through the hedge bordering the field. X was leaning on the inside of the hedge watching the show. Y is a passer-by. Both are injured. Who can sue A?

Note
For an example of the 'heat of the moment' defence applied to the police, see **Marshall v Osmond** [1983] QB 1034, where a police car was chasing a suspect car and, in drawing up alongside it, braked too hard and skidded into it. This was held to be an error of judgment but not negligence.

6 CAUSATION AND REMOTENESS OF DAMAGE

Causation and remoteness of damage are separate but related topics. Once it has been shown that a defendant owed the plaintiff a duty to take care and was in breach of that duty, liability can still be avoided if it can be shown that the breach did not cause the damage or that the damage was too remote a consequence of the breach.

A causation problem usually occurs when we look at the damage and see that it was actually caused by a number of different factors, or, to put it another way, that a number of factors combining together brought about the damage. The problem is to determine which, if any, of these factors were legally relevant, so as to be able to say that the person responsible for that factor should be liable, perhaps to the exclusion of people responsible for other factors.

A remoteness problem can arise in two different situations: that is where the plaintiff is a foreseeable plaintiff and the damage has in fact been caused by the defendant's act, but where the damage is either unpredictable in extent or unpredictable in nature. Injury to a haemophiliac might be an example of the former, and *Re Polemis* (below), where the dropping of a plank into the hold of a ship caused it to explode, is an example of the latter.

Section 1: causation

There is no simple formula which can test whether an act or event is a legally relevant cause of the damage, and many books and cases content themselves with asking whether the act was a 'substantial' factor in bringing about the harm. The solution is pragmatic rather than theoretical, and is founded as much on social policy as on logic. However, one test which will solve a number of cases, but not all, is the 'but for' test, illustrated by the first case.

Barnett v *Chelsea and Kensington Hospital*
Queen's Bench Division [1969] 1 QB 428; [1968] 1 All ER 1068;
[1968] 2 WLR 422

The plaintiff, William Barnett, and two other men were nightwatchmen at the Chelsea College of Science and Technology. At 5.00 a.m. on the morning of New Year's Day 1966, all three shared some tea, and about 20 minutes later they began vomiting. At 8.00 a.m. they went to the defendant hospital and were seen by a nurse who telephoned the doctor on duty. He replied 'Well, I am vomiting myself and I have not been drinking. Tell them to go home and go to bed and call their own doctors . . .'. The three men returned to the college but continued to feel ill, and by 2.00 p.m. the plaintiff had died. It was shown that he had been poisoned with arsenic, and a coroner's verdict of murder by persons unknown was returned. His widow said the hospital failed to treat her husband. Held: the hospital was not liable.

NEILD J: Without doubt the casualty officer should have seen and examined the deceased. His failure to do either cannot be described as an excusable error as has been submitted. It was negligence. It is unfortunate that he was himself at the time a tired and unwell doctor, but there was no one else to do that which it was his duty to do. Having examined the deceased I think the first and provisional diagnosis would have been one of food poisoning. . . .

It remains to consider whether it is shown that the deceased's death was caused by that negligence or whether, as the defendants have said, the deceased must have died in any event. In his concluding submission Mr Pain submitted that the casualty officer should have examined the deceased and had he done so he would have caused tests to be made which would have indicated the treatment required and that, since the defendants were at fault in these respects, therefore the onus of proof passed to the defendants to show that the appropriate treatment would have failed, and authorities were cited to me. I find myself unable to accept that argument, and I am of the view that the onus of proof remains upon the plaintiff, and I have in mind (without quoting it) the decision cited by Mr Wilmers in *Bonnington Castings Ltd* v *Wardlaw* [1956] AC 613. However, were it otherwise and the onus did pass to the defendants, then I would find that they have discharged it, as I would proceed to show.

There has been put before me a timetable which I think is of much importance. The deceased attended at the casualty department at five or 10 minutes past eight in the morning. If the casualty officer had got up and dressed and come to see the three men and examined them and decided to admit them, the deceased (and Dr Lockett agreed with this) could not have been in bed in a ward before 11 a.m. I accept Dr Goulding's evidence that an intravenous drip would not have been set up before 12 noon, and if potassium loss was suspected it could not have been discovered until 12.30 p.m. Dr Lockett, dealing with this, said: 'If this man had not been treated until after 12 noon the chances of survival were not good.'

Without going in detail into the considerable volume of technical evidence which has been put before me, it seems to me to be the case that when death results from arsenical poisoning it is brought about by two conditions; on the one hand dehydration and on the other disturbance of the enzyme processes. If the principal condition is one of enzyme disturbance — as I am of the view it was here — then the only method of treatment which is likely to succeed is the use of the specific antidote which is commonly called B.A.L. Dr Goulding said in the course of his evidence:

The only way to deal with this is to use the specific B.A.L. I see no reasonable prospect of the deceased being given B.A.L. before the time at which he died — and at a later point in his evidence — I feel that even if fluid loss had been discovered death would have been caused by the enzyme disturbance. Death might have occurred later.

I regard that evidence as very moderate, and it might be a true assessment of the situation to say that there was no chance of B.A.L. being administered before the death of the deceased.

For those reasons, I find that the plaintiff has failed to establish, on the balance of probabilities, that the defendants' negligence caused the death of the deceased.

Note

The 'but for' test is perhaps the simplest, and should be tried first, but it cannot solve all problems. For example, Fleming (*Law of Torts*, 7th ed.) puts the case of two people carrying candles independently and simultaneously approaching a leaking gas pipe, causing an explosion. Can each claim that the explosion would have happened anyway, even if he had not been there?

Hotson v East Berkshire Health Authority
House of Lords [1987] AC 750; [1987] 2 WLR 232; [1987] 2 All ER 909

Stephen Hotson fell out of a tree and sustained an 'acute traumatic fracture of the left femoral epiphysis' (i.e. an injury to his hip). The trial judge assessed that at that point there was a 75 per cent probability that sufficient blood vessels had been destroyed that avascular necrosis would develop. The defendant hospital negligently delayed treatment so that even if sufficient blood vessels had survived Hotson would have developed avascular necrosis. The trial judge said that the 75 per cent probability of the disability developing had been translated by the hospital into a certainty, and awarded the plaintiff 25 per cent of the full damages. Held: allowing the appeal, that on a balance of probabilities the disability was caused solely by the fall and the health authority was not liable.

LORD ACKNER: [The trial judge] thus found that immediately after the fall, that is before admission to hospital and therefore *before* the duty was imposed upon the defendants properly to diagnose and treat, the epiphysis was doomed. Accordingly the judge had determined as a matter of fact, on the balance of probabilities, that the compression and blocking of the blood vessels had had no effect on the plaintiff's ultimate condition. In determining what happened in the past the court decides on the balance of probabilities. Anything that is more probable than not is treated as certainty: *Mallet* v *McMonagle* [1970] AC 166, 176, *per* Lord Diplock.

In the result the judge had by his clear findings decided that the negligence of the defendants in failing to diagnose and treat for a period of five days had not caused the deformed left hip. The judge, in agreement with the submission made to your Lordships by counsel for the defendants, said in terms that in the end the problem came down to one of classification [1985] 1 WLR 1036, 1043–1044:

Is this on true analysis a case where the plaintiff is concerned to establish causative negligence or is it rather a case where the real question is the proper quantum of damage?

The judge thought, at p. 1044, that the case 'hovers near the border.' To my mind, the first issue which the judge had to determine was an issue of causation — did the breach of duty cause the damage alleged. If it did not, as the judge so held, then no question of quantifying damage arises. The debate on the loss of a chance cannot arise where there has been a positive finding that before the duty arose the damage complained of had already been sustained or had become inevitable.

Kitchen v *Royal Air Force Association* [1978] 1 WLR 563 has no relevance to this appeal. In that case there was an undoubted breach of contract which caused the plaintiff to suffer more than nominal damages. By reason of the solicitor's negligence, she had lost a worthwhile action. What the court there had to do was to value that action. It is, of course, obvious that it is not only actions that are bound to succeed that have a value. Every action with a prospect of success has a value and it is a familiar task for the court to assess that value where negligence has prevented such an action being brought. Again, *Chaplin* v *Hicks* [1911] 2 KB 786, strongly relied upon by the plaintiff, provides no assistance. In that case a young lady actress-to-be had made a contract with the defendant under which she had an opportunity of appearing in a competition in which, if successful, she would have obtained a remunerative engagement as an actress. In the words of Fletcher Moulton LJ, at p. 797:

> The contract gave the plaintiff a right of considerable value, one for which many people would give money; therefore to hold that the plaintiff was entitled to no damages for being deprived of such a right because the final result depended on a contingency or chance would have been a misdirection.

In a sentence, the plaintiff was not entitled to any damages in respect of the deformed hip because the judge had decided that this was not caused by the admitted breach by the defendants of their duty of care but was caused by the separation of the left femoral epiphysis when he fell some 12 feet from a rope on which he had been swinging.

On this simple basis I would allow this appeal. I have sought to stress that this case was a relatively simple case concerned with the proof of causation, upon which the plaintiff failed, because he was unable to prove, on the balance of probabilities, that his deformed hip was caused by the defendants' breach of duty in delaying over a period of five days a proper diagnosis and treatment. Where *causation* is in issue, the judge decides that issue on the balance of the probabilities. Unless there is some special situation, e.g. joint defendants where the apportionment of liability between them is required, there is no point or purpose in expressing in percentage terms the certainty or near certainty which the plaintiff has achieved in establishing his cause of action.

Once liability is established, on the balance of probabilities, the loss which the plaintiff has sustained is payable in full. It is not discounted by reducing his claim by the extent to which he has failed to prove his case with 100 per cent certainty. The decision by Simon Brown J in the subsequent case of *Bagley* v *North Herts Health Authority*, reported only in (1986) 136 NLJ 1014, in which he discounted an award for a stillbirth, because there was a five per cent risk that the plaintiff would have had a stillborn child even if the hospital had not been negligent, was clearly wrong. In that case, the plaintiff had established on a balance of probabilities, indeed with near certainty, that the hospital's negligence had caused the stillbirth. Causation was thus fully established. Such a finding does not permit any discounting — to do so would be to propound a wholly new doctrine which has no support in principle or authority and would give rise to many complications in the search for mathematical or statistical exactitude.

Question

Could it be argued that when Stephen Hotson presented himself at the hospital there was a 25 per cent chance that he was not so severely injured that the disability would develop and that the hospital had deprived him of the chance that avascular necrosis would not develop?

Smith v Littlewoods
House of Lords [1987] AC 1; [1987] 1 All ER 710; [1987] 2 WLR 480

The Littlewoods Organisation purchased the Regal Cinema in Dunfermline, with right of entry from 31 May 1976. Thereafter the cinema remained empty, but by the middle of June it was regularly being broken into, mainly by children, and damage was being caused. On one occasion a small fire had been started. Contractors employed by Littlewoods knew about the vandalism but Littlewoods did not. On 5 July 1976 a fire was deliberately started by vandals inside the cinema, and the fire spread to the property of the two pursuers, owners of the Maloco Cafe, and the minister of St Paul's Church. It was alleged that the defenders should have prevented the vandals gaining access to the cinema. Held: dismissing the appeal, that the defenders were not liable as they did not know of the earlier acts of vandalism and were thus not under any duty to the pursuers.

LORD GOFF: My Lords, the Lord President founded his judgment on the proposition that the defenders, who were both owners and occupiers of the cinema, were under a general duty to take reasonable care for the safety of premises in the neighbourhood.

Now if this proposition is understood as relating to a general duty to take reasonable care *not to cause damage* to premises in the neighbourhood (as I believe that the Lord President intended it to be understood) then it is unexceptionable. But it must not be overlooked that a problem arises when the pursuer is seeking to hold the defender responsible for having failed to *prevent* a third party from causing damage to the pursuer or his property by the third party's own deliberate wrongdoing. In such a case, it is not possible to invoke a general duty of care: for it is well recognised that there is no *general* duty of care to prevent third parties from causing such damage. The point is expressed very clearly in *Hart and Honoré, Causation in the Law*, 2nd ed. (1985), when the authors state, at pp. 196-197:

> The law might acknowledge a general principle that, whenever the harmful conduct of another is reasonably foreseeable, it is our duty to take precautions against it . . . But, up to now, no legal system has gone so far as this . . .

The same point is made in *Fleming, The Law of Torts*, 6th ed. (1983), where it is said, at p. 200: 'there is certainly no *general* duty to protect others against theft or loss.' I wish to add that no such general duty exists even between those who are nieghbours in the sense of being occupiers of adjoining premises. There is no general duty upon a householder that he should act as a watchdog, or that his house should act as a bastion, to protect his neighbour's house. . . .

Another statement of principle, which has been much quoted, is the observation of Lord Sumner in *Weld-Blundell* v *Stephens* [1920] AC 956, when he said, at p. 986: 'In general . . . even though A is in fault he is not responsible for injury to C which B, a stranger to him, deliberately chooses to do.' This dictum may be read as expressing the general idea that the voluntary act of another, independent of the defender's fault, is regarded as a novus actus interveniens which, to use the old metaphor, 'breaks the chain of causation.' But it also expresses a general perception that we ought not to be held responsible in law for the deliberate wrongdoing of others. Of course, if a duty of care is imposed to guard against deliberate wrongdoing by others, it can hardly be said that the harmful effects of such wrongdoing are not caused by such breach of duty. We are therefore thrown back to the duty of care. But one thing is clear, and that is that liability in negligence for harm caused by the deliberate wrongdoing of others cannot be founded simply upon foreseeability that the pursuer will suffer loss or damage by reason of such wrongdoing. There is no such general principle. We have therefore to identify the circumstances in which such liability may be imposed.

That there are special circumstances in which a defender may be held responsible in law for injuries suffered by the pursuer through a third party's deliberate wrongdoing is not in doubt. For example, a duty of care may arise from a relationship between the parties, which gives rise to an imposition or assumption of responsibility upon or by the defender, as in *Stansbie* v *Troman* [1948] 2 KB 48, where such responsibility was held to arise from a contract. In that case a decorator, left alone on the premises by the householder's wife, was held liable when he went out leaving the door on the latch, and a thief entered the house and stole property. Such responsibility might well be held to exist in other cases where there is no contract, as for example where a person left alone in a house has entered as a licensee of the occupier. . . .

These are all special cases. But there is a more general circumstance in which a defender may be held liable in negligence to the pursuer although the immediate cause of the damage suffered by the pursuer is the deliberate wrongdoing of another. This may occur where the defender negligently causes or permits to be created a source of danger, and it is reasonably foreseeable that third parties may interfere with it and, sparking off the danger, thereby cause damage to persons in the position of the pursuer. The classic example of such a case is, perhaps, *Haynes* v *Harwood* [1935] 1 KB 146, where the defendant's carter left a horse-drawn van unattended in a crowded street, and the horses bolted when a boy threw a stone at them. A police officer who suffered injury in stopping the horses before they injured a woman and children was held to be entitled to recover damages from the defendant. There, of course, the defendant's servant had created a source of danger by leaving his horses unattended in a busy street. Many different things might have caused them to bolt — a sudden noise or movement, for example, or, as happened, the deliberate action of a mischievous boy. But all such events were examples of the very sort of thing which the defendant's servant ought reasonably to have foreseen and to have guarded against by taking appropriate precautions. In such a case, Lord Sumner's dictum (*Weld-Blundell* v *Stephens* [1920] AC 956, 986) can have no application to exclude liability.

Haynes v *Harwood* was a case concerned with the creation of a source of danger in a public place. We are concerned in the present case with an allegation that the defenders should be held liable for the consequences of deliberate wrongdoing by others who were trespassers on the defenders' property. In such a case it may be said that the defenders are entitled to use their property as their own and so should not be held liable if, for example, trespassers interfere with dangerous things on their land. But this is, I consider, too sweeping a proposition. It is well established that an occupier of land may be liable to a trespasser who has suffered injury on his land; though in *Herrington* v *British Railways Board* [1972] AC 877, in which the nature and scope of such liability was reconsidered by your Lordships' House, the standard of care so imposed on occupiers was drawn narrowly so as to take proper account of the rights of occupiers to enjoy the use of their land. It is, in my opinion, consistent with the existence of such liability that an occupier who negligently causes or permits a source of danger to be created on his land, and can reasonably foresee that third parties may trespass on his land and, interfering with the source of danger, may spark it off, thereby causing damage to the person or property of those in the vicinity, should be held liable to such a person for damage so caused to him. It is useful to take the example of a fire hazard, not only because that is the relevant hazard which is alleged to have existed in the present case, but also because of the intrinsically dangerous nature of fire hazards as regards neighbouring property. Let me give an example of circumstances in which an occupier of land might be held liable for damage so caused. Suppose that a person is deputed to buy a substantial quantity of fireworks for a village fireworks display on Guy Fawkes night. He stores them, as usual, in an unlocked garden shed abutting onto a neighbouring house. It is well known that he does this. Mischievous boys from the village enter as trespassers and, playing with the fireworks, cause a serious fire which spreads to and burns down the neighbouring house. Liability might well be imposed in such a case; for, having regard to the dangerous and tempting nature of fireworks, interference by naughty children was the very thing which, in the circumstances, the purchaser of the fireworks ought to have guarded against.

But liability should only be imposed under this principle in cases where the defender has negligently caused or permitted the creation of a source of danger on his land, and where it is foreseeable that third parties may trespass on his land and spark it off, thereby damaging the pursuer or his property. Moreover it is not to be forgotten that, in ordinary households in this country, there are nowadays many things which might be described as possible sources of fire if interfered with by third parties, ranging from matches and firelighters to electric irons and gas cookers and even oil-fired central heating systems. These are commmonplaces of modern life; and it would be quite wrong if householders were to be held liable in negligence for acting in a socially acceptable manner. No doubt the question whether liability should be imposed on defenders in a case where a source of danger on his land has been sparked off by the deliberate wrongdoing of a third party is a question to be decided on the facts of each case, and it would, I think, be wrong for your Lordships' House to anticipate the manner in which the law may develop: but I cannot help thinking that cases where liability will be so imposed are likely to be very rare.

There is another basis upon which a defender may be held liable for damage to neighbouring property caused by a fire started on his (the defender's) property by the deliberate wrongdoing of a third party. This arises where he has knowledge or means of knowledge that a third party has created or is creating a risk of fire, or indeed has started a fire, on his premises, and then fails to take such steps as are reasonably open to him (in the limited sense explained by Lord Wilberforce in *Goldman* v *Hargrave* [1967] 1 AC 645, 663-664) to prevent any such fire from damaging neighbouring property. If, for example, an occupier of property has knowledge, or means of knowledge, that intruders are in the habit of trespassing upon his property and starting fires there, thereby creating a risk that fire may spread to and damage neighbouring property, a duty to take reasonable steps to prevent such damage may be held to fall upon him. He could, for example, take reasonable steps to keep the intruders out. He could also inform the police; or he could warn his neighbours and invite their assistance. If the defender is a person of substantial means, for example a large public company, he might even be expected to employ some agency to keep a watch on the premises. What is reasonably required would, of course, depend on the particular facts of the case. I observe that, in *Goldman* v *Hargrave,* such liability was held to sound in nuisance; but it is difficult to belive that, in this respect, there can be any material distinction between liability in nuisance and liability in negligence. . . .

I wish to emphasise that I do not think that the problem in these cases can be solved simply through the mechanism of foreseeability. When a duty *is* cast upon a person to take precautions against the wrongdoing of third parties, the ordinary standard of foreseeability applies and so the possibility of such wrongdoing does not have to be very great before liability is imposed. I do not myself subscribe to the opinion that liability for the wrongdoing of others is limited because of the unpredictability of human conduct. So, for example, in *Haynes* v *Harwood* [1935] 1 KB 146, liability was imposed although it cannot have been at all likely that a small boy would throw a stone at the horses left unattended in the public road; and in *Stansbie* v *Troman* [1948] 2 KB 48, liability was imposed although it cannot have been at all likely that a thief would take advantage of the fact that the defendant left the door on the latch while he was out. Per contra, there is at present no general duty at common law to prevent persons from harming others by their deliberate wrongdoing, however foreseeable such harm may be if the defender does not take steps to prevent it.

Notes
1.   In *Stansbie* v *Troman* [1948] 2 KB 48, mentioned above, a decorator (Stansbie) was working alone in Mr Troman's house, and he left to get some wallpaper, leaving the door unlocked. While he was away a thief entered the property and stole £334. The decorator was held liable on the basis that he had increased the risk of theft. The chances of a thief appearing at that time were presumably small, and anyway, even if the door had been locked, a persistent thief could have broken in. Would this case be decided the same way today and, if so, on what basis? If a guest of the householder had property stolen could he sue?
2.   There have been a number of other cases on this problem of liability for the intervening act of a third party. See *Lamb* v *Camden Borough Council* [1981] QB 625 and *Knightley* v *Johns* [1982] 1 WLR 349.

Jobling v *Associated Dairies Ltd*
House of Lords [1982] AC 794; [1981] 2 All ER 752; [1981] 3 WLR 155

The plaintiff was the manager of the defendants' butchers shop in Newcastle, and in 1973 he slipped on the floor of a meat refrigerator and damaged his back. The defendants were liable for the fall. The plaintiff's injury reduced his earnings capacity by 50 per cent, but in 1976 he became totally disabled when he suffered from a condition known as spondylotic myelopathy which was wholly unrelated to the 1973 accident. The question was whether he should be awarded damages only for his loss between 1973 and 1976 on the ground that the illness of 1976 meant that the original injury ceased to be an effective cause of his disability, or whether he was entitled to damages for his reduced capacity for ever on the ground that he was still suffering from that reduced capacity, together with a further reduction caused by the 1976 illness. Held: dismissing the appeal, that he was only entitled to damages for his loss from 1973 to 1976.

Note
There is much discussion in *Jobling* of *Baker* v *Willoughby* [1970] AC 467, where the plaintiff, George Baker, was injured in a car accident in 1964 due to the negligence of the defendant, and he suffered injuries to his leg which

resulted in a permanently stiff ankle. In 1967 he was working in a scrap yard when he was shot by a robber and his leg was amputated. The House of Lords held that he was entitled to damages for the stiff leg for ever and not just for the period 1964-67, because after 1967 the causes of his lost capacity were concurrent. Thus the robber, if sued, would only have had to pay for the loss of an already damaged leg.

LORD KEITH: It was argued for the respondent [in *Baker* v *Willoughby* [1970] AC 467] that the second injury removed the very limb from which the earlier disability had stemmed, and that therefore no loss suffered thereafter could be attributed to the respondent's negligence. In rejecting this argument Lord Reid, whose speech was concurred in by Lord Guest, Viscount Dilhorne and Lord Donovan, said at p. 492:

> If it were the case that in the eye of the law an effect could only have one cause then the respondent might be right. It is always necessary to prove that any loss for which damages can be given was caused by the defendant's negligent act. But it is a commonplace that the law regards many events as having two causes: that happens whenever there is contributory negligence for then the law says that the injury was caused both by the negligence of the defendant and by the negligence of the plaintiff. And generally it does not matter which negligence occurred first in point of time.

Lord Reid took the view that the appellant's disability could be regarded as having two causes, and he found support for this view in *Harwood* v *Wyken Colliery Co.* [1913] 2 KB 158. That was a workmen's compensation case in which the Court of Appeal held the plaintiff entitled to compensation, notwithstanding that there had supervened upon the incapacity resulting from an accident at work an incapacity of similar extent resulting from heart disease. Lord Reid later went on to distinguish the case where damages might properly fall to be diminished by reason of the death of the plaintiff before trial, upon the basis that in such a case the supervening event had reduced the plaintiff's loss. He said at p. 494:

> If the later injury suffered before the date of the trial either reduces the disabilities from the injury for which the defendant is liable, or shortens the period during which they will be suffered by the plaintiff, then the defendant will have to pay less damages. But if the later injuries merely become a concurrent cause of the disabilities caused by the injury inflicted by the defendant, then in my view they cannot diminish the damages. Suppose that the plaintiff has to spend a month in bed before the trial because of some illness unconnected with the original injury, the defendant cannot say that he does not have to pay anything in respect of that month: during that month the original injuries and the new illness are concurrent causes of his inability to work and that does not reduce the damages.

It seems clear from this passage that the principle of concurrent causes which Lord Reid selected as the ratio decidendi of the case would, if sound, apply with the same force where the supervening event is natural disease, as in the present case, as it does where the supervening event is a tortious act.

Lord Pearson's main reason for rejecting the respondent's argument was that it would produce manifest injustice. He said at p. 495:

> The supervening event has not made the plaintiff less lame nor less disabled nor less deprived of amenities. It has not shortened the period over which he will be suffering.

It has made him more lame, more disabled, more deprived of amenities. He should not have less damages through being worse off than might have been expected.

Lord Pearson went on to illustrate the nature of the injustice by pointing out that, where the supervening event was a tortious act, the later tortfeasor, upon the principle that he takes his victim as he finds him, would be liable for damages in respect of loss of earnings only to the extent that the act had caused an additional diminution of earning capacity. If the earlier incapacity were treated, in a question with the first tortfeasor, as submerged by the later, the plaintiff would be left in the position of being unable to recover from anyone a substantial part of the loss suffered after the date of the second tort. So he would not be fully compensated in respect of the combined effects of both torts. It is to be observed that this was the consideration which had been principally urged in the argument for the appellant.

A notable feature of the speeches in *Baker* v *Willoughby* [1970] AC 467 is the absence of any consideration of the possible implications of what may be termed the 'vicissitudes' principle. The leading exposition of this principle is to be found in the judgment of Brett LJ in *Phillips* v *London and South Western Railway Co.* (1879) 5 CPD 280, 291-292:

> . . . if no accident had happened, nevertheless many circumstances might have happened to prevent the plaintiff from earning his previous income; he may be disabled by illness, he is subject to the ordinary accidents and vicissitudes of life; and if all these circumstances of which no evidence can be given are looked at, it will be impossible to exactly estimate them; yet if the jury wholly pass them over they will go wrong, because these accidents and vicissitudes ought to be taken into account. It is true that the chances of life cannot be accurately calculated, but the judge must tell the jury to consider them in order that they may give a fair and reasonable compensation.

This principle is to be applied in conjunction with the rule that the court will not speculate when it knows, so that when an event within its scope has actually happened prior to the trial date, that event will fall to be taken into account in the assessment of damages. . . .

It is implicit in [*Baker* v *Willoughby*] that the scope of the 'vicissitudes' principle is limited to supervening events of such a nature as either to reduce the disabilities resulting from the accident or else to shorten the period during which they will be suffered. I am of opinion that failure to consider or even advert to this implication weakens the authority of the ratio decidendi of the case, and must lead to the conclusion that in its full breadth it is not acceptable. The assessment of damages for personal injuries involves a process of restitutio in integrum. The object is to place the injured plaintiff in as good a position as he would have been in but for the accident. He is not to be placed in a better position. The process involves a comparison between the plaintiff's circumstances as regards capacity to enjoy the amenities of life and to earn a living as they would have been if the accident had not occurred and his actual circumstances in those respects following the accident. In considering how matters might have been expected to turn out if there had been no accident, the 'vicissitudes' principle says that it is right to take into account events, such as illness, which not uncommonly occur in the ordinary course of human life. If such events are not taken into account, the damages may be greater than are required to compensate the plaintiff for the effects of the accident, and that result would be unfair to the defendant. . . .

I am therefore of opinion that the majority in *Baker* v *Willoughby* were mistaken in approaching the problems common to the case of a supervening tortious act and to that of supervening illness wholly from the point of view of causation. While it is logically correct to say that in both cases the original tort and the supervening event may be concurrent causes of incapacity, that does not necessarily, in my view, provide the correct solution. In the case of supervening illness, it is appropriate to keep in view that this is one of the ordinary vicissitudes of life, and when one is comparing the situation resulting from the accident with the situation had there been no accident, to recognise that the illness would have overtaken the plaintiff in any event, so that it cannot be disregarded in arriving at proper compensation, and no more than proper compensation.

Additional considerations come into play when dealing with the problems arising where the plaintiff has suffered injuries from two or more successive and independent tortious acts. In that situation it is necessary to secure that the plaintiff is fully compensated for the aggregate effects of all his injuries. As Lord Pearson noted in *Baker* v *Willoughby* it would clearly be unjust to reduce the damages awarded for the first tort because of the occurrence of the second tort, damages for which are to be assessed on the basis that the plaintiff is already partially incapacitated. I do not consider it necessary to formulate any precise juristic basis for dealing with this situation differently from the case of supervening illness. It might be said that a supervening tort is not one of the ordinary vicissitudes of life, or that it is too remote a possibility to be taken into account, or that it can properly be disregarded because it carries its own remedy. None of these formulations, however, is entirely satisfactory. The fact remains that the principle of full compensaton requires that a just and practical solution should be found. In the event that damages against two successive tortfeasors fall to be assessed at the same time, it would be highly unreasonable if the aggregate of both awards were less than the total loss suffered by the plaintiff. The computation should start from an assessment of that total loss. The award against the second tortfeasor cannot in fairness to him fail to recognise that the plaintiff whom he injured was already to some extent incapacitated. In order that the plaintiff may be fully compensated, it becomes necessary to deduct the award so calculated from the assessment of the plaintiff's total loss and award the balance against the first tortfeasor. If that be a correct approach, it follows that, in proceedings against the first tortfeasor alone, the occurrence of the second tort cannot be successfully relied on by the defendant as reducing the damages which he must pay. That, in substance, was the result of the decision in *Baker* v *Willoughby*, where the supervening event was a tortious act, and to that extent the decision was, in my view, correct.

Before leaving the case, it is right to face up to the fact that, if a non-tortious supervening event is to have the effect of reducing damages but a subsequent tortious act is not, there may in some cases be difficulty in ascertaining whether the event in question is or is not of a tortious character, particularly in the absence of the alleged tortfeasor. Possible questions of contributory negligence may cause additional complications. Such difficulties are real, but are not sufficient, in my view, to warrant the conclusion that the distinction between tortious and non-tortious supervening events should not be accepted. The court must simply do its best to arrive at a just assessment of damages in a pragmatical way in the light of the whole circumstances of the case.

Notes
1.   For a useful discussion of this and other problems in causation, see Fraser and Howarth, 'More concern for cause' (1984) 4 LS 131.
2.   In *Jobling* the House of Lords did not overrule *Baker* v *Willoughby*, but said that it was correct on its facts. However, the House did not say what principle should govern it. In particular, Lord Bridge rejected the distinction adopted by Lord Keith between tortious and non-tortious supervening events.

Cook v *Lewis*
Supreme Court of Canada [1951] SCR 830; [1952] 1 DLR 1

While out shooting grouse on Vancouver Island, the plaintiff, Lewis, was shot by either Cook or Akenhead. The jury found that one of the two shot the plaintiff, but were unable to decide which. The Supreme Court of Canada ordered a new trial, but the judgment of Rand J included some interesting comments on how the burden of proof could be reversed so as to possibly render both defendants liable.

RAND J: What, then, the culpable actor had done by his intitial negligent act is, first, to have set in motion a dangerous force which embraces the injured person within the scope of its probable mischief; and next, in conjunction with circumstances which he must be held to contemplate, to have made more difficult if not impossible the means of proving the possible damaging results of his own act or the similar results of the act of another. He has violated not only the victim's substantive right to security, but he has also culpably impaired the latter's remedial right of establishing liability. By confusing his act with environmental conditions, he has, in effect, destroyed the victim's power of proof.

The legal consequence of that is, I should say, that the onus is then shifted to the wrongdoer to exculpate himself; it becomes in fact a question of proof between him and other and innocent member of the alternatives, the burden of which he must bear. The onus attaches to culpability, and if both acts bear that taint, the onus or *prima facie* transmisson of responsibility attaches to both, and the question of the sole responsibility of one is a matter between them. . . .

Assuming, then, that the jury have found one or both of the defendants here negligent, as on the evidence I think they must have, and at the same time have found that the consequences of the two shots, whether from a confusion in time or in area, cannot be segregated, the onus on the guilty person arises. This is a case where each hunter would know of or expect the shooting by the other and the negligent actor has culpably participated in the proof-destroying fact, the multiple shooting and its consequences. No liability will, in any event, attach to an innocent act of shooting, but the culpable actor, as against innocence, must bear the burden of exculpation.

Notes
1.   Do you agree with Rand J that the person who did not shoot Lewis had, acting negligently, deprived Lewis of a remedy against the person who did shoot, and should thus be required to prove he was not the person who shot the plaintiff?
2.   The principle suggested by Rand J in *Cook* v *Lewis* was taken further in the American case of *Sindell* v *Abbott Laboratories* (1980) 2 ALR 4th 1061, where the plaintiff suffered a malignant tumour, allegedly due to the fact that her mother had taken a drug called DES during pregnancy. DES was manufactured by a large number of companies and the plaintiff could not prove whose pills her mother had taken. The Supreme Court of California suggested that each manufacturer could be made a defendant and could be made liable for the proportion of the damages represented by its share in the market for DES. If this were so, some manufacturers would be liable even though they did not cause the damage. Can this be justified?

If one company made 51 per cent of DES, could it be liable *alone* on the ground that it is more likely than not that it was its pills which caused the damage?

Section 2: remoteness of damage

Even if the defendant's act caused the damage, liability can still be excluded if the damage was too remote, that is if the *kind* of damage was an unforeseeable consequence of the act. There has been a great deal of argument about this subject, but it may be that the different theories do not lead to very different results.

One problem is the relationship between this concept and duty of care, for some cases can be decided by application of either concept (e.g. *Tremain* v *Pike* [1969] 3 All ER 1303), and a number of cases on such topics as economic loss and nervous shock were once regarded as remoteness cases, whereas now they are seen as duty cases. One way to illustrate the difference is by the facts (but not the decision) in *Smith* v *London South Western Rly* (1870) LR 6 CP 14. The defendant's employees had cut some hedge trimmings which were laid in heaps alongside a railway line, and a passing locomotive set fire to one of the heaps. The fire spread across a stubble field 200 yards wide, across a road, and finally burnt the plaintiff's cottage. If we assume that the fire at the cottage was unforeseeable, for example because the road would have acted as a fire break, the position is this: if the plaintiff did *not* own the field there is no liability because no duty was owed to him since he was not a foreseeable plaintiff, having no property that was likely to be damaged. But if he did own the field he becomes a foreseeable plaintiff, and the question becomes one of remoteness: for how much damage can he recover?

Re Polemis
Court of Appeal [1921] 3 KB 560; 90 LJKB 1353; 126 LJ 154

Messrs Polemis and Boyazides chartered a ship called the *Thrasyvoulos* to Furness, Withy & Co. At Lisbon the ship loaded cargo for Casablanca, which included a number of drums of petrol, some of which leaked on the voyage due to heavy weather. At Casablanca some stevedores negligently dislodged a plank which fell into the hold, and a spark ignited the petrol vapour from the drums and a fire started, which ultimately destroyed the ship. The arbitrators found that 'the causing of the spark could not reasonably have been anticipated from the falling of the board, though some damage to the ship might reasonably have been anticipated'. Held: dismissing the appeal, that the charterers (as employers of the stevedores) were liable for the destruction of the ship.

BANKES LJ: In the present case the arbitrators have found as a fact that the falling of the plank was due to the negligence of the defendants' servants. The fire appears to me to have been directly caused by the falling of the plank. Under these circumstances I consider that it is immaterial that the causing of the spark by the falling of the plank could not have been reasonably anticipated. The appellants' junior counsel sought to draw a distinction between the anticipation of the extent of damage resulting from a negligent act, and the anticipation of the type of damage resulting from such an act. He admitted that it could not lie in the mouth of a person whose negligent act had caused damage to say that he could not reasonably have foreseen the extent of the damage, but he contended that the negligent person was entitled to rely upon the fact that he could not reasonably have anticipated the type of damage which resulted from his negligent act. I do not think that the distinction can be admitted. Given the breach of duty which constitutes the negligence, and given the damage as a direct result of that negligence, the anticipations of the person whose negligent act has produced the damage appear to me to be irrelevant. I consider that the damages claimed are not too remote. . . .

SCRUTTON LJ: The second defence is that the damage is too remote from the negligence, as it could not be reasonably foreseen as a consequence. On this head we were referred to a number of well known cases in which vague language, which I cannot think to be really helpful, has been used in an attempt to define the point at which damage becomes too remote from, or not sufficiently directly caused by, the breach of duty, which is the original cause of action, to be recoverable. For instance, I cannot think it useful to say the damage must be the natural and probable result. This suggests that there are results which are natural but not probable, and other results which are probable but not natural. I am not sure what either adjective means in this connection; if they mean the same thing, two need not be used; if they mean different things, the difference between them should be defined. And as to many cases of fact in which the distinction has been drawn, it is difficult to see why one case should be decided one way and one another. . . . To determine whether an act is negligent, it is relevant to determine whether any reasonable person would foresee that the act would cause damage; if he would not, the act is not negligent. But if the act would or might probably cause damage, the fact that the damage it in fact causes is not the exact kind of damage one would expect is immaterial, so long as the damage is in fact directly traceable to the negligent act, and not due to the operation of independent causes having no connection with the negligent act, except that they could not avoid its results. Once the act is negligent, the fact that its exact operation was not foreseen is immaterial. . . . In the present case it was negligent in discharging cargo to knock down the planks of the temporary staging, for they might easily cause some damage either to workmen, or cargo, or the ship. The fact that they did directly produce an unexpected result, a spark in an atmosphere of petrol vapour which caused a fire, does not relieve the person who was negligent from the damage which his negligent act directly caused.

Notes
1. This case is no longer regarded as law following the decision in *The Wagon Mound* (below), but it is necessary to know about it because of the extensive debate on the subject of remoteness and the various tests which have been adopted. Note also the dictum of Lord Sumner in *Weld Blundell* v *Stephens* [1920] AC 956, where he said that foresight 'goes to culpability, not to compensation', a view which was condemned in *The Wagon Mound*. For a discussion of the *Polemis* rule see Davies, 'The Road from Morocco' (1982) 45 MLR 534.
2. This test required *some* damage to be foreseeable and to have occurred, for otherwise there would be no duty or breach of duty. Thus the charterers were at least liable for the dent in the steel plating in the hold when the plank fell, but

the question was whether they were liable for more. It would not have applied if the plaintiffs had suffered no foreseeable damage at all. For a discussion of this problem, see Goodhart, 'The imaginary necktie and the rule in Re Polemis' (1952) 68 LQR 514.

The Wagon Mound (No. 1)
Privy Council [1961] AC 388; [1961] 1 All ER 404; [1961] 2 WLR 126

The defendants, Overseas Tankship (UK) Ltd, were charterers of the SS Wagon Mound, which was moored at the Caltex Wharf in Sydney harbour. On 30 October 1951 they negligently allowed a quantity of bunkering oil to spill into the harbour, and some of this drifted over to the Sheerlegs Wharf which was owned by the plaintiffs, Morts Dock and Engineering Co. The manager of the wharf asked the manager of Caltex Oil whether it was safe to continue welding operations and was told that the flammability of bunkering oil in sea water was such that it was. However, later that day a fire broke out at the wharf, apparently caused by molten metal falling on some cotton waste which was lying on a piece of debris, which set fire to the surrounding oil. The trial judge found that the defendant could not reasonably be expected to have known that the oil was capable of being set on fire when spread on water. The plaintiffs not only suffered loss by fire, but also suffered foreseeable loss caused by oil congealing on their slipways. Held: allowing the appeal, that the defendants were not liable.

VISCOUNT SIMONDS: Enough has been said to show that the authority of *Polemis* has been severely shaken though lip-service has from time to time been paid to it. In their Lordships' opinion it should no longer be regarded as good law. It is not probable that many cases will for that reason have a different result, though it is hoped that the law will be thereby simplified, and that in some cases, at least, palpable injustice will be avoided. For it does not seem consonant with current ideas of justice or morality that for an act of negligence, however slight or venial, which results in some trivial foreseeable damage the actor should be liable for all consequences however unforeseeable and however grave, so long as they can be said to be 'direct.' It is a principle of civil liability, subject only to qualifications which have no present relevance that a man must be considered to be responsible for the probable consequences of his act. To demand more of him is too harsh a rule, to demand less is to ignore that civilised order requires the observance of a minimum standard of behaviour.

This concept applied to the slowly developing law of negligence has led to a great variety of expressions which can, as it appears to their Lordships, be harmonised with little difficulty with the single exception of the so-called rule in *Polemis*. For, if it is asked why a man should be responsible for the natural or necessary or probable consequences of his act (or any other similar description of them) the answer is that it is not because they are natural or necessary or probable, but because, since they have this quality, it is judged by the standard of the reasonable man that he ought to have foreseen them. Thus it is that over and over again it has happened that in different judgments in the same case, and sometimes in a single judgment, liability for a consequence has been imposed on the ground that it was reasonably foreseeable or, alternatively, on the ground that it was natural or necessary or probable. The two grounds have been treated as coterminous, and so they largely are. But, where they are not, the question arises to which the wrong answer was given in *Polemis*. For, if some limitation must be imposed upon the consequences for which the negligent actor is to be held responsible — and all are agreed that some limitation there must be — why should that test (reasonable foreseeability) be rejected which, since he is judged by what the reasonable man ought to foresee, corresponds with the common conscience of mankind, and a test (the 'direct' consequence) be substituted which leads to nowhere but the never-ending and insoluble problems of causation. 'The lawyer,' said Sir Frederick Pollock, 'cannot afford to adventure himself with philosophers in the logical and metaphysical controversies that beset the idea of cause.' Yet this is just what he has most unfortunately done and must continue to do if the rule in *Polemis* is to prevail. A conspicuous example occurs when the actor seeks to escape liability on the ground that the 'chain of causation' is broken by a 'nova causa' or 'novus actus interveniens.' . . .

At an early stage in this judgment their Lordships intimated that they would deal with the proposition which can best be stated by reference to the well-known dictum of Lord Sumner: 'This however goes to culpability not to compensation.' It is with the greatest respect to that very learned judge and to those who have echoed his words, that their Lordships find themselves bound to state their view that this proposition is fundamentally false.

It is, no doubt, proper when considering tortious liability for negligence to analyse its elements and to say that the plaintiff must prove a duty owed to him by the defendant, a breach of that duty by the defendant, and consequent damage. But there can be no liability until the damage has been done. It is not the act but the consequences on which tortious liability is founded. Just as (as it has been said) there is no such thing as negligence in the air, so there is no such thing as liability in the air. Suppose an action brought by A for damage caused by the carelessness (a neutral word) of B, for example, a fire caused by the careless spillage of oil. It may, of course, become relevant to know what duty B owed to A, but the only liability that is in question is the liability for damage by fire. It is vain to isolate the liability from its context and to say that B is or is not liable, and then to ask for what damage he is liable. For his liability is in respect of that damage and no other. If, as admittedly it is, B's liability (culpability) depends on the reasonable foreseeability of the consequent damage, how is that to be determined except by the foreseeability of the damage which in fact happened — the damage in suit? And, if that damage is unforeseeable so as to displace liability at large, how can the liability be restored so as to make compensation payable?

But, it is said, a different position arises if B's careless act has been shown to be negligent and has caused some foreseeable damage to A. Their Lordships have already observed that to hold B liable for conequences however unforeseeable of a careless act, if, but only if, he is at the same time liable for some other damage however trivial, appears to be neither logical nor just. This becomes more clear if it is supposed that similar unforeseeable damage is suffered by A and C but other foreseeable damage, for which B is liable, by A only. A system of law which would hold B liable to A but not to C for the similar damage suffered by each of them could not easily be defended. Fortunately, the attempt is not necessary. For the same fallacy is at the root of the proposition. It is irrelevant to the question whether B is liable for unforeseeable damage that he is liable for foreseeable damage, as irrelevant as would the fact that he had trespassed on Whiteacre be to the question whether he has trespassed on Blackacre. Again, suppose a claim by A for damage by fire by the careless act of B. Of what relevance is it to that claim that he has another claim arising out of the same careless act? It would surely not prejudice his claim if that other claim failed: it cannot assist it if it succeeds. Each of them rests on its own bottom, and will fail if it can be established that the damage could not reasonably be foreseen. We have come back to the plain common sense stated by Lord Russell of Killowen in *Bourhill* v *Young* [1943] AC 92, 101. As Denning LJ said in *King* v *Phillips* [1953] 1 QB 429: 'there can be no doubt since *Bourhill* v *Young* that the test of *liability for shock* is foreseeability of *injury by shock.*' Their Lordships substitute the word 'fire' for 'shock' and endorse this statement of the law.

Notes

1. For a discussion of this and the following case, see Dias, 'Remoteness of Damages and Legal Policy' [1962] CLJ 178, and 'Trouble on Oiled Waters' [1967] CLJ 62.

2. It may be that foreseeability by itself is not the whole story, for other, often unexpressed, factors may also be relevant (see below). Thus, in **March v Stramare** (1991) ALR 423, McHugh J said (in a minority judgment):

Once it is recognised that foreseeability is not the exclusive test of remoteness and that policy-based rules, disguised as causation principles, are also being used to limit responsibility for occasioning damage, the rationalisation of the rules concerning remoteness of damage requires an approach which incorporates the issue of foreseeability but also enables other policy factors to be articulated and examined.

One such approach, and the one I favour, is the 'scope of the risk' test which has much support among academic writers as well as the support of Denning LJ in *Roe* v *Minister of Health* [1954] 2 QB 66 at 85, where his Lordship said:

'Starting with the proposition that a negligent person should be liable, within reason, for the consequences of his conduct, the extent of his liability is to be found by asking the one question: Is the consequence *fairly* to be regarded as within the risk created by the negligence? If so, the negligent person is liable for it: but otherwise not' (my emphasis).

Damage will be a consequence of the risk if it is the kind of damage which should have been reasonably foreseen. However, the precise damage need not have been foreseen. It is sufficient if damage of the kind which occurred could have been foreseen in a general way: *Hughes* v *Lord Advocate* [1963] AC 837. But the 'scope of the risk' test enables more than foreseeability of damage to be considered. As Fleming points out (*The Law of Torts*, 7th ed, p. 193), it also enables allowance to:

'. . . be made to such other pertinent factors as the purpose of the legal rule violated by the defendant, analogies drawn from accepted patterns of past decisions, general community notions regarding the allocation of "blame" as well as supervening considerations of judicial policy bearing on accident prevention, loss distribution and insurance.'

3. The Privy Council left open the question whether the foresight test applies to torts of strict liability, and there is some doubt whether it applies in trespass. In the Canadian case of **Allen v Mount Sinai Hospital** (1980) 109 DLR 3d 634 (a case of medical battery), Linden J said 'In battery, however, any and all damage is recoverable, if it results from the wrongful act, whether it is

foreseeable or not.' However, in the New Zealand case of **Mayfair v Pears** [1987] 1 NZLR 459, the Court of Appeal agreed that the foresight test may in some cases be too benevolent to a trespasser, but refused to lay down any hard and fast rule of remoteness, saying the rules of remoteness are intended to 'limit the amounts recoverable by the plaintiff to those that are not only connected to the act but which are reasonable having regard to its nature and the interests of the parties and society.' (The defendant was held not liable for a fire which burnt down a building owned by the plaintiff. The fire started accidentally in the defendant's car which was unlawfully parked on the plaintiff's land.)

The Wagon Mound (No. 2)
Privy Council [1967] 1 AC 617; [1966] 1 All ER 709; [1966] 3 WLR 498

This case arose out of the same fire as in *Wagon Mound No. 1*, but the plaintiff here, Miller Steamship Pty, was the owner of the ships, The Corrimal and the Audrey D., which were lying alongside Sheerlegs Wharf. The trial judge in this action made significantly different findings of fact, and the Privy Council held the defendants were liable.

LORD REID: The findings of the learned trial judge are as follows:

(1) Reasonable people in the position of the officers of the *Wagon Mound* would regard the furnace oil as very difficult to ignite upon water. (2) Their personal experience would probably have been that this had very rarely happened. (3) If they had given attention to the risk of fire from the spillage, they would have regarded it as a possibility, but one which could become an actuality only in very exceptional circumstances. (4) They would have considered the chances of the required exceptional circumstances happening whilst the oil remained spread on the harbour waters as being remote. (5) I find that the occurrence of damage to the plaintiff's property as a result of the spillage was not reasonably foreseeable by those for whose acts the defendant would be responsible. (6) I find that the spillage of oil was brought about by the careless conduct of persons for whose acts the defendant would be responsible. (7) I find that the spillage of oil was a cause of damage to the property of each of the plaintiffs. (8) Having regard to those findings, and because of finding (5), I hold that the claim of each of the plaintiffs, framed in negligence, fails.

. . .

The crucial finding of Walsh J in this case is in finding (5): that the damage was 'not reasonably foreseeable by those for whose acts the defendant would be responsible.' That is not a primary finding of fact but an inference from the other findings, and it is clear from the learned judge's judgment that in drawing this inference he was to a large extent influenced by his view of the law. The vital parts of the findings of fact which have already been set out in full are (1) that the officers of the *Wagon Mound* [1961] AC 388 'would regard furnace oil as very difficult to ignite upon water' — not that they would regard this as impossible; (2) that their experience would probably have been 'that this had very rarely happened' — not that they would never have heard of a case where it had happened, and (3) that they would have regarded it as a 'possibility, but one which could become an actuality only in very exceptional circumstances' — not, as in *The Wagon Mound (No. 1)*, that they could not reasonably be expected to have known that this oil was capable of being set afire when spread on water. The question which must now be determined is whether these differences between the findings in the two cases do or do not lead to different results in law.

In *The Wagon Mound (No. 1)* the Board were not concerned with degrees of foreseeability because the finding was that the fire was not foreseeable at all. So Lord Simonds had no cause to amplify the statement that the 'essential factor in determining liability is whether the damage is of such a kind as the reasonable man should have foreseen.' But here the findings show that some risk of fire would have been present to the mind of a reasonable man in the shoes of the ship's chief engineer. So the first question must be what is the precise meaning to be attached in this context to the words 'foreseeable' and 'reasonably foreseeable.'

Before *Bolton v Stone* [1951] AC 850 the cases had fallen into two classes: (1) those where, before the event, the risk of its happening would have been regarded as unreal either because the event would have been thought to be physically impossible or because the possibility of its happening would have been regarded as so fantastic or far-fetched that no reasonable man would have paid any attention to it — 'a mere possibility which would never occur to the mind of a reasonable man' (*per* Lord Dunedin in *Fardon v Harcourt-Rivington*) (1932) 146 LT 391 — or (2) those where there was a real and substantial risk or chance that something like the event which happens might occur, and then the reasonable man would have taken the steps necessary to eliminate the risk.

Bolton v Stone [1951] AC 850 posed a new problem. There a member of a visiting team drove a cricket ball out of the ground onto an unfrequented adjacent public road and it struck and severely injured a lady who happened to be standing in the road. That it might happen that a ball would be driven onto this road could not have been said to be a fantastic or far-fetched possibility: according to the evidence it had happened about six times in 28 years. And it could not have been said to be a far-fetched or fantastic possibility that such a ball would strike someone in the road: people did pass along the road from time to time. So it could not have been said that, on any ordinary meaning of the words, the fact that a ball might strike a person in the road was not foreseeable or reasonably foreseeable — it was plainly foreseeable. But the chance of its happening in the foreseeable future was infinitesimal. A mathematician given the data could have worked out that it was only likely to happen once in so many thousand years. The House of Lords held that the risk was so small that in the circumstances a reasonable man would have been justified in disregarding it and taking no steps to eliminate it.

But it does not follow that, no matter what the circumstances may be, it is justifiable to neglect a risk of such a small magnitude. A reasonable man would only neglect such a risk if he had some valid reason for doing so, e.g., that it would involve considerable expense to eliminate the risk. He would weigh the risk against the difficulty of eliminating it. If the activity which caused the injury to Miss Stone had been an unlawful activity, there can be little doubt but that *Bolton v Stone* would have been decided differently. In their Lordships' judgment *Bolton v Stone* did not alter the general principle that a person must be regarded as negligent if he does not take steps to eliminate a risk which he knows or ought to know is a real risk and not a mere possibility which would never influence the mind of a reasonable man. What that decision did was to recognise and give effect to the qualification that it is justifiable not to take steps to eliminate a real risk if it is small and if the circumstances are such that a reasonable man, careful of the safety of his neighbour, would think it right to neglect it.

In the present case there was no justification whatever for discharging the oil into Sydney Harbour. Not only was it an offence to do so, but it involved considerable loss financially. If the ship's engineer had thought about the matter, there could have been no question of balancing the advantages and disadvantages. From every point of view it was both his duty and his interest to stop the discharge immediately. . . .

In their Lordships' view a properly qualified and alert chief engineer would have realised there was a real risk here and they do not understand Walsh J to deny that. But he appears to have held that if a real risk can properly be described as remote it must then be held to be not reasonably foreseeable. That is a possible interpretation of some of the authorities. But this is still an open question and on principle their Lordships cannot accept this view. If a real risk is one which would occur to the mind of a reasonable man in the position of the defendant's servant and which he would not brush aside as far-fetched, and if the criterion is to be what that reasonable man would have done in the circumstances, then surely he would not neglect such a risk if action to eliminate it presented no difficulty, involved no disadvantage, and required no expense.

Notes

1. The reason for the different evidence and findings of fact may be that when No. 1 was decided the contributory negligence rules in New South Wales meant that if a plaintiff was contributorily negligent at all he lost his case entirely: naturally, therefore, the plaintiffs would have been wary of saying that the fire was foreseeable. By the time of No. 2 the rules had changed, so that in a case of contributory negligence the damages could be apportioned between the parties, thus providing less risk to the plaintiff.

2. The procedure in No. 2 was complex, and in the event the Privy Council found the defendants were liable in negligence but not in nuisance. The explanation for this is complicated, and is discussed by Hoffman in (1967) 83 LQR 13.

3. The oddest case on remoteness is *Falkenham v Zwicker* (1979) 90 DLR 3d 289. On 1 February 1977 the defendant was driving her car in Nova Scotia when she slammed on her brakes to avoid a cat in the road. The car left the road and ran into wire fencing alongside the road. This caused the fence to 'unzip', in that a number of staples sprung out of the fence into the field. There were no cows in the field at the time. On 24 May the plaintiff put his cows into the field: they ate the staples. The staples caused the cows to contract 'hardware disease'. The vet put magnets in their stomachs, but five of the cows never recovered and were sent to the meat packer. MacIntosh J, in the Supreme Court of Nova Scotia, held the defendant liable for the reduced value of the cows. How could this be?

A: Subsequent interpretations — the egg shell skull rule

The Wagon Mound changed the theory of remoteness of damage, but did it make any practical difference? One area where this arose was the so-called 'egg shell skull' rule, whereby, in personal injury cases at least, you take your victim as you find him — i.e. if the plaintiff has a thin skull and therefore suffers extensive injury, a defendant is liable for the whole loss and not just for the damage which might have been expected to occur to a normal person.

Robinson v Post Office
Court of Appeal [1974] 1 WLR 1176; [1974] 2 All ER 737; 16 KIR 12

The plaintiff slipped on an oily ladder and cut his shin. He went to a doctor who gave him an anti-tetanus injection. The plaintiff was allergic to the serum and contracted encephalitis. Held: dismissing the appeal, that the defendants were liable for the entire damage.

ORR LJ: Mr Newey's main argument, however, was that the onset of encephalitis was not reasonably foreseeable and that on the basis of the decision of the Privy Council in *Overseas Tankship (UK) Ltd v Morts Dock and Engineering Co. Ltd (The Wagon Mound)* [1961] AC 388, the Post Office should not be held liable for that consequence of the injury. In answer to this argument the plaintiff relied on the judgment of Lord Parker C J in *Smith v Leech Brain & Co. Ltd* [1962] 2 QB 405. In that case an employee already suffering from premalignant changes had, as a result of his employers' negligence, sustained a burn which the judge found to have been the promoting agent in the development of cancer from which the employee died, and in a fatal accident claim by his widow it was argued for the defendant employers that the development of cancer was unforeseeable and that on the basis of *The Wagon Mound* decision the claim should be dismissed. Lord Parker CJ, however, rejected this argument in the following passages from his judgment, at pp. 414-415, which are quoted in the judgment now under appeal:

> For my part, I am quite satisfied that the Judicial Committee in *The Wagon Mound* case did not have what I may call, loosely, the thin-skull cases in mind. It has always been the law of this country that a tortfeasor takes his victim as he finds him . . . The test is not whether these employers could reasonably have foreseen that a burn would cause cancer and that he would die. The question is whether these employers could reasonably foresee the type of injury he suffered, namely, the burn. What, in the particular case, is the amount of damage which he suffers as a result of that burn, depends upon the characteristics and constitution of the victim.

It is to be noted, as pointed out in the judgment under appeal, that the last of these passages is supported by very similar language used by Lord Reid in the later case of *Hughes v Lord Advocate* [1963] AC 837, 845.

On this appeal Mr Newey did not challenge the correctness of Lord Parker CJ's reasoning and conclusion in the *Leech Brain* case and accepted that some at least of the subsequent decisions fell within the same principle, but he claimed that an essential link which was missing in the present case was that it was not foreseeable that administration of a form of anti-tetanus prophylaxis would itself give rise to a rare serious illness. In our judgment, however, there was no missing link and the case is governed by the principle that the Post Office had to take their victim as they found him, in this case with an allergy to a second dose of ATS. . . . In our judgment the principle that a defendant must take the plaintiff as he finds him involves that if a wrongdoer ought reasonably to foresee that as a result of his wrongful act the victim may require medical treatment he is, subject to the principle of novus actus interveniens, liable for the consequences of the treatment applied although he could not reasonably foresee those consequences or that they could be serious.

Question

The plaintiff was here suffering from a 'pre-existing susceptibility' to greater damage than normal. Was the ship in *Re Polemis* also suffering from such a defect?

Note

This case is also a good example of the application of the 'but for' test of causation. The plaintiff also sued the doctor. When the plaintiff saw him he was given a test to see if there would be adverse reaction to the serum. The doctor was supposed to wait half an hour, but in fact waited only half a minute to see if there was a reaction. Thus, although negligent, the doctor was not liable because the reaction did not become apparent for nine days. The test, even if performed properly, would have made no difference.

Stephenson v *Waite Tileman Ltd*
New Zealand Court of Appeal [1973] 1 NZLR 153

The plaintiff cut his hand on a wire rope. Medical evidence was given that an 'unknown virus' had entered the wound, causing brain damage. Held: allowing the appeal, the defendants were liable for the whole damage.

RICHMOND J: It would seem to me that if the principle of the eggshell skull cases is still part of English law, then it must follow both on grounds of logic and practical policy that the principle of new risk created by injury must also be part of the law. It would be illogical to allow recovery in respect of disease latent in the plaintiff's body but activated by physical injury and at the same time to deny recovery in respect of illness caused by an infection entering the plaintiff's system as the result of a wound. On the more practical side, it may in any given case be quite impossible to decide in which category a particular consequence of an accident lies. Thus in the case of the present appeal, it is common ground that an infection entered the appellant's system through the wound caused by the wire rope. It is not however possible to say whether the virus was of an unusually virulent kind against which the appellant put up a normal resistance or whether the virus was one to which the appellant was unusually susceptible. . . .

The result of this lengthy review of the authorities is to disclose the existence of a very strong body of judicial opinion both in England and in Commonwealth jurisdictions in favour of the view that the eggshell skull rule remains part of our law notwithstanding the decision in *The Wagon Mound (No. 1)*. As already indicated, I accept that view myself and for reasons which I have endeavoured to express I am also satisfied that similar principles must be applied to cases where a foreseeable kind of physical injury gives rise to some new risk or state of susceptibility in the victim. I have also found it helpful to consider the various fact situations which have arisen in the reported cases while endeavouring to arrive at some general principle which may be fairly and properly applied. I now summarise my conclusions:

1   In cases of damage by physical injury to the person the principles imposing liability for consequences flowing from the pre-existing special susceptibility of the victim and/or from new risk or susceptibility created by the initial injury remain part of our law.

2   In such cases the question of foreseeability should be limited to the initial injury. The tribunal of fact must decide whether that injury is of a kind, type or character which the defendant ought reasonably to have foreseen as a real risk.

3   If the plaintiff establishes that the initial injury was within a reasonably foreseeable kind, type or character of injury, then the necessary link between the ultimate consequences of the initial injury and the negligence of the defendant can be forged simply as one of cause and effect — in other words by establishing an adequate relationship of cause and effect between the initial injury and the ultimate consequence.

Question
In this case the plaintiff was *not* suffering from a pre-existing susceptibility, and therefore it is not strictly an 'egg shell skull' case at all. Does the view of Richmond J mean that the *Polemis* test now applies to personal injuries?

B: Subsequent interpretations — the kind of damage

In *The Wagon Mound* Viscount Simonds said that 'the essential factor in determining liability is whether the damage is of such a kind as the reasonable man should have foreseen'. Obviously the answer to such a question will often depend on how wide a category of 'kind of damage' is adopted as the test.

Hughes v Lord Advocate
House of Lords [1963] AC 837; [1963] 2 WLR 779; [1963] 1 All ER 705

Some Post Office employees erected a shelter tent over a manhole in Russell Road, Edinburgh. At about 5.30 p.m. they went for their tea, leaving the tent unattended. It had four red paraffin lamps, one at each corner, and the men pulled the ladder out of the manhole. The pursuer, aged eight and his uncle, aged ten, approached the shelter. They picked up one of the paraffin lamps and took the ladder into the shelter. They tied the lamp to a rope and lowered it into the hole and they followed. When they emerged from the hole, the lamp was knocked back into it and there was an enormous explosion, causing flames to reach 30 feet. The pursuer fell back into the hole and was badly burnt. It was thought that when the lamp fell into the hole, some paraffin escaped and vaporised. This was so unlikely as to be unforeseeable. Held: allowing the appeal, that the defendant was liable.

LORD REID: This accident was caused by a known source of danger, but caused in a way which could not have been foreseen, and, in my judgment, that affords no defence. I would therefore allow the appeal.

LORD JENKINS: It is true that the duty of care expected in cases of this sort is confined to reasonably foreseeable dangers, but it does not necessarily follow that liability is escaped because the danger actually materialising is not identical with the danger reasonably foreseen and guarded against. Each case much depends on its own particular facts. For example (as pointed out in the opinions), in the present case the paraffin did the mischief by exploding, not burning, and it is said that while a paraffin fire (caused, for example, by the upsetting of the lighted lamp or otherwise allowing its contents to leak out) was a reasonably foreseeable risk so soon as the pursuer got access to the lamp, an explosion was not.

To my mind, the distinction drawn between burning and explosion is too fine to warrant acceptance. Supposing the pursuer had on the day in question gone to the site and taken one of the lamps, and upset it over himself, thus setting his clothes alight, the person to be considered responsible for protecting children from the dangers to be found there would presumably have been liable. On the other hand, if the lamp, when the boy upset it, exploded in his face, he would have had no remedy because the explosion was an event which could not reasonably be foreseen. This does not seem to me to be right.

LORD MORRIS: My Lords, in my view, there was a duty owed by the defenders to safeguard the pursuer against the type or kind of occurrence which in fact happened and which resulted in his injuries, and the defenders are not absolved from liability because they did not envisage 'the precise concatenation of circumstances which led up to the accident.'. . .

LORD GUEST: In dismissing the appellant's claim the Lord Ordinary and the majority of the judges of the First Division reached the conclusion that the accident which happened was not reasonably foreseeable. In order to establish a coherent chain of causation it is not necessary that the precise details leading up to the accident should have been reasonably foreseeable; it is sufficient if the accident which occurred is of a type which should have been foreseeable by a reasonably careful person . . . or as Lord Mackintosh expressed it in the *Harvey* case, 1960 SC 155, the precise concatenation of circumstances need not be envisaged. Concentration has been placed in the courts below on the explosion which, it was said, could not have been foreseen because it was caused in a unique fashion by the paraffin forming into vapour and being ignited by the naked flame of the wick. But this, in my opinion, is to concentrate on what is really a non-essential element in the dangerous situation created by the allurement. The test might better be put thus: Was the igniting of paraffin outside the lamp by the flame a foreseeable consequence of the breach of duty? In the circumstances, there was a combination of potentially dangerous circumstances against which the Post Office had to protect the appellant. If these formed an allurement to children it might have been foreseen that they would play with the lamp, that it might tip over, that it might be broken, and that when broken the paraffin might spill and be ignited by the flame. All these steps in the chain of causation seem to have been accepted by all the judges in the courts below as foreseeable. But because the explosion was the agent which caused the burning and was unforeseeable, therefore the accident, according to them, was not reasonably foreseeable. In my opinion, this reasoning is fallacious. An explosion is only one way in which burning can be caused. Burning can also be caused by the contact between liquid paraffin and a naked flame. In the one case paraffin vapour and in the other case liquid paraffin is ignited by fire. I cannot see that these are two different types of accident. They are both burning accidents and in both cases the injuries would be burning injuries. Upon this view the explosion was an immaterial event in the chain of causation. It was simply one way in which burning might be caused by the potentially dangerous paraffin lamp. . . .

LORD PEARCE: The obvious risks were burning and conflagration and a fall. All these in fact occurred, but unexpectedly the mishandled lamp instead of causing an ordinary conflagration produced a violent explosion. Did the explosion create an accident and damage of a different type from the misadventure and damage that could be foreseen? In my judgment it did not. The accident was but a variant of the foreseeable.

Question
What was foreseeable?
    (a)   damage by paraffin? (in which case would the defendants have been liable if the boys had drunk the paraffin?);
    (b)   damage by lamp? (in which case would the defendants have been liable if the plaintiff had dropped the lamp on his foot?);
    (c)   damage by burning? (how was the plaintiff supposed to have burnt himself?). If it is supposed that there was a risk that the boy might touch the lamp and burn himself (how badly?) is that a variant of being sucked into the hole by an unforeseeable explosion?

Notes
1.   *Hughes* is not inconsistent with the theory behind *The Wagon Mound,* that is that remoteness should be tested by probability rather than by cause;

nevertheless, it is based on probability of result rather than probability of the method of bringing about the result.
2. In *Tremain* v *Pike* [1969] 3 All ER 1303, the defendant operated a farm at Beer in Devon, where there were too many rats. The plaintiff, a herdsman employed by the defendant, contracted a rare disease, Weil's disease, from contact with rats' urine. Payne J held, *inter alia*, that this was different from the foreseeable damage such as injury by rat bites, and therefore it was too remote. Injury by rat bites is foreseeable: injury by rats' urine is not. But if the test was injury by rats the result might have been different. Which is the appropriate category?

Doughty v *Turner Manufacturing Co.*
Court of Appeal [1964] 1 QB 518; [1964] 1 All ER 98; [1964] 2 WLR 248

The defendants had two cauldrons containing sodium cyanide powder, which became liquid when heated to 800C by electrodes. Each bath had a cover made of an asbestos compound. What was not known was that the compound, when heated above 500C underwent a chemical change and emitted steam. Due to negligence one of the covers slid into the liquid, which then erupted, injuring the plaintiff who was standing near the bath. Held: allowing the appeal, that the defendants were not liable.

HARMAN LJ: The plaintiff's argument most persuasively urged by Mr James rested, as I understood it, on admissions made that, if this lid had been dropped into the cauldron with sufficient force to cause the molten material to splash over the edge, that would have been an act of negligence or carelessness for which the defendants might be vicariously responsible. Reliance was put upon *Hughes* v *Lord Advocate* [1963] AC 837, where the exact consequences of the lamp overturning were not foreseen, but it was foreseeable that, if the manhole were left unguarded, boys would enter and tamper with the lamp, and it was not unlikely that serious burns might ensue for the boys. Their Lordships' House distinguished *The Wagon Mound* case [1961] AC 388 on the ground that the damage which ensued, though differing in degree, was the same in kind as that which was foreseeable. So it is said here that a splash causing burns was foreseeable and that this explosion was really only a magnified splash which also caused burns and that, therefore, we ought to follow *Hughes* v *Lord Advocate* and hold the defendants liable. I cannot accept this. In my opinion, the damage here was of entirely different kind from the foreseeable splash. Indeed, the evidence showed that any disturbance of the material resulting from the immersion of the hard-board was past an appreciable time before the explosion happened. This latter was caused by the disintegration of the hard-board under the great heat to which it was subjected and the consequent release of the moisture enclosed within it. This had nothing to do with the agitation caused by the dropping of the board into the cyanide. I am of opinion that it would be wrong on these facts to make another inroad on the doctrine of foreseeability which seems to me to be a satisfactory solvent of this type of difficulty.

Question
If an explosion is a variant of fire, why is not an eruption a variant of a splash?

Note
A better solution to this case is that taken by Diplock LJ, and is based on duty. The foreseeable risk was burning people by splashing if the cover was dropped from a height into the bath. However, as the chemical change in the cover was unknown, there was no duty to prevent the cover being *in* the bath: thus, if the cover slides gently in, the defendants are not in breach of any duty. Note also that if the plaintiff had been outside the range of potential splashing (said to be about one foot) he would have been an unforeseeable plaintiff anyway.

7 SPECIAL DUTY PROBLEMS: OMISSIONS

The common law took the view that it would be too great a burden to impose liability upon a person for a mere omission. The law could not require a person to love his neighbour, but could only ask that he should avoid injuring him, and so there is, for example, no liability for failing to prevent a blind man walking over a cliff. Given that position, the next problem was whether a person who volunteers to help, although under no duty to do so, is liable if he assists negligently? For example, can a doctor who voluntarily assists at a road accident be liable for negligent medical attention?

Even though the common law took the view that mere inaction did not give rise to liability, duties can in fact be imposed in two ways. The first is terminological, that is interpreting an omission as a negligent act. Thus, in *Kelly* v *Metropolitan Rly* [1895] 1 QB 944 the plaintiff was injured in a railway accident where a train was driven into a wall at Baker Street station. The defendants admitted this was a breach of contract, but claimed that it was not a tort because there was only an omission, in that the engine driver had merely failed to turn off the steam. The court naturally held that this amounted to the positive act of driving the train negligently.

The second way of imposing a duty is by the reliance of the plaintiff upon the defendant. This can come about either by the previous conduct of the defendant, which induces reliance by the plaintiff that the defendant will continue to act in that way, or by reliance which comes out of a relationship of dependence between the parties.

Mercer v *South Eastern and Chatham Rly*
Queen's Bench Division [1922] 2 KB 549; 92 LJKB 25; 127 LT 723

The plaintiff was a jogger who approached a level crossing near Slade Green in Kent. The main gates were closed and he waited for a train (the down train) to pass. He then found that the small gate at the side for pedestrian use was unlocked, and he passed through and was knocked down by a train going the other way (the up train). The plaintiff used the crossing two or three times a week and was accustomed to finding the small gate locked if a train was due. Held: the defendants owed the plaintiff a duty and were liable.

LUSH J: What in the present case is the true inference to be drawn from the facts as I have stated them?

I should certainly hesitate to hold that if in a case of this kind a person wishing to use the level crossing were, merely because he found the gate unlocked, to omit to look and see whether the way was clear when there was nothing to prevent him from doing so, and were to walk on, reading a newspaper, for example, he could make the company liable if he were run down by a train that he could easily have seen or heard. The railway company may have tacitly invited him to cross the line, but they did not invite him to leave his common sense behind him. There are however special circumstances in this case, inasmuch as, owing to the position of the down train, the plaintiff could neither see nor hear the up train.

I come to the conclusion on these facts that the plaintiff got in front of the up train because he was thrown off his guard by what the signalman did, that the danger was not an obvious one, and that he was injured while taking what was in the circumstances ordinary and reasonable care. . . .

In this case I think that the defendants gave a tacit invitation, and that it was in consequence of his acting upon that invitation that the plaintiff was injured.

It may seem a hardship on a railway company to hold them responsible for the omission to do something which they were under no legal obligation to do, and which they only did for the protection of the public. They ought, however, to have contemplated that if a self-imposed duty is ordinarily performed, those who know of it will draw an inference if on a given occasion it is not performed. If they wish to protect themselves against the inference being drawn they should do so by giving notice, and they did not do so in this case.

R v Instan
Court for Crown Cases Reserved [1893] 1 QB 450

Kate Instan lived with her aunt, who was 73. Towards the end of her life the aunt suffered from gangrene in the leg, but the defendant failed to give her any medical or nursing attention, nor did she give her any food. The cause of death was gangrene, accelerated by neglect and lack of food. Held: the defendant was guilty of manslaughter.

LORD COLERIDGE CJ: We are all of opinion that this conviction must be affirmed. It would not be correct to say that every moral obligation involves a legal duty; but every legal duty is founded on a moral obligation. A legal common law duty is nothing else than the enforcing by law of that which is a moral obligation without legal enforcement. There can be no question in this case that it was the clear duty of the prisoner to impart to the deceased so much as was necessary to sustain life of the food which she from time to time took in, and which was paid for by the deceased's own money for the purpose of the maintenance of herself and the prisoner; it was only through the instrumentality of the prisoner that the deceased could get the food. There was, therefore, a common law duty imposed upon the prisoner which she did not discharge.

Note
Although this is a criminal case, there is no doubt the defendant would have been liable in tort for a breach of duty arising from the relationship of dependence by the aunt upon the niece. For a discussion of the liability of the operator of a boat towards a passenger who falls overboard, see *The Ogopogo (Horsley v MacLaren)* [1971] 2 Lloyds Rep 410. (A passenger fell overboard without any negligence by the defendant operator: the operator owes a duty to rescue him. Also, the operator could have been liable to a person who attempted to rescue the passenger in the water, if the operator's method of going about the rescue had been negligent, which it had not.)

Question
A enters B's bar and becomes drunk. B ejects A from the bar because he is becoming a nuisance. B knows that A will be walking home, and on the way home A is run over by a car. Is B liable to A for failing to call a taxi or the police? See *Jordan House Ltd v Menow* (1974) 38 DLR 3d 105 where liability was imposed in such circumstances. Compare *Barrett v Ministry of Defence* [1995] 3 All ER 87 where the Ministry was not liable for failing to prevent a naval airman becoming so drunk at a naval base that he eventually died.

8 SPECIAL DUTY PROBLEMS: EXERCISE OF STATUTORY POWERS

The difficulty which arises here is the extent of liability of a person, usually a local authority, who has the *power,* but not the duty, to do something, and he either fails to do it or does it badly. This issue is fully discussed in *Anns* v *London Borough of Merton* (below), but it is not certain that these principles are universally accepted, and much remains to be worked out. One complication is the growing distinction between private and public law, and *O'Reilly* v *Mackman* [1983] 2 AC 237 and cases which followed it take the view that where the allegation raises an issue of public law, for example that a local authority had no power to do what it did, then only public law remedies may be appropriate, and a private action in negligence cannot be pursued.

Anns v *Merton London Borough Council*
House of Lords [1978] AC 728; [1977] 2 WLR 1024; [1977] 2 All ER 492

The plaintiffs were lessees of flats in a building in Wimbledon, and in 1970 there were structural movements which caused walls to crack. This was due to inadequate foundations. In 1962 the builders had deposited plans with the predecessors of the defendant local authority, which showed that the foundations would be at least three feet deep, but in fact they were only two feet six inches. The plaintiffs sued the local authority on the ground that their predecessors' inspectors had either not inspected the foundations, or, if they had, had done so negligently. The Public Health Act 1936 required the local authority to pass building regulations, and they had the power to inspect any foundations to see if they complied with the regulations. Held: dismissing the appeal, that the local authority owed a duty of care. (This case has now been overruled by the House of Lords in *Murphy* v *Brentwood District Council* [1991] 1 AC 398, but it is thought that this has not affected the validity (or otherwise) of the dicta of Lord Wilberforce relating to the exercise of powers.)

LORD WILBERFORCE: What then is the extent of the local authority's duty towards these persons? Although, as I have suggested, a situation of 'proximity' existed between the council and owners and occupiers of the houses, I do not think that a description of the council's duty can be based upon the 'neighbourhood' principle alone or upon merely any such factual relationship as 'control' as suggested by the Court of Appeal. So to base it would be to neglect an essential factor which is that the local authority is a public body, discharging functions under statute: its powers and duties are definable in terms of public not private law. The problem which this type of action creates, is to define the circumstances in which the law should impose, over and above, or perhaps alongside, these public law powers and duties, a duty in private law towards individuals such that they may sue for damages in a civil court. It is in this context that the distinction sought to be drawn between duties and mere powers has to be examined.

Most, indeed probably all, statutes relating to public authorities or public bodies, contain in them a large area of policy. The courts call this 'discretion' meaning that the decision is one for the authority or body to make, and not for the courts. Many statutes also prescribe or at least presuppose the practical execution of policy decisions: a convenient description of this is to say that in addition to the area of policy or discretion, there is an operational area. Although this distinction between the policy area and the operational area is convenient, and illuminating, it is probably a distinction of degree; many 'operational' powers or duties have in them some element of 'discretion.' It can safely be said that the more 'operational' a power or duty may be, the easier it is to superimpose upon it a common law duty of care.

I do not think that it is right to limit this to a duty to avoid causing extra or additional damage beyond what must be expected to arise from the exercise of the power or duty. That may be correct when the act done under the statute *inherently* must adversely *affect* the interest of individuals. But many other acts can be done without causing any harm to anyone — indeed may be directed to preventing harm from occurring. In these cases the duty is the normal one of taking care to avoid harm to those likely to be affected.

Let us examine the Public Health Act 1936 in the light of this. Undoubtedly it lays out a wide area of policy. It is for the local authority, a public and elected body, to decide upon the scale of resources which it can make available in order to carry out its functions under Part II of the Act — how many inspectors, with what expert qualifications, it should recruit, how often inspections are to be made, what tests are to be carried out, must be for its decision. It is no accident that the Act is drafted in terms of functions and powers rather than in terms of positive duty. As was well said, public authorities have to strike a balance between the claims of efficiency and thrift (du Parcq LJ in *Kent* v *East Suffolk Rivers Catchment Board* [1940] 1 KB 319, 338): whether they get the balance right can only be decided through the ballot box, not in the courts. It is said — there are reflections of this in the judgments in *Dutton* v *Bognor Regis Urban District Council* [1972] 1 QB 373 — that the local authority is under no duty to inspect, and this is used as the foundation for an argument, also found in some of the cases, that if it need not inspect at all, it cannot be liable for negligent inspection: if it were to be held so liable, so it is said, councils would simply decide against inspection. I think that this is too crude an argument. It overlooks the fact that local authorities are public bodies operating under statute with a clear responsibility for public health in their area. They must, and in fact do, make their discretionary decisions responsibly and for reasons which accord with the statutory purpose; see *Ayr Harbour Trustees* v *Oswald* (1883) 8 App Cas 623, 639, *per* Lord Watson:

the powers which [section 10] confers are discretionary . . . But it is the plain import of the clause that the harbour trustees . . . shall be vested with, and shall avail themselves of, these discretionary powers, whenever and as often as they may be of opinion that the public interest will be promoted by their exercise.

If they do not exercise their discretion in this way they can be challenged in the courts. Thus, to say that councils are under no duty to inspect, is not a sufficient statement of the position. They are under a duty to give proper consideration to the question whether they should inspect or not. Their immunity from attack, in the event of failure to inspect, in other words, though great is not absolute. And because it is not absolute, the necessary premise for the proposition 'if no duty to inspect, then no duty to take care in inspection' vanishes.

Passing then to the duty as regards inspection, if made. On principle there must surely be a duty to exercise reasonable care. The standard of care must be related to the duty to be performed — namely to ensure compliance with the byelaws. It must be related to the fact that the person responsible for construction in accordance with the byelaws is the builder, and that the inspector's function is supervisory. It must be related to the fact that once the inspector has passed the foundations they will be covered up, with no subsequent opportunity for inspection. But this duty, heavily operational though it may be, is still a duty arising under the statute. There may be a discretionary element in its exercise — discretionary as to the time and manner of inspection, and the techniques to be used. A plaintiff complaining of negligence must prove, the burden being on him, that action taken was not within the limits of a discretion bona fide exercised, before he can begin to rely upon a common law duty of care. But if he can do this, he should, in principle, be able to sue.

Is there, then, authority against the existence of any such duty or any reason to restrict it? It is said that there is an absolute distinction in the law between statutory duty and statutory power — the former giving rise to possible liability, the latter not, or at least not doing so unless the exercise of the power involves some positive act creating some fresh or additional damage.

My Lords, I do not believe that any such absolute rule exists . . .

In [*Dorset Yacht Co. Ltd* v *Home Office* [1970] AC 1004] the Borstal officers, for whose actions the Home Office was vicariously responsible, were acting, in their control of the boys, under statutory powers. But it was held that, nevertheless they were under a duty of care as regards persons who might suffer damage as the result of their carelessness — see *per* Lord Reid, at pp. 1030-1031, Lord Morris of Borth-y-Gest, at p. 1036, Lord Pearson, at p. 1055: 'The existence of the statutory duties does not exclude liability at common law for negligence in the performance of the statutory duties.' Lord Diplock in his speech gives this topic extended consideration with a view to relating the officers' responsibility under public law to their liability in damages to members of the public under private, civil law: see pp. 1064 et seq. My noble and learned friend points out that the accepted principles which are applicable to Powers conferred by a private Act of Parliament, as laid down in *Geddis* v *Bann Reservoir Proprietors*, 3 App Cas 430, cannot automatically be applied to public statutes which confer a large measure of discretion upon public authorities. As regards the latter, for a civil action based on negligence at common law to succeed, there must be acts or omissions taken outside the limits of the delegated discretion: in such a case 'Its actionability falls to be determined by the civil law principles of negligence': see [1970] AC 1004, 1068.

It is for this reason that the law, as stated in some of the speeches in *East Suffolk Rivers Catchment Board* v *Kent* [1941] AC 74, but not in those of Lord Atkin or Lord Thankerton, requires at the present time to be understood and applied with the recognition that, quite apart from such consequences as may flow from an examination of the duties laid down by the particular statute, there may be room, once one is outside the area of legitimate discretion or policy, for a duty of care at common law. It is irrelevant to the existence of this duty of care whether what is created by the statute is a duty or a power: the duty of care may exist in either case. The difference between the two lies in this, that, in the case of a power, liability cannot exist unless the act complained of lies outside the ambit of the power. In *Dorset Yacht Co. Ltd* v *Home Office* [1970] AC 1004 the officers may (on the assumed facts) have acted outside any discretion delegated to them and having disregarded their instructions as to the precautions which they should take to prevent the trainees from escaping: see *per* Lord Diplock, at p. 1069. So in the present case, the allegations made are consistent with the council or its inspector having acted outside any delegated discretion either as to the making of an inspection, or as to the manner in which an inspection was made. Whether they did so must be determined at the trial. . . .

Notes
1. For a full discussion of this case, see Bailey and Bowman, 'The policy/operational dichotomy — a cuckoo in the nest' [1986] CLJ 430. See also *Sutherland Shire Council* v *Heyman* (1985) 157 CLR 424, where, on similar facts to *Anns*, the High Court of Australia held that a local authority did owe a duty to take care, but on the facts was not in breach of it. The court differed from *Anns*, in saying that the ordinary principles of negligence applied to public bodies, and that the issue was one of proximity or reliance.
2. *Anns* has been considered in a number of cases and the position now seems to be that: (1) the distinction between policing and operational matters is one of degree; (2) that if an issue is classed as one of policy, i.e. not justiciable in a private law action, there is no duty of care; (3) that if a matter is classed as operational there may or may not be a duty of care depending on whether the other criteria for a duty are present, and particularly relevant will be the question whether it is fair and reasonable for a duty to be imposed. (See *X* v *Bedfordshire C.C.* [1995] 3 All ER 353.)
3. In **Sheppard** v **Glossop Corporation** [1921] 3 KB 132 a local authority had power to put up street lights. The defendants did so, but resolved to extinguish the light at 9.00 p.m. The plaintiff was injured by falling over a retaining wall at 11.30 p.m. The court held the defendants not liable as they were not obliged to light the streets. How would this be regarded now? Was this a policy or an operational decision? Would it matter what the reasons were for turning off the lights at 9.00 p.m.?
4. The distinction between private and public law has not been worked out, but it seems clear that if the issue is classified as one of public law, a plaintiff may not evade the restrictions placed upon public law remedies by bringing a private action. In *O'Reilly* v *Mackman* [1983] 2 AC 237, at p. 285, Lord Diplock said:

> it would in my view as a general rule be contrary to public policy, and as such an abuse of the process of the court, to permit a person seeking to establish that a decision of a public authority infringed rights to which he was entitled to protection under public law to proceed by way of an ordinary action and by this means to evade the provision of Order 53 for the protection of such authorities.

An example of this principle is *Cocks v Thanet DC* [1983] 2 AC 286, where the plaintiff claimed to be homeless and requested the defendants to house him under the Housing (Homeless Persons) Act 1977. He was turned down and began an action for a declaration and damages, alleging the council were in breach of their duty under the Act. The House of Lords held that he could only use public law remedies to quash the council's decision, and could not use private law remedies. See also *Jones v Department of Employment* [1988] 1 All ER 725, where a person who was turned down for unemployment benefit successfully appealed to a Social Security Appeal Tribunal and was allowed benefit. He then tried to sue the adjudicating officer for negligently denying him benefit, claiming expenses and damages for distress. It was held that he had no action in negligence.

However, in *Roy v Kensington and Chelsea Family Practitioner Committee* [1992] 1 All ER 705 the House of Lords warned that the *O'Reilly v Mackman* principles should not be applied too strictly. Lord Bridge said 'It is appropriate that an issue which depends exclusively on the existence of a purely public law right should be determined in judicial review proceedings and not otherwise. But where a litigant asserts his entitlement to a subsisting right in private law, whether by way of a claim or defence, the circumstance that the existence and the extent of the private right asserted may incidentally involve the examination of a public law issue cannot prevent the litigant from seeking to establish his right by action commenced by writ or originating summons...' (the defendants had reduced the plaintiffs 'basic practice allowance' as they believed he was not devoting a substantial amount of his time to the NHS. The plaintiff was permitted to sue on the basis that the defendants were in breach of contract and was not limited to a public law claim that they had acted *ultra vires* or unreasonably).

5.   One particular problem arises where a public body *voluntarily* exercises its powers but subsequently causes damage through negligence. Such a problem arose in *East Suffolk Rivers Catchment Board v Kent* [1941] AC 74 (where the defendants were held not liable for incompetently repairing a river bank). That case has now been explained away on the ground that the cause of the damage was natural forces rather than incompetence, but a similar problem arose in *Stovin v Wise* [1994] 3 All ER 467 where a local authority voluntarily agreed to remove an earth bank on British Rail land which obscured visibility for road users. The defendants approached British Rail but nothing further was done, and three years later an accident occurred due to poor visibility caused by the earth bank. The defendants were held liable as they had already decided the policy issue, that is to spend money on removing the bank, and they were operationally negligent in failing to pursue that decision.

X v Bedfordshire C.C.
House of Lords [1995] 2 AC 633; [1995] 3 WLR 152; [1955] 3 All ER 353

This case involved a number of actions against various local authorities. In the 'abuse' cases (Bedfordshire and Newham) it was alleged that the authorities had, in one case, failed to diagnose abuse, and in the other had identified the wrong person as the abuser. In the 'education' cases (Dorset, Hampshire and Bromley) it was alleged that the authorities had failed properly to identify and provide for the special educational needs of the plaintiffs. Held: that no duty was owed in either the abuse or education cases in pursuance of the authorities' statutory obligations.

LORD BROWNE-WILKINSON: . . .

The common law duty of care
In this category, the claim alleges either that a statutory duty gives rise to a common law duty of care owed to the plaintiff by the defendant to do or refrain from doing a particular act or (more often) that in the course of carrying out a statutory duty the defendant has brought about such a relationship between himself and the plaintiff as to give rise to a duty of care at common law. A further variant is a claim by the plaintiff that, whether or not the authority is itself under a duty of care to the plaintiff, its servant in the course of performing the statutory function was under a common law duty of care for breach of which the authority is vicariously liable.

Mr Munby, in his reply in the *Newham* case, invited your Lordships to lay down the general principles applicable in determining the circumstances in which the law would impose a common law duty of care arising from the exercise of statutory powers or duties. I have no doubt that, if possible, this would be most desirable. But I have found it quite impossible either to detect such principle in the wide range of authorities and academic writings to which we were referred or to devise any such principle de novo. The truth of the matter is that statutory duties now exist over such a wide range of diverse activities and take so many different forms that no one principle is capable of being formulated applicable to all cases. However, in my view it is possible in considering the problems raised by these particular appeals to identify certain points which are of significance.

1. Co-existence of statutory duty and common law duty of care
It is clear that a common law duty of care may arise in the performance of statutory functions. But a broad distinction has to be drawn between: (a) cases in which it is alleged that the authority owes a duty of care in the manner in which it exercises a statutory discretion; (b) cases in which a duty of care is alleged to arise from the manner in which the statutory duty has been implemented in practice.

An example of (a) in the educational field would be a decision whether or not to exercise a statutory discretion to close a school, being a decision which necessarily involves the exercise of a discretion. An example of (b) would be the actual running of a school pursuant to the statutory duties. In such latter case a common law duty to take reasonable care for the physical safety of the pupils will arise. The fact that the school is being run pursuant to a statutory duty is not necessarily incompatible with a common law duty of care arising from the proximate relationship between a school and the pupils it has agreed to accept. The distinction is between (a) taking care in exercising a statutory discretion whether or not to do an act and (b) having decided to do that act, taking care in the manner in which you do it.

2. Discretion: justiciability and the policy/operational test
(a) Discretion
Most statutes which impose a statutory duty on local authorities confer on the authority a discretion as to the extent to which, and the methods by which, such statutory duty is to be performed. It is clear both in principle and from the decided cases that the local

authority cannot be liable in damages for doing that which Parliament has authorised. Therefore if the decisions complained of fall within the ambit of such statutory discretion they cannot be actionable in common law. However if the decision complained of is so unreasonable that it falls outside the ambit of the discretion conferred upon the local authority, there is no a priori reason for excluding all common law liability.

That this is the law is established by the decision in the *Dorset Yacht* case [1970] AC 1004 and by that part of the decision in *Anns v Merton London Borough Council* [1978] AC 728 which, so far as I am aware, has largely escaped criticism in later decisions. In the *Dorset Yacht* case Lord Reid said [1970] AC 1004, 1031:

> Where Parliament confers a discretion the position is not the same. Then there may, and almost certainly will, be errors of judgment in exercising such a discretion and Parliament cannot have intended that members of the public should be entitled to sue in respect of such errors. But there must come a stage when the discretion is exercised so carelessly or unreasonably that there has been no real exercise of the discretion which Parliament has conferred. The person purporting to exercise his discretion has acted in abuse or excess of his power. Parliament cannot be supposed to have granted immunity to persons who do that.

See also per Lord Morris, at p. 1037F.

Lord Diplock, as I have said, took a rather different line, making it a condition precedent to any common law duty arising that the decision impugned should be shown to be ultra vires in the public law sense. For myself, I do not believe that it is either helpful or necessary to introduce public law concepts as to the validity of a decision into the question of liability at common law for negligence. In public law a decision can be ultra vires for reasons other than *Wednesbury* unreasonableness (*Associated Provincial Picture Houses Ltd* v *Wednesbury Corporation* [1948] 1 KB 223) (e.g. breach of the rules of natural justice) which have no relevance to the question of negligence. Moreover it leads, in my judgment mistakenly, to the contention that claims for damages for negligence in the exercise of statutory powers should for procedural purposes be classified as public law claims and therefore, under *O'Reilly* v *Mackman* [1983] 2 AC 237 should be brought in judicial review proceedings: see *Lonrho Plc* v *Tebbit* [1992] 4 All ER 280. However, although I consider that the public law doctrine of ultra vires has, as such, no role to play in the subject under discussion, the remarks of Lord Diplock were plainly directed to the fact that the exercise of a statutory discretion cannot be impugned unless it is so unreasonable that it falls altogether outside the ambit of the statutory discretion. He said [1970] AC 1004, 1068:

> These considerations lead me to the conclusion that neither the intentional release of a Borstal trainee under supervision, nor the unintended escape of a Borstal trainee still under detention which was the consequence of the application of a system of relaxed control intentionally adopted by the Home Office as conducive to the reformation of trainees, can have been intended by Parliament to give rise to any cause of action on the part of any private citizen unless the system adopted was so unrelated to any purpose of reformation that no reasonable person could have reached a bona fide conclusion that it was conducive to that purpose. Only then would the decision to adopt it be ultra vires in public law.

Exactly the same approach was adopted by Lord Wilberforce in *Anns v Merton London Borough Council* [1978] AC 728 who, speaking of the duty of a local authority which had in fact inspected a building under construction, said, at p. 755:

But this duty, heavily operational though it may be, is still a duty arising under the statute. There may be a discretionary element in its exercise — discretionary as to the time and manner of inspection, and the techniques to be used. A plaintiff complaining of negligence must prove, the burden being on him, that action taken was not within the limits of a discretion bona fide exercised, before he can begin to rely upon a common law duty of care.

It follows that in seeking to establish that a local authority is liable at common law for negligence in the exercise of a discretion conferred by statute, the first requirement is to show that the decision was outside the ambit of the discretion altogether: if it was not, a local authority cannot itself be in breach of any duty of care owed to the plaintiff.

In deciding whether or not this requirement is satisfied, the court has to assess the relevant factors taken into account by the authority in exercising the discretion. Since what are under consideration are discretionary powers conferred on public bodies for public purposes the relevant factors will often include policy matters, for example social policy, the allocation of finite financial resources between the different calls made upon them or (as in *Dorset Yacht*) the balance between pursuing desirable social aims as against the risk to the public inherent in so doing. It is established that the courts cannot enter upon the assessment of such 'policy' matters. The difficulty is to identify in any particular case whether or not the decision in question is a 'policy' decision.

(b)   Justiciability and the policy/operational dichotomy
. . . As Lord Wilberforce [in *Anns*] appreciated, this approach did not prove a hard and fast test as to those matters which were open to the court's decision. In *Rowling* v *Takaro Properties Ltd* [1988] AC 473 the Privy Council reverted to the problem. In that case the trial judge had found difficulty in applying the policy/operational test, but having classified the decision in question as being operational, took the view that as a result there was a common law duty of care. Commenting on the judge's view, Lord Keith of Kinkel said, at p. 501:

> Their Lordships feel considerable sympathy with Quilliam J's difficulty in solving the problem by reference to this distinction. They are well aware of the references in the literature to this distinction (which appears to have originated in the United States of America), and of the critical analysis to which it has been subjected. They incline to the opinion, expressed in the literature, that this distinction does not provide a touchstone of liability, but rather is expressive of the need to exclude altogether those cases in which the decision under attack is of such a kind that a question whether it has been made negligently is unsuitable for judicial resolution, of which notable examples are discretionary decisions on the allocation of scarce resources or the distribution of risks: see especially the discussion in *Craig on Administrative Law* (1983), pp. 534–538. If this is right, classification of the relevant decision as a policy or planning decision in this sense may exclude liability; but a conclusion that it does not fall within that category does not, in their Lordships' opinion, mean that a duty of care will *necessarily* exist. (Emphasis added.)

From these authorities I understand the applicable principles to be as follows. Where Parliament has conferred a statutory discretion on a public authority, it is for that authority, not for the courts, to exercise the discretion: nothing which the authority does within the ambit of the discretion can be actionable at common law. If the decision complained of falls outside the statutory discretion, it *can* (but not necessarily will) give rise to common law liability. However, if the factors relevant to the exercise of the discretion include matters of policy, the court cannot adjudicate on such policy matters and therefore cannot reach the conclusion that the decision was outside the ambit of the statutory discretion. Therefore a common law duty of care in relation to the taking of decisions involving policy matters cannot exist.

3. If justiciable, the ordinary principles of negligence apply

If the plaintiff's complaint alleges carelessness, not in the taking of a discretionary decision to do some act, but in the practical manner in which that act has been performed (e.g. the running of a school) the question whether or not there is a common law duty of care falls to be decided by applying the usual principles i.e. those laid down in *Caparo Industries Plc* v *Dickman* [1990] 2 AC 605, 617–618. Was the damage to the plaintiff reasonably foreseeable? Was the relationship between the plaintiff and the defendant sufficiently proximate? Is it just and reasonable to impose a duty of care? See *Rowling* v *Takaro Properties Ltd* [1988] AC 473; *Hill* v *Chief Constable of West Yorkshire* [1989] AC 53.

However the question whether there is such a common law duty and if so its ambit, must be profoundly influenced by the statutory framework within which the acts complained of were done. The position is directly analogous to that in which a tortious duty of care owed by A to C can arise out of the performance by A of a contract between A and B. In *Henderson* v *Merrett Syndicates Ltd* [1994] 3 WLR 761 your Lordships held that A (the managing agent) who had contracted with B (the members' agent) to render certain services for C (the Names) came under a duty of care to C in the performance of those services. It is clear that any tortious duty of care owed to C in those circumstances could not be inconsistent with the duty owed in contract by A to B. Similarly, in my judgment a common law duty of care cannot be imposed on a statutory duty if the observance of such common law duty of care would be inconsistent with, or have a tendency to discourage, the due performance by the local authority of its statutory duties.

4.   Direct liability and vicarious liability

In certain of the appeals before the House, the local authorities are alleged to be under a direct duty of care to the plaintiff not only in relation to the exercise of a statutory discretion but also in relation to the operational way in which they performed that duty.

This allegation of a direct duty of care owed by the authority to the plaintiff is to be contrasted with those claims which are based on the vicarious liability of the local authority for the negligence of its servants, i.e. for the breach of a duty of care owed by the servant to the plaintiff, the authority itself not being under any relevant duty of care to the plaintiff. Thus, in the *Newham* case the plaintiffs' claim is wholly based on allegations that two professionals, a social worker and a psychiatrist, individually owed professional duties of care to the plaintiff for the breach of which the authorities as their employers are vicariously liable. It is not alleged that the authorities were themselves under a duty of care to the plaintiff.

This distinction between direct and vicarious liability can be important since the authority may not be under a direct duty of care at all or the extent of the duty of care owed directly by the authority to the plaintiff may well differ from that owed by a professional to a patient. However, it is important not to lose sight of the fact that, even in the absence of a claim based on vicarious liability, an authority under a direct duty of care to the plaintiff will be liable for the negligent acts or omissions of its servant which constitute a breach of that direct duty. The authority can only act through its servants.

The position can be illustrated by reference to the hospital cases. It is established that those conducting a hospital are under a direct duty of care to those admitted as patients to the hospital (I express no view as to the extent of that duty). They are liable for the negligent acts of a member of the hospital staff which constitute a breach of that duty, whether or not the member of the staff is himself in breach of a separate duty of care owed by him to the plaintiff.

Common law duty of care — direct [the education cases]

. . . As to the claim based on the negligent failure to comply with the statutory requirements of the [Education] Act of 1981, it is in essence a claim that the authority was negligent in the exercise of the statutory discretions conferred on the defendant authority by the Act of 1981. The claim cannot be struck out as being not justiciable. Although it is very improbable, it may be that the exercise of the statutory discretions involved in operating the special needs machinery of the Act of 1981 involved policy decisions. The decision as to what should be included in the statement and what provision should be made is, by statute, a decision conferred on the defendant authority. Therefore, even if such decisions were made carelessly, the claim will fail unless the plaintiff can show that the decisions were so careless that no reasonable education authority could have reached them. Again, although it seems most improbable that this requirement can be satisfied, it is impossible to be certain until all the facts are known. Therefore the claim cannot be struck out at this stage on the grounds that it is not justiciable or the acts complained of fell within the statutory discretion.

The question, then, is whether it is right to superimpose on the statutory machinery for the investigation and treatment of the plaintiff's special educational needs a duty of care to exercise the statutory discretions carefully? I find this a difficult question on which my views have changed from time to time. In favour of imposing a duty of care is the fact that it was plainly foreseeable that if the powers were exercised carelessly a child with special educational needs might be harmed in the sense that he would not obtain the advantage that the statutory provisions were designed to provide for him. Further, for the reasons that I have given, a common law duty of care in the exercise of statutory discretions can only arise in relation to an authority which has decided an issue so carelessly that no reasonable authority could have reached that decision. Why, it may be asked, should such a grossly delinquent authority escape liability? However, I have reached the conclusion that, powerful though those considerations may be, they are outweighed by other factors.

First, in relation to the special statutory duties imposed by sections 2, 4, 5 and 7 of the Act of 1981, the exercise of the discretions involves the close participation of the parents who are themselves under a duty to cause the child to receive 'efficient full-time education suitable to his . . . ability and aptitude:' section 36 of the Education Act 1944. The parents are themselves involved in the process of decision making and can appeal against decisions which they think to be erroneous. Although in the *Dorset* case the parents availed themselves of all the advantages of the statutory machinery, in the generality of cases to allow either the parents (on behalf of the child) or the child when he attains his majority to bring a claim alleging negligence by the authority in the making of the decision would be to duplicate remedies. Although in the present case this factor is not directly in point, if a duty of care is to be held to exist it must apply as much in relation to actions brought by a parent or child who has not used the statutory machinery as in the case of parents or a child who have.

Next, the number of cases which could successfully be brought for breach of such a duty of care would be very small since, as I have said, it would have to be shown that the decision impugned was taken so carelessly that no authority could have reached it. Yet, if a common law duty of care is held to exist, there is a very real risk that many hopeless (and possibly vexatious) cases will be brought, thereby exposing the authority to great expenditure of time and money in their defence. If there were no other remedy open, this is a price which might have to be paid in the interests of justice. But, in almost every case which could give rise to a claim for the negligent exercise of the statutory discretions, it is probable that, as in the present case, there will be an alternative remedy by way of a claim against the authority on the grounds of its vicarious liability for the negligent advice on the basis of which it exercises its discretion: as to which see below.

We were not referred to any category of case by analogy with which, in accordance with the *Caparo* principles [1990] 2 AC 605, it would be right to impose a direct duty of care on the authority in the exercise of its statutory discretions. It was suggested that *Ministry of Housing and Local Government* v *Sharp* [1970] 2 QB 223 was such a case, but I cannot agree. In that case a most precise statutory duty was imposed to search the local land charges register and issue a certificate as to the entries on it. That statutory duty was imposed on the clerk to the authority as persona designata. A negligent search was conducted, not by the clerk himself, but by an employee of the authority. As a result a certificate was issued which failed to disclose an existing entry on the register. The claim was brought against the clerk personally for damages for breach of statutory duty (i.e. a Category (A) claim) and against the authority as being vicariously liable for the breach of a common law duty of care owed by the employee who actually made the search. The claim against the clerk failed: the claim against the authority based on vicarious liability succeeded. That case is in no way analogous to the present. First, the statutory duty in question was mandatory and in no way discretionary. Second, the statutory duty was not imposed on the authority but on the clerk. Therefore the person under the statutory duty (the clerk) was not held liable either directly or vicariously for common law negligence. A third party (the authority) which was under no statutory duty was the only party held vicariously liable for the negligence of its employee.

In my judgment, as in the child abuse cases, the courts should hesitate long before imposing a common law duty of care in the exercise of discretionary powers or duties conferred by Parliament for social welfare purposes. The aim of the Act of 1981 was to provide, for the benefit of society as a whole, an administrative machinery to help one disadvantaged section of society. The statute provides its own detailed machinery for securing that the statutory purpose is performed. If, despite the complex machinery for consultation and appeals contained in the Act, the scheme fails to provide the benefit intended that is a matter more appropriately remedied by way of the Ombudsman looking into the administrative failure than by way of litigation.

For these reasons I reach the conclusion that an education authority owes no common law duty of care in the exercise of the powers and discretions relating to children with special educational needs specifically conferred on them by the Act of 1981.

Notes
1.   There was also a claim that the authorities were providing a 'psychology' service and that professionals employed by the authorities had negligently advised the parents who had relied on their advice. These claims were not struck out, but it was pointed out that the plaintiffs would have to establish that the authorities were indeed providing such a service to the public rather than using such professionals to perform their statutory obligations.
2.   One valuable point is the separation of public and private law and that it is unhelpful 'to introduce public law concepts as to the validity of a decision into the question of liability at common law'. The question is solely whether the decision is properly within the discretion of the public body, but there can be liability if the decision is so unreasonable as to take it outside the ambit of that discretion.

3. This was an application to strike out the statements of claim and much remained to be proved. For example, the 'education' claims were not thrown out on the 'non-justiciable' ground, but they could only have passed this barrier if at trial it could have been shown that no reasonable education authority could have taken those decisions.

4. In relation to special needs education there is now an appeal tribunal which hears appeals from the decisions of local authorities. See the Special Educational Needs Tribunal Regulations 1995 (SI 1995 No. 3113). This is surely a better way to resolve these problems, and the existence of an alternative remedy would now preclude a private law action anyway (see *Jones* v *Dept. of Employment* [1988] 2 WLR 493).

9 SPECIAL DUTY PROBLEMS: NERVOUS SHOCK

The essential question to be asked in this chapter is the degree of proximity which is required when a person has suffered psychiatric damage as a result of the act of the defendant. This issue has an interesting history, for it was thought at first that a plaintiff could only succeed if he was also within the range of physical impact (*Dulieu* v *White* [1901] 2 KB 669). In other words, only the 'primary' victim could sue, that is the person who would foreseeably suffer physical damage. Liability was later extended to secondary victims, that is where the plaintiff was not at risk of physical injury, but saw or heard the accident which caused the shock with his own unaided senses (*Hambrook* v *Stokes* [1925] 1 KB 141). After *Bourhill* v *Young* [1943] AC 92, the appropriate test became foreseeability of injury by shock, but the problem is, when is shock foreseeable? It is suggested that the courts in effect created 'sub-rules' or guide-lines which indicated the kind of case where proximity in the legal sense would exist. The issue which arose in *McLoughlin* v *O'Brian* [1983] 1 AC 410, was whether duty was to be tested by these sub-rules or by foresight alone. The members of the House of Lords took different views on this question, but in the more recent case of *Alcock* v *Chief Constable of South Yorkshire* [1991] 3 WLR 1057, the House seems to have adopted a compromise position whereby the test is one of foresight but one where foresight has a coded meaning. Thus, where the plaintiff has suffered psychiatric damage, the test of proximity which is required to establish a duty of care is 'foresight', as determined in the light of the relevant guidelines.

Section 1: the primary victim

If a person has or might have suffered physical damage, the problem that has arisen is whether a duty must be shown to have existed in relation to the psychiatric damage separate from the duty owed in relation to the physical damage: or is it sufficient that if the duty can be shown to exist in relation to actual or potential physical damage, then damages for psychiatric injury can be recovered so long as they are not too remote? In *Dulieu* v *White* [1901] 2 KB 669, the court allowed recovery for the plaintiff when a horse van burst into the pub where she was working, even though she suffered no actual physical injury but was in the range of potential impact. This has now been affirmed in *Page* v *Smith* (below).

Page v *Smith*
House of Lords [1996] 1 AC 155; [1995] 2 WLR 655; [1995] 2 All ER 736

The plaintiff was involved in a car accident negligently caused by the defendant. Although the plaintiffs car was damaged he was physically unhurt but the accident caused a revival of chronic fatigue syndrome which he had suffered from some years before. The Court of Appeal had held that the illness was not foreseeable independently from the potential physical injury. Held: allowing the appeal, that the defendant was liable for the psychiatric illness.

LORD LLOYD: . . . Otton J [at first instance] adopted the same line of reasoning:

> Once it is established that CFS exists and that a relapse or recrudescence can be triggered by the trauma of an accident and that nervous shock was suffered by the plaintiff who is actually involved in the accident, it becomes a foreseeable consequence. The nervous shock cases relied on by Mr Priest, in my judgment, have no relevance. The plaintiff was not a spectator of the accident who suffered shock from what he witnessed happening to another. He was directly involved and suffered the shock directly from experiencing the accident. The remoteness argument, therefore, must be rejected.

Since physical injury to the plaintiff was clearly foreseeable, although it did not in the event occur, the judge did not consider, as a separate question, whether the defendant should have foreseen injury by nervous shock.

When the case got to the Court of Appeal [1994] 4 All ER 522, the approach became more complicated. Mr Priest's argument was as follows, as summarised by Ralph Gibson LJ, at p. 540:

> If a plaintiff establishes that he has suffered some physical injury, he may advance a claim in respect of a recognised psychiatric illness which has resulted from that physical injury. If a plaintiff has suffered no physical injury, and his only injuries are a recognised form of psychiatric illness, he may succeed if the court decides that psychiatric illness was foreseeable in the case of a person of reasonable fortitude. There is no difference in this respect, it was submitted, between a bystander and a person directly involved in an event, except that the consequences are more likely to be foreseeable in the case of the latter than in the case of the former. . . .

Are there any disadvantages in taking the simple approach adopted by Otton J? It may be said that it would open the door too wide, and encourage bogus claims. As for opening the door, this is a very important consideration in claims by secondary victims. It is for this reason that the courts have, as a matter of policy, rightly insisted on a number of control mechanisms. Otherwise, a negligent defendant might find himself being made liable to all the world. Thus in the case of secondary victims, foreseeability of injury by shock is not enough. The law also requires a degree of proximity: see *Alcock's* case [1992] 1 AC 310 *per* Lord Keith of Kinkel, at p. 396, and the illuminating judgment of Stuart-Smith LJ in *McFarlane* v *EE Caledonia Ltd* [1994] 2 All ER 1, 14. This means not only proximity to the event in time and space, but also proximity of relationship between the primary victim and the secondary victim. A further control mechanism is that the secondary victim will only recover damages for nervous shock if the defendant should have foreseen injury by shock to a person of normal fortitude or 'ordinary phlegm'.

None of these mechanisms are required in the case of a primary victim. Since liability depends on foreseeability of physical injury, there could be no question of the defendant finding himself liable to all the world. Proximity of relationship cannot arise, and proximity in time and space goes without saying.

Nor in the case of a primary victim is it appropriate to ask whether he is a person of 'ordinary phlegm.' In the case of physical injury there is no such requirement. The negligent defendant, or more usually his insurer, takes his victim as he finds him. The same should apply in the case of psychiatric injury. There is no difference in principle, as Geoffrey Lane J pointed out in *Malcolm* v *Broadhurst* [1970] 3 All ER 508, between an eggshell skull and an eggshell personality. Since the number of potential claimants is limited by the nature of the case, there is no need to impose any further limit by reference to a person of ordinary phlegm. Nor can I see any justification for doing so.

As for bogus claims, it is sometimes said that if the law were such as I believe it to be, the plaintiff would be able to recover damages for a fright. This is not so. Shock by itself is not the subject of compensation, any more than fear or grief or any other human emotion occasioned by the defendant's negligent conduct. It is only when shock is followed by recognisable psychiatric illness that the defendant may be held liable.

There is another limiting factor. Before a defendant can be held liable for psychiatric injury suffered by a primary victim, he must at least have foreseen the risk of physical injury. So that if, to take the example given by my noble and learned friend, Lord Jauncey of Tullichettle, the defendant bumped his neighbour's car while parking in the street, in circumstances in which he could not reasonably foresee that the occupant would suffer any physical injury at all, or suffer injury so trivial as not to found an action in tort, there could be no question of his being held liable for the onset of hysteria. Since he could not reasonably foresee any injury, physical or psychiatric, he would owe the plaintiff no duty of care. That example is, however, very far removed from the present.

So I do not foresee any great increase in unmeritorious claims. The court will, as ever, have to be vigilant to discern genuine shock resulting in recognised psychiatric illness. But there is nothing new in that. The floodgates argument has made regular appearances in this field, ever since it first appeared in *Victorian Railways Commissioners* v *Coultas* (1888) 13 App Cas 222. I do not regard it as a serious obstacle here.

My provisional conclusion, therefore, is that Otton J's approach was correct. The test in every case ought to be whether the defendant can reasonably foresee that his conduct will expose the plaintiff to risk of personal injury. If so, then he comes under a duty of care to that plaintiff. If a working definition of 'personal injury' is needed, it can be found in section 38(1) of the Limitation Act 1980: '"personal injuries" includes any disease and any impairment of a person's physical or mental condition . . .' There are numerous other statutory definitions to the same effect. In the case of a secondary victim, the question will usually turn on whether the foreseeable injury is psychiatric, for the reasons already explained. In the case of a primary victim the question will almost always turn on whether the foreseeable injury is physical. But it is the same test in both cases, with different applications. There is no justification for regarding physical and psychiatric injury as different 'kinds' of injury. Once it is established that the defendant is under a duty of care to avoid causing personal injury to the plaintiff, it matters not whether the injury in fact sustained is physical, psychiatric or both. The utility of a single test is most apparent in those cases such as *Schneider* v *Eisovitch* [1960] QB 430, *Malcolm* v *Broadcast* [1970] 3 All ER 508 and *Brice* v *Brown* [1984] 1 All ER 997, where the plaintiff is both primary and secondary victim of the same accident.

Applying that test in the present case, it was enough to ask whether the defendant should have reasonably foreseen that the plaintiff might suffer physical injury as a result of the defendant's negligence, so as to bring him within the range of the defendant's duty of care. It was unnecessary to ask, as a separate question, whether the defendant should reasonably have foreseen injury by shock; and it is irrelevant that the plaintiff did not, in fact, suffer any external physical injury. . . .

In conclusion, the following propositions can be supported. 1. In cases involving nervous shock, it is essential to distinguish between the primary victim and secondary victims. 2. In claims by secondary victims the law insists on certain control mechanisms, in order as a matter of policy to limit the number of potential claimants. Thus, the defendant will not be liable unless psychiatric injury is foreseeable in a person of normal fortitude. These control mechanisms have no place where the plaintiff is the primary victim. 3. In claims by secondary victims, it may be legitimate to use hindsight in order to be able to apply the test of reasonable foreseeability at all. Hindsight, however, has no part to play where the plaintiff is the primary victim. 4. Subject to the above qualifications, the approach in all cases should be the same, namely, whether the defendant can reasonably foresee that his conduct will expose the plaintiff to the risk of personal injury, whether physical or psychiatric. If the answer is yes, then the duty of care is established, even though physical injury does not, in fact, occur. There is no justification for regarding physical and psychiatric injury as different 'kinds of damage.' 5. A defendant who is under a duty of care to the plaintiff, whether as primary or secondary victim, is not liable for damages for nervous shock unless the shock results in some recognised psychiatric illness. It is no answer that the plaintiff was predisposed to psychiatric illness. Nor is it relevant that the illness takes a rare form or is of unusual severity. The defendant must take his victim as he finds him.

Notes

1. Lords Keith and Jauncey dissented. Lord Keith said that the defendant can only be liable if the hypothetical reasonable man in his position should have foreseen that the plaintiff, regarded as a man of normal fortitude, might suffer nervous shock leading to an identifiable illness. He thought that on the facts nervous shock was not foreseeable and the fact that he might have suffered direct personal injury was irrelevant. Lord Jauncey also noted that there should be foreseeability of the kind of damage that actually occurred, not which might have occurred. The majority felt that there was no distinction between direct personal injury and psychiatric illness and that they are the same 'kind of damage', so that all that had to be foreseen was either one or the other. Do you agree that they are the same 'kind' of damage?

2. There is also a problem with regard to duty of care and remoteness. It might be thought that if a different level of proximity is required in relation to different interests, then where two such interests arise out of one event the requisite level of proximity should be established in relation to each interest. The House of Lords has said this is not so, but this could cause injustice as between a plaintiff who happens to be a foreseeable plaintiff in relation to some damage (which did not actually occur) and one who is not. This is the kind of thing *The Wagon Mound* was supposed to prevent. Also, there could be a remoteness problem unless both interests are said to involve the same 'kind' of damage, for otherwise part of the damage will be too remote.

Section 2: the secondary victim

It is generally agreed that where the person suffers psychiatric illness as a result of witnessing injury to another, special rules of proximity apply. There has been considerable debate about what is required, but the argument is often about how the rules should be presented. The test is still one of foreseeability, but judges such as Lord Wilberforce prefer to lay down guidelines as to when such liability will arise: in effect saying when such damage is or is not foreseeable.

McLoughlin v O'Brian
House of Lords [1983] AC 410; [1982] 2 WLR 982; [1982] 2 All ER 298

The plaintiff's husband, Thomas McLoughlin, and three of her children (George, Kathleen and Gillian) were injured in a car accident caused by the negligence of the defendant. The plaintiff was told of the accident by a friend and taken to the appropriate hospital, where she saw her husband and George before they had been attended to. She saw Kathleen after she had been cleaned up, and she was told that Gillian had died. She alleged that she suffered severe shock, organic depression and a change of personality. Held: allowing the appeal, that on the facts alleged by the plaintiff, the defendant was liable.

LORD WILBERFORCE: Although we continue to use the hallowed expression 'nervous shock,' English law, and common understanding, have moved some distance since recognition was given to this symptom as a basis for liability. Whatever is unknown about the mind-body relationship (and the area of ignorance seems to expand with that of knowledge), it is now accepted by medical science that recognisable and severe physical damage to the human body and system may be caused by the impact, through the senses, of external events on the mind. There may thus be produced what is as identifiable an illness as any that may be caused by direct physical impact. It is safe to say that this, in general terms, is understood by the ordinary man or woman who is hypothesised by the courts in situations where claims for negligence are made. Although in the only case which has reached this House (*Bourhill* v *Young* [1943] AC 92) a claim for damages in respect of 'nervous shock' was rejected on its facts, the House gave clear recognition to the legitimacy, in principle, of claims of that character. As the result of that and other cases, assuming that they are accepted as correct, the following position has been reached:

1. While damages cannot, at common law, be awarded for grief and sorrow, a claim for damages for 'nervous shock' caused by negligence can be made without the necessity of showing direct impact or fear of immediate personal injuries for oneself. The reservation made by Kennedy J in *Dulieu* v *White & Sons* [1901] 2 KB 669, though taken up by Sargant LJ in *Hambrook* v *Stokes Brothers* [1925] 1 KB 141, has not gained

acceptance, and although the respondents, in the courts below, reserved their right to revive it, they did not do so in argument. I think that it is now too late to do so. The arguments on this issue were fully and admirably stated by the Supreme Court of California in *Dillon* v *Legg* (1968) 29 ALR 3d 1316.

2. A plaintiff may recover damages for 'nervous shock' brought on by injury caused not to him — or herself but to a near relative, or by the fear of such injury. So far (subject to 5 below), the cases do not extend beyond the spouse or children of the plaintiff (*Hambrook* v *Stokes Brothers* [1925] 1 KB 141, *Boardman* v *Sanderson* [1964] 1 WLR 1317, *Hinz* v *Berry* [1970] 2 QB 40 — including foster children — (where liability was assumed) and see *King* v *Phillips* [1953] 1 QB 429).

3. Subject to the next paragraph, there is no English case in which a plaintiff has been able to recover nervous shock damages where the injury to the near relative occurred out of sight and earshot of the plaintiff. In *Hambrook* v *Stokes Brothers* an express distinction was made between shock caused by what the mother saw with her own eyes and what she might have been told by bystanders, liability being excluded in the latter case.

4. An exception from, or I would prefer to call it an extension of, the latter case, has been made ` here the plaintiff does not see or hear the incident but comes upon its immediate aftermath. In *Boardman* v *Sanderson* the father was within earshot of the accident to his child and likely to come upon the scene: he did so and suffered damage from what he then saw. In *Marshall* v *Lionel Enterprises Inc.* [1972] 2 QR 177, the wife came immediately upon the badly injured body of her husband. And in *Benson* v *Lee* [1972] VR 879, a situation existed with some similarity to the present case. The mother was in her home 100 yards away, and, on communication by a third party, ran out to the scene of the accident and there suffered shock. Your Lordships have to decide whether or not to validate these extensions.

5. A remedy on account of nervous shock has been given to a man who came upon a serious accident involving numerous people immediately thereafter and acted as a rescuer of those involved (*Chadwick* v *British Railways Board* [1967] 1 WLR 912). 'Shock' was caused neither by fear for himself nor by fear or horror on account of a near relative. The principle of 'rescuer' cases was not challenged by the respondents and ought, in my opinion, to be accepted. But we have to consider whether, and how far, it can be applied to such cases as the present.

Throughout these developments, as can be seen, the courts have proceeded in the traditional manner of the common law from case to case, upon a basis of logical necessity. If a mother, with or without accompanying children, could recover on account of fear for herself, how can she be denied recovery on account of fear for her accompanying children? If a father could recover had he seen his child run over by a backing car, how can he be denied recovery if he is in the immediate vicinity and runs to the child's assistance? If a wife and mother could recover if she had witnessed a serious accident to her husband and children, does she fail because she was a short distance away and immediately rushes to the scene (cf. *Benson* v *Lee*)? I think that unless the law is to draw an arbitrary line at the point of direct sight and sound, these arguments require acceptance of the extension mentioned above under 4 in the interests of justice.

If one continues to follow the process of logical progression, it is hard to see why the present plaintiff also should not succeed. She was not present at the accident, but she came very soon after upon its aftermath. If, from a distance of some 100 yards (cf. *Benson* v *Lee*), she had found her family by the roadside, she would have come within principle 4 above. Can it make any difference that she comes upon them in an ambulance, or, as here, in a nearby hospital, when, as the evidence shows, they were in the same condition, covered with oil and mud, and distraught with pain? If Mr

Chadwick can recover when, acting in accordance with normal and irresistible human instinct, and indeed moral compulsion, he goes to the scene of an accident, may not a mother recover if, acting under the same motives, she goes to where her family can be found?

I could agree that a line can be drawn above her case with less hardship than would have been apparent in *Boardman* v *Sanderson* [1964] 1 WLR 1317 and *Hinz* v *Berry* [1970] 2 QB 40, but so to draw it would not appeal to most people's sense of justice. To allow her claim may be, I think it is, upon the margin of what the process of logical progression would allow. But where the facts are strong and exceptional, and, as I think, fairly analogous, her case ought, prima facie, to be assimilated to those which have passed the test.

To argue from one factual situation to another and to decide by analogy is a natural tendency of the human and the legal mind. But the lawyer still has to inquire whether, in so doing, he has crossed some critical line behind which he ought to stop. That is said to be the present case. . . .

We must then consider the policy arguments. In doing so we must bear in mind that cases of 'nervous shock,' and the possibility of claiming damages for it, are not necessarily confined to those arising out of accidents on public roads. To state, therefore, a rule that recoverable damages must be confined to persons on or near the highway is to state not a principle in itself, but only an example of a more general rule that recoverable damages must be confined to those within sight and sound of an event caused by negligence or, at least, to those in close, or very close, proximity to such a situation.

The policy arguments against a wider extension can be stated under four heads.

First, it may be said that such extension may lead to a proliferation of claims, and possibly fraudulent claims, to the establishment of an industry of lawyers and psychiatrists who will formulate a claim for nervous shock damages, including what in America is called the customary miscarriage, for all, or many, road accidents and industrial accidents.

Secondly, it may be claimed that an extension of liability would be unfair to defendants, as imposing damages out of proportion to the negligent conduct complained of. In so far as such defendants are insured, a large additional burden will be placed on insurers, and ultimately upon the class of persons insured — road users or employers.

Thirdly, to extend liability beyond the most direct and plain cases would greatly increase evidentiary difficulties and tend to lengthen litigation.

Fourthly, it may be said — and the Court of Appeal agreed with this — that an extension of the scope of liability ought only to be made by the legislature, after careful research. This is the course which has been taken in New South Wales and the Australian Capital Territory.

The whole argument has been well summed up by Dean Prosser (*Prosser, Torts*, 4th ed. (1971), p. 256):

> The reluctance of the courts to enter this field even where the mental injury is clearly foreseeable, and the frequent mention of the difficulties of proof, the facility of fraud, and the problem of finding a place to stop and draw the line, suggest that here it is the nature of the interest invaded and the type of damage which is the real obstacle.

Since he wrote, the type of damage has, in this country at least, become more familiar and less deterrent to recovery. And some of the arguments are susceptible of answer. Fraudulent claims can be contained by the courts, who, also, can cope with evidentiary difficulties. The scarcity of cases which have occurred in the past, and the modest sums recovered, give some indication that fears of a flood of litigation may be exaggerated — experience in other fields suggests that such fears usually are. If some increase does occur, that may only reveal the existence of a genuine social need: that legislation has been found necessary in Australia may indicate the same thing.

But, these discounts accepted, there remains, in my opinion, just because 'shock' in its nature is capable of affecting so wide a range of people, a real need for the law to place some limitation upon the extent of admissible claims. It is necessary to consider three elements inherent in any claim: the class of persons whose claims should be recognised; the proximity of such persons to the accident; and the means by which the shock is caused. As regards the class of persons, the possible range is between the closest of family ties — of parent and child, or husband and wife — and the ordinary bystander. Existing law recognises the claims of the first: it denies that of the second, either on the basis that such persons must be assumed to be possessed of fortitude sufficient to enable them to endure the calamities of modern life, or that defendants cannot be expected to compensate the world at large. In my opinion, these positions are justifiable, and since the present case falls within the first class, it is strictly unnecessary to say more. I think, however, that it should follow that other cases involving less close relationships must be very carefully scrutinised. I cannot say that they should never be admitted. The closer the tie (not merely in relationship, but in care) the greater the claim for consideration. The claim, in any case, has to be judged in the light of the other factors, such as proximity to the scene in time and place, and the nature of the accident.

As regards proximity to the accident, it is obvious that this must be close in both time and space. It is, after all, the fact and consequence of the defendant's negligence that must be proved to have caused the 'nervous shock.' Experience has shown that to insist on direct and immediate sight or hearing would be impractical and unjust and that under what may be called the 'aftermath' doctrine one who, from close proximity, comes very soon upon the scene should not be excluded. In my opinion, the result in *Benson* v *Lee* [1972] VR 879 was correct and indeed inescapable. It was based, soundly, upon

> direct perception of some of the events which go to make up the accident as an entire event, and this includes . . . the immediate aftermath . . . (p.880).

The High Court's majority decision in *Chester* v *Waverley Corporation* (1939) 62 CLR 1, where a child's body was found floating in a trench after a prolonged search, may perhaps be placed on the other side of a recognisable line (Evatt J in a powerful dissent placed it on the same side), but, in addition, I find the conclusion of Lush J to reflect developments in the law.

Finally, and by way of reinforcement of 'aftermath' cases, I would accept, by analogy with 'rescue' situations, that a person of whom it could be said that one could expect nothing else than that he or she would come immediately to the scene — normally a parent or a spouse — could be regarded as being within the scope of foresight and duty. Where there is not immediate presence, account must be taken of the possibility of alterations in the circumstances, for which the defendant should not be responsible.

Subject only to these qualifications, I think that a strict test of proximity by sight or hearing should be applied by the courts.

Lastly, as regards communication, there is no case in which the law has compensated shock brought about by communication by a third party. In *Hambrook* v *Stokes Brothers* [1925] 1 KB 141, indeed, it was said that liability would not arise in such a case and this is surely right. It was so decided in *Abramzik* v *Brenner* (1967) 65 DLR (2d) 651. The shock must come through sight or hearing of the event or of its immediate aftermath. Whether some equivalent of sight or hearing, e.g., through simultaneous television, would suffice may have to be considered.

My Lords, I believe that these indications, imperfectly sketched, and certainly to be applied with common sense to individual situations in their entirety, represent either the existing law, or the existing law with only such circumstantial extension as the common law process may legitimately make. They do not introduce a new principle. Nor do I see any reason why the law should retreat behind the lines already drawn. I find on this appeal that the appellant's case falls within the boundaries of the law so drawn. . . .

Notes

1. As often happens in the law of negligence, the issue largely turns on what we can be expected to put up with. Seeing one's daughter run over by a car is different from seeing a stranger run over. In *Bourhill* v *Young* [1943] AC 92, Lord Parker said:

the driver of a car or vehicle even though careless is entitled to assume that the ordinary frequenter of the streets has sufficient fortitude to endure such incidents as may from time to time be expected to occur in them . . . and is not to be considered negligent towards one who does not possess the customary phlegm.

Is Lord Wilberforce in effect laying down the degree of 'customary phlegm' which a person ought to possess?

2. Lord Wilberforce points out that damages cannot be awarded for grief and sorrow (see also *Hinz* v *Berry* [1970] 1 All ER 1084), as that is something we are expected to put up with (customary phlegm). However, it may be difficult to say when only grief is foreseeable and when mental illness is foreseeable. Now that there is greater recognition of post-traumatic stress disorder and pathological grief disorder it may be that illness as the result of bereavement in sudden circumstances is more likely to be foreseeable than in the past. See *Vernon* v *Bosley* (1996) 146 NLJ 589 where the plaintiff saw his children drown.

Question

Would Mrs McLoughlin have won if she had seen her family only after they had been attended to and were in ward beds?

Alcock v *Chief Constable of South Yorkshire*
House of Lords [1991] 3 WLR 1057; [1991] 4 All ER 907

Shortly before the start of a football match between Liverpool and Nottingham Forest at the Hillsborough Stadium in Sheffield, the police negligently allowed a large number of spectators to have access to the stadium which was already full. In the resulting crush 95 spectators were killed and more than 400 were injured. The match was due to be televised and the disaster was shown live on television. The plaintiffs all claimed they suffered psychiatric damage and fell into various groups. Some were present at the match (but not in the vicinity of the disaster), some saw the events on television and some heard about them on the radio. The relationship between the plaintiffs and the victims also varied, some being relatives of varying degrees and others being friends. Held: dismissing the appeal, that the defendant was not liable to any of the plaintiffs.

LORD ACKNER: In *Bourhill* v *Young* [1943] AC 92, 103, Lord Macmillan said:

in the case of mental shock there are elements of greater subtlety than in the case of an ordinary physical injury and these elements may give rise to debate as to the precise scope of the legal liability.

It is now generally accepted that an analysis of the reported cases of nervous shock establishes that it is a type of claim in a category of its own. Shock is no longer a variant of physical injury but a separate kind of damage. Whatever may be the pattern of the future development of the law in relation to this cause of action, the following propositions illustrate that the application simpliciter of the reasonable foreseeability test is, today, far from being operative.

(1)   Even though the risk of psychiatric illness is reasonably foreseeable, the law gives no damages if the psychiatric injury was not induced by shock. Psychiatric illnesses caused in other ways, such as from the experience of having to cope with the deprivation consequent upon the death of a loved one, attracts no damages. Brennan J in *Jaensch* v *Coffey*, 155 CLR 549, 569, gave as examples, the spouse who has been worn down by caring for a tortiously injured husband or wife and who suffers psychiatric illness as a result, but who, nevertheless, goes without compensation; a parent made distraught by the wayward conduct of a brain-damaged child and who suffers psychiatric illness as a result also has no claim against the tortfeasor liable to the child.

(2)   Even where the nervous shock and the subsequent psychiatric illness caused by it could both have been reasonably foreseen, it has been generally accepted that damages for merely being informed of, or reading, or hearing about the accident are not recoverable. In *Bourhill* v *Young* [1943] AC 92, 103, Lord Macmillan only recognised the action lying where the injury by shock was sustained 'through the medium of the eye or the ear without direct contact.' Certainly Brennan J in his judgment in *Jaensch* v *Coffey*, 155 CLR 549, 567, recognised:

A psychiatric illness induced by mere knowledge of a distressing fact is not compensable; perception by the plaintiff of the distressing phenomenon is essential.

That seems also to have been the view of Banks LJ in *Hambrook* v *Stokes Brothers* [1925] 1 KB 141, 152 . . .

(3)   Mere mental suffering, although reasonably foreseeable, if unaccompanied by physical injury, is not a basis for a claim for damages. To fill this gap in the law a very limited category of relatives are given a statutory right by the Administration of Justice Act 1982, section 3 inserting a new section 1A into the Fatal Accidents Act 1976, to bring an action claiming damages for bereavement.

(4)   As yet there is no authority establishing that there is liability on the part of the injured person, his or her estate, for mere psychiatric injury which was sustained by another by reason of shock, as a result of a self-inflicted death, injury or peril of the negligent person, in circumstances where the risk of such psychiatric injury was reasonably foreseeable. On the basis that there must be a limit at some reasonable point to the extent of the duty of care owed to third parties which rests upon everyone in all his actions, Lord Robertson, the Lord Ordinary, in his judgment in the *Bourhill* case,

1941 SC 395, 399, did not view with favour the suggestion that a negligent window-cleaner who loses his grip and falls from a height, impaling himself on spiked railings, would be liable for the shock-induced psychiatric illness occasioned to a pregnant woman looking out of the window of a house situated on the opposite side of the street.

(5) 'Shock', in the context of this cause of action, involves the sudden appreciation by sight or sound of a horrifying event, which violently agitates the mind. It has yet to include psychiatric illness caused by the accumulation over a period of time of more gradual assaults on the nervous system.

I do not find it surprising that in this particular area of the tort of negligence, the reasonable foreseeability test is not given a free rein. As Lord Reid said in *McKew* v *Holland & Hannen & Cubitts (Scotland) Ltd* [1969] 3 All ER 1621, 1623:

> A defender is not liable for a consequence of a kind which is not foreseeable. But it does not follow that he is liable for every consequence which a reasonable man could foresee.

Deane J pertinently observed in *Jaensch* v *Coffey*, 155 CLR 549, 583:

> Reasonable foreseeability on its own indicates no more than that such a duty of care will exist if, and to the extent that, it is not precluded or modified by some applicable overriding requirement or limitation. It is to do little more than to state a truism to say that the essential function of such requirements or limitations is to confine the existence of a duty to take reasonable care to avoid reasonably foreseeable injury to the circumstances or classes of case in which it is the policy of the law to admit it. Such overriding requirements or limitations shape the frontiers of the common law of negligence.

Although it is a vital step towards the establishment of liability, the satisfaction of the test of reasonable foreseeability does not, in my judgment, ipso facto satisfy Lord Atkin's well known neighbourhood principle enunciated in *Donoghue* v *Stevenson* [1932] AC 562, 580. For him to have been reasonably in contemplation by a defendant he must be:

> so closely and directly affected by my act that I ought reasonably to have them in contemplation as being so affected when I am directing my mind to the acts or omissions which are called in question.

The requirement contained in the words 'so closely and directly affected . . . that' constitutes a control upon the test of reasonable foreseeability of injury. Lord Atkin was at pains to stress, at pp. 580–582, that the formulation of a duty of care, merely in the general terms of reasonable foreseeability, would be too wide unless it were 'limited by the notion of proximity' which was embodied in the restriction of the duty of care to one's 'neighbour.'

The three elements

Because 'shock' in its nature is capable of affecting such a wide range of persons, Lord Wilberforce in *McLoughlin* v *O'Brian* [1983] 1 AC 410, 422, concluded that there was a real need for the law to place some limitation upon the extent of admissible claims and in this context he considered that there were three elements inherent in any claim. It is common ground that such elements do exist and are required to be considered in connection with all these claims. The fundamental difference in approach is that on behalf of the plaintiffs it is contended that the consideration of these three elements is merely part of the process of deciding whether, as a matter of fact, the reasonable foreseeability test has been satisfied. On behalf of the defendant it is contended that these elements operate as a control of limitation on the mere application of the reasonable foreseeability test. They introduce the requirement of 'proximity' as conditioning the duty of care.

The three elements are (1) the class of persons whose claims should be recognised; (2) the proximity of such persons to the accident — in time and space; (3) the means by which the shock has been caused.

I will deal with those three elements seriatim.

(1)   *The class of persons whose claim should be recognised*
When dealing with the possible range of the class of persons who might sue, Lord Wilberforce in *McLoughlin* v *O'Brian* [1983] 1 AC 410 contrasted the closest of family ties — parent and child and husband and wife — with that of the ordinary bystander. He said that while existing law recognised the claims of the first, it denied that of the second, either on the basis that such persons must be assumed to be possessed with fortitude sufficient to enable them to endure the calamities of modern life, or that defendants cannot be expected to compensate the world at large. He considered that these positions were justified, that other cases involving less close relationships must be very carefully considered, adding, at p. 422:

> The closer the tie (not merely in relationship, but in care) the greater the claim for consideration. The claim, in any case, has to be judged in the light of the other factors, such as proximity to the scene in time and place, and the nature of the accident.

I respectfully share the difficulty expressed by Atkin LJ in *Hambrook* v *Stokes Brothers* [1925] 1 KB 141, 158–159 — how do you explain why the duty is confined to the case of parent or guardian and child and does not extend to other relations of life also involving intimate associations; and why does it not eventually extend to bystanders? As regards the latter category, while it may be very difficult to envisage a case of a stranger, who is not actively and foreseeably involved in a disaster or its aftermath, other than in the role of rescuer, suffering shock-induced psychiatric injury by the mere observation of apprehended or actual injury of a third person in circumstances that could be considered reasonably foreseeable, I see no reason in principle why he should not, if in the circumstances, a reasonably strong-nerved person would have been so shocked. In the course of argument your Lordships were given, by way of an example, that of a petrol tanker careering out of control into a school in session and bursting into flames. I would not be prepared to rule out a potential claim by a passer-by so shocked by the scene as to suffer psychiatric illness.

As regards claims by those in the close family relationships referred to by Lord Wilberforce, the justification for admitting such claims is the presumption, which I would accept as being rebuttable, that the love and affection normally associated with persons in those relationships is such that a defendant ought reasonably to contemplate that they may be so closely and directly affected by his conduct as to suffer shock resulting in psychiatric illness. While as a generalisation more remote relatives and, a fortiori, friends, can reasonably be expected not to suffer illness from the shock, there can well be relatives and friends whose relationship is so close and intimate that their love and affection for the victim is comparable to that of the normal parent, spouse or child of the victim and should for the purpose of this cause of action be so treated. . . .

The proximity of the plaintiff to the accident
It is accepted that the proximity to the accident must be close both in time and space. Direct and immediate sight or hearing of the accident is not required. It is reasonably foreseeable that injury by shock can be caused to a plaintiff, not only through the sight or hearing of the event, but of its immediate aftermath.

Only two of the plaintiffs before us were at the ground. However, it is clear from *McLoughlin* v *O'Brian* [1963] 1 AC 410 that there may be liability where subsequent identification can be regarded as part of the 'immediate aftermath' of the accident. Mr Alcock identified his brother-in-law in a bad condition in the mortuary at about midnight, that is some eight hours after the accident. This was the earliest of the identification cases. Even if this identification could be described as part of the 'aftermath,' it could not in my judgment be described as part of the *immediate* aftermath. *McLoughlin's* case was described by Lord Wilberforce as being upon the margin of what the process of logical progression from case to case would allow. Mrs McLoughlin had arrived at the hospital within an hour or so after the accident. Accordingly in the post-accident identification cases before your Lordships there was not sufficient proximity in time and space to the accident.

The means by which the shock is caused
Lord Wilberforce concluded that the shock must come through sight or hearing of the event or its immediate aftermath but specifically left for later consideration whether some equivalent of sight or hearing, e.g. through simultaneous television, would suffice . . . . Of course it is common ground that it was clearly foreseeable by the defendant that the scenes at Hillsborough would be broadcast live and that amongst those who would be watching would be parents and spouses and other relatives and friends of those in the pens behind the goal at the Leppings Lane end. However he would also know of the code of ethics which the television authorities televising this event could be expected to follow, namely that they would not show pictures of suffering by recognisable individuals. Had they done so, Mr Hytner accepted that this would have been a 'novus actus' breaking the chain of causation between the defendant's alleged breach of duty and the psychiatric illness. As the defendant was reasonably entitled to expect to be the case, there were no such pictures. Although the television pictures certainly gave rise to feelings of the deepest anxiety and distress, in the circumstances of this case the simultaneous television broadcasts of what occurred cannot be equated with the 'sight or hearing of the event or its immediate aftermath.' Accordingly shocks sustained by reason of these broadcasts cannot found a claim. I agree, however, with Nolan LJ that simultaneous broadcasts of a disaster cannot in all cases by ruled out as providing the equivalent of the actual sight or hearing of the event or its immediate aftermath. Nolan LJ gave . . . an example of a situation where it was reasonable to anticipate that the television cameras, whilst filming and transmitting pictures of a special event of children travelling in a balloon, in which there was media interest, particularly amongst the parents, showed the balloon suddenly bursting into flames. Many other such situations could be imagined where the impact of the simultaneous television pictures would be as great, if not greater, than the actual sight of the accident.

Conclusion
Only one of the plaintiffs, who succeeded before Hidden J, namely Brian Harrison, was at the ground. His relatives who died were his two brothers. The quality of brotherly love is well known to differ widely — from Cain and Abel to David and Jonathan. I assume that Mr Harrison's relationship with his brothers was not an abnormal one. His claim was not presented upon the basis that there was such a close and intimate relationship between them, as gave rise to that very special bond of affection which would make his shock-induced psychiatric illness reasonably foreseeable by the defendant. Accordingly, the judge did not carry out the requisite close scrutiny of their relationship. Thus there was no evidence to establish the necessary proximity which would make his claim reasonably foreseeable and, subject to the other factors, to which I have referred, a valid

one. The other plaintiff who was present at the ground, Robert Alcock, lost a brother-in-law. He was not, in my judgment, reasonably foreseeable as a potential sufferer from shock-induced psychiatric illness, in default of very special facts and none was established. Accordingly their claims must fail, as must those of the other plaintiffs who only learned of the disaster by watching simultaneous television. . . .

Notes

1. It is clear from *Alcock* v *Chief Constable of South Yorkshire* that 'nervous shock' or psychiatric damage cannot be regarded as a variant of physical injury, and therefore special rules of proximity apply. To this extent Lord Ackner agrees with the view of Lord Wilberforce in *McLoughlin* v *O'Brian* above, but does he wholly agree with the limitations Lord Wilberforce places on proximity in this area?

2. People who are not related to the victim of an accident may be able to sue, but there must be some close involvement with the event. A mere bystander probably could not sue, as he will be assumed to have sufficient fortitude to overcome distress at witnessing an accident (*McFarlane* v *E. E. Caledonia Ltd* [1994] 2 All ER 1 — witness of the Piper Alpha oil rig disaster). In **Chadwick v British Railways Board** [1967] 2 All ER 945, the plaintiff assisted in the rescue operations at the Lewisham train crash in 1957. The circumstances were particularly difficult, as two trains had collided under a bridge, which compressed the wreckage. Mr Chadwick, who lived near the line, was a fairly small man, and he was asked to crawl into the wreckage to give injections to trapped passengers. It was held that he could recover damages for the anxiety neurosis which he developed.

3. It is agreed that an ordinary person might suffer psychiatric illness as the result of injury to close relatives, but what degree of fortitude is expected of a person who sees his property destroyed? In **Attia v British Gas** [1988] QB 304, the plaintiff returned home to find her house on fire, and claimed that she suffered nervous shock as a result. The Court of Appeal held that such a claim was not automatically excluded and should proceed to trial to determine whether it was foreseeable that a reasonable householder, exposed to the experience undergone by the plaintiff, might suffer psychiatric illness, as opposed to grief and sorrow at the loss of his home. Would it be relevant to know whether the house was insured, or whether the defendants made an instant offer of reparation?

4. The 'egg shell skull' rule applies to cases of nervous shock, but it still needs to be proved that a person of reasonable fortitude who possesses the 'customary phlegm' would have suffered *some* psychiatric damage, for the duty of care needs to be established. The egg shell skull rule relates only to remoteness, and brings in damage which is greater than would normally have been suffered. In **Brice v Brown** [1984] 1 All ER 997, Mrs Brice was in a taxi which was in collision with a bus, and while she suffered only slight injury, her daughter was quite seriously hurt. The plaintiff became mentally ill. It was held that an ordinary person might have suffered psychiatric damage and therefore a duty was owed, and the fact that, due to a personality disorder, her illness was much

more severe than might have been expected did not render the damage too remote.

5.   See further Teff, 'Liability for psychiatric illness after Hillsborough' (1992) OJLS 440, and Murphy, 'Negligently inflicted psychiatric harm: a re-appraisal' (1996) 15 LS 415.

10 SPECIAL DUTY PROBLEMS: NEGLIGENT STATEMENTS

This chapter deals with negligently made statements which cause economic loss. There are therefore two peculiarities in this area: the first is due to the fact that liability for statements has always been restricted, and the second is that economic loss by itself is rarely protected.

The harmful effects of a statement can carry further than the effects of an act, and it is probably easier to make a careless statement than commit a negligent act. This subject is therefore one where fairly stringent limitations have been placed on the notion of proximity, and it is said that there must be 'a special relationship' between the parties before a duty of care can arise. Indeed, until 1963 there was no duty at all in this area, but after *Hedley Byrne* v *Heller* in that year, the range of liability steadily expanded, although the ever increasing complexity and interrelation of communication means that new problems are always presenting themselves — the most recent being the question of the range of potential liability of accountants. This area of law is developing rapidly. The traditional view of *Hedley Byrne* liability is that it depends upon a voluntary assumption of responsibility by the defendant when giving advice or exercising skills, and the plaintiff acts to his detriment when relying on that advice or skill. However, as will be seen in section 3 that may now extend to cases where the advice is not given to the plaintiff but rather to a third party who acts to the detriment of the plaintiff (*Spring* v *Guardian Assurance*, below). Also, there may be cases where reliance is not necessary at all because the defendant has assumed a responsibility which is analogous to a fiduciary obligation (*White* v *Jones*, below). One point to note is that if a defendant is liable for a negligent statement, the plaintiff may recover his losses, even though these may be purely economic losses. The extent to which a person who suffers pure economic loss as the result of an act may recover is discussed in the next chapter. This chapter does not deal with other wrongs which may result from a statement, such as the tort of deceit or breach of a fiduciary obligation.

The particular issues which need to be addressed are: (a) when is a person under a duty to be careful in making a statement?; (b) to whom is that duty owed?; (c) when can there be liability to a third party, i.e. to a person who is not a recipient of the information but is a person who suffers damage because of the act of a person who is?; and (d) to what extent can a person absolve himself of responsibility?

Section 1: by whom a duty is owed

It would be too onerous a burden to hold a person responsible whenever he carelessly makes a statement which turns out to be wrong, and someone else has suffered loss as a result, for otherwise a person could be liable for a casual statement made at a party. The courts have established that special rules of proximity apply in this area, so that a 'special relationship' must be established between the parties, and to a large extent this depends on the defendant knowing that the plaintiff is justifiably relying upon him for his special skill or expertise or knowledge.

Hedley Byrne & Co. Ltd v Heller and Partners Ltd
House of Lords [1964] AC 465; [1963] 3 WLR 100; [1963] 2 All ER 575

The plaintiffs, Hedley Byrne & Co., were advertising agents who intended to engage in an advertising programme for Easipower Ltd which would cost about £100,000. They asked their own bankers, National Provincial Bank Ltd, to obtain a reference about Easipower, and National Provincial wrote to the defendants, Heller and Partners, who were Easipower's bankers. They replied in a letter which said that it was 'For your private use and without responsibility of the part of the bank or its officials' and went on to say that Easipower was a 'respectably constituted company, considered good for its ordinary business engagements. Your figures are larger than we are accustomed to see.' Easipower went into liquidation, and the plaintiffs lost some £17,000. Held: dismissing the appeal, that there could be a duty not to make a statement carelessly which causes only economic loss, but that in the circumstances the disclaimer prevented a duty arising and the defendants were not liable.

LORD REID: A reasonable man, knowing that he was being trusted or that his skill and judgment were being relied on, would, I think, have three courses open to him. He could keep silent or decline to give the information or advice sought: or he could give an answer with a clear qualification that he accepted no responsibility for it or that it was given without that reflection or inquiry which a careful answer would require: or he could simply answer without any such qualification. If he chooses to adopt the last course he must, I think, be held to have accepted some responsibility for his answer being given carefully, or to have accepted a relationship with the inquirer which requires him to exercise such care as the circumstances require.

LORD MORRIS: My Lords, I consider that it follows and that it should now be regarded as settled that if someone possessed of a special skill undertakes, quite irrespective of contract, to apply that skill for the assistance of another person who relies upon such skill, a duty of care will arise. The fact that the service is to be given by means of or by the instrumentality of words can make no difference. Furthermore, if in a sphere in which a person is so placed that others could reasonably rely upon his judgment or his skill or upon his ability to make careful inquiry, a person takes it upon himself to give information or advice to, or allows his information or advice to be passed on to, another person who, as he knows or should know, will place reliance upon it, then a duty of care will arise.

LORD DEVLIN: I think, therefore, that there is ample authority to justify your Lordships in saying now that the categories of special relationships which may give rise to a duty to take care in word as well as in deed are not limited to contractual relationships or to relationships of fiduciary duty, but include also relationships which in the words of Lord Shaw in *Nocton* v *Lord Ashburton* [1914] AC 932, 972 are 'equivalent to contract,' that is, where there is an assumption of responsibility in circumstances in which, but for the absence of consideration, there would be a contract. Where there is an express undertaking, an express warranty as distinct from mere representation, there can be little difficulty. The difficulty arises in discerning those cases in which the undertaking is to be implied. In this respect the absence of consideration is not irrelevant. Payment for information or advice is very good evidence that it is being relied upon and that the informer or adviser knows that it is. Where there is no consideration, it will be necessary to exercise greater care in distinguishing between social and professional relationships and between those which are of a contractual character and those which are not. It may often be material to consider whether the adviser is acting puely out of good nature or whether he is getting his reward in some indirect form. The service that a bank performs in giving a reference is not done simply out of a desire to assist commerce. It would discourage the customers of the bank if their deals fell through because the bank had refused to testify to their credit when it was good.

I have had the advantage or reading all the opinions prepared by your Lordships and of studying the terms which your Lordships have framed by way of definition of the sort of relationship which gives rise to a responsibility towards those who act upon information or advice and so creates a duty of care towards them. I do not understand any of your Lordships to hold that it is a responsibility imposed by law upon certain types of persons or in certain sorts of situations. It is a responsibility that is voluntarily accepted or undertaken, either generally where a general relationship, such as that of solicitor and client or banker and customer, is created, or specifically in relation to a particular transaction. In the present case the appellants were not, as in *Woods* v *Martins Bank Ltd* [1959] 1 QB 55, the customers or potential customers of the bank. Responsibility can attach only to the single act, that is, the giving of the reference, and only if the doing of that act implied a voluntary undertaking to assume responsibility. This is a point of great importance because it is, as I understand it, the foundation for the ground on which in the end the House dismisses the appeal. I do not think it possible to formulate with exactitude all the conditions under which the law will in a specific case imply a voluntary undertaking any more than it is possible to formulate those in which the law will imply a contract. . . .

I shall therefore content myself with the proposition that wherever there is a relationship equivalent to contract, there is a duty of care. Such a relationship may be either general or particular. Examples of a general relationship are those of solicitor and client and of banker and customer. For the former *Nocton* v *Lord Ashburton* has long stood as the authority and for the latter there is the decision of Salmon J in *Woods* v

Martins Bank Ltd, which I respectfully approve. There may well be others yet to be established. Where there is a general relationship of this sort, it is unnecessary to do more than prove its existence and the duty follows. Where, as in the present case, what is relied on is a particular relationship created ad hoc, it will be necessary to examine the particular facts to see whether there is an express or implied undertaking of responsibility.

I regard this proposition as an application of the general conception of proximity. Cases may arise in the future in which a new and wider proposition, quite independent of any notion of contract, will be needed. There may, for example, be cases in which a statement is not supplied for the use of any particular person, any more than in *Donoghue* v *Stevenson* [1932] AC 562, the ginger beer was supplied for consumption by any particular person; and it will then be necessary to return to the general conception of proximity and to see whether there can be evolved from it, as was done in *Donoghue* v *Stevenson,* a specific proposition to fit the case. . . .

LORD PEARCE: The law of negligence has been deliberately limited in its range by the courts' insistence that there can be no actionable negligence in vacuo without the existence of some duty to the plaintiff. For it would be impracticable to grant relief to everybody who suffers damage through the carelessness of another.

The reason for some divergence between the law of negligence in word and that of negligence in act is clear. Negligence in word creates problems different from those of negligence in act. Words are more volatile than deeds. They travel fast and far afield. They are used without being expended and take effect in combination with innumerable facts and other words. Yet they are dangerous and can cause vast financial damage. How far they are relied on unchecked (by analogy with there being no probability of intermediate inspection — see *Grant* v *Australian Knitting Mills Ltd,* [1936] AC 85) must in many cases be a matter of doubt and difficulty. If the mere hearing or reading of words were held to create proximity, there might be no limit to the persons to whom the speaker or writer could be liable. Damage by negligent acts to persons or property on the other hand is more visible and obvious; its limits are more easily defined, and it is with this damage that the earlier cases were more concerned. It was not until 1789 that *Pasley* v *Freeman,* 100 ER 450, recognised and laid down a duty of honesty in words to the world at large — thus creating a remedy designed to protect the economic as opposed to the physical interests of the community. Any attempts to extend this remedy by imposing a duty of care as well as a duty of honesty in representations by word were curbed by *Derry* v *Peek* 14 App Cas 337.

. . . There is also, in my opinion, a duty of care created by special relationships which, though not fiduciary, give rise to an assumption that care as well as honesty is demanded.

Was there such a special relationship in the present case as to impose on the defendants a duty of care to the plaintiffs as the undisclosed principals for whom the National Provincial Bank was making the inquiry? The answer to that question depends on the circumstances of the transaction. If, for instance, they disclosed a casual social approach to the inquiry no such special relationship or duty of care would be assumed . . . To import such a duty the representation must normally, I think, concern a business or professional transaction whose nature makes clear the gravity of the inquiry and the importance and influence attached to the answer. It is conceded that Salmon J rightly found a duty of care in *Woods* v *Martins Bank Ltd* but the facts in that case were wholly different from those in the present case. A most important circumstance is the form of the inquiry and of the answer. Both were here plainly stated to be without liability. Mr Gardiner argues that those words are not sufficiently precise to exclude liability for negligence. Nothing, however, except negligence could, in the facts of this case, create a liability (apart from fraud, to which they cannot have been intended to refer and against which the words would be no protection, since they would be part of the fraud). I do not, therefore, accept that even if the parties were already in contractual or other special relationship the words would give no immunity to a negligent answer. But in any event they clearly prevent a special relationship from arising. They are part of the material from which one deduces whether a duty of care and a liability for negligence was assumed. If both parties say expressly (in a case where neither is deliberately taking advantage of the other) that there shall be no liability, I do not find it possible to say that a liability was assumed.

Notes

1.   For a further discussion of the elements of *Hedley Byrne* liability see also *Spring* v *Guardian Assurance* and *White* v *Jones* (below, section 3).

2.   In *Caparo* v *Dickman* (below) Lord Oliver said that 'voluntary assumption of responsibility' is a convenient phrase but not intended to be a test for the existence of the duty, for it means no more than that the act of the defendant was voluntary and the law attributes to it an assumption of responsibility. However, in *Spring* v *Guardian Assurance* (below), Lord Goff speaks of an assumption or undertaking of responsibility coupled with reliance by the plaintiff. The issue could be important in determining whether (apart from the Unfair Contract Terms Act 1977) a disclaimer will always be effective. Note also that it was said in *Mutual Life Citizens Assurance Co.* v *Evatt* [1971] AC 793 that a duty will also be owed if the defendant has a financial interest in the transaction about which the advice was sought.

3.   In *Mutual Life Citizens Assurance Co.* v *Evatt* [1971] AC 793, the Privy Council held that a defendant could not be liable if he was not in the business of giving advice (the plaintiff had asked MLC about the wisdom of investing in a company called HG Palmer Ltd because both were subsidiaries of the same holding company). This case was doubted in *Esso* v *Mardon* [1976] 1 QB 801 and ignored (or referred to as not binding) in *Spring* v *Guardian Assurance* [1995] 2 AC 296. There was a strong dissent by Lords Reid and Morris, the first ever dissent in the Privy Council.

4.   An example of it being unreasonable to rely on advice is **Kleine v Canadian Propane** (1967) 64 DLR 2d 338, where there was a smell of gas which was attributed to low fuel in the tank. A delivery was made and a drop in pressure was discovered, but the tanker driver thought this might be due to an unlit pilot light. The pilot was lit and an explosion occurred one and a half hours later. It was held that it would have been unreasonable for the householder to rely on the advice of the tanker driver.

5.   Can silence ever be a breach of duty? According to Slade LJ in **Banque Keyser SA v Skandia (UK) Insurance** [1989] 3 WLR 25, at p. 101 it can. He says 'Can a mere failure to speak ever give rise to liability in negligence under *Hedley Byrne* principles? In our view it can, subject to the all important proviso that there has been on the facts a voluntary assumption of responsibility in the relevant sense and reliance on that assumption.' He cites *Al-Kandari* v *Brown* [1988] QB 665 as a possible example, and gives the hypothetical example of a father employing an estate agent to advise his son about the proposed purchase of a house, and the agent negligently fails to tell the son that a motorway is to be built nearby. The son could sue. 'To draw a distinction on those particular facts between misinformation and a failure to inform would be to perpetuate the sort of nonsense in the law which Lord Devlin condemned in *Hedley Byrne* v *Heller*.' The point was not discussed on appeal ([1990] 2 All ER 947), where Lord Templeman merely said 'that there was no negligent misstatement and the silence of [A] did not amount to an assertion that [B] was trustworthy and the banks did not rely on the silence of [A]'.

Section 2:   to whom the duty is owed

Information can spread far beyond the person to whom it is given, and this section is addressed to the problem of the range of potential plaintiffs. In basic negligence the question is answered by the foreseeable plaintiff rule, but such an answer would not be appropriate in the area where more stringent proximity is required. Thus the question is: Who can be within a 'special relationship' with the defendant even though the information is not strictly addressed to him?

Smith v *Eric Bush*
House of Lords [1990] 1 AC 831; [1989] 2 WLR 790; [1989] 2 All ER 514

Mrs Smith wanted to buy a house in Norwich and approached the Abbey National Building Society for a mortgage, and they asked the defendants, Eric Bush, to do a valuation. The valuation was negligently carried out, in that, while the surveyor noticed that the chimney breasts had been removed downstairs, he did not check whether the brickwork above had also been removed or was properly supported. It was not, and the chimney later fell into the main bedroom. The contract for the valuation was between the Abbey National and the defendants, although the plaintiff was obliged to reimburse the Abbey National for the fee. The purpose of the valuation was to protect the security of the building society and was not strictly to advise the plaintiff on the value of the house, although it was foreseeable that she would rely on it. Held: dismissing the appeal, that the surveyors owed the plaintiff a duty. Note: the case also deals with the effect of the Unfair Contract Terms Act 1977 on the disclaimer in the contract between the surveyor and the building society. This is dealt with below in section 3.

LORD TEMPLEMAN: The common law imposes on a person who contracts to carry out an operation an obligation to exercise reasonable skill and care. A plumber who mends a burst pipe is liable for his incompetence or negligence whether or not he has been expressly required to be careful. The law implies a term in the contract which requires the plumber to exercise reasonable skill and care in his calling. The common law also imposes on a person who carries out an operation an obligation to exercise reasonable skill and care where there is no contract. Where the relationship between the operator and a person who suffers injury or damage is sufficiently proximate and where

the operator should have foreseen that carelessness on his part might cause harm to the injured person, the operator is liable in the tort of negligence. . . .
These two appeals are based on allegations of negligence in circumstances which are akin to contract. . . . Mrs Smith paid £36.89 to the Abbey National for a report and valuation and the Abbey National paid the appellants for the report and valuation. . . . the valuer knew or ought to have known that the purchaser would only contract to purchase the house if the valuation was satisfactory and that the purchaser might suffer injury or damage or both if the valuer did not exercise reasonable skill and care. In these circumstances I would expect the law to impose on the valuer a duty owed to the puchaser to exercise reasonable skill and care in carrying out the valuation.

A valuer who values property as a security for a mortgage is liable either in contract or in tort to the mortgagee for any failure on the part of the valuer to exercise reasonable skill and care in the valuation. The valuer is liable in contract if he receives instructions from and is paid by the mortgagee. The valuer is liable in tort if he receives instruction from and is paid by the mortgagor but knows that the valuation is for the purpose of a mortgage and will be relied upon by the mortgagee. . . .

In *Candler* v *Crane, Christmas & Co.* [1951] 2 KB 164, the accountants of a company showed their draft accounts to and discussed them with an investor who, in reliance on the accounts, subscribed for shares in the company. Denning LJ, whose dissenting judgment was subsequently approved in the *Hedley Byrne* case [1964] AC 465, found that the accountants owed a duty to the investor to exercise reasonable skill and care in preparing the draft accounts. Denning LJ said, at p. 176:

> If the matter were free from authority, I should have said that they clearly did owe a duty of care to him. They were professional accountants who prepared and put before him these accounts, knowing that he was going to be guided by them in making an investment in the company. On the faith of those accounts he did make the investment, whereas if the accounts had been carefully prepared, he would not have made the investment at all. The result is that he has lost his money.

Denning LJ, at pp. 178-179 rejected the argument that:

> a duty to take care only arose where the result of a failure to take care will cause physical damage to person or property. . . . I can understand that in some cases of financial loss there may not be a sufficiently proximate relationship to give rise to a duty of care; but, if once the duty exists, I cannot think that liability depends on the nature of the damage.

The duty of professional men 'is not merely a duty to use care in their reports. They have also a duty to use care in their work which results in their reports,' p. 179. The duty of an accountant is owed:

> to any third person to whom they themselves show the accounts, or to whom they know their employer is going to show the accounts, so as to induce him to invest money or take some other action on them. But I do not think the duty can be extended still further so as to include strangers of whom they have heard nothing and to whom their employer, without their knowledge may choose to show their accounts . . . . The test of proximity in these cases is: did the accountants know that the accounts were required for submission to the plaintiff and use by him?: pp. 180-181.

Subject to the effect of any disclaimer of liability, these considerations appear to apply to the valuers in the present appeals.

. . . I agree that by obtaining and disclosing a valuation, a mortgagee does not assume responsibility to the purchaser for that valuation. But in my opinion the valuer assumes responsibility to both mortgagee and purchaser by agreeing to carry out a valuation for mortgage purposes knowing that the valuation fee has been paid by the purchaser and knowing that the valuation will probably be relied upon by the purchaser in order to decide whether or not to enter into a contract to purchase the house. The valuer can escape the responsibility to exercise reasonable skill and care by an express exclusion clause, provided the exclusion clause does not fall foul of the Unfair Contract Terms Act 1977. . . .

. . . The contractual duty of a valuer to value a house for the Abbey National did not prevent the valuer coming under a tortious duty to Mrs Smith who was furnished with a report of the valuer and relied on the report.

In general I am of the opinion that in the absence of a disclaimer of liability the valuer who values a house for the purpose of a mortgage, knowing that the mortgagee will rely and the mortgagor will probably rely on the valuation, knowing that the purchaser mortgagor has in effect paid for the valuation, is under a duty to exercise reasonable skill and care and that duty is owed to both parties to the mortgage for which the valuation is made. Indeed, in both the appeals now under consideration the existence of such a dual duty is tacitly accepted and acknowledged because notices excluding liability for breach of the duty owed to the purchaser were drafted by the mortgagee and imposed on the purchaser. In these circumstances it is necessary to consider the second question which arises in these appeals, namely, whether the disclaimers of liability are notices which fall within the Unfair Contract Terms Act 1977.

Note
For an earlier example of liability on similar facts, see *Yianni* v *Evans* [1982] 2 QB 438, which was approved in *Smith* v *Bush*.

Question
What did the valuer know about the use to which his valuation would be put? Is a valuation for the purposes of the building society's security any different from a valuation for a purchaser? Was it relevant that the plaintiff in the end paid for the valuation?

Caparo v *Dickman*
House of Lords [1990] 2 AC 605; [1990] 2 WLR 358; [1990] 1 All ER 568

The plaintiffs were shareholders in Fidelity plc and after the accounts for 1984 (which were audited by the defendants) were published they purchased further shares, ultimately making a take-over bid which was successful. They alleged that they had relied on the accounts for 1984 which should have shown a loss of £465,000 rather than a profit of £1.3 million. Held: allowing the appeal, that the defendant auditors owed no duty to the plaintiffs.

LORD BRIDGE: The salient feature of all these cases is that the defendant giving advice or information was fully aware of the nature of the transaction which the plaintiff had in contemplation, knew that the advice or information would be communicated to him directly or indirectly and knew that it was very likely that the plaintiff would rely on that advice or information in deciding whether or not to engage in the transaction in contemplation. In these circumstances the defendant could clearly be expected, subject always to the effect of any disclaimer of responsibility, specifically to anticipate that the plaintiff would rely on the advice or information given by the defendant for the very purpose for which he did in the event rely on it. So also the plaintiff, subject again to the effect of any disclaimer, would in that situation reasonably suppose that he was entitled to rely on the advice or information communicated to him for the very purpose for which he required it. The situation is entirely different where a statement is put into more or less general circulation and may foreseeably be relied on by strangers to the maker of the statement for any one of a variety of different purposes which the maker of the statement has no specific reason to anticipate. To hold the maker of the statement to be under a duty of care in respect of the accuracy of the statement to all and sundry for any purpose for which they may choose to rely on it is not only to subject him, in the classic words of Cardozo CJ to 'liability in an indeterminate amount for an indeterminate time to an indeterminate class:' see *Ultramares Corporation* v *Touche* (1931) 174 NE 441, 444; it is also to confer on the world at large a quite unwarranted entitlement to appropriate for their own purposes the benefit of the expert knowledge or professional expertise attributed to the maker of the statement. Hence, looking only at the circumstances of these decided cases where a duty of care in respect of negligent statements has been held to exist, I should expect to find that the 'limit or control mechanism . . . imposed upon the liability of a wrongdoer towards those who have suffered economic damage in consequence of his negligence' rested in the necessity to prove, in this category of the tort of negligence, as an essential ingredient of the 'proximity' between the plaintiff and the defendant, that the defendant knew that his statement would be communicated to the plaintiff, either as an individual or as a member of an identifiable class, specifically in connection with a particular transaction or transactions of a particular kind (e.g. in a prospectus inviting investment) and that the plaintiff would be very likely to rely on it for the purpose of deciding whether or not to enter upon that transaction or upon a transaction of that kind. . . .

Some of the speeches in the *Hedley Byrne* case derive a duty of care in relation to negligent statements from a voluntary assumption of responsibility on the part of the maker of the statements. In his speech in *Smith* v *Eric S. Bush* [1990] 1 AC 831, 862, Lord Griffiths emphatically rejected the view that this was the true ground of liability and concluded that:

> The phrase 'assumption of responsibility' can only have any real meaning if it is understood as referring to the circumstances in which the law will deem the maker of the statement to have assumed responsibility to the person who acts upon the advice.

I do not think that in the context of the present appeal anything turns upon the difference between these two approaches.

These considerations amply justify the conclusion that auditors of a public company's accounts owe no duty of care to members of the public at large who rely upon the accounts in deciding to buy shares in the company. If a duty of care were owed so widely, it is difficult to see any reason why it should not equally extend to all who rely on the accounts in relation to other dealings with a company as lenders or merchants extending credit to the company. A claim that such a duty was owed by auditors to a bank lending to a company was emphatically and convincingly rejected by Millett J in *Al Saudi Banque* v *Clarke Pixley* [1990] Ch 313. The only support for an unlimited duty of care owed by auditors for the accuracy of their accounts to all who may foreseeably rely upon them is to be found in some jurisdictions in the United States of America where there are striking differences in the law in different states. In this jurisdiction I have no doubt that the creation of such an unlimited duty would be a legislative step which it would be for Parliament, not the courts, to take. . . .

No doubt these provisions [of the Companies Act 1985] establish a relationship between the auditors and the shareholders of a company on which the shareholder is entitled to rely for the protection of his interest. But the crucial question concerns the extent of the shareholder's interest which the auditor has a duty to protect. The shareholders of a company have a collective interest in the company's proper management and in so far as a negligent failure of the auditor to report accurately on the state of the company's finances deprives the shareholders of the opportunity to exercise their powers in general meeting to call the directors to book and to ensure that errors in management are corrected, the shareholders ought to be entitled to a remedy. But in practice no problem arises in this regard since the interest of the shareholders in the proper management of the company's affairs is indistinguishable from the interest of the company itself and any loss suffered by the shareholders, e.g. by the negligent failure of the auditor to discover and expose a misappropriation of funds by a director of the company, will be recouped by a claim against the auditors in the name of the company, not by individual shareholders.

I find it difficult to visualise a situation arising in the real world in which the individual shareholder could claim to have sustained a loss in respect of his existing shareholding referable to the negligence of the auditor which could not be recouped by the company. But on this part of the case your Lordships were much pressed with the argument that such a loss might occur by a negligent undervaluation of the company's assets in the auditor's report relied on by the individual shareholder in deciding to sell his shares at an undervalue. The argument then runs thus. The shareholder, qua shareholder, is entitled to rely on the auditor's report as the basis of his investment decision to sell his existing shareholding. If he sells at an undervalue he is entitled to recover the loss from the auditor. There can be no distinction in law between the shareholder's investment decision to sell the shares he has or to buy additional shares. It follows, therefore, that the scope of the duty of care owed to him by the auditor extends to cover any loss sustained consequent on the purchase of additional shares in reliance on the auditor's negligent report.

I believe this argument to be fallacious. Assuming without deciding that a claim by a shareholder to recover a loss suffered by selling his shares at an undervalue attributable to an undervaluation of the company's assets in the auditor's report could be sustained at all, it would not be by reason of any reliance by the shareholder on the auditor's report in deciding to sell; the loss would be referable to the depreciatory effect of the report on the market value of the shares before ever the decision of the shareholder to sell was taken. A claim to recoup a loss alleged to flow from the purchase of overvalued shares, on the other hand, can only be sustained on the basis of the purchaser's reliance on the report. The specious equation of 'investment decisions' to sell or to buy as giving rise to parallel claims thus appears to me to be untenable. Moreover, the loss in the case of the sale would be of a loss of part of the value of the shareholder's existing holding, which, assuming a duty of care owed to individual shareholders, it might sensibly lie within the scope of the auditor's duty to protect. A loss, on the other hand, resulting from the purchase of additional shares would result from a wholly independent transaction having no connection with the existing shareholding.

I believe it is this last distinction which is of critical importance and which demonstrates the unsoundness of the conclusion reached by the majority of the Court of Appeal. It is never sufficient to ask simply whether A owes B a duty of care. It is always necessary to determine the scope of the duty by reference to the kind of damage from which A must take care to save B harmless. 'The question is always whether the defendant was under a duty to avoid or prevent that damage, but the actual nature of the damage suffered is relevant to the existence and extent of any duty to avoid or prevent it:' see *Sutherland Shire Council* v *Heyman*, 60 ALR 1, 48, *per* Brennan J. Assuming for the purpose of the argument that the relationship between the auditor of a company and individual shareholders is of sufficient proximity to give rise to a duty of care, I do not understand how the scope of that duty can possibly extend beyond the protection of any individual shareholder from losses in the value of the shares which he holds. As a purchaser of additional shares in reliance on the auditor's report, he stands in no different position from any other investing member of the public to whom the auditor owes no duty. . . .

LORD OLIVER: . . . What can be deduced from the *Hedley Byrne* case, therefore, is that the necessary relationship between the maker of a statement or giver of advice ('the adviser') and the recipient who acts in reliance upon it ('the advisee') may typically be held to exist where (1) the advice is required for a purpose, whether particularly specified or generally described, which is made known, either actually or inferentially, to the adviser at the time when the advice is given; (2) the adviser knows, either actually or inferentially, that his advice will be communicated to the advisee, either specifically or as a member of an ascertainable class, in order that it should be used by the advisee for that purpose; (3) it is known either actually or inferentially, that the advice so communicated is likely to be acted upon by the advisee for that purpose without independent inquiry, and (4) it is so acted upon by the advisee to his detriment. That is not, of course, to suggest that these conditions are either conclusive or exclusive, but merely that the actual decision in the case does not warrant any broader propositions. . . .

In seeking to ascertain whether there should be imposed on the adviser a duty to avoid the occurrence of the kind of damage which the advisee claims to have suffered it is not, I think, sufficient to ask simply whether there existed a 'closeness' between them in the sense that the advisee had a legal entitlement to receive the information upon the basis of which he has acted or in the sense that the information was intended to serve his interest or to protect him. One must, I think, go further and ask, in what capacity was his interest to be served and from what was he intended to be protected? A company's annual accounts are capable of being utilised for a number of purposes and if one thinks about it it is entirely foreseeable that they may be so employed. But many of such purposes have absolutely no connection with the recipient's status or capacity, whether as a shareholder, voting or non-voting, or as a debenture-holder. Before it can be concluded that the duty is imposed to protect the recipient against harm which he suffers by reason of the particular use that he chooses to make of the information which he receives, one must, I think. first ascertain the purpose for which the information is required to be given. Indeed the paradigmatic *Donoghue* v *Stevenson* case of a manufactured article requires, as an essential ingredient of liability, that the article has been used by the consumer in the manner in which it was intended to be used: see *Grant* v *Australian Knitting Mills Ltd* [1936] AC 85, 104 and *Junior Books Ltd* v *Veitchi Co. Ltd* [1983] 1 AC 520, 549, 552. I entirely follow that if the conclusion is reached that the very purpose of providing the information is to serve as the basis for making investment decisions or giving investment advice, it is not difficult then to conclude also that the duty imposed upon the adviser extends to protecting the recipient against loss occasioned by an unfortunate investment decision which is based on carelessly inaccurate information. . . . I do not believe and I see no grounds for believing that, in enacting the statutory provisions [of the Companies Act 1985], Parliament had in mind the provision of information for the assistance of purchasers of shares or debentures in the market, whether they be already the holders of shares or other securities or persons having no previous proprietary interest in the company. It is unnecessary to decide the point on this appeal, but I can see more force in the contention that one purpose of providing the statutory information might be to enable the recipient to exercise whatever rights he has in relation to his proprietary interest by virtue of which he receives it, by way, for instance, of disposing of that interest. I can, however, see no ground for supposing that the legislature was intending to foster a market for the existing holders of shares or debentures by providing information for the purpose of enabling them to acquire such securities from other holders who might be minded to sell.

For my part, I think that the position as regards the auditor's statutory duty was correctly summarised by O'Connor LJ, in his dissenting judgment when he said, at p. 714:

> The statutory duty owed by auditors to shareholders is, I think, a duty owed to them as a body. I appreciate that it is difficult to see how the over-statement of the accounts can cause damage to the shareholders as a body; it will be the underlying reasons for the over-statement which cause damage, for example fraudulent abstraction of assets by directors or servants, but such loss is recoverable by the company. I am anxious to limit the present case to deciding whether the statutory duty operates to protect the individual shareholder as a potential buyer of further shares. If I am wrong in thinking that under the statute no duty is owed to shareholders as individuals, then I think the duty must be confined to transactions in which the shareholder can only participate because he is a shareholder. The Companies Act 1985 imposes a duty to shareholders as a class and the duty should not extend to an individual save as a member of the class in respect of some class activity. Buying shares in a company is not such an activity.

In my judgment, accordingly, the purpose for which the auditors' certificate is made and published is that of providing those entitled to receive the report with information to enable them to exercise in conjunction those powers which their respective proprietary interests confer upon them and not for the purposes of individual speculation with a view to profit. The same considerations as limit the existence of a duty of care also, in my judgment, limit the scope of the duty and I agree with O'Connor LJ that the duty of care is one owed to the shareholders as a body and not to individual shareholders.

To widen the scope of the duty to include loss caused to an individual by reliance upon the accounts for a purpose for which they were not supplied and were not intended would be to extend it beyond the limits which are so far deducible from the decisions of this House. It is not, as I think, an extension which either logic requires or policy dictates and I, for my part, am not prepared to follow the majority of the Court of Appeal in making it. In relation to the purchase of shares of other shareholders in a company, whether in the open market or as a result of an offer made to all or a majority of the existing shareholders, I can see no sensible distinction, so far as a duty of care is concerned, between a potential purchaser who is, vis-à-vis the company, a total outsider and one who is already the holder of one or more shares. . . .

Notes

1. There were two grounds for this decision: first that there was not sufficient proximity between the plaintiffs and the defendants and secondly that the accounts were produced for the purpose of informing the members of the company in order to assist the members (i.e. the shareholders) in directing the company, and not for the purpose of advising the shareholders as to further speculation. Is this a realistic distinction? If a shareholder receives accounts which show the company to be in a poor state does he think first of attending the AGM to try to influence the direction of the company or of selling his shares?

2.   In *Smith* v *Eric Bush* (above) the survey was directed to the building society to advise them whether the house was good security for the loan. Was this the same purpose as advising the purchaser as to the value of his house? If the functions are different, how can *Smith* v *Bush* be explained? In *Morgan Crucible* v *Hill Samuel* [1991] Ch 295, the Court of Appeal pointed out that at first instance the judge had distinguished *Smith* v *Bush* on the ground of 'the different economic relationships between the parties and the nature of the markets' but went on to say that 'we would not think it right by reference to economic considerations to dismiss as unarguable an otherwise arguable case'. Does this mean that the fact that Mrs Smith paid for the survey and was a 'consumer' is not the distinguishing feature?

3.   Subsequent cases have analysed and applied *Caparo* v *Dickman*. Thus in *Al-Nakib Investments* v *Longcroft* [1990] 3 All ER 321, a company issued a prospectus to existing shareholders in relation to a rights issue. The plaintiffs both subscribed to the rights issue and also bought shares in the market. It was held that a duty was owed in relation to the subscription to the rights issue but not in relation to the shares the plaintiffs had bought in the open market, on the ground that the purpose of the prospectus was limited to inviting existing shareholders to subscribe to the rights issue. Again, in *McNaughton Papers Group* v *Hicks Anderson* [1991] 2 QB 113, the plaintiffs were negotiating to take over a company called MK. Draft accounts were hurriedly drawn up by the defendants and given to MK, and these were used in the negotiations. The defendants were not liable, one ground being that the accounts had been supplied to MK and not to the plaintiffs. In addition, the accounts were only draft accounts and the defendants could not have expected reliance on them by the plaintiffs.

4,   In *Galoo* v *Bright Grahame Murray* [1995] 1 All ER 16, the defendants audited the accounts of a company called Gamine which was purchased by Hillsdown Holdings. The auditors failed to detect that Gamine was insolvent. The terms of the agreement to sell Gamine were that the price would be 5.2 times the net profits for 1986. The defendants knew that this was how the price was to be fixed and were to deliver a set of the audited completion accounts direct to Hillsdown Holdings. Accordingly, it was held that as there was sufficient proximity on the special facts, the claim would not be struck out.

5.   A potential ground of liability has been exposed in *Morgan Crucible* v *Hill Samuel* [1991] Ch 295. The plaintiff was engaged in a hostile take over bid for a company called First Castle Electronics (FCE). The defendants were the directors of FCE and their financial advisers and publicly issued a number of statements. It was said that *if* the object of these statements was to encourage the plaintiffs to increase their bid, a duty of care could be owed to them. It has been said that the intention of the defendants to influence the plaintiffs is significant and this intention must be objectively determined. Thus in *Possfund Custodian Trustee* v *Diamond* [1996] 2 All ER 774 it was argued that a prospectus issued in pursuance of a flotation on the unlisted securities

market may be directed not only to the recipients of the prospectus but may also be designed 'to inform and encourage after-market purchasers'. Accordingly an action by a subsequent purchaser of shares based on negligent misrepresentations in the prospectus was not struck out.

Question

If a house surveyor realises that his report will be relied on by purchasers of a house (even though they are not clients of his) he may be liable if the report is negligently prepared. Even if an auditor realises that accounts he has audited may be relied on by the purchasers of the company he will not be liable. Can you explain this?

Section 3: liability to third parties

This section deals with the situation where A makes a statement to B but damage is caused to C (usually by B acting on A's statement). One problem is can there be liability to C when no statement was ever made to him? In which case, how should 'proximity' be defined? Also *Hedley Byrne* is said largely to depend on 'reliance'. It is true that in this situation C relies on A making a non-negligent statement to B, but he does not *act* in reliance on the statement. Despite these conceptual problems liability has in fact been extended into this area and this makes it difficult to establish the true basis of *Hedley Byrne* liability. Furthermore, *White* v *Jones* below suggests that there may be cases, analogous to fiduciary duties, where reliance is not necessary at all.

Ministry of Housing v *Sharp*
Court of Appeal [1970] 2 QB 223; [1970] 1 All ER 7009; [1970] 2 WLR 802

In 1960 Mr Neale was refused planning permission, and as a result he was paid compensation of about £1,800. The Ministry of Housing and Local Government registered this fact in the register of local land charges maintained by the Hemel Hempstead RDC, the second defendant, whose clerk was Mr Sharp, the first defendant. In 1962 planning permission was granted, and this meant that the £1,800 should have been repaid to the Ministry by Mr Neal's successor in title, Parsons Ltd. However, Parsons Ltd had called for a search of the register and were given a clear certificate to the effect that there were no encumbrances on the land. This meant that the Ministry could not claim the £1,800 from Parsons Ltd, and they sued Mr Sharp and the council for negligently providing the clear certificate. Held: the council was liable for the negligence of their clerk.

LORD DENNING MR: I have no doubt that the clerk is liable. He was under a duty at common law to use due care. That was a duty which he owed to any person — incumbrancer or purchaser — whom he knew, or ought to have known, might be injured if he made a mistake. The case comes four square within the principles which are stated in *Candler* v *Crane, Christmas & Co.* [1951] 2 KB 164, 179–185, and which were approved by the House of Lords in *Hedley Byrne & Co. Ltd* v *Heller & Partners Ltd* [1964] AC 465.

Mr Hunter submitted to us, however, that the correct principle did not go to that length. He said that a duty to use due care (where there was no contract) only arose when there was a voluntary assumption of responsibility. I do not agree. He relied particularly on the words of Lord Reid in *Hedley Byrne's* case [1964] AC 465, 487, and of Lord Devlin at p. 529. I think they used those words because of the special circumstances of that case (where the bank disclaimed responsibility). But they did not in any way mean to limit the general principle.

In my opinion the duty to use due care in a statement arises, not from any voluntary assumption of responsibility, but from the fact that the person making it knows, or ought to know, that others, being his neighbours in this regard, would act on the faith of the statement being accurate. That is enough to bring the duty into being. It is owed, of course, to the person to whom the certificate is issued and whom he knows is going to act on it, see the judgment of Cardozo J in *Glanzer* v *Shepard* (1922) 233 NY 236. But it also is owed to any person whom he knows, or ought to know, will be injuriously affected by a mistake, such as the incumbrancer here.

Notes
1. This is a difficult case, as no statement was made by the clerk to the Ministry and they did not act in reliance on anything he said. It has been said to stand for the proposition that where A makes a statement to B whereby B does an act to the detriment of C, A is liable to C, and this is the issue which is discussed at some length in the next two cases which have given rise to considerable diversity of opinion. Note also that there is a contractual element to some of these cases which is discussed in chapter 12. For example, if A is under a contractual duty to B to exercise his skills and the object of the transaction is to benefit C, could C sue A in contract? The answer is not yet: see *White* v *Jones* in Chapter 12.
2. Did the registrar 'voluntarily' assume a responsibility? In most cases an adviser either can not make a statement or can make it 'without responsibility' as in *Hedley Byrne*. But here the registrar could not refuse to issue a certificate nor could he disclaim responsibility.

Spring v *Guardian Assurance*
[1995] 2 AC 296; [1994] 3 WLR 354; [1994] 3 All ER 129

Mr Spring was employed by a company which among other things sold Guardian Assurance policies. The company was taken over by Guardian Assurance and subsequently Mr Spring was dismissed. He tried to set up a new business selling Scottish Amicable policies but it refused to appoint him as one of its representatives. The reason was that Guardian Assurance had negligently given a highly unfavourable reference to Scottish Amicable about Mr Spring. The regulatory body (Lautro) required that all persons appointed as representatives for insurance companies must provide a reference and previous employers are obliged to provide one. Held: allowing the appeal that the defendants were liable.

LORD GOFF: . . . The wide scope of the principle recognised in *Hedley Byrne* is reflected in the broad statements of principle which I have quoted. All the members of the Appellate Committee in this case spoke in terms of the principle resting upon an assumption or undertaking of responsibility by the defendant towards the plaintiff, coupled with reliance by the plaintiff on the exercise by the defendant of due care and skill. Lord Devlin, in particular, stressed that the principle rested upon an assumption of responsibility when he said, at p. 531, that 'the essence of the matter in the present case and in others of the same type is the acceptance of responsibility.' For the purpose of the case now before your Lordships it is, I consider, legitimate to proceed on the same basis. Furthermore, although *Hedley Byrne* itself was concerned with the provision of information and advice, it is clear that the principle in the case is not so limited and extends to include the performance of other services, as for example the professional services rendered by a solicitor to his client (see in particular, Lord Devlin, at pp. 529–530). Accordingly where the plaintiff entrusts the defendant with the conduct of his affairs, in general or in particular, the defendant may be held to have assumed responsibility to the plaintiff, and the plaintiff to have relied on the defendant to exercise due skill and care, in respect of such conduct.

For present purposes, I wish also to refer to the nature of the 'special skill' to which Lord Morris referred in his statement of principle. It is, I consider, clear from the facts of *Hedley Byrne* itself that the expression 'special skill' is to be understood in a broad sense, certainly broad enough to embrace special knowledge. Furthermore Lord Morris himself, when speaking of the provision of a statement in the form of information or advice, referred to the defendant's judgment or skill or ability to make careful inquiry, from which it appears that the principle may apply in a case in which the defendant has access to information and fails to exercise due care (and skill, to the extent that this is relevant) in drawing on that source of information for the purposes of communicating it to another.

The fact that the inquiry in *Hedley Byrne* itself was directed, in a case concerned with liability in respect of a negligent misstatement (in fact a reference), to whether the maker of the statement was liable to a recipient of it who had acted in reliance upon it, may have given the impression that this is the only way in which liability can arise under the principle in respect of a misstatement. But, having regard to the breadth of the principle as stated in *Hedley Byrne* itself, I cannot see why this should be so. Take the case of the relationship between a solicitor and his client, treated implicitly by Lord Morris and expressly by Lord Devlin as an example of a relationship to which the principle may apply. I can see no reason why a solicitor should not be under a duty to his client to exercise due care and skill when making statements to third parties, so that if he fails in that duty and his client suffers damage in consequence, he may be liable to his client in damages. The question whether a person who gives a reference to a third party may, if the reference is negligently prepared be liable in damages not to the recipient but to the subject of the reference, did not arise in *Hedley Byrne* and so was not addressed in that case. That is the central question with which we are concerned in the present case; and I propose first to consider it in the context of an ordinary relationship between employer and employee, and then to turn to apply the relevant principles to the more complex relationships which existed in the present case.

Prima facie (i.e., subject to the point on defamation, which I will have to consider later), it is my opinion that an employer who provides a reference in respect of one of his employees to a prospective future employer will ordinarily owe a duty of care to his employee in respect of the preparation of the reference. The employer is possessed of special knowledge, derived from his experience of the employee's character, skill and diligence in the performance of his duties while working for the employer. Moreover, when the employer provides a reference to a third party in respect of his employee, he does so not only for the assistance of the third party, but also, for what it is worth, for the assistance of the employee. Indeed, nowadays it must often be very difficult for an employee to obtain fresh employment without the benefit of a reference from his present or a previous employer. It is for this reason that, in ordinary life, it may be the employee, rather than a prospective future employer, who asks the employer to provide the reference; and even where the approach comes from the prospective future employer, it will (apart from special circumstances) be made with either the express or the tacit authority of the employee. The provision of such references is a service regularly provided by employers to their employees; indeed, references are part of the currency of the modern employment market. Furthermore, when such a reference is provided by an employer, it is plain that the employee relies upon him to exercise due skill and care in the preparation of the reference before making it available to the third party. In these circumstances, it seems to me that all the elements requisite for the application of the *Hedley Byrne* [1964] AC 465 principle are present. I need only add that, in the context under consideration, there is no question of the circumstances in which the reference is provided being, for example, so informal as to negative an assumption of responsibility by the employer. . . .

I wish however to add that, in considering the duty of care owed by the employer to the employee, although it can and should be expressed in broad terms, nevertheless the central requirement is that reasonable care and skill should be exercised by the employer in ensuring the accuracy of any facts which either (1) are communicated to the recipient of the reference from which he may form an adverse opinion of the employee, or (2) are the basis of an adverse opinion expressed by the employer himself about the employee. I wish further to add that it does not necessarily follow that, because the employer owes such a duty of care to his employee, he also owes a duty of care to the recipient of the reference. The relationship of the employer with the recipient is by no means the same as that with his employee; and whether, in a case such as this, there should be held (as was prima facie held to be so on the facts of the *Hedley Byrne* case itself) a duty of care owed by the maker of the reference to the recipient is a point on which I do not propose to express an opinion, and which may depend on the facts of the particular case before the court.

At this point I must face the possibility that the conclusion which I have expressed may be thought to be inconsistent with the decision of the Privy Council in *Mutual Life and Citizens' Assurance Co. Ltd* v *Evatt* [1971] AC 793. There a claim was made against a company for damages arising from negligent advice gratuitously supplied by the company to the plaintiff in respect of a particular investment. The company was not engaged in the business of giving advice about investments; and it was held that a person who renders services gratuitously in circumstances where he is not engaged in the business or profession of rendering such services owes no duty to exercise skill or competence, or indeed care, in so doing. Quite apart however from the fact that the decision, which is not binding on your Lordships' House, has attracted serious criticism particularly in the light of the formidable dissenting opinion of Lord Reid and Lord Morris of Borth-y-Gest (both of whom were members of the Appellate Committee in *Hedley Byrne*), I do not consider that it stands in the way of the approach which I favour in the present case, since the skill of preparing a reference in respect of an employee falls as much within the expertise of an employer as the skill of preparing a bank reference fell within the expertise of the defendant bank in *Hedley Byrne* itself. . . .

[*Note*: it had been argued that the appropriate tort for a misleading reference was the tort of defamation, and that there would have been no liability in defamation because the reference would have attracted qualified privilege which meant there could be no liability unless the writer was in law malicious. The Court of Appeal had agreed that if there was no liability in defamation there should not be in negligence, for otherwise the defence of qualified privilege would be subverted. This issue is dealt with by Lord Slynn.]

LORD SLYNN: . . . It seems to me that on the basis of these authorities two questions therefore arise. The first is whether the nature of the tort of defamation and the tort of injurious falsehood is such that it would be wrong to recognise the possibility of a duty of care in negligence for a false statement. The second question is whether, independently of the existence of the other two torts, and taking the tests adopted by Lord Bridge of Harwich in *Caparo Industries Plc v Dickman* [1990] 2 AC 605, a duty of care can in any event arise in relation to the giving of a reference. If the answer to the first is 'No,' and to the second 'Yes' then it remains to consider whether in all the circumstances such a duty of care was owed in this case by an employer to an ex-employee.

As to the first question the starting-point in my view is that the suggested claim in negligence and the torts of defamation and injurious and malicious falsehood do not cover the same ground, as Mr Tony Weir shows in his note in [1993] CLJ 376. They are separate torts, defamation not requiring a proof by the plaintiff that the statement was untrue (though justification may be a defence) or that he suffered economic damage, but being subject to defences quite different from those in negligence, such as the defence of qualified privilege which makes it necessary to prove malice. Malicious falsehood requires proof that the statement is false, that harm has resulted and that there was express malice. Neither of these involves the concept of a duty of care. The essence of a claim in defamation is that a person's reputation has been damaged; it may or not involve the loss of a job or economic loss. A claim that a reference has been given negligently is essentially based on the fact, not so much that reputation has been damaged, as that a job, or an opportunity, has been lost. A statement carelessly made may not be defamatory — a statement that a labourer is 'lame,' a secretary 'very arthritic' when neither statement is true, though they were true of some other employee mistakenly confused with the person named.

I do not consider that the existence of either of these two heads of claim, defamation and injurious falsehood, a priori prevents the recognition of a duty of care where, but for the existence of the other two torts, it would be fair, just and reasonable to recognise it in a situation where the giver of a reference has said or written what is untrue and where he has acted unreasonably and carelessly in what he has said.

The policy reasons underlying the requirement that the defence of qualified privilege is only dislodged if express malice is established do not necessarily apply in regard to a claim in negligence. There may be other policy reasons in particular situations which should prevail. Thus, in relation to a reference given by an employer in respect of a former employee or a departing employee (and assuming no contractual obligation to take care in giving a reference) it is relevant to consider the changes which have taken place in the employer-employee relationship, with far greater duties imposed on the employer than in the past, whether by statute or by judicial decision, to care for the physical, financial and even psychological welfare of the employee.

As to the second question it is a relevant circumstance that in many cases an employee will stand no chance of getting another job, let alone a better job, unless he is given a reference. There is at least a moral obligation on the employer to give it. This is not necessarily true when the claim is laid in defamation even if on an occasion of qualified privilege. In the case of an employee or ex-employee the damage is clearly foreseeable if a careless reference is given; there is as obvious a proximity of relationship in this context as can be imagined. The sole question therefore, in my view, is whether balancing all the factors (per Lord Bridge of Harwich in *Caparo Industries Plc* v *Dickman* [1990] 2 AC 605, 618):

> the situation should be one in which the court considers it fair, just and reasonable that the law should impose a duty of a given scope upon the one party for the benefit of the other.

Hedley Byrne & Co. Ltd v *Heller & Partners Ltd* [1964] AC 465 does not decide the present case, but I find it unacceptable that the person to whom a reference is given about an employee X should be able to sue for negligence if he relies on the statement (and, for example, employs X who proves to be inadequate for the job) as it appears to be assumed that he can; but that X who is refused employment because the recipient relies on a reference negligently given should have no recourse unless he can prove express malice as defined by Lord Diplock in *Horrocks* v *Lowe* [1975] AC 135, 149–151.
. . .

I do not accept the in terrorem arguments that to allow a claim in negligence will constitute a restriction on freedom of speech or that in the employment sphere employers will refuse to give references or will only give such bland or adulatory ones as is forecast. They should be and are capable of being sufficiently robust as to express frank and honest views after taking reasonable care both as to the factual content and as to the opinion expressed. They will not shrink from the duty of taking reasonable care when they realise the importance of the reference both to the recipient (to whom it is assumed that a duty of care exists) and to the employee (to whom it is contended on existing authority there is no such duty). They are not being asked to warrant absolutely the accuracy of the facts or the incontrovertible validity of the opinions expressed but to take reasonable care in compiling or giving the reference and in verifying the information on which it is based. The courts can be trusted to set a standard which is not higher than the law of negligence demands. Even if it is right that the number of references given will be reduced, the quality and value will be greater and it is by no means certain that to have more references is more in the public interest than to have more careful references.

Those giving such references can make it clear what are the parameters within which the reference is given such as stating their limited acquaintance with the individual either as to time or as to situation. This issue does not arise in the present case but it may be that employers can make it clear to the subject of the reference that they will only give one if he accepts that there will be a disclaimer of liability to him and to the recipient of the reference.

Notes

1. Lord Goff bases *Hedley Byrne* liability on voluntary assumption of responsibility and reliance, but does not link the two. *Hedley Byrne* was a case where the plaintiff was both the person to whom the statement was made as a result of the assumption of responsibility and who acted on it to his detriment. However, Lord Goff says that *Hedley Byrne* can extend to cases where there is (a) an assumption of responsibility by the defendant to the plaintiff and (b) the plaintiff 'relies' on the defendant not being negligent. This is so even if the statement is made to someone else who then acts to the detriment of the plaintiff. In what sense did the plaintiff 'rely' on the defendant? Presumably, he had no choice but to use the defendant as a referee but no doubt was entitled to expect him to act without negligence. For a different explanation of this type of liability see *White* v *Jones* (below).

2. The 'defamation' issue has been very controversial. It was argued that as the defendant would not have been liable in defamation because of the defence of qualified privilege, that defence should not be subverted by allowing the plaintiff to sue in negligence. Lord Slynn says there is no conflict between the two torts because defamation is about reputation and negligence, in this case, is about employability and the two may not coincide (e.g. his example of a statement that a secretary has arthritis).

3. Should, or will, referees now refuse to give a reference, or at least give one so bland as to be of little use?

4. If A negligently gives an unjustifiably excellent reference to B about C and B employs C, can B sue A for any damage done by C to B's business? Lord Slynn assumes he could but Lord Goff leaves the matter open. For an example, see *T* v *Surrey County Council* [1994] 4 All ER 577.

White v Jones
[1995] 2 AC 207; [1995] 2 WLR 187; [1995] 1 All ER 691

In 1986 the testator cut his daughters out of his will, but he later relented and in July he instructed the defendant solicitors to draw up a new will giving the daughters £9,000 each. The new will had not been drawn up by 14 September when the testator died. The daughters sued the solicitors. Held: dismissing the appeal, that the defendants were liable.

LORD BROWNE-WILKINSON: My Lords, I have read the speech of my noble and learned friend, Lord Goff of Chieveley, and agree with him that this appeal should be dismissed. In particular, I agree that your Lordships should hold that the defendant solicitors were under a duty of care to the plaintiffs arising from an extension of the principle of assumption of responsibility explored in *Hedley Byrne and Co. Ltd* v *Heller & Partners Ltd* [1964] AC 465. In my view, although the present case is not directly covered by the decided cases, it is legitimate to extend the law to the limited extent proposed using the incremental approach by way of analogy advocated in *Caparo Industries Plc* v *Dickman* [1990] 2 AC 605. To explain my reasons requires me to attempt an analysis of what is meant by 'assumption of responsibility' in the law of negligence. To avoid misunderstanding I must emphasise that I am considering only whether some duty of care exists, not with the extent of that duty which will vary according to the circumstances.

Far from that concept having been invented by your Lordships' House in *Hedley Byrne*, its genesis is to be found in *Nocton* v *Lord Ashburton* [1914] AC 932. It is impossible to analyse what is meant by 'assumption of responsibility' or 'the *Hedley Byrne* principle' without first having regard to *Nocton's* case. . . .

In my judgment, there are three points relevant to the present case which should be gathered from *Nocton's* case. First, there can be special relationships between the parties which give rise to the law treating the defendant as having assumed a duty to be careful in circumstances where, apart from such relationship, no duty of care would exist. Second, a fiduciary relationship is one of those special relationships. Third, a fiduciary relationship is not the only such special relationship: other relationships may be held to give rise to the same duty.

The second of those propositions merits further consideration, since if we can understand the nature of one 'special relationship' it may cast light on when, by analogy, it is appropriate for the law to treat other relationships as being 'special.' The paradigm of the circumstances in which equity will find a fiduciary relationship is where one party, A, has assumed to act in relation to the property or affairs of another, B. A, having assumed responsibility, pro tanto, for B's affairs, is taken to have assumed certain duties in relation to the conduct of those affairs, including normally a duty of care. Thus, a trustee assumes responsibility for the management of the property of the beneficiary, a company director for the affairs of the company and an agent for those of his principal. By so assuming to act in B's affairs, A comes under fiduciary duties to B. Although the extent of those fiduciary duties (including duties of care) will vary from case to case some duties (including a duty of care) arise in each case. The importance of these considerations for present purposes is that the special relationship (i.e. a fiduciary relationship) giving rise to the assumption of responsibility held to exist in *Nocton's* case does not depend on any mutual dealing between A and B, let alone on any relationship akin to contract. Although such factors may be present, equity imposes the obligation because A has assumed to act in B's affairs. Thus, a trustee is under a duty of care to his beneficiary whether or not he has had any dealing with him: indeed he may be as yet unborn or unascertained and therefore any direct dealing would be impossible.

Moreover, this lack of mutuality in the typical fiduciary relationship indicates that it is not a necessary feature of all such special relationships that B must in fact rely on A's actions. If B is unaware of the fact that A has assumed to act in B's affairs (e.g. in the case of B being an unascertained beneficiary) B cannot possibly have relied on A. What is important is not that A knows that B is consciously relying on A, but A knows that B's economic well being is dependent upon A's careful conduct of B's affairs. Thus, in my judgment *Nocton* demonstrates that there is at least one special relationship giving rise to the imposition of a duty of care that is dependent neither upon mutuality of dealing nor upon actual reliance by the plaintiff on the defendant's actions.

I turn then to consider the *Hedley Byrne* case [1964] AC 465. In that case this House had to consider the circumstances in which there could be liability for negligent misstatement in the absence of either a contract or a fiduciary relationship between the parties. The first, and for present purposes perhaps the most important, point is that there is nothing in the *Hedley Byrne* case to cast doubt on the decision in *Nocton's* case. On the contrary, each of their Lordships treated *Nocton's* case as their starting point and asked the question 'in the absence of any contractual or fiduciary duty, what circumstances give rise to a special relationship between the plaintiff and the defendant sufficient to justify the imposition of the duty of care in the making of statements?' The House was seeking to define a further special relationship in addition to, not in substitution for, fiduciary relationships: see *per* Lord Reid, at p. 486; *per* Lord Morris of Borth-y-Gest, at p. 502; *per* Lord Hodson, at p. 511; *per* Lord Devlin, at p. 523; *per* Lord Pearce, at p. 539.

Second, since this House was concerned with cases of negligent misstatement or advice, it was inevitable that any test laid down required both that the plaintiff should rely on the statement or advice and that the defendant could reasonably foresee that he would do so. In the case of claims based on negligent statements (as opposed to negligent actions) the plaintiff will have no cause of action at all unless he can show damage and he can only have suffered damage if he has relied on the negligent statement. Nor will a defendant be shown to have satisfied the requirement that he should foresee damage to the plaintiff unless he foresees such reliance by the plaintiff as to give rise to the damage. Therefore although reliance by the plaintiff is an essential ingredient in a case based on negligent misstatement or advice, it does not follow that in all cases based on negligent action or inaction by the defendant it is necessary in order to demonstrate a special relationship that the plaintiff has in fact relied on the defendant or the defendant has foreseen such reliance. If in such a case careless conduct can be foreseen as likely to cause and does in fact cause damage to the plaintiff that should be sufficient to found liability.

Third, it is clear that the basis on which (apart from the disclaimer) the majority would have held the bank liable for negligently giving the reference was that, were it not for the disclaimer, the bank would have assumed responsibility for such reference. Although there are passages in the speeches which may point the other way, the reasoning of the majority in my judgment points clearly to the fact that the crucial element was that, by choosing to answer the enquiry, the bank had assumed to act, and thereby created the special relationship on which the necessary duty of care was founded. Thus Lord Reid, at p.486, pointed out that a reasonable man knowing that he was being trusted, had three possible courses open to him: to refuse to answer, to answer but with a disclaimer of responsibility, or simply to answer without such disclaimer. . . .

Just as in the case of fiduciary duties, the assumption of responsibility referred to is the defendants' assumption of responsibility for the task not the assumption of legal liability. Even in cases of ad hoc relationships, it is the undertaking to answer the question posed which creates the relationship. If the responsibility for the task is assumed by the defendant he thereby creates a special relationship between himself and the plaintiff in relation to which the law (not the defendant) attaches a duty to carry out carefully the task so assumed. If this be the right view, it does much to allay the doubts about the utility of the concept of assumption of responsibility voiced by Lord Griffiths in *Smith* v *Eric S. Bush* [1990] 1 AC 831, 862 and by Lord Roskill in *Caparo Industries Plc* v *Dickman* [1992] AC 605, 628: see also Barker in 'Unreliable Assumptions in the Modern Law of Negligence' (1993) 109 LQR 461. As I read those judicial criticisms they proceed on the footing that the phrase 'assumption of responsibility' refers to the defendant having assumed legal responsibility. I doubt whether the same criticisms would have been directed at the phrase if the words had been understood, as I think they should be, as referring to a conscious assumption of responsibility for the task rather than a conscious assumption of legal liability to the plaintiff for its careful performance. Certainly, the decision in both cases is consistent with the view I take. . . .

Let me now seek to bring together these various strands so far as is necessary for the purposes of this case: I am not purporting to give any comprehensive statement of this aspect of the law. The law of England does not impose any general duty of care to avoid negligent misstatements or to avoid causing pure economic loss even if economic damage to the plaintiff was foreseeable. However, such a duty of care will arise if there is a special relationship between the parties. Although the categories of cases in which such special relationship can be held to exist are not closed, as yet only two categories have been identified, viz. (1) where there is a fiduciary relationship and (2) where the defendant has voluntarily answered a question or tenders skilled advice or services in circumstances where he knows or ought to know that an identified plaintiff will rely on his answers or advice. In both these categories the special relationship is created by the defendant voluntarily assuming to act in the matter by involving himself in the plaintiff's affairs or by choosing to speak. If he does so assume to act or speak he is said to have assumed responsibility for carrying through the matter he has entered upon. In the words of Lord Reid in *Hedley Byrne* [1964] AC 465, 486 he has 'accepted a relationship . . . which requires him to exercise such care as the circumstances require,' i.e. although the extent of the duty will vary from category to category, *some* duty of care arises from the special relationship. Such relationship can arise even though the defendant has acted in the plaintiff's affairs pursuant to a contract with a third party. . . .

The solicitor who accepts instructions to draw a will knows that the future economic welfare of the intended beneficiary is dependent upon his careful execution of the task.

It is true that the intended beneficiary (being ignorant of the instructions) may not rely on the particular solicitor's actions. But, as I have sought to demonstrate, in the case of a duty of care flowing from a fiduciary relationship liability is not dependent upon actual reliance by the plaintiff on the defendant's actions but on the fact that, as the fiduciary is well aware, the plaintiff's economic well-being is dependent upon the proper discharge by the fiduciary of his duty. Second, the solicitor by accepting the instructions has entered upon, and therefore assumed responsibility for, the task of procuring the execution of a skilfully drawn will knowing that the beneficiary is wholly dependent upon his carefully carrying out his function. That assumption of responsibility for the task is a feature of both the two categories of special relationship so far identified in the authorities. It is not to the point that the solicitor only entered on the task pursuant to a contract with the third party (i.e. the testator). There are therefore present many of the features which in the other categories of special relationship have been treated as sufficient to create a special relationship to which the law attaches a duty of care. In my judgment the analogy is close.

Notes
1.   See chapter 12 for the contractual aspects of this case. It was argued that there was a contract between the testator and the solicitor which was intended to benefit the daughters and that they ought to be able to sue directly in contract. The invitation to evade the doctrine of privity was declined for the time being but the issue is certain to be raised again.
2.   Lord Browne-Wilkinson admits that this case did not fit in with traditional views of the nature of *Hedley Byrne* liability. As *Spring* v *Guardian Assurance* (above) showed there is a problem in these third party cases with 'reliance'. His Lordship has neatly avoided this problem by suggesting that there may be cases where reliance is not necessary, and this can be done by analogy with fiduciary duties where that element of 'mutuality' is not required. This was not a case of an actual fiduciary obligation,but was close enough to it. Accordingly, if the views of Lord Browne-Wilkinson are adopted there is now a new category of *Hedley Byrne* liability which has not yet been fully defined, but which places an obligation upon a person who voluntarily undertakes a task knowing that another will be directly affected if he fails to exercise proper skill and there is no other way the loss can be avoided.
3.   For a discussion of this and other recent cases, see McBride and Hughes, '*Hedley Byrne* in the House of Lords' (1996) 15 LS 376.

Section 4:   the effect of a clause disclaiming responsibility

In theory a clause which disclaims responsibility is not one which excludes an existing duty, but rather one which prevents that duty arising in the first place, since, according to *Hedley Byrne*, liability is based on a voluntary assumption of responsibility. However, the position has changed considerably since 1963, and it may be that a different view of the nature of the disclaimer clause should now be taken. In *Mutual Life Citizens Assurance Co.* v *Evatt* (1970) 122 CLR 556, Barwick CJ in the High Court of Australia took the view that liability was imposed and not voluntarily undertaken and that the disclaimer clause was merely one of the factors which was relevant to determine whether a duty of care had come about. This seems a sensible solution and one which accords with the view of Lord Griffiths, who said in *Smith v Eric Bush* (below) that assumption of responsibility 'can only have any real meaning if it is understood as referring to the circumstances in which the law will deem the maker of the statement to have assumed responsibility to the person who acts on the advice'.

Another issue is the degree of notice of a disclaimer which is necessary for it to be effective. Thus 'E & O. E.' is commonly printed on commercial documents, but how many lay people know what it means? The matter was touched on briefly by Lord Reid in *Hedley Byrne,* where he pointed out that denying a voluntary assumption of responsibility was different from excluding a contractual obligation. However, the issue has never been resolved.

Another issue is whether a disclaimer is caught by the Unfair Contract Terms Act 1977, and this is dealt with by *Smith v Bush* (below).

Smith v Eric Bush
House of Lords [1990] AC 831; [1989] 2 WLR 790; [1989] 2 All ER 514

For the facts and decision, see section 2 above. These extracts deal only with the application of the Unfair Contract Terms Act 1977. The argument for the surveyor was that liability is based on a voluntary assumption of responsibility, and as the disclaimer prevented that assumption of responsi-bility being made, there was therefore no liability in the first place to be excluded and the Act only applied to existing liability which was thereafter disclaimed. Held: dismissing the appeal, that the 1977 Act did apply and the exclusion clause was unreasonable.

LORD GRIFFITHS: At common law, whether the duty to exercise reasonable care and skill is founded in contract or tort, a party is as a general rule free, by the use of appropriate wording, to exclude liability for negligence in discharge of the duty. The disclaimer of liability in the present case is prominent and clearly worded and on the authority of *Hedley Byrne & Co. Ltd v Heller & Partners Ltd* [1964] AC 465, in so far as the common law is concerned effective to exclude the surveyors' liability for negligence. The question then is whether the Unfair Contract Terms Act 1977 bites upon such a disclaimer. In my view it does.

The Court of Appeal, however, accepted an argument based upon the definition of negligence contained in section 1(1) of the Act of 1977 which provides:

For the purposes of this part of this Act, 'negligence' means the breach — (*a*) of any obligation, arising from the express or implied terms of a contract, to take reasonable care or exercise reasonable skill in the performance of the contract: (*b*) of any common law duty to take reasonable care or exercise reasonable skill (but not any stricter duty); (*c*) of the common duty of care imposed by the Occupiers' Liability Act 1957 or the Occupiers' Liability Act (Northern Ireland) 1957.

They held that, as the disclaimer of liability would at common law have prevented any duty to take reasonable care arising between the parties, the Act had no application. In my view this construction fails to give due weight to the provisions of two further sections of the Act. Section 11(3) provides:

In relation to a notice (not being a notice having contractual effect), the requirement of reasonableness under this Act is that it should be fair and reasonable to allow reliance on it, having regard to all the circumstances obtaining when the liability arose or (but for the notice) would have arisen.

And section 13(1):

To the extent that this Part of this Act prevents the exclusion or restriction of any liability it also prevents — (a) making the liability or its enforcement subject to restrictive or onerous conditions; (b) excluding or restricting any right or remedy in respect of the liability, or subjecting a person to any prejudice in consequence of his pursuing any such right or remedy; (c) excluding or restricting rules of evidence or procedure; and (to that extent) sections 2 and 5 to 7 also prevent excluding or restricting liability by reference to terms and notices which exclude or restrict the relevant obligation or duty.

I read these provisions as introducing a 'but for' test in relation to the notice excluding liability. They indicate that the existence of the common law duty to take reasonable care, referred to in section 1(1)(b), is to be judged by considering whether it would exist 'but for' the notice excluding liability. The result of taking the notice into account when assessing the existence of a duty of care would result in removing all liability for negligent mis-statements from the protection of the Act. It is permissible to have regard to the second report of the Law Commission on Exemption Clauses (1975) (Law Com. No. 69) which is the genesis of the Unfair Contract Terms Act 1977 as an aid to the construction of the Act. Paragraph 127 of that report reads:

Our recommendations in this part of the report are intended to apply to exclusions of liability for negligence where the liability is incurred in the course of a person's business. We consider that they should apply even in cases where the person seeking to rely on the exemption clause was under no legal obligation (such as a contractual obligation) to carry out the activity. This means that, for example, conditions attached to a licence to enter on to land, and disclaimers of liability made where information or advice is given, should be subject to control. . . .

I have no reason to think that Parliament did not intend to follow this advice and the wording of the Act is, in my opinion, apt to give effect to that intention. This view of the construction of the Act is also supported by the judgment of Slade LJ in *Phillips Products Ltd* v *Hyland (Note)* [1987] 1 WLR 659, when he rejected a similar argument in relation to the construction of a contractual term excluding negligence.

11 SPECIAL DUTY PROBLEMS: ECONOMIC LOSS

While the recovery of economic loss caused by statements is covered by the concept of 'special relationship' spelt out in *Hedley Byrne* v *Heller,* it is rather more difficult to say when, if at all, a plaintiff can recover for pure economic loss caused by an act. A simple example of an economic loss case is the Canadian case of *Star Village Tavern* v *Nield* (1976) 71 DLR 3d 439, where the defendant collided with a bridge across the Red River near Selkirk in Manitoba, causing it to be closed for one month for repairs. The plaintiff owned a pub on the far side of the bridge from Selkirk, which meant that customers from there had to travel 15 miles rather than under two miles. The plaintiff sued for the decrease in his profits, but failed because he had suffered only economic loss.

The basic rule is that a person may sue for economic loss which is consequent on physical loss which he has suffered, but may not sue if he has only suffered economic loss by itself. To this rule there may be exceptions where there is sufficient proximity between the parties, and one element in this may be reliance by the one on the other. However, despite the large number of cases on this subject at a very high level, no case spells out what degree of proximity would be necessary, and so far no plaintiff has succeeded in claiming pure economic loss, except possibly in one case which has been explained away and subsequently ignored (*Junior Books* v *Veitchi* [1982] 3 All ER 201).

Although in the past this issue was sometimes regarded as one of remoteness of damage, it is now always regarded as a duty issue. A number of cases on this subject also involve the effect of contractual terms on the standard of care, but this problem is dealt with elsewhere.

For discussion of this difficult topic see MacGrath, 'The recovery of economic loss in negligence — an emerging dichotomy' (1985) OJLS 350; Cane, *Tort Law and Economic Interests* (1996); Atiyah, 'Negligence and economic loss' (1967) 83 LQR 248.

Cattle v *Stockton Waterworks*
Court of Queen's Bench (1875) LR 10 QBD 453; 44 LJQB 139; 133 LT 475

The plaintiff was a contractor who was employed, for a fixed sum, to dig a tunnel under a road, through ground that belonged to one Knight. Unfortunately a water main belonging to the defendants was defective and caused flooding of the works, and this meant that the plaintiff lost money on his contract. Held: the defendants were not liable.

BLACKBURN J: In the present case the objection is technical and against the merits, and we should be glad to avoid giving it effect. But if we did so, we should establish an authority for saying that, in such a case as that of *Fletcher* v *Rylands* LR 1 Ex 265 the defendant would be liable, not only to an action by the owner of the drowned mine, and by such of his workmen as had their tools or clothes destroyed, but also to an action by every workman and person employed in the mine, who in consequence of its stoppage made less wages that he would otherwise have done. And many similar cases to which this would apply might be suggested. It may be said that it is just that all such persons should have compensation for such a loss, and that, if the law does not give them redress, it is imperfect. Perhaps it may be so. But, as was pointed out by Coleridge J, in *Lumley* v *Gye* (1853) 2 E & B 216, at p. 252, Courts of justice should not 'allow themselves, in the pursuit of perfectly complete remedies for all wrongful acts, to transgress the bounds, which our law, in a wise consciousness as I conceive of its limited powers, has imposed on itself, of redressing only the proximate and direct consequences of wrongful acts.' In this we quite agree. No authority in favour of the plaintiff's right to sue was cited, and, as far as our knowledge goes, there was none that could have been cited. . . .

In the present case there is no pretence for saying that the defendants were malicious or had any intention to injure anyone. They were, at most, guilty of a neglect of duty, which occasioned injury to the property of Knight, but which did not injure any property of the plaintiff. The plaintiff's claim is to recover the damage which he has sustained by his contract with Knight becoming less profitable, or, it may be, a losing contract, in consequence of this injury to Knight's property. We think this does not give him any right of action.

Note

This case encapsulates the problems which the courts have experienced with economic loss. The objection may be technical and against the merits, but it has always succeeded, partly because of the floodgates argument and partly because of the realisation that foreseeability is not by itself a sufficient limitation on the range of potential plaintiffs. If Mr Cattle could sue, could his workmen who were temporarily laid off also claim? What about the local shopkeepers and pub owners who would have taken less money while the men were laid off?

Spartan Steel v *Martin & Co.*
Court of Appeal [1973] QB 27; [1972] 3 All ER 557; [1972] 3 WLR 502

The defendants negligently cut a power cable supplying electricity to the plaintiffs, who manufactured steel alloys. At the time of the power cut there was a 'melt' in progress, and in order to stop the steel solidifying the plaintiffs had to add oxygen to it and run it off. This reduced its value by £368. Also, they would have made a profit of £400 on that melt had it been completed. They also claimed £1,767 for the profit they would have made on melts they could have processed during the time when the power was cut off. Held: allowing the appeal, that the plaintiffs could only recover for the physical damage to the melt in progress (£368), plus loss of profit on that melt (£400), but not for the profits they would have made (£1,767) while the power was off.

LORD DENNING MR: At bottom I think the question of recovering economic loss is one of policy. Whenever the courts draw a line to mark out the bounds of *duty*, they do it as matter of policy so as to limit the responsibility of the defendant. Whenever the courts set bounds to the *damages* recoverable — saying that they are, or are not, too remote — they do it as matter of policy so as to limit the liability of the defendant.

The more I think about these cases, the more difficult I find it to put each into its proper pigeon-hole. Sometimes I say: 'There was no duty.' In others I say: 'The damage was too remote.' So much so that I think the time has come to discard those tests which have proved so elusive. It seems to me better to consider the particular relationship in hand, and see whether or not, as a matter of policy, economic loss should be recoverable, or not. Thus in *Weller & Co.* v *Foot and Mouth Disease Research Institute* [1966] 1 QB 569 it was plain that the loss suffered by the auctioneers was not recoverable, no matter whether it is put on the ground that there was no duty or that the damage was too remote. Again in *Electrochrome Ltd* v *Welsh Plastics Ltd* [1968] 2 All ER 205, it is plain that the economic loss suffered by the plaintiffs' factory (due to the damage to the fire hydrant) was not recoverable, whether because there was no duty or that it was too remote.

So I turn to the relationship in the present case. It is of common occurrence. . . .

The first consideration is the position of the statutory undertakers. If the board do not keep up the voltage or pressure of electricity, gas or water — or, likewise, if they shut it off for repairs — and thereby cause economic loss to their consumers, they are not liable in damages, not even if the cause of it is due to their own negligence. The only remedy (which is hardly ever pursued) is to prosecute the board before the magistrates. . . .

The second consideration is the nature of the hazard, namely, the cutting of the supply of electricity. This is a hazard which we all run. It may be due to a short circuit, to a flash of lightning, to a tree falling on the wires, to an accidental cutting of the cable, or even to the negligence of someone or other. And when it does happen, it affects a multitude of persons: not as a rule by way of physical damage to them or their property, but by putting them to inconvenience, and sometimes to economic loss. The supply is usually restored in a few hours, so the economic loss is not very large. Such a hazard is regarded by most people as a thing they must put up with — without seeking compensation from anyone. Some there are who instal a stand-by system. Others seek refuge by taking out an insurance policy against breakdown in the supply. But most people are content to take the risk on themselves. When the supply is cut off, they do not go running round to their solicitor. They do not try to find out whether it was anyone's fault. They just put up with it. They try to make up the economic loss by doing more work next day. This is a healthy attitude which the law should encourage.

The third consideration is this: if claims for economic loss were permitted for this particular hazard, there would be no end of claims. Some might be genuine, but many might be inflated, or even false. A machine might not have been in use anyway, but it would be easy to put it down to the cut in supply. It would be well-nigh impossible to check the claims. If there was economic loss on one day, did the claimant do his best to mitigate it by working harder next day? And so forth. Rather than expose claimants to such temptation and defendants to such hard labour — on comparatively small claims — it is better to disallow economic loss altogether, at any rate when it stands alone, independent of any physical damage.

The fourth consideration is that, in such a hazard as this, the risk of economic loss should be suffered by the whole community who suffer the losses — usually many but comparatively small losses — rather than on the one pair of shoulders, that is, on the contractor on whom the total of them, all added together, might be very heavy.

The fifth consideration is that the law provides for deserving cases. If the defendant is guilty of negligence which cuts off the electricity supply and causes actual physical damage to person or property, that physical damage can be recovered . . . .

These considerations lead me to the conclusion that the plaintiffs should recover for the physical damage to the one melt (£368), and the loss of profit on that melt consequent thereon (£400): but not for the loss of profit on the four melts (£1,767), because that was economic loss independent of the physical damage. I would, therefore, allow the appeal and reduce the damages to £768.

EDMUND DAVIES LJ, *dissenting*: Having considered the intrinsic nature of the problem presented in this appeal, and having consulted the relevant authorities, my conclusion, as already indicated, is that an action lies in negligence for damages in respect of purely economic loss, provided that it was a reasonably foreseeable and direct consequence of failure in a duty of care. The application of such a rule can undoubtedly give rise to difficulties in certain sets of circumstances, but so can the suggested rule that economic loss may be recovered *provided* it is directly consequential upon physical damage. Many alarming situations were conjured up in the course of counsel's arguments before us. In their way, they were reminiscent of those formerly advanced against awarding damages for nervous shock; for example, the risk of fictitious claims and expensive litigation, the difficulty of disproving the alleged cause and effect, and the impossibility of expressing such a claim in financial terms. But I suspect that they . . . would for the most part be resolved either on the ground that no duty of care was owed to the injured party or that the damages sued for were irrecoverable *not* because they were simply financial but because they were too remote.

. . . Such good sense as I possess guides me to the conclusion that it would be wrong to draw in the present case any distinction between the first, spoilt 'melt' and the four 'melts' which, but for the defendants' negligence, would admittedly have followed it. That is simply another way of saying that I consider the plaintiffs are entitled to recover the entirety of the financial loss they sustained.

I should perhaps again stress that we are here dealing with economic loss which was both reasonably foreseeable and a direct consequence of the defendants' negligent act. What the position should or would be were the latter feature lacking (as in *Weller & Co. v Foot and Mouth Disease Research Institute* [1966] 1 QB 569) is not our present concern. By stressing this point one is not reviving the distinction between direct and indirect consequences which is generally thought to have been laid at rest by *The Wagon Mound* [1961] AC 388, for, in the words of Professor Atiyah, *Negligence and Economic Loss*, 83 LQR 263, that case

> was solely concerned with the question whether the directness of the damage is a *sufficient* test of liability, . . . In other words, *The Wagon Mound* merely decides that a plaintiff cannot recover for unforeseeable consequences even if they are direct; it does not decide that a plaintiff can always recover for foreseeable consequences even if they are indirect.

Both directness and foreseeability being here established, it follows that I regard Faulks J as having rightly awarded the sum of £2,535.

Notes
1. The point made in the above case can be illustrated by contrasting two cases. The first is **British Celanese v Hunt Capacitors** [1969] 2 All ER 1253, where strips of metal foil escaped from the defendant's premises and struck an electricity sub-station, causing a power cut. The plaintiffs made synthetic yarn, and material in their machines solidified. They were able to recover damages for their physical loss, together with consequent economic loss. On the other hand, in **Electrochrome v Welsh Plastics** [1968] 2 All ER 205, the defendants struck a fire hydrant which caused the water supply to the plaintiffs' factory to be cut off for some hours. (The hydrant did not belong to the plaintiffs.) The plaintiffs were engaged in electroplating hardware, and the factory was closed for a day as the process depended on the supply of water. However, as they suffered no physical damage they were unable to sue.
2. This decision has been rejected in similar circumstances in New Zealand. In **New Zealand Forest Products v A-G** [1986] 1 NZLR 14, an electricity cable which supplied only the plaintiffs (as did the cable in *Spartan Steel*) was cut by the negligence of the defendants, causing pumps to stop and the plaintiffs' mill came to a standstill. The plaintiffs were able to recover all their loss of profit even though no physical damage had been caused. The *Caltex Oil* principle (below) was applied, and it seems to have been significant that the defendants knew that the cable supplied only the plaintiffs. However, this factor was not regarded as decisive in *Mainguard Packaging* v *Hilton Haulage* [1990] 1 NZLR 360, where liability was imposed because the defendants should have realised the damage to the relevant cable would cut off the plaintiffs amongst others.

'The Willemstad': Caltex Oil Ltd v The Dredge Willemstad
High Court of Australia (1976-77) 136 CLR 529; (1976) 11 ALR 227

Australian Oil Refining Ltd (AOR) owned a pipeline across Botany Bay which led from the Caltex Oil terminal to the AOR refinery. The oil in the pipeline belonged to Caltex, but the risk of loss was, by contract, on AOR. On 26 October 1971 the dredge Willemstad negligently broke the pipeline. Caltex claimed the extra expense caused by having to transport oil round the bay while the pipeline was being repaired. *Held:* allowing the appeal, that the defendants were liable even though the plaintiffs had suffered only economic loss.

GIBBS J: In my opinion it is still right to say that as a general rule damages are not recoverable for economic loss which is not consequential upon injury to the plaintiff's person or property. The fact that the loss was foreseeable is not enough to make it recoverable. However, there are exceptional cases in which the defendant has knowledge or means of knowledge that the plaintiff individually, and not merely as a member of an unascertained class, will be likely to suffer economic loss as a consequence of his negligence, and owes the plaintiff a duty to take care not to cause him such damage by his negligent act. It is not necessary, and would not be wise, to attempt to formulate a principle that would cover all cases in which such a duty is owed; to borrow the words of Lord Diplock in *Mutual Life & Citizens' Assurance Co. Ltd* v *Evatt*, [1971] AC 793: 'Those will fall to be ascertained step by step as the facts of particular cases which come before the courts make it necessary to determine them.' All the facts of the particular case will have to be considered. It will be material, but not in my opinion sufficient, that some property of the plaintiff was in physical proximity to the damaged property, or that the plaintiff, and the person whose property was injured, were engaged in a common adventure.

In the present case the persons interested in the dredge and the employees of Decca (in particular Mr Austin) knew that the pipeline led directly from the refinery to Caltex's terminal. They should have known that, whatever the contractual or other relationship between Caltex and AOR might have been, the pipeline was the physical means by which the products flowed from the refinery to the terminal. Moreover, the pipeline appeared to be designed to serve the terminal particularly (although no doubt it would have been possible for it to serve other persons as well) and was not like a water main or electric cable serving the public generally. In these circumstances the persons interested in the dredge, and Decca, should have had Caltex in contemplation as a person who would probably suffer economic loss if the pipes were broken. Further, the officers navigating the dredge had a particular obligation to take care to avoid damage to the pipeline, which was shown on the drawing supplied to them for the very purpose of enabling them to avoid it. Decca had a similar obligation to draw the lines on the track plotter chart, in such a way that the navigators would not sail the dredge over the pipeline. In all these circumstances the particular relationship between the dredge and Decca on the one hand, and Caltex on the other, was such that both the dredge and Decca owed a duty to Caltex to take reasonable care to avoid causing damage to the pipeline and thereby causing economic loss to Caltex. It should therefore in my opinion be concluded that Caltex is entitled to recover the economic loss resulting from the breach of that duty of care. . . .

MASON J: It is preferable, then, as Mr P. P. Craig suggests in his illuminating article, 'Negligent Misstatements, Negligent Acts and Economic Loss' *Law Quarterly Review*, vol. 92 (1976), p. 213, that the delimitation of the duty of care in relation to economic damage through negligent conduct be expressed in terms which are related more closely to the principal factor inhibiting the acceptance of a more generalized duty of care in relation to economic loss, that is, the apprehension of an indeterminate liability. A defendant would then be liable for economic damage due to his negligent conduct when he can reasonably foresee that a specific individual, as distinct from a general class of persons, will suffer financial loss as a consequence of his conduct. This approach eliminates or diminishes the prospect that there will come into existence liability to an indeterminate class of persons; it ensures that liability is confined to those individuals whose financial loss falls within the area of foreseeability; and it accords with the decision in *Rivtow*, [1973] 40 DLR 3d 530.

On the facts of the present case (which are comprehensively narrated in the reasons for judgment of Stephen J) the dredge and Decca were aware of the situation of the pipeline, that it linked the AOR refinery and the Caltex terminal at Banksmeadow on the other side of Botany Bay. They should have known, if they did not know, that the pipeline carried refined petroleum products from the refinery to the terminal and that the oil was used by Caltex in its business operations as an oil company. Moreover, they should have foreseen, as the primary judge found, that negligence on their parts resulting in a severance of the pipeline would involve not only loss of oil from the pipeline but an interruption in supply which would necessitate the expense of making alternative transport and delivery arrangements, which included the expense of modifying the terminal.

In these circumstances both the dredge and Decca owed a duty of care not only to the owner of the pipeline but to Caltex whose oil . . . was flowing through the pipeline. It was a duty to take reasonable care to avoid damage, whether physical or financial, as might result from negligent navigation of the dredge in the vicinity of the pipeline. This duty was breached and Caltex sustained economic damage in the form of the expenditure to which I have referred and which by agreement amounted to $95,000.

Note
This method of solving the problem of economic loss has not been accepted in this country: see *The Mineral Transporter* below.

The Mineral Transporter: Candlewood Navigation v Mitsui OSK Lines
Privy Council [1986] AC 1; [1985] 3 WLR 381; [1985] 2 All ER 935

The Ibaraki Maru and The Mineral Transporter collided off Port Kembla in New South Wales due to the fault of The Mineral Transporter. Mitsui Lines (the plaintiffs) owned the Ibaraki Maru but had let it under a bareboat charter, or charter by demise (i.e. like a lease) to Matsuoka Steamship Co. Matsuoka then let the ship under a time charter back to the plaintiffs, Mitsui Lines. Under the various charters Matsuoka were responsible for the cost of repairs, and the plaintiffs remained liable to pay for the hire of the ship, although at a reduced rate. Matsuoka could sue for the physical damage to the ship, as they had a property interest in it under the bareboat charter. The question was whether the plaintiffs, as time charterers, could sue for the hire payments they had to pay while the ship was idle. (Note: the fact that the plaintiffs were also owners of the ship was irrelevant because they were suing for losses incurred as time charterers and the time charter gave them no property rights in the ship.) Held: allowing the appeal, that the defendants were not liable for the economic loss.

LORD FRASER: Their Lordships have carefully considered these reasons for the decision in the *Caltex* case, 136 CLR 529. With regard to the reasons given by Gibbs and Mason JJ, their Lordships have difficulty in seeing how to distinguish between a plaintiff as an individual and a plaintiff as a member of an unascertained class. The test can hardly be whether the plaintiff is known by name to the wrongdoer. Nor does it seem logical for the test to depend upon the plaintiff being a single individual. Further, why should there be a distinction for this purpose between a case where the wrongdoer knows (or has the means of knowing) that the persons likely to be affected by his negligence consist of a definite number of persons whom he can identify either by name or in some other way (for example as being the owners of particular factories or hotels) and who may therefore be regarded as an ascertained class, and a case where the wrongdoer knows only that there are several persons, the exact number being to him unknown, and some or all of whom he could not identify by name or otherwise, and who may therefore be regarded as an unascertained class? Moreover much of the argument in favour of an ascertained class seems to depend upon the view that the class would normally consist of only a few individuals. But would it be different if the class, though ascertained, was large? Suppose for instance that the class consisted of all the pupils in a particular school. If it was a kindergarten school with only six pupils they might be regarded as constituting an ascertained class, even if their names were unknown to the wrongdoer. If the school was a large one with over a thousand pupils it might be suggested that they were not an ascertained class. But it is not easy to see a distinction in principle merely because the number of possible claimants is larger in one case than in the other. Apart from cases of negligent misstatement, with which their Lordships are not here concerned, they do not consider that it is practicable by reference to an ascertained class to find a satisfactory control mechanism which could be applied in such a way as to give reasonable certainty in its results. . . .

In these circumstances their Lordships have concluded that they are entitled, and indeed bound, to reach their own decision without the assistance of any single ratio decidendi to be found in the *Caltex* case. . . .

Their Lordships consider that some limit or control mechanism has to be imposed upon the liability of a wrongdoer towards those who have suffered economic damage in consequence of his negligence. The need for such a limit has been repeatedly asserted in the cases, from *Cattle's* case, LR 10 QB 453, to *Caltex*, 136 CLR 529, and their Lordships are not aware that a view to the contrary has ever been judicially expressed. . . .

Almost any rule will have some exceptions, and the decision in the *Caltex* case may perhaps be regarded as one of the 'exceptional cases' referred to by Gibbs J in the passage already quoted from his judgment. . . . Certainly the decision in *Caltex* does not appear to have been based upon a rejection of the general rule stated in *Cattle's* case. For these reasons their Lordships are of the opinion that Yeldham J erred in holding that the time charterer was entitled to recover damages from the defendant in this case.

Note

A similar conclusion was reached in *The Aliakmon , Leigh and Sillivan Ltd v Aliakmon Shipping* [1986] AC 785, which is the latest in a long series of cases dealing with the problem where goods are damaged which do not belong to the plaintiff, but for which he has to bear the risk of damage. In that case the plaintiffs were buyers of steel coil which was damaged on its voyage in the Aliakmon. The effect of the contractual arrangements was such that the sellers reserved title to the steel, whereas it was at the plaintiffs' risk. Thus the sellers owned the steel, but the buyers had to take the risk of its being damaged. The House of Lords held that the buyers could not sue for the loss, since it was purely economic loss. Lord Brandon said that:

there is a long line of authority for the principle that, in order to enable a person to claim in negligence for loss caused to him by reason of loss of or damage to property, he must have had either the legal ownership of or a possessory title to the property concerned at the time when the loss or damage occurred, and it is not enough for him to have only had contractual rights in relation to such property which have been adversely affected by the loss or damage to it.

The result is that the sellers could sue, but would not bother to do so because they have received full price from the buyers. The buyers have paid the full price for damaged steel, but are unable to recover from the person who damaged it. However, as the House of Lords pointed out, the buyers could have so ordered their contractual arrangements so as to avoid this result, and the best solution to the problem probably lies in contract rather than tort. The case is further discussed in the next chapter.

Murphy v *Brentwood District Council*
House of Lords [1991] AC 398; [1990] 3 WLR 414; [1990] 2 All ER 908

In 1970, the plaintiff purchased a house which was constructed on a concrete raft foundation over an in-filled site. From 1981 cracks began appearing in the internal walls of the house and it was found that the concrete raft had subsided. In an action against the local authority for negligently approving the design of the concrete raft (for which see chapter 12 below), the question was whether the plaintiff had suffered only economic loss. The House of Lords held that he had, as the house had only damaged itself and was therefore merely a defective house which was a bad bargain. Lord Oliver made the following comments about the nature of the economic loss problem and the circumstances in which such loss might be recoverable.

LORD OLIVER: It does not, of course, at all follow as a matter of necessity from the mere fact that the only damage suffered by a plaintiff in an action for the tort of negligence is pecuniary or 'economic' that this claim is bound to fail. It is true that, in an uninterrupted line of cases since 1875, it has consistently been held that a third party cannot successfully sue in tort for the interference with his economic expectations or advantage resulting from injury to the person or property of another person with whom he has or is likely to have a contractual relationship: see *Cattle* v *Stockton Waterworks Co.* (1875) LR 10 QB 453; *Simpson & Co.* v *Thomson* (1877) 3 App Cas 279; *Société Anonyme de Remorquage á Hélice* v *Bennetts* [1911] 1 KB 243. That principle was applied more recently by Widgery J in *Weller & Co.* v *Foot and Mouth Disease Research Institute* [1966] QB 569 and received its most recent reiteration in the decision of this House in *Leigh and Sillavan Ltd* v *Aliakmon Shipping Co. Ltd* [1986] AC 785. But it is far from clear from these decisions that the reason for the plaintiff's failure was simply that the only loss sustained was 'economic.' Rather they seem to have been based either upon the remoteness of the damage as a matter of direct causation or, more probably, upon the 'floodgates' argument of the impossibility of containing liability within any acceptable bounds if the law were to permit such claims to succeed. The decision of this House in *Morrison Steamship Co. Ltd* v *Greystoke Castle (Cargo Owners)* [1947] AC 265 demonstrates that the mere fact that the primary damage suffered by a plaintiff is pecuniary is no necessary bar to an action in negligence given the proper circumstances — in that case, what was said to be the 'joint venture' interest of shipowners and the owners of cargo carried on board — and if the matter remained in doubt that doubt was conclusively resolved by the decision of this House in *Hedley Byrne & Co. Ltd* v *Heller & Partners Ltd* [1964] AC 465 where Lord Devlin, at p. 517, convincingly demonstrated the illogicality of a distinction between financial loss caused directly and financial loss resulting from physical injury to personal property.

The critical question, as was pointed out in the analysis of Brennan J in his judgment in *Council of the Shire of Sutherland* v *Heyman* (1985) 157 CLR 424, is not the nature of the damage in itself, whether physical or pecuniary, but whether the scope of the duty

of care in the circumstances of the case is such as to embrace damage of the kind which
the plaintiff claims to have sustained: see *Caparo Industries Plc* v *Dickman* [1990] 2 WLR
358. The essential question which has to be asked in every case, given that damage
which is the essential ingredient of the action has occurred, is whether the relationship
between the plaintiff and the defendant is such — or, to use the favoured expression,
whether it is of sufficient 'proximity' — that it imposes upon the latter a duty to take care
to avoid or prevent that loss which has in fact been sustained. That the requisite degree
of proximity may be established in circumstances in which the plaintiff's injury results
from his reliance upon a statement or advice upon which he was entitled to rely and
upon which it was contemplated that he would be likely to rely is clear from *Hedley Byrne*
and subsequent cases, but *Anns* [1978] AC 728 was not such a case and neither is the
instant case. It is not, however, necessarily to be assumed that the reliance cases form
the only possible category of cases in which a duty to take reasonable care to avoid or
prevent pecuniary loss can arise. *Morrison Steamship Co. Ltd* v *Greystoke Castle (Cargo
Owners)*, for instance, clearly was not a reliance case. Nor indeed was *Ross* v *Caunters*
[1980] Ch 297 so far as the disappointed beneficiary was concerned. Another example
may be *Ministry of Housing and Local Government* v *Sharp* [1980] 2 QB 223, although
this may, on analysis, properly be categorised as a reliance case.

Nor is it self-evident logically where the line is to be drawn. Where, for instance, the
defendant's careless conduct results in the interruption of the electricity supply to
business premises adjoining the highway, it is not easy to discern the logic in holding that
a sufficient relationship of proximity exists between him and a factory owner who has
suffered loss because material in the course of manufacture is rendered useless but that
none exists between him and the owner of, for instance, an adjoining restaurant who
suffers the loss of profit on the meals which he is unable to prepare and sell. In both cases
the real loss is pecuniary. The solution to such borderline cases has so far been achieved
pragmatically (see *Spartan Steel & Alloys Ltd* v *Martin & Co. (Contractors) Ltd* [1973]
QB 27) not by the application of logic but by the perceived necessity as a matter of policy
to place some limits — perhaps arbitrary limits — to what would otherwise be an
endless, cumulative causative chain bounded only by theoretical foreseeability.

I frankly doubt whether, in searching for such limits, the categorisation of the damage
as 'material', 'physical', 'pecuniary' or 'economic' provides a particularly useful
contribution. Where it does, I think, serve a useful purpose is in identifying those cases
in which it is necessary to search for and find something more than the mere reasonable
foreseeability of damage which has occurred as providing the degree of 'proximity'
necessary to support the action. In his classical exposition in *Donoghue* v *Stevenson*
[1932] AC 562, 580–581, Lord Atkin was expressing himself in the context of the
infliction of direct physical injury resulting from a carelessly created latent defect in a
manufactured product. In his analysis of the duty in those circumstances he clearly
equated 'proximity' with the reasonable foresight of damage. In the straightforward case
of the direct infliction of physical injury by the act of the plaintiff there is, indeed, no
need to look beyond the foreseeability by the defendant of the result in order to establish
that he is in a 'proximate' relationship with the plaintiff. But, as was pointed out by Lord
Diplock in *Dorset Yacht Co. Ltd* v *Home Office* [1970] AC 1004, 1060, Lord Atkin's test,
though a useful guide to characteristics which will be found to exist in conduct and
relationships giving rise to a legal duty of care, is manifestly false if misused as a
universal; and Lord Reid, in the course of his speech in the same case, recognised that
the statement of principle enshrined in that test necessarily required qualification in
cases where the only loss caused by the defendant's conduct was economic. The
infliction of physical injury to the person or property of another universally requires to
be justified. The causing of economic loss does not. If it is to be categorised as wrongful

it is necessary to find some factor beyond the mere occurrence of the loss and the fact that its occurrence could be foreseen. Thus the categorisation of damage as economic serves at least the useful purpose of indicating that something more is required . . . .

Notes
1. For an explanation as to why the loss in *Murphy* v *Brentwood District Council* was regarded as economic loss see the discussion of that case in Chapter 13 (liability for defective structures).
2. In *Murphy* v *Brentwood DC*, Lord Oliver suggests that 'economic' loss may be recoverable where there is sufficient proximity, but does not say what criteria will be used to bring about that necessary degree of proximity. In the search for an appropriate test to allow the recovery of economic loss in restricted circumstances, a number of factors have been discussed, but none has yet won the day. These include close proximity, as in *Caltex Oil*, reliance, as in *Junior Books* and *Muirhead Tank*, and voluntary assumption of responsibility, as in *Hedley Byrne*. The *Caltex Oil* test has been rejected in this country and the idea that *Hedley Byrne* liability is based on a voluntary assumption of responsibility was denied in *Smith* v *Eric Bush*. As to reliance, it was said by Dillon LJ in *Simaan* v *Pilkington Ltd* [1988] 1 QB 758, at p. 784, 'Indeed I find it difficult to see that future citation from the *Junior Books* case can ever serve any useful purpose', and yet in *Murphy* v *Brentwood DC* Lord Bridge said, citing *Junior Books*, that 'there may be situations where, even in the absence of contract, there is a special relationship of proximity . . . which is sufficiently akin to contract to introduce the element of reliance so that the scope of the duty of care owed . . . is wide enough to embrace purely economic loss'. It seems, therefore, that reliance may be the way forward, but it is too early to say in what circumstances reliance will give rise to the duty to avoid economic loss. However see Stapleton, 'Duty of Care and Economic Loss: A Wider Agenda' (1991) 107 LQR 249, where it is argued that reliance is not the answer but that the courts should adopt a policy-based approach whereby plaintiffs must establish their worthiness to be protected by satisfying various conditions, including the absence of indeterminate liability, the inadequacy of alternative means of protection, that the area is not one more appropriate to Parliamentary action and that a duty would not allow a circumvention of a positive arrangement regarding the allocation of the risk which had been accepted by the plaintiff.
3. The contractual problems which often arise in economic loss cases, such as *Simaan*, are dealt with in the next chapter.

Canadian National Railway v Norsk Pacific Steamship Co.
Supreme Court of Canada [1992] 1 SCR 1021; (1992) 91 DLR 4th 289

The New Westminster Railway Bridge spans the Fraser river in British Columbia. It is owned by the Canadian Government through Public Works Canada (PWC) and is used by four different railway companies including the plaintiffs. On November 28th 1987 the barge Crown Forest No. 4 collided with the bridge and damaged it. As a result the plaintiffs had to re-route their trains for several weeks and sued for that additional cost. Held: the economic loss was recoverable as there was sufficient proximity between the plaintiffs and defendants.

McLACHLIN J:

Implications of the comparative review
The foregoing comparative review suggests that in some cases damages for economic loss should be available where the plaintiff has neither suffered physical damage nor relied in the sense of *Hedley Byrne*. Civil law jurisdictions, far from precluding such recovery, require it where it is direct and certain. The common law jurisdictions started from a narrow rule excluding most pure economic loss, but found themselves in a situation where judges on a case-by-case basis persisted in awarding damages for economic loss outside the categories. Even in the United States, where fear of the floodgates of unlimited liability has held the strongest sway, courts have been forced to make exceptions in the interests of justice. The fact is that situations arise, other than those falling within the old exclusionary rule, where it is manifestly fair and just that recovery of economic loss be permitted. Faced with these situations, courts will strain to allow recovery, provided they are satisfied that the case will not open the door to a plethora of undeserving claims. They will refuse to accept injustice merely for the sake of the doctrinal tidiness which is the motivating spirit of *Murphy* v *Brentwood District Council*. This is in the best tradition of the law of negligence, the history of which exhibits a sturdy refusal to be confined by arbitrary forms and rules where justice indicates otherwise. It is the tradition to which this Court has adhered in suggesting in *Kamloops* v *Nielsen* [1984] 2 SCR 2 that the search should not be for a universal rule but for the elaboration of categories where recovery of economic loss is justifiable on a case-by-case basis.

If a comparative review suggests that economic loss should be recoverable in circumstances not covered by the traditional exclusionary rule, it also suggests that the need for some limit on such recovery is universally recognized. To permit all economic loss related to a negligent act to be recovered would be to subject potential defendants to liability which is not only unfair, but which may cripple their ability to do business.

The search then must be for a legal formulation which will permit recovery of economic loss in appropriate cases, while excluding frivolous and remote claims. The comparative jurisprudence indicates that this may be accomplished in different ways. In the civil law, a direct connection test appears to provide appropriate limits. At common law, two approaches present themselves: the 'exhaustive rule' solution typified by *Murphy* and the incremental approach adopted in *Kamloops*. I turn next to a consideration of which of these two approaches should prevail.

3.   *The approach which should be adopted to recovery of pure economic Loss*
     (a)   *Doctrinal consideration*
     Murphy makes an important point. It is not enough that a rule of law be defensible on moral and economic terms. It should, in addition, provide a logical basis upon which individuals can predicate their conduct and courts can decide future cases. The history of the problem in different jurisdictions demonstrates a clear need to allow recovery of economic loss for negligence in some cases where the criteria of physical damage and reliance do not apply. On the other hand, a fair and functional legal system cannot accept that all economic loss related to negligence should be recoverable. Judges seem able to pick out deserving cases when they see them. The difficulty lies in formulating a

rule which explains why judges allow recovery of economic loss in some cases and not in others. . . .

The matter may be put thus: before the law will impose liability there must be a connection between the defendant's conduct and plaintiff's loss which makes it just for the defendant to indemnify the plaintiff. In contract, the contractual relationship provides this link. In trust, it is the fiduciary obligation which establishes the necessary connection. In tort, the equivalent notion is proximity. Proximity may consist of various forms of closeness — physical, circumstantial, causal or assumed — which serve to identify the categories of cases in which liability lies.

Viewed thus, the concept of proximity may be seen as an umbrella, covering a number of disparate circumstances in which the relationship between the parties is so close that it is just and reasonable to permit recovery in tort. The complexity and diversity of the circumstances in which tort liability may arise defy identification of a single criterion capable of serving as the universal hallmark of liability. The meaning of 'proximity' is to be found rather in viewing the circumstances in which it has been found to exist and determining whether the case at issue is similar enough to justify a similar finding.

In summary, it is my view that the authorities suggest that pure economic loss is *prima facie* recoverable where, in addition to negligence and foreseeable loss, there is sufficient proximity between the negligent act and the loss. Proximity is the controlling concept which avoids the spectre of unlimited liability. Proximity may be established by a variety of factors, depending on the nature of the case. To date, sufficient proximity has been found in the case of negligent misstatements where there is an undertaking and correlative reliance (*Hedley Byrne*); where there is a duty to warn (*Rivtow*); and where a statute imposes a responsibility on a municipality towards the owners and occupiers of land (*Kamloops*). But the categories are not closed. As more cases are decided, we can expect further definition on what factors give rise to liability for pure economic loss in particular categories of cases. In determining whether liability should be extended to a new situation, courts will have regard to the factors traditionally relevant to proximity such as the relationship between the parties, physical propinquity, assumed or imposed obligations and close causal connection. And they will insist on sufficient special factors to avoid the imposition of indeterminate and unreasonable liability. The result will be a principled, yet flexible, approach to tort liability for pure economic loss. It will allow recovery where recovery is justified, while excluding indeterminate and inappropriate liability, and it will permit the coherent development of the law in accordance with the approach initiated in England by *Hedley Byrne* and followed in Canada in *Rivtow*, *Kamloops* and *Hofstrand*.

I add the following observations on proximity. The absolute exclusionary rule adopted in *Stockton* and affirmed in *Murphy* (subject to *Hedley Byrne*) can itself be seen as an indicator of proximity. Where there is physical injury or damage, one posits proximity on the ground that if one is close enough to someone or something to do physical damage to it, one is close enough to be held legally responsible for the consequences. Physical injury has the advantage of being a clear and simple indicator of proximity. The problem arises when it is taken as the *only* indicator of proximity. As the cases amply demonstrate, the necessary proximity to found legal liability fairly in tort may well arise in circumstances where there is no physical damage.

Viewed in this way, proximity may be seen as paralleling the requirement in civil law that damages be direct and certain. Proximity, like the requirement of directness, posits a close link between the negligent act and the resultant loss. Distant losses which arise from collateral relationships do not qualify for recovery.

In many of the cases discussed above, the judiciary has focused upon the relationship between the tortfeasor and the plaintiff as an indication of proximity, a focus closely related to the foreseeability analysis inherent to all negligence actions. In the classic case of *Hedley Byrne*, the reliance analysis focused upon the connection between the party who made the negligent misstatement and the injured party, i.e., is that plaintiff a party that the tortfeasor ought reasonably to have foreseen would rely on his or her statement? The judgments below focused on the relationship between the tortfeasor Norsk and the plaintiff CN both within and outside their discussion of proximity. A more comprehensive, and I submit objective, consideration of proximity requires that the court review all of the factors connecting the negligent act with the loss; this includes not only the relationship between the parties but all forms of proximity — physical, circumstantial, causal or assumed indicators of closeness. While it is impossible to define comprehensively what will satisfy the requirements of proximity or directness, precision may be found as types of relationships or situations are defined in which the necessary closeness between negligence and loss exists.

While proximity is critical to establishing the right to recover pure economic loss in tort, it does not always indicate liability. It is a necessary but not necessarily sufficient condition of liability. Recognizing that proximity is itself concerned with policy, the approach adopted in *Kamloops* (paralleled by the second branch of *Anns*) requires the Court to consider the purposes served by permitting recovery as well as whether there are any residual policy considerations which call for a limitation on liability. This permits courts to reject liability for pure economic loss where indicated by policy reasons not taken into account in the proximity analysis.

I conclude that, from a doctrinal point of view, this Court should continue on the course charted in *Kamloops* rather than reverting to the narrow exclusionary rule as the House of Lords did in *Murphy*.

4. *Application to this case*
The plaintiff CN suffered economic loss as a result of being deprived of its contractual right to use the bridge damaged by the defendants' negligence. Applying the *Kamloops* approach, its right to recover depends on: (1) whether it can establish sufficient proximity or 'closeness', and (2) whether extension of recovery to this type of loss is desirable from a practical point of view.

The first question is whether the evidence in this case establishes the proximity necessary to found liability. The case does not fall within any of the categories where proximity and liability have been hitherto found to exist. So we must consider the matter afresh . . .

In addition to focusing upon the relationship between the appellant Norsk and CN — a significant indicator of proximity in and of itself — the trial judge based his conclusion that there was sufficient proximity on a number of factors related to CN's connection with the property damaged, the bridge, including the fact that CN's property was in close proximity to the bridge, which was an integral part of its railway system and that CN supplied materials, inspection and consulting services for the bridge, was its preponderant user, and was recognized in the periodic negotiations surrounding the closing of the bridge.

MacGuigan JA summarized the trial judge's findings on proximity as follows, at p. 167:

> In effect, the Trial Judge found that the CNR was so closely assimilated to the position of PWC that it was very much within the reasonable ambit of risk of the appellants at the time of the accident. That, it seems to me, is sufficient proximity: in Deane J's language, it is both physical and circumstantial closeness.

Such a characterization brings the situation into the 'joint' or 'common venture' category under which recovery for purely economic loss has heretofore been recognized in maritime law cases from the United Kingdom (*The Greystoke Castle*, [1947] AC 265) and the United States (*Amoco Transport,* 768 F2d 659 (1985)). The reasoning, as I apprehend it, is that where the plaintiff's operations are so closely allied to the operations of the party suffering physical damage and to its property (which — as damaged — causes the plaintiff's loss) that it can be considered a joint venturer with the owner of the property, the plaintiff can recover its economic loss even though the plaintiff has suffered no physical damage to its own property. To deny recovery in such circumstances would be to deny it to a person who for practical purposes is in the same position as if he or she owned the property physically damaged.

The second question is whether extension of recovery to this type of loss is desirable from a practical point of view. Recovery serves the purpose of permitting a plaintiff whose position for practical purposes, vis-à-vis the tortfeasor, is indistinguishable from that of the owner of the damaged property, to recover what the actual owner could have recovered. This is fair and avoids an anomalous result. Nor does the recovery of economic loss in this case open the floodgates to unlimited liability. The category is a limited one. It has been applied in England and the United States without apparent difficulty. It does not embrace casual users of the property or those secondarily and incidentally affected by the damage done to the property. Potential tortfeasors can gauge in advance the scope of their liability. Businesses are not precluded from self-insurance or from contracting for indemnity, nor are they 'penalized' for not so doing. Finally, frivolous claims are not encouraged.

I conclude that here, as in *Kamloops*, the necessary duty and proximity are established, that valid purposes are served by permitting recovery, and that recovery will not open the floodgates to unlimited liability. In such circumstances, recovery should be permitted.

Note
The above represents the view of the majority in the Supreme Court of Canada. Stevenson J decided the case in favour of the plaintiff on the basis of the *Caltex Oil* principles and La Forest J dissented on the ground that economic loss should not be recoverable where it arises out of damage to the property of a third party with whom the plaintiff has a contractual arrangement.

12 SPECIAL DUTY PROBLEMS: CONTRACT AND DUTY OF CARE

There are two classes of problem concerning the relationship of contract and tort. The first is whether there can be a duty in tort when there is a contract between the same parties, and the second is whether a contract between A and B can affect a duty owed by A to C.

The first issue has been a matter of debate for many years but now appears to have been settled by *Henderson v Merrett Syndicates* (below). There will not be many cases where it will be beneficial to sue in tort rather than contract, but there are some. These include extended limitation periods, less restricted remoteness rules, more liberal rules on suing out of the jurisdiction and different rules on contribution.

The second problem to be dealt with in this chapter occurs where a duty is owed by the defendant to the plaintiff, but the content of that duty is also the subject of a contractual relationship with a third party. Thus, where there is a contract between A and B and between B and C it may be that because of the connection, C owes a duty in tort to A. The question is whether any term in the contract between A and B or between B and C can affect the duty owed by C to A?

The problem is essentially one of privity of contract and it may be that a contractual solution to the problem is preferable. One way round privity is the use of a 'Himalaya clause' (see *The Eurymedon* [1975] AC 154) whereby C authorises B to enter into an exemption clause on his behalf in the contract between B and A, whereby the clause becomes effective between A and C. However this is of limited effect.

An example of the problem could occur if a company (A) engages a builder (B) to build an extension to its factory, and the builder engages an electrician (C) to do the electrical work. Both the main contract between the owner and the builder, and the sub-contract between the builder and the electrician contain exemption clauses excluding liability for damage caused to the main building by any work on the extension. Thus C (the electrician) has a contract with B (the builder) in relation to the same issue in relation to which he owes a duty in tort to the building owner (A). Presumably, under such an arrangement both the builder and the electrician have tendered at a lower price because they will not be bearing the risk of damage. If the electrician causes damage to the factory, would it be right in such circumstances to make him owe a higher duty in tort to A than he owes under his contract with B, or for A to have greater rights in tort against C than he has under his contract with B? The problem will only matter where for some reason the owner is unable to enforce his contractual rights against the builder, either because the builder is bankrupt or because there is an exclusion clause in the contract between them.

The problem could occur not only where there are exemption clauses, but also where there are other terms which might affect the degree of care owed. In relation to the example above, suppose the main contract between the factory owner (A) and the builder (B), stipulates that wire of a certain thickness be used, and this is installed by the electrician (C). If the wire turns out to be too thin and causes a fire, could A turn round and sue C for installing inadequate wire? Should not the terms of the contract between A and B determine the degree of care owed by C to A?

For a proposed solution to the problems discussed in this chapter see Adams and Brownsword, 'Privity and the concept of a network contract' (1990) 10 LS 12.

Section 1: concurrent liability

Henderson v Merrett Syndicates
House of Lords [1995] 2 AC 145; [1994] 3 WLR 761; [1994] 3 All ER 506; [1994] 2 Lloyds Rep 468

The plaintiffs were Lloyd's underwriters (names) who were suing defendants for the negligent management of syndicates to which they belonged. Sometimes the names' agents themselves managed the syndicate which made the names 'direct names'. In other cases the names' agent placed the name in a syndicate managed by a different agent by way of a sub-agency agreement. These were 'indirect names'. The names wished to take advantage of more liberal limitation periods in tort and thus the question arose whether there could be liability in tort at the same time as there were contractual relationships in place between the parties. Held: dismissing the appeal, that the defendants were liable in tort to both the direct and indirect names.

LORD GOFF: . . .

The impact of the contractual context
All systems of law which recognise a law of contract and a law of tort (or delict) have to solve the problem of the possibility of concurrent claims arising from breach of duty under the two rubrics of the law. Although there are variants, broadly speaking two possible solutions present themselves: either to insist that the claimant should pursue his

remedy in contract alone, or to allow him to choose which remedy he prefers. As my noble and learned friend, Lord Mustill, and I have good reason to know (see *J. Bracconot et Cie* v *Compagnie des Messageries Maritimes (The Sindh)* [1975] 1 Lloyd's Rep 372), France has adopted the former solution in its doctrine of non cumul, under which the concurrence of claims in contract and tort is outlawed (see Tony Weir in XI *Int. Encycl. Comp. L.*, ch. 12. paras. 47–72, at para. 52). The reasons given for this conclusion are (1) respect for the will of the legislator, and (2) respect for the will of the parties to the contract (see: para. 53). The former does not concern us; but the latter is of vital importance. It is however open to various interpretations. For such a policy does not necessarily require the total rejection of concurrence, but only so far as a concurrent remedy in tort is inconsistent with the terms of the contract. It comes therefore as no surprise to learn that the French doctrine is not followed in all civil law jurisdictions, and that concurrent remedies in tort and contract are permitted in other civil law countries, notably Germany (see: para. 58). I only pause to observe that it appears to be accepted that no perceptible harm has come to the German system from admitting concurrent claims.

The situation in common law countries, including of course England, is exceptional, in that the common law grew up within a procedural framework uninfluenced by Roman law. The law was categorised by reference to the forms of action, and it was not until the abolition of the forms of action by the Common Law Procedure Act 1852 (15 & 16 Vict. c. 76) that it became necessary to reclassify the law in substantive terms. The result was that common lawyers did at last segregate our law of obligations into contract and tort, though in so doing they relegated quasi-contractual claims to the status of an appendix to the law of contract, thereby postponing by a century or so the development of a law of restitution. Even then, there was no systematic reconsideration of the problem of concurrent claims in contract and tort. We can see the courts rather grappling with unpromising material drawn from the old cases in which liability in negligence derived largely from categories based upon the status of the defendant. In a sense, we must not be surprised; for no significant law faculties were established at our universities until the late 19th century, and so until then there was no academic opinion available to guide or stimulate the judges. Even so, it is a remarkable fact that there was little consideration of the problem of concurrent remedies in our academic literature until the second half of the 20th century, though in recent years the subject has attracted considerable attention.

In the result, the courts in this country have until recently grappled with the problem very largely without the assistance of systematic academic study. At first, as is shown in particular by cases concerned with liability for solicitors' negligence, the courts adopted something very like the French solution, holding that a claim against a solicitor for negligence must pursued in contract, and not in tort (see, e.g., *Bean* v *Wade* (1885) 2 TLR 157); and in *Groom* v *Crocker* [1939] 1 KB 194, this approach was firmly adopted.
. . .

Moreover I myself perceive at work in these decisions not only the influence of the dead hand of history, but also what I have elsewhere called the temptation of elegance. Mr Tony Weir (XI *Int. Encycl. Comp. L.* ch. 12., para. 55) has extolled the French solution for its elegance, and we can discern the same impulse behind the much-quoted observation of Lord Scarman when delivering the judgment of the Judicial Committee of the Privy Council in *Tai Hing Cotton Mill Ltd* v *Liu Chong Hing Bank Ltd* [1986] AC 80, 107:

> their Lordships do not believe that there is anything to the advantage of the law's
> development in searching for a liability in tort where the parties are in a contractual

relationship. This is particularly so in a commercial relationship. Though it is possible as a matter of legal semantics to conduct an analysis of the rights and duties inherent in some contractual relationships including that of banker and customer either as a matter of contract law when the question will be what, if any, terms are to be implied or as a matter of tort law when the task will be to identify a duty arising from the proximity and character of the relationship between the parties, their Lordships believe it to be correct in principle and necessary for the avoidance of confusion in the law to adhere to the contractual analysis: on principle because it is a relationship in which the parties have, subject to a few exceptions, the right to determine their obligations to each other, and for the avoidance of confusion because different consequences do follow according to whether liability arises from contract or tort, e.g. in the limitation of action.

It is however right to stress, as did Sir Thomas Bingham MR in the present case, that the issue in the *Tai Hing* case was whether a tortious duty of care could be established which was more extensive than that which was provided for under the relevant contract. . . .

The judgment of Oliver J in the *Midland Bank Trust Co.* case [1979] Ch 384 provided the first analysis in depth of the question of concurrent liability in tort and contract. Following upon *Esso Petroleum Co. Ltd* v *Mardon* [1976] QB 801, it also broke the mould, in the sense that it undermined the view which was becoming settled that, where there is an alternative liability in tort, the claimant must pursue his remedy in contract alone. The development of the case law in other common law countries is very striking. In the same year as the *Midland Bank Trust Co.* case, the Irish Supreme Court held that solicitors owed to their clients concurrent duties in contract and tort: see *Finley* v *Murtagh* [1979] IR 249. Next, in *Central Trust Co.* v *Rafuse* (1986) 31 DLR (4th) 481, Le Dain J, delivering the judgment of the Supreme Court of Canada, conducted a comprehensive and most impressive survey of the relevant English and Canadian authorities on the liability of solicitors to their clients for negligence, in contract and in tort, in the course of which he paid a generous tribute to the analysis of Oliver J in the *Midland Bank Trust Co.* case. His conclusions are set out in a series of propositions at pp. 521–522; but his general conclusion was to the same effect as that reached by Oliver J. He said, at p. 522:

> A concurrent or alternative liability in tort will not be admitted if its effect would be to permit the plaintiff to circumvent or escape a contractual exclusion or limitation of liability for the act or omission that would constitute the tort. Subject to this qualification, where concurrent liability in tort and contract exists the plaintiff has the right to assert the cause of action that appears to be the most advantageous to him in respect of any particular legal consequences.

I respectfully agree. . . .

So far as *Hedley Byrne* itself is concerned, Mr Kaye ['Liability of Solicitors in Tort' (1984) 100 LQR 84] reads the speeches as restricting the principle of assumption of responsibility there established to cases where there is no contract; indeed, on this he tolerates no dissent, stating (at p. 706) that 'unless one reads [*Hedley Byrne*] with deliberate intent to find obscure or ambiguous passages' it will not bear the interpretation favoured by Oliver J. I must confess however that, having studied yet again the speeches in *Hedley Byrne* [1964] AC 465 in the light of Mr Kaye's critique, I remain of the opinion that Oliver J's reading of them is justified. It is, I suspect, a matter of the angle of vision with which they are read. For here, I consider, Oliver J was influenced not only by what he read in the speeches themselves, notably the passage from Lord

Devlin's speech at pp. 528–529 (quoted above), but also by the internal logic reflected in that passage, which led inexorably to the conclusion which he drew. Mr Kaye's approach involves regarding the law of tort as supplementary to the law of contract, i.e. as providing for a tortious liability in cases where there is no contract. Yet the law of tort is the general law, out of which the parties can, if they wish, contract; and, as Oliver J demonstrated, the same assumption of responsibility may, and frequently does, occur in a contractual context. Approached as a matter of principle, therefore, it is right to attribute to that assumption of responsibility, together with its concomitant reliance, a tortious liability, and then to inquire whether or not that liability is excluded by the contract because the latter is inconsistent with it. This is the reasoning which Oliver J, as I understand it, found implicit, where not explicit, in the speeches in *Hedley Byrne*. With his conclusion I respectfully agree. But even if I am wrong in this, I am of the opinion that this House should now, if necessary, develop the principle of assumption of responsibility as stated in *Hedley Byrne* to its logical conclusion so as to make it clear that a tortious duty of care may arise not only in cases where the relevant services are rendered gratuitously, but also where they are rendered under a contract. This indeed is the view expressed by my noble and learned friend, Lord Keith of Kinkel, in *Murphy* v *Brentwood District Council* [1991] 1 AC 398, 466, in a speech with which all the other members of the Appellate Committee agreed.

An alternative approach, which also avoids the concurrence of tortious and contractual remedies, is to be found in the judgment of Deane J, in *Hawkins* v *Clayton*, 164 CLR 539, 582–586, in which he concluded, at p. 585:

> On balance, however, it seems to me to be preferable to accept that there is neither justification nor need for the implication of a contractual term which, in the absence of actual intention of the parties, imposes upon a solicitor a contractual duty (with consequential liability in damages for its breach) which is coextensive in content and concurrent in operation with a duty (with consequential liability in damages for its breach) which already exists under the common law of negligence.

It is however my understanding that by the law in this country contracts for services do contain an implied promise to exercise reasonable care (and skill) in the performance of the relevant services; indeed, as Mr Tony Weir has pointed out (XI *Int. Encycl. Comp. L.*, ch. 12, para. 67), in the 19th century the field of concurrent liabilities was expanded 'since it was impossible for the judges to deny that contracts contained an implied promise to take reasonable care, at the least not to injure the other party.' My own belief is that, in the present context, the common law is not antipathetic to concurrent liability, and that there is no sound basis for a rule which automatically restricts the claimant to either a tortious or a contractual remedy. The result may be untidy; but, given that the tortious duty is imposed by the general law, and the contractual duty is attributable to the will of the parties, I do not find it objectionable that the claimant may be entitled to take advantage of the remedy which is most advantageous to him, subject only to ascertaining whether the tortious duty is so inconsistent with the applicable contract that, in accordance with ordinary principle, the parties must be taken to have agreed that the tortious remedy is to be limited or excluded.

In the circumstances of the present case, I have not regarded it as necessary or appropriate to embark upon yet another detailed analysis of the case law, choosing rather to concentrate on those authorities which appear to me to be here most important. I have been most anxious not to overburden an inevitably lengthy opinion with a discussion of an issue which is only one (though an important one) of those which fall for decision; and, in the context of the relationship of solicitor and client, the task of surveying the authorities has already been admirably performed by both Oliver J and Le Dain J. But, for the present purposes more important, in the present case liability can, and in my opinion should, be founded squarely on the principle established in *Hedley Byrne* itself, from which it follows that an assumption of responsibility coupled with the concomitant reliance may give rise to a tortious duty of care irrespective of whether there is a contractual relationship between the parties, and in consequence, unless his contract precludes him from doing so, the plaintiff, who has available to him concurrent remedies in contract and tort, may choose that remedy which appears to him to be the most advantageous.

Note
This case decides that there is no reason in principle why there should not be concurrent liability in contract and tort. Usually, the substantive liability derived from an implied term will be the same as the tort duty, but this need not be so. As was said in *Holt* v *Payne Shillington, The Times*, 22 December 1995, the duties may be concurrent but need not be co-extensive. 'The difference in scope between the two would reflect the more limited factual basis which gave rise to the contract and the absence of any term in the contract which precluded or restricted the duty of care in tort.'

Section 2:   liability to third parties

The Aliakmon: Leigh and Sillavan Ltd v *Aliakmon Ltd*

The plaintiffs bought coils of steel from Japanese sellers which were shipped aboard *The Aliakmon*, owned by the defendants. During the voyage the steel was damaged due to poor ventilation and storage. There was a contract of carriage between the defendant shipowners and the sellers, and a contract of sale between the sellers and the plaintiff buyers. For various reasons the contractual arrangements meant that the sellers retained title to the steel, whereas the risk of its being damaged was upon the buyers. In the event it was held by both the Court of Appeal and the House of Lords that, as the buyers did not own the steel at the time of its damage, they had suffered only pure economic loss and could not sue. One complication was that the contract between the defendant shipowners and the sellers was subject to the terms of the bill of lading, and this incorporated internationally agreed terms which limited the liability of the shipowner (the Hague rules). Hence, one issue was, assuming the shipowners could be liable to the buyers (which they were not), would their liability be subject to the Hague rules contained in the contract between the shipowners and the sellers? Held: that both the Court of Appeal and the House of Lords doubted that the duty in tort could be limited in this way, and this was one factor in deciding against the buyers.

Court of Appeal
[1985] 1 QB 350; [1985] 2 All ER 44; [1985] 2 WLR 289

SIR JOHN DONALDSON MR: Mr Sumption's second and third considerations can be taken together. They are:

The existence of a duty of care owed to others than the owners of cargo would impose on a shipowner most of the liabilities which he will generally assume by contract by virtue of the Hague Rules without the protection which those Rules afford and which it is recognised as a matter of international and domestic public policy that he should have.

And:

> if it be accepted that a shipowner is liable to others than the owners of the goods at the relevant time, then he is potentially exposed to liability to anyone who may suffer loss because the nature of his contractual arrangements prevent him from recovering from anyone other than the shipowner, e.g., the purchaser (whenever the purchase occurs) of goods suffering from a latent defect acquired on board ship, or of goods sold 'as is where is.'

Mr Sumption might, perhaps, have added that without some limitation the shipowner would also be liable to cargo underwriters, although Mr Clarke, who has appeared for the plaintiff buyers, did not seek to contend that the shipowner's liability was as extensive as this.

I find these considerations wholly compelling. The relationship between buyer and seller on the one hand and cargo-owner and shipowner on the other are quite distinct. In each case the parties seek to establish an economic balance, but there is no reason why it should be the same balance. The buyer may well be able to obtain the goods more cheaply if he undertakes not to hold the seller liable if the goods are lost or damaged after shipment and before they are delivered to him and to pay the price in any event. The shipowner may well charge a lower freight if, in return, he is to enjoy the protection of exceptions and limitations upon his liability. Indeed he may be unwilling to accept the goods for carriage at all, if to do so will involve him in assuming any more extended duty of care or more extended liability for breach of that duty.

In the instant case the buyers claim the right to impose upon the shipowners a higher duty of care than the shipowners owed to the seller under the bill of lading contract or, as the case may be, the charter and to do so without the shipowners' leave or licence, by means of a contract with the sellers.

I have, of course, considered whether any duty of care owed in tort to the buyer could in some way be equated to the contractual duty of care owed to the shipper, but I do not see how this could be done. The commonest form of contract of carriage by sea is one on the terms of the Hague Rules. But this is an intricate blend of responsibilities and liabilities (Article III), rights and immunities (Article IV), limitations in the amount of damages recoverable (Article IV, r. 5), time bars (Article III, r. 6), evidential provisions (Article III, rr. 4 and 6), indemnities (Article III, r. 5 and Article IV, r. 6) and liberties (Article IV, rr. 4 and 6). I am quite unable to see how these can be synthesised into a standard of care.

House of Lords
[1986] AC 785; [1986] 2 WLR 902; [1986] 2 All ER 145

LORD BRANDON: Mr Clarke sought to rely also on *Junior Books Ltd* v *Veitchi Co. Ltd* [1983] 1 AC 520. That was a case in which it was held by a majority of your Lordships' House that, when a nominated sub-contractor was employed by a head contractor under the standard form of RIBA building contract, the sub-contractor was not only under a contractual obligation to the head contractor, under the sub-contract between them, not to lay a defective factory floor, but also owed a duty of care in tort to the building owner not to do so and thereby cause him economic loss. The decision is of no direct help to the buyers in the present case, for the plaintiffs who were held to have a good cause of action in negligence in respect of a defective floor were the legal owners of it. But Mr Clarke relied on certain observations in the speech of Lord Roskill as supporting the proposition that a duty of care in tort might, as he submitted it should be in the present case, be qualified by reference to the terms of a contract to which the defendant was not a party. In this connection Lord Roskill said, at p. 546:

> During the argument it was asked what the position would be in a case when there was a relevant exclusion clause in the main contract. My Lords, that question does not arise for decision in the instant appeal, but in principle I would venture the view that such a claim according to the manner in which it was worded might in some circumstances limit the duty of care just as in the *Hedley Byrne* case the plaintiffs were ultimately defeated by the defendants' disclaimer of responsibility.

As is apparent this observation was no more than an obiter dictum. Moreover, with great respect to Lord Roskill there is no analogy between the disclaimer in *Hedley Byrne & Co. Ltd* v *Heller & Partners Ltd* [1964] AC 465, which operated directly between the plaintiffs and the defendants, and an exclusion of liability clause in a contract to which the plaintiff is a party but the defendant is not. I do not therefore find in the observation of Lord Roskill relied on any convincing legal basis for qualifying a duty of care owed by A to B by reference to a contract to which A is, but B is not, a party.

As I said earlier, Mr Clarke submitted that your Lordships should hold that a duty of care did exist in the present case, but that it was subject to the terms of the bill of lading. With regard to this suggestion Sir John Donaldson MR said in the present case [1985] QB 350, 368: [His Lordship quoted from the extract above.]

I find myself suffering from the same inability to understand how the necessary synthesis could be made as the Master of the Rolls . . .

Ground (5): the judgment of Robert Goff LJ
My Lords, after a full examination of numerous authorities relating to the law of negligence Robert Goff LJ (now Lord Goff of Chieveley) said [1985] QB 350, 399:

> In my judgment, there is no good reason in principle or in policy, why the c. and f. buyer should not have . . . a direct cause of action. The factors which I have already listed point strongly towards liability. I am particularly influenced by the fact that the loss in question is of a character which will ordinarily fall on the goods owner who will have a good claim against the shipowner, but in a case such as the present the loss may, in practical terms, fall on the buyer. It seems to me that the policy reasons pointing towards a direct right of action by the buyer against the shipowner in a case of this kind outweigh the policy reasons which generally preclude recovery for purely economic loss. There is no question of any wide or indeterminate liability being imposed on wrongdoers; on the contrary, the shipowner is simply held liable to the buyer in damages for loss for which he would ordinarily be liable to the goods owner. There is a recognisable principle underlying the imposition of liability, which can be called the principle of transferred loss. Further, that principle can be formulated. For the purposes of the present case, I would formulate it in the following deliberately narrow terms, while recognising that it may require modification in the light of experience. Where A owes a duty of care in tort not to cause physical damage to B's property, and commits a breach of that duty in circumstances in which the loss of or physical damage to the property will ordinarily fall on B but (as is reasonably foreseeable by A) such loss or damage, by reason of a contractual relationship

between B and C, falls upon C, then C will be entitled, subject to the terms of any contract restricting A's liability to B, to bring an action in tort against A in respect of such loss or damage to the extent that it falls on him, C. To that proposition there must be exceptions. In particular, there must, for the reasons I have given, be an exception in the case of contracts of insurance. I have also attempted to draw the principle as to exclude the case of the time charterer who remains liable for hire for the chartered ship while under repair following collision damage, though this could if necessary be treated as another exception having regard to the present state of the authorities.

With the greatest possible respect to Lord Goff the principle of transferred loss which he there enunciated, however useful in dealing with special factual situations it may be in theory, is not only not supported by authority, but is on the contrary inconsistent with it. Even if it were necessary to introduce such a principle in order to fill a genuine lacuna in the law, I should myself, perhaps because I am more faint-hearted than Lord Goff, be reluctant to do so. As I have tried to show earlier, however, there is in truth no such lacuna in the law which requires to be filled. Neither Sir John Donaldson MR nor Oliver LJ (now Lord Oliver of Aylmerton) was prepared to accept the introduction of such a principle and I find myself entirely in agreement with their unwillingness to do so.

Note
The problem here is essentially one of privity of contract. Under normal circumstances in international trade, the bill of lading would have been transferred from the seller to the buyer, putting the buyer into a contractual relationship with the shipowner by virtue of what is now the Carriage of Goods by Sea Act 1992. Thus the problem arose only because things did not work out as planned, and this would occur only rarely. However, the point of the judgments is that, as the shipowner should not be under any greater obligation to the buyer in tort than he is to the seller under the contract, and as the terms of the contract cannot be easily translated into a duty of care, therefore no duty at all should be owed to the buyer.

White v Jones
[1995] 2 AC 207; [1995] 2 WLR 187; [1995] 1 All ER 691

In 1986 the testator cut his daughters out of his will, but he later relented and in July he instructed the defendant solicitors to draw up a new will giving the daughters £9,000 each. The new will had not been drawn up by 14 September when the testator died. The daughters sued the solicitors. It was held that the solicitors were liable on the *Hedley Byrne* principle (see Chapter 10), but the extracts below deal with contractual issues which arose. The particular difficulty arises where A makes a contract with B and B's breach of contract causes loss to C but not to A. In pure contract A could sue but has suffered no loss, whereas C has suffered loss but cannot sue because of lack of privity with B.

LORD GOFF: . . .

Transferred loss in English law
I can deal with this topic briefly. The problem of transferred loss has arisen in particular in maritime law, when a buyer of goods seeks to enforce against a shipowner a remedy

in tort in respect of loss of or damage to goods at his risk when neither the rights under the contract nor the property in the goods has passed to him (see *Leigh and Sillavan Ltd* v *Aliakmon Shipping Co. Ltd* [1985] QB 350, 399, *per* Robert Goff LJ and [1986] AC 785, 820, *per* Lord Brandon of Oakbrook). In cases such as these (with all respect to the view expressed by Lord Brandon [1986] AC 785, 819) there was a serious lacuna in the law, as was revealed when all relevant interests in the city of London called for reform to make a remedy available to the buyers who under the existing law were without a direct remedy against the shipowners. The problem was solved, as a matter of urgency, by the Carriage of Goods by Sea Act 1992, I myself having the honour of introducing the Bill into your Lordships' House (acting in its legislative capacity) on behalf of the Law Commission. The solution adopted by the Act was to extend the rights of suit available under section 1 of the Bills of Lading Act 1855 (there restricted to cases where the property in the goods had passed upon or by reason of the consignment or endorsement of the relevant bill of lading) to all holders of bills of lading (and indeed other documents): see section 9(1) of the Act of 1992. Here is a sweeping statutory reform, powered by the needs of commerce, which has the effect of enlarging the circumstances in which contractual rights may be transferred by virtue of the transfer of certain documents. For present purposes, however, an important consequence is the solution in this context of a problem of transferred loss, the lacuna being filled by statute rather than by the common law. Moreover this result has been achieved, as in German law, by vesting in the plaintiff, who has suffered the relevant loss, the contractual rights of the person who has stipulated for the carrier's obligation but has suffered no loss.

I turn next to English law in relation to cases such as the present. Here there is a lacuna in the law, in the sense that practical justice requires that the disappointed beneficiary should have a remedy against the testator's solicitor in circumstances in which neither the testator nor his estate has in law suffered a loss. Professor Lorenz (*Essays in Memory of Professor F. H. Lawson*, p. 90) has said that 'this is a situation which comes very close to the cases of "transferred loss," the only difference being that the damage due to the solicitor's negligence could never have been caused to the testator or to his executor.' In the case of the testator, he suffers no loss because (in contrast to a gift by an inter vivos settlor) a gift under a will cannot take effect until after the testator's death, and it follows that there can be no depletion of the testator's assets in his lifetime if the relevant asset is, through the solicitors' negligence, directed to a person other than the intended beneficiary. The situation is therefore not one in which events have subsequently occurred which have resulted in the loss falling on another. It is one in which the relevant loss could never fall on the testator to whom the solicitor owed a duty, but only on another; and the loss which is suffered by that other, i.e. an expectation loss, is of a character which in any event could never have been suffered by the testator. Strictly speaking, therefore, this is not a case of transferred loss.

Even so, the analogy is very close. In practical terms, part or all of the testator's estate has been lost because it has been dispatched to a destination unintended by the testator. Moreover, had a gift been similarly misdirected during the testator's lifetime, he would either have been able to recover it from the recipient or, if not, he could have recovered the full amount from the negligent solicitor as damages. In a case such as the present, no such remedies are available to the testator or his estate. The will cannot normally be rectified: the testator has of course no remedy: and his estate has suffered no loss, because it has been distributed under the terms of a valid will. In these circumstances, there can be no injustice if the intended beneficiary has a remedy against the solicitor for the full amount which he should have received under the will, this being no greater than the damage for which the solicitor could have been liable to the donor if the loss had occurred in his lifetime.

A contractual approach
It may be suggested that, in cases such as the present, the simplest course would be to solve the problem by making available to the disappointed beneficiary, by some means or another, the benefit of the contractual rights (such as they are) of the testator or his estate against the negligent solicitor, as is for example done under the German principle of Vertrag mit Schutzwirkung für Dritte. Indeed that course has been urged upon us by Professor Markesinis, 103 LQR 354, 396–397, echoing a view expressed by Professor Fleming in (1986) 4 OJLS 235, 241. Attractive though this solution is, there is unfortunately a serious difficulty in its way. The doctrine of consideration still forms part of our law of contract, as does the doctrine of privity of contract which is considered to exclude the recognition of a jus quaesitum tertio. To proceed as Professor Markesinis has suggested may be acceptable in German law, but in this country could be open to criticism as an illegitimate circumvention of these long established doctrines; and this criticism could be reinforced by reference to the fact that, in the case of carriage of goods by sea, a contractual solution to a particular problem of transferred loss, and to other cognate problems, was provided only by recourse to Parliament. Furthermore, I myself do not consider that the present case provides a suitable occasion for reconsideration of doctrines so fundamental as these.

The Albazero principle
Even so, I have considered whether the present problem might be solved by adding cases such as the present to the group of cases referred to by Lord Diplock in *The Albazero* [1977] AC 774, 846–847. In these cases, a person may exceptionally sue in his own name to recover a loss which he has not in fact suffered, being personally accountable for any damages so recovered to the person who has in fact suffered the loss. Lord Diplock was prepared to accommodate within this group the so-called rule in *Dunlop* v *Lambert* (1839) 6 Cl & F 600, on the principle that:

> in a commercial contract concerning goods where it is in the contemplation of the parties that the proprietary interests in the goods may be transferred from one owner to another after the contract has been entered into and before the breach which causes loss or damage to the goods, an original party to the contract, if such be the intention of them both, is to be treated *in law* as having entered into the contract for the benefit of all persons who have or may acquire an interest in the goods before they are lost or damaged, and is entitled to recover by way of damages for breach of contract the actual loss sustained by those for whose benefit the contract is entered into. (Emphasis supplied.)

Furthermore in *Linden Gardens Trust* v *Lenesto Sludge Disposals Ltd* [1994] 1 AC 85, your Lordships' House extended this group of cases to include a case in which work was done by the defendants under a contract with the first plaintiffs who, despite a contractual bar against assignment of their contractual rights without the consent of the defendants, had without consent assigned them to the second plaintiffs who suffered damage by reason of defective work carried out by the defendants. It was held that, by analogy with the cases referred to in *The Albazero* [1977] AC 774 the first plaintiffs could recover the damages from the defendants for the benefit of the second plaintiffs. In so holding, your Lordships' House relied upon a passage in Lord Diplock's speech, at p. 847:

> there may still be occasional cases in which the rule [in *Dunlop* v *Lambert*] would provide a remedy where no other would be available to a person sustaining loss which

under a rational legal system ought to be compensated by the person who has caused it.

The decision is noteworthy in a number of respects. First, this was a case of transferred loss; and Lord Diplock's dictum, as applied by your Lordships' House, reflects a clear need for the law to find a remedy in cases of this kind. Second, your Lordships' House felt able to do so in a case in which there was a contractual bar against assignment without consent: and as a result, unlike Lord Diplock, did not find it necessary to look for a common intention that the contract was entered into for the benefit of persons such as the second plaintiffs, which in this case, having regard to the prohibition against assignment, it plainly was not. Third, the consequence was that your Lordships' House simply made the remedy available as a matter of law in order to solve the problem of transferred loss in the case before them.

Even so, the result was only to enable a person to recover damages in respect of loss which he himself had not suffered, for the benefit of a third party. In the present case, there is the difficulty that the third party (the intended beneficiary) is seeking to recover damages for a loss (expectation loss) which the contracting party (the testator) would not himself have suffered. In any event, under this principle, the third party who has suffered the loss is not able to compel the contracting party to sue for his benefit, or to transfer the right of action to him; still less is he entitled to sue in his own name. In the last analysis, this is because any such right would be contrary to the doctrine of privity of contract. In consequence a principle such as this, if it could be extended to cases such as the present, would be of limited value because, quite apart from any other difficulties, the family relationship may be such that the executors may be unwilling to assist the disappointed beneficiary by pursuing a claim of this kind for his benefit. Certainly, it could not assist the plaintiffs in the present case, who very understandably are proceeding against the solicitors by a direct action in their own name.

Note
Again, this is a privity problem but the House of Lords was unwilling to change such a fundamental contract doctrine and preferred to use tort to solve the problem (see Chapter 10 for the tort aspects of this case). The Law Commission looked at privity in 1991 (Consultation Paper No. 121) and concluded that a third party should only be able to enforce a contract where the parties intended that he should receive the benefit and also intended to create a legal obligation enforceable by him. It follows that the creation of a right should not be inferred from the mere fact that he will derive a benefit from performance of the contract (para. 5.10). On the specific problem of disappointed beneficiaries they expressed no view (para. 5.44), although the general principle suggested above would rule out a contractual claim.

Questions
1. Considering the point in *The Aliakmon*, what would have happened in *White* v *Jones* if either the solicitor had excluded liability for any delay or the testator had agreed that the matter could wait until the clerk returned from his holidays? (See the speech of Lord Goff in Chapter 10.)
2. If a contract between A and B is ineffective to give C any contractual rights, why should the terms of that contract affect the duty of care?

Simaan Contracting Co. v *Pilkington Glass*
Court of Appeal [1988] QB 758; [1988] 1 All ER 791; [1988] 2 WLR 761

Simaan had a contract with Sheikh Al-Oteiba to build a building in Abu Dhabi. The erection of some curtain walling was sub-contracted to a company called Feal. Feal contracted with Pilkington for the supply of certain coloured glass. The glass was defective, in that it was the wrong colour, and the Sheikh withheld money from Simaan, the main contractor. Simaan sued Pilkington in tort for negligently causing the withholding of the money. Held: that this was pure economic loss and not recoverable. The extracts below deal with the possible effects of the contractual arrangements on any duty of care.

BINGHAM LJ: . . . I do not think it just and reasonable to impose on the defendants a duty of care towards the plaintiffs of the scope contended for. (a) Just as equity remedied the inadequacies of the common law, so has the law of torts filled gaps left by other causes of action where the interests of justice so required. I see no such gap here, because there is no reason why claims beginning with the Sheikh should not be pursued down the contractual chain, subject to any short-cut which may be agreed upon, ending up with a contractual claim against the defendants. That is the usual procedure. It must be what the parties contemplated when they made their contracts. I see no reason for departing from it. (b) Although the defendants did not sell subject to exempting conditions, I fully share the difficulty which others have envisaged where there were such conditions. Even as it is, the defendants' sale may well have been subject to terms and conditions imported by the Sale of Goods Act 1979. Some of those are beneficial to the seller. If such terms are to circumscribe a duty which would be otherwise owed to a party not a party to the contract and unaware of its terms, then that could be unfair to him. But if the duty is unaffected by the conditions on which the seller supplied the goods, it is in my view unfair to him and makes a mockery of contractual negotiation.

DILLON LJ: It might at first glance seem reasonable that, if the plaintiffs have a right of action in contract against Feal and Feal has in respect of the same general factual matters a claim in contract — albeit a different contract — against the defendants, the plaintiffs should be allowed a direct claim against the defendants. But in truth to allow the plaintiffs a direct claim against the defendants where there is no contract between them would give rise to formidable difficulties.

If the plaintiffs have a direct claim against the defendants so equally or a fortiori has the Sheikh. Feal has its claim in contract also. All three claims should be raised in separate proceedings, whether by way of arbitration or litigation, and possibly in separate jurisdictions. The difficulties of awarding damages to any one claimant would be formidable, in view of the differing amounts of retentions by the Sheikh against the plaintiffs and by the plaintiffs against Feal and other possibilities of set off, and in view, even more, of the fact that none of the parties has yet actually incurred the major cost of replacing the defendants' (assumedly) defective glass panels with new panels of the correct colour. It would not be practicable, in my view, for the court to award damages against the defendants in a global sum for all possible claimants and for the court subsequently to apportion that fund between all claimants and administer it accordingly.

Moreover, if in principle it were to be established in this case that a main contractor or an owner has a direct claim in tort against the nominated supplier to a sub-contractor for economic loss occasioned by defects in the quality of the goods supplied, the formidable question would arise, in future cases if not in this case, as to how far exempting clauses in the contract between the nominated supplier and the sub-contractor were to be imported into the supposed duty in tort owed by the supplier to those higher up the chain. Such difficulties were dismissed by Lord Brandon in *Leigh and Sillavan Ltd* v *Aliakmon Shipping Co. Ltd* [1986] 785, 817-819, and provided, as I read his speech, part of his reasoning for maintaining the established principle which I have set out at the beginning of his judgment.

If, by contrast, the court does not extend — and in my judgment it would be an extension — the principle of the *Hedley Byrne* case [1964] AC 465 to cover a direct claim by the plaintiffs against the defendants, no party will be left without a remedy, by English law at any rate, which is the only system of law we have been asked to consider. There will be the 'normal chain of liability,' as Lord Pearce called it in *Young & Marten Ltd* v *McManus Childs Ltd* [1969] 1 AC 454, 470, in that the Sheikh can sue the plaintiffs on the main building contract, the plaintiffs can sue Feal on the sub-contract and Feal can sue the defendants. Each liability would be determined in the light of such exemptions as applied contractually at that stage. There is thus no warrant for extending the law of negligence to impose direct liability on the defendants in favour of the plaintiffs.

Note
A somewhat similar situation arose in *Greater Nottingham Co-operative Society* v *Cementation Piling and Foundations Ltd* [1989] QB 71, but it was resolved by rather different means. There, a contract was entered into between the plaintiffs, Nottingham Co-op, and main contractors, Shepherd Constructions, who in turn sub-contracted piling work to the defendants, Cementation. The piling work was negligently done, but what made this case different was that there was a direct collateral contract between the plaintiffs and the sub-contractors. Thus this was in effect a two-party and not a three-party case, and hence the relationship between the plantiffs and the sub-contractors was governed by the collateral contract, and tort duties were irrelevant. Mann LJ said 'I ask myself whether it is just and reasonable to impose a duty in tort where the parties are united by a contract which is notably silent upon the liability which it is sought to enforce by tort. In my judgment it is not', and he cited Cumming-Bruce LJ who said, in *William Hill* v *Bernard Sunley & Sons* (1982) 22 BLR 1, that 'the plaintiffs are not entitled to claim a remedy in tort which is wider than the obligations assumed by the defendants under their contract'.

Norwich City Council v *Harvey*
Court of Appeal [1989] 1 WLR 828; [1989] 1 All ER 1180

Norwich City Council, the plaintiffs, entered into a contract with Bush Builders (Norwich) Ltd to build an extension to the swimming pool at St Augustines. They in turn entered into a sub-contract with Briggs Amasco, the second defendant, for some roofing work. One of their employees, the first defendant, while using a blow torch, set fire to the building, damaging both the new and the existing structures. Clause 20[C] of the main contract stated that the existing structures 'shall be at the sole risk of the employer [i.e.

Norwich Council] as regards loss or damage by fire and the employer shall maintain adequate insurance against those risks.' The sub-contract incorporated the terms of the main contract. The plaintiffs sued both the subcontractors and their employee. Held: dismissing the appeal, that the defendants were not liable.

MAY LJ: I trust I do no injustice to the plaintiff's argument in this appeal if I put it shortly in this way. There is no dispute between the employer and the main contractor that the former accepted the risk of fire damage: see *James Archdale & Co. Ltd* v *Comservices Ltd* [1954] 1 WLR 459 and *Scottish Special Housing Association* v *Wimpey Construction UK Ltd* [1986] 1 WLR 995. However clause 20[C] does not give rise to any obligation on the employer to indemnify the subcontractor. That clause is primarily concerned to see that the works were completed. It was intended to operate only for the mutual benefit of the employer and the main contractor. If the judge and the subcontractor are right, the latter obtains protection which the rules of privity do not provide. Undoubtedly the subcontractor owed duties of care in respect of damage by fire to other persons and in respect of other property (for instance the lawful visitor, employees of the employer, or other buildings outside the site); in those circumstances it is impracticable juridically to draw a sensible line between the plaintiff on the one hand and others on the other to whom a duty of care was owed. The employer had no effective control over the terms upon which the relevant subcontract was let and no direct contractual control over either the subcontractor or any employee of its.

In addition, the plaintiff pointed to the position of the first defendant, the subcontractor's employee. Ex hypothesi he was careless and even if his employer be held to have owed no duty to the building employer, on what grounds can it be said that the employee himself owed no such duty? In my opinion, however, this particular point does not take the matter very much further. If in principle the subcontractor owed no specific duty to the building owner in respect of damage by fire, then neither in my opinion can any of its employees have done so.

In reply the defendants contend that the judge was right to hold that in all the circumstances there was no duty of care on the subcontractor in this case. Alternatively they submit that the employer's insurers have no right of subrogation to entitle them to maintain this litigation against the subcontractor. . . .

In my opinion the present state of the law on the question whether or not a duty of care exists is that, save where there is already good authority that in the circumstances there is such a duty, it will only exist in novel situations where not only is there foreseeability of harm, but also such a close and direct relation between the parties concerned, not confined to mere physical proximity, to the extent contemplated by Lord Atkin in his speech in *Donoghue* v *Stevenson* [1932] AC 562. Further, a court should also have regard to what it considers just and reasonable in all the circumstances and facts of the case.

In the instant case it is clear that as between the plaintiff and the main contractor the former accepted the risk of damage by fire to its premises arising out of and in the course of the building works. Further, although there was no privity between the plaintiff and the subcontractor, it is equally clear from the documents passing between the main contractor and the subcontractor to which I have already referred that the subcontractor contracted on a like basis . . . Approaching the question on the basis of what is just and reasonable I do not think that the mere fact that there is no strict privity between the employer and the subcontractor should prevent the latter from relying upon the clear basis upon which all the parties contracted in relation to damage to the employer's building casused by fire, even when due to the negligence of the contractors or subcontractors.

Notes

1. This is therefore a clear case where an exemption clause in a contract between A and B was effective to prevent a duty being owed by C, but it is important to note that it was clear to all parties that by virtue of the contractual arrangements the risk of fire was on the plaintiffs. A much more difficult case would be where there is no exemption clause in the contract between A and B, but there is in the contract between B and C. Could C be liable to A? On the one hand it could be argued that A has not voluntarily taken the risk upon himself and therefore should be able to sue. On the other hand C could argue that he should not be under any greater duty to A in tort than he is to B in contract. See generally Beyleveld and Brownsword, 'Privity, Transitivity and Rationality' (1991) 54 MLR 48, which argues that in a three-party case A should be able to sue C and C could rely on exemption clauses in the contract between A and B or between B and C.

2. Another example is *Southern Water Authority* v *Carey* [1985] 2 All ER 1077, where the predecessors of Southern Water entered into a main contract for the construction of a sewage works with Mather & Platt, who entered into sub-contracts with Simon Hartley Ltd and Vokes Ltd. The main contract contained a clause limiting liability. The sewage works proved to be defective. Judge Smout held that, even though the main contract stated that the contractors were deemed to have contracted on their own behalf and on behalf of the sub-contractors, the sub-contractors could not take the benefit of this in contract due to the rules of privity. Nevertheless, he held that the sub-contractors were not liable to the plaintiffs. He said:

We must look to see the nature of such limitation clause to consider whether or not it is relevant in defining the scope of the duty in tort. The contractual setting may not necesarily be overriding, but it is relevant in the consideration of the scope of the duty in tort for it indicates the extent of the liability which the plaintiff's predecessor wished to impose. To put it more crudely . . . the contractual setting defines the area of risk which the plaintiff's predecessor chose to accept and for which it may or may not have sought commercial insurance.

13 SPECIAL DUTY PROBLEMS: DEFECTIVE STRUCTURES

The question of liability for negligently constructed buildings has always caused problems. At one time it was said that the tort of negligence did not apply to a builder of defective premises, but it is now clear that it does, at least where a defect causes physical injury (see *Murphy* v *Brentwood District Council* [1991] 1 AC 398). There is also statutory liability in the Defective Premises Act 1972 (below), but by far the most difficult question has been the liability of builders and others where the defect is one of quality which affects only the building itself, on which see *Murphy* v *Brentwood DC*, below. Other issues relate to whether the damage is economic or physical loss, and whether there can be liability where one part of a building damages another part (because there can be liability only if the defective part damages 'other' property).

DEFECTIVE PREMISES ACT 1972

1. Duty to build dwellings properly

(1) A person taking on work for or in connection with the provisions of a dwelling (whether the dwelling is provided by the erection or by the conversion or enlargement of a building) owes a duty—

    (a)   if the dwelling is provided to the order of any person, to that person; and

    (b)   without prejudice to paragraph (a) above, to every person who acquires an interest (whether legal or equitable) in the dwelling;

to see that the work which he takes on is done in a workmanlike or, as the case may be, professional manner, with proper materials and so that as regards that work the dwelling will be fit for habitation when completed.

(2) A person who takes on any such work for another on terms that he is to do it in accordance with instructions given by or on behalf of that other shall, to the extent to which he does it properly in accordance with those instructions, be treated for the purposes of this section as discharging the duty imposed on him by subsection (1) above

except where he owes a duty to that other to warn him of any defects in the instructions and fails to discharge that duty.

(3) A person shall not be treated for the purposes of subsection (2) above as having given instructions for the doing of work merely because he has agreed to the work being done in a specified manner, with specified materials or to a specified design.

(4) A person who—

(a) in the course of a business which consists of or includes providing or arranging for the provision of dwellings or installations in dwellings; or

(b) in the exercise of a power of making such provision or arrangements conferred by or by virtue of any enactment;

arranges for another to take on work for or in connection with the provision of a dwelling shall be treated for the purposes of this section as included among the persons who have taken on the work.

(5) Any cause of action in respect of a breach of the duty imposed by this section shall be deemed, for the purposes of the Limitation Act 1939, the Law Reform (Limitation of Actions, &c.) Act 1954 and the Limitation Act 1963, to have accrued at the time when the dwelling was completed, but if after that time a person who has done work for or in connection with the provision of the dwelling does further work to rectify the work he has already done, any such cause of action in respect of that further work shall be deemed for those purposes to have accrued at the time when the further work was finished.

2. Cases excluded from the remedy under section 1

(1) Where—

(a) in connection with the provision of a dwelling or its first sale or letting for habitation any rights in respect of defects in the state of the dwelling are conferred by an approved scheme to which this section applies on a person having or acquiring an interest in the dwelling; and

(b) it is stated in a document of a type approved for the purposes of this section that the requirements as to design or construction imposed by or under the scheme have, or appear to have, been substantially complied with in relation to the dwelling;

no action shall be brought by any person having or acquiring an interest in the dwelling for breach of the duty imposed by section 1 above in relation to the dwelling.

(2) A scheme to which this section applies—

(a) may consist of any number of documents and any number of agreements or other transactions between any number of persons; but

(b) must confer, by virtue of agreements entered into with persons having or acquiring an interest in the dwellings to which the scheme applies, rights on such persons in respect of defects in the state of the dwellings.

(3) In this section 'approved' means approved by the Secretary of State, and the power of the Secretary of State to approve a scheme or document for the purposes of this section shall be exercisable by order, except that any requirements as to construction or design imposed under a scheme to which this section applies may be approved by him without making any order or, if he thinks fit, by order.

(4)–(6) . . .

(7) Where an interest in a dwelling is compulsorily acquired—

(a) no action shall be brought by the acquiring authority for breach of the duty imposed by section 1 above in respect of the dwelling; and

(b) if any work for or in connection with the provision of the dwelling was done otherwise than in the course of a business by the person in occupation of the dwelling at the time of the compulsory acquisition, the acquiring authority and not that person shall be treated as the person who took on the work and accordingly as owing that duty.

3.   Duty of care with respect to work done on premises not abated by disposal of premises

(1)   Where work of construction, repair, maintenance or demolition or any other work is done on or in relation to premises, any duty of care owed, because of the doing of the work, to persons who might reasonably be expected to be affected by defects in the state of the premises created by the doing of the work shall not be abated by the subsequent disposal of the premises by the person who owed the duty.

(2)   This section does not apply—

(a)   in the case of premises which are let, where the relevant tenancy of the premises commenced, or the relevant tenancy agreement of the premises was entered into, before the commencement of this Act;

(b)   in the case of premises disposed of in any other way, when the disposal of the premises was completed, or a contract for their disposal was entered into, before the commencement of this Act; or

(c)   in either case, where the relevant transaction disposing of the premises is entered into in pursuance of an enforceable option by which the consideration for the disposal was fixed before the commencement of this Act.

5.   Application to Crown
This Act shall bind the Crown, but as regards the Crown's liability in tort shall not bind the Crown further than the Crown is made liable in tort by the Crown Proceedings Act 1947.

6.   Supplemental
(1)   In this Act—
'disposal', in relation to premises, includes a letting, and an assignment or surrender of a tenancy, of the premises and the creation by contract of any other right to occupy the premises, and 'dispose' shall be construed accordingly;
'personal injury' includes any disease and any impairment of a person's physical or mental condition;
'tenancy' means—

(a)   a tenancy created either immediately or derivatively out of the freehold, whether by a lease or underlease, by an agreement for a lease or underlease or by a tenancy agreement, but not including a mortgage term or any interest arising in favour of a mortgagor by his attorning tenant to his mortgagee; or

(b)   a tenancy at will or a tenancy on sufferance; or

(c)   a tenancy, whether or not constituting a tenancy at common law, created by or in pursuance of any enactment;
and cognate expressions shall be construed accordingly.

(2)   Any duty imposed by or enforceable by virtue of any provision of this Act is in addition to any duty a person may owe apart from that provision.

(3)   Any term of an agreement which purports to exclude or restrict, or has the effect of excluding or restricting, the operation of any of the provisions of this Act, or any liability arising by virtue of any such provision, shall be void.

Notes

1.   It appears that the NHBC Vendor-Purchaser Insurance Scheme is no longer an approved scheme under s. 2: see Wallace, '*Anns* beyond repair' (1991) 107 LQR 230.

2. In *Andrews* v *Schooling* [1991] 3 All ER 723 the defendants converted two houses into flats and granted a long lease of a ground floor flat to the plaintiff. While converting the property the defendants did no work to the cellar and because they had failed to put in a damp proofing system, damp came up to the plaintiff's flat from the cellar. The plaintiff sought damages but the defendants claimed that s. 1 of the 1972 Act did not apply to omissions. The Court of Appeal held that the Act applied both to a failure to carry out necessary work as well as to carrying out work badly.

BUILDING ACT 1984

38. Civil Liability
  (1) Subject to this section—
    (a) breach of a duty imposed by building regulations, so far as it causes damage, is actionable, except in so far as the regulations provide otherwise, and
    (b) as regards such a duty, building regulations may provide for a prescribed defence to be available in an action for breach of that duty brought by virtue of this subsection.
  (2) Subsection (1) above, and any defence provided for in regulations made by virtue of it, do not apply in the case of a breach of such a duty in connection with a building erected before the date on which that subsection comes into force unless the regulations imposing the duty apply to or in connection with the building by virtue of section 2(2) above or paragraph 8 of Schedule 1 to this Act.
  (3) This section does not affect the extent (if any) to which breach of—
    (a) a duty imposed by or arising in connection with this Part of this Act or any other enactment relating to building regulations, or
    (b) a duty imposed by building regulations in a case to which subsection (1) above does not apply,
is actionable, or prejudice a right of action that exists apart from the enactments relating to building regulations.
  (4) In this section, 'damage' includes the death of, or injury to, any person (including any disease and any impairment of a person's physical or mental condition).

Note
This section is not yet in force.

Murphy v *Brentwood District Council*
House of Lords [1991] 1 AC 398; [1990] 3 WLR 414; [1990] 2 All ER 908

In 1970, the plaintiff purchased 38 Vineway, Brentwood. The house had been built by ABC Homes and was constructed on a concrete raft foundation over an in-filled site. The design of the raft was submitted to the defendant council for approval under the Public Health Act 1936, and, after seeking the advice of consulting engineers, the design was approved. From 1981 cracks began appearing in the internal walls of the house and it was found that the concrete raft had subsided. This also caused breakage of soil and gas pipes. The plaintiff eventually sold the house for £35,000 less than its value in good condition and sued the council as being responsible for the negligent approval of the design by the consulting engineers. Held: allowing the appeal and overruling *Anns* v *London Borough of Merton*, that the council was not liable.

LORD BRIDGE: If a manufacturer negligently puts into circulation a chattel containing a latent defect which renders it dangerous to persons or property, the manufacturer, on the well known principles established by *Donoghue* v *Stevenson* [1932] AC 562, will be liable in tort for injury to persons or damage to property which the chattel causes. But if a manufacturer produces and sells a chattel which is merely defective in quality, even to the extent that it is valueless for the purpose for which it is intended, the manufacturer's liability at common law arises only under and by reference to the terms of any contract to which he is a party in relation to the chattel; the common law does not impose on him any liability in tort to persons to whom he owes no duty in contract but who, having acquired the chattel, suffer economic loss because the chattel is defective in quality. If a dangerous defect in a chattel is discovered before it causes any personal injury or damage to property, because the danger is now known and the chattel cannot safely be used unless the defect is repaired, the defect becomes merely a defect in quality. The chattel is either capable of repair at economic cost or it is worthless and must be scrapped. In either case the loss sustained by the owner or hirer of the chattel is purely economic. It is recoverable against any party who owes the loser a relevant contractual duty. But it is not recoverable in tort in the absence of a special relationship of proximity imposing on the tortfeasor a duty of care to safeguard the plaintiff from economic loss. There is no such special relationship between the manufacturer of a chattel and a remote owner or hirer.

I believe that these principles are equally applicable to buildings. If a builder erects a structure containing a latent defect which renders it dangerous to persons or property, he will be liable in tort for injury to persons or damage to property resulting from that dangerous defect. But if the defect becomes apparent before any injury or damage has been caused, the loss sustained by the building owner is purely economic. If the defect can be repaired at economic cost, that is the measure of the loss. If the building cannot be repaired, it may have to be abandoned as unfit for occupation and therefore valueless. These economic losses are recoverable if they flow from breach of a relevant contractual duty, but, here again, in the absence of a special relationship of proximity they are not recoverable in tort. The only qualification I would make to this is that, if a building stands so close to the boundary of the building owner's land that after discovery of the dangerous defect it remains a potential source of injury to persons or property on neighbouring land or on the highway, the building owner ought, in principle, to be entitled to recover in tort from the negligent builder the cost of obviating the danger, whether by repair or by demolition, so far as that cost is necessarily incurred in order to protect himself from potential liability to third parties.

The fallacy which, in my opinion, vitiates the judgments of Lord Denning MR and Sachs LJ in *Dutton* [1972] 1 QB 373 is that they brush these distinctions aside as of no consequence . . . Stamp LJ on the other hand, fully understood and appreciated them and his statement of the applicable principles as between the building owner and the builder . . . seems to me unexceptionable. He rested his decision in favour of the plaintiff against the local authority on a wholly distinct principle which will require separate examination.

The complex structure theory
In my speech in *D. & F. Estates* [1989] AC 177, 206G-207H I mooted the possibility that in complex structures or complex chattels one part of a structure or chattel might,

when it caused damage to another part of the same structure or chattel, be regarded in the law of tort as having caused damage to 'other property' for the purpose of the application of *Donoghue* v *Stevenson* principles. I expressed no opinion as to the validity of this theory, but put it forward for consideration as a possible ground on which the facts considered in *Anns* [1978] AC 728 might be distinguishable from the facts which had to be considered in *D. & F. Estates* itself. I shall call this for convenience 'the complex structure theory' and it is, so far as I can see, only if and to the extent that this theory can be affirmed and applied that there can be any escape from the conclusions I have indicated above under the rubric 'Dangerous defects and defects of quality.'

. . . The reality is that the structural elements in any building form a single indivisible unit of which the different parts are essentially interdependent. To the extent that there is any defect in one part of the structure it must to a greater or lesser degree necessarily affect all other parts of the structure. Therefore any defect in the structure is a defect in the quality of the whole and it is quite artificial, in order to impose a legal liability which the law would not otherwise impose, to treat a defect in an integral structure, so far as it weakens the structure, as a dangerous defect liable to cause damage to 'other property.'

A critical distinction must be drawn here between some part of a complex structure which is said to be a 'danger' only because it does not perform its proper function in sustaining the other parts and some distinct item incorporated in the structure which positively malfunctions so as to inflict positive damage on the structure in which it is incorporated. Thus, if a defective central heating boiler explodes and damages a house or a defective electrical installation malfunctions and sets the house on fire, I see no reason to doubt that the owner of the house, if he can prove that the damage was due to the negligence of the boiler manufacturer in the one case or the electrical contractor on the other, can recover damages in tort on *Donoghue* v *Stevenson* [1932] AC 562 principles. But the position in law is entirely different where, by reason of the inadequacy of the foundations of the building to support the weight of the superstructure, differential settlement and consequent cracking occurs. Here, once the first cracks appear, the structure as a whole is seen to be defective and the nature of the defect is known. Even if, contrary to my view, the initial damage could be regarded as damage to other property caused by a latent defect, once the defect is known the situation of the building owner is analogous to that of the car owner who discovers that the car has faulty brakes. He may have a house which, until repairs are effected, is unfit for habitation, but, subject to the reservation I have expressed with respect to ruinous buildings at or near the boundary of the owner's property, the building no longer represents a source of danger and as it deteriorates will only damage itself.

For these reasons the complex structure theory offers no escape from the conclusion that damage to a house itself which is attributable to a defect in the structure of the house is not recoverable in tort on *Donoghue* v *Stevenson* principles, but represents purely economic loss which is only recoverable in contract or in tort by reason of some special relationship of proximity which imposes on the tortfeasor a duty of care to protect against economic loss.

The relative positions of the builder and the local authority
I have so far been considering the potential liability of a builder for negligent defects in the structure of a building to persons to whom he owes no contractual duty. Since the relevant statutory function of the local authority is directed to no other purpose than securing compliance with building byelaws or regulations by the builder, I agree with the view expressed in *Anns* [1978] AC 728 and by the majority of the Court of Appeal in *Dutton* [1972] 1 QB 373 that a negligent performance of that function can attract no greater liability than attaches to the negligence of the builder whose fault was the

primary tort giving rise to any relevant damage. I am content for present purposes to assume, though I am by no means satisfied that the assumption is correct, that where the local authority, as in this case or in *Dutton*, have in fact approved the defective plans or inspected the defective foundations and negligently failed to discover the defect, their potential liability in tort is coextensive with that of the builder.

Only Stamp LJ in *Dutton* was prepared to hold that the law imposed on the local authority a duty of care going beyond that imposed on the builder and extending to protection of the building owner from purely economic loss. I must return later to consider the question of liability for economic loss more generally, but here I need only say that I cannot find in *Hedley Byrne & Co. Ltd* v *Heller & Partners Ltd* [1964] AC 465 or *Dorset Yacht Co. Ltd* v *Home Office* [1970] AC 1004 any principle applicable to the circumstances of *Dutton* or the present case that provides support for the conclusion which Stamp LJ sought to derive from those authorities.

Imminent danger to health or safety
A necessary element in the building owner's cause of action against the negligent local authority, which does not appear to have been contemplated in *Dutton* but which, it is said in *Anns*, must be present before the cause of action accrues, is that the state of the building is such that there is present or imminent danger to the health or safety of persons occupying it. Correspondingly the damages recoverable are said to include the amount of expenditure necessary to restore the building to a condition in which it is no longer such a danger, but presumably not any further expenditure incurred in any merely qualitative restoration. I find these features of the *Anns* doctrine very difficult to understand. The theoretical difficulty of reconciling this aspect of the doctrine with previously accepted legal principle was pointed out by Lord Oliver of Aylmerton in *D. & F. Estates* [1989] AC 177, 212D–213D. But apart from this there are, as it appears to me, two insuperable difficulties arising from the requirement of imminent danger to health or safety as an ingredient of the cause of action which lead to quite irrational and capricious consequences in the application of the *Anns* doctrine. The first difficulty will arise where the relevant defect in the building, when it is first discovered, is not a present or imminent danger to health or safety. What is the owner to do if he is advised that the building will gradually deteriorate, if not repaired, and will in due course become a danger to health and safety, but that the longer he waits to effect repairs the greater the cost will be? Must he spend £1,000 now on the necessary repairs with no redress against the local authority? Or is he entitled to wait until the building has so far deteriorated that he has a cause of action and then to recover from the local authority the £5,000 which the necessary repairs are now going to cost? I can find no answer to this conundrum. A second difficulty will arise where the latent defect is not discovered until it causes the sudden and total collapse of the building, which occurs when the building is temporarily unoccupied and causes no damage to property except to the building itself. The building is now no longer capable of occupation and hence cannot be a danger to health or safety. It seems a very strange result that the building owner should be without remedy in this situation if he would have been able to recover from the local authority the full cost of repairing the building if only the defect had been discovered before the building fell down.

Liability for economic loss
All these considerations lead inevitably to the conclusion that a building owner can only recover the cost of repairing a defective building on the ground of the authority's negligence in performing its statutory function of approving plans or inspecting buildings in the course of construction if the scope of the authority's duty of care is wide enough to embrace purely economic loss. The House has already held in *D. & F. Estates*

that a builder, in the absence of any contractual duty or of a special relationship of proximity introducing the *Hedley Byrne* principle of reliance, owes no duty of care in tort in respect of the quality of his work. As I pointed out in *D. & F. Estates*, to hold that the builder owed such a duty of care to any person acquiring an interest in the product of the builder's work would be to impose upon him the obligations of an indefinitely transmissible warranty of quality.

By section 1 of the Defective Premises Act 1972 Parliament has in fact imposed on builders and others undertaking work in the provision of dwellings the obligations of a transmissible warranty of the quality of their work and of the fitness for habitation of the completed dwelling. But besides being limited to dwellings, liability under the Act is subject to a limitation period of six years from the completion of the work and to the exclusion provided for by section 2. It would be remarkable to find that similar obligations in the nature of a transmissible warranty of quality, applicable to buildings of every kind and subject to no such limitations or exclusions as are imposed by the Act of 1972, could be derived from the builder's common law duty of care or from the duty imposed by building byelaws or regulations. In *Anns* Lord Wilberforce expressed the opinion that a builder could be held liable for a breach of statutory duty in respect of buildings which do not comply with the byelaws. But he cannot, I think, have meant that the statutory obligation to build in conformity with the byelaws by itself gives rise to obligations in the nature of transmissible warranties of quality. If he did mean that, I must respectfully disagree. I find it impossible to suppose that anything less than clear express language such as is used in section 1 of the Act of 1972 would suffice to impose such a statutory obligation.

As I have already said, since the function of a local authority in approving plans or inspecting buildings in course of construction is directed to ensuring that the builder complies with building byelaws or regulations, I cannot see how. in principle, the scope of the liability of the authority for a negligent failure to ensure compliance can exceed that of the liability of the builder for his negligent failure to comply.

There may, of course, be situations where, even in the absence of contract, there is a special relationship of proximity between builder and building owner which is sufficiently akin to contract to introduce the element of reliance so that the scope of the duty of care owed by the builder to the owner is wide enough to embrace purely economic loss. The decision in *Junior Books Ltd* v *Veitchi Co. Ltd* [1983] 1 AC 520 can I believe, only be understood on this basis.

Notes

1. *Murphy* was applied in **Department of Environment v T. Bates Ltd** [1990] 3 WLR 457, where the defendants had built a two-storey building with a flat roof and an 11-storey office block. The plaintiffs were sub-lessees of the buildings and discovered that some of the concrete in the buildings was soft, and they sued the builder for the cost of the remedial work and the cost of alternative accommodation while the work was carried out. The House of Lords held that there was no liability, since the buildings were not unsafe but rather suffered a defect of quality in that they could not be loaded to their designed capacity unless repaired. The loss resulted from the quality of the building itself and was therefore pure economic loss and irrecoverable.

2. An example of the line between liability and non-liability is **Nitrigin Eireann Teoranta v Inco Alloys** [1992] 1 All ER 854, where the plaintiffs operated a chemical factory. In 1983 they discovered a crack in a steel pipe

supplied by the defendants. The pipe was repaired but it was held that no cause of action arose as the pipe had merely damaged itself and the loss was economic loss. However, in 1984 the pipe burst, and this caused damage to surrounding parts of the factory. This did give rise to a cause of action as 'other' property was damaged.

3. In *Junior Books* v *Veitchi* [1983] 1 AC 520, mentioned by Lord Bridge, Ogilvie Builders Ltd (the main contractors) built a factory for Junior Books Ltd. The architects of Junior Books nominated Veitchi Co. Ltd to lay a floor, and they as subcontractors entered into a contract with the main contractors (Ogilvie). The floor turned out to be inadequate for the required purpose and Junior Books successfully sued for the cost of its replacement. This case has often been doubted (and never followed) but has not been overruled. It is now explained on the basis that the relationship between Junior Books and the subcontractors (Veitchi) was so close as to be as good as a contract, so that a duty based on reliance came about.

4. *Murphy* has been rejected in most Commonwealth countries. In *Bryan* v *Maloney* (1994) 128 ALR 163, the High Court of Australia held that there was sufficient proximity between a builder and subsequent purchasers because the house was a permanent structure intended to be used indefinitely (liability for subsidence caused by inadequate foundations). In *Invercargill City Council* v *Hamlin* [1996] 1 All ER 756 the Privy Council accepted that the law in New Zealand was different, saying that policy conditions were such as to lead to liability, although this did not cast doubt on the correctness of *Murphy* in England and Wales. The New Zealand Court of Appeal, [1994] 3 NZLR 519, had said that house buyers rely on building inspectors to ensure compliance by builders with building regulations. Accordingly, the Council was liable for negligent inspection of foundations when subsidence later occurred. In Canada the Supreme Court held in *Winnipeg Condominium Corporation* v *Bird Construction* (1995) 121 DLR 193, that a builder or architect could be liable where negligence caused the building to be dangerous. Liability was limited to the cost of making the building safe.

5. In England it was suggested in *The Orjula* [1995] 2 Lloyd's Rep 395 at 403 that where dangerous property was put into circulation, the person who was obliged to make it safe could sue even though no damage to other property had yet occurred. It was said that this principle has survived *Murphy*. The case concerned contaminated containers but presumably it would also apply to premises that are dangerous rather than merely of poor quality.

6. The rejection of *Murphy* has led to a loosening of the bonds of the common law. In *Invercargill* v *City Council* (above) Cooke P said, 'While the disharmony may be regrettable, it is inevitable now that the Commonwealth jurisdictions have gone on their own paths without taking English decisions as the invariable starting point. The ideal of a uniform Common-law has proved as unattainable as any ideal of a uniform law. It could not survive the independence of the United States; constitutional evolution in the Commonwealth has done the rest. What of course is both desirable and feasible . . . is to take account and learn from decisions in other jurisdictions.'

7. For a full discussion of the effect of *Murphy* v *Brentwood DC* on the liability of builders and others, see Wallace, '*Anns* beyond repair' (1991) 107 LQR 230.

14 SPECIAL DUTY PROBLEMS: UNBORN CHILDREN, WRONGFUL LIFE AND WRONGFUL BIRTH

The problem of whether a duty was owed to a foetus which suffered damage before birth was brought to the fore by the Thalidomide tragedy in the 1960s, when the initial settlement with the manufacturers (Distillers) involved a payment of only 40 per cent of the damages because of the uncertainty of liability (see *S v Distillers Co. Ltd* [1969] 3 All ER 1412). Due to public pressure the settlement was later substantially increased, but that did not solve the legal problem, although other common law jurisdictions had found in favour of liability to unborn children — see, for example, *Watt v Rama* [1972] VR 353 and *Duval v Seguin* (1972) 26 DLR 3d 418. In 1991, the English courts finally followed suit, and held in *B v Islington Health Authority* [1992] 3 All ER 833, that injury to an unborn child could give rise to an action at common law. However, this only applies to births before 22 July 1976, because under the Congenital Disabilities (Civil Liability) Act 1976, s. 4(5), all births after that date are covered by that Act, which supplants the common law and which may be narrower in effect. (In 1974 the Law Commission had recommended legislation to establish liability (see Report No. 60, *Injuries to Unborn Children*) and this became the Congenital Disabilities (Civil Liability) Act 1976.)

Section 1: injuries to unborn children

CONGENITAL DISABILITIES (CIVIL LIABILITY) ACT 1976

1. Civil liability to child born disabled
   (1) If a child is born disabled as the result of such an occurrence before its birth as is mentioned in subsection (2) below, and a person (other than the child's own mother) is under this section answerable to the child in respect of the occurrence, the child's

disabilities are to be regarded as damage resulting from the wrongful act of that person and actionable accordingly at the suit of the child.

(2)   An occurrence to which this section applies is one which—

(a)   affected either parent of the child in his or her ability to have a normal, healthy child; or

(b)   affected the mother during her pregnancy, or affected her or the child in the course of its birth, so that the child is born with disabilities which would not otherwise have been present.

(3)   Subject to the following subsections, a person (here referred to as 'the defendant') is answerable to the child if he was liable in tort to the parent or would, if sued in due time, have been so; and it is no answer that there could not have been such liability because the parent suffered no actionable injury, if there was a breach of legal duty which, accompanied by injury, would have given rise to the liability.

(4)   In the case of an occurrence preceding the time of conception, the defendant is not answerable to the child if at that time either or both of the parents knew the risk of their child being born disabled (that is to say, the particular risk created by the occurrence); but should it be the child's father who is the defendant, this subsection does not apply if he knew of the risk and the mother did not.

(5)   The defendant is not answerable to the child, for anything he did or omitted to do when responsible in a professional capacity for treating or advising the parent, if he took reasonable care having due regard to then received professional opinion applicable to the particular class of case; but this does not mean that he is answerable only because he departed from received opinion.

(6)   Liability to the child under this section may be treated as having been excluded or limited by contract made with the parent affected, to the same extent and subject to the same restrictions as liability in the parent's own case; and a contract term which could have been set up by the defendant in an action by the parent, so as to exclude or limit his liability to him or her, operates in the defendant's favour to the same, but no greater, extent in an action under this section by the child.

(7)   If in the child's action under this section it is shown that the parent affected shared the responsibility for the child being born disabled, the damages are to be reduced to such extent as the court thinks just and equitable having regard to the extent of the parent's responsibility.

1A.   Extension of section 1 to cover infertility treatments

(1)   In any case where —

(a)   a child carried by a woman as the result of the placing in her of an embryo or of sperm and eggs or her artificial insemination is born disabled,

(b)   the disability results from an act or omission in the course of the selection, or the keeping or use outside the body, of the embryo carried by her or of the gametes used to bring about the creation of the embryo, and

(c)   a person is under this section answerable to the child in respect of the act or omission,

the child's disabilities are to be regarded as damage resulting from the wrongful act of that person and actionable accordingly at the suit of the child.

(2)   Subject to subsection (3) below and the applied provisions of section 1 of this Act, a person (here referred to as 'the defendant') is answerable to the child if he was liable in tort to one or both of the parents (here referred to as 'the parent or parents concerned') or would, if sued in due time, have been so; and it is no answer that there could not have been such liability because the parent or parents concerned suffered no actionable injury, if there was a breach of legal duty which, accompanied by injury, would have given rise to the liability.

(3)   The defendant is not under this section answerable to the child if at the time the embryo, or the sperm and eggs, are placed in the woman or the time of her insemination (as the case may be) either or both of the parents knew the risk of the child being born disabled (that is to say, the particular risk created by the act or omission).

(4)   Subsections (5) to (7) of section 1 of this Act apply for the purposes of this section as they apply for the purposes of that but as if references to the parent or the parent affected were references to the parent or parents concerned.

2.   Liability of woman driving when pregnant

A woman driving a motor vehicle when she knows (or ought reasonably to know) herself to be pregnant is to be regarded as being under the same duty to take care for the safety of her unborn child as the law imposes on her with respect to the safety of other people; and if in consequence of her breach of that duty her child is born with disabilities which would not otherwise have been present, those disabilities are to be regarded as damage resulting from her wrongful act and actionable accordingly at the suit of the child.

3.   Disabled birth due to radiation

(1)   Section 1 of this Act does not affect the operation of the Nuclear Installations Act 1965 as to liability for, and compensation in respect of, injury or damage caused by occurrences involving nuclear matter or the emission of ionising radiations.

(2)   For the avoidance of doubt anything which—
  (a)   affects a man in his ability to have a normal, healthy child; or
  (b)   affect a woman in that ability, or so affects her when she is pregnant that her
child is born with disabilities which would not otherwise have been present,
is an injury for the purposes of that Act.

(3)   If a child is born disabled as the result of an injury to either of its parents caused in breach of a duty imposed by any of sections 7 to 11 of that Act (nuclear site licensees and others to secure that nuclear incidents do not cause injury to persons, etc.), the child's disabilities are to be regarded under the subsequent provisions of that Act (compensation and other matters) as injuries caused on the same occasion, and by the same breach of duty, as was the injury to the parent.

(4)   As respects compensation to the child, section 13(6) of that Act (contributory fault of person injured by radiation) is to be applied as if the reference there to fault were to the fault of the parent.

(5)   Compensation is not payable in the child's case if the injury to the parent preceded the time of the child's conception and at that time either or both of the parents knew the risk of their child being born disabled (that is to say, the particular risk created by the injury).

4.   Interpretation and other supplementary provisions

(1)   References in this Act to a child being born disabled or with disabilities are to its being born with any deformity, disease or abnormality, including predisposition (whether or not susceptible of immediate prognosis) to physical or mental defect in the future.

(2)   In this Act—
  (a)   'born' means born alive (the moment of a child's birth being when it first has a life separate from its mother), and 'birth' has a corresponding meaning; and
  (b)   'motor vehicle' means a mechanically propelled vehicle intended or adapted for use on roads,
and references to embryos shall be construed in accordance with section 1 of the Human Fertilisation and Embryology Act 1990.

(3)   Liability to a child under section 1, 1A or 2 of this Act is to be regarded—

(a)   as respects all its incidents and any matters arising or to arise out of it; and
(b)   subject to any contrary context or intention, for the purpose of construing references in enactments and documents to personal or bodily injuries and cognate matters,
as liability for personal injuries sustained by the child immediately after its birth.

(4)   No damage shall be recoverable under any of those sections in respect of any loss of expectation of life, nor shall any such loss be taken into account in the compensation payable in respect of a child under the Nuclear Installations Act 1965 as extended by section 3, unless (in either case) the child lives for at least 48 hours.

(5)   This Act applies in respect of births after (but not before) its passing, and in respect of any such birth it replaces any law in force before its passing, whereby a person could be liable to a child in respect of disabilities with which it might be born; but in section 1(3) of this Act the expression 'liable in tort' does not include any reference to liability by virtue of this Act, or to liability by virtue of any such law.

Notes
1.   For commentaries on the Act, see Pace, 'Civil Liability for Pre-Natal Injuries' (1977) 40 MLR 141, and Cave, 'Injuries to Unborn Children' (1977) 51 ALJ 704.
2.   The issue of ante-natal injury was discussed by the Pearson Commission (Cmnd. 7054), who suggested the following changes to the 1976 Act:
(a)   The law of tort should continue to apply in the case of a child born alive and suffering from the effects of ante-natal injury (such liability is excluded by s. 4(5)).
(b)   A child should not have a right of action against either parent for ante-natal injury, except where the claim arises out of an activity where insurance is compulsory.
(c)   Section 1(7) of the Act should be repealed — i.e. the contributory negligence of the parent should not be visited on the child.

Section 2:   wrongful life

An action for wrongful *life* means an action whereby a child claims that he or she would not have been born at all, but for the defendant's negligence. On the other hand, an action for wrongful *birth* is one by the parents claiming *their* losses arising from having to bring up a child which they claim would not have been born. The courts have rejected wrongful life cases, but have accepted wrongful birth ones.

McKay v Essex Health Authority
Court of Appeal [1982] QB 1166; [1982] 2 All ER 771; [1982] 2 WLR 890

The plaintiff, Mary McKay, was born in 1975. The defendants were the mother's doctor and the Health Authority. In April 1975 the mother saw her doctor and told him that she was pregnant and that she had been in contact with rubella (German measles), which can cause a child to be born disabled. The doctor took a blood sample and the mother was subsequently told (wrongly) that her unborn child had not been infected with rubella. The mother alleged that if she had been told that the child had been infected she would have had an abortion. The plaintiff was born in August 1975 and was partly blind and deaf. Held: allowing the appeal, that the defendants were not liable at common law, as in essence the plaintiff's claim was that the defendants had negligently allowed her to be born alive and this could not be actionable. It was also noted that the terms of the 1976 Act would prevent any such cases in the future.

Note: it is important to bear in mind that the plaintiff's disabilities were caused by the rubella and not by the defendants. The claim discussed here was not for the disabilities the plaintiff suffered, but only for failing to give the mother the chance to have an abortion.

ACKNER LJ: . . . The Congenital Disabilities (Civil Liability) Act 1976 received the Royal Assent on July 22, 1976. Section 1, which deals with civil liability to a child born disabled, was in the terms of clause 1 of a draft annexed to the Law Commission Report on Injuries to Unborn Children (1974) (Law Com. No. 60) (Cmnd. 5709). . . . Subsection (2)(b) is so worded as to import the assumption that, but for the occurrence giving rise to a disabled birth, the child would have been born normal and healthy — not that it would not have been born at all. Thus, the object of the Law Commission that the child should have no right of action for 'wrongful life' is achieved. In paragraph 89 of the Report the Law Commission stated that they were clear in their opinion that no cause of action should lie:

> Such a cause of action, if it existed, would place an almost intolerable burden on medical advisers in their socially and morally exacting role. The danger that doctors would be under subconscious pressures to advise abortions in doubtful cases through fear of an action for damages is, we think, a real one.

This view was adopted by the Royal Commission on Civil Liability and Compensation for Personal Injury (1978) (Cmnd. 7054-1), paragraph 1485.

(4)   Section 4(5) of the Act provides: 'This Act applies in respect of births after (but not before) its passing, and in respect of any such birth it replaces any law in force before its passing, whereby a person could be liable to a child in respect of disabilities with which it might be born; . . .'

Thus, there can be no question of such a cause of action arising in respect of births after July 22, 1976. This case therefore raises no point of general public importance. It can, for all practical purposes, be considered as a 'one-off' case.

Note

For a discussion of wrongful life cases, see Teff, 'Wrongful life in England and the United States' (1985) 34 ICLQ 423.

Section 3:   wrongful birth

This section deals with cases where the *parents* are claiming that, but for the negligence of the defendant, they would not have had the child in question. The most obvious example of such a case is where a sterilisation operation is ineffective and a child is born unexpectedly. Liability can follow in both contract and tort, and damages can be awarded for the cost of upkeep of the unexpected child.

Thake v *Maurice*
Court of Appeal [1986] QB 644; [1986] 1 All ER 497; [1986] 2 WLR 337

Mr and Mrs Thake had five children and, accordingly, Mr Thake had a vasectomy which was done by the defendant. Some three years later Mrs Thake began to miss her periods, but, believing her husband to be sterile, thought that she could not be pregnant. When she finally went to the doctor she discovered that she was four months pregnant. Mr Thake's vasectomy had reversed itself naturally, and the plaintiffs sued on the basis that the defendant had failed to warn them of the small chance that this might occur. If Mrs Thake had been aware of the possibility she would have realised she was pregnant sooner and would have been in time to have an abortion. Held: dismissing the appeal, that the defendant was liable.

KERR LJ: The plaintiffs' claim was pleaded both in contract and in tort, i.e., what was for convenience referred to as 'contractual negligence' as well as negligence simpliciter resulting from the duty of care owed by a surgeon to his patient. For present purposes I do not think that it is necessary to distinguish between them. On both aspects the issue turned on the defendant's failure — found by the judge — to give his usual warning of the slight risk that 'late recanalisation' might lead to defeat by nature of a vasectomy operation performed properly, and even after two successful sperm tests. The only issue raised explicitly by the pleadings in this connection was whether or not this warning had been given. . . .

Foreseeability and causation
The plaintiffs' case was not that Mr Thake would not have had the operation if they had been warned of a risk that it might not render him permanently sterile; they said that he would still have had the operation, but that Mrs Thake would then have been alert to the risk that she might again become pregnant and would then have had an abortion at an early stage. In the circumstances, however, it never occurred to her that she might be pregnant when she missed a number of her periods, attributing this to her age and the 'change of life.' In the result, as explained by the judge, she was astonished and very upset on being told that she was five months pregnant and that it was too late for an abortion.

On behalf of the defendant it was not suggested that Mrs Thake should have realised earlier that she was pregnant, nor that she could possibly have had an abortion when she became aware of the position. Two points were taken. First, so far as the claim in contract was concerned, it was submitted that it could not have been in the reasonable contemplation of the defendant that a failure to give his usual warning might have the result that Mrs Thake would not appreciate, at a sufficiently early stage to enable her to have an abortion if she wished, that she had again become pregnant. In this connection the defendant relied on the principles laid down by the House of Lords in *C. Czarnikow Ltd* v *Koufos* [1969] 1 AC 350. In so far as the claim lay in tort, it was accepted on his behalf that this consequence was reasonably foreseeable as liable to happen and not too remote: see the remarks of Lord Reid, at pp. 385 and 386. Having held that the plaintiffs succeeded in contract, the judge only dealt with this aspect on this basis, but we permitted the plaintiffs to amend their respondents' notice, without opposition on behalf of the defendant, to contend that the judge's decision on this aspect should be upheld in tort in any event. Accordingly, this particular issue became largely academic on the appeal, but I respectfully agree with the judge when he concluded that the risk of

Mrs Thake failing to appreciate at an early stage that she had once again become pregnant must have been in the reasonable contemplation of the defendant. Indeed, in his evidence he virtually conceded this himself.

The second point taken on behalf of the defendant was that the plaintiffs had not proved on a balance of probability that Mrs Thake would have been able to have a lawful abortion even if she had become aware of her renewed pregnancy as soon as this occurred. The plaintiffs accepted that the test was not whether she could have secured an abortion, but whether she could have secured one which would have been lawful under section 1 of the Abortion Act 1967. The judge dealt with this issue on the same page; again I agree, and again this was virtually frankly conceded by the defendant himself. Having regard to Mrs Thake's age, her family, financial and housing situation, and also bearing in mind that her general practitioner had already put her on the National Health Service list for sterilisation, I do not see how one can realistically reach any different conclusion on the probabilities. That disposes of the appeal.

Notes
1.   In another case the plaintiff succeeded in a similar situation, even though she could have had an abortion. In *Emeh* v *Kensington Area Health Authority* [1985] QB 1012, the plaintiff underwent a sterilisation operation, but she later discovered that she was 20 weeks pregnant. It was held that her failure to have an abortion 'was not so unreasonable as to eclipse the defendant's wrongdoing'. Would this be so if she was only eight weeks pregnant?
2.   Who can sue? In *Goodwill* v *Pregnancy Advisory Service* [1996] 2 All ER 161, Mr M had a vasectomy in 1985 which later reversed itself. In 1988 he began sexual relations with the plaintiff who became pregnant in 1989. It was argued on the basis of *White* v *Jones* [1995] 2 AC 107 (see Chapter 10) that just as there the solicitor was engaged to confer a benefit on the intended beneficiaries of the will, so here the doctor was engaged to confer a benefit (non-pregnancy) on future sexual partners of M. (The case was based on the doctor's failure to warn M of the possibility of reversal.) The claim was rejected on the grounds that no duty could be owed to all future potential partners of M.

Would a duty be owed to the current wife or partner of M in 1985? (See *Thake* v *Maurice* (above).) Would the doctor need to know that M was married or had a regular partner? What if M told the doctor that the reason M wanted the vasectomy was because he was promiscuous and had a number of partners?
3.   For the assessment of damages in such cases see *Allen* v *Bloomsbury Health Authority* [1993] 1 All ER 651, where it was said that damages would include:

(a)   compensation for the discomfort and pain associated with the pregnancy offset by the benefit of not having to undergo an abortion;

(b)   future loss of earnings of the mother and the cost of maintaining the child to adulthood;

(c)   damages in appropriate cases for stress in bringing up a handicapped child but not the stress associated with bringing up a healthy child. In that case the general damages came to £62,342.
4.   For a discussion of 'wrongful birth' cases, see Symmons, 'Policy factors in actions for wrongful birth' (1987) 50 MLR 269.

15 DEFENCES TO NEGLIGENCE

Section 1: contributory negligence

The principle of contributory negligence is that the damages awarded to a plaintiff who has himself been at fault should be reduced to the extent that his fault contributed to the accident or the damage. It might seem logical that if a defendant is to be held responsible for his fault, then so should a plaintiff for his, but it should be borne in mind that in practice the effect of a finding of contributory negligence on the part of the plaintiff is entirely different from a finding of fault on the part of the defendant. The reason is that, at least in personal injury cases, a defendant will usually be insured, or may be able to distribute his loss in some other way. Thus a defendant who is made liable will not often bear the burden himself. But where a *plaintiff* is held to be contributorily negligent and his damages are reduced, he will almost always bear the burden himself. Why should we deliberately undercompensate people in this way? It is doubtful whether the doctrine has any deterrent effect: for example, it is highly unlikely that in the past the fact that a person who was not wearing a seat belt would be held contributorily negligent had any effect on the numbers of people who wore seat belts. (Television advertising was not very successful either, and it was not until the criminal law was used that wearing seat belts became common.) See generally on the problems associated with contributory negligence, Atiyah, *Accidents, Compensation and the Law,* 4th ed., pp. 116-126.

The cases below show that the rules for establishing contributory negligence on the part of the plaintiff are not the same as the rules for establishing liability for negligence on the part of the defendant. There is, for example, no room for the concept of duty of care, and the question is rather simply whether the plaintiff has taken proper care for his own safety. One of the most difficult problems relates to causation, i.e. was the act of the plaintiff merely the background against which the negligence of the defendant operated, or did it causally contribute to the accident?

LAW REFORM (CONTRIBUTORY NEGLIGENCE) ACT 1945

1. Apportionment of liability in case of contributory negligence
Where any person suffers damage as the result partly of his own fault and partly of the fault of any other person or persons, a claim in respect of that damage shall not be defeated by reason of the fault of the person suffering the damage, but the damages recoverable in respect thereof shall be reduced to such extent as the court thinks just and equitable having regard to the claimant's share in the responsibility for the damage . . . .

4. Interpretation
The following expressions have the meanings hereby respectively assigned to them, that is to say—
'court' means, in relation to any claim, the court or arbitrator by or before whom the claim falls to be determined;
'damage' includes loss of life and personal injury;
. . .
'fault' means negligence, breach of statutory duty or other act or omission which gives rise to a liability in tort or would apart from this Act, give rise to the defence of contributory negligence.

Note
It is not possible under this Act to say that a person has been 100 per cent contributorily negligent. In *Pitts* v *Hunt* [1991] 1 QB 24, Balcombe LJ referred to such a view as logically unsupportable, and Beldam LJ said:

> Section 1 begins with the premise that the person 'suffers damage as the result partly of his own fault and partly of the fault of any other person or persons . . .' Thus before the section comes into operation, the court must be satisfied that there is fault on the part of both parties which has caused damage. It is then expressly provided that the claim 'shall not be defeated by reason of the fault of the person suffering the damage . . .' To hold that he is himself entirely responsible for the damage effectively defeats his claim. It is then provided that 'the damages recoverable in respect thereof' — that is, the damage suffered partly as a result of his own fault and partly the fault of any other person — 'shall be reduced . . .' It therefore presupposes that the person suffering the damage will recover some damages. Finally, reduction is to be 'to such extent as the court thinks just and equitable having regard to the claimant's share in the responsibility for the damage: . . .' To hold that the claimant is 100 per cent responsible is not to hold that he shared in the responsibility for the damage.

Jones v Livox Quarries Ltd
Court of Appeal [1952] 2 QB 608; [1952] 1 TLR 1377

The plaintiff worked in a quarry and was riding on the back of a 'traxcavator', 'very much in the position in which a footman stood at the back of an eighteenth century carriage'. The traxcavator, which had a speed of two mph, rounded an obstruction and stopped to change gear, when it was run into from behind by a dumper truck and the plaintiff was injured. Held: dismissing the appeal, that the plaintiff was contributorily negligent.

DENNING LJ: . . . The case of *Davies* v *Swan Motor Co. (Swansea) Ltd* [1949] 2 KB 291 has been much discussed before us. It has been said that the three judgments in the case do not proceed on precisely the same lines. That is true, but it is, I suggest, quite understandable, because the court was there feeling its way in difficult country. Since that time, however, the ground has been cleared considerably. It can now be safely asserted that the doctrine of last opportunity is obsolete; and also that contributory negligence does not depend on the existence of a duty. But the troublesome problem of causation still remains to be solved.

Although contributory negligence does not depend on a duty of care, it does depend on foreseeability. Just as actionable negligence requires the foreseeability of harm to others, so contributory negligence requires the foreseeability of harm to oneself. A person is guilty of contributory negligence if he ought reasonably to have foreseen that, if he did not act as a reasonable, prudent man, he might be hurt himself; and in his reckonings he must take into account the possibility of others being careless.

Once negligence is proved, then no matter whether it is actionable negligence or contributory negligence, the person who is guilty of it must bear his proper share of responsibility for the consequences. The consequences do not depend on foreseeability, but on causation. The question in every case is: What faults were there which caused the damage? Was his fault one of them? The necessity of causation is shown by the word 'result' in section 1(1) of the Act of 1945, and it was accepted by this court in *Davies* v *Swan Motor Co. (Swansea) Ltd.*

There is no clear guidance to be found in the books about causation. All that can be said is that causes are different from the circumstances in which, or on which, they operate. The line between the two depends on the facts of each case. It is a matter of common sense more than anything else. In the present case, as the argument of Mr Arthian Davies proceeded, it seemed to me that he sought to make foreseeability the decisive test of causation. He relied on the trial judge's statement that a man who rode on the towbar of the traxcavator 'ran the risk of being thrown off and no other risk.' That is, I think, equivalent to saying that such a man could reasonably foresee that he might be thrown off the traxcavator, but not that he might be crushed between it and another vehicle.

In my opinion, however, foreseeability is not the decisive test of causation. It is often a relevant factor, but it is not decisive. Even though the plaintiff did not foresee the possibility of being crushed, nevertheless in the ordinary plain common sense of this business the injury suffered by the plaintiff was due in part to the fact that he chose to ride on the towbar to lunch instead of walking down on his feet. If he had been thrown off in the collision, Mr Arthian Davies admits that his injury would be partly due to his own negligence in riding on the towbar; but he says that, because he was crushed, and not thrown off, his injury is in no way due to it. That is too fine a distinction for me. I cannot believe that that purely fortuitous circumstance can make all the difference to the case. As Scrutton LJ said in *In re Polemis and Another and Furness , Withy & Co. Ld* [1921] 3 KB 560, 577 'Once the act is negligent, the fact that its exact operation was not foreseen is immaterial.'

In order to illustrate this question of causation, I may say that if the plaintiff, whilst he was riding on the towbar, had been hit in the eye by a shot from a negligent sportsman, I should have thought that the plaintiff's negligence would in no way be a cause of his injury. It would only be the circumstance in which the cause operated. It would only be part of the history. But I cannot say that in the present case. The man's negligence here was so much mixed up with his injury that it cannot be dismissed as mere history. His dangerous position on the vehicle was one of the causes of his damage just as it was in *Davies* v *Swan Motor Co. (Swansea) Ltd.*

The present case is a good illustration of the practical effect of the Act of 1945. In the course of the argument my Lord suggested that before the Act of 1945 he would have regarded this case as one where the plaintiff should recover in full. That would be because the negligence of the dumper driver would then have been regarded as the predominant cause. Now, since the Act, we have regard to all the causes, and one of them undoubtedly was the plaintiff's negligence in riding on the towbar of the traxcavator. His share in the responsibility was not great — the trial judge assessed it at one-fifth — but, nevertheless, it was his share, and he must bear it himself. . . .

It all comes to this: If a man carelessly rides on a vehicle in a dangerous position, and subsequently there is a collision in which his injuries are made worse by reason of his position than they otherwise would have been, then his damage is partly the result of his own fault, and the damages recoverable by him fall to be reduced accordingly.

Note

Another case on the causation problem is **Stapley** v **Gypsum Mines Ltd** [1953] AC 663, where the plaintiff, Seagull Gladys Stapley, was the widow of John Stapley who worked in a gypsum mine. He and another miner, Dale, had been told to take down a dangerous part of the roof in a stope where they were working. They tried to do so, but after about half an hour they gave up and decided to carry on with their normal work. Later the roof fell and killed Stapley. The House of Lords held that the employers were vicariously liable for the negligence of Dale, and that Stapley was 80 per cent contributorily negligent. Dale was negligent in that, if he had not agreed with Stapley to cease trying to bring the roof down, Stapley would not have stood out against him and so would not have started to work under the dangerous roof. Lord Reid said:

> One may find that as a matter of history several people have been at fault and that if any one of them had acted properly the accident would not have happened, but that does not mean that the accident must be regarded as having been caused by the faults of all of them. One must discriminate between those faults which must be discarded as being too remote and those hich must not.

He went on to say that the question is whether Dale's fault was 'so much mixed up with the state of things brought about by Stapley that in the ordinary plain commonsense of this business it must be regarded as having contributed to the accident'.

Questions

1. A leaves his car parked near a sharp bend in a 30 mph area where the view is obstructed. B, driving at 45 mph, crashes into it. Had B been driving at 30 mph he could have stopped in time. Is A contributorily negligent, i.e. is the fact that the car is badly parked merely the background against which the

negligence of B operates, or did it contribute to the accident? See the comments about *Davies* v *Mann* (1842) 152 ER 588 in *Davies* v *Swan Motor Co.* [1949] 2 KB 291.

2.   What degree of carelessness by others is foreseeable? Note the comment of Lord Uthwatt in *LPTB* v *Upson* [1949] AC 155, at p. 173 that 'a driver is not of course bound to anticipate folly in all its forms but he is not, in my opinion, entitled to put out of consideration the teachings of experience as to the form these follies commonly take'.

Froom v *Butcher*
Court of Appeal [1976] QB 286; [1975] 3 WLR 379; [1975] 3 All ER 520

The plaintiff was involved in a collision due to the defendant's negligence. He was not wearing a seat belt. He suffered injuries to his head and chest which would not have occurred had he been wearing a belt. He also suffered injury to his finger, which would have happened anyway. Held: allowing the appeal, that the plaintiff was contributorily negligent.

LORD DENNING MR: . . .

The cause of the damage
In the seat belt cases, the injured plaintiff is in no way to blame for the accident itself. Sometimes he is an innocent passenger sitting beside a negligent driver who goes off the road. At other times he is an innocent driver of one car which is run into by the bad driving of another car which pulls out on to its wrong side of the road. It may well be asked: why should the injured plaintiff have his damages reduced? The accident was solely caused by the negligent driving of the defendant. Sometimes outrageously bad driving. It should not lie in his mouth to say: 'You ought to have been wearing a seat belt.' That point of view was strongly expressed in *Smith* v *Blackburn (Note)* [1974] RTR 533, 536 by O'Connor J: '. . . the idea that the insurers of a grossly negligent driver should be relieved in any degree from paying what is proper compensation for injuries is an idea that offends ordinary decency. Until I am forced to do so by higher authority I will not so rule.' I do not think that is the correct approach. The question is not what was the cause of the accident. It is rather what was the cause of the damage. In most accidents on the road the bad driving, which causes the accident, also causes the ensuing damage. But in seat belt cases the cause of the accident is one thing. The cause of the damage is another. The *accident* is caused by the bad driving. The *damage* is caused in part by the bad driving of the defendant, and in part by the failure of the plaintiff to wear a seat belt. If the plaintiff was to blame in not wearing a seat belt, the damage is in part the result of his own fault. He must bear some share in the responsibility for the damage: and his damages fall to be reduced to such extent as the court thinks just and equitable. . . .

The share of responsibility
Whenever there is an accident, the negligent driver must bear by far the greater share of responsibility. It was his neglience which caused the accident. It also was a prime cause of the whole of the damage. But in so far as the damage might have been avoided or lessened by wearing a seat belt, the injured person must bear some share. But how much should this be? Is it proper to inquire whether the driver was grossly negligent or only slightly negligent? or whether the failure to wear a seat belt was entirely inexcusable or

almost forgivable? If such an inquiry could easily be undertaken, it might be as well to do it. In *Davies* v *Swan Motor Co. (Swansea) Ltd* [1949] 2 KB 291, 326, the court said that consideration should be given not only to the causative potency of a particular factor, but also its blameworthiness. But we live in a practical world. In most of these cases the liability of the driver is admitted, the failure to wear a seat belt is admitted, the only question is: what damages should be payable? This question should not be prolonged by an expensive inquiry into the degree of blameworthiness on either side, which would be hotly disputed. Suffice it to assess a share of responsibility which will be just and equitable in the great majority of cases.

Sometimes the evidence will show that the failure made no difference. The damage would have been the same, even if a seat belt had been worn. In such case the damages should not be reduced at all. At other times the evidence will show that the failure made all the difference. The damage would have been prevented altogether if a seat belt had been worn. In such cases I would suggest that the damages should be reduced by 25 per cent. But often enough the evidence will only show that the failure made a considerable difference. Some injuries to the head, for instance, would have been a good deal less severe if a seat belt had been worn, but there would still have been some injury to the head. In such case I would suggest that the damages attributable to the failure to wear a seat belt should be reduced by 15 per cent.

Note
The important point here is that the negligence of the plaintiff in no way contributed to the accident happening, but rather only to the extent of the damage. If we assume that a driver is 100 per cent responsible for the accident occurring, and the plaintiff is 100 per cent responsible for the extent of the damage, how can these different factors be balanced? To what extent has each contributed to the damage?

Question
Who gains and who loses from the rule that failure to wear a seat belt amounts to contributory negligence? What makes people wear seat belts? Is the contributory negligence rule a factor in making people wear seat belts? If not, what is its function?

Owens v *Brimmell*
Queen's Bench Division [1977] QB 859; [1977] 2 WLR 943;
[1976] 3 All ER 765

The plaintiff and defendant went out drinking together in Cardiff, and each consumed eight or nine pints of beer. On the way home at about 2 a.m. the defendant negligently drove into a lamp post. Held: the plaintiff was 20 per cent contributorily negligent in getting in the car with a driver whom he knew to be drunk.

WATKINS J: The other allegation of contributory negligence gives rise to very different considerations, although it is based upon the same fundamental principle as explained by Lord Denning MR in *Froom's* case. He said, at p. 291: 'Contributory negligence is a man's carelessness in looking after his own safety. He is guilty of contributory negligence if he ought reasonably to have foreseen that, if he did not act as a reasonable prudent man, he might be hurt himself: . . .'

But, is a man who voluntarily allows himself to be carried as a passenger in a motor car, driven by someone whom he knows has consumed a substantial quantity of alcohol which, as he must have been aware, reduced his capacity to drive properly, guilty of contributory negligence if the driver does drive negligently and the passenger is thereby injured? . . .

In the American Law Institution Restatement of the Law of Torts [*Restatement, Second, Torts*], section 466, it is stated that a plaintiff's contributory negligence may consist in an intentional and unreasonable exposure of himself to danger created by the defendant's negligence, of which danger the plaintiff knows or has reason to know. In subsection (e) it is stated, in illustration of this rule, that if a plaintiff rides a car knowing that the driver is drunk or that the car has insufficient brakes or headlights, he is ordinarily guilty of contributory negligence unless there are special circumstances which may make such conduct reasonable.

In Australia it seems to be accepted that contributory negligence can successfully be established upon this basis: see *Insurance Commissioner* v *Joyce*, 77 CLR 39. In that case Latham CJ expressed himself, at p. 47, of the opinion that he found himself in this dilemma:

> If . . . the plaintiff was sober enough to know and understand the danger of driving with [the defendant] in a drunken condition, he was guilty of contributory negligence . . . . But if he was not sober enough to know and understand such a danger . . . if he drank himself into a condition of stupidity or worse, he thereby disabled himself from avoiding the consequences of negligent driving by [the defendant], and his action fails on the ground of contributory negligence.

Thus, it appears to me that there is widespread and weighty authority for the proposition that a passenger may be guilty of contributory negligence if he rides with the driver of a car whom he knows has consumed alcohol in such quantity as is likely to impair to a dangerous degree that driver's capacity to drive properly and safely. So, also, may a passenger be guilty of contributory negligence if he, knowing that he is going to be driven in a car by his companion later, accompanies him upon a bout of drinking which has the effect, eventually, of robbing the passenger of clear thought and perception and diminishes the driver's capacity to drive properly and carefully. Whether this principle can be relied upon successfully is a question of fact and degree to be determined in the circumstances out of which the issue is said to arise.

In the instant case the plaintiff and the defendant drank a fairly considerable amount of beer, much of it within a relatively short period before the beginning of the fateful journey. They were both reasonably intelligent young men and the plaintiff, in particular, must have appreciated at some part of the evening, in my view, that to continue the bout of drinking would be to expose himself to the risk of being driven later by someone who would be so much under the influence of drink as to be incapable of driving safely. I think it more than likely, however, that the two of them were bent on a kind of what is known as a pub crawl and gave little, if any, thought to the possible consequences of it, or were recklessly indifferent to them.

I think this is a clear case on the facts of contributory negligence, either upon the basis that the minds of the plaintiff and the defendant, behaving recklessly, were equally befuddled by drink so as to rid them of clear thought and perception, or, as seems less likely, the plaintiff remained able to, and should have if he actually did not, foresee the risk of being hurt by riding with the defendant as passenger. In such a case as this the degree of blameworthiness is not, in my opinion, equal. The driver, who alone controls the car and has it in him, therefore, to do, whilst in drink, great damage, must bear by far the greater responsibility. I, therefore, adjudge the plaintiff's fault to be of the degree of 20 per cent. . . .

Notes

1.   The idea that a person may be contributorily negligent either in getting into a car knowing the driver is drunk or in going out with the defendant knowing that he will be driven back by him later when he is drunk, does not solve one problem: what if a person meets a driver when both he and the driver are drunk, and then he is unable to appreciate what he ought to do for his own safety? An extreme form of this occurred in New Zealand in *Dixon* v *King* [1925] 2 NZLR 357, where the plaintiff was so drunk that he was unconscious, and he was loaded into the defendant's van. The court logically held that the defence of consent could not apply, and, although it was not raised, contributory negligence could not apply either. Thus, a plaintiff who accepts a lift, not having made previous arrangements, is better off if he is very drunk rather than slightly drunk, because his judgment is impaired and he is unable to appreciate the risk he runs or what he ought to do about it.

2.   The defence of consent has been raised in this context, but it is clear from *Pitts* v *Hunt* [1991] 1 QB 24 that the Road Traffic Act 1988, s. 149(3) prevents that defence operating in relation to motor vehicles where compulsory insurance is required: see section 3 below. However, it can apply in other situations: see *Morris* v *Murray* [1991] 2 QB 6, where the plaintiff was a passenger on a plane the pilot of which was drunk.

Jones v *Boyce*
Nisi Prius (1816) 1 Stark 492; 171 ER 540

The plaintiff was a passenger on the defendant's coach. A defective coupling rein broke while the coach was going downhill. The driver forced the coach into the side of the road and it was stopped by a post. However, the plaintiff, fearing a crash, had thrown himself from the coach and broke a leg. Had he stayed where he was he would have been safe. *Held*: the plaintiff was not contributorily negligent.

LORD ELLENBOROUGH: This case presents two questions for your consideration; first, whether the proprietor of the coach was guilty of any default in omitting to provide the safe and proper means of conveyance, and if you should be of that opinion, the second question for your consideration will be, whether that default was conducive to the injury which the plaintiff has sustained; for if it was not so far conducive as to create such a reasonable degree of alarm and apprehension in the mind of the plaintiff, as rendered it necessary for him to jump down from the coach in order to avoid immediate danger, the action is not maintainable. To enable the plaintiff to sustain the action, it is not necessary that he should have been thrown off the coach; it is sufficient if he was placed by the misconduct of the defendant in such a situation as obliged him to adopt the alternative of a dangerous leap, or to remain at certain peril; if that position was occasioned by the default of the defendant, the action may be supported. On the other hand, if the plaintiff's act resulted from a rash apprehension of danger, which did not exist, and the injury which he sustained is to be attributed to rashness and imprudence, he is not entitled to recover. The question is, whether he was placed in such a situation as to render what he did a prudent precaution, for the purpose of self-preservation . . . . Therefore it is for your consideration, whether the plaintiff's act was the measure of an unreasonably alarmed mind, or such as a reasonable and prudent mind would have adopted. If I place a man in such a situation that he must adopt a perilous alternative, I am responsible for the consequences; if, therefore, you should be of opinion, that the reins were defective, did this circumstance create a necessity for what he did, and did he use proper caution and prudence in extricating himself from the apparently impending peril. If you are of that opinion, then, since the original fault was in the proprietor, he is liable to the plaintiff for the injury which his misconduct has occasioned. This is the first case of the kind which I recollect to have occurred. A coach proprietor certainly is not to be responsible for the rashness and imprudence of a passenger; it must appear that there existed a reasonable cause for alarm.

Note
A modern example of this principle is *Holomis* v *Dubuc* (1975) 56 DLR 3d 351. The defendant landed a seaplane in which the plaintiff was travelling on a remote lake in British Columbia, and the plane hit a submerged object. Water began to pour into the passenger compartment and the plaintiff leaped out and was drowned. Had he remained in the plane he would have been safe, as the plane was successfully beached. However, the plaintiff was held to be 50 per cent responsible for his own death, not for jumping out, but for jumping out without a life jacket. Is it contributorily negligent to panic?

Fitzgerald v *Lane and Patel*
House of Lords [1989] AC 328; [1988] 2 All ER 961; [1988] 3 WLR 365

The plaintiff was a pedestrian who carelessly stepped into the road and was hit by a car driven by the first defendant. This propelled him further into the road and he was struck again by a car driven by the second defendant. The trial judge determined that all three were equally to blame, and gave judgment for the plaintiff for two-thirds of his damages. The Court of Appeal held that the trial judge's finding meant that the plaintiff should have judgment for only 50 per cent of his damages. Held: dismissing the appeal, that the plaintiff should receive 50 per cent of his damages.

LORD ACKNER:

The correct approach to the determination of contributory negligence, apportionment and contribution
It is axiomatic that whether the plaintiff is suing one or more defendants, for damages for personal injuries, the first question which the judge has to determine is whether the plaintiff has established liability against one or other or all the defendants, i.e. that they, or one or more of them, were negligent (or in breach of statutory duty) and that the negligence (or breach of statutory duty) caused or materially contributed to his injuries. The next step, of course, once liability has been established, is to assess what is the total of the damage that the plaintiff has sustained as a result of the established negligence. It is only after these two decisions have been made that the next question arises, namely, whether the defendant or defendants have established (for the onus is upon them) that

the plaintiff, by his own negligence, contributed to the damage which he suffered. If, and only if, contributory negligence is established does the court then have to decide, pursuant to section 1 of the Law Reform (Contributory Negligence) Act 1945, to what extent it is just and equitable to reduce the damages which would otherwise be recoverable by the plaintiff, having regard to his 'share in the responsibility for the damage.'

All the decisions referred to above are made in the main action. Apportionment of liability in a case of contributory neglience between plaintiff and defendants must be kept separate from apportionment of *contribution between the defendants inter se.* Although the defendants are each liable to the plaintiff for the whole amount for which he has obtained judgment, the proportions in which, as between themselves, the defendants must meet the plaintiff's claim, do not have any direct relationship to the extent to which the total damages have been reduced by the contributory negligence, although the facts of any given case may justify the proportions being the same.

Once the questions referred to above in the main action have been determined in favour of the plaintiff to the extent that he has obtained a judgment against two or more defendants, then and only then should the court focus its attention on the claims which may be made between those defendants for contribution pursuant to the Civil Liability (Contribution) Act 1978, re-enacting and extending the court's powers under section 6 of the Law Reform (Married Women and Tortfeasors) Act 1935. In the contribution proceedings, whether or not they are heard during the trial of the main action or by separate proceedings, the court is concerned to discover what contribution is just and equitable, having regard to the responsibility between the tortfeasors inter se, for the damage which the plaintiff has been adjudged entitled to recover. That damage may, of course, have been subject to a reduction as a result of the decision in the main action that the plaintiff, by his own negligence, contributed to the damage which he sustained.

Thus, where the plaintiff successfully sues more than one defendant for damages for personal injuries, and there is a claim between co-defendants for contribution, there are two distinct and different stages in the decision-making process — the one in the main action and the other in the contribution proceedings.

The trial judge's error
Mr Stewart accepts that the judge telescoped or elided the two separate stages referred to above into one when he said: 'I find that it is impossible to say that one of the parties is more or less to blame than the other and hold that the responsibility should be borne equally by all three.' The judge, in my judgment, misdirected himself by thinking in tripartite terms, instead of pursuing separately the two stages — phase 1: was the plaintiff guilty of contributory negligence and, if so, to what extent should the recoverable damages be reduced, issues which concerned the plaintiff on the one hand and the defendants jointly on the other hand; and phase 2: the amount of the contribution recoverable between the two defendants having regard to the extent of their responsibility for the damage recovered by the plaintiff — an issue which affected only the defendants inter se and in no way involved the plaintiff.

Note
This case makes clear that one should first assess the degree of responsibility of the plaintiff for his own loss in relation to the totality of the actions of the defendants, and only at a later stage should one assess the responsibility of the defendants as between themselves. This solves one version of the 'relativities' problem, in that a plaintiff is no better off being injured by two defendants than

by one. However, other problems remain. The difficulty arises from the fact that the plaintiff's responsibility is assessed relative to that of the defendant, so that a plaintiff is better off if he is injured by a grossly negligent defendant. For example, a plaintiff acts carelessly: this carelessness will have a lower relative value in relation to a very negligent defendant than in relation to a slightly negligent defendant. Thus the *same* conduct by the plaintiff will be assessed at, say, 50 per cent in relation to a slightly negligent defendant, but at only 25 per cent in relation to a very negligent defendant. Can this problem be solved? See further Atiyah, *Accidents, Compensation and the Law*, 4th ed., p. 122.

Section 2:   consent

Consent or, as it is sometimes referred to, *volenti non fit injuria*, provides a complete defence to an action, and, if successful, the plaintiff gets nothing. The defence is based on the view that a person cannot sue if he *consents* to the risk of damage. It is not enough merely to *know* of the risk, but no doubt where the risk is extremely obvious the plaintiff will be taken to have consented. This presumption should be used sparingly. An example where it was perhaps justified was *O'Reilly* v *National Rail and Tramway Appliances* [1966] 1 All ER 499, where the plaintiff and others were sorting scrap when they found a live ammunition shell nine inches long and one inch in diameter. After it had been rolled about, someone said to the plaintiff, who was holding a sledgehammer, 'Hit it: what are you scared of?', and the plaintiff did so, suffering severe injuries.

The defence of consent is fairly rare, especially in cases involving employees, but sometimes a similar device is used: that is that there was no breach of duty, either because there was no breach to that particular plaintiff (for example as between competitors in a sport) or because the plaintiff would have been injured even if the duty had been fulfilled. The relationship between duty, breach of duty and consent is illustrated by *McGinlay* v *British Railways Board* (below).

For a general discussion of this defence, where it is argued that the defence should not apply in the absence of an agreement to absolve the defendant, see Jaffey, 'Volenti non fit injuria' [1985] CLJ 87.

Morris v *Murray*
Court of Appeal [1991] 2 QB 6; [1991] 2 WLR 195; [1990] 3 All ER 801

The plaintiff and the defendant spent the afternoon drinking, during which time the defendant consumed the equivalent of 17 whiskies, the alcohol concentration in his blood being more than three times that permitted for a car driver. The defendant then suggested that they go for a flight in his light aircraft for which he held a pilot's licence. The defendant took off down wind rather than up wind as he should have done, and the plane climbed to 300 feet, stalled and dived into the ground. The pilot was killed and the plaintiff passenger injured. Held: allowing the appeal, that the defendant was not liable as the plaintiff had consented to the risk.

FOX LJ: *Nettleship* v *Weston* [1971] 2 QB 691 was a case of a driving instructor injured by the negligent driving of the pupil. It is not, as a decision, of much relevance to the present case since, before giving the lesson, the instructor had asked for and obtained an assurance that there was in existence a policy of insurance. He was in fact shown a comprehensive policy which covered a passenger. That was unhopeful ground for a volens plea. There are, however, observations of Lord Denning MR and Salmon LJ to which I should refer. Lord Denning said, at p. 701:

> Knowledge of the risk of injury is not enough. . . . Nothing will suffice short of an agreement to waive any claim for negligence. The plaintiff must agree, expressly or impliedly, to waive any claim for any injury that may befall him due to the lack of reasonable care by the defendant: or, more accurately, due to the failure by the defendant to measure up to the standard of care which the law requires of him.

Salmon LJ, at p. 704, adopted, in a dissenting judgment, a different approach. He said that if, to the knowledge of the passenger, the driver was so drunk as to be incapable of driving safely, a passenger having accepted a lift could not expect the driver to drive other than dangerously. The duty of care, he said, sprang from relationship. The relationship which the passenger has created in accepting a lift in such circumstances cannot entitle him to expect the driver to discharge a duty of care which the passenger knows that he is incapable of discharging. The result is that no duty is owed by the driver to the passenger to drive safely. The difficulty about this analysis is that it may tend to equate 'sciens' with 'volens' which is not the law. However, there must be cases where the facts are so strong that 'volens' is the only sensible conclusion. Salmon LJ said that, alternatively, if there is a duty owed to the passenger to drive safely, the passenger by accepting the lift clearly assumed the risk of the driver failing to discharge that duty.

I doubt whether the gap between Lord Denning MR's approach and that of Salmon LJ is a very wide one. On the one hand, you may have an implicit waiver of any claims by reason of an exhibited notice as to the assumption of risk: see *Bennett* v *Tugwell* [1987] QB 267, which was decided before the Road Traffic Act 1972. On the other hand, if it is evident to the passenger from the first that the driver is so drunk that he is incapable of driving safely, the passenger must have accepted the obvious risk of injury. You may say that he is volens or that he has impliedly waived the right to claim or that the driver is impliedly discharged from the normal duty of care. In general, I think that the volenti doctrine can apply to the tort of negligence, though it must depend upon the extent of the risk, the passenger's knowledge of it and what can be inferred as to his acceptance of it. The passenger cannot be volens (in the absence of some form of express disclaimer) in respect of acts of negligence which he had no reason to anticipate and he must be free from compulsion. Lord Pearce in *Imperial Chemical Industries Ltd* v *Shatwell* [1965] AC 656, 687–688, said:

> as concerns common law negligence, the defence of volenti non fit injuria is clearly applicable if there was a genuine full agreement, free from any kind of pressure, to assume the risk of loss. In *Williams* v *Port of Liverpool Stevedoring Co. Ltd* [1956] 1 WLR 551 Lynskey J rejected the defence where one stevedore was injured by the deliberate negligence of the whole gang (to which the plaintiff gave 'tacit consent') in adopting a dangerous system of unloading. There was an overall duty on the master to provide a safe system of work, and it is difficult for one man to stand out against his gang. In such circumstances one may not have that deliberate free assumption of risk which is essential to the plea and which makes it as a rule unsuitable in master and servant cases owing to the possible existence of indefinable social and economic pressure. If the plaintiff had been shown to be a moving spirit in the decision to unload

in the wrong manner it would be different. But these matters are questions of fact and degree.

. . . I think that in embarking upon the flight the plaintiff had implicitly waived his rights in the event of injury consequent on Mr Murray's failure to fly with reasonable care. . . .

Considerations of policy do not lead me to any different conclusion. Volenti as a defence has, perhaps, been in retreat during this century — certainly in relation to master and servant cases. It might be said that the merits could be adequately dealt with by the application of the contributory negligence rules. The judge held that the plaintiff was only 20 per cent to blame (which seems to me to be too low) but if that were increased to 50 per cent so that the plaintiff's damages were reduced by half, both sides would be substantially penalised for their conduct. It seems to me, however, that the wild irresponsibility of the venture is such that the law should not intervene to award damages and should leave the loss where it falls. Flying is intrinsically dangerous and flying with a drunken pilot is great folly. . . .

Notes

1.   One issue that arose was whether the plaintiff was so drunk that he could not appreciate and therefore consent to the risk he was running. It was held that in fact he was capable of understanding the risks. See further *Dixon* v *King* [1975] 2 NZLR 357 and *Kirkham* v *Chief Constable of Manchester* [1990] 2 QB 283, in both of which the plaintiffs were unable to appreciate the risk and therefore did not consent.

2.   This case does not apply to drunk drivers of motor vehicles, as by the Road Traffic Act 1988, s. 149(3), volenti cannot be pleaded by a person driving a motor vehicle in circumstances where compulsory insurance applies: see section 3 below.

Question

Do you agree with Fox LJ that contributory negligence is not the appropriate principle to apply? Does this mean that the greater the fault of the defendant the less he has to pay?

McGinlay (or Titchener) v *British Railways Board*
House of Lords [1983] 1 WLR 1427; [1983] 3 All ER 770

The pursuer and her friend, John Grimes, were struck by a train near Shettleston in Glasgow. There was a fence alongside the railway consisting of old sleepers, but this was in disrepair, and the pursuer and her friend had climbed up the embankment, through the broken fence and on to the railway line in order to get to a disused brickworks which was popular with courting couples. The pursuer was injured and her friend killed. The defendants knew that the fence was in disrepair and that people often crossed the line at that point. The House of Lords held: dismissing the appeal, (1) that the defendants had discharged their duty to the pursuer since the fence, although in disrepair, was a sufficient warning to the plaintiff to keep off the railway,

(2) alternatively, that there was no breach of duty because the pursuer would have crossed the line even if the fence had been in good repair, and (3) alternatively, that the pursuer consented to the risk of injury within the terms of s. 2(3) of the Occupiers' Liability (Scotland) Act 1960 which absolves a defendant from liability to a person 'in respect of risks which that person has willingly accepted as his'.

LORD FRASER: . . . The existence and extent of a duty to fence will depend on the circumstances of the case including the age and intelligence of the particular person entering upon the premises; the duty will tend to be higher in a question with a very young or a very old person than in the question with a normally active and intelligent adult or adolescent. The nature of the locus and the obviousness or otherwise of the railway may also be relevant. In the circumstances of this case, and in a question with this appellant, I have reached the opinion that the Lord Ordinary was well entitled to hold, as he did, that the respondents owed no duty to her to do more than they in fact did to maintain the fence along the line. I reach that view primarily because the appellant admitted that she was fully aware that the line existed, that there was danger in walking across it or along it, that she ought to have kept a look out for trains, and that she had done so when crossing the line on previous occasions.

If I am right so far, that would be enough to dispose of this appeal in favour of the respondents. But the Lord Ordinary and the Division based their decisions also on other grounds and I ought briefly to consider those additional grounds. In the first place the Lord Ordinary held that, even if the respondents were at fault in failing to maintain the fence and to repair the gaps in it, the appellant had failed to prove, as a matter of probability, that if the respondents had performed their duty in those respects, the accident would have been prevented. The Lord Ordinary expressed himself strongly on this point and concluded that the appellant and her companion would not have been stopped by anything short of an impenetrable barrier. No doubt he reached that conclusion mainly because of the appellant's evidence in cross-examination, that the respondents should have put up an impenetrable barrier which would have been 'impossible to get through.' That extreme view is clearly untenable; even in the *M'Glone* case, 1966 SC(HL) 1, where the danger (from a transformer) was at least as great as the danger in this case and where the injured intruder was a boy aged only 12, Lord Reid, at p. 11, described the suggestion that the defenders owed him a duty to surround the transformer with an impenetrable and unclimbable fence as 'quite unreasonable.' But the appellant also said that even an ordinary post and wire fence would have been enough to prevent her from crossing the line because she could not have climbed over it. This was at least partly because she was wearing platform shoes. . . . Having regard to the fact that the appellant, helped perhaps by her boyfriend, was apparently able to climb up the embankment and walk across the line, platform shoes and all, I consider that the Lord Ordinary was fully entitled to conclude that she had failed to satisfy him that a post and wire fence would have deterred her. It follows that the respondents' failure to maintain the fence in a reasonable condition, even assuming that it was their duty to have done so, did not cause the accident. The respondents aver that post and wire fencing was the type of fencing mainly relied on by them near the locus and that it was subject to frequent vandalism, but these matters were not explored in evidence.

Secondly the Lord Ordinary held that the respondents had established a defence under section 2(3) of the Act of 1960 by proving that the appellant had willingly accepted the risks of walking across the line. As Lord Reid said in the *M'Glone* case, 1966 SC(HL) 1, 13, subsection (3), merely puts in words the principle volenti non fit injuria. That principle is perhaps less often relied upon in industrial accident cases at the present time than formerly, but so far as cases under the Act of 1960 are concerned, the principle is expressly stated in subsection (3) and there is no room for an argument that it is out of date or discredited. If the Lord Ordinary was entitled to sustain this defence, the result would be that, whether the respondents would otherwise have been in breach of their duty to the appellant or not, the appellant had exempted them from any obligation towards her: see *Salmond & Heuston on Torts,* 18th ed. (1981), p. 467. On this matter I am of opinion, in agreement with Lord Hunter, that the Lord Ordinary was well founded in sustaining this defence. The reasons for doing so are in the main the same as the reasons for holding that the respondents were not in breach of their duty. The appellant admitted that she was fully aware that this was a line along which trains ran, and that it would be dangerous to cross the line because of the presence of the trains. She said in cross-examination 'it was just a chance I took,' and the Lord Ordinary evidently accepted that she understood what she was saying. She was in a different position from the boy in the *M'Glone* case, 1966, SC(HL) 1, who did not have a proper appreciation of the danger from live wires: see Lord Reid at p. 13 and Lord Pearce at p. 18. As I have said already the appellant did not suggest that the train which injured her had been operated in an improper or unusual way. The importance of that is that the chance which she took was no doubt limited to the danger from the train operated properly, in the 'ordinary and accustomed way': see *Slater* v *Clay Cross Co. Ltd* [1956] 2 QB 264, 271, *per* Denning LJ. Had there been evidence to show that the train which injured the appellant was driven negligently, like the train in *Slater's* case, the risk which materialised would not have been within the risks that the appellant had accepted. But there is nothing of that kind here. In my opinion therefore the defence under section 2(3) is established.

In these circumstances no question of apportioning the blame on the ground of contributory negligence arises.

Note
Rescuers might be thought to consent to the risks that their rescue involves, but this has never been a defence for the defendant who created the initial risk. In *Baker* v *Hopkins* [1959] 1 WLR 966 the defendant had adopted a dangerous system of working, in cleaning a well by lowering a petrol engine which emitted poisonous fumes. Two of his workmen were overcome by fumes, and the plaintiff, a doctor, volunteered to go down the well, knowing of the existence of fumes. He too was overcome, but he could not be pulled out of the well because the rope which was tied to his waist became caught. The defendants were liable and unable to rely on consent. Morris LJ said:

> If C, activated by an impulsive desire to save life, acts bravely and promptly and subjugates any timorous over-concern for his own well being or comfort, I cannot think it would be either rational or seemly to say that he freely and voluntarily agreed to incur the risks of the situation which had been created by A's negligence.

Question
Is a person justified in exposing himself to danger to recover a dead body, or a live dog?

Section 3:   exclusion clauses and notices

Tortious liability can be excluded by the term of a contract, but this is subject to the effect of the Unfair Contract Terms Act 1977 (below). For the effect of exclusion notices on occupiers' liability, see Chapter 19 below, and for the effect of the 1977 Act on a disclaimer of liability for a negligent statement, see Chapter 9.

UNFAIR CONTRACT TERMS ACT 1977

PART I

1.   Scope of Part I

(1)   For the purposes of this Part of this Act, 'negligence' means the breach—

    (a)   of any obligation, arising from the express or implied terms of a contract, to take reasonable care or exercise reasonable skill in the performance of the contract;

    (b)   of any common law duty to take reasonable care or exercise reasonable skill (but not any stricter duty);

    (c)   of the common duty of care imposed by the Occupiers' Liability Act 1957 or the Occupiers' Liability Act (Northern Ireland) 1957.

. . .

(3)   In the case of both contract and tort, sections 2 to 7 apply . . . only to business liability, that is liability for breach of obligations or duties arising—

    (a)   from things done or to be done by a person in the course of a business (whether his own business or another's); or

    (b)   from the occupation of premises used for business purposes of the occupier; and references to liability are to be read accordingly, but liability of an occupier of premises for breach of an obligation or duty towards a person obtaining access to the premises for recreational or educational purposes, being liability for loss or damage suffered by reason of the dangerous state of the premises, is not a business liability of the occupier unless granting that person such access for the purposes concerned falls within the business purposes of the occupier.

(4)   In relation to any breach of duty or obligation, it is immaterial for any purpose of this Part of this Act whether the breach was inadvertent or intentional, or whether liability for it arises directly or vicariously.

Avoidance of liability for negligence, breach of contract, etc.

2.   Negligence liability

(1)   A person cannot by reference to any contract term or to a notice given to persons generally or to particular persons exclude or restrict his liability for death or personal injury resulting from negligence.

(2)   In the case of other loss or damage, a person cannot so exclude or restrict his liability for negligence except in so far as the term or notice satisfies the requirement of reasonableness.

(3)   Where a contract term or notice purports to exclude or restrict liability for negligence a person's agreement to or awareness of it is not of itself to be taken as indicating his voluntary acceptance of any risk.

Liability arising from sale or supply of goods

5.   'Guarantee' of consumer goods

(1)   In the case of goods of a type ordinarily supplied for private use or consumption, where loss or damage—

(a)   arises from the goods proving defective while in consumer use; and

(b)   results from the negligence of a person concerned in the manufacture or distribution of the goods,

liability for the loss or damage cannot be excluded or restricted by reference to any contract term or notice contained in or operating by reference to a guarantee of the goods.

(2)   For these purposes—

(a)   goods are to be regarded as 'in consumer use' when a person is using them, or has them in his possession for use, otherwise than exclusively for the purposes of a business; and

(b)   anything in writing is a guarantee if it contains or purports to contain some promise or assurance (however worded or presented) that defects will be made good by complete or partial replacement, or by repair, monetary compensation or otherwise.

(3)   This section does not apply as between the parties to a contract under or in pursuance of which possession or ownership of the goods passed.

Explanatory provisions

11.   The 'reasonableness' test

(1)   In relation to a contract term, the requirement of reasonableness for the purposes of this Part of this Act, . . . is that the term shall have been a fair and reasonable one to be included having regard to the circumstances which were, or ought reasonably to have been, known to or in the contemplation of the parties when the contract was made.

. . .

(3)   In relation to a notice (not being a notice having contractual effect), the requirement of reasonableness under this Act is that it should be fair and reasonable to allow reliance on it, having regard to all the circumstances obtaining when the liability arose or (but for the notice) would have arisen.

(4)   Where by reference to a contract term or notice a person seeks to restrict liability to a specified sum of money, and the question arises (under this or any other Act) whether the term or notice satisfies the requirement of reasonableness, regard shall be had in particular (but without prejudice to subsection (2) above in the case of contract terms) to—

(a)   the resources which he could expect to be available to him for the purpose of meeting the liability should it arise; and

(b)   how far it was open to him to cover himself by insurance.

(5)   It is for those claiming that a contract term or notice satisfies the requirement of reasonableness to show that it does.

13.   Varieties of exemption clause

(1)   To the extent that this Part of this Act prevents the exclusion or restriction of any liability it also prevents—

(a)   making the liability or its enforcement subject to restrictive or onerous conditions;

(b)   excluding or restricting any right or remedy in respect of the liability, or subjecting a person to any prejudice in consequence of his pursuing any such right or remedy;

(c)   excluding or restricting rules of evidence or procedure;

and (to that extent) sections 2 and 5 to 7 also prevent excluding or restricting liability by reference to terms and notices which exclude or restrict the relevant obligation or duty.

(2) But an agreement in writing to submit present or future differences to arbitration is not to be treated under this Part of this Act as excluding or restricting any liability.

14. Interpretation of Part I
In this Part of this Act—
'business' includes a profession and the activities of any government department or local or public authority;
'goods' has the same meaning as in the Sale of Goods Act 1979;
. . .
'negligence' has the meaning given by section 1(1);
'notice' includes an announcement, whether or not in writing, and any other communication or pretended communication; and
'personal injury' includes any disease and any impairment of physical or mental condition.

ROAD TRAFFIC ACT 1988

149. Avoidance of certain agreements as to liability towards passengers
(1) This section applies where a person uses a motor vehicle in circumstances such that under section 143 of this Act there is required to be in force in relation to his use of it such a policy of insurance or such a security in respect of third-party risks as complies with the requirements of this Part of this Act.

(2) If any other person is carried in or upon the vehicle while the user is so using it, any antecedent agreement or understanding between them (whether intended to be legally binding or not) shall be of no effect so far as it purports or might be held—

(a) to negative or restrict any such liability of the user in respect of persons carried in or upon the vehicle as is required by section 145 of this Act to be covered by a policy of insurance, or

(b) to impose any conditions with respect to the enforcement of any such liability of the user.

(3) The fact that a person so carried has willingly accepted as his the risk of negligence on the part of the user shall not be treated as negativing any such liability of the user.

(4) For the purposes of this section—

(a) references to a person being carried in or upon a vehicle include references to a person entering or getting on to, or alighting from, the vehicle, and

(b) the reference to an antecedent agreement is to one made at any time before the liability arose.

Notes
1. This important provision prevents a driver excluding liability where insurance is compulsory. One problem was that drivers put exclusion notices in their cars, believing that this excluded only their personal liability and not that of the insurance company, but of course if the liability of the owner is excluded so is that of the insurance company.
2. In *Pitts v Hunt* [1991] 1 QB 24, it was made clear that this statute applies to all cases of consent, including that of a passenger who gets into a car driven by a drunk driver. Beldam LJ said that 'it is no longer open to the driver of a motor vehicle to say that the fact of his passenger travelling in circumstances in

which for one reason or another it could be said that he had willingly accepted a risk of negligence on the driver's part, relieves him of liability for such negligence'. However it should be noted that s. 149(3) does not prevent the operation of the defence of participation in an unlawful act (below).

3.   Restrictions on the application of the defence of consent cannot be avoided by saying that the defendant was 100 per cent contributorily negligent. *Pitts* v *Hunt* [1991] 1 QB 24 makes it clear that the doctrine presupposes that the plaintiff will recover some of his damages: see section 1 above.

Section 4:   participating in an unlawful act

This defence, sometimes referred to as *ex turpi causa non oritur actio,* is ill defined, at least in relation to tort. The difficulty is to distinguish between those unlawful acts which do and those which do not preclude recovery by the victim, but different tests have been suggested. These are discussed in *Pitts* v *Hunt* but no clear view has yet emerged.

Pitts v *Hunt*
Court of Appeal [1991] QB 24; [1990] 3 WLR 542; [1990] 3 All ER 344

The plaintiff, Andrew Pitts, was a pillion pasenger on a motorbike driven by the defendant, Mark Hunt. The defendant was 16, did not have a driving licence and was not insured. Both parties went to a disco where they were drinking, and on the way home the bike was driven at about 50 mph and was weaving from side to side of the road when it collided with a car. The trial judge found that the defendant was unfit to drive through drink and was deliberately trying to frighten others on the road. He also found that the plaintiff aided and abetted the defendant and 'was fully in agreement with and was encouraging the way in which the [defendant] was manipulating the controls'. Held: dismissing the appeal, that the defendant was not liable as the damage to the plaintiff arose from a joint unlawful act.

DILLON LJ: Mr Peppitt for the plaintiff founds on certain recent authorities in this country which he relied on as establishing a 'conscience test' to be applied in cases of illegality. The starting point is the judgment of Hutchison J in *Thackwell* v *Barclays Bank plc* [1986] 1 All ER 676. In that case the plaintiff claimed damages from the bank for having paid a cheque drawn in favour of the plaintiff to a third party in reliance on a forgery of the plaintiff's signature on an endorsement of the cheque. The claim was rejected on the ground that the cheque represented the proceeds of a fraud on a fourth party, to which the plaintiff, the drawer of the cheque, and the forger of the endorsement were all parties. Hutchison J, at p. 689, treated the case as one in which public policy would prevent the plaintiff suing:

> just as it would prevent a burglar from whom the stolen goods were snatched by a third party just as the burglar left the victim's house from maintaining an action in conversion against the third party.

The judge in reaching that conclusion seems to have accepted a submission from counsel for the defendants that there were two distinct but related lines of authority running through the cases on illegality, the second of which laid down the 'conscience test.' That test was put as follows, at p. 687:

That test, [counsel] suggested, involved the court looking at the quality of the illegality relied on by the defendant and all the surrounding circumstances, without fine distinctions, and seeking to answer two questions: first, whether there had been illegality of which the court should take notice and, second, whether in all the circumstances it would be an affront to the public conscience if by affording him the relief sought the court was seen to be indirectly assisting or encouraging the plaintiff in his criminal act.

. . . I find a test that depends on what would or would not be an affront to the public conscience very difficult to apply, since the public conscience may well be affected by factors of an emotional nature, e.g., that these boys by their reckless and criminal behaviour happened to do no harm to anyone but themselves. Moreover if the public conscience happened to think that the plaintiff should be compensated for his injuries it might equally think that the deceased driver of the motor cycle, had he survived and merely been injured, ought to be compensated, and that leads into the much-debated question whether there ought to be a universal scheme for compensation for the victims of accidents without regard to fault.

Beyond that, appeal to the public conscience would be likely to lead to a graph of illegalities according to moral turpitude, and I am impressed by the comments of Mason J in *Jackson* v *Harrison*, 138 CLR 438, 455:

there arises the difficulty, which I regard as insoluble, of formulating a criterion which would separate cases of serious illegality from those which are not serious. Past distinctions drawn between felonies and misdemeanours, malum in se and malum prohibitum, offences punishable by imprisonment and those which are not, non-statutory and statutory offences offer no acceptable discrimen.

Bingham LJ's dichotomy in *Saunders* v *Edwards* [1987] 1 WLR 1116 between cases where the plaintiff's action in truth arises directly ex turpi causa and cases where the plaintiff has suffered a genuine wrong to which allegedly unlawful conduct is incidental avoids this difficulty, in that it does not involve grading illegalities according to moral turpitude. . . .

I find it, at this stage, both necessary and helpful to examine the principal Australian cases.

In *Smith* v *Jenkins*, 44 ALJR 78 a group of four youths all about 16 years of age, who had been drinking, robbed a man, stole his car keys, and then, having found out where his car was, stole the car and drove it off on a joyride. The plaintiff was the first driver, but after a couple of changes of driver he was merely a passenger; a relatively few miles from the scene of the theft the car left the road at 80 or 90 mph and hit a tree. The plaintiff was seriously injured and sued the youth who had been the driver at the time of the accident; it was held that he could not recover anything.

In *Bondarenko* v *Sommers* (1968) 69 SR (NSW) 269, a decision of the Court of Appeal of New South Wales, a group of youths stole a car and proceeded to race the stolen car against a car one of them owned along a rough and fairly narrow road containing potholes and ruts. The result of such reckless driving was that the stolen car turned over. One of the youths who was a passenger in the stolen car at the time of that accident claimed damages for his injuries, but was held not entitled to recover.

Then in *Jackson* v *Harrison*, 138 CLR 438 a passenger was injured through the neglient driving of a motor car by a driver who was at the time of the accident and to the

passenger's knowledge disqualified from driving. It was held by the majority of the High
Court, Barwick CJ dissenting, that the passenger was not thereby disabled from
recovering damages from the driver. The view of the majority, Mason Jacobs and Aickin
JJ, was that the illegality did not bear on the standard of care reasonably to be expected
of the driver. . . .

Barwick CJ held in *Smith* v *Jenkins*, 44 ALJR 78, 78–79, that the failure of the plaintiff
to recover damages was to be attributable to a refusal of the law to erect a duty of care
as between persons jointly participating in the performance of an illegal act, rather than
to a refusal of the courts, upon grounds of public policy, to lend their assistance to the
recovery of damages for breach, in those circumstances, of a duty of care owed by the
one to the other because of the criminally illegal nature of the act out of which the harm
arose. The other members of the High Court seem to have taken the same view. Owen
J commented, at p. 89, that:

> It would . . . be an odd state of affairs if in a case such as that put by Lord Asquith in
> *National Coal Board* v *England* [1954] AC 403, at p. 429, a court was called upon to
> consider and decide the standard of care to be expected, in particular circumstances,
> of a prudent safebreaker or whether in the case suggested by Scrutton LJ in *Hillen* v
> *ICI (Alkali) Ltd* [1934] 1 KB 455, at p. 467, the smuggler who had not warned his
> confederates of a defect in the rope which they were using in the course of hiding
> smuggled goods had acted with the degree of care to be expected in the circumstan-
> ces, of a reasonably careful smuggler.

The court considered that the doctrine of volenti did not provide a satisfactory solution
of the problem.

On the facts of *Progress and Properties Ltd* v *Craft*, 135 CLR 651 it became clear that
merely to say that if the parties were engaging in a joint illegal act neither would owe any
duty of care to the other was to put the proposition too widely. The distillation of the
law by the High Court of Australia rests therefore now on the judgment of Jacobs J, with
which the other members of the majority of the court concurred, in *Progress and
Properties Ltd* v *Craft* and in the judgments of Mason and Jacobs JJ, with whom Aickin J
concurred, in *Jackson* v *Harrison*, 138 CLR 438. For relief to be denied on the ground
of the illegality, the circumstances of the joint illegal venture in the course of which the
accident which caused the plaintiff's injuries occurred must be such as to negate, as
between the two of them, any ordinary standard of care. Thus Mason J said in *Jackson*
v *Harrison*, at p. 456:

> A plaintiff will fail when the joint illegal enterprise in which he and the defendant are
> engaged is such that the court cannot determine the particular standard of care to be
> observed

and Jacobs J said in *Progress and Properties Ltd* v *Craft*, 135 CLR 651, 668:

> Where there is a joint illegal activity the actual act of which the plaintiff in a civil action
> may be complaining as done without care may itself be a criminal act of a kind in
> respect of which a court is not prepared to hear evidence for the purpose of
> establishing the standard of care which was reasonable in the circumstances.

This formulation would clearly cover the instances given in the authorities of the
careless smuggler or safebreaker, or the reckless driving, to escape capture, of the
getaway car after a robbery, as in the English case of *Ashton* v *Turner* [1981] QB 137. It
was regarded in *Jackson* v *Harrison* as also covering the factual situations in *Bondarenko*
v *Sommers*, 69 SR (NSW) 269 where there was, in the words of Mason J in *Jackson* v

Harrison, an agreement to drive the stolen car recklessly for the purpose of racing on the highway, and the factual situation in *Smith* v *Jenkins*, 44 ALJR 78. In reference to *Smith* v *Jenkins*, Jacobs J said in *Jackson* v *Harrison*, 138 CLR 438, 460:

> It was a jaunt, an escapade, a joyride even though of a most serious kind from the beginning to the end. How could a standard of care be determined for such a course of criminal activity?

I feel unable to draw any valid distinction between the reckless riding of the motor cycle in the present case by the deceased boy Hunt and the plaintiff under the influence of drink, and the reckless driving of the cars, albeit stolen, in *Smith* v *Jenkins* and *Bondarenko* v *Sommers*. The words of Barwick CJ in *Smith* v *Jenkins*, 44 ALJR 78:

> The driving of the car by the appellant, the manner of which is the basis of the respondent's complaint, was in the circumstances as much a use of the car by the respondent as it was a use by the appellant. That use was their joint enterprise of the moment

apply with equal force to the riding of the motor cycle in the present case. This is a case in which, in Bingham LJ's words in *Saunders* v *Edwards* [1987] 1 WLR 1116, 1134, the plaintiff's action in truth arises directly ex turpi causa.

Notes

1.   The public conscience test (doubted by Dillon LJ) was used by Beldam LJ in *Pitts* v *Hunt*, on the ground that the plaintiff was jointly engaged in an activity which, if it had caused the death of a person other than the defendant driver, would have amounted to manslaughter. It has also been accepted in New Zealand in *Brown* v *Dunsmuir* [1994] 3 NZLR 485. However, in *Tinsley* v *Milligan* [1993] 3 All ER 65 the House of Lords rejected the test, at least in so far as it might apply in contract.

2.   In **Gala v Preston** (1991) 172 CLR 243 the High Court of Australia adopted the 'proximity' approach to cases involving illegality. In that case four men had stolen a car to travel north and over four hours later the plaintiff passenger (one of the four) was injured due to the defendant's careless driving. The majority held that since 'proximity' was the test of whether a duty of care was owed and as this involved policy issues, a relevant factor would be the inappropriateness of trying to define the content of a duty of care where the parties were involved in joint criminal activity. In other words the relationship between the parties determines whether a duty is owed, and one thief does not owe another a duty of care. The majority said that 'to conclude that he should have observed the ordinary standard of care to be expected of a competent driver would be to disregard the actual relationship between the parties. To seek to define a more limited duty of care by reference to the exigencies of the particular case would involve a weighing and adjusting of the conflicting demands of the joint criminal activity and the safety of the participants in which it would be neither appropriate nor feasible for the courts to engage'. Is this too harsh a rule? What connection was there between the theft and the standard of driving?

3.   The Supreme Court of Canada has rejected the 'proximity' view, saying that 'the legality or morality of the plaintiff's conduct is an extrinsic

consideration' to the question whether a duty arises on the basis of foreseeable harm. In *Hall* v *Hebert* (1993) 101 DLR 4th 129 the court preferred to see *ex turpi causa* as a proper defence rather than as an element in the duty of care equation, and also criticised the proximity view on the ground that it was an 'all or nothing' approach. The majority preferred the view that 'there is a need in the law of tort for a principle which permits judges to deny recovery to a plaintiff on the ground that to do so would undermine the integrity of the justice system. The power is a limited one. Its use is justified where allowing the plaintiff's claim would introduce inconsistency into the fabric of the law either by permitting the plaintiff to profit from an illegal or wrongful act, or to evade a penalty prescribed by criminal law. Its use is not justified where the plaintiff's claim is merely for compensation for personal injuries sustained as a consequence of the negligence of the defendant'.

4. Most cases of *ex turpi causa* will also be cases of consent, but in one area there is an important difference. The Road Traffic Act 1988, s. 149(3), prevents the defence of consent applying where the defendant has negligently driven a motor vehicle when insurance is compulsory (see section 3). That section does not, however, prevent the *ex turpi causa* doctrine applying (*Pitts* v *Hunt*), and care will need to be taken that the *ex turpi causa* doctrine is not used as a way of avoiding s. 149(3). In this situation, what extra factors need to be shown, over and above consent, for the *ex turpi causa* doctrine to apply?

5. A trespasser who is engaged in criminal activities is not barred from making a claim for personal injuries against the occupier because to do so would be to make him an outlaw. It is one thing to deny him any fruits of his illegal conduct but another to deprive him of compensation for injury. See *Revill* v *Newbery* [1996] 1 All ER 291 where the plaintiff who was attempting to break into the defendant's allotment shed was shot. The defendant was liable (see further Chapter 21).

16 DAMAGES FOR DEATH AND PERSONAL INJURIES

The law relating to damages for personal injuries is a large and complicated subject, and only a few of the topics can be dealt with here, and even then only in outline. The object of this chapter is to give some idea of what damages are awarded for and how they are calculated, but the subject is highly unscientific and can really only be understood by experience.

Section 1: types of action for damages

Where a live plaintiff sues, the award will usually be for a lump sum to compensate for such matters as loss of future income, loss of amenity and pain and suffering. This once and for all payment has the advantage of finality and is preferred by plaintiffs, but there may be occasions where it is inappropriate. Accordingly, by consent damages can be paid by way of periodic payments, and in cases where the prognosis is uncertain there can be an interim payment. Furthermore, a plaintiff may prefer to negotiate a structured settlement which essentially is a lump sum commuted to an annuity. This has considerable tax advantages.

Where a person dies as the result of a tort there are two methods of claiming damages and their relationship can be complicated. First, there is an action by the deceased himself through his estate under the Law Reform (Miscellaneous Provisions) Act 1934. Secondly, there can be an action by the dependants of the deceased. This is independent of the action by the estate, for the dependants sue for their own loss, although their right to sue is conditional upon the deceased having had a right of action. There can be an action both by the estate and by the dependants for their separate losses, but it should be remembered that any damages received by the estate will be distributed according to the deceased's will (or on his intestacy), and the money may not have been left to the dependants.

DAMAGES BILL 1996

2. Consent orders for periodical payments

(1) A court awarding damages in an action for personal injury may, with the consent of the parties, make an order under which the damages are wholly or partly to take the form of periodical payments.

(2) In this section 'damages' includes an interim payment which the court, by virtue of rules of court in that behalf, orders the defendant to make to the plaintiff (or, in the application of this section to Scotland, the defender to make to the pursuer).

(3) This section is without prejudice to any powers exercisable apart from this section.

Note

This provision is different from (but includes) interim payments (see below) and from structured settlements (see below). The court may make an order for the direct payment from the defendant to the plaintiff of periodic payments, but only with the consent of both parties. The power of the court to order periodic payments without consent has been much discussed. It was approved by the Pearson Commission but opposed by earlier studies. (See the Winn Committee on Personal Injuries Litigation, Cmnd. 3691 and the Law Commission Report No. 56.)

SUPREME COURT ACT 1981

32A. Orders for provisional damages for personal injuries

(1) This section applies to an action for damages for personal injuries in which there is proved or admitted to be a chance that at some definite or indefinite time in the future the injured person will, as a result of the act or omission which gave rise to the cause of action, develop some serious disease or suffer some serious deterioration in his physical or mental condition.

(2) Subject to subsection (4) below, as regards any action for damages to which this section applies in which a judgment is given in the High Court, provision may be made by rules of court for enabling the court, in such circumstances as may be prescribed, to award the injured person—

(a) damages assessed on the assumption that the injured person will not develop the disease or suffer the deterioration in his condition; and

(b) further damages at a future date if he develops the disease or suffers the deterioration.

(3) [omitted]

(4) Nothing in this section shall be construed—

(a) as affecting the exercise of any power relating to costs, including any power to make rules of court relating to costs; or

(b) as prejudicing any duty of the court under any enactment or rule of law to reduce or limit the total damages which would have been recoverable apart from any such duty.

Note

This provision is intended for the cases where liability is clear but the medical prognosis is not. In that situation the plaintiff may apply for the loss known at the time of the trial and return to court for a further award if his condition deteriorates as a result of the tort. By RSC Order 29, r. 11 the section only applies if: (a) the defendant has admitted liability; or (b) the plaintiff has obtained judgment for damages to be assessed; or (c) if the action proceeded to trial the plaintiff would obtain substantial damages. Furthermore, the defendant must either: (a) be insured; or (b) be a public authority; or (c) be a person whose resources are such as to enable him to make the interim payment. Note also that where a plaintiff has been awarded provisional damages and he subsequently dies within three years of the original cause of action arising, then the defendants may still claim under the Fatal Accidents Act 1976. (See the Damages Bill 1996.)

DAMAGES BILL 1996

5. Meaning of structured settlement

(1)   In section 4 above a 'structured settlement' means an agreement settling a claim or action for damages for personal injury on terms whereby—

(a)   the damages are to consist wholly or partly of periodical payments; and

(b)   the person to whom the payments are to be made is to receive them as the annuitant under one or more annuities purchased for him by the person against whom the claim or action is brought or, if he is insured against the claim, by his insurer.

(2)   The periodical payments may be for the life of the claimant, for a specified period or of a specified number or minimum number or include payments of more than one of those descriptions.

(3)   The amounts of the periodical payments (which need not be at a uniform rate or payable at uniform intervals) may be—

(a)   specified in the agreement, with or without provision for increases of specified amounts or percentages; or

(b)   subject to adjustment in a specified manner so as to preserve their real value; or

(c)   partly specified as mentioned in paragraph (a) above and partly subject to adjustment as mentioned in paragraph (b) above.

(4)   The annuity or annuities must be such as to provide the annuitant with sums which as to amount and time of payment correspond to the periodical payments described in the agreement.

(5)   Payments in respect of the annuity or annuities may be received on behalf of the annuitant by another person or received and held on trust for his benefit under a trust of which he is, during his lifetime, the sole beneficiary.

(6)   The Lord Chancellor may by an order made by statutory instrument provide that there shall for the purposes of this section be treated as an insurer any body specified in the order, being a body which, though not an insurer, appears to him to fulfil corresponding functions in relation to damages for personal injury claimed or awarded against persons of any class or description, and the reference in subsection (1)(b) above to a person being insured against the claim and his insurer shall be construed accordingly.

(7)   In the application of subsection (6) above to Scotland for the reference to the Lord Chancellor there shall be substituted a reference to the Secretary of State.

Notes

1.   Section 4 referred to in this section relates to the protection of a plaintiff for the purposes of the Policyholders Protection Act 1975, but s. 5 is included as a

useful definition of a structured settlement. For the tax benefits of a structured settlement see the Taxes Act 1988, s. 329A as inserted by the Finance Act 1995, s. 142.

2. A structured settlement is an arrangement whereby a plaintiff purchases an annuity from an insurance company with the damages he has been awarded or is entitled to. It works in the same way as any insurance policy whereby the insurer agrees to make a regular payment to the insured. If the policy is to last for the life of the plaintiff, the insurance company will make the usual actuarial assessments of his life expectancy. The advantage of a structured settlement is the tax benefit, but in negotiations with the insurance company as to the amount of the annuity some of this benefit may well accrue to them rather than to the plaintiff. See generally Law Commission Report No. 24 'Structured settlements and interim and provisional damages'.

LAW REFORM (MISCELLANEOUS PROVISIONS) ACT 1934

1. Effect of death on certain causes of action

(1) Subject to the provisions of this section, on the death of any person after the commencement of this Act all causes of action subsisting against or vested in him shall survive against, or, as the case may be, for the benefit of, his estate. Provided that this subsection shall not apply to causes of action for defamation . . .

(1A) The right of a person to claim under section 1A of the Fatal Accidents Act 1976 (bereavement) shall not survive for the benefit of his estate on his death.

(2) Where a cause of action survives as aforesaid for the benefit of the estate of a deceased person, the damages recoverable for the benefit of the estate of that person—

    (a) shall not include:

        (i) any exemplary damages;

        (ii) any damages for loss of income in respect of any period after that person's death;

    (c) Where the death of that person has been caused by the act or omission which gives rise to the cause of action, shall be calculated without reference to any loss or gain to his estate consequent on his death, except that a sum in respect of funeral expenses may be included.

(4) Where damage has been suffered by reason of any act or omission in respect of which a cause of action would have subsisted against any person if that person had not died before or at the same time as the damage was suffered, there shall be deemed, for the purposes of this Act, to have been subsisting against him before his death such cause of action in respect of that act or omission as would have subsisted if he had died after the damage was suffered.

(5) The rights conferred by this Act for the benefit of the estates of deceased persons shall be in addition to and not in derogation of any rights conferred on the dependants of deceased persons by the Fatal Accidents Act 1976, and so much of this Act as relates to causes of action against the estates of deceased persons shall apply in relation to causes of action under the said Act as it applies in relation to other causes of action not expressly excepted from the operation of subsection (1) of this section.

(6) In the event of the insolvency of an estate against which proceedings are maintainable by virtue of this section, any liability in respect of the cause of action in respect of which the proceedings are maintainable shall be deemed to be a debt provable in the administration of the estate, notwithstanding that it is a demand in the nature of unliquidated damages arising otherwise than by a contract, promise or breach of trust.

Note

The question of 'lost years' has caused considerable difficulty. This refers to the years the plaintiff would have lived but for the act of the defendant. If the estate is suing under the 1934 Act, damages for those lost years are not recoverable, but rather the dependants will have an action under the Fatal Accidents Act 1976 for the years they would have been supported by the deceased had he remained alive. Note that if a victim sues while he is alive he is able to recover for the lost years, because in those circumstances the dependants will not have an action and the damages for the lost years will be needed to support them after the plaintiff's death.

FATAL ACCIDENTS ACT 1976

1. Right of action for wrongful act causing death

(1) If death is caused by any wrongful act, neglect or default which is such as would (if death had not ensued) have entitled the person injured to maintain an action and recover damages in respect thereof, the person who would have been liable if death had not ensued shall be liable to an action for damages, notwithstanding the death of the person injured.

(2) Subject to section 1A(2) below, every such action shall be for the benefit of the dependants of the person ('the deceased') whose death has been so caused.

(3) In this Act 'dependant' means—

(a) the wife or husband or former wife or husband of the deceased;

(b) any person who—

(i) was living with the deceased in the same household immediately before the date of the death; and

(ii) had been living with the deceased in the same household for at least two years before that date; and

(iii) was living during the whole of that period as the husband or wife of the deceased;

(c) any parent or other ascendant of the deceased;

(d) any person who was treated by the deceased as his parent;

(e) any child or other descendant of the deceased;

(f) any person (not being a child of the deceased) who, in the case of any marriage to which the deceased was at any time a party, was treated by the deceased as a child of the family in relation to that marriage;

(g) any person who is, or is the issue of, a brother, sister, uncle or aunt of the deceased.

(4) The reference to the former wife or husband of the deceased in subsection (3)(a) above includes a reference to a person whose marriage to the deceased has been annulled or declared void as well as a person whose marriage to the deceased has been dissolved.

(5) In deducing any relationship for the purposes of subsection (3) above—

(a) any relationship by affinity shall be treated as a relationship by consanguinity, any relationship of the half blood as a relationship of the whole blood, and the stepchild of any person as his child, and

(b) an illegitimate person shall be treated as the legitimate child of his mother and reputed father.

(6) Any reference in this Act to injury includes any disease and any impairment of a person's physical or mental condition.

1A. Bereavement

(1) An action under this Act may consist of or include a claim for damages for bereavement.

(2) A claim for damages for bereavement shall only be for the benefit—
  (a) of the wife or husband of the deceased; and
  (b) where the deceased was a minor who was never married—
    (i) of his parents, if he was legitimate; and
    (ii) of his mother, if he was illegitimate.

(3) Subject to subsection (5) below, the sum to be awarded as damages under this section shall be £3,500.

(4) Where there is a claim for damages under this section for the benefit of both the parents of the deceased, the sum awarded shall be divided equally between them (subject to any deduction falling to be made in respect of costs not recovered from the defendant).

(5) The Lord Chancellor may by order made by statutory instrument, subject to annulment in pursuance of a resolution of either House of Parliament, amend this section by varying the sum for the time being specified in subsection (3) above.

2. Persons entitled to bring the action

(1) The action shall be brought by and in the name of the executor or administrator of the deceased.

(2) If—
  (a) there is no executor or administrator of the deceased, or
  (b) no action is brought within six months after the death by and in the name of an executor or administrator of the deceased,
the action may be brought by and in the name of all or any of the persons for whose benefit an executor or administrator could have brought it.

(3) Not more than one action shall lie for and in respect of the same subject matter of complaint.

(4) The plaintiff in the action shall be required to deliver to the defendant or his solicitor full particulars of the persons for whom and on whose behalf the action is brought and of the nature of the claim in respect of which damages are sought to be recovered.

3. Assessment of damages

(1) In the action such damages, other than damages for bereavement, may be awarded as are proportioned to the injury resulting from the death to the dependants respectively.

(2) After deducting the costs not recovered from the defendant any amount recovered otherwise than as damages for bereavement shall be divided among the dependants in such shares as may be directed.

(3) In an action under this Act where there fall to be assessed damages payable to a widow in respect of the death of her husband there shall not be taken account the re-marriage of the widow or her prospects of re-marriage.

(4) In an action under this Act where there fall to be assessed damages payable to a person who is a dependant by virtue of section 1(3)(b) above in respect of the death of the person with whom the dependant was living as husband or wife there shall be taken into account (together with any other matter that appears to the court to be relevant to the action) the fact that the dependant had no enforceable right to financial support by the deceased as a result of their living together.

(5) If the dependants have incurred funeral expenses in respect of the deceased, damages may be awarded in respect of those expenses.

(6)   Money paid into court in satisfaction of a cause of action under this Act may be in one sum without specifying any person's share.

4.   Assessment of damages: disregard of benefits
In assessing damages in respect of a person's death in an action under this Act, benefits which have accrued or will or may accrue to any person from his estate or otherwise as a result of his death shall be disregarded.

5.   Contributory negligence
Where any person dies as the result partly of his own fault and partly of the fault of any other person or persons, and accordingly if an action were brought for the benefit of the estate under the Law Reform (Miscellaneous Provisions) Act 1934 the damages recoverable would be reduced under section 1(1) of the Law Reform (Contributory Negligence) Act 1945, any damages recoverable in an action under this Act shall be reduced to a proportionate extent.

Notes
1.   Prospects of re-marriage.   Section 3(3) states that the chances of a widow re-marrying are not to be taken into account in assessing damages. This rule was introduced because it was felt to be disparaging for a woman's looks and character to be assessed by judges with a view to her eligibility in the marriage market. Nevertheless, the rule does have some absurd consequences: in *Thompson* v *Price* [1973] 2 All ER 846 the widow had already re-married before the trial, and this fact was ignored in assessing damages. Thus she received damages for the support she would have received from the deceased, even though her new husband was now legally obliged to support her. Further oddities are that the widow's chances of re-marriage *can* be taken into account when assessing the children's damages, and that, where the deceased is the wife, the husband's chances of marrying again can be taken into account.

A related problem is whether a widow's prospects of earning should be taken into account. Should a widow of 25 who has no children be provided with the equivalent of income for the rest of her life, even though she is able to earn for herself? In fact such issues are ignored (see *Howitt* v *Heads* below).
2.   Bereavement.   The statute now provides for a fixed sum of £7,500 for bereavement. One function of this is to provide damages where no other loss is apparent. Thus, in the case of the death of a young child this will be the only loss. There has been much criticism by parents in such cases that this grossly undervalues a life, but the fact remains that the purpose of damages here is to compensate for a pecuniary loss, and such parents have in fact suffered no monetary loss. (The hard hearted would point out that, economically speaking, the parents have made a gain by the loss of their child, in that they will no longer be put to the expense of its upbringing.)

Section 2:   calculation of loss of earnings

This is the most difficult part of the subject, for the principles involved are wholly unscientific, and assessments are made on the basis of assumptions which need to be explained. The problem is to calculate a future income stream as a lump sum, and the situation is the same in the case of both fatal accident cases and claims by living plaintiffs.

The objective of an award of damages is to provide the equivalent of the income which would have been received by the plaintiff (whether the victim himself or the dependants of a deceased victim) for the period during which he is unable to earn due to the tort committed by the defendant. There are three steps in the calculation:

(1)   Work out the period for which the earnings have been lost, or, in a fatal accident case, the period during which the dependants would have been supported by the deceased.

(2)   Secondly, work out the amount of loss, or the dependency, in weekly, monthly or annual terms.

(3)   Work out the present capital value of that future loss.

It is the third step which produces the problems: obviously you do not simply multiply the amount of the loss by the number of years for which it will occur, because when you give the plaintiff a lump sum he will be able to earn interest on that money, and that must be taken into account. Thus, if a person has lost £10,000 per year for ten years, he would be overcompensated if he were awarded £100,000, for he would be able to earn, say, £6,000 per year interest on this sum. What is needed is to work out a capital sum from which he can, after investing it, withdraw £10,000 per year, and which will be exhausted at the end of the period of loss. What this sum will be will depend to a great extent on the assumed rate of interest he will gain on the capital sum, and at present this is assumed to be about 4 per cent or 5 per cent. (This relatively low figure is used to take some account of inflation, as is explained in *Mallet* v *McMonagle* below).

In practice, the judges talk about a 'multiplier'. This is the figure which, when multiplied by the amount of annual loss, will produce a capital sum from which the amount of the loss may be drawn (net of tax) for the period of loss. For example, in the first case, *Howitt* v *Heads*, the loss was £936 per year for 40 years, and the judge awarded a capital sum of £16,848, that is 18 times the annual loss. The figure 18 was chosen because if the capital sum (18 × 936) is invested at about 5 per cent, then £936 could be drawn out of the fund each year for 40 years. Another way to explain the multiplier is to say that if A gives B £18 he should be able to draw out £1 per year for 40 years, assuming that it is invested at about 5 per cent net of tax.

The actual multiplier selected will also be affected by other uncertainties about the future: for example, a slight reduction will be made for what are called 'the vicissitudes of life', that is the chance that the plaintiff will not survive for the period of the loss or that some other injury will occur to him. In the past calculating these chances was often a matter of intuition and guess-work but now, by virtue of the Civil Evidence Act 1995, s. 10, actuarial tables prepared by the government actuary (the so-called 'Ogden tables') may be used in assessing the chance of future risks materialising.

The first case, *Howitt* v *Heads* is given as a simple example of the application of the Fatal Accidents Act and of the calculation of the multiplier.

Howitt v *Heads*
Queen's Bench Division [1973] 1 QB 64; [1972] 2 WLR 183;
[1972] 1 All ER 491

The plaintiff was a widow aged 21 who had a young son, and she was suing under the Fatal Accidents Act for the loss of her husband. The dependency was calculated at £936 per year for a period of 40 years. Held: neither prospects of re-marriage nor of the plaintiff being able to earn should be taken into account, and a multiplier of 18 should be applied, giving damages of £16,848.

CUMMING-BRUCE J: On the basis of that dependency [of £18 per week] I approach the next problem, which is the problem of the capital sum which fairly represents the injury to the wife occurring from the death. I have to do it with rather less guidance from authority than has for many years been possible in fatal accident cases, as a consequence of the new situation flowing from the effect of section 4(1) of the Law Reform (Miscellaneous Provisions) Act 1971. Here is a young lady now, I think, 21, with one child. Her prospects of remarriage are not to be taken into account. The situation as I see it is this: on the wife's evidence it is likely, being evidently a lady of ability, that when it is convenient for her to make suitable arrangements for their son, she probably will at some stage — perhaps when the boy starts going to school — resume employment, not only to have the advantage of the money, but also because obviously it is likely to make life more interesting for her. And so, peering into the future, I envisage a situation in which it is likely that after a period of years, probably not very far ahead, she will resume employment and make a good deal of money every week as a result. That, of course, is upon the contingency that she does not remarry with all the implications that that might have — implications which I have to leave out of account.

What is the correct approach in a Fatal Accidents Act case to the situation of a widow who has an earning capacity which she will probably use after a fairly short period of years? As far as I know there is no explicit authority in English cases, though there is a good deal of authority to the effect that a wife's private means are not to be taken into account. There is a useful discussion in the well known textbook of *Kemp and Kemp, The Quantum of Damages*, 2nd ed., vol. 2 (1962), p. 272, upon the relevance or otherwise of a widow's capacity to support herself, and there have been two cases in Australia, which were approved in the High Court of Australia, dealing with the matter: see *Carroll* v *Purcell* (1927) 35 ALJR 384. And in *Goodger* v *Knapman* [1924] SASR 347 (and I rely on the citation from that case given in the textbook to which I have referred) Murray CJ said, at p. 358:

'Mr Thomson asked me to make a further reduction by reason of the widow being relieved from the heavier part of her domestic duties, and thereby set free to go out and earn something on her own account. I do not accede to the suggestion, as I am unable to see how liberty to work can reasonably be brought within the description of a pecuniary advantage she has derived from the death of her husband. Any money she might earn would be the result of her labour, not of his death.' The same decision was made by Wolff J in Western Australia in *Usher* v *Williams* (1955) 60 WALR 69, 80: 'The argument for the diminution of the claim by some allowance of the widow's earning potential proceeds on the theory that the husband's death has released a flood of earning capacity. . . . In my opinion the plaintiff's ability to earn is not a gain resulting from the death of her husband within the principle established by *Davies* v

Powell Duffryn Collieries Ltd [1942] AC 601. The widow's ability to work was always there and she could perhaps, as many women do — particularly in professions — have preferred to work after marriage. The same argument that is put forward for the defendants could be applied to any woman who goes out to work through necessity to support herself and her children following her husband's death; and if it can be applied to the widow there is no reason why it should not be used to diminish or extinguish the children's claims in a case where, by her efforts, she is able to support them as well as her husband did in his lifetime. . . . I therefore hold that the widow's earning capacity is not to be taken into account in diminution of damages.'

I agree with the principle enunciated in those cases and I follow them. I therefore make no deduction in respect of the widow's capacity to earn, even though I am satisfied as a matter of probability that she will fairly soon be obtaining a significant degree of financial independence. . . .

The exercise upon which I embark, in seeking to capitalise her loss therefore, has two elements of some artificiality, but by statute I consider that I am bound to postulate one artificiality and on principle, having regard to the approach of the court to the widow's own capacity to earn, I think it is my duty to introduce the second artificiality. Having regard to the age and good health of the husband, subject to what is commonly described as the changes and chances of life, he had a prospect of remunerative employment of not less than 40 years, and having regard to the lady's health and youth, her expectation of life is at least as good as his. And so, subject as I say to changes and chances of the unknown future, this widow has been deprived of the prospect of a settled and stable financial future afforded by her husband over a period of some 40 years.

The reason that there is very little to guide me upon the capitalisation of the financial loss is that in past years, through the whole experience of the Fatal Accidents Acts, in such a case the courts, inevitably taking into account the prospect of remarriage of the young lady of 20 or 21 with one child, or sometimes two or more children, have taken the view that that was a real element in the future which should be given great significance according to the facts of the particular case, in curtailing the probable period for which the injury following the death would continue. Now, for the reasons stated, I have to disregard that very important factor.

Mr Cobb put in, as an aid to testing the effect of an award of £15,000 some tables showing what the effect would be if such a sum was invested to yield either 3 per cent or 4 per cent and I approach the case on the basis of the guidance given in the House of Lords in *Taylor* v *O'Connor* [1971] AC 115. I cite in particular a passage from the speech of Lord Pearson, which I think Mr Cobb had in mind when he caused to be prepared the tables that he put before me. Lord Pearson said, at p. 143:

'The fund of damages is not expected to be preserved intact. It is expected to be used up gradually over the relevant period — 15 or 18 years in this case — so as to be exhausted by the end of the period.' The case with which their Lordships were dealing was a case where the deceased was 53 at the time of death and the respondent 52. 'Therefore, what the widow received annually — £3,750 in this case — is made up partly of income and partly of capital. As the fund is used up, the income becomes less and less and the amounts withdrawn from the capital of the fund become greater and greater, because the total sum to be provided in each year — £3,750 — is assumed (subject to what is said below) to remain constant throughout the relevant period. It is not difficult, though somewhat laborious, to work out without expert assistance how long a given fund will last with a given rate of interest and a given sum of money to be provided in each year.'

Then he gives the first few lines of such a calculation to show the method, which was the method Mr Cobb presented to me. And when one looks at Mr Cobb's figures showing the consequences of an award of £15,000 invested at 3 per cent on the basis that the loss of dependency was £1,000, so that that is the income one is seeking to afford the widow throughout the future, it appears that on that investment of 3 per cent the fund disappears altogether in the 20th year. And at 4 per cent it disappears in the 23rd year. . . . On an £18 a week dependency the annual loss of dependency is £936. So that I seek by my award to provide the widow with capital that will afford her and her son over the foreseeable future an income of £936, and I find in the speeches of the House of Lords in *Taylor* v *O'Connor,* an indication that it is by the management of the capital fund that the widow may reasonably expect to counteract the probable fall in the value of money as a consequence of inflation. I have looked at annuity tables and I have taken them into account as providing one test of the appropriateness of the calculations, but I accept unhesitatingly the view frequently expressed that the actual evidence of such computations (and there is no evidence in this case of an actuarial character), is of limited value in assistance in a fatal accidents case.

I hope that I have thus indicated the factors that have affected my mind, and I have decided that the capital value that should be placed on the loss of dependency by this widow is the sum of £16,848. If my arithmetic is correct it will be found that can be represented as a multiplier of 18. . . .

Note
It is unlikely that the widow would merely invest the money and draw out £936 per year, but if she had, would the capital sum be likely to provide for the widow and her child until the year 2010? [Today's equivalent of £936 is about £6,200, and £16,848 would today be about £110,000.]

Mallett v *McMonagle*
House of Lords [1970] AC 166; [1969] 2 WLR 767; [1969] 2 All ER 178

The extract below deals only with the way in which inflation should be dealt with in an award of damages.

LORD DIPLOCK: My Lords, the purpose of an award of damages under the Fatal Accidents Acts is to provide the widow and other dependants of the deceased with a capital sum which with prudent management will be sufficient to supply them with material benefits of the same standard and duration as would have been provided for them out of the earnings of the deceased had he not been killed by the tortious act of the defendant, credit being given for the value of any material benefits which will accrue to them (otherwise than as the fruits of insurance) as a result of his death.

To assess the damages it is necessary to form a view upon three matters each of which is in greater or less degree one of speculation: (1) the value of the material benefits for his dependants which the deceased would have provided out of his earnings for each year in the future during which he would have provided them, had he not been killed; (2) the value of any material benefits which the dependants will be able to obtain in each such year from sources (other than insurance) which would not have been available to them had the deceased lived but which will become available to them as a result of his death; (3) the amount of the capital sum which with prudent management will produce annual amounts equal to the difference between (1) and (2) (that is 'the dependency') for each of the years during which the deceased would have provided material benefits for the dependants, had he not been killed.

Since the essential arithmetical character of this assessment is the calculation of the present value of an annuity it has become usual both in England and in Northern Ireland to arrive at the total award by multiplying a figure assessed as the amount of the annual 'dependency' by a number of 'years' purchase.' If the figure for the annual 'dependency' remained constant and could be assessed with certainty and if the number of years for which it would have continued were also ascertainable with certainty it would be possible in times of stable currency, interest rates and taxation to calculate with certainty the number of years' purchase of the dependency which would provide a capital sum sufficient to produce an annuity equal in amount to the dependency for the number of years for which it would have continued. If the estimated 'dependency' did not remain constant, but altered at intervals during the period of its enjoyment, an accurate assessment of the appropriate award would involve calculating the present value of a series of annuities for fixed periods progressively deferred. For reasons to which I shall advert this is seldom, if ever, done. Anticipated future variations in 'dependency' are normally dealt with by an adjustment in the multiplicand to be multiplied by the single multiplier — the number of years' purchase.

During the last twenty years, however, sterling has been subject to continuous inflation. Its purchasing power has fallen at an average rate of 3 per cent to 3F per cent per annum and the increase in wage rates has more than kept pace with the fall in the value of money. It has been strongly contended on behalf of the appellant that inflation and increased wage rates are irreversible phenomena in the modern world and that in assessing damages under the Fatal Accidents Acts the 'dependency' should be calculated as a continuously increasing amount to allow for the increasing cost in a depreciating currency of equivalent material benefits which the deceased would have provided for his dependants out of his rising wages. But this is to isolate but one of many interrelated factors. The damages will be paid in currency which has the value of sterling at the date of the judgment. Experience of the twenty years of inflation has shown that its effects can be offset to some extent at any rate by prudent investment in buying a home, in growth stocks, or in the short term high-interest bearing securities.

A simple example will illustrate the effect of high interest rates: the sum which represents the capital value of an annuity of £100 per annum for five years at compound interest rates of 4F per cent per annum would purchase an annuity for the same period of about £110 per annum at current short term interest rates of 8 per cent per annum. During the same five years at a rate of inflation of 3F per cent per annum compound the purchasing power of the pound would fall progressively until at the end of the five year period about £119 would be needed to buy the equivalent of £100 at the beginning of the period. During the first part of the five year period an annuity of £110 would more than compensate for inflation and the excess, invested at 8 per cent, would largely compensate for the short fall at the end of the period.

Fiscal policy, too, may have a considerable effect upon the annual amounts which can be produced by a given capital sum. The changes in income tax and the introduction of capital gains tax during the last twenty years would themselves have been sufficient to falsify actuarial calculations of the capital value of an annuity made before those changes were introduced; and it would be unwise to assume that fiscal policy will not alter further in the coming years.

In my view, the only practicable course for courts to adopt in assessing damages awarded under the Fatal Accidents Acts is to leave out of account the risk of further inflation, on the one hand, and the high interest rates which reflect the fear of it and capital appreciation of property and equities which are the consequence of it, on the other hand. In estimating the amount of the annual dependency in the future, had the deceased not been killed, money should be treated as retaining its value at the date of the judgment, and in calculating the present value of annual payments which would have been received in future years, interest rates appropriate to times of stable currency such as 4 per cent to 5 per cent should be adopted.

Note

1. In *Taylor* v *O'Connor* [1971] AC 115, Lord Reid took a rather different line, saying:

> I am well aware that there is a school of thought which holds that the law should refuse to have any regard to inflation, but that calculations should be based on stable prices, steady or slowly increasing rates of remuneration and low rates of interest. That must, I think, be based either on an expectation of an early return to a period of stability or on a nostalgic reluctance to recognise change. To take account of future inflation will no doubt cause complications and make estimates even more uncertain. No doubt we should not assume the worst, but it would, I think, be quite unrealistic to refuse to take it into account at all.

However the stricter view has prevailed and in *Lim* v *Camden Area Health Authority* [1980] AC 174 Lord Scarman said that inflation should generally not be taken into account because (i) future inflation rates are pure speculation, (ii) inflation is best dealt with by investment policy, and (iii) a person in receipt of damages should be in no better position than anyone else who has to live off capital.

2. The Pearson Commission (Chapter 15) studied the method of calculation and by a majority recommended a more scientific approach, but one which still depended on assumptions about future inflation. The very high multipliers which would have resulted from this system meant that it has not been implemented. (For example, on the assumption of a rate of inflation of 5 per cent and a return net of tax of 8 per cent over the period of the loss, the multiplier in *Howitt* v *Heads* (above) would have been in the region of 33 rather than 18, and multipliers as high as 78 would have been possible to cover a 40-year period if the rate of inflation were considerably higher than the rate of return on the investment.)

DAMAGES BILL 1996

1.   Assumed rate of return on investment of damages

(1)   In determining the return to be expected from the investment of a sum awarded as damages for future pecuniary loss in an action for personal injury the court shall, subject to and in accordance with rules of court made for the purposes of this section, take into account such rate of return if any as may from time to time be prescribed by an order made by the Lord Chancellor.

(2)   Subsection (1) above shall not however prevent the court taking a different rate of return into account if any party to the proceedings shows that it is more appropriate in the case in question.

(3)   An order under subsection (1) above may prescribe different rates for different classes of case.

(4)   Before making an order under subsection (1) above the Lord Chancellor shall consult the Government Actuary and the Treasury; and any order under that subsection shall be made by statutory instrument subject to annulment in pursuance of a resolution of either House of Parliament.

(5)   In the application of this section to Scotland for references to the Lord Chancellor there shall be substituted references to the Secretary of State.

Note

This provision would make a significant change in the law as the rate of return which is assumed in calculating damages would be set by government order, apart from exceptional cases. There are a number of ways this could be done, but one of the simplest would be to adopt the view of Kemp ('Discounting compensation for future loss' (1985) LQR 550) that the most appropriate rate would be that available on Index-Linked Government Securities (ILGS). The important point to note is that the lower the rate the higher will be the damages. The courts at the moment assume a rate of 4–5 per cent, but the current rate in ILGS is $2\frac{1}{2}$ per cent. If that rate were adopted, this would produce a considerable increase in damages.

Section 3:   intangible losses

Intangible losses include damages for pain and suffering and loss of amenity, and the amounts awarded tend to be conventional and are arrived at on the basis of experience. Thus *Kemp and Kemp, Quantum of damages* lists awards under these heads, and these are used as guide-lines in any given case.

'Loss of amenity' means loss by the plaintiff of the ability to enjoy life to the full. However one issue over which there has been disagreement is whether damages should be awarded under this head for a person who is unable to appreciate his loss, such as someone in a coma. Are the damages for the deprivation or for the awareness of the deprivation? *West* v *Shepherd* deals with that problem.

West v *Shepherd*
House of Lords [1964] AC 326; [1963] 2 WLR 1359; [1963] 2 All ER 625

The plaintiff, aged 41, was injured in a road accident and she suffered from 'post-traumatic spastic quadriplegia and intellectual deficit'. She may have been aware of her condition to a slight degree, but the House of Lords discussed the question of the basis of awards for loss of amenities. Held: that a person would be entitled to damages even if unaware of the loss.

LORD PEARCE: My Lords, the appellants seek to use the plaintiff's condition as the foundation for two arguments in extinction or diminution of damages claimed in respect of her injuries and pain and loss of amenities.

First it is argued that such damages are given as compensation or consolation, and therefore, when the plaintiff's condition is so bad that they cannot be used by her to compensate or console they should either be greatly reduced or should not be awarded at all. No authority is cited in favour of such a proposition nor can I see any principle of common law that supports it.

The argument contains the assumption, which in my opinion is fallacious, that the court is concerned with what happens to the damages when they have been awarded. The court has to perform the difficult and artificial task of converting into monetary damages the physical injury and deprivation and pain and to give judgment for what it considers to be a reasonable sum. It does not look beyond the judgment to the spending of the damages. If it did so, many difficult problems would arise. Similar sums awarded for similar suffering may produce wholly different results. To a poor man who is thereby enabled to achieve some cherished object such as the education of his family the sum awarded may prove to be a more than adequate consolation. To a man who already has more money than he wants, it may be no consolation at all. But these are matters with which the court is not concerned. Whether the sum awarded is spent or how it is spent is entirely a matter for the plaintiff or the plaintiff's legal representatives. If the plaintiff's personal ability to use or enjoy the damages awarded for injury and pain and loss of amenity were a condition precedent to their award, it would be impossible for the executors of an injured person to obtain such damages. Yet they did so in *Rose v Ford* [1937] AC 826 and *Benham v Gambling* [1941] AC 157 and many other cases.

The second argument is founded on *Benham v Gambling* and would affect the whole basis of damages awarded for personal injury, apart, of course, from economic loss with which the argument is not concerned. Substantial damages are not awarded, it is said, for physical injury simpliciter, but only for the pain and suffering and general loss of happiness which it occasions. Therefore the deprivation of a limb can only command any substantial compensation in so far as it results in suffering or loss of happiness; and where there is little or no consciousness of deprivation there can be little or no damages. For this argument the appellants rely on *Benham v Gambling* and on the minority judgment of Diplock LJ in *Wise v Kaye* [1962] 1 QB 368.

The practice of the courts hitherto has been to treat bodily injury as a deprivation which in itself entitles a plaintiff to substantial damages according to its gravity. In *Phillips v London and South Western Railway Co.* 4 QBD 406 Cockburn CJ in enumerating the heads of damage which the jury must take into account and in respect of which a plaintiff is entitled to compensation, said: 'These are the bodily injury sustained; the pain undergone; the effect on the health of the sufferer, according to its degree and its probable duration as likely to be temporary or permanent; the expenses incidental to attempts to effect a cure, or to lessen the amount of injury; the pecuniary loss.' In *Rose v Ford* Lord Roche said: 'I regard impaired health and vitality not merely as a cause of pain and suffering but as a loss of a good thing in itself.' If a plaintiff has lost a leg, the court approaches the matter on the basis that he has suffered a serious physical deprivation no matter what his condition or temperament or state of mind may be. That deprivation may also create future economic loss which is added to the assessment. Past and prospective pain and discomfort increase the assessment. If there is loss of amenity apart from the obvious and normal loss inherent in the deprivation of the limb — if, for instance, the plaintiff's main interest in life was some sport or hobby from which he will in future be debarred, that too increases the assessment. If there is a particular consequential injury to the nervous system, that also increases the assessment. So, too, with other personal and subjective matters that fall to be decided in the light of common sense in particular cases. These considerations are not dealt with as separate items but are taken into account by the court in fixing one inclusive sum for general damages. . . .

The loss of happiness of the individual plaintiffs is not, in my opinion, a practicable or correct guide to reasonable compensation in cases of personal injury to a living plaintiff. A man of fortitude is not made less happy because he loses a limb. It may alter the scope of his activities and force him to seek his happiness in other directions. The cripple by the fireside reading or talking with friends may achieve happiness as great as that which, but for the accident, he would have achieved playing golf in the fresh air of the links. To some ancient philosopher the former kind of happiness might even have seemed of a higher nature than the latter, provided that the book or the talk were such as they would approve. Some less robust persons, on the other hand, are prepared to attribute a great loss of happiness to a quite trivial event. It would be lamentable if the trial of a personal injury claim put a premium on protestations of misery and if a long face was the only safe passport to a large award. Under the present practice there is no call for a parade of personal unhappiness. A plaintiff who cheerfully admits that he is happy as ever he was, may yet receive a large award as reasonable compensation for the grave injury and loss of amenity over which he has managed to triumph.

Note

The Pearson Commission (para. 398) disagreed with this view, saying that non pecuniary damages should not be recoverable for permanent unconsciousness. They took the view that damages should only be paid under this head where they can serve some useful purpose, such as providing some alternative source of satisfaction to replace one that has been lost. The High Court of Australia, in *Skelton* v *Collins* (1966) 39 AJLR 480, also, by a majority, took this view, saying that the subjective element could not be ignored, although some damages should be awarded for the objective elements.

Section 4:   deduction of other benefits

The law of tort may not be the only source of compensation available to an injured person, and a difficult question is the extent to which benefits received from other quarters should be deducted from the damages. It is agreed that gifts to the plaintiff should not be deducted, nor should the proceeds of private insurance taken out by the plaintiff, since these are the result of the plaintiff's own payments and are not caused by the defendant's negligence. Also it would be odd if the defendant's liability to pay damages is reduced because of the plaintiff's payment of premiums. It is also agreed (*Parry* v *Cleaver* [1970] AC 1) that a pension is not deductible from damages, for a pension is different from lost wages. Also, in fatal accident cases, s. 4 of the 1976 Act makes it clear that insurance payments or pensions are not to be deducted from damages payable to the dependants.

However, two important areas of collateral benefit remain: sick pay and social security payments. *Hussain* v *New Taplow Mills* deals with the first, and statutory provisions deal with the second.

Hussain v *New Taplow Paper Mills*
House of Lords [1988] AC 514; [1988] 2 WLR 266; [1988] 1 All ER 541

The plaintiff was injured at work and his left arm was amputated below the elbow. Under his contract of employment the plaintiff was entitled to receive full pay for 13 weeks and, if fully incapacitated, half pay thereafter. Held: dismissing the appeal, that the sick pay should be deducted from the damages.

LORD BRIDGE: In *Parry* v *Cleaver* [1970] AC 1, Lord Reid, discussing the general principles applicable to the assessment of damages for financial loss said, at p. 13:

Two questions can arise. First, what did the plaintiff lose as a result of the accident? What are the sums which he would have received but for the accident but which by reason of the accident he can no longer get? And secondly, what are the sums which he did in fact receive as a result of the accident? And then the question arises whether the latter sums must be deducted from the former in assessing the damages. *British Transport Commission* v *Gourley* [1956] AC 185 did two things. With regard to the first question it made clear, if it had not been clear before, that it is a universal rule that the plaintiff cannot recover more than he has lost. And, more important, it established the principle that in this chapter of the law we must have regard to realities rather than technicalities. The plaintiff would have had to pay tax in respect of the income which he would have received but for the accident. So what he really lost was what would have remained to him after payment of tax . . . . But *Gourley's* case had nothing whatever to do with the second question.

This dichotomy, however, must not be allowed to obscure the rule that prima facie the only recoverable loss is the net loss. Financial gains accruing to the plaintiff which he would not have received but for the event which constitutes the plaintiff's cause of action are prima facie to be taken into account in mitigation of losses which that event occasions to him. In many, perhaps most cases, both losses and gains will come into the calculation. Just as in a claim for damages for wrongful dismissal the plaintiff must, if he can, mitigate his damage by securing other employment, so also a plaintiff disabled by personal injury from continuing his pre-accident occupation mitigates his damage suffered by the loss of the whole of his earnings in that occupation by exercising some other skill, which he already possesses or acquires by training, to earn money in a new occupation which, but for the accident, he would never have pursued. One may ask either 'What is his real loss?' or 'Is the gain accruing from earnings in the new occupation deductible from the loss of earnings of the old occupation?' to arrive at the same answer. But to the prima facie rule there are two well established exceptions. First, where a plaintiff recovers under an insurance policy for which he has paid the premiums, the insurance moneys are not deductible from damages payable by the tortfeasor: *Bradburn* v *Great Western Railway Co.* (1864) LR 10 EX 1. Secondly, when the plaintiff receives money from the benevolence of third parties prompted by sympathy for his misfortune, as in the case of a beneficiary from a disaster fund, the amount received is again to be disregarded: *Redpath* v *Belfast and County Down Railways* [1967] NI 147. In both these cases there is in one sense double recovery. If the award of damages adequately compensates the plaintiff, as it should, the additional amounts received from the insurer or from third party benevolence may be regarded as a net gain to the plaintiff resulting from his injury. But in both cases the common sense of the exceptions stares one in the face. It may be summed up in the rhetorical question: 'Why should the tortfeasor derive any benefit, in the one case, from the premiums which the plaintiff has paid to insure himself against some contingency, however caused, in the other case, from the money provided by the third party with the sole intention of benefiting the injured plaintiff?'

Given the inevitable divergencies of judicial opinion as to what justice, reasonableness and public policy require, it is not surprising that courts in different common law jurisdictions should sometimes have solved similar problems in this field in different ways, nor that, in the leading case of *Parry* v *Cleaver* [1970] AC 1 itself, this House should have reversed the Court of Appeal by a majority of three to two in holding that a disability pension payable to a police officer compelled to retire from the police force by injury caused by the defendant's negligence was not to be taken into account in mitigation of his loss of earnings and loss of earning capacity up to the date of police retiring age, but only in mitigation of his loss of police retirement pension after that age. Lord Reid said, at p. 15: 'Surely the distinction between receipts which must be brought into account and those which must not must depend not on their source but on their intrinsic nature.'

He went on to consider the nature of the police disability pension and concluded, in effect, that it was the fruit of a form of insurance for which the plaintiff had in substance contributed the premiums by his pre-accident service. He contrasted it with sick pay in the following passage, at p. 16:

Then it is said that instead of getting a pension he may get sick pay for a time during his disablement — perhaps his whole wage. That would not be deductible, so why should a pension be different? But a man's wage for a particular week is not related to the amount of work which he does during that week. Wages for the period of a man's holiday do not differ in kind from wages paid to him during the rest of the year. And neither does sick pay; it is still wages. So during the period when he receives sick pay he has lost nothing. We never reach the second question of how to treat sums of a different kind which he would never have received but for his accident.

Later he said, pp. 20-21:

As regards police pension, his loss after reaching police retiring age would be the difference between the full pension which he would have received if he had served his full time and his ill-health pension. It has been asked why his ill-health pension is to be brought into account at this point if not brought into account for the earlier period. The answer is that in the earlier period we are not comparing like with like. He lost wages but gained something different in kind, a pension. But with regard to the period after retirement we are comparing like with like. Both the ill-health pension and the full retirement pension are the products of the same insurance scheme; his loss in the later period is caused by his having been deprived of the opportunity to continue in insurance so as to swell the ultimate product of that insurance from an ill-health to a retirement pension. There is no question as regards that period of a loss of one kind and a gain of a different kind. . . .

Mr Andrew Collins, for the plaintiff, seeks to apply by analogy a principle said to be established by *Parry* v *Cleaver* [1970] AC 1 in support of the argument that all payments to an employee enjoying the benefit of the defendants' permanent health insurance scheme are effectively in the nature of the fruits of insurance accruing to the benefit of the employee in consideration of the contributions he has made by his work for the defendants prior to incapacity. Much emphasis was laid on the long term nature of the scheme payments to which the plaintiff has become entitled and it was submitted that they are strictly comparable to a disability pension. Both these arguments fall to the ground, as it seems to me, in the light of the concession rightly made at an early stage that the nature of payments under the scheme is unaffected by the duration of the incapacity which determines the period for which payments will continue to be made. The question whether the scheme payments are or are not deductible in assessing damages for loss of earnings must be answered in the same way whether, after the first 13 weeks of incapacity, the payments fall to be made for a few weeks or for the rest of an employee's working life. Looking at the payments made under the scheme by the defendants in the first weeks after the expiry of the period of 13 weeks of continuous incapacity, they seem to me indistinguishable in character from the sick pay which the employee receives during the first 13 weeks. They are payable under a term of the employee's contract by the defendants to the employee qua employee as a partial substitute for earnings and are the very antithesis of a pension, which is payable only after employment ceases. The fact that the defendants happen to have insured their liability to meet these contractual commitments as they arise cannot affect the issue in any way.

. . . From the point of view of justice, reasonableness and public policy the case seems to me far removed from the principle underlying the insurance cases stemming from *Bradburn* v *Great Western Railway Co.*, LR 10 Ex 1. It positively offends my sense of justice that a plaintiff, who has certainly paid no insurance premiums as such, should receive full wages during a period of incapacity to work from two different sources, his employer and the tortfeasor. It would seem to me still more unjust and anomalous where, as here, the employer and the tortfeasor are one and the same.

Note
Hussain was distinguished in *McCamley* v *Cammell Laird* [1990] 1 WLR 963, where the plaintiff was injured at work and his employers had a group accident policy for the benefit of their employees. The employees did not pay anything towards the premium, and although the benefits were limited to the amount earned by the employee they were paid as a lump sum. It was held that the lump sum should not be deducted from the damages. The court noted that the benefit was 'not paid in substitution for loss of wages', and that it was 'a payment by way of benevolence, even though the mechanics required the use of an insurance policy'. Why did the employers pay the premiums? (Note that in this case the employers were also the defendants, so that if the money had been deducted this would only have gone to reduce the amount payable, not by the employers but by their liability insurers.)

Questions
1.   If the plaintiff is dismissed and becomes eligible for a disability pension rather than sick pay, should this be deducted?
2.   Lord Bridge said that in *Hussain* the plaintiff had not paid insurance premiums as such. If an employee was given a choice of being covered by a sick pay scheme or receiving higher wages, would this alter the situation? If he is not given a choice, could the provision of cover be regarded as foregone wages?
3.   If the contract of employment had stated that if the plaintiff recovered damages from a tortfeasor he must re-pay the sick pay to the employer, should the sick pay have been deducted?

ADMINISTRATION OF JUSTICE ACT 1982

5.   Maintenance at public expense to be taken into account in assessment of damages
In an action under the law of England and Wales or the law of Northern Ireland for damages for personal injuries (including any such action arising out of a contract) any saving to the injured person which is attributable to his maintenance wholly or partly at public expense in a hospital, nursing home or other institution shall be set off against any income lost by him as a result of his injuries.

SOCIAL SECURITY ADMINISTRATION ACT 1992

PART IV
RECOVERY FROM COMPENSATION PAYMENTS

81. Interpretation of Part IV

(1) In this Part of this Act—

'benefit' means any benefit under the Contributions and Benefits Act except child benefit and, subject to regulations under subsection (2) below, the 'relevant benefits' are such of those benefits as may be prescribed for the purposes of this Part of this Act;

'certificate of deduction' means a certificate given by the compensator specifying the amount which he has deducted and paid to the Secretary of State in pursuance of section 82(1) below;

'certificate of total benefit' means a certificate given by the Secretary of State in accordance with this Part of this Act;

'compensation payment' means any payment falling to be made (whether voluntarily, or in pursuance of a court order or an agreement, or otherwise)—

(a)   to or in respect of the victim in consequence of the accident, injury or disease in question, and

(b)   either—

(i)   by or on behalf of a person who is, or is alleged to be, liable to any extent in respect of that accident, injury or disease; or

(ii)   in pursuance of a compensation scheme for motor accidents,

but does not include benefit or an exempt payment or so much of any payment as is referable to costs incurred by any person;

'compensation scheme for motor accidents' means any scheme or arrangement under which funds are available for the payment of compensation in respect of motor accidents caused, or alleged to have been caused, by uninsured or unidentified persons;

'compensator', 'victim' and 'intended recipient' shall be construed in accordance with section 82(1) below;

'payment' means payment in money or money's worth, and cognate expressions shall be construed accordingly;

'relevant deduction' means the deduction required to be made from the compensation payment in question by virtue of this Part of this Act;

'relevant payment' means the payment required to be made to the Secretary of State by virtue of this Part of this Act;

'relevant period' means—

(a)   in the case of a disease, the period of 5 years beginning with the date on which the victim first claims a relevant benefit in consequence of the disease; or

(b)   in any other case, the period of 5 years immediately following the day on which the accident or injury in question occurred;

but where before the end of that period the compensator makes a compensation payment in final discharge of any claim made by or in respect of the victim and arising out of the accident, injury or disease, the relevant period shall end on the date on which that payment is made; and

'total benefit' means the gross amount referred to in section 82(1)(a) below.

(2) [repealed]

(3) For the purposes of this Part of this Act the following are the 'exempt payments'—

(a) any small payment, as defined in section 85 below;

(b) any payment made to or for the victim under section 35 of the Powers of Criminal Courts Act 1973 or section 58 of the Criminal Justice (Scotland) Act 1980;

(c) any payment to the extent that it is made—

(i) in consequence of an action under the Fatal Accidents Act 1976; or

(ii) in circumstances where, had an action been brought, it would have been brought under that Act;

(d) any payment to the extent that it is made in respect of a liability arising by virtue of section 1 of the Damages (Scotland) Act 1976;

(e) without prejudice to section 6(4) of the Vaccine Damage Payments Act 1979 (which provides for the deduction of any such payment in the assessment of any award of damages), any payment made under that Act to or in respect of the victim;

(f) any award of compensation made to or in respect of the victim by the Criminal Injuries Compensation Board under section 111 of the Criminal Justice Act 1988;

(g) any payment made in the exercise of a discretion out of property held subject to a trust in a case where no more than 50 per cent by value of the capital contributed to the trust was directly or indirectly provided by persons who are, or are alleged to be, liable in respect of—

(i) the accident, injury or disease suffered by the victim in question; or

(ii) the same or any connected accident, injury or disease suffered by another;

(h) any payment made out of property held for the purposes of any prescribed trust (whether the payment also falls within paragraph (g) above or not);

(i) any payment made to the victim by an insurance company within the meaning of the Insurance Companies Act 1982 under the terms of any contract of insurance entered into between the victim and the company before—

(i) the date on which the victim first claims a relevant benefit in consequence of the disease in question; or

(ii) the occurrence of the accident or injury in question;

(j) any redundancy payment falling to be taken into account in the assessment of damages in respect of an accident, injury or disease.

(4) Regulations may provide that any prescribed payment shall be an exempt payment for the purposes of this Part of this Act.

(5) Except as provided by any other enactment, in the assessment of damages in respect of an accident, injury or disease the amount of any relevant benefits paid or likely to be paid shall be disregarded.

(6) If, after making the relevant deduction from the compensation payment, there would be no balance remaining for payment to the intended recipient, any reference in this Part to the making of the compensation payment shall be construed in accordance with regulations.

82. Recovery from damages etc. of sums equivalent to benefit

(1) A person (the 'compensator') making a compensation payment, whether on behalf of himself or another, in consequence of an accident, injury or disease suffered by any other person (the 'victim') shall not do so until the Secretary of State has furnished him with a certificate of total benefit and shall then—

(a) deduct from the payment an amount, determined in accordance with the certificate of total benefit, equal to the gross amount of any relevant benefits paid or likely to be paid to or for the victim during the relevant period in respect of that accident, injury or disease;

(b) pay to the Secretary of State an amount equal to that which is required to be so deducted; and

(c)   furnish the person to whom the compensation payment is or, apart from this section, would have been made (the 'intended recipient') with a certificate of deduction.

(2)   Any right of the intended recipient to receive the compensation payment in question shall be regarded as satisfied to the extent of the amount certified in the certificate of deduction.

Note

By the Social Security (Recoupment) Regulations 1990 (SI 1990 No. 322) the following are 'relevant benefits' for the purposes of s. 22: attendance allowance; disablement benefit; family credit; income support; incapacity benefit; invalidity pension and allowance; mobility allowance; benefits payable under schemes made by the Old Cases Act; reduced earnings allowance; retirement allowance; severe disablement allowance; sickness benefit; unemployment benefit; disability living allowance and disability working allowance.

A 'small payment' is defined as one which does not exceed £2,500.

Exempt payments include any contractual amount paid to an employee by an employer of his in respect of a day of incapacity for work.

LAW REFORM (PERSONAL INJURIES) ACT 1948

2.   Measure of damages

(1)   In an action for damages for personal injuries (including any such action arising out of a contract), where this section applies there shall in assessing those damages be taken into account, against them, one half of the value of any rights which have accrued or probably will accrue to the injured person from the injuries in respect of—

(a)   any of the relevant benefits, within the meaning of section 81 of the Social Security Administration Act 1992, or

(b)   any corresponding benefits payable in Northern Ireland,

for the five years beginning with the time when the cause of action accrued.

(1A)   This section applies in any case where the amount of the damages that would have been awarded apart from any reduction under subsection (1) above is less than the sum for the time being prescribed under section 85(1) of the Social Security Administration Act 1992 (recoupment of benefit: exception for small payments).

(3)   The reference in subsection (1) of this section to assessing the damages for personal injuries shall, in cases where the damages otherwise recoverable are subject to reduction under the law relating to contributory negligence or are limited by or under any Act or by contract, be taken as referring to the total damages which would have been recoverable apart from the reduction or limitation.

(4)   In an action for damages for personal injuries (including any such action arising out of a contract), there shall be disregarded, in determining the reasonableness of any expenses, the possibility of avoiding those expenses or part of them by taking advantage of facilities available under the National Health Service Act 1977 or the National Health Service (Scotland) Act 1978, or of any corresponding facilities in Northern Ireland.

(6)   For the purposes of this section disablement benefit in the form of a gratuity is to be treated as benefit for the period taken into account by the assessment of the extent of the disablement in respect of which it is payable.

3.   Definition of 'personal injury'

In this Act the expression 'personal injury' includes any disease and any impairment of a person's physical or mental condition, and the expression 'injured' shall be construed accordingly.

17   VICARIOUS LIABILITY

Vicarious liability is a system whereby an employer is liable for the torts of his employees committed in the course of employment. This is the usual case, but there may be other examples, and these will be dealt with in section 3. The principle of placing liability on the employer as well as upon the individual tortfeasor is mainly justified by the concept of loss distribution, that is that the employer will usually be better able to distribute the loss, either through insurance or through his customers. Other factors have also been put forward (see *Atiyah, Vicarious Liability in the Law of Torts,* 1967, Chapter 2): these include encouraging an employer to exercise proper control over his employees, thus supporting a policy of accident prevention; encouraging an employer to be careful in the selection of his employees; and the fact that as an employer gets the benefit of the work done by his employees he should also take the risks attached to that activity.

There are also problems as to the legal theory behind vicarious liability. It may be too simplistic to say that the employer is liable because the employee is liable, although in most cases this will be so. The problem can be illustrated by **Broom v Morgan** [1953] 1 QB 597, where a husband and wife were both employed by the same employer, and the husband negligently injured the wife. At that time, but no longer, a wife could not sue her husband, but nevertheless the employer was held vicariously liable for the husband's negligence, even though the husband himself could not be sued. It is probable that this case does not alter the theory of vicarious liability, but rather only means that an employer cannot take advantage of a procedural bar available to the employee.

A more difficult case would be where the employee is absolved because of insanity, as in *Buckley v Smith Transport* [1946] 4 DLR 721, where a Canadian court said that an employer would not be liable for the negligence of an insane employee, because an employer could not be liable if the employee was not liable, but the point was not argued. It is not clear, therefore, whether liability is imposed because the employee is liable, or because the acts and state of mind of the employee are attributed to the employer, or whether the acts are attributed to the employer, which if done by him would render him liable.

An alternative theory, advanced by Lord Denning in particular, is the 'master's tort' theory, whereby it is said that the duty is owed by the employer which he performs through others, but this view has not found favour in recent years.

Section 1:   who is an employee?

The need to define an employee arises in many areas of the law, and it can mean different things for different purposes. Accordingly, while cases, for example, on the definition for the purposes of social security, are analogous and relevant, care must be taken to ensure that there are no special factors which render it inapplicable for the purposes of vicarious liability. The function of the definition here is to determine who should bear the risks created in the course of the enterprise, and a wider view may be more appropriate than in other areas of the law.

The main technical function is to distinguish employees, for whom an employer generally is vicariously liable, from independent contractors, for whom he is usually not liable. The distinction is sometimes said to be between a contract of service (employee) and a contract for services (independent contractor). Also, it should be noted that some of the older cases use the words 'master' and 'servant' instead of 'employer' and 'employee'.

Performing Right Society v *Mitchell and Booker* *(Palais De Danse) Ltd*
King's Bench Division [1924] 1 KB 762; 93 LJKB 306; 131 LT 243

The defendants engaged a band called 'The Original Lyrical Five' to play at their dance hall, and the band played two songs without the permission of the plaintiffs, the owners of the copyright. Held: the members of the band were employees of the defendants who were liable for the breach of copyright.

MCCARDIE J: The nature of the task undertaken, the freedom of action given, the magnitude of the contract amount, the manner in which it is to be paid, the powers of dismissal and the circumstances under which payment of the reward may be withheld, all these bear on the solution of the question. . . . It seems, however, reasonably clear that the final test, if there be a final test, and certainly the test to be generally applied, lies in the nature and degree of detailed control over the person alleged to be a servant. This circumstance is, of course, one only of several to be considered, but it is usually of vital importance. The point is put well in Pollock on Torts, 12th ed., pp. 79, 80.

The relation of master and servant exists only between persons of whom the one has the order and control of the work done by the other. A master is one who not only prescribes to the workman the end of his work, but directs or at any moment may direct the means also, or, as it has been put, 'retains the power of controlling the work': see per Crompton J in *Sadler* v *Henlock*, 119 ER 209. A servant is a person subject to the command of his master as to the manner in which he shall do his work: see per Bramwell LJ in *Yewens* v *Noakes* (1880) 6 QBD 530, 532, and the master is liable for his acts, neglects and defaults, to the extent to be specified. An independent contractor is one who undertakes to produce a given result, but so that in the actual execution of the work he is not under the order or control of the person for whom he does it, and may use his own discretion in things not specified beforehand.

Note
The factor of control is not the only test of employment. A further factor may be the extent to which the job is integrated into the organisation. In *Stevenson v MacDonald* [1952] 1 TLR 101, at p. 111 Denning LJ said:

It is often easy to recognise a contract of service when you see it, but difficult to say wherein the difference lies. A ship's master, a chauffeur, and a reporter on the staff of a newspaper are all employed under a contract of service; but a ship's pilot, a taxi-man and a newspaper contributor are employed under a contract for services. One feature which seems to run through the instances is that, under a contract of service, a man is employed as part of the business, and his work is done as an integral part of the business; whereas, under a contract for services, his work, although done for the business, is not integrated into it but is only accessory to it.

Market Investigations Ltd v Ministry of Social Security
Queens Bench Division [1969] 2 QB 173; [1969] 1 WLR 1;
[1968] 3 All ER 732

The question was whether a Mrs Irving was an employed person for the purposes of social security legislation. She was engaged as an interviewer by a company involved in market research and was free to work when she wanted. Held: Mrs Irving was an employee.

COOKE J: If control is not a decisive test, what then are the other considerations which are relevant? No comprehensive answer has been given to this question but assistance is to be found in a number of cases.

In *Montreal* v *Montreal Locomotive Works Ltd* [1947] 1 DLR 161, Lord Wright said, at p. 169:

In earlier cases a single test, such as the presence or absence of control, was often relied on to determine whether the case was one of master and servant, mostly in order to decide issues of tortious liability on the part of the master or superior. In the more complex conditions of modern industry, more complicated tests have to be applied. It has been suggested that a fourfold test would in some cases be more appropriate, a complex involving (1) control; (2) ownership of the tools; (3) chance of profit; (4) risk of loss. Control in itself is not always conclusive. Thus the master of a chartered vessel is generally the employee of the shipowner though the charterer can direct the employment of the vessel. Again the law often limits the employer's right to interfere with the employee's conduct, as also do trade union regulations. In many cases the question can only be settled by examining the whole of the various elements which constitute the relationship between the parties. In this way it is in some cases possible to decide the issue by raising as the crucial question whose business is it, or in other words by asking whether the party is carrying on the business, in the sense of carrying it on for himself or on his own behalf and not merely for a superior.

In *Bank voor Handel en Scheepvaart NV* v *Slatford* [1953] 1 QB 248, Denning LJ said, at p. 295:

The test of being a servant does not rest nowadays on submission to orders. It depends on whether the person is part and parcel of the organisation.

In *United States of America* v *Silk* (1946) 3312 US 704, the question was whether certain men were 'employees' within the meaning of that word in the Social Security Act 1935. The judges of the Supreme Court decided that the test to be applied was not 'power of control, whether exercised or not, over the manner of performing service to the undertaking', but whether the men were employees 'as a matter of economic reality.'

The observations of Lord Wright, of Denning LJ and of the judges of the Supreme Court suggest that the fundamental test to be applied is this: 'Is the person who has engaged himself to perform these services performing them as a person in business on his own account?' If the answer to that question is 'yes', then the contract is a contract for services. If the answer is 'no', then the contract is a contract of service. No exhaustive list has been compiled and perhaps no exhaustive list can be compiled of the considerations which are relevant in determining that question, nor can strict rules be laid down as to the relative weight which the various considerations should carry in particular cases. The most that can be said is that control will no doubt always have to be considered, although it can no longer be regarded as the sole determining factor; and that factors which may be of importance are such matters as whether the man performing the services provides his own equipment, whether he hires his own helpers, what degree of financial risk he takes, what degree of responsibility for investment and management he has, and whether and how far he has an opportunity of profiting from sound management in the performance of his task.

The application of the general test may be easier in a case where the person who engages himself to perform the services does so in the course of an already established business of his own; but this factor is not decisive, and a person who engages himself to perform services for another may well be an independent contractor even though he has not entered into the contract in the course of an existing business carried on by him.

Note
The nature of employment is changing for there are now more part time workers, agency workers, home workers, contract workers and trainees. The traditional 'control' test may be inadequate to determine whether such persons are 'employees'. The question is what risks are properly attributable to the enterprise and for this purpose it makes sense to ask whether or not the worker was working on his own account (the entrepreneur test) — i.e. is he taking the financial risk with the chance of loss as well as profit? Such a test may mean that 'employer' means different things for different purposes: see further Kidner, 'Vicarious liability: for whom should the employer be liable?' (1995) 15 Legal Studies 47.

Mersey Docks and Harbour Board v Coggins and Griffith Ltd
House of Lords [1947] AC 1; [1946] 2 All ER 345; 175 LJ 270

The Harbour Board hired out a mobile crane, together with a driver, Mr Newall, to the defendant stevedores. Mr Newall was paid and liable to be dismissed by the Board, but the contract of hire stated that he was to be regarded as the employee of the stevedores. The stevedores could tell him what to do, but not how he was to operate the crane. Mr Newall negligently injured a Mr McFarlane. Held: on the question whether the Board or the stevedores were to be held vicariously liable for the negligence of Mr Newall, dismissing the appeal, that the Board was liable.

LORD PORTER: Many factors have a bearing on the result. Who is paymaster, who can dismiss, how long the alternative service lasts, what machinery is employed, have all to be kept in mind. The expressions used in any individual case must always be considered in regard to the subject matter under discussion but amongst the many tests suggested I think that the most satisfactory, by which to ascertain who is the employer at any particular time, is to ask who is entitled to tell the employee the way in which he is to do the work upon which he is engaged. If someone other than his general employer is authorized to do this he will, as a rule, be the person liable for the employee's negligence. But it is not enough that the task to be performed should be under his control, he must also control the method of performing it. It is true that in most cases no orders as to how a job should be done are given or required: the man is left to do his own work in his own way. But the ultimate question is not what specific orders, or whether any specific orders, were given but who is entitled to give the orders as to how the work should be done. Where a man driving a mechanical device, such as a crane, is sent to perform a task, it is easier to infer that the general employer continues to control the method of performance since it is his crane and the driver remains responsible to him for its safe keeping. In the present case if the appellants' contention were to prevail, the crane driver would change his employer each time he embarked on the discharge of a fresh ship. Indeed, he might change it from day to day, without any say as to who his master should be and with all the concomitant disadvantages of uncertainty as to who should be responsible for his insurance in respect of health, unemployment and accident. I cannot think that such a conclusion is to be drawn from the facts established. . . .

Notes

1. The question in this case was not whether Mr Newall was an employee, but rather who was to be responsible. It shows that it is possible, although it was not actually so in this case, for a person to be vicariously liable, even though he would not for other purposes, such as employment law, be regarded as the employer. Such a case could occur if a labourer is hired out without any accompanying machinery. Further, the point of the case is not who pays in the end, for that might be settled by the terms of the hiring contract, but rather who the plaintiff should sue. Why should this depend on contracts of which he knows nothing?

2. The case also illustrates the difficulty with the control test: in evidence Mr Newall said 'I take no orders from anybody.' As Lord Parker pointed out, this 'sturdy reply' meant that he was a skilled man, but nevertheless the Board had the power to give him directions as to how he should carry out the work, and could dismiss him if he refused to carry them out. Does the control test make sense, for example, when applied to a surgeon? See *Cassidy* v *Ministry of Health* [1951] 2 KB 343.

Question

Is the control test based on a circular argument? (Who is a servant? A person the employer can direct: Who can the employer direct? A servant.)

Section 2: liability of the employee

It is generally assumed that even if the employer is liable the employee can also be sued. This may be thought to flow from the idea that the employer is liable because the employee is liable but it may produce wholly inequitable results where for example, the employer is bankrupt or an exemption clause limits his liability. In *Lister* v *Romford Ice and Cold Storage Co.* [1957] AC 533, the House of Lords went so far as to hold that an employee may even be required to indemnify an employer if he has had to pay damages, but companies which insure employers have refused to take advantage of so unfair a rule.

Where there is a limitation clause in the contract between the plaintiff and the employer an express term may be sufficient to extend the benefit of such a clause to certain agents of the employer (commonly called a 'Himalaya Clause': see *The Eurymedon* [1975] AC 154) but this principle is of limited effect. In *London Drugs* v *Kuehne & Nagel International* (below) the Supreme Court of Canada said that certain employees may be impliedly exempted. However, in his dissenting judgment in *London Drugs* La Forest J has proposed the radical solution that in some circumstances the employee should not *as a matter of tort law* be liable at all — ie, that an employer can be vicariously liable but the employee is not directly liable. The judgment raises fundamental issues about the nature and function of vicarious liability.

London Drugs v *Kuehne & Nagel International*
Supreme Court of Canada [1992] 3 SCR 299; (1993) 97 DLR 4th 261

London Drugs bought a transformer and arranged for it to be stored by Kuehne and Nagel International (KNI). The contract between London Drugs and KNI limited liability to $40 and London Drugs refused to purchase insurance through KNI but preferred to arrange their own insurance. Two employees of KNI, Dennis Brassart and Hank Vanwinkel negligently damaged the transformer causing damage worth $33,955.41. London Drugs sued KNI but obtained only $40 by virtue of the limitation clause. They then sued the two employees for the full damages. The High Court allowed the full claim but the British Columbia Court of Appeal limited it to $40. Held: dismissing the appeal, that the liability of the employees was limited to $40.

Note: the majority decided the case on the basis that the employees were impliedly entitled to take advantage of the limitation clause between the plaintiffs and their employers. (In the absence of an express term this result is unlikely to be reached in England.) La Forest J dissented on the ground that in the circumstances the employees should not be liable in tort at all. MacLachlin J limited damages to $40 on the ground that in tort the plaintiffs had taken the risk of further damage.

LA FOREST J (dissenting):

Vicarious Liability
. . . In my opinion, the vicarious liability regime is best seen as a response to a number of policy concerns. In its traditional domain, these are primarily linked to compensation,

deterrence and loss internalization. In addition, in a case like the one at bar, which involves a planned transaction or a contractual matrix, the issue of tort liability in the context of contractual relations involves a wider range of policy concerns. Alongside those respecting compensation, deterrence and loss internalization, there are important concerns regarding planning and agreed risk allocation.

The most important policy considerations lying behind the doctrine of vicarious liability are based on the perception that the employer is *better* placed to incur liability, both in terms of fairness and effectiveness, than the employee. Fleming admirably summarizes the policy concerns in the following passage from *The Law of Torts* (7th ed. 1987), at p. 340:

> Despite the frequent invocation of such tired tags as *Respondeat superior* or *Qui facit per alium, facit per se*, the modern doctrine of vicarious liability cannot parade as a deduction from legalistic premises, but should be frankly recognised as having its basis in a combination of policy considerations. Most important of these is the belief that a person who employs others to advance his own economic interest should in fairness be placed under a corresponding liability for losses incurred in the course of the enterprise; that the master is a more promising source for recompense than his servant who is apt to be a man of straw; and that the rule promotes wide distribution of tort losses, the employer being a most suitable channel for passing them on through liability insurance and higher prices. The principle gains additional support for its admonitory value in accident prevention. In the first place, deterrent pressures are most effectively brought to bear on larger units like employers who are in a strategic position to reduce accidents by efficient organisation and supervision of their staff. Secondly, the fact that employees are, as a rule, not worth suing because they are rarely financially responsible, removes from them the spectre of tort liability as a discouragement of wrongful conduct. By holding the master liable, the law furnishes an incentive to discipline servants guilty of wrongdoing, if necessary by insisting on an indemnity or contribution.

It is useful to separate out the various policy concerns identified by Fleming.

First, the vicarious liability regime allows the plaintiff to obtain compensation from someone who is financially capable of satisfying a judgment. As Lord Wilberforce noted in *Kooragang Investments Pty Ltd* v *Richardson & Wrench Ltd* [1981] 3 All ER 65 (PC), at p. 68, the manner in which the common law has dealt with the liability of employers for acts of employees (masters for servants, principals for agents) has been progressive; the tendency has been toward more liberal protection of innocent third parties; see also Fridman, at pp. 315–16. The plaintiff benefits greatly from the doctrine of vicarious liability, which allows access to the deep pocket of the company, even where the company is blameless in any ordinary sense.

Second, a person, typically a corporation, who employs others to advance its own economic interest should in fairness be placed under a corresponding liability for losses incurred in the course of the enterprise. As Lord Denning noted in *Morris* v *Ford Motor Co.* [1973] 1 QB 792 (CA) at p. 798, the courts 'would not find negligence so readily — or award sums of such increasing magnitude — except on the footing that the damages are to be borne, not by the man himself, but by an insurance company' through coverage purchased by the employer.

Third, the regime promotes a wide distribution of tort losses since the employer is a most suitable channel for passing them on through liability insurance and higher prices. In *Hamilton* v *Farmers' Ltd* [1953] 3 DLR 382 (NSSC), MacDonald J noted, at p. 393, that the principle of vicarious liability 'probably reflects a conclusion of public policy that the master should be held liable for the incidental results of the conduct of his business by means of his servants as a means of distributing the social loss arising from the conduct of his enterprises'.

Fourth, vicarious liability is also a coherent doctrine from the perspective of deterrence. KNI is in a much better situation than Vanwinkel and Brassart to adopt policies with respect to the use of cranes, the inspection of stickers and so on in order to prevent accidents of this type. Given that it will either be held liable or its customers' insurance costs will reflect its carefulness, KNI has every incentive to encourage its employees to perform well on the job and to discipline those who are guilty of wrongdoing.

It is apparent that the vicarious liability regime is not merely a mechanism by which the employer guarantees the employee's primary liability. The regime responds to wider policy concerns than simply the desire to protect the plaintiff from the consequences of the possible and indeed likely incapacity of the employee to afford sufficient compensation, although obviously that concern remains of primary importance. Vicarious liability has the broader function of transferring to the enterprise itself the risks created by the activity performed by its agents.

The question in this case is whether the elimination of the employee's liability would significantly impact on the policies advanced by vicarious liability. In my view, it would impact favourably on the second and third considerations set out above and have negligible impact on the fourth. Again, Fleming, *supra*, at pp. 340–41, sets out the reasons why the elimination of the employee's liability is generally desirable:

> As already noted, the master's vicarious liability does not displace the servant's personal liability to the tort victim. But this conclusion is neither self-evident nor beyond all objection. For one thing, *ordinarily it is positively desirable that the master absorb the cost as a matter of sound resource allocation rather than that he be considered merely as guaranteeing the servant's primary responsibility to pay for the damage.* For another, to hold the servant liable will either tend to overtax his financial resources (especially under modern conditions when these have become increasingly unequal to his capacity for causing great loss) or require double insurance, covering both him and his employer against the same risk. For these reasons, there is now a growing momentum in many countries for 'channelling' liability to the employer alone; the employee being freed altogether from claims by third parties and liable at most to his employer for a limited contribution when this is justified on disciplinary grounds. This mostly corresponds with our own *practices* — damages are rarely collected from employees by their tort victims or indemnity sought by their employers — but except in South Australia and the Northern Territory, the popular notion that the primary responsibility should be the employer's rather than the employee's is as yet hardly reflected by the law in books. [Emphasis added.]

In my view, not only is the elimination of the possibility of the employee bearing the loss logically compatible with the vicarious liability regime, it is practically compelled by the developing logic of that regime. . . .

Furthermore, the decision of this Court today with respect to the application of contractual clauses excluding or limiting liability will remove one of the principal reasons to sue employees, since such an approach will no longer offer a convenient way around such a contractual clause. In light of the Court's decision today on the applicability of the contractual clause, the issue of an employee's liability will arise principally when the employer is unable to satisfy a judgment, most often because it is bankrupt.

Nonetheless, for one reason or another, the employer may not be available as a source of compensation. In my view, in what may be termed a 'classic' or non-contractual vicarious liability case, in which there are no 'contractual overtones' concerning the plaintiff, the concern over compensation for loss caused by the fault of another requires that *as between the plaintiff and the negligent employee*, the employee must be held liable for property damage and personal injury caused to the plaintiff. An example of such a case is a plaintiff who is injured by an employee while the employee, acting in the course of employment, is driving on the road. In this context, the plaintiff obviously never chose to deal with a limited liability company. I do not find it necessary here to consider the vexing question of the possible impact of clauses in the defendant's contract with a third party, i.e., in this example, a clause in the contract between the employee and the employer, on liability to a plaintiff; see Atiyah, *An Introduction to the Law of Contract* (4th ed. 1989), at pp. 394–95; B. J. Reiter, 'Contracts, Torts, Relations and Reliance' in B. J. Reiter and J. Swan, eds., *Studies in Contract Law* (1980), 235, at p. 301. *As between the plaintiff and the employee*, there is no reason to excuse the employee in such a case. Even if a contractual clause as described above could in some circumstances act to modify the tort duty, a question I expressly reserve, it could obviously never do so with respect to the duty to drive carefully.

However, the policy arguments set out above strongly support the idea that, as between the *employee and employer*, the employer should still bear the risk even in this kind of case. The best solution to such 'classic', non-contractual, cases would probably be an indemnity regime operating between employer and employee along the lines of that which exists, as a result of judicial innovation, in Germany . . .

I referred earlier to classic, non-contractual, vicarious liability cases. These cases can be distinguished from those like the case at bar, that involve a planned transaction. Such cases may perhaps best be described as commercial vicarious liability claims. Professor Blom sets forth a simple definition of a planned transaction as one in which someone acquires or disposes of property of any kind or services of any kind; see 'Fictions and Frictions', *supra*. As Blom notes, whenever a planned transaction is involved, there are foreseeable risks — to someone's person, land, goods, or financial interests — and thus the possibility of allocating or otherwise dealing with those risks in advance. This circumstance must be taken into account, even if the plaintiff's action is in tort. He states, at p. 159:

> Wherever there is a planned transaction there are foreseeable risks — to someone's person, land, goods, or financial interests — and thus the possibility of allocating or otherwise dealing with those risks in advance. Where the risk materializes, and there is a tort claim for the loss that results, it is relevant to ask what expectations it was reasonable to have about that risk, and what planning the victim and the negligent party could have done with regard to their respective exposures to loss or liability. In short, the proper approach to the tort claim may need to be coordinated with these contractual or contract-like features of the situation.

This Court has increasingly recognized the importance of such considerations in recent tort cases; see my reasons (at pp. 1125–27), and those of McLachlin J (at p. 1164) in *Norsk* which hold that contractual concerns were a relevant consideration. The opinions of both my colleagues in the present case also attest to the importance of this type of consideration.

In my view, where the plaintiff has suffered injury to his property pursuant to contractual relations with the company, he can be considered to have chosen to deal *with a company*. Company legislation typically provides for notice and publicity of the fact that a company is under a limited liability regime; customers and creditors are thereby put on notice that in ordinary circumstances they can only look to the company for the satisfaction of their claims. In British Columbia, corporations are also required to set out their name in all contracts, invoices, negotiable instruments and orders for goods and services; see British Columbia *Company Act*, RSBC 1979, c. 59, ss. 16 and 130.

In my view, in contracting for services to be provided by a business corporation like KNI in the circumstances of the present case, London Drugs can fairly be regarded as relying upon performance by the corporation, and upon the liability of that body if the services are negligently performed. As Reiter, *supra*, suggests, at p. 290:

> The plaintiff did not rely, or cannot be regarded as having relied reasonably, upon the liability of any individual where the individual is acting in furtherance of a contract between plaintiff and a principal or employer of the individual: the individual defendant cannot reasonably be regarded as appreciating that he is being looked to (personally) to satisfy the expectations of the plaintiff.

Nor can Vanwinkel and Brassart be taken on the facts of this case to appreciate that the plaintiff is relying on *them* for compensation at all. As Reiter underlines, the intention to transfer the responsibility to the corporation or association is a most explicit risk allocation by contract in the three-party enterprise. . . .

The Test: Reliance, Undertakings and Insurance

In my view, a requirement of specific and reasonable reliance on the defendant employees is justified in this type of case. I find it to be a necessary condition for recovery in cases of employee negligence where the law provides for the possibility of compensation through recourse to the employer and where, accordingly, the plaintiff's interest in compensation for its loss caused by the fault of another is substantially looked after. I also find it to be necessary in cases in which the defendant has no real opportunity to decline the risk.

In my view, there is no reason to limit the requirement of reasonable reliance to employee torts involving negligent misrepresentation. In the case of negligent misrepresentations, the requirement of reasonable reliance exists in part to respond to policy concerns about potentially indeterminate liability in the context of negligent words and economic loss. Here, the policy concerns are different, but a requirement of reasonable reliance is equally justified in light of my analysis of the situation of the employees in this case and the policies underlying vicarious liability. Reliance has been found to be relevant to findings of proximity by this Court in cases not involving negligent misrepresentations; see *Hofstrand, supra*.

Reliance on an ordinary employee will rarely if ever be reasonable. In most if not all situations, reliance on an employee will not be reasonable in the absence of an express or implied undertaking of responsibility by the employee to the plaintiff. Mere performance of the contract by the employee, without more, is not evidence of the existence of such an undertaking since such performance is required under the terms of the employee's contract with his employer. It may well be, as Blom argues, 'Fictions and Frictions', at p. 179, that the further one moves away from a wholly commercial type of case, the more scope there is for asserting reasonable reliance on something less than promises. This case, at any rate, is wholly commercial. With respect for those of a contrary opinion, I find any reliance by London Drugs on Vanwinkel and Brassart was certainly not reasonable in this case . . .

Subject to consideration by this Court of the arguments put forward by Fleming and others with respect to employee liability generally under the vicarious liability regime, the employee also remains liable to the plaintiff for his independent torts. The employer may also be vicariously liable for some independent torts in accordance with the general rules for establishing the employer's liability. The term 'independent tort' has been used with different meanings in different contexts. I should make clear that by independent tort in this context I mean a tort that is unrelated to the performance of the contract. It is not necessary in this case to consider the question of the definition of independent tort at length, since the tort in question was obviously not unrelated to the performance of the contract between London Drugs and KNI. Furthermore, since it is very likely that the only time a plaintiff will need to allege an independent tort is when the company is unable to satisfy a judgment, it can be expected that the issue will not arise with great frequency. . . .

It may be helpful to set out an appropriate approach to cases of this kind. The first question to be resolved is whether the tort alleged against the employee is an independent tort or a tort related to a contract between the employer and the plaintiff. In answering this question, it is legitimate to consider the scope of the contract, the nature of the employee's conduct and the nature of the plaintiff's interest. If the alleged tort is independent, the employee is liable to the plaintiff if the elements of the tort action are proved. The liability of the company to the plaintiff is determined under the ordinary rules applicable to cases of vicarious liability. If the tort is related to the contract, the next question to be resolved is whether any reliance by the plaintiff on the employee was reasonable. The question here is whether the plaintiff reasonably relied on the eventual legal responsibility of the defendants under the circumstances.

In this case, as I noted, the tort was related to the contract and any reliance by the plaintiff on Vanwinkel and Brassart was not reasonable.

Questions
1.   Do you think the employees should have paid $33,955.41, $40 or nothing?
2.   If you believe it should not be $33,955.41 would you prefer to resolve the question by extending the benefit of the exemption clause to the employees (as the majority did) or by adopting La Forest J's suggestion about vicarious liability?
3.   Do you think any of the proposed rules in *London Drugs* are likely to be adopted in England?

Section 3:   the course of employment

An employer is only liable for the torts of his employee if the act is committed 'in the course of his employment'. This is one of the most litigated phrases in the English language, and it has many functions. Again, it may mean something different for the purposes of vicarious liability than for other purposes, and one must bear in mind that its function is to limit the liability to those risks which can properly be seen as a function of the enterprise. There are two basic issues: first, was the employee in the course of his employment as regards time and space, and, secondly, was what he was doing, or the way he was doing it, within his employment?

A: Time and space

Compton v McClure
Queen's Bench Division [1975] ICR 378

The first defendant, McClure, was late for work and, in an effort to 'clock in' in time, he drove onto the premises of his employer, the second defendants, too fast and negligently injured the plaintiff. Held: the employers were vicariously liable.

MAY J: Most of the decided cases on this issue are ones in which there was no question that the course of the employment prima facie existed, but where the issue was whether the servant or agent had gone outside the course of that employment, whether he had gone, as it is said, 'on a frolic of his own.' In the present case the question is whether the course of the employment had in fact started.

The facts of *Staton v National Coal Board* [1957] 1 WLR 893, were these. One of the National Coal Board's employees, having finished his week's work, was riding his bicycle across their premises in order to collect his wages from a part of those premises different from the part on which he worked. While he was doing so he knocked over and killed another employee of the National Coal Board. The question was whether the National Coal Board was liable vicariously for the negligence of the cyclist employee. It was contended on behalf of the National Coal Board that they were not liable because the course of that employee's employment had ceased when he had finished work: the fact that he was merely going to collect his wages was neither here nor there; that did not, as it were, keep the chain of the course of employment in existence. On behalf of the plaintiff it was asked, what could be more part of the course of a person's employment than collecting his wages? The employee was still on the National Coal Board's premises; he was merely going to collect his wages from a place also on those premises; it could not in those circumstances be said that the course of employment had ceased.

Finnemore J, in a long judgment in which he considered all the cases to which he had been referred, came to the conclusion that the course of employment had not ceased, that the chain had not been broken, and that accordingly the board was vicariously liable for the negligent cyclist. . . .

Mr Wolton, on the second defendants' behalf, also referred me to *Nottingham v Aldridge* [1971] 2 QB 739, a decision at first instance of Eveleigh J. However, I do not propose to deal with that case in any great detail because, once again, I think that its facts can equally easily be distinguished from the facts of the present case as can those in *Staton's* case. In *Nottingham v Aldridge* the relevant accident occurred on a Sunday/Monday night. One employee of the employers was driving another back to the town in which on the Monday both of them had to go to work in the course of their apprenticeships. The driver of the car in which the plaintiff apprentice was being driven was entitled to claim from his employers petrol and mileage allowance for the journey he was making, and he was, as I have said, taking his fellow-apprentice back to the place at which the following morning they were both to do their work. Nevertheless the accident happened hours before they were due to re-start such work and on the public highway. It was held that the accident did not happen in the course of the driver's employment. . . .

Doing the best I can on the authorities to which I have been referred, I find myself driven to the conclusion that the least artificial place at which to draw the line in the circumstances of the present case is at the boundary of the factory premises; at the gates where employees coming in find that control by the employers starts; where the 5 mph speed limit begins; where there are security officers to see that the traffic is proceeding properly; where employees at this point are clearly coming to work — providing, of course, that that is the purpose for which they cross the boundary. I see the force of Mr Wolton's contrary argument, that at this time the employee is still using the roadway for his own purposes and not for his employers' purposes, but I do not think that it is straining language to say that in fact it is for the employers' purposes that an employee is on the former's premises when he is coming to work. Thus in cases such as the present, unless the circumstances of the entry to the employers' premises are such as, for instance, to make it a frolic of the employee's own, or unless the purposes of the entry were, as Mr Wolton suggested, that he was merely coming back to collect a coat which he had left behind, then in my judgment the course of the employment prima facie begins and the conditions giving rise to vicarious liability are fulfilled when the employee comes onto his employers' premises in order to start the work that he is employed to do. For these reasons I have come to the conclusion in the present case that the second defendants must be held to be vicariously liable for the clear negligence of the first defendant and, accordingly, that there must be judgment for the plaintiff against both defendants for whatever sum I consider to be the appropriate award by way of damages.

Question
What if McClure had been early for work by 30 minutes because he wanted to play cards before the shift started?

B: *Unauthorised modes of doing authorised things*
Jefferson v Derbyshire Farmers Ltd
Court of Appeal [1921] 2 KB 281; 90 LJKB 1361; 124 LJ 775

Charles Booth, aged 16, was told by his employer to fill some tins with petrol from a drum. He turned on the tap on the drum and then lit a cigarette and threw the match on the floor. The garage where he was working, owned by the plaintiff, was destroyed. Held: dismissing the appeal, that the employers were vicariously liable.

WARRINGTON LJ: There is no doubt or question that the fire was caused by the negligent act of Booth. It would have been a negligent act to smoke at all in the immediate neighbourhood of the spirit. Still more was it a negligent act to light a match while the spirit was flowing from the drum. Horridge J decided in favour of the defendants on this point on the ground that what the boy did in lighting and throwing away the match was not in the scope of his employment. In one sense it was not; he was not employed to light the match and throw it away; but that is not the way in which to approach the question. It was in the scope of his employment to fill the tin with motor spirit from the drum. That work required special precautions. The act which caused the damage was an act done while he was engaged in this dangerous operation, and it was an improper act in the circumstances. That is to say, the boy was doing the work of his employers in an improper way and without taking reasonable precautions; and in that case the employers are liable. . . .

Note
Even skylarking may be within the course of employment. In **Harrison v Michelin Tyre Co.** [1985] ICR 696 Mr Smith in the proper course of his employment was wheeling a hand truck along a passageway when he deliberately, as a matter of ordinary horseplay, turned the truck a couple of inches and pushed the edge of it under a duck board on which the plaintiff was standing. The plaintiff fell and was injured. It was held that the employer was vicariously liable. Does this follow from the principle in *Jefferson* above? Compare the *Keppel Bus* case below. Was this a risk properly attributable to the enterprise?

Keppel Bus Co. v *Sa'ad bin Ahmad*
Privy Council [1974] 1 WLR 1082; [1974] 2 All ER 700; [1974] RTR 504

The plaintiff took exception to a bus conductor's treatment of another passenger and an altercation broke out, each trying to hit the other. The other passenger got off, and the conductor began collecting fares. He abused the plaintiff in Chinese 'using a very rude expression of which an English translation has not been furnished'. The plaintiff objected and the conductor hit him in the eye with his ticket punch. Held: allowing the appeal, that the bus company was not vicariously liable.

LORD KILBRANDON: It is necessary, accordingly, in the present appeal to examine the grounds upon which the judge held that, on the facts, this assault was committed in the course of carrying out, by a wrong mode, work which the conductor was expressly or impliedly authorised and therefore employed to do, and to see whether there is any evidene to support them. If there be no evidence, it is matter of law that his conclusions could not stand. The passage in which those grounds are stated is as follows:

I find that the conductor when he hit the plaintiff was acting in the course of his duties. He was then maintaining order among the passengers in the bus. He was in effect telling the plaintiff by his act not to interfere with him in his due performance of his duties. He may have acted in a very high handed manner but nonetheless I am of the opinion that he was acting in the due performance of his duties then.

Upon the facts as found by the judge, and after examining, with the assistance of counsel, the testimony of those witnesses whom the judge accepted as credible, their Lordships are unable to find any evidence which, if it had been under the consideration of a jury, could have supported a verdict for the plaintiff. It may be accepted that the keeping of order among the passengers is part of the duties of a conductor. But there was no evidence of disorder among the passengers at the time of the assault. The only sign of disorder was that the conductor had gratuitously insulted the plaintiff, and the plaintiff had asked him in an orderly manner not to do it again. The Lordships do not consider the question whether the events of that morning are to be regarded as one incident, or as two incidents separated by a gap, to be of much importance. Certainly the end result can be related back to the treatment of the Malay lady: on the other hand she had by now left the bus, normalcy had been restored, except, apparently, for some simmering resentment in the conductor which caused him to misbehave himself. But to describe what he did in these circumstances as an act of quelling disorder seems to their Lordships to be impossible on the evidence; on the story as a whole, if anyone was keeping order in the bus it was the passengers. The evidence falls far short of establishing an implied authority to take violent action where none was called for. . . .

A similar criticism can be levelled at the second ground upon which the judge found that the conductor was acting under authority. There is no evidence that the plaintiff was interfering with the conductor in his due performance of his duty. His interference, if so it could be described, was a protest against the conductor's insulting language. Insults to passengers are not part of the due performance of a conductor's duty, as the judge seems to recognise in the paragraph of his judgment which follows.

The function of a bus conductor, from which could be deduced the scope of the authority committed to him, was attractively put by counsel for the respondent as 'managing the bus'; it was said that what he did arose out of that power and duty of management. But this concept, it seems, if pushed to its extreme, could serve to bring anything which the conductor did during his employment within the class of things done in the course of it. There must be room for some distinction between the acts of a manager, however foreign to his authority, and acts of management properly so called. Probably this way of putting the case is fundamentally no different from that which the trial judge adopted and their Lordships reject, because there is no evidence of circumstances which would suggest that what the manager actually did was, although wrongful, within the scope of his authority, express or implied, and thus an act of management.

Although each case on this branch of the law must stand upon its own facts, it was natural and proper that their Lordships should have been referred to other cases by way of analogy. . . . As regards the two public house cases cited, *Deatons Pty Ltd v Flew* (1949) 79 CLR 370 and *Petterson v Royal Oak Hotel Ltd* [1948] NZLR 136, their Lordships have some difficulty in reconciling them, except on the possible ground that while in both the servant was retaliating for a personal affront, in the latter, though not the former, he was also encouraging the undesirable he assaulted to leave the premises. If either of those cases assist by analogy, the present, it would seem that more assistance might be obtained from the former.

Notes

1. The approach to the problem of 'personal' acts of employees has varied, and is exemplified by the 'barmaid' cases mentioned above in *Keppel Bus*. In *Deatons v Flew* (1949) 79 CLR 370, referred to above, a barmaid threw a glass of beer and then the glass at the plaintiff, allegedly because the plaintiff had struck her. Her employer was held not liable as the response was a personal and independent act of the barmaid. See also *Griggs v Southside Hotel* [1947] 4 DLR 49. In *Petterson v Royal Oak Hotel* [1948] NZLR 136 a barman refused a drink to a customer, who thereupon threw a glass at the barman. The barman picked up a piece of the broken glass and threw it at the customer, but a piece of the glass struck a bystander in the eye. It was held that the barman's employer was vicariously liable, as he was engaged in an improper mode of keeping order. Who should pay for the torts of irascible (or provoked) barmen?

2. In *General Engineering Ltd v Kingston Corporation* [1989] ICR 88 firemen were engaged in an industrial dispute and conducting a 'go slow'. The plaintiff's property caught fire and the fire brigade took 17 rather than the normal three minutes to arrive. The Privy Council held that the local authority, as employer of the firemen, was not liable, as the strike was a repudiation of the contract of employment. Does it matter that the repudiation had not been accepted by the employer? Why was driving slowly not merely regarded as a wrongful mode of driving fast?

Rose v Plenty
Court of Appeal [1976] 1 WLR 141; [1976] 1 All ER 97;
[1976] 1 Lloyd's Rep 263

Christopher Plenty was a milkman. At his depot was a notice saying 'Children and young persons must not in any circumstances be employed by you in the performance of your duties.' Nevertheless, Mr Plenty engaged Leslie Rose, aged 13, to help him on his rounds, and injured him by driving the milk float negligently. Held: allowing the appeal, that the employers were vicariously liable.

LORD DENNING MR: This raises a nice point on the liability of a master for his servant. I will first take the notices to the roundsmen saying they must not take the boys on. Those do not necessarily exempt the employers from liability. The leading case is *Limpus* v *London General Omnibus Co.* (1862) 1 H & C 526. The drivers of omnibuses were furnished with a card saying they 'must not on any account race with or obstruct another omnibus.' Nevertheless the driver of one of the defendants' omnibuses did obstruct a rival omnibus and caused an accident in which the plaintiff's horses were injured. Martin B directed the jury that, if the defendants' driver did it for the purposes of his employer, the defendants were liable, but if it was an act of his own, and in order to effect a purpose of his own, the defendants were not responsible. The jury found for the plaintiff. The Court of Exchequer Chamber held that the direction was correct. It was a very strong court which included Willes J and Blackburn J. Despite the prohibition, the employers were held liable because the injury resulted from an act done by the driver in the course of his service and for his masters' purposes. The decisive point was that it was *not* done by the servant for his own purposes, but for his masters' purposes. . . .

In considering whether a prohibited act was within the course of the employment, it depends very much on the purpose for which it is done. If it is done for his employers' business, it is usually done in the course of his employment, even though it is a prohibited act. That is clear from *Limpus* v *London General Omnibus Co.*, 1 H & C 526; *Young* v *Edward Box & Co. Ltd* [1951] 1 TLR 789 and *Ilkiw* v *Samuels* [1963] 1 WLR 991. But if it is done for some purpose other than his masters' business, as, for instance, giving a lift to a hitchhiker, such an act, if prohibited, may not be within the course of his employment. Both *Twine* v *Bean's Express Ltd* (1946) 62 TLR 458 and *Conway* v *George Wimpey & Co. Ltd (No. 2)* [1951] 2 KB 266 are to be explained on their own facts as cases where a driver had given a lift to someone else, contrary to a prohibition and not for the purposes of the employers. *Iqbal* v *London Transport Executive* (1973) 16 KIR 329 seems to be out of line and should be regarded as decided on its own special circumstances. In the present case it seems to me that the course of the milk roundsman's employment was to distribute the milk, collect the money and to bring back the bottles to the van. He got or allowed this young boy to do part of that business which was the employers' business. It seems to me that although prohibited, it was conduct which was within the course of the employment; and on this ground I think the judge was in error. . . .

SCARMAN LJ: . . . The next question, as Lord Denning MR has said, is whether the employer should shoulder the liability for compensating the person injured by the tort. With all respect to the points developed by Lawton LJ it does appear to me to be clear, since the decision of *Limpus* v *London General Omnibus Co.*, 1 H & C 526 that that question has to be answered by directing attention to what the servant was employed to do when he committed the tort that has caused damage to the plaintiff. The servant was, of course, employed at the time of the accident to do a whole number of operations. He was certainly not employed to give the boy a lift, and if one confines one's analysis of the facts to the incident of injury to the plaintiff, then no doubt one would say that carrying the boy on the float — giving him a lift — was not in the course of the servant's employment. But in *Ilkiw* v *Samuels* [1963] 1 WLR 991 Diplock LJ indicated that the proper approach to the nature of the servant's employment is a broad one. He says, at p. 1004:

'As each of these nouns implies' — he is referring to the nouns used to describe course of employment, sphere, scope and so forth — 'the matter must be looked at broadly, not dissecting the servant's task into its component activities — such as driving, loading, sheeting and the like — by asking: what was the job on which he was engaged for his employer? and answering that question as a jury would.'

Applying those words to the employment of this servant, I think it is clear from the evidence that he was employed as a roundsman to drive his float round his round and to deliver milk, to collect empties and to obtain payment. That was his job. He was under an express prohibition — a matter to which I shall refer later — not to enlist the help of anyone doing that work. And he was also under an express prohibition not to give lifts on the float to anyone. How did he choose to carry out the task which I have analysed. He chose to disregard the prohibition and to enlist the assistance of the plaintiff. As a matter of common sense, that does seem to me to be a mode, albeit a prohibited mode, of doing the job with which he was entrusted. Why was the plaintiff being carried on the float when the accident occurred? Because it was necessary to take him from point to point so that he could assist in delivering milk, collecting empties and, on occasions, obtaining payment. The plaintiff was there because it was necessary that he should be there in order that he could assist, albeit in a way prohibited by the employers, in the job entrusted to the servant by his employers.

. . . in *Plumb* v *Cobden Flour Mills Co. Ltd* [1914] AC 62, . . . Lord Dunedin said, at p. 67: 'there are prohibitions which limit the sphere of employment, and prohibitions which only deal with conduct within the sphere of employment'. . . . And, coming right down to today, one finds the same idea being followed and developed by this court in *Iqbal* v *London Transport Executive* (1973) 16 KIR 329. In that case the Court of Appeal had to consider whether the London Transport Executive was liable for the action of a bus conductor in driving contrary to his express instructions a motor bus a short distance in a garage. Of course, the court had no difficulty at all in distinguishing between the spheres of employment of a driver and a conductor in the London Transport. Accordingly, it treated the prohibition upon the conductors acting as drivers of motor buses as a prohibition which defined their sphere of employment. Now there was nothing of that sort in the prohibition in this case. The prohibition is twofold: (1) that the milk roundsman was not to give lifts on his float, and (2) that he was not to employ others to help him in delivering the milk and so forth. There was nothing in those prohibitions which defined or limited the sphere of his employment. The sphere of his employment remained precisely the same after as before the prohibitions were brought to his notice. The sphere was as a milk roundsman to go round the rounds delivering milk, collecting empties and obtaining payment. Contrary to instructions, he chose to do what he was employed to do in an improper way. But the sphere of his employment was in no way affected by his express instructions not to enlist the help of a stranger.

Notes

1. The reasoning of Scarman LJ in *Rose* v *Plenty* is generally preferred to that of Lord Denning.

2. In *Limpus* v *London General Omnibus Company,* referred to above, a bus driver deliberately obstructed a rival bus, despite being prohibited from doing so. (Willis J pointed out that 'He was employed not only to drive the omnibus, . . . but also to get as much money as he could for his master and to do it in rivalry with other omnibuses on the road'.) The Court of Exchequer Chamber approved a direction to the jury that:

in doing that which he believed to be for the interest of the defendants, then the defendants were responsible for the act of their servant: that if the act of the defendants' driver, in driving as he did across the road to obstruct the plaintiff's omnibus, although reckless driving on his part, was nevertheless an act done by him in the course of his service, and to do that which he thought best to suit the interest of his employers and so to interfere with the trade and business of the other omnibuses, the defendants were responsible.

Alternatively, the case can be explained by saying that driving recklessly is merely a wrongful mode of driving, i.e. an unauthorised mode of doing an authorised thing.

3.   In *Iqbal* v *LTE* (referred to above), and in **Beard** v **London General Omnibus Co.** [1900] 2 QB 530, a bus conductor turned a bus round negligently and injured somebody. In both cases it was held that the employer was not liable, as driving a bus is not what a conductor is employed to do. *Iqbal* was criticised by Lord Denning, but approved by Scarman LJ in *Rose* v *Plenty* (above). Do you think it was rightly decided?

C: *Criminal acts done for the employee's own benefit*

Morris v C W Martin & Sons Ltd
Court of Appeal [1966] 1 QB 716; [1965] 3 WLR 276; [1965] 2 All ER 725

Mrs Lily Morris sent a fur coat to a furrier, who in turn sent it to the defendants to be cleaned. They gave it to one of their employees, called Morrissey, to clean and he stole it. Held: allowing the appeal, that the defendants were liable.

LORD DENNING MR: The law on this subject has developed greatly over the years. During the 19th century it was accepted law that a master was liable for the dishonesty or fraud of his servant if it was done in the course of his employment *and* for his master's benefit. Dishonesty or fraud by the servant for his *own* benefit took the case out of the course of his employment. The judges took this simple view: No servant who turns thief and steals is acting in the course of his employment. He is acting outside it altogether. But in 1912 the law was revolutionised by *Lloyd* v *Grace, Smith & Co.* [1912] AC 716, where it was held that a master was liable for the dishonesty or fraud of his servant if it was done within the course of his employment, no matter whether it was done for the benefit of the master or for the benefit of the servant. Nevertheless there still remains the question: What is meant by the phrase 'in the course of his employment'? When can it be said that the dishonesty or fraud of a servant, done for his *own* benefit, is in the course of his employment? . . .

If you go through the cases on this difficult subject, you will find that, in the ultimate analysis, they depend on the nature of the duty owed by the master towards the person whose goods have been lost or damaged. If the master is under a duty to use due care to keep goods safely and protect them from theft and depredation, he cannot get rid of his responsibility by delegating his duty to another. If he entrusts that duty to his servant, he is answerable for the way in which the servant conducts himself therein. No matter whether the servant be negligent, fraudulent, or dishonest, the master is liable. But not when he is under no such duty. . . .

From all these instances we may deduce the general proposition that when a principal has in his charge the goods or belongings of another in such circumstances that he is under a duty to take all reasonable precautions to protect them from theft or depredation, then if he entrusts that duty to a servant or agent, he is answerable for the manner in which that servant or agent carries out his duty. If the servant or agent is careless so that they are stolen by a stranger, the master is liable. So also if the servant or agent himself steals them or makes away with them. . . .

DIPLOCK LJ: If the bailee in the present case had been a natural person and had converted the plaintiff's fur by stealing it himself, no one would have argued that he was not liable to her for its loss. But the defendant bailees are a corporate person. They could not perform their duties to the plaintiffs to take reasonable care of the fur and not to convert it otherwise than vicariously by natural persons acting as their servants or agents. It was one of their servants to whom they had entrusted the care and custody of the fur for the purpose of doing work upon it who converted it by stealing it. Why should they not be vicariously liable for this breach of their duty by the vicar whom they had chosen to perform it? Sir John Holt, I think, would have answered that they were liable 'for seeing that someone must be the loser by this deceit it is more reason that he who employs and puts a trust and confidence in the deceiver should be the loser than a stranger': *Hern* v *Nichols* (1701) 1 Salk 289.

. . . *Lloyd* v *Grace, Smith & Co.* [1912] AC 716, . . . was a further landmark in this branch of the law. It rejected the view that a dishonest act committed by a servant for his own benefit was, as Collins MR thought, ipso facto 'outside the scope of his employment.' Whether the act of the servant be honest or dishonest, the ground of the master's liability is: 'he [the master] has put the agent in his place to do that class of acts and he must be answerable for the manner in which that agent has conducted himself in doing the business which it was the act of his master to place him in.' This explanation of the master's liability taken from the judgment of Willes J in *Barwick's* case (1867) LR 2 Exch 259, was understandably preferred by Lord Macnaghten in *Lloyd* v *Grace, Smith & Co.* to the commoner expressions 'acting within his authority,' 'acting in the course of his employment,' or 'acting within the scope of his agency,' all of which, he said, mean the same thing and must be construed liberally. . . .

If the principle laid down in *Lloyd* v *Grace, Smith & Co.* is applied to the facts of the present case, the defendants cannot in my view escape liability for the conversion of the plaintiff's fur by their servant Morrissey. They accepted the fur as bailees for reward in order to clean it. They put Morrissey as their agent in their place to clean the fur and to take charge of it while doing so. The manner in which he conducted himself in doing that work was to convert it. What he was doing, albeit dishonestly, he was doing in the scope or course of his employment in the technical sense of that infelicitous but time-honoured phrase. The defendants as his masters are responsible for his tortious act. . . .

Nor are we concerned with what would have been the liability of the defendants if the fur had been stolen by another servant of theirs who was not employed by them to clean the fur or to have the care or custody of it. The mere fact that his employment by the defendants gave him the opportunity to steal it would not suffice. . . .

SALMON LJ: I accordingly agree with my Lords that the appeal should be allowed. I am anxious, however, to make it plain that the conclusion which I have reached depends upon Morrissey being the servant through whom the defendants chose to discharge their duty to take reasonable care of the plaintiff's fur. The words of Willes J in *Barwick's* case are entirely applicable to these facts. The defendants 'put the agent (Morrissey) in (the defendants') place to do that class of acts and . . . must be answerable for the manner in which that agent has conducted himself in doing the business which it was the act of his master to put him in.' A bailee for reward is not answerable for a theft by any of his servants but only for a theft by such of them as are deputed by him to discharge some part of his duty of taking reasonable care. A theft by any servant who is not employed to do anything in relation to the goods bailed is entirely outside the scope of his employment and cannot make the master liable. So in this case, if someone employed by the defendants in another depot had broken in and stolen the fur, the defendants would not have been liable. Similarly in my view if a clerk employed in the same depot had seized the opportunity of entering the room where the fur was kept and had stolen it, the defendants would not have been liable. The mere fact that the master, by employing a rogue, gives him the opportunity to steal or defraud does not make the master liable for his depredations: *Ruben* v *Great Fingall Consolidated* [1906] AC 439. It might be otherwise if the master knew or ought to have known that his servant was dishonest, because then the master could be liable in negligence for employing him.

Note
In *Heasmans* v *Clarity Cleaning Co.* [1987] ICR 949 the defendants provided office cleaning services and employed one Bonsu as a cleaner. He cleaned the plaintiffs' offices, and while doing so made international telephone calls costing £1,411. His duties included cleaning the telephone. It was held that the defendants were not vicariously liable on the ground (per Purchas LJ) that merely providing the opportunity to commit a tort or a crime was not sufficient to render the employer liable, but rather a closer connection must exist between the nature of the employment and the act of the employee, or (per Nourse LJ) that using a telephone is not merely an unauthorised mode of cleaning it.

Questions
1. What if in *Morris* v *Martin* the coat had been stolen by (a) an accounts clerk, or (b) the person on the counter?
2. What if in *Clarity Cleaning* the phone had been used by the nightwatchman who was authorised to use the telephone to make emergency calls?

Section 4: liability for independent contractors and others

The principle whereby one person may be liable for the acts of another is not limited to the relationship of employer and employee, but outside that category the law is vague and undeveloped. As to the engagement of independent contractors, the rule is that the 'employer' may be liable if he has himself been negligent, for example in selecting the contractor, or if he has authorised the tort or if the law imposes upon him a 'non-delegable' duty of care, as in the case of inherently hazardous activities.

There is probably no liability for a mere agent, unless the degree of control is sufficient to make him both an agent and a 'servant' at the same time. However, there may be cases where a person is engaged in an activity for the mutual benefit of himself and another whereby that other is held responsible.

A: *Independent contractors*
Salsbury v Woodland
Court of Appeal [1970] 1 QB 324; [1969] 3 All ER 863; [1969] 3 WLR 29

Mr Woodland wanted a hawthorn tree cut down. The tree was 25 feet high and stood 28 feet from the road, and running across the garden diagonally was a pair of telephone wires. Mr Woodland engaged Terence Coombe to cut the tree down and he did so negligently. The tree hit the telephone wires which landed in the roadway. The plaintiff intended to coil up the wires, but on seeing the third defendant, Mr Waugh, approaching too fast in his Morris Cooper, he flung himself to the ground to avoid being hit by the wires (which would have whipped around on being struck by the car). The plaintiff had a tumour on his spine and the falling to the ground dislodged this and caused damage to the plaintiff. Held: allowing the appeal by Mr Woodland, that he was not liable for the negligence of his independent contractor. (Note: the driver was held partly responsible as he was driving too fast.)

WIDGERY LJ: It is trite law that an employer who employs an independent contractor is not vicariously responsible for the negligence of that contractor. He is not able to control the way in which the independent contractor does the work, and the vicarious obligation of a master for the negligence of his servant does not arise under the relationship of employer and independent contractor. I think that it is entirely accepted that those cases — and there are some — in which an employer has been held liable for injury done by the negligence of an independent contractor are in truth cases where the employer owes a direct duty to the person injured, a duty which he cannot delegate to the contractor on his behalf. The whole question here is whether the occupier is to be judged by the general rule, which would result in no liability, or whether he comes within one of the somewhat special exceptions — cases in which a direct duty to see that care is taken rests upon the employer throughout the operation.

This is clear from authority; and for convenience I take from *Salmond on Torts,* 14th ed. (1965), p. 687, this statement of principle:

> One thing can, however, be said with confidence: the mere fact that the work entrusted to the contractor is of a character which may cause damage to others unless precautions are taken is not sufficient to impose liability on the employer. There are few operations entrusted to an agent which are not capable, if due precautions are not observed, of being sources of danger and mischief to others; and if the principal was responsible for this reason alone, the distinction between servants and independent contractors would be practically eliminated from the law.

I am satisfied that that statement is supported by authority, and I adopt it for the purposes of this judgment. . . .

In truth, according to the authorities there are a number of well-determined classes of case in which this direct and primary duty upon an employer to see that care is taken exists. Two such classes are directly relevant for consideration in the present case. The first class concerns what have sometimes been described as 'extra-hazardous acts' — acts commissioned by an employer which are so hazardous in their character that the law has thought it proper to impose this direct obligation on the employer to see that care is taken. An example of such a case is *Honeywill & Stein Ltd v Larkin Bros (London's Commercial Photographers) Ltd* [1934] 1 KB 191. Other cases which one finds in the books are cases where the activity commissioned by the employer is the keeping of dangerous things within the rule in *Rylands* v *Fletcher* (1868) LR 3 HL 330 and where liability is not dependent on negligence at all.

I do not propose to add to the wealth of authority on this topic by attempting further to define the meaning of 'extra-hazardous acts'; but I am confident that the act commissioned in the present case cannot come within that category. The act commissioned in the present case, if done with ordinary elementary caution by skilled men, presented no hazard to anyone at all.

The second class of case, which is relevant for consideration, concerns dangers created in a highway. There are a number of cases on this branch of the law, a good example of which is *Holliday* v *National Telephone Co.* [1899] 2 QB 392. These, on analysis, will all be found to be cases where work was being done in a highway and was work of a character which would have been a nuisance unless authorised by statute. It will be found in all these cases that the statutory powers under which the employer commissioned the work were statutory powers which left upon the employer a duty to see that due care was taken in the carrying out of the work, for the protection of those who passed on the highway. In accordance with principle, an employer subject to such a direct and personal duty cannot excuse himself, if things go wrong, merely because the direct cause of the injury was the act of the independent contractor.

This again is not a case in that class. It is not a case in that class because in the instant case no question of doing work in the highway, which might amount to a nuisance if due care was not taken, arises. In my judgment, the present case is clearly outside the well defined limit of the second class to which I have referred. Mr Bax, accordingly, invited us to say that there is a third class into which the instant case precisely falls, and he suggested that the third class comprised those cases where an employer commissions work to be done *near* a highway in circumstances in which, if due care is not taken, injury to passers-by on the highway may be caused. If that be a third class of case to which the principle of liability of the employer applies, no doubt the present case would come within that description. The question is, is there such a third class?

Reliance was placed primarily on three authorities. . . .

The second case relied upon was *Tarry* v *Ashton* (1876) 1 QBD 314. That was a case where a building adjoining the highway had attached to it a heavy lamp, which was suspended over the footway and which was liable to be a source of injury to passers-by if allowed to fall into disrepair. It fell into disrepair, and injury was caused. The defendant sought to excuse himself by saying that he had employed a competent independent contractor to put the lamp into good repair and that the cause of the injury was the fault of the independent contractor. Mr Bax argued that that case illustrated the special sympathy with which the law regards passers-by on the highway. He said that it demonstrated that the law has always been inclined to give special protection to persons in that category and so supported his argument that any action adjacent to the highway might be subject to special rights. But, in my judgment, that is not so. *Tarry* v *Ashton* seems to me to be a perfectly ordinary and straightforward example of a case where the employer was under a positive and continuing duty to see that the lamp was kept in repair. That duty was imposed upon him before the contractor came and after the contractor had gone; and on the principle that such a duty cannot be delegated the responsibility of the employer in that case seems to me to be fully demonstrated. I cannot find that it produces on a side-wind, as it were, anything in support of Mr Bax's contention.

Notes

1.   An example where a person was liable on the basis of extra-hazardous activities is ***Honeywill & Stein Ltd v Larkin*** [1934] 1 KB 191, where the

plaintiffs engaged the defendants, Larkin Brothers, to take photographs of the interior of the cinema. In those days this involved igniting magnesium powder in a metal tray. The defendants did this some four feet from a curtain which caught fire. In an action in which the question arose whether the plaintiffs would have been liable to the cinema owners, it was held they would. Slesser LJ referred to 'acts which in their very nature involve in the eyes of the law special danger to others'. The difficulty is that the taking of the photograph would have been quite safe if it had not been done negligently. What does extra-hazardous mean? Does it mean a greater risk of damage or a risk of greater damage, or both?

2. It is sometimes said that under this head there can be no liability on the 'employer' for acts of 'collateral' negligence by the contractor — for example, if the camera tripod in *Honeywill* had been placed so as to render it likely that someone would trip over it. In *Salsbury* v *Woodland* (above) Sachs LJ said:

> I derived no assistance at all from any distinction between 'collateral and casual' negligence and other negligence. Such a distinction provides too many difficulties for me to accept without question, unless it simply means that one must ascertain exactly what was the occupier's duty and then treat any act that is not part of that duty as giving rise to no liability on his part.

B: Mutual benefit

Ormrod v Crosville Motor Services: Murphie, Third Party
[1953] 1 WLR 1120; [1953] 2 All ER 5753

Mr Murphie intended to take part in the Monte Carlo rally and then go on holiday with Mr and Mrs Ormrod. The arrangement was that the Ormrods would drive Murphie's car to Monte Carlo, which would then be used for the joint holiday (Murphie was using a different car for the rally). The Ormrods set off but soon ran into a Crosville bus. Held: dismissing the appeal, that Murphie, the owner of the car, was liable for the negligent driving of Mr Ormrod.

DENNING LJ: It has often been supposed that the owner of a vehicle is only liable for the negligence of the driver if that driver is his servant acting in the course of his employment. But that is not correct. The owner is also liable if the driver is his agent, that is to say, if the driver is, with the owner's consent, driving the car on the owner's business or for the owner's purposes. In the present case the driver was, by mutual arrangement, driving the car partly for his own purposes and partly for the owner's purposes. The owner wanted the car taken to Monte Carlo, and the driver himself wanted to go with his wife to Monte Carlo, and he intended to visit friends in Normandy on the way. On this account he started two or three days earlier than he would have done if he had been going solely for the owner's purposes. Mr Scholefield Allen says that this should exempt the owner from liability for the driver's negligence, because the accident might never have happened if he had started later. He says that the owner would not have been liable for any negligence of the driver on the trip from Calais to Normandy and should not be liable for negligence on the early start. I do not think that this argument is correct. The law puts an especial responsibility on the owner of a vehicle who allows it out on to the road in charge of someone else, no matter whether it is his servant, his friend, or anyone else. If it is being used wholly or partly on the owner's business or for the owner's purposes, then the owner is liable for any negligence on the part of the driver. The owner only escapes liability when he lends it out or hires it out to a third person to be used for purposes in which the owner has no interest or concern: see *Hewitt* v *Bonvin* [1940] 1 KB 188. That is not this case. The trip to Monte Carlo must be considered as a whole, including the proposed excursion to Normandy, and, as such, it was undertaken with the owner's consent for the purposes of both of them, and the owner is liable for any negligence of the driver in the course of it. . . .

Notes
1.   In the past this principle has mainly been used in cases where a car driver is uninsured. The existence of the Motor Insurers Bureau and changes in the rules of insurance law have meant that this principle is not often needed to provide compensation of victims of uninsured drivers, except perhaps where compulsory insurance is not required.
2.   That the mutual benefit argument is still alive, and perhaps capable of extension, is illustrated by the strange case of *Moynihan* v *Moynihan* [1975] IR 192, where the defendant grandmother invited the plaintiff, aged 2, her parents and her aunt for a meal. After the meal the aunt made a pot of tea and, covering it with a brightly coloured tea-cosy, placed it on the table. The plaintiff upset the teapot and was scalded. The court held that the grandmother was liable for the negligence of the aunt on the ground that the negligence of the aunt was not the casual negligence of a fellow guest, but rather the negligence of a person engaged in one of the duties of the grandmother's household. The grandmother's power of control was not dependent on the relationshp of mother and daughter, but upon the relationship of the head of a household with a person to whom some of the duties of the head of the household had been delegated by that head. Do you agree? Was the aunt an independent contractor, or an agent in a mutually beneficial enterprise? If the former, was the teapot extra-hazardous? If the latter, would it have mattered if either the aunt or the grandmother did not intend to have any tea? Should the head of a household be liable for acts committed by others in the running of the household? Who do you think was insured in *Moynihan*?

18 BREACH OF STATUTORY DUTY

The idea behind the form of liability discussed in this chapter is that there may be cases where a statute renders a certain activity a crime, and the law imposes an additional civil liability towards a person harmed by the act. Some statutes state this directly: for example, the Consumer Protection Act 1987 makes it an offence to supply goods, such as flammable nightdresses, which contravene the safety regulations, and s. 41 expressly states that a person contravening the regulations will also be liable to pay compensation to a person harmed by the breach. On the other hand, the Guard Dogs Act 1975 (which makes it an offence to have a guard dog free to roam about the premises or not under the control of a handler), in s. 5 states that no civil liability will arise from a breach of the Act. Most statutes, however, make no mention of potential civil liability, but nevertheless liability may be imposed if the court believes that Parliament impliedly intended there to be a remedy. (In 1969 the Law Commission, in Report No. 21 on the Interpretation of Statutes, recommended that rather than courts trying to answer this impossible question, it should be presumed, unless stated to the contrary, that any statute which imposes a duty is intended to give rise to a civil remedy. This was never implemented.)

Not only are there difficulties about when a civil duty will be spelt out of a criminal or regulatory statute, but there are also problems about the role and function of the tort of statutory duty, and, as will be seen, different jurisdictions in the Common Law have taken different views on this. The main importance of the tort lies in its application to breaches of the factories regulations, but how useful it is outside this sphere is a matter of current debate, for the decisions are rather haphazard.

For thorough discussion of the tort outside the standard textbooks, see K. M. Stanton, *Breach of Statutory Duty in Tort* (1985) and Buckley, 'Liability in Tort for Breach of Statutory Duty' (1984) 100 LQR 204.

Phillips v *Britannia Hygienic Laundry*
Court of Appeal [1923] 2 KB 832

The axle of a lorry owned by the defendants was defective and broke. A wheel came off and damaged the plaintiff's van. The Motor Cars (Use and Construction) Order 1904 stated that 'the motor car and all the fittings thereof shall be in such a condition as not to cause, or to be likely to cause, danger to any person in the motor car or on any highway'. Held: dismissing the appeal, that the regulations did not give rise to any civil liability.

ATKIN LJ: . . . This is an important question, and I have felt some doubt upon it, because it is clear that these regulations are in part designed to promote the safety of the public using highways. The question is whether they were intended to be enforced only by the special penalty attached to them in the Act. In my opinion, when an Act imposes a duty of commission or omission, the question whether a person aggrieved by a breach of the duty has a right of action depends on the intention of the Act. Was it intended to make the duty one which was owed to the party aggrieved as well as to the State, or was it a public duty only? That depends on the construction of the Act and the circumstances in which it was made and to which it relates. One question to be considered is, does the Act contain reference to a remedy for breach of it? Prima facie if it does that is the only remedy. But that is not conclusive. The intention as disclosed by its scope and wording must still be regarded, and it may still be that, though the statute creates the duty and provides a penalty, the duty is nevertheless owed to individuals. Instances of this are *Groves* v *Lord Wimborne*, [1898] 2 QB 402, and *Britannic Merthyr Coal Co.* v *David* [1910] AC 74. To my mind, and in this respect I differ from McCardie J, the question is not to be solved by considering whether or not the person aggrieved can bring himself within some special class of the community or whether he is some designated individual. The duty may be of such paramount importance that it is owed to all the public. It would be strange if a less important duty, which is owed to a section of the public, may be enforced by an action, while a more important duty owed to the public at large cannot. The right of action does not depend on whether a statutory commandment or prohibition is pronounced for the benefit of the public or for the benefit of a class. It may be conferred on any one who can bring himself within the benefit of the Act, including one who cannot be otherwise specified than as a person using the highway. Therefore I think McCardie J is applying too strict a test when he says ([1923] 1 KB 547): 'The Motor Car Acts and Regulations were not enacted for the benefit of any particular class of folk. They are provisions for the benefit of the whole public, whether pedestrians or vehicle users, whether aliens or British citizens, and whether working or walking or standing upon the highway.' Kelly CB in stating the argument for the defendant in *Gorris* v *Scott* LR 9 Ex 125, refers to the obligation imposed upon railway companies by s. 47 of the Railways Clauses Consolidation Act, 1845, to erect gates across public carriage roads crossed by the railway on the level, and to keep the gates closed except when the crossing is being actually and properly used, under the penalty of 40s. for every default. It was never doubted that if a member of the public crossing the railway were injured by the railway company's breach of duty, either in not erecting a gate or in not keeping it closed, he would have a right of action. Therefore the question is whether these regulations, viewed in the circumstances in which they were made and to which they relate, were intended to impose a duty which is a public duty only or whether they were intended, in addition to the public duty, to impose a duty enforceable by an individual aggrieved. I have come to the conclusion that the duty they were intended to impose was not a duty enforceable by individuals injured, but a public duty only, the sole remedy for which is the remedy provided by way of a fine. They impose obligations of various kinds, some are concerned more with the maintenance of the highway than with the safety of passengers; and they are of varying degrees of importance; yet for breach of any regulation a fine not exceeding 10*l.* is the penalty. It is not likely that the Legislature, in empowering a department to make regulations for the use and construction of motor cars, permitted the department to impose new duties in favour of individuals and new causes of action for breach of them in addition to the obligations already well provided for and regulated by the common law of those who bring vehicles upon highways. In particular it is not likely that the Legislature intended by these means to impose on the owners of vehicles an absolute obligation to have them roadworthy in all events even in the absence of negligence. . . .

Notes
1.   This seems a surprising decision, as it may be thought that the purpose of the regulation was to protect other road users; but at the time the control of motor cars was a highly contentious and political issue, and it may be that the court felt inhibited from entering such an arena. A more important reason may have been that compulsory insurance had not yet been introduced.
2.   An earlier case, where liability was imposed for a breach of the Factory and Workshop Act 1878 (in fact for failing to fence machinery), was *Groves* v *Lord Wimborne* [1898] 2 QB 402, where it was said that the Act was clearly passed for the protection of workmen. A. L. Smith LJ said that it was material to ask whether the Act was passed for the protection of a particular class of persons or in the interests of the public at large. This is not to say that a statute creating general public rights cannot give rise to civil liability, but only that it will be *easier* to show that the aim of the statute was to provide a right of action where a particular group is selected.
3.   In *R* v *Deputy Governor of Parkhurst, ex parte Hague* [1991] 3 WLR 341, Lord Jauncey said, in relation to breach of statutory duty, that:

> it must always be a matter for consideration whether the legislature intended that private law rights of action should be conferred upon individuals in respect of breaches of the relevant statutory provision. The fact that a particular provision was intended to protect certain individuals is not of itself sufficient to confer private law rights of action upon them. Something more is required to show that the legislature intended such conferment.

The 'more' that is required is the intention of the legislature to provide a right of action, and according to Lord Bridge that is a matter of statutory construction like any other. But how can that be when the problem arises only because the statute says nothing about the issue? On this approach see further the *Saskatchewan Wheat Pool* case, below. In *Hague* itself it was held that the Prison Rules were administrative only and gave rise to no right of action (the plaintiff had claimed that segregation in breach of the Prison Rules gave him an action in private law).

Lonrho v *Shell Petroleum (No. 2)*
House of Lords [1982] AC 173; [1981] 3 WLR 33; [1981] 2 All ER 456

After the unilateral declaration of independence by the government of Southern Rhodesia, Parliament passed the Southern Rhodesia (Petroleum) Order 1965, which prohibited the supply of oil to Southern Rhodesia. Lonrho owned a pipeline from Mozambique to Rhodesia, which was thereupon closed. They alleged that the defendants and others had maintained the supply of oil to Rhodesia, thereby prolonging the period of unconstitutional government and lengthening the period of closure of the plaintiff's pipeline. One of the arguments related to liability for the breach of statutory duty arising from the order. Held: dismissing the appeal, that the order did not give rise to civil liability.

LORD DIPLOCK: The sanctions Order thus creates a statutory prohibition upon the doing of certain classes of acts and provides the means of enforcing the prohibition by prosecution for a criminal offence which is subject to heavy penalties including imprisonment. So one starts with the presumption laid down originally by Lord Tenterden CJ in *Doe d. Murray* v *Bridges* (1831) 1 B & Ad 847, 859, where he spoke of the 'general rule' that 'where an Act creates an obligation, and enforces the performance in a specified manner . . . that performance cannot be enforced in any other manner' — a statement that has frequently been cited with approval ever since, including on several occasions in speeches in this House. Where the only manner of enforcing performance for which the Act provides is prosecution for the criminal offence of failure to perform the statutory obligation or for contravening the statutory prohibition which the Act creates, there are two classes of exception to this general rule.

The first is where upon the true construction of the Act it is apparent that the obligation or prohibition was imposed for the benefit or protection of a particular class of individuals, as in the case of the Factories Acts and similar legislation. As Lord Kinnear put it in *Butler (or Black)* v *Fife Coal Co. Ltd* [1912] AC 149, 165, in the case of such a statute:

There is no reasonable ground for maintaining that a proceeding by way of penalty is the only remedy allowed by the statute . . . . We are to consider the scope and purpose of the statute and in particular for whose benefit it is intended. Now the object of the present statute is plain. It was intended to compel mine owners to make due provision for the safety of the men working in their mines, and the persons for whose benefit all these rules are to be enforced are the persons exposed to danger. But when a duty of this kind is imposed for the benefit of particular persons there arises at common law a correlative right in those persons who may be injured by its contravention.

The second exception is where the statute creates a public right (i.e. a right to be enjoyed by all those of Her Majesty's subjects who wish to avail themselves of it) and a particular member of the public suffers what Brett J in *Benjamin* v *Storr* (1874) LR 9 CP 400, 407, described as 'particular, direct, and substantial' damage 'other and different from that which was common to all the rest of the public.' Most of the authorities about this second exception deal not with public rights created by statute but with public rights existing at common law, particularly in respect of use of highways. *Boyce* v *Paddington Borough Council* [1903] 1 Ch 109 is one of the comparatively few cases about a right conferred upon the general public by statute. It is in relation to that class of statute only that Buckley J's oft-cited statement at p. 114 as to the two cases in which a plaintiff, without joining the Attorney-General, could himself sue in private law for interference with that public right, must be understood. The two cases he said were: '. . . first, where the interference with the public right is such as that some private right of his is at the same time interfered with . . . and, secondly, where no private right is interfered with, but the plaintiff, in respect of his public right, suffers special damage peculiar to himself from the interference with the public right.' The first case would not appear to depend upon the existence of a public right in addition to the private one; while to come within the second case at all it has first to be shown that the statute, having regard to its scope and language, does fall within that class of statutes which creates a legal right to be enjoyed by all of Her Majesty's subjects who wish to avail themselves of it. A mere prohibition upon members of the public generally from doing what it would otherwise be lawful for them to do, is not enough.

In agreement with all those present and former members of the judiciary who have considered the matter I can see no ground on which contraventions by Shell and BP of the sanctions Order though not amounting to any breach of their contract with Lonrho, nevertheless constituted a tort for which Lonrho could recover in a civil suit any loss caused to them by such contraventions.

Notes
1.   In *X* v *Bedfordshire C.C* [1995] 2 AC 633 (see Chapter 8), various plaintiffs claimed that certain local authorities had failed in their statutory obligation as regards (a) the welfare of children and (b) the provision of special educational needs. It was said that usually a breach of statutory duty does not give rise to a private right of action, but may do so if as a matter of construction it can be shown that the statute was for the protection of a limited class of the public and that impliedly a private right of action was intended. If the statute does not provide any means of enforcing the duty that will tend to suggest a private right, but the provision of means of enforcement does not necessarily rule out a private right, as the factory cases show. It was also said that usually regulatory or welfare legislation which involves the exercise of administrative discretion would not give rise to a private right, and the actions in this case were struck out.
2.   An example of a civil action in a non-industrial sphere is *Rickless* v *United Artists* [1988] QB 40, where the Dramatic and Musical Performers' Protection Act 1958 made it an offence to make use of a film without the consent of the performers. The defendants made a film called 'Trail of the Pink Panther', which, after the death of Peter Sellers, incorporated 'out-takes' from his previous five Pink Panther films. It was held that the statute gave a civil remedy in addition to the fine of £400, and damages of $1,000,000 were granted to the personal representatives of Peter Sellers.

Gorris v *Scott*
Court of Exchequer (1874) LR 9 Exch 125

The defendant owned a ship called the *Hastings,* on which he carried the plaintiff's sheep from Hamburg to Newcastle. On the voyage some of the sheep were washed overboard. The Animals Order 1871 required sheep to be kept in pens. If they had been, which they had not, they would not have been lost. Held: the defendants were not liable.

PIGOTT B: For the reasons which have been so exhaustively stated by the Lord Chief Baron, I am of opinion that the declaration shews no cause of action. It is necessary to see what was the object of the legislature in this enactment, and it is set forth clearly in the preamble as being 'to prevent the introduction into Great Britain of contagious or infectious diseases among cattle, sheep, or other animals,' and the 'spread of such diseases in Great Britain.' The purposes enumerated in s. 75 are in harmony with this preamble, and it is in furtherance of that section that the order in question was made. The object, then, of the regulations which have been broken was, not to prevent cattle from being washed overboard, but to protect them against contagious disease. The legislature never contemplated altering the relations between the owners and carriers of cattle, except for the purposes pointed out in the Act; and if the Privy Council had gone out of their way and made provisions to prevent cattle from being washed overboard, their act would have been ultra vires. If, indeed, by reason of the neglect complained of, the cattle had contracted a contagious disease, the case would have been different. But as the case stands on this declaration, the answer to the action is this: Admit there has been a breach of duty; admit there has been a consequent injury; still the legislature was not legislating to protect against such an injury, but for an altogether different purpose; its object was not to regulate the duty of the carrier for all purposes, but only for one particular purpose.

The Queen v Saskatchewan Wheat Pool
Supreme Court of Canada [1983] 1 SCR 205; (1983) 143 DLR 3d 9

The Canadian Grain Commission received from the Wheat Pool a consignment of grain which turned out to be infected with rusty beetle larvae, and the Board had to pay $98,261 for unloading, fumigation and re-loading. Section 86(c) of the Canada Grain Act prohibited the delivery of infested grain. Held: dismissing the appeal, that the Act by itself gave no civil remedy.

DICKSON J: (a)   *General*
The uncertainty and confusion in relation between breach of statute and a civil cause of action for damages arising from the breach is of long standing. The commentators have little but harsh words for the unhappy state of affairs, but arriving at a solution, from the disarray of cases, is extraordinarily difficult. It is doubtful that any general principle or rationale can be found in the authorities to resolve all of the issues or even those which are transcendent.

There does seem to be general agreement that the breach of a statutory provision which causes damage to an individual should in some way be pertinent to recovery of compensation for the damage. Two very different forces, however, have been acting in opposite directions. In the United States the civil consequences of breach of statute have been subsumed in the law of negligence. On the other hand, we have witnessed in England the painful emergence of a new nominate tort of statutory breach. . . .

(b)   *The English position*
In 1948 in the case of *London Passenger Transport Board* v *Upson*, [1949] AC 155, . . . the House of Lords affirmed the existence of a tort of statutory breach distinct from any issue of negligence. The statute prescribes the duty owed to the plaintiff who need only show (i) breach of the statute, and (ii) damage caused by the breach. . . .

As Street puts it 'The effect of the leading cases in the nineteenth century (which remain important authorities) however, was to make the cause of action rest on proof that the legislature intended that violation of the right or interest conferred by the statute was to be treated as tortious' (Street, *Law of Torts*, 2nd ed., p. 273). Fricke pointed out (76 LQR, at p. 260) that that doctrine leads to many difficulties. In the first place it is not clear what the *prima facie* rule or presumption should be. Some of the cases suggest that *prima facie* an action is given by the statement of a statutory duty, and that it exists unless it can be said to be taken away by any provisions to be found in the Act. Other authorities suggest the *prima facie* rule is that the specific statement of a certain manner of enforcement excludes any other means of enforcement. Sometimes the courts jump one way, sometimes the other. . . .

This fragmentation of approach has given rise to some theoretical, and some not-so-theoretical, difficulties. The pretence of seeking what has been called a 'will o' the wisp', a non-existent intention of Parliament to create a civil cause of action, has been harshly criticized. It is capricious and arbitrary, 'judicial legislation' at its very worst.

> Not only does it involve an unnecessary fiction, but it may lead to decisions being made on the basis of insignificant details of phraseology instead of matters of substance. If the question whether a person injured by breach of a statutory obligation is to have a right of action for damages is in truth a question to be decided by the court, let it be acknowledged as such and some useful principles of law developed.

Winfield & Jolowicz, *supra*, at p. 159 [*Torts*, 11th ed. (1979)]. It is a 'bare faced fiction' at odds with accepted canons of statutory interpretation: 'the legislature's silence on the question of civil liability rather points to the conclusion that it either did not have it in mind or deliberately omitted to provide for it' (Fleming, *The Law of Torts*, 5th ed. (1977), at p. 123). Glanville Williams is now of the opinion that the 'irresolute course' of the judicial decisions 'reflect no credit on our jurisprudence' and with respect, I agree. He writes:

> The failure of the judges to develop a governing attitude means that it is almost impossible to predict, outside the authorities, when the courts will regard a civil duty as impliedly created. In effect the judge can do what he likes, and then select one of the conflicting principles stated by his predecessors in order to justify his decision.

. . . Various presumptions or guidelines sprang up. 'Thus, it has often been tediously repeated that the crucial test is whether the duty created by the statute is owed primarily to the State, and only incidentally to the individual, or vice versa' (Fleming, *supra*, at p. 125). A duty to all the public (ratepayers, for example) does not give rise to a private cause of action whereas a duty to an individual (an injured worker, for example) may. The purpose of the statute must be the protection of a certain 'class' of individuals of whom the plaintiff is one and the injury suffered must be of a kind which it was the object of the legislation to prevent. Both requirements have, in the past, been fairly narrowly construed and fairly heavily criticized.

Although '[i]t is doubtful, indeed, if any general principle can be found to explain all the cases on the subject' (*Salmond on Torts*, 7th ed. (1977), at p. 243) several justifications are given for the tort of statutory breach. It provides fixed standards of negligence and replaces the judgment of amateurs (the jury) with that of professionals in highly technical areas. In effect, it provides for absolute liability in fields where this has been found desirable such as industrial safety. Laudable as these effects are, the state of the law remains extremely unsatisfactory. . . .

(c) *The American position*
Professor Fleming prefers the American approach which has assimilated civil responsibility for statutory breach into the general law of negligence (*The Law of Torts, supra*, at
p. 124):

> Intellectually more acceptable, because less arcane, is the prevailing American theory
> which frankly disclaims that the civil action is in any sure sense a creature of the
> statute, for the simple enough reason that the statute just does not contemplate, much
> less provide, a civil remedy. Any recovery of damages for injury due to its violation
> must, therefore, rest on common law principles. But though the penal statute does
> not create civil liability the court may think it proper to adopt the legislative
> formulation of a specific standard in place of the unformulated standard of reasonable
> conduct, in much the same manner as when it rules peremtorily [*sic*] that certain acts
> or omissions constitute negligence of the law.

There are, however, differing views of the effect of this assimilation: at one end of the
spectrum, breach of a statutory duty may constitute negligence *per se* or, at the other, it
may merely be evidence of negligence. . . .
The majority view in the United States has been that statutory breach constitutes
negligence *per se* — in certain circumstances (Prosser, *The Law of Torts, supra*, at
p. 200):

> Once the statute is determined to be applicable — which is to say, once it is
> interpreted as designed to protect the class of persons in which the plaintiff is
> included, against the risk of the type of harm which had in fact occurred as a result of
> its violation — the great majority of the courts hold that an unexcused violation is
> conclusive on the issue of negligence, and that the court must so direct the jury. The
> standard of conduct is taken over by the court from that fixed by the legislature, and
> 'jurors have no dispensing power by which to relax it', except in so far as the court may
> recognize the possibility of a valid excuse for disobedience of the law. This usually is
> expressed by saying that the unexcused violation is negligence 'per se', or in itself. The
> effect of such a rule is to stamp the defendant's conduct as negligence, with all of the
> effects of common law negligence, but with no greater effect.

The so-called 'minority view' in the United States considers breach of a statute to be
merely evidence of negligence. There are, however, varying degrees of evidence.
Statutory breach may be considered totally irrelevant, merely relevant, or *prima facie*
evidence of negligence having the effect of reversing the onus of proof (Prosser, *supra*, at
p. 201):

(d) *The Canadian position*
    . . . The use of breach of statute as evidence of negligence as opposed to recognition
of a nominate tort of statutory breach is, as Professor Fleming has put it, more
intellectually acceptable. It avoids, to a certain extent, the fictitious hunt for legislative
intent to create a civil cause of action which has been so criticized in England. It also
avoids the inflexible application of the legislature's criminal standard of conduct to a
civil case. Glanville Williams is of the opinion, with which I am in agreement, that where
there is no duty of care at common law, breach of non-industrial penal legislation should
not affect civil liability unless the statute provides for it. As I have indicated above,
industrial legislation historically has enjoyed special consideration. Recognition of the
doctrine of absolute liability under some industrial statutes does not justify extension of
such doctrine to other fields, particularly when one considers the jejune reasoning
supporting the juristic invention.

Regarding statutory breach as part of the law of negligence is also more consonant with other developments which have taken place in the law. More and more the legislator is heeding the admonition of Lord du Parcq given many years ago in *Cutler* v *Wandsworth Stadium Ltd,* [1949] AC 398 at p. 410, [1949] 1 All ER 544 at p. 549:

> To a person unversed in the science, or art, of legislation it may well seem strange that Parliament has not by now made it a rule to state explicitly what its intention is in a matter which is often of no little importance, instead of leaving it to the courts to discover, by a careful examination and analysis of what is expressly said, what that intention may be supposed probably to be. There are, no doubt, reasons which inhibit the legislature from revealing its intention in plain words. I do not know, and must not speculate, what those reasons may be. I trust, however, that it will not be thought impertinent, in any sense of that word, to suggest respectfully that those who are responsible for framing legislation might consider whether the traditional practice, which obscures, if it does not conceal, the intention which Parliament has, or must be presumed to have, might not safely be abandoned.

Statutes are increasingly speaking plainly to civil responsibility: consumer protection acts, rental acts, business corporations acts, securities acts. Individual compensation has become an active concern of the legislator.

In addition, the role of tort liability in compensation and allocation of loss is of less and less importance:

> [I]nstead of tort liability being the sole source of potential compensation (as it was throughout most of our history) it is now but one of several such sources, and (at that) carrying an ever diminishing share of the economic burden of compensating the injured.

Fleming, 'More Thoughts on Loss Distribution', 4 Osgoode HLJ 161 (1966).

Tort law itself has undergone a major transformation in this century with nominate torts being eclipsed by negligence, the closest the common law has come to a general theory of civil responsibility. The concept of duty of care, embodied in the neighbour principle has expanded into areas hitherto untouched by tort law.

One of the main reasons for shifting a loss to a defendant is that he has been at fault, that he has done some act which should be discouraged. There is then good reason for taking money from the defendant as well as a reason for giving it to the plaintiff who has suffered from the fault of the defendant. But there seems little in the way of defensible policy for holding a defendant who breached a statutory duty unwittingly to be negligent and obligated to pay even though not at fault. The legislature has imposed a penalty on a strictly admonitory basis and there seems little justification to add civil liability when such liability would tend to produce liability without fault. The legislature has determined the proper penalty for the defendant's wrong but if tort admonition of liability without fault is to be added, the financial consequences will be measured, not by the amount of the penalty, but by the amount of money which is required to compensate the plaintiff. Minimum fault may subject the defendant to heavy liability. Inconsequential violations should not subject the violator to any civil liability at all but should be left to the criminal courts for enforcement of a fine. . . .

In sum I conclude that:

1. Civil consequences of breach of statute should be subsumed in the law of negligence.

2. The notion of a nominate tort of statutory breach giving a right to recovery merely on proof of breach and damages should be rejected, as should the view that unexcused breach constitutes negligence *per se* giving rise to absolute liability.

3.   Proof of statutory breach, causative of damages, may be evidence of negligence.
4.   The statutory formulation of the duty may afford a specific, and useful, standard of reasonable conduct.
5.   In the case at bar negligence is neither pleaded nor proven. The action must fail.

Notes
1.   This case raises wide and important issues. Undoubtedly the British view of breach of statutory duty is haphazard and based on an unsatisfactory fiction, but it is an attempt to distinguish those statutes which should give rise to a remedy and those which should not. Unfortunately, the real reason for the difference is never explained. One well accepted rule is that legislation passed for the safety of workmen does give rise to civil liability, but beyond that there is little agreement. Perhaps the only solution is for each statute to state whether a civil action arises (as an increasing number nowadays do) or, in order to encourage that, provide a statutory presumption in favour of liability as the Law Commission recommended in 1969.
2.   Dissatisfaction with the present state of affairs should not lead us to reject the whole tort because of some structural inadequacies. In the *Wheat Pool* case one argument against a separate tort was the dominance of fault liability, but fault is not nowadays universally regarded as the only touchstone of liability, and it may be thought that, at least so far as personal safety is concerned, failure to adhere to statutory standards might also be a ground for liability. Much of the sting is taken out of the criticism in the *Wheat Pool* case by the fact that many statutes only require certain standards to be achieved, 'so far as is reasonably practicable'. This is close to fault, but in many cases will allow the court to look at the structures of the defendant authority or company for monitoring statutory standards.
3.   For further discussion of the basis of the tort of breach of statutory duty, see Matthews (1984) 4 Oxf JLS 429 and Buckley (1984) 100 LQR 204.

Questions
Which of the following provisions give rise to additional civil liability?
    (a)   A requirement to maintain water in the mains at a certain pressure, the plaintiff being a person whose house burnt down because of insufficient supply of water. (*Atkinson* v *Newcastle Waterworks Co.* (1877) LR 2 Ex D 441.)
    (b)   A duty on racetrack owners, so long as a 'totalisator' is being operated, to allow bookmakers onto the course, the plaintiff being a bookmaker who was excluded. (*Cutler* v *Wandsworth Stadium* [1949] AC 398.)
    (c)   A rule prohibiting a person from lending his car to a person who is not insured, the plaintiff being a person injured by the uninsured driver. (*Monk* v *Warbey* [1935] 1 KB 75.)
    (d)   An obligation on the Law Society to consider complaints by individuals against the conduct of solicitors, the plaintiff being a person who alleges that the Law Society failed to investigate her complaint adequately. (*Wood* v *The Law Society* (1993) 143 NLJ 1475.)

19 PRODUCT LIABILITY

This chapter deals with damage caused by defective products, and the topic is covered by two separate legal regimes. The first is the ordinary law of negligence (with some qualifications) and the second is the system of strict liability introduced by the Consumer Protection Act 1987, as required by an EC Directive. The latter is limited to personal injuries and to damage to private property, so there will still be a number of cases where a plaintiff will have to rely on negligence — for example, where there is damage to goods used for commercial purposes. Also, the Act only applies to certain kinds of defendants ('producers'), and a plaintiff will need to use negligence if, for example, he is injured by a defectively repaired product.

One important point is that both systems only apply to damage to goods other than the defective product and not to damage which the defective product causes to itself: that is a matter solely for the law of contract.

Section 1: liability for negligence

Donoghue v *Stevenson* was important, not only for establishing a general concept of duty of care in negligence (the wide rule) but also for laying down the qualifications of that broad concept when applied to liability for damage caused by a defective product (the narrow rule). The relevant passages are reproduced below.

Donoghue v *Stevenson*
House of Lords [1932] AC 562; 147 LT 281; 48 TLR 494

The facts are given above in Chapter 4. Held: that a manufacturer owes a duty of care to the consumer of a product which he has produced negligently, even though there is no contractual relationship between them.

LORD ATKIN: There will no doubt arise cases where it will be difficult to determine whether the contemplated relationship is so close that the duty arises. But in the class of case now before the Court I cannot conceive any difficulty to arise. A manufacturer puts up an article of food in a container which he knows will be opened by the actual consumer. There can be no inspection by any purchaser and no reasonable preliminary inspection by the consumer. Negligently, in the course of preparation, he allows the contents to be mixed with poison. It is said that the law of England and Scotland is that the poisoned consumer has no remedy against the negligent manufacturer. If this were the result of the authorities, I should consider the result a grave defect in the law, and so contrary to principle that I should hesitate long before following any decision to that effect which had not the authority of this House. I would point out that, in the assumed state of the authorities, not only would the consumer have no remedy against the manufacturer, he would have none against any one else, for in the circumstances alleged there would be no evidence of negligence against any one other than the manufacturer; and, except in the case of a consumer who was also a purchaser, no contract and no warranty of fitness, and in the case of the purchase of a specific article under its patent or trade name, which might well be the case in the purchase of some articles of food or drink, no warranty protecting even the purchaser-consumer. There are other instances than of articles of food and drink where goods are sold intended to be used immediately by the consumer, such as many forms of goods sold for cleaning purposes, where the same liability must exist. The doctrine supported by the decision below would not only deny a remedy to the consumer who was injured by consuming bottled beer or chocolates poisoned by the negligence of the manufacturer, but also to the user of what should be a harmless proprietary medicine, an ointment, a soap, a cleaning fluid or cleaning powder. I confine myself to articles of common household use, where every one, including the manufacturer, knows that the articles will be used by other persons than the actual ultimate purchaser — namely, by members of his family and his servants, and in some cases his guests. I do not think so ill of our jurisprudence as to suppose that its principles are so remote from the ordinary needs of civilized society and the ordinary claims it makes upon its members as to deny a legal remedy where there is so obviously a social wrong.

It will be found, I think, on examination that there is no case in which the circumstances have been such as I have just suggested where the liability has been negatived. There are numerous cases, where the relations were much more remote, where the duty has been held not to exist. There are also dicta in such cases which go further than was necessary for the determination of the particular issues, which have caused the difficulty experienced by the Courts below. I venture to say that in the branch of the law which deals with civil wrongs, dependent in England at any rate entirely upon the application by judges of general principles also formulated by judges, it is of particular importance to guard against the danger of stating propositions of law in wider terms than is necessary, lest essential factors be omitted in the wider survey and the inherent adaptability of English law be unduly restricted. For this reason it is very necessary in considering reported cases in the law of torts that the actual decision alone should carry authority, proper weight, of course, being given to the dicta of the judges.

In my opinion several decided cases support the view that in such a case as the present the manufacturer owes a duty to the consumer to be careful. . . .

My Lords, if your Lordships accept the view that this pleading discloses a relevant cause of action you will be affirming the proposition that by Scots and English law alike a manufacturer of products, which he sells in such a form as to show that he intends them to reach the ultimate consumer in the form in which they left him with no reasonable possibility of intermediate examination, and with the knowledge that the absence of reasonable care in the preparation or putting up of the products will result in an injury to the consumer's life or property, owes a duty to the consumer to take that reasonable care.

LORD MACMILLAN: . . . . The question is: Does he owe a duty to take care, and to whom does he owe that duty? Now I have no hesitation in affirming that a person who for gain engages in the business of manufacturing articles of food and drink intended for consumption by members of the public in the form in which he issues them is under a duty to take care in the manufacture of these articles. That duty, in my opinion, he owes to those whom he intends to consume his products. He manufactures his commodities for human consumption; he intends and contemplates that they shall be consumed. By reason of that very fact he places himself in a relationship with all the potential consumers of his commodities, and that relationship which he assumes and desires for his own ends imposes upon him a duty to take care to avoid injuring them. He owes them a duty not to convert by his own carelessness an article which he issues to them as wholesome and innocent into an article which is dangerous to life and health. It is sometimes said that liability can only arise where a reasonable man would have foreseen and could have avoided the consequences of his act or omission. In the present case the respondent, when he manufactured his ginger-beer, had directly in contemplation that it would be consumed by members of the public. Can it be said that he could not be expected as a reasonable man to foresee that if he conducted his process of manufacture carelessly he might injure those whom he expected and desired to consume his ginger-beer? The possibility of injury so arising seems to me in no sense so remote as to excuse him from foreseeing it. Suppose that a baker, through carelessness, allows a large quantity of arsenic to be mixed with a batch of his bread, with the result that those who subsequently eat it are poisoned, could he be heard to say that he owed no duty to the consumers of his bread to take care that it was free from poison, and that, as he did not know that any poison had got into it, his only liability was for breach of warranty under his contract of sale to those who actually bought the poisoned bread from him? Observe that I have said 'through carelessness,' and thus excluded the case of a pure accident such as may happen where every care is taken. I cannot believe, and I do not believe, that neither in the law of England nor in the law of Scotland is there redress for such a case. . . .

. . . It must always be a question of circumstances whether the carelessness amounts to negligence, and whether the injury is not too remote from the carelessness. I can readily conceive that where a manufacturer has parted with his product and it has passed into other hands it may well be exposed to vicissitudes which may render it defective or noxious, for which the manufacturer could not in any view be held to be to blame. It may be a good general rule to regard responsibility as ceasing when control ceases. So, also, where between the manufacturer and the user there is interposed a party who has the means and opportunity of examining the manufacturer's product before he re-issues it to the actual user. But where, as in the present case, the article of consumption is so prepared as to be intended to reach the consumer in the condition in which it leaves the manufacturer, and the manufacturer takes steps to ensure this by sealing or otherwise closing the container so that the contents cannot be tampered with, I regard his control as remaining effective until the article reaches the consumer and the container is opened by him. The intervention of any exterior agency is intended to be excluded, and was in fact in the present case excluded. . . .

Notes

1. The above principle was applied in *Grant v Australian Knitting Mills Ltd* [1936] AC 85, where the plaintiff contracted dermatitis from wearing underpants manufactured by the defendants and which contained an excess of sulphites. It was pointed out that the use of the word 'control' by Lord

Macmillan was misleading ('I regard his control as remaining effective until the article reaches the consumer'). According to the Privy Council, all that was meant was that 'the consumer must use the article exactly as it left the maker, that is in all material features, and use it as it was intended to be used.'

2.   The principle has been extended to repairers of goods (*Haseldine* v *Daw* [1941] 2 KB 343), and also to distributors where they might be expected to test the product before passing it on. Thus, in **Watson v Buckley, Osborne Garrett & Co. and Wyrovoys Products** [1940] 1 All ER 174 the plaintiff had his hair dyed by Mrs Buckley with dye which she had obtained from the distributors, Osborne Garrett & Co., who had bought it from Mr Wyrovoys ('a gentleman who had emerged unexpectedly from Spain'). The dye was delivered in carboys and packaged by Osborne Garrett. Stable J held Mrs Buckley liable in contract and Osborne Garrett in tort. Wyrovoys Products had ceased to exist. Liability was based on the fact that by packaging the dye the defendants had brought themselves into a relationship with the ultimate consumer. However, the principle is not limited to situations where the defendant has packaged the goods as his own, for it will extend to cases where the goods remain in the same form, but where it is expected that the distributor or retailer will have tested them. Thus, in *Andrews* v *Hopkinson* [1957] 1 QB 229 it was held that a commercial seller of a secondhand car was liable in negligence for not testing the car for safety before selling it.

Question
In *Grant* (above) the harm could have been avoided if the underpants had been washed before use, but Lord Wright forthrightly pointed out that 'it was not contemplated that they should first be washed'. What if the packet said 'Warning: these underpants should be washed before use'? If the plaintiff had not done so, would that have been a complete defence to the manufacturer, or a matter of contributory negligence on the part of the plaintiff? What if it is shown that nobody takes any notice of such ultra-cautious notices, thinking they are only designed to remove the manufacturer's responsibility for producing safe goods?

Note
A defendant is only liable if the defective product damages property other than itself. The problem is, what is 'other property'? In **Aswan Engineering v Lupdine Ltd** [1987] 1 WLR 1 the plaintiffs bought a quantity of waterproofing compound called Lupguard from the first defendants, Lupdine Ltd. The Lupguard was packed in pails which had been manufactured by the second defendants, Thurgar Bolle Ltd. The Lupguard was exported to Kuwait where the pails were stacked five high on the quayside in full sunshine, and the pails collapsed. The whole consignment was lost. It was held that there was no liability on the sellers in contract as the pails were of merchantable quality, and no liability in tort because the type of damage was unforeseeable. One issue was whether the product had merely damaged itself, or whether the pails (assuming they were defective, which they were not) had damaged other property of the

plaintiff, i.e. the Lupguard in the pails. It was thought, *obiter,* that the contents of the pails were 'other property'.

A similar problem arises under s. 5(2) of the Consumer Protection Act 1987 (below), which says that there is no liability under the Act for damage to the product itself or to the whole or any part of any product which has been supplied with the product in question comprised in it.

Section 2: strict liability

Strict liability for products has long been accepted in the United States (see Restatement 2nd, s. 402A), and there had been numerous recommendations, both in Britain and in Europe, for its adoption. These were the Law Commission Report No. 82, The Pearson Commission (Cmnd 70054, 1978 Ch. 22), The European Convention on Products Liability (The Strasbourg Convention), and finally the EEC Directive (85/374) on liability for defective products. As a result of the mandatory nature of the Directive, strict liability was finally adopted in this country by the Consumer Protection Act 1987.

This section reproduces The Consumer Protection Act 1987, which imposes strict liability in tort in certain limited circumstances, together with the EC Directive. The reason for providing the text of the Directive is that the Act is intended to give effect to the Directive, and therefore the Directive will be useful in interpreting the Act: for example s. 2(4) of the Act speaks of agricultural produce which has not undergone an 'industrial' process, whereas the Directive speaks of an 'initial' process. In this case either the Act is in conflict with the Directive, or it will need to be interpreted so as to comply with it. It is also thought that s. 4(1)(e) (the development risks defence) might be in conflict with the Directive. For an analysis of the Act, see Miller, *Product Liability and Safety Encyclopaedia.* Also included is the proposed Directive on liability for supplies of services which although based on fault proposes a reversal of the burden of proof.

CONSUMER PROTECTION ACT 1987

PART I PRODUCT LIABILITY

1. Purpose and construction of Part I
   (1) This Part shall have effect for the purpose of making such provision as is necessary in order to comply with the product liability Directive and shall be construed accordingly.
   (2) In this Part, except in so far as the context otherwise requires—
      'agricultural produce' means any produce of the soil, of stock-farming or of fisheries;
      'dependant' and 'relative' have the same meaning as they have in, respectively, the Fatal Accidents Act 1976 and the Damages (Scotland) Act 1976;
      'producer', in relation to a product, means—
      (a) the person who manufactured it;
      (b) in the case of a substance which has not been manufactured but has been won or abstracted, the person who won or abstracted it;

(c)   in the case of a product which has not been manufactured, won or abstracted but essential characteristics of which are attributable to an industrial or other process having been carried out (for example, in relation to agricultural produce), the person who carried out that process;

'product' means any goods or electricity and (subject to subsection (3) below) includes a product which is comprised in another product, whether by virtue of being a component part or raw material or otherwise; and

'the product liability Directive' means the Directive of the Council of the European Communities, dated 25th July 1985, (No. 85/374/EEC) on the approximation of the laws, regulations and administrative provisions of the member States concerning liability for defective products.

(3)   For the purposes of this Part a person who supplies any product in which products are comprised, whether by virtue of being component parts or raw materials or otherwise, shall not be treated by reason only of his supply of that product as supplying any of the products so comprised.

2.   Liability for defective products

(1)   Subject to the following provisions of this Part, where any damage is caused wholly or partly by a defect in a product, every person to whom subsection (2) below applies shall be liable for the damage.

(2)   This subsection applies to—

(a)   the producer of the product;

(b)   any person who, by putting his name on the product or using a trade mark or other distinguishing mark in relation to the product, has held himself out to be the producer of the product;

(c)   any person who has imported the product into a member State from a place outside the member States in order, in the course of any business of his, to supply it to another.

(3)   Subject as aforesaid, where any damage is caused wholly or partly by a defect in a product, any person who supplied the product (whether to the person who suffered the damage, to the producer of any product in which the product in question is comprised or to any other person) shall be liable for the damage if—

(a)   the person who suffered the damage requests the supplier to identify one or more of the persons (whether still in existence or not) to whom subsection (2) above applies in relation to the product;

(b)   that request is made within a reasonable period after the damage occurs and at a time when it is not reasonably practicable for the person making the request to identify all those persons; and

(c)   the supplier fails, within a reasonable period after receiving the request, either to comply with the request or to identify the person who supplied the product to him.

(4)   Neither subsection (2) nor subsection (3) above shall apply to a person in respect of any defect in any game or agricultural produce if the only supply of the game or produce by that person to another was at a time when it had not undergone an industrial process.

(5)   Where two or more persons are liable by virtue of this Part for the same damage, their liability shall be joint and several.

(6)   This section shall be without prejudice to any liability arising otherwise than by virtue of this Part.

3.   Meaning of 'defect'

(1)   Subject to the following provisions of this section, there is a defect in a product for the purposes of this Part if the safety of the product is not such as persons generally

are entitled to expect; and for those purposes 'safety', in relation to a product, shall include safety with respect to products comprised in that product and safety in the context of risks of damage to property, as well as in the context of risks of death or personal injury.

(2)   In determining for the purposes of subsection (1) above what persons generally are entitled to expect in relation to a product all the circumstances shall be taken into account, including—

(a)   the manner in which, and purposes for which, the product has been marketed, its get-up, the use of any mark in relation to the product and any instructions for, or warnings with respect to, doing or refraining from doing anything with or in relation to the product;

(b)   what might reasonably be expected to be done with or in relation to the product; and

(c)   the time when the product was supplied by its producer to another;

and nothing in this section shall require a defect to be inferred from the fact alone that the safety of a product which is supplied after that time is greater than the safety of the product in question.

4.   Defences

(1)   In any civil proceedings by virtue of this Part against any person ('the person proceeded against') in respect of a defect in a product it shall be a defence for him to show—

(a)   that the defect is attributable to compliance with any requirement imposed by or under any enactment or with any Community obligation; or

(b)   that the person proceeded against did not at any time supply the product to another; or

(c)   that the following conditions are satisfied, that is to say—

(i)   that the only supply of the product to another by the person proceeded against was otherwise than in the course of a business of that person's; and

(ii)   that section 2(2) above does not apply to that person or applies to him by virtue only of things done otherwise than with a view to profit; or

(d)   that the defect did not exist in the product at the relevant time; or

(e)   that the state of scientific and technical knowledge at the relevant time was not such that a producer of products of the same description as the product in question might be expected to have discovered the defect if it had existed in his products while they were under his control; or

(f)   that the defect—

(i)   constituted a defect in a product ('the subsequent product') in which the product in question had been comprised; and

(ii)   was wholly attributable to the design of the subsequent product or to compliance by the producer of the product in question with instructions given by the producer of the subsequent product.

(2)   In this section 'the relevant time', in relation to electricity, means the time at which it was generated, being a time before it was transmitted or distributed, and in relation to any other product, means—

(a)   if the person proceeded against is a person to whom subsection (2) of section 2 above applies in relation to the product, the time when he supplied the product to another:

(b)   if that subsection does not apply to that person in relation to the product, the time when the product was last supplied by a person to whom that subsection does apply in relation to the product.

5. Damage giving rise to liability

(1) Subject to the following provisions of this section, in this Part 'damage' means death or personal injury or any loss of or damage to any property (including land).

(2) A person shall not be liable under section 2 above in respect of any defect in a product for the loss of or any damage to the product itself or for the loss of or any damage to the whole or any part of any product which has been supplied with the product in question comprised in it.

(3) A person shall not be liable under section 2 above for any loss of or damage to any property which, at the time it is lost or damaged, is not—

(a) of a description of property ordinarily intended for private use, occupation or consumption; and

(b) intended by the person suffering the loss or damage mainly for his own private use, occupation or consumption.

(4) No damages shall be awarded to any person by virtue of this Part in respect of any loss of or damage to any property if the amount which would fall to be so awarded to that person, apart from this subsection and any liability for interest, does not exceed £275.

(5) In determining for the purposes of this Part who has suffered any loss of or damage to property and when any such loss or damage occurred, the loss or damage shall be regarded as having occurred at the earliest time at which a person with an interest in the property had knowledge of the material facts about the loss or damage.

(6) For the purposes of subsection (5) above the material facts about any loss of or damage to any property are such facts about the loss or damage as would lead a reasonable person with an interest in the property to consider the loss or damage sufficiently serious to justify his instituting proceedings for damages against a defendant who did not dispute liability and was able to satisfy a judgment.

(7) For the purposes of subsection (5) above a person's knowledge includes knowledge which he might reasonably have been expected to acquire —

(a) from facts observable or ascertainable by him; or

(b) from facts ascertainable by him with the help of appropriate expert advice which it is reasonable for him to seek;

but a person shall not be taken by virtue of this subsection to have knowledge of a fact ascertainable by him only with the help of expert advice unless he has failed to take all reasonable steps to obtain (and, where appropriate, to act on) that advice.

(8) Subsections (5) to (7) above shall not extend to Scotland.

6. Application of certain enactments etc.

(1) Any damage for which a person is liable under section 2 above shall be deemed to have been caused—

(a) for the purposes of the Fatal Accidents Act 1976, by that person's wrongful act, neglect or default;

(b) for the purposes of section 3 of the Law Reform (Miscellaneous Provisions) (Scotland) Act 1940 (contribution among joint wrongdoers), by that person's wrongful act or negligent act or omission;

(c) for the purposes of section 1 of the Damages (Scotland) Act 1976 (rights of relatives of a deceased), by that person's act or omission; and

(d) for the purposes of Part II of the Administration of Justice Act 1982 (damages for personal injuries, etc. — Scotland), by an act or omission giving rise to liability in that person to pay damages.

(2) Where—

(a) a person's death is caused wholly or partly by a defect in a product, or a person dies after suffering damage which has been so caused;

(b)   a request such as mentioned in paragraph (a) of subsection (3) of section 2 above is made to a supplier of the product by that person's personal representatives or, in the case of a person whose death is caused wholly or partly by the defect, by any dependant or relative of that person; and

(c)   the conditions specified in paragraphs (b) and (c) of that subsection are satisfied in relation to that request,
this Part shall have effect for the purposes of the Law Reform (Miscellaneous Provisions) Act 1934, the Fatal Accidents Act 1976 and the Damages (Scotland) Act 1976 as if liability of the supplier to that person under that subsection did not depend on that person having requested the supplier to identify certain persons or on the said conditions having been satisfied in relation to a request made by that person.

(3)   Section 1 of the Congenital Disabilities (Civil Liability) Act 1976 shall have effect for the purposes of this Part as if—

(a)   a person were answerable to a child in respect of an occurrence caused wholly or partly by a defect in a product if he is or has been liable under section 2 above in respect of any effect of the occurrence on a parent of the child, or would be so liable if the occurrence caused a parent of the child to suffer damage;

(b)   the provisions of this Part relating to liability under section 2 above applied in relation to liability by virtue of paragraph (a) above under the said section 1; and

(c)   subsection (6) of the said section 1 (exclusion of liability) were omitted.

(4)   Where any damage is caused partly by a defect in a product and partly by the fault of the person suffering the damage, the Law Reform (Contributory Negligence) Act 1945 and section 5 of the Fatal Accidents Act 1976 (contributory negligence) shall have effect as if the defect were the fault of every person liable by virtue of this Part for the damage caused by the defect.

(5)   In subsection (4) above 'fault' has the same meaning as in the said Act of 1945.

(7)   It is hereby declared that liability by virtue of this Part is to be treated as liability in tort for the purposes of any enactment conferring jurisdiction on any court with respect to any matter.

(8)   Nothing in this Part shall prejudice the operation of section 12 of the Nuclear Installations Act 1965 (rights to compensation for certain breaches of duties confined to rights under that Act).

7.   Prohibition on exclusions from liability
The liability of a person by virtue of this Part to a person who has suffered damage caused wholly or partly by a defect in a product, or to a dependant or relative of such a person, shall not be limited or excluded by any contract term, by any notice or by any other provision.

PART V

45.   Interpretation
(1)   In this Act, except in so far as the context otherwise requires—
'aircraft' includes gliders, balloons and hovercraft;
'business' includes a trade or profession and the activities of a professional or trade association or of a local authority or other public authority;
'goods' includes substances, growing crops and things comprised in land by virtue of being attached to it and any ship, aircraft or vehicle;
'personal injury' includes any disease and any other impairment of a person's physical or mental condition;
'ship' includes any boat and any other description of vessel used in navigation;

'substance' means any natural or artificial substance, whether in solid, liquid or gaseous form or in the form of a vapour, and includes substances that are comprised in or mixed with other goods.

46. Meaning of 'supply'

(1) Subject to the following provisions of this section, references in this Act to supplying goods shall be construed as references to doing any of the following, whether as principal or agent, that is to say—

    (a) selling, hiring out or lending the goods;

    (b) entering into a hire-purchase agreement to furnish the goods;

    (c) the performance of any contract for work and materials to furnish the goods;

    (d) providing the goods in exchange for any consideration (including trading stamps) other than money;

    (e) providing the goods in or in connection with the performance of any statutory function; or

    (f) giving the goods as a prize or otherwise making a gift of the goods;

and, in relation to gas or water, those references shall be construed as including references to providing the service by which the gas or water is made available for use.

(2) For the purposes of any reference in this Act to supplying goods, where a person ('the ostensible supplier') supplies to another person ('the customer') under a hire-purchase agreement, conditional sale agreement or credit-sale agreement or under an agreement for the hiring of goods (other than a hire-purchase agreement) and the ostensible supplier—

    (a) carries on the business of financing the provision of goods for others by means of such agreements; and

    (b) in the course of that business acquired his interest in the goods supplied to the customer as a means of financing the provision of them for the customer by a further person ('the effective supplier'),

the effective supplier and not the ostensible supplier shall be treated as supplying the goods to the customer.

(3) Subject to subsection (4) below, the performance of any contract by the erection of any building or structure on any land or by the carrying out of any other building works shall be treated for the purposes of this Act as a supply of goods in so far as, but only in so far as, it involves the provision of any goods to any person by means of their incorporation into the building, structure or works.

(4) Except for the purposes of, and in relation to, notices to warn or any provision made by or under Part III of this Act, references in this Act to supplying goods shall not include references to supplying goods comprised in land where the supply is effected by the creation or disposal of an interest in the land.

LIMITATION ACT 1980

11A. Actions in respect of defective products

(1) This section shall apply to an action for damages by virtue of any provision of Part I of the Consumer Protection Act 1987.

(2) None of the time limits given in the preceding provisions of this Act shall apply to an action to which this section applies.

(3) An action to which this section applies shall not be brought after the expiration of the period of ten years from the relevant time, within the meaning of section 4 of the said Act of 1987; and this subsection shall operate to extinguish a right of action and shall do so whether or not that right of action had accrued, or time under the following provisions of this Act had begun to run, at the end of the said period of ten years.

(4)   Subject to subsection (5) below, an action to which this section applies in which the damages claimed by the plaintiff consist of or include damages in respect of personal injuries to the plaintiff or any other person or loss of or damage to any property, shall not be brought after the expiration of the period of three years from whichever is the later of—
    (a)   the date on which the cause of action accrued; and
    (b)   the date of knowledge of the injured person or, in the case of loss of or damage to property, the date of knowledge of the plaintiff or (if earlier) of any person in whom his cause of action was previously vested.

Notes
1.   In relation to s. 2(4) (liability for agricultural produce), the Act imposes liability only if the article has undergone an 'industrial' process. The EC Directive on which the Act is based uses the words 'initial process'. Does the Act comply with the Directive?
2.   In relation to s. 4(1)(e), the EC Commission has instituted an action against the United Kingdom on the ground that this section does not comply with art 7(e) of the Directive (below). In addition, the question whether any country should be allowed to use this defence is currently being considered by the EC.

EC COUNCIL DIRECTIVE
on the approximation of the laws, regulations and administrative provisions of the Member States concerning liability for defective products

OJ L 210/29 (25.7.1985)

Article 1

The producer shall be liable for damage caused by a defect in his product.

Article 2

For the purpose of this Directive 'product' means all movables, with the exception of primary agricultural products and game, even though incorporated into another movable or into an immovable. 'Primary agricultural products' means the products of the soil, of stock-farming and of fisheries, excluding products which have undergone initial processing. 'Product' includes electricity.

Article 3

1.   'Producer' means the manufacturer of a finished product, the producer of any raw material or the manufacturer of a component part and any person who, by putting his name, trade mark or other distinguishing feature on the product presents himself as its producer.
2.   Without prejudice to the liability of the producer, any person who imports into the Community a product for sale, hire, leasing or any form of distribution in the course of his business shall be deemed to be a producer within the meaning of this Directive and shall be responsible as a producer.
3.   Where the producer of the product cannot be identified, each supplier of the product shall be treated as its producer unless he informs the injured person, within a reasonable time, of the identity of the producer or of the person who supplied him with

the product. The same shall apply, in the case of an imported product, if this product does not indicate the identity of the importer referred to in paragraph 2, even if the name of the producer is indicated.

Article 4

The injured person shall be required to prove the damage, the defect and the causal relationship between defect and damage.

Article 5

Where, as a result of the provisions of this Directive, two or more persons are liable for the same damage, they shall be liable jointly and severally, without prejudice to the provisions of national law concerning the rights of contribution or recourse.

Article 6

1.   A product is defective when it does not provide the safety which a person is entitled to expect, taking all circumstances into account, including:
   (a)   the presentation of the product;
   (b)   the use to which it could reasonably be expected that the product would be put;
   (c)   the time when the product was put into circulation.
2.   A product shall not be considered defective for the sole reason that a better product is subsequently put into circulation.

Article 7

The producer shall not be liable as a result of this Directive if he proves:
   (a)   that he did not put the product into circulation; or
   (b)   that, having regard to the circumstances, it is probable that the defect which caused the damage did not exist at the time when the product was put into circulation by him or that this defect came into being afterwards; or
   (c)   that the product was neither manufactured by him for sale or any form of distribution for economic purpose nor manufactured or distributed by him in the course of his business; or
   (d)   that the defect is due to compliance of the product with mandatory regulations issued by the public authorities; or
   (e)   that the state of scientific and technical knowledge at the time when he put the product into circulation was not such as to enable the existence of the defect to be discovered; or
   (f)   in the case of a manufacturer of a component, that the defect is attributable to the design of the product in which the component has been fitted or to the instructions given by the manufacturer of the product.

Article 8

1.   Without prejudice to the provisions of national law concerning the right of contribution or recourse, the liability of the producer shall not be reduced when the damage is caused both by a defect in product and by the act or omission of a third party.
2.   The liability of the producer may be reduced or disallowed when, having regard to all the circumstances, the damage is caused both by a defect in the product and by the fault of the injured person or any person for whom the injured person is responsible.

Article 9

For the purpose of Article 1, 'damage' means:
  (a) damage caused by death or by personal injuries;
  (b) damage to, or destruction of, any item of property other than the defective product itself, with a lower threshold of 500 ECU, provided that the item of property:
    (i)   is of a type ordinarily intended for private use or consumption, and
    (ii) was used by the injured person mainly for his own private use or consumption.

This Article shall be without prejudice to national provisions relating to non-material damage.

Article 10

1. Member States shall provide in their legislation that a limitation period of three years shall apply to proceedings for the recovery of damages as provided for in this Directive. The limitation period shall begin to run from the day on which the plaintiff became aware, or should reasonably have become aware, of the damage, the defect and the identity of the producer.

2. The laws of Member States regulating suspension or interruption of the limitation period shall not be affected by this Directive.

Article 11

Member States shall provide in their legislation that the rights conferred upon the injured person pursuant to this Directive shall be extinguished upon the expiry of a period of 10 years from the date on which the producer put into circulation the actual product which caused the damage, unless the injured person has in the meantime instituted proceedings against the producer.

Article 12

The liability of the producer arising from the Directive may not, in relation to the injured person, be limited or excluded by a provision limiting his liability or exempting him from liability.

Article 13

This Directive shall not affect any rights which an injured person may have according to the rules of the law of contractual or non-contractual liability or a special liability system existing at the moment when this Directive is notified.

Proposed EC Directive on the liability of suppliers of services

OJ C 12/8 (18.1.91)

Article 1

Principle

1. The supplier of a service shall be liable for damage to the health and physical integrity of persons or the physical integrity of movable or immovable property, including the persons or property which were the object of the service, caused by a fault committed by him in the performance of the service.

2. The burden of proving the absence of fault shall fall upon the supplier of the service.

3. In assessing the fault, account shall be taken of the behaviour of the supplier of the service, who, in normal and reasonably foreseeable conditions, shall ensure the safety which may reasonably be expected.

4. Whereas the mere fact that a better service existed or might have existed at the moment of performance or subsequently shall not constitute a fault.

Article 2

Definition of service

For the purpose of this Directive, 'service' means any transaction carried out on a commercial basis or by way of a public service and in an independent manner, whether or not in return for payment, which does not have as its direct and exclusive object the manufacture of movable property or the transfer of rights *in rem* or intellectual property rights.

This Directive shall not apply to public services intended to maintain public safety. It shall not apply to package travel or to waste services.

Nor shall it apply to damage covered by liability arrangements governed by international agreements ratified by the Member States or by the Community.

Article 3

Definition of supplier of services

1. The term 'supplier of services' means any natural or legal person governed by private or public law who, in the course of his professional activities or by way of a public service, provides a service referred to in Article 2.

2. Any person who provides a service by using the services of a representative or other legally independent intermediary shall continue to be deemed to be a supplier of services within the meaning of this Directive.

3. If the supplier of the service referred to in paragraph 1 is not established within the Community, and without prejudice to his liability, the person carrying out the service in the Community shall be considered as the supplier of that service for the purpose of this Directive.

Article 4

Definition of damage

The term 'damage' means:
  (a) death or any other direct damage to the health or physical integrity of persons;
  (b) any direct damage to the physical integrity of movable or immovable property, including animals, provided that this property:
    (i) is of a type normally intended for private use or consumption, and
    (ii) was intended for or used by the injured person, principally for his private use or consumption;
  (c) any financial material damage resulting directly from the damage referred to at (a) or (b).

Article 5

Proof

The injured person shall be required to provide proof of the damage and the causal relationship between the performance of the service and the damage.

Article 6

Third parties and joint liability

1. The liability of the supplier of the service shall not be reduced where the damage is caused jointly by a fault on his part and by the intervention of a third party.

2. The liability of the supplier of the service may be reduced, or even waived, where the damage is caused jointly by a fault on his part and by the fault of the injured person, or a person for whom the injured person is responsible.

Article 7
Exclusion of liability
The supplier of a service may not, in relation to the injured person, limit or exclude his liability under this Directive.

Article 8
Joint and several liability
1. If, in applying this Directive, several people are liable for a given damage, they shall be jointly liable, without prejudice to the provisions of national law relating to the law of recourse of one supplier against another.

2. The franchisor, the master franchisee and the franchisee, within the meaning of Commission Regulation (EEC) No 4087/88 of 30 November 1988 on the application of Article 85(3) of the Treaty to categories of franchise agreements shall be deemed to be jointly and severally liable within the meaning of paragraph 1.

However, the franchisor and the master franchisee may absolve themselves of liability if they can prove that the damage is due to a product which, on the basis of Regulation (EEC) No 4087/88, they themselves had not been able to supply or impose.

Article 9
Extinction of rights
The Member States shall provide in their legislation that the rights conferred upon the injured person pursuant to this Directive shall be extinguished upon the expiry of a period of five years from the date on which the supplier of services provided the service which caused the damage, unless in the meantime the injured person has instituted legal, administrative or arbitration proceedings against that person.

However, this period shall be extended to 20 years where the service relates to the design or construction of immovable property.

Article 10
Limitation period
1. Member States shall provide in their legislation that a limitation period of three years shall apply to proceedings for the recovery of damages as provided for in this Directive, beginning on the day on which the plaintiff became aware or should reasonably have become aware of the damage, the service and the identity of the supplier of the service.

However, this period shall be extended to 10 years where the service relates to the design or construction of immovable property.

2. The laws of Member States regulating suspension or interruption of the limitation period shall not be affected by this Directive.

20 OCCUPIERS' LIABILITY

This chapter deals with the liability of an occupier to persons who are injured on his premises. (If the damage is caused by something on the premises but the damage occurs *off* the premises, that is dealt with by the law of negligence or nuisance.) The basis of liability is fault, and to visitors at least the duty differs little from the requirements of negligence, but there are sufficient differences to make it subject to a special chapter. These differences arise partly for historical reasons, but also because of the need to balance the rights of the occupier to deal with his property as he wishes and the need to protect entrants from injury. Property rights still make a difference.

The character of the entrant also makes a difference, and rather than subject this to the usual tests of proximity in negligence, a clear distinction is made between visitors and other entrants. The draconian rules relating to trespassers have been ameliorated, and the duty owed is now flexible enough to distinguish between kinds of trespassers, e.g. the burglar and the wandering child.

Some jurisdictions have abandoned these distinctions based on status. The Occupiers' Liability (Scotland) Act 1960 makes no distinction between trespassers and visitors, and in Australia the High Court has abandoned the separate rules of occupiers' liability altogether and has subjected all issues to the ordinary rules of negligence. In *Australian Safeway Stores* v *Zaluzna* (1987) 162 CLR 479 the court approved the view of Deane J in *Hackshaw* v *Shaw* (1984) 155 CLR 614, where he said:

> It is not necessary, in an action in negligence against an occupier, to go through the procedure of considering whether either one or other or both of a special duty *qua* occupier and an ordinary duty of care was owed. All that is necessary is to determine whether, in all the relevant circumstances including the fact of the defendant's occupation of premises and the manner of the plaintiff's entry upon them, the defendant owed a duty of care under the ordinary principles of negligence to the plaintiff. A prerequisite of any such duty is that there be the necessary degree of proximity of relationship.

That, however, is not a step which has been taken in this country, and the law is governed by the Occupiers' Liability Act 1957 in relation to visitors, and by the Occupiers' Liability Act 1984 in relation to trespassers and other non-visitors.

OCCUPIERS' LIABILITY ACT 1957

1. Preliminary

(1) The rules enacted by the two next following sections shall have effect, in place of the rules of the common law, to regulate the duty which an occupier of premises owes to his visitors in respect of dangers due to the state of the premises or to things done or omitted to be done on them.

(2) The rules so enacted shall regulate the nature of the duty imposed by law in consequence of a person's occupation or control of premises and of any invitation or permission he gives (or is to be treated as giving) to another to enter or use the premises, but they shall not alter the rules of the common law as to the persons on whom a duty is so imposed or to whom it is owed; and accordingly for the purpose of the rules so enacted the persons who are to be treated as an occupier and as his visitors are the same (subject to subsection (4) of this section) as the persons who would at common law be treated as an occupier and as his invitees or licensees.

(3) The rules so enacted in relation to an occupier of premises and his visitors shall also apply, in like manner and to the like extent as the principles applicable at common law to an occupier of premises and his invitees or licensees would apply, to regulate—

(a) the obligations of a person occupying or having control over any fixed or moveable structure, including any vessel, vehicle or aircraft; and

(b) the obligations of a person occupying or having control over any premises or structure in respect of damage to property, including the property of persons who are not themselves his visitors.

(4) A person entering any premises in exercise of rights conferred by virtue of an access agreement or order under the National Parks and Access to the Countryside Act 1949, is not, for the purposes of this Act, a visitor of the occupier of those premises.

2. Extent of occupier's ordinary duty

(1) An occupier of premises owes the same duty, the 'common duty of care', to all his visitors, except in so far as he is free to and does extend, restrict, modify or exclude his duty to any visitor or visitors by agreement or otherwise.

(2) The common duty of care is a duty to take such care as in all the circumstances of the case is reasonable to see that the visitor will be reasonably safe in using the premises for the purposes for which he is invited or permitted by the occupier to be there.

(3) The circumstances relevant for the present purpose include the degree of care, and of want of care, which would ordinarily be looked for in such a visitor, so that (for example) in proper cases—

(a) an occupier must be prepared for children to be less careful than adults; and

(b) an occupier may expect that a person, in the exercise of his calling, will appreciate and guard against any special risks ordinarily incident to it, so far as the occupier leaves him free to do so.

(4) In determining whether the occupier of premises has discharged the common duty of care to a visitor, regard is to be had to all the circumstances, so that (for example)—

(a)   where damage is caused to a visitor by a danger of which he had been warned by the occupier, the warning is not to be treated without more as absolving the occupier from liability, unless in all the circumstances it was enough to enable the visitor to be reasonably safe; and

(b)   where damage is caused to a visitor by a danger due to the faulty execution of any work of construction, maintenance or repair by an independent contractor employed by the occupier, the occupier is not to be treated without more as answerable for the danger if in all the circumstances he had acted reasonably in entrusting the work to an independent contractor and had taken such steps (if any) as he reasonably ought in order to satisfy himself that the contractor was competent and that the work had been properly done.

(5)   The common duty of care does not impose on an occupier any obligation to a visitor in respect of risks willingly accepted as his by the visitor (the question whether a risk was so accepted to be decided on the same principles as in other cases in which one person owes a duty of care to another).

(6)   For the purposes of this section, persons who enter premises for any purpose in the exercise of a right conferred by law are to be treated as permitted by the occupier to be there for that purpose, whether they in fact have his permission or not.

3.   Effect of contract on occupier's liability to third party

(1)   Where an occupier of premises is bound by contract to permit persons who are strangers to the contract to enter or use the premises, the duty of care which he owes to them as his visitors cannot be restricted or excluded by that contract, but (subject to any provision of the contract to the contrary) shall include the duty to perform his obligations under the contract, whether undertaken for their protection or not, in so far as those obligations go beyond the obligations otherwise involved in that duty.

(2)   A contract shall not by virtue of this section have the effect, unless it expressly so provides, of making an occupier who has taken all reasonable care answerable to strangers to the contract for dangers due to the faulty execution of any work of construction, maintenance or repair or other like operation by persons other than himself, his servants and persons acting under his direction and control.

(3)   In this section 'stranger to the contract' means a person not for the time being entitled to the benefit of the contract as a party to it or as the successor by assignment or otherwise of a party to it, and accordingly includes a party to the contract who has ceased to be so entitled.

(4)   Where by the terms or conditions governing any tenancy (including a statutory tenancy which does not in law amount to a tenancy) either the landlord or the tenant is bound, though not by contract, to permit persons to enter or use premises of which he is the occupier, this section shall apply as if the tenancy were a contract between the landlord and the tenant.

5.   Implied term in contracts

(1)   Where persons enter or use, or bring or send goods to, any premises in exercise of a right conferred by contract with a person occupying or having control of the premises, the duty he owes them in respect of dangers due to the state of the premises, or to things done or omitted to be done on them, in so far as the duty depends on a term to be implied in the contract by reason of its conferring that right, shall be the common duty of care.

(2)   The foregoing subsection shall apply to fixed and moveable structures as it applies to premises.

(3)   This section does not affect the obligations imposed on a person by or by virtue of any contract for the hire of, or for the carriage for reward of persons or goods in, any

vehicle, vessel, aircraft or other means of transport, or by virtue of any contract of bailment.

Section 1: occupiers' liability and negligence

One consequence of adopting duties based on the status of the entrant is the need to distinguish between a person's duty under the *Donoghue* v *Stevenson* principle not to injure another and his duties under the Occupiers' Liability Act 1957. In practice the problem does not matter very much, as the two duties are very similar, but although there has been some doubt about the question, the usual view is that activity duties are dealt with by the rules of ordinary negligence, and occupancy duties by the special rules of occupiers' liability. The distinction is not easy, but it is usually asked whether the premises themselves have been rendered unsafe.

New Zealand Insurance Co. v *Prudential Assurance Ltd*
Court of Appeal, New Zealand [1976] NZLR 84

Mrs Woods committed suicide by drinking arsenic. On the following day, after the body had been taken away, Mr Woods and his son Roger entered the house. In the kitchen Roger saw what appeared to be a glass of lemon juice and he drank some of it. The glass contained arsenic and Roger died. Mrs Woods was covered by an insurance policy: one clause dealt with personal liability and limited a claim to $10,000 whereas another clause (cl. 2C(1)) dealt with liability as occupier and limited the claim to $50,000. The question therefore arose whether the liability of Mrs Woods was based on occupiers' liability or not. In a dispute concerning indemnities it was held: that the procedure adopted by the parties was inappropriate, but Richmond J also indicated, without deciding, that the matter probably was one of occupiers' liability.

RICHMOND J: I return now to the judgment of O'Regan J. He did not advert to any procedural difficulties, and I sympathise with his evident desire to assist the parties. He dealt with the case in the following way. First, and very importantly, he said that section 2C(1) 'has to do with the insured's legal liability "as occupier"'. He then referred to the distinction drawn by Denning LJ in *Dunster* v *Abbott* [1954] 1 WLR 58, 62; [1953] 2 All ER 1572, 1574, between duties arising out of the particular relationship between an occupier and an invitee or licensee, on the one hand, and the duties arising out of the general duty of care. Denning LJ thought that the former duty related only to the static condition of the premises and not to current operations on the premises. This distinction is often described as one between 'occupancy' duties and 'activity' duties. O'Regan J came to the conclusion that an 'activity' duty was outside the scope of the Occupiers' Liability Act 1962. He noted that s.3(1) prima facie appeared to relate to both duties, as it refers to the duty, which an occupier owes to his visitors in his capacity as an occupier, in respect of dangers 'due to the state of the premises or *to things done or omitted to be done on them*'. He thought, however, that s.3(2) made it clear that only 'occupancy' duties were covered because that subsection states that 'The rules so enacted shall regulate the nature of the duty imposed by law *in consequence of a person's occupation or control of premises*'. The Judge then said:

Relating the view I have taken to the facts of the case, I consider that the liability in tort for the act of the elder Mrs Woods leaving a glass of poisonous substance on the sink bench is the same as if such act was done by a trespasser or an overnight guest in the house. Such liability is in no way dependent on her occupation of the premises; it arises *qua neighbour* and not *qua occupier*.

From what I have said it will be seen that the Judge really decided two things:

(1)   A question of construction of the policy, namely, that section 2C(1) 'has to do with the insured's legal liability "as occupier" '. Although he did not elaborate on this, or discuss any alternative construction, I think he meant that section 2C(1) is concerned only with cases where the fact of occupancy is an essential legal ingredient of the cause of action.

(2)   A question of liability as between the widow and the New Zealand Insurance Co. Ltd. He held, on such evidence as he had before him, and as a mixed question of fact and law, that the widow could not succeed in a claim under the Occupiers' Liability Act.

On the hearing of this appeal Mr Clark challenged both the foregoing conclusions. I propose to deal with them in reverse order.

In the passage from the judgment in *Dunster's* case upon which O'Regan J relied, Denning LJ appears to have treated dangers in the 'static condition of the premises' as the equivalent of dangers 'which have been present for some time in the physical structure of the premises'. It is probable that the Judge based his conclusion in the present case upon the fact that the presence of a glass of poison obviously did not affect the 'physical structure of the premises'. While sympathising with the position in which O'Regan J found himself I think that he allowed himself to become involved in a question of mixed fact and law which was quite outside the type of question which can be dealt with on an originating summons under the Declaratory Judgments Act. Accordingly, I do not myself propose to deal with this question by attempting a definite answer to it. I am inclined to think, however, that it is impossible to say that current operations which do not affect the physical structure of the premises are outside the scope of the Act. The problem may rather be to draw the line between those 'current operations' or 'activities' which do, and those which do not, result in a state of affairs falling within the scope of the Act. The point is discussed in *Street's Law of Torts* (5th ed) 180-181, and also in *North's Occupiers' Liability* (1971) 80-82. Both the learned authors are agreed that the Act is not limited in the way which I believe found favour with O'Regan J. This because of the words in subs (1), 'or to things done or omitted to be done on them'. Both also agree that the Act only replaces the common law in respect of duties consequent upon occupation. But because of the words in subs (1) to which I have just referred it is said in *Street* at p. 180: 'At the very least, then, the Act covers acts or omissions which have created a dangerous condition of a continuing nature which later causes harm'.

Likewise it is said in *North* at p. 80: 'This would include conduct on the land which causes a continuing source of danger and thereby renders the premises or structure unsafe'.

But it is clear that both authors find difficulty in drawing a satisfactory line between those activities which are relevant under the Act and those which are not. Professor Street thinks that an activity such as the shooting of arrows would be outside the Act 'for the duty of care is imposed on the actor because he is himself performing an act which is foreseeably likely to cause harm to others present on the premises, and not because the occupier occupies the land' (p. 181). In *North's Occupiers' Liability* at p. 81 it is suggested that an activity on the premises which does not affect the safety of the premises as a structure falls outside the Act.

These difficulties are also discussed in *Clerk & Lindsell on Torts* (13th ed) pp. 595-596. It is there said:

It is clear that the duty under the Act covers dangers due to the static condition of the premises, and dangers due to the condition of the premises at the time of the visitor's entry, although the condition has been temporarily brought about by 'things done or omitted to be done' thereon. It is suggested that it does not cover 'superadded negligence' such as dropping a sack of sugar on the visitor from a crane, running into him in a car or locomotive, shooting him, or pouring tea over him, where these acts are done by the occupier or his servants.

Roles v *Nathan* [1963] 1 WLR 117; [1963] 2 All ER 908 suggests that the presence of carbon monoxide gas in a building may be an occupiers' liability situation. Pearson LJ (at p. 1131; 917) seems to have regarded the lighting of the fire in that case as the breach of the occupier's duty. As to whether it may be possible to draw an analogy between the presence of carbon monoxide and the continuing presence of a glass of poison I express no opinion. But I have referred to the views of three textbook writers as being in agreement at least to the point that the Act extends to cover conduct which causes a continuing source of danger and thereby renders the premises unsafe. At the same time they are all in agreement that the Act does not extend to every activity of the occupier. As I have said, the present proceedings are quite inappropriate to enable the Court to express any final opinion on this question. But I am inclined to think that O'Regan J took too narrow a view of the scope of the Act.

Notes
1.   See also *Revill* v *Newbery* [1996] 1 All ER 291, where an occupier shot an intruder trying to enter his allotment shed. It was said this was not a matter of occupiers' liability but rather was to be decided under the general tort of negligence. Occupiers' liability is limited to liability as occupier and the Occupiers' Liability Acts are concerned with only the safety of the premises and with dangers due to things done on the premises. However, it was also held that the special duty in the Occupiers' Liability Act 1984 was the appropriate level of duty for ordinary negligence in the circumstances. In the event the defendant was liable as he had used greater force than was justified although the trespasser was held to be two-thirds contributorily negligent.
2.   Some insurance policies provide cover for a person's liability 'as owner', and people might be misled into thinking that this provides cover for accidents occurring on their land. It does not: a person who is insured 'as owner' is not covered for liability as 'occupier'.

Section 2:   who is an occupier?

Liability is imposed on a person not because he is the owner of the land but because he is the occupier, and indeed, as will be seen, it may not be necessary for a person to have property rights over the land at all (see *Collier* v *Anglian Water Authority* below). Conversely, a person may be the occupier if he merely has the right to occupy (*Harris* v *Birkenhead Corporation* below). The principal test is one of control on the grounds that the person to be liable should be the person who could prevent the damage, and it is possible for two people to be

occupiers of either different parts of the premises, or of the same part at the
same time.

Wheat v *E. Lacon & Co. Ltd*
House of Lords [1966] AC 552; [1966] 2 WLR 581; [1966] 1 All ER 582

Lacon & Co. owned the Golfers Arms at Great Yarmouth and employed Mr
Richardson as their manager. He and his wife lived on the upper floor, and
they had a lodger, Mr Wheat. One evening at about 9.00 p.m. Mr Wheat was
coming down the stairs when he fell and was killed. The hand rail on the
stairs ended just above the third step from the bottom and there was no knob
on the end of the rail. At the top of the stairs was a light fitting but it had no
bulb and the stairs were dark. Held: dismissing the appeal, that Lacon & Co.
owed a duty of care as occupiers of the stairs, but on the facts were not in
breach of that duty.

LORD DENNING: The case raises this point of law: did the brewery company owe any
duty to Mr Wheat to see that the handrail was safe to use or to see that the stairs were
properly lighted? That depends on whether the brewery company was 'an occupier' of
the private portion of the 'Golfers' Arms,' and Mr Wheat its 'visitor' within the
Occupiers' Liability Act, 1957: for, if so, the brewery company owed him the 'common
duty of care.'
    In order to determine this question we must have resort to the law before the Act: for
it is expressly enacted [in section 1(2)] that the Act

> shall not alter the rules of the common law as to the persons on whom a duty is so
> imposed or to whom it is owed; and accordingly . . . the persons who are to be treated
> as an occupier and as his visitors are the same . . . as the persons who would at
> common law be treated as an occupier and as his invitees or licensees.

    At the outset, I would say that no guidance is to be obtained from the use of the word
'occupier' in other branches of the law: for its meaning varies according to the
subject-matter.
    In the Occupiers' Liability Act, 1957, the word 'occupier' is used in the same sense as
it was used in the common law cases on occupiers' liability for dangerous premises. It
was simply a convenient word to denote a person who had a sufficent degree of control
over premises to put him under a duty of care towards those who came lawfully on to
the premises. Those persons were divided into two categories, invitees and licensees:
and a higher duty was owed to invitees than to licensees. But by the year 1956 the
distinction between invitees and licensees had been reduced to vanishing point. The
duty of the occupier had become simply a duty to take reasonable care to see that the
premises were reasonably safe for people coming lawfully on to them: and it made no
difference whether they were invitees or licensees: see *Slater* v *Clay Cross Co. Ltd* [1956]
2 QB 264. The Act of 1957 confirmed the process. It did away, once and for all, with
invitees and licensees and classed them all as 'visitors', and it put upon the occupier the
same duty to all of them, namely, the common duty of care. This duty is simply a
particular instance of the general duty of care which each man owes to his 'neighbour'.
. . . Translating this general principle into its particular application to dangerous
premises, it becomes simply this: wherever a person has a sufficient degree of control
over premises that he ought to realise that any failure on his part to use care may result

in injury to a person coming lawfully there, then he is an 'occupier' and the person coming lawfully there is his 'visitor': and the 'occupier' is under a duty to his 'visitor' to use reasonable care. In order to be an 'occupier' it is not necessary for a person to have entire control over the premises. He need not have exclusive occupation. Suffice it that he has some degree of control. He may share the control with others. Two or more may be 'occupiers.' And whenever this happens, each is under a duty to use care towards persons coming lawfully on to the premises, dependent on his degree of control. If each fails in his duty, each is liable to a visitor who is injured in consequence of his failure, but each may have a claim to contribution from the other.

In *Salmond on Torts*, 14th ed. (1965), p. 372, it is said that an 'occupier' is 'he who has the immediate supervision and control and the power of permitting or prohibiting the entry of other persons.' This definition was adopted by Roxburgh J in *Hartwell* v *Grayson, Rollo and Clover Docks Ltd*, [1947] KB 901, and by Diplock LJ in the present case. There is no doubt that a person who fulfils that test is an 'occupier.' He is the person who says 'come in.' But I think that test is too narrow by far. There are other people who are 'occupiers,' even though they do not say 'come in.' If a person has any degree of control over the state of the premises it is enough. . . .

. . . I ask myself whether the brewery company had a sufficient degree of control over the premises to put them under a duty to a visitor. Obviously they had complete control over the ground floor and were 'occupiers' of it. But I think that they had also sufficient control over the private portion. They had not let it out to Mr Richardson by a demise. They had only granted him a licence to occupy it, having a right themselves to do repairs. That left them with a residuary degree of control which was equivalent to that retained by the Chelsea Corporation in *Greene's* case [1954] 2 QB 127. They were in my opinion 'an occupier' within the Act of 1957. Mr Richardson, who had a licence to occupy, had also a considerable degree of control. So had Mrs Richardson, who catered for summer guests. All three of them were, in my opinion, 'occupiers' of the private portion of the 'Golfer's Arms.' There is no difficulty in having more than one occupier at one and the same time, each of whom is under a duty of care to visitors. The Court of Appeal so held in the recent case of *Crockfords Club* (*Fisher* v *CHT Ltd*) [1965] 1 WLR 1093).

What did the common duty of care demand of each of these occupiers towards their visitors? Each was under a duty to take such care as 'in all the circumstances of the case' is reasonable to see that the visitor will be reasonably safe. So far as the brewery company are concerned, the circumstances demanded that on the ground floor they should, by their servants, take care not only of the structure of the building, but also the furniture, the state of the floors and lighting, and so forth, at all hours of day or night when the premises were open. But in regard to the private portion, the circumstances did not demand so much of the brewery company. They ought to see that the structure was reasonably safe, including the handrail, and that the system of lighting was efficient. But I doubt whether they were bound to see that the lights were properly switched on or the rugs laid safely on the floor. The brewery company were entitled to leave those day-to-day matters to Mr and Mrs Richardson. They, too, were occupiers. The circumstances of the case demanded that Mr and Mrs Richardson should take care of those matters in the private portion of the house. And of other matters, too. If they had realised the handrail was dangerous, they should have reported it to the brewery company.

We are not concerned here with Mr and Mrs Richardson. The judge has absolved them from any negligence and there is no appeal. We are only concerned with the brewery company. They were, in my opinion, occupiers and under a duty of care. In this respect I agree with Sellers LJ and Winn J, but I come to a different conclusion on the facts. I can see no evidence of any breach of duty by the brewery company. So far as the handrail was concerned, the evidence was overwhelming that no one had any reason before this accident to suppose that it was in the least dangerous. So far as the light was concerned, the proper inference was that it was removed by some stranger shortly before Mr Wheat went down the staircase. Neither the brewery company nor Mr and Mrs Richardson could be blamed for the act of a stranger.

Notes
1.   In *Collier* v *Anglian Water Authority*, *The Times*, 26 March 1983, the plaintiff tripped over an uneven paving slab on the promenade at Mablethorpe. The promenade was owned by the local authority who kept it clean and granted leases to shop owners on it, but they did no repair work on it. The repairs were conducted by the water authority (who appeared to have no property interest in the promenade) as part of their duty to maintain adequate sea defences. It was held that both the local authority and the water authority were occupiers, the latter because, by maintaining the promenade as part of their statutory duty, they exercised control over it.

2.   In *Harris* v *Birkenhead Corporation* [1976] 1 All ER 279 the defendants were held to be occupiers, even though they had never exercised control over the property, because they had the *right* to do so. The defendants compulsorily purchased a house which was owned by Mrs Gledhill and let to Mrs Redmond. Mrs Redmond left without telling the defendants, and the house became vacant and derelict. The plaintiff, aged 4, entered the house and fell from the second floor. It was held that the defendants were occupiers, even though they had never entered the property, because the compulsory purchase order gave them the immediate right to enter.

Question
A owns land on which buildings are to be demolished. He engages B to do the demolition work, and B sub-contracts the work to C. Who occupies the land? (See *Ferguson* v *Welsh* [1987] 1 WLR 1553.)

DEFECTIVE PREMISES ACT 1972

4.   Landlord's duty of care in virtue of obligation or right to repair premises demised
    (1)   Where premises are let under a tenancy which puts on the landlord an obligation to the tenant for the maintenance or repair of the premises, the landlord owes to all persons who might reasonably be expected to be affected by defects in the state of the premises a duty to take such care as is reasonable in all the circumstances to see that they are reasonably safe from personal injury or from damage to their property caused by a relevant defect.
    (2)   The said duty is owed if the landlord knows (whether as the result of being notified by the tenant or otherwise) or if he ought in all the circumstances to have known of the relevant defect.
    (3)   In this section 'relevant defect' means a defect in the state of the premises existing at or after the material time and arising from, or continuing because of, an act or omission by the landlord which constitutes or would if he had had notice of the defect, have constituted a failure by him to carry out his obligation to the tenant for the

maintenance or repair of the premises; and for the purposes of the foregoing provision 'the material time' means—

    (a)   where the tenancy commenced before this Act, the commencement of this Act; and

    (b)   in all other cases, the earliest of the following times, that is to say—

        (i)   the time when the tenancy commences;

        (ii)   the time when the tenancy agreement is entered into;

        (iii)   the time when possession is taken of the premises in contemplation of the letting.

    (4)   Where premises are let under a tenancy which expressly or impliedly gives the landlord the right to enter the premises to carry out any description of maintenance or repair of the premises, then, as from the time when he first is, or by notice or otherwise can put himself, in a position to exercise the right and so long as he is or can put himself in that position, he shall be treated for the purposes of subsections (1) to (3) above (but for no other purpose) as if he were under an obligation to the tenant for that description of maintenance or repair of the premises; but the landlord shall not owe the tenant any duty by virtue of this subsection in respect of any defect in the state of the premises arising from, or continuing because of, a failure to carry out an obligation expressly imposed on the tenant by the tenancy.

    (5)   For the purposes of this section obligations imposed or rights given by any enactment in virtue of a tenancy shall be treated as imposed or given by the tenancy.

    (6)   This section applies to a right of occupation given by contract or any enactment and not amounting to a tenancy as if the right were a tenancy, and 'tenancy' and cognate expressions shall be construed accordingly.

Note

In *McCauley* v *Bristol City Council* [1991] 1 All ER 749 the plaintiff, a council tenant, fell and injured her ankle when an unstable concrete step in the garden moved under her. The council was only obliged to repair the structure and exterior of the house and the tenant was responsible, inter alia, for the garden. However, clause 6(c) of the tenancy agreement entitled the council to enter the premises for any purpose. The court held that for the purposes of s. 4(4) of the 1972 Act there was an implied right for the council to enter any part of the premises for the purpose of maintenance as they could insist on doing so if the tenant refused to maintain the property. Accordingly the council was liable under the Act. If the council had inserted in the tenancy agreement an express provision that they should have no right to do repairs to the garden they would not have been liable.

Section 3:   who is a visitor?

Section 1 of the Occupiers' Liability Act 1957 merely defines a visitor as a person who could have been either an 'invitee' or a 'licensee' at common law. An invitee was a person you asked to come onto your land for your purposes, and a licensee was a person you permitted to enter. It is no longer necessary to distinguish between them, but it is still necessary to define the outer limits of the two categories. Thus, visitor = invitee + licensee. It does not include trespassers or those using rights of way.

Edwards v Railway Executive
House of Lords [1952] AC 737; [1952] 2 All ER 430; [1952] 2 TLR 237

For a number of years children had been accustomed to climb through a fence beside a railway line and toboggan down the embankment. The defendants repaired the fence whenever they found it broken. The plaintiff was injured by a train when he was playing on the line. Held: dismissing the appeal, that the plaintiff was a trespasser and not an implied visitor.

LORD PORTER: The first matter for decision accordingly is whether there was any evidence from which it could be inferred that children from the recreation ground had become licensees to enter the respondents' premises and toboggan down the embankment.

The appellants support their claim on the authority of such cases as *Cooke* v *Midland Great Western Railway of Ireland* [1909] AC 229 and *Lowery* v *Walker* [1911] AC 10. I refrain from referring to the many cases which have not reached your Lordships' House inasmuch as the principle is, I think, clear — the application alone difficult. There must, I think, be such assent to the user relied upon as amounts to a licence to use the premises. Whether that result can be inferred or not must, of course, be a question of degree, but in my view a court is not justified in lightly inferring it. In *Cooke's* case [1909] AC 229 there was an open and well worn pathway leading to a turntable on which children could ride and which was an allurement to them. Apparently the whole station staff in that case knew of the practice of children to congregate there and ride upon the turntable and no attempt was made to stop them. Similar considerations apply to *Lowery* v *Walker* [1911] AC 10. The ground of the decision is best set out in the words of Lord Loreburn LC. The facts of the case were that the defendant put a dangerous horse into a field through which he knew the public were accustomed to pass as a short cut to the station. Lord Loreburn says: 'I think in substance it' (i.e., the county court judge's finding) 'amounts to this: that the plaintiff was not proved to be in this field of right; that he was there as one of the public who habitually used the field to the knowledge of the defendant; that the defendant did not take steps to prevent that user; and in those circumstances it cannot be lawful that the defendant should with impunity allow a horse which he knew to be a savage and dangerous beast to be loose in that field without giving any warning whatever, either to the plaintiff or to the public, of the dangerous character of the animal.'

I mention these cases because they deal with circumstances having some resemblance to the present case, but each case must be determined on its own facts. The onus is on the appellants to establish their licence, and in my opinion they do not do so merely by showing that, in spite of a fence now accepted as complying with the Act requiring the respondents to fence, children again and again broke their way through. What more, the appellants were asked, could the respondents do? Report to the corporation? But their caretaker knew already. Prosecute? First you have to catch your children and even then would that be more effective? In any case I cannot see that the respondents were under any obligation to do more than keep their premises shut off by a fence which was duly repaired when broken and obviously intended to keep intruders out.

It will be observed that in expressing this opinion I have assumed that the servants of the Railway Executive had knowledge that children were accustomed to go there. I am not convinced that they had this knowledge, but it may have been legitimate for the jury to find that the ganger who repaired the fence must have known, although I am not prepared to accept the proposition that any inference can be drawn from the fact that trains passed up or down, or to hold that their drivers ought or must be taken to have seen the children. However that may be, and even assuming that the respondents had knowledge of the intrusion of children onto the embankment, the suggestion that that knowledge of itself constitutes the children licensees, in my opinion, carries the doctrine of implied licence much too far, though no doubt where the owner of the premises knows that the public or some portion of it is accustomed to trespass over his land he must take steps to show that he resents and will try to prevent the invasion.

An open pathway, as in *Cooke* v *Midland Great Western Railway of Ireland* [1909] AC 229, or a knowledge that a track is and has long been constantly used, coupled with a failure to take any steps to indicate that ingress is not permitted, as in *Lowery* v *Walker* [1911] AC 10, may well amount to a tacit licence. But I do not accept the theory that every possible step to keep out intruders must be taken and, if it is not, a licence may be inferred. . . .

Notes
1. Another way of trying to turn a trespasser into an implied visitor was the doctrine of allurement, whereby a person, usually a child, was tempted away from where he was allowed to be to somewhere where he was not. In *Glasgow Corporation* v *Taylor* [1922] 1 AC 44 a boy aged 7 entered the herb garden in the Botanic Gardens, Glasgow, where he picked berries from a belladonna bush and ate them. He died. The defendants were liable, although technically permission to enter the gardens did not include permission to meddle with the plants. (Until recently there was a notice by the herb garden saying that children under 10 were not admitted unless accompanied by a responsible adult. Would this have made any difference as to the status of the entrant?)
2. Now that trespassers are owed a duty under the Occupiers' Liability Act 1984, the 'device' of implied permission may no longer be necessary, and the principles discussed above may no longer apply. See *Herrington* v *British Rlys Board* [1972] AC 877, at p. 933, per Lord Diplock.

Question
In *The Calgarth* [1927] P 93, Scrutton LJ said 'When you invite a person into your house to use the staircase you do not invite him to slide down the bannisters'. From whose point of view is a limitation of what an entrant is allowed to do judged? The reasonable occupier, the reasonable entrant, or the reasonable bystander?

Section 4:   the duty owed to visitors

The nature of the duty owed by an occupier to his visitors is dealt with in s. 2 of the Occupiers' Liability Act 1957, and this has generally been equated with the ordinary rules of negligence, subject to the particular conditions in s. 2(3) and (4), which relate to children and to skilled entrants and to the role of warnings. It should be noted that the statute does not require the premises themselves to be safe, but only that the visitor is enabled to be safe. This can be achieved not only by making the premises safe, but also by warning the entrant of dangers or otherwise enabling him to avoid them.

Roles v *Nathan*
Court of Appeal [1963] 1 WLR 1117; [1963] 2 All ER 908

Donald and Joseph Roles were chimney sweeps who were working on the flues of the Manchester Assembly Rooms. There was a boiler with lengthy flues and, the fire being difficult to light, a boiler engineer was consulted. He advised that two vent holes should be sealed up, and warned the Roles brothers of the dangers of working on the flues with the fires lit and of the risk of carbon monoxide poisoning. One day the men were working on the flue (with the fire lit) in the presence of the engineer and the manager. The work had not been finished, and the two returned later that evening to complete it. They died of carbon monoxide poisoning, and at first instance the judge held the occupier liable for not having the fire drawn or at least damped down. Held: allowing the appeal, that the occupier was not liable.

LORD DENNING MR: The occupier now appeals and says that it is not a case of negligence and contributory negligence, but that, on the true application of the Occupiers' Liability Act, 1957, the occupier was not liable at all. This is the first time we have had to consider that Act. It has been very beneficial. It has rid us of those two unpleasant characters, the invitee and the licensee, who haunted the courts for years, and it has replaced them by the attractive figure of a visitor, who has so far given no trouble at all. The Act has now been in force six years, and hardly any case has come before the courts in which its interpretation has had to be considered. The draftsman expressed the hope that 'the Act would replace a principle of the common law with a new principle *of the common law;* instead of having the judgment of Willes J construed as if it were a statute, one is to have a statute which can be construed as if it were a judgment of Willes J.' It seems that his hopes are being fulfilled. All the fine distinctions about traps have been thrown aside and replaced by the common duty of care.

'The common duty of care,' the Act says, 'is a duty to take such care as in all the circumstances of the case is reasonable to see that the visitor' — note the visitor, not the premises — 'will be reasonably safe in using the premises for the purposes for which he is invited or permitted by the occupier to be there.' That is comprehensive. All the circumstances have to be considered. But the Act goes on to give examples of the circumstances that are relevant. The particular one in question here is in subsection (3) of section 2:

> The circumstances relevant for the present purpose include the degree of care, and of want of care, which would ordinarily be looked for in such a visitor, so that (for example) in proper cases . . . (b) an occupier may expect that a person, in the exercise of his calling, will appreciate and guard against any special risks ordinarily incident to it, so far as the occupier leaves him free to do so.

. . . Likewise in the case of a chimney sweep who comes to sweep the chimneys or to seal up a sweep-hole. The householder can reasonably expect the sweep to take care of himself so far as any dangers from the flues are concerned. These chimney sweeps ought to have known that there might be dangerous fumes about and ought to have taken steps to guard against them. They ought to have known that they should not attempt to seal up a sweep-hole whilst the first was still alight. They ought to have had the fire withdrawn before they attempted to seal it up, or at any rate they ought not to have stayed in the alcove too long when there might be dangerous fumes about. All this was known to these two sweeps; they were repeatedly warned about it, and it was for them to guard against the danger. It was not for the occupier to do it, even though he was present and heard the warnings. When a householder calls in a specialist to deal with a defective installation on his premises, he can reasonably expect the specialist to appreciate and guard against the dangers arising from the defect. The householder is not bound to watch over him to see that he comes to no harm. I would hold, therefore, that the occupier here was under no duty of care to these sweeps, at any rate in regard to the dangers which caused their deaths. If it had been a different danger, as for instance if the stairs leading to the cellar gave way, the occupier might no doubt be responsible, but not for these dangers which were special risks ordinarily incidental to their calling.

Even if I am wrong about this point, and the occupier was under a duty of care to these chimney sweeps, the question arises whether the duty was discharged by the warning that was given to them. This brings us to subsection (4) which states:

In determining whether the occupier of premises has discharged the common duty of care to a visitor, regard is to be had to all the circumstances, so that (for example) — (a) where damage is caused to a visitor by a danger of which he had been warned by the occupier, the warning is not to be treated without more as absolving the occupier from liability, unless in all the circumstances it was enough to enable the visitor to be reasonably safe.

We all know the reason for this subsection. It was inserted so as to clear up the unsatisfactory state of the law as it had been left by the decision of the House of Lords in *London Graving Dock Co.* v *Horton* [1951] AC 737. That case was commonly supposed to have decided that, when a person comes onto premises as an invitee, and is injured by the defective or dangerous condition of the premises (due to the default of the occupier), it is nevertheless a complete defence for the occupier to prove that the invitee knew of the danger, or had been warned of it. Suppose for instance, that there was only one way of getting into and out of premises, and it was by a footbridge over a stream which was rotten and dangerous. According to *Horton's* case, the occupier could escape all liability to any visitor by putting up a notice. 'This bridge is dangerous' even though there was no other way by which the visitor could get in or out, and he had no option but to go over the bridge. In such a case, section 2(4) makes it clear that the occupier would nowadays be liable. But if there were two footbridges, one of which was rotten, and the other safe a hundred yards away, the occupier could still escape liability even today, by putting up a notice: 'Do not use this footbridge. It is dangerous. There is a safe one further upstream.' Such a warning is sufficient because it does enable the visitor to be reasonably safe.

I think that the law would probably have developed on these lines in any case; see *Greene* v *Chelsea Borough Council* [1954] 2 QB 127 where I ventured to say 'knowledge or notice of the danger is only a defence when the plaintiff is free to act upon that knowledge or notice so as to avoid the danger.' But the subsection has now made it clear. A warning does not absolve the occupier, unless it is enough to enable the visitor to be reasonably safe.

Apply subsection (4) to this case. I am quite clear that the warnings which were given to the sweeps were enough to enable them to be reasonably safe. The sweeps would have been quite safe if they had heeded these warnings. They should not have come back that evening and attempted to seal up the sweep-hole while the fire was still alight. They ought to have waited till next morning, and then they should have seen that the fire was out before they attempted to seal up the sweep-hole. In any case they should not have stayed too long in the sweep-hole. In short, it was entirely their own fault. The judge held that it was contributory negligence. I would go further and say that under the Act the occupier has, by the warnings, discharged his duty.

Phipps v Rochester Corporation
Queen's Bench Division [1955] 1 QB 450; [1955] 2 WLR 23;
[1955] 1 All ER 129

Yvonne Phipps, aged 7, and her brother Ian, aged 5, entered land which was being developed for building, in order to collect blackberries. On the site was a trench eight or nine feet deep and two feet wide, and Ian fell into it, breaking his leg. As children were known to play on the site the plaintiff was an implied visitor. Held: the occupier was not liable.

DEVLIN J: The cases which deal with the licensor's duty towards children in general are well known. The law recognizes for this purpose a sharp difference between children and adults. But there might well, I think, be an equally well-marked distinction between 'big children' and 'little children.' I shall use those broad terms to denote broadly the difference between children who know what they are about and children who do not. The latter are sometimes referred to in the cases as 'children of tender years.' Not having reached the age of reason or understanding, they present a special problem. When it comes to taking care of themselves, there is a greater difference between big and little children than there is between big children and adults, and much justification for putting little children into a separate category. Adults and big children can be guilty of contributory negligence; a little child cannot.

I have not been able to find in the cases which have been cited to me any clearly authoritative formulation of the licensor's duty towards little children. I think that the cases do show that judges have not allowed themselves to be driven to the conclusion that licensors must make their premises safe for little children; but they have chosen different ways of escape from that conclusion. . . . A third way is to treat the licence as being conditional upon the little child being accompanied by a responsible adult. That is a solution for which Mr O'Connor contends in the alternative. A fourth way is to frame the duty so as to compromise between the robustness that would make children take the world as they found it and the tenderness which would give them nurseries wherever they go. On this view the licensor is not entitled to assume that all children will, unless they are allured, behave like adults; but he is entitled to assume that normally little children will in fact be accompanied by a responsible person and to discharge his duty of warning accordingly.

I think that it would be an unjustifiable restriction of the principle if one were to say that although the licensor may in determining the extent of his duty have regard to the fact that it is the habit, and also the duty, of prudent people to look after themselves, he may not in that determination have a similar regard to the fact that it is the habit, and also the duty, of prudent people to look after their little children. If he is entitled, in the absence of evidence to the contrary, to assume that parents will not normally allow their little children to go out unaccompanied, he can decide what he should do and consider what warnings are necessary on that basis. He cannot then be made liable for the exceptional child that strays, nor will he be required to prove that any particular parent has been negligent. It is, I think, preferable that this result should be achieved by allowing the general principle to expand in a natural way rather than by restricting its influence and then having to give it artificial aids in order to make it work at all in the case of little children.

The principle I am seeking to express is that contained in the passage I have quoted from the speech of Lord Shaw in *Glasgow Corporation* v *Taylor*, [1922] 1 AC 44, where he says that the municipality is entitled to take into account that reasonable parents will not permit their children to be sent into danger without protection; that the guardians of the child and of the park must each act reasonably; and that each is entitled to assume of the other that he will. That passage was not spoken in reference to the English law of licence, but nevertheless it seems to me to express perfectly the way in which the English law can reasonably be applied. A licensor who tacitly permits the public to use his land without discriminating between its members must assume that the public may include little children. But as a general rule he will have discharged his duty towards them if the dangers which they may encounter are only those which are obvious to a guardian or of which he has given a warning comprehensible by a guardian. To every general rule there are, of course, exceptions. A licensor cannot divest himself of the obligation of finding out something about the sort of people who are availing themselves of his permission and the sort of use they are making of it. He may have to take into account the social habits of the neighbourhood. No doubt there are places where little children go to play unaccompanied. If the licensor knows or ought to anticipate that, he may have to take steps accordingly. But the responsibility for the safety of little children must rest primarily upon the parents; it is their duty to see that such children are not allowed to wander about by themselves, or at the least to satisfy themselves that the places to which they do allow their children to go unaccompanied are safe for them to go to. It would not be socially desirable if parents were, as a matter of course, able to shift the burden of looking after their children from their own shoulders to those of persons who happen to have accessible bits of land. Different considerations may well apply to public parks or to recognized playing grounds where parents allow their children to go unaccompanied in the reasonable belief that they are safe.

Note
In *Simkiss* v *Rhondda BC* (1983) 81 LGR 460 Catherine Simkiss, aged 7, and a friend, aged 10, went to picnic on a hillside occupied by the defendants. They came there as visitors, and the picnic spot was visible from Catherine's parents' flat. After the picnic they walked up the mountain and then slid down the slope on a blanket. The plaintiff fell down a natural bluff for some 30 feet and was injured. The defendants were not liable because (a) the occupiers were entitled to assume that parents would have warned their children of the dangers, and (b) the standard applicable to the occupier was that of a reasonably prudent parent, and they could not be expected to fence off every natural hazard which provided an opportunity to children to injure themselves.

Question
In evidence in *Simkiss* v *Rhondda BC* Mr Simkiss was asked whether he, as a reasonably prudent parent, regarded the bluff as a danger. What are the legal consequences of his answering 'Yes' or 'No' to this question?

Section 5:   the duty owed to trespassers and other non-visitors

The issue of the level of duty which should be owed to trespassers has had a turbulent history, but following the Law Commission Report No. 75 on

Liability for Damage or Injury to Trespassers and Related Questions of Occupiers' Liability (Cmnd 6429, 1976), the matter was settled by the Occupiers' Liability Act 1984. However, it is important to realise the limits of the Act, and the position now is as follows:

(a) the 1984 Act applies only to personal injuries incurred by trespassers and other non-visitors, but the Act does not apply to highway users;

(b) property damage to all non-visitors is covered, if at all, by the common law, as expressed in *Herrington* v *British Railways Board*;

(c) users of *adopted* highways are covered by the Highways Act 1980, s. 41;

(d) injury to users of *unadopted* highways is covered by the tort of public nuisance, or possibly the duty in *Herrington* v *British Railways Board*. However, an occupier of land over which such a public right of way runs is not under any obligation to maintain the path or road and thus is not liable in negligence for failure to maintain: see *McGeown* v *Northern Ireland Housing Executive* [1994] 3 All ER 53.

OCCUPIERS' LIABILITY ACT 1984

1. Duty of occupier to persons other than his visitors

(1) The rules enacted by this section shall have effect, in place of the rules of the common law, to determine —

(a) whether any duty is owed by a person as occupier of premises to persons other than his visitors in respect of any risk of their suffering injury on the premises by reason of any danger due to the state of the premises or to things done or omitted to be done on them; and

(b) if so, what that duty is.

(2) For the purposes of this section, the persons who are to be treated respectively as an occupier of any premises (which, for those purposes, include any fixed or movable structure) and as his visitors are —

(a) any person who owes in relation to the premises the duty referred to in section 2 of the Occupiers' Liability Act 1957 (the common duty of care), and

(b) those who are his visitors for the purposes of that duty.

(3) An occupier of premises owes a duty to another (not being his visitor) in respect of any such risk as is referred to in subsection (1) above if —

(a) he is aware of the danger or has reasonable grounds to believe that it exists;

(b) he knows or has reasonable grounds to believe that the other is in the vicinity of the danger concerned or that he may come into the vicinity of the danger (in either case, whether the other has lawful authority for being in that vicinity or not); and

(c) the risk is one against which, in all the circumstances of the case, he may reasonably be expected to offer the other some protection.

(4) Where, by virtue of this section, an occupier of premises owes a duty to another in respect of such a risk, the duty is to take such care as is reasonable in all the circumstances of the case to see that he does not suffer injury on the premises by reason of the danger concerned.

(5) Any duty owed by virtue of this section in respect of a risk may, in an appropriate case, be discharged by taking such steps as are reasonable in all the circumstances of the case to give warning of the danger concerned or to discourage persons from incurring the risk.

(6) No duty is owed by virtue of this section to any person in respect of risks willingly accepted as his by that person (the question whether a risk was so accepted to be decided

on the same principles as in other cases in which one person owes a duty of care to another).

(7)   No duty is owed by virtue of this section to persons using the highway, and this section does not affect any duty owed to such persons.

(8)   Where a person owes a duty by virtue of this section, he does not, by reason of any breach of the duty, incur any liability in respect of any loss of or damage to property.

(9)   In this section —
    'highway' means any part of a highway other than a ferry or waterway;
    'injury' means anything resulting in death or personal injury, including any disease and any impairment of physical or mental condition; and
    'movable structure' includes any vessel, vehicle or aircraft.

HIGHWAYS ACT 1980

41.   Duty to maintain highways maintainable at public expense
The authority who are for the time being the highway authority for a highway maintainable at the public expense are under a duty . . . to maintain the highway.

58.   Special defence in action against a highway authority for damages for non-repair of highway
(1)   In an action against a highway authority in respect of damage resulting from their failure to maintain a highway maintainable at the public expense it is a defence (without prejudice to any other defence or the application of the law relating to contributory negligence) to prove that the authority had taken such care as in all the circumstances was reasonably required to secure that the part of the highway to which the action relates was not dangerous for traffic.

(2)   For the purposes of a defence under subsection (1) above, the court shall in particular have regard to the following matters: —
    (a)   the character of the highway, and the traffic which was reasonably to be expected to use it;
    (b)   the standard of maintenance appropriate for a highway of that character and used by such traffic;
    (c)   the state of repair in which a reasonable person would have expected to find the highway;
    (d)   whether the highway authority knew, or could reasonably have been expected to know, that the condition of the part of the highway to which the action relates was likely to cause danger to users of the highway;
    (e)   where the highway authority could not reasonably have been expected to repair that part of the highway before the cause of action arose, what warning notices of its condition had been displayed;
but for the purposes of such a defence it is not relevant to prove that the highway authority had arranged for a competent person to carry out or supervise the maintenance of the part of the highway to which the action relates unless it is also proved that the authority had given him proper instructions with regard to the maintenance of the highway and that he had carried out the instructions.

British Railways Board v *Herrington*
House of Lords [1972] AC 877; [1972] 2 WLR 537; [1972] 1 All ER 749

The plaintiff, aged 6, went to play in Bunces Meadow, a National Trust property, near Mitcham in Surrey. Alongside the field was an electrified railway line protected by a chain link fence. The fence had fallen into disrepair and had been trodden down to about ten inches from the ground. The plaintiff went through the fence and was injured by touching the electrified rail. Held: dismissing the appeal, that the defendants were liable. (Note: liability to trespassers is now almost wholly governed by the Occupiers' Liability Act 1984, but this case is included for its potential residual liability in cases not covered by that Act and for the justification given by Lord Pearson for treating trespassers differently from visitors.)

LORD REID: Normally the common law applies an objective test. If a person chooses to assume a relationship with members of the public, say by setting out to drive a car or to erect a building fronting a highway, the law requires him to conduct himself as a reasonable man with adequate skill, knowledge and resources would do. He will not be heard to say that in fact he could not attain that standard. If he cannot attain that standard he ought not to assume the responsibility which that relationship involves. But an occupier does not voluntarily assume a relationship with trespassers. By trespassing they force a 'neighbour' relationship on him. When they do so he must act in a humane manner — that is not asking too much of him — but I do not see why he should be required to do more.

So it appears to me that an occupier's duty to trespassers must vary according to his knowledge, ability and resources. It has often been said that trespassers must take the land as they find it. I would rather say that they must take the occupier as they find him.

So the question whether an occupier is liable in respect of an accident to a trespasser on his land would depend on whether a conscientious humane man with his knowledge, skill and resources could reasonably have been expected to have done or refrained from doing before the accident something which would have avoided it. If he knew before the accident that there was a substantial probability that trespassers would come I think that most people would regard as culpable failure to give any thought to their safety. He might often reasonably think, weighing the seriousness of the danger and the degree of likelihood of trespassers coming against the burden he would have to incur in preventing their entry or making his premises safe, or curtailing his own activities on his land, that he could not fairly be expected to do anything. But if he could at small trouble and expense take some effective action, again I think that most people would think it inhumane and culpable not to do that. If some such principle is adopted there will no longer be any need to strive to imply a fictitious licence.

It would follow that an impecunious occupier with little assistance at hand would often be excused from doing something which a large organisation with ample staff would be expected to do.

LORD PEARSON: There are several reasons why an occupier should not have imposed upon him onerous obligations to a trespasser —

(1)   There is the unpredictability of the possible trespasser both as to whether he will come on the land at all and also as to where he will go and what he will do if he does come on the land. I enlarged on this point in *Videan v British Transport Commission* [1963] 2 QB 650, 679, and I will only summarise it shortly here. As the trespasser's presence and movements are unpredictable, he is not within the zone of reasonable contemplation (*Bourhill v Young* [1943] AC 92) and he is not a 'neighbour'(*Donoghue v Stevenson*) to the occupier, and the occupier cannot reasonably be required to take precautions for his safety. Occupiers are entitled to farm lands, operate quarries and factories, run express trains at full speed through stations, fell trees and fire shots without regard to the mere general possibility that there might happen to be in the

vicinity a trespasser who might be injured. The occupiers do not have to cease or restrict their activities in view of that possibility, which is too remote to be taken into account and could not fairly be allowed to curtail their freedom of action.

(2) Even when his presence is known or reasonably to be anticipated, so that he becomes a neighbour, the trespasser is rightly to be regarded as an under-privileged neighbour. . . .

(3) . . . It would in many, if not most, cases be impracticable to take effective steps to prevent (instead of merely endeavouring to deter) trespassers from going into or remaining in situations of danger. The cost of erecting and maintaining an impenetrable and unclimbable or, as it has been put, 'boy-proof' fence would be prohibitive, if it could be done at all. . . .

(4) There is also a moral aspect. Apart from trespasses which are inadvertent or more or less excusable, trespassing is a form of misbehaviour, showing lack of consideration for the rights of others. It would be unfair if trespassers could by their misbehaviour impose onerous obligations on others. One can take the case of a farmer. He may know well from past experience that persons are likely to trespass on his land for the purpose of tearing up his primroses and bluebells, or picking his mushrooms or stealing his turkeys, or for the purpose of taking country walks in the course of which they will tread down his grass and leave gates open and watch their dogs chasing the farmer's cattle and sheep. It would be intolerable if a farmer had to take expensive precautions for the protection of such persons in such activities.

Section 6: exclusion of liability

Section 2(1) of the Occupiers' Liability Act 1957 allows an occupier to exclude liability 'in so far as he is free to and does extend, restrict, modify or exclude his duty to any visitor or visitors by agreement or otherwise'. This, of course, is subject to the restrictions imposed by the Unfair Contract Terms Act 1977, for which see Chapter 14. As can be seen from *White* v *Blackmore* (below), it is necessary to distinguish between an exclusion notice, which is subject to the Unfair Contract Terms Act, and a warning notice, which is subject to the test of adequacy in s. 2(4) of the Occupiers' Liability Act 1957.

It is generally assumed that an exclusion clause is valid because it varies the terms of the licence granted to the visitor, but if this is the rationale, it is difficult to see how such a notice would restrict liability to trespassers. This creates an anomaly because it could mean that a non-business occupier could exclude liability to visitors but not to trespassers. See Mesher, 'Occupiers, Trespassers and The Unfair Contract Terms Act 1977', (1979) Conv 58.

White v *Blackmore*
Court of Appeal [1972] 2 QB 651; [1972] 3 WLR 296; [1972] 3 All ER 158

Mr White was a member of a jalopy racing club. One morning he took his jalopy car to a field where races were to be held and signed on as a competitor. In the afternoon he went to the field with his family. At the entrance was a notice saying 'Warning to the Public: Motor Racing is Dangerous' and excluding liability to 'spectators or ticket holders'. Mr White paid for his family to enter, but he himself entered free as a competitor. On each programme was a notice excluding liability 'to you'.

After finishing his race Mr White went to stand by the ropes to watch other races. About one-third of a mile away a car collided with the ropes, and the rear wheel acted as a winch and pulled all the safety ropes tight, pulling out the stakes. Mr White was catapulted into the air and later died. Held: dismissing the appeal, that the defendants were not liable.

LORD DENNING MR, *dissenting:* Section 2(4)(a) of the Occupiers' Liability Act 1957 says explicitly: 'where damage is caused to a visitor by a danger of which he had been warned by the occupier, the warning is not to be treated without more as absolving the occupier from liability, unless in all the circumstances it was enough to enable the visitor to be reasonably safe; . . .'

During the argument we were not referred to that subsection: nor was the judge below. But I think it is decisive. The warning notices in this case do not enable the visitor to be reasonably safe. They do not tell him anything about any danger except that 'motor racing is dangerous.' They do not tell him to avoid the danger by going away — for that is the very last thing the organisers want him to do. They want him to come and stay and see the races. By inviting him to come, they are under a duty of care to him: which they cannot avoid by telling him that it is dangerous.

I appreciate, of course, that the warning notices go on to say: 'The organisers will not be liable for any accident howsoever caused.' But that does not make any difference. Or, at any rate, it ought not to do so. It does no more than underline the warning about danger. It is just another attempt to avoid their responsibilities. Suppose there was a stream running through this field with a rotten footbridge across it. A warning 'This bridge is dangerous' would not exempt the occupiers from liability for negligence — see the illustration I gave in *Roles* v *Nathan* [1963] 1 WLR 1117, 1124. It follows that a warning 'Visitors cross this bridge at their own risk' equally does not exempt him. An occupier cannot get round the statute by such a change of wording. It is a warning still and within the statute.

BUCKLEY LJ: When the deceased returned with his family in the afternoon, the notice to which Lord Denning MR has referred was prominently displayed near the entrance to the ground. The judge found as a fact that the deceased saw that notice and appreciated that it was a notice governing the conditions under which people were to be admitted to watch the racing.

No argument was addressed to us based upon the Occupiers' Liability Act 1957, s. 2(4). This, I think, was right. To the extent that the notice at the entrance was a warning of a danger, I agree with Lord Denning MR that it did not enable a visitor to be reasonably safe, but the notice was more than a warning of danger: it was designed to subject visitors to a condition that the classes of persons mentioned in it should be exempt from liability arising out of accidents. Section 2(4) has, it seems to me, no application to this aspect of the notice.

What then was the effect of the situation which arose when the deceased returned to the field in the afternoon? It is clear that the occupier of land, who permits someone else to enter upon that land as his licensee, can by imposing suitable conditions limit his own liability to the licensee in respect of any risks which may arise while the licensee is on the land (*Ashdown* v *Samuel Williams & Sons Ltd* [1957] 1 QB 409). The Occupiers' Liability Act 1957, which in section 2(1) refers to an occupier excluding his duty of care to any visitor 'by agreement or otherwise' has not altered the law in this respect. Mr Griffiths concedes that in the present case the notice displayed at the entrance to the ground was sufficient to exclude liability on the part of the organisers of the meeting to all spectators properly so-called, but he contends that a distinction is to be drawn between competitors and spectators for this purpose. It is common ground that the deceased was not a ticket holder within the meaning of the notice, but, in my judgment, he was a spectator. The judge so held, and I think that he was right in doing so. The notice was, in my opinion, sufficiently explicit in its application to the deceased. I feel unable to accept the suggestion that the heading 'Warning to the Public' should be read in a restrictive sense excluding competitors.

Notes
1. This case would now be decided differently, as under the Unfair Contract Terms Act 1977, the occupier of business premises is no longer permitted to exclude liability for personal injuries, but an occupier of private premises may do so.
2. In *Burnett* v *British Waterways Board* [1973] 1 WLR 700 the plaintiff worked on a barge on the river Thames, and was injured when a rope pulling his barge into a lock snapped. The defendants admitted this was due to the negligence of their staff, but claimed that liability was excluded by a notice at the entrance to the lock. Nevertheless, the defendants were held liable on the grounds that they could not exclude liability where the plaintiff had no choice whether to enter the lock, because he was bound to do so by his contract of employment. (He was not employed by the defendants but by another company.)

Questions
1. A is a postman delivering mail to a private house. On the gate is a notice saying 'Beware of falling slates. No liability is accepted under the Occupiers' Liability Act 1957 for any injury caused to any entrant.' A is hit by a falling slate. Is the occupier liable?
2. How would you deal with the question of whether an exclusion notice affects trespassers? If it does not, how would you resolve the anomaly thereby created in relation to visitors? Should the duty in the 1984 Act or in *Herrington* be an irreducible minimum?

21 NUISANCE

Private nuisance is an ancient wrong designed as an action between neighbouring landowners to protect a person's interest in land from being adversely affected by the activities of his neighbour. The harm is usually indirect, as the tort of trespass protects a person against direct invasion. The tort protects only a limited range of interests such as physical harm to the land or interference with quiet enjoyment of it, and generally a defendant's activity must be unreasonable. The tort therefore defines two things: first, what kinds of interests a person has in his land (e.g. does he have the right to receive television or to have an uninterrupted view), and secondly , if such an interest has been interfered with, whether the level of the interference is unreasonable and has been caused by an unreasonable activity.

Confusion is sometimes caused by the analogous wrong of public nuisance, which has entirely different antecedents, but which covers similar subject matter. The distinction between public and private nuisance will be dealt with first, and public nuisance can then be left to one side.

Section 1:   public and private nuisance

Private nuisance deals with the rights between two landowners, and generally the harm must affect private land. Public nuisance is a crime to which a civil remedy has been attached, and the harm need not emanate from or affect private land. However, a civil action will only be allowed where an individual has suffered harm over and above that experienced by the general public. The various heads of damage claimed in *Halsey* v *Esso Petroleum* (below) neatly illustrate which kinds of harm can be claimed in private and which in public nuisance.

Halsey* v *Esso Petroleum
Queen's Bench Division [1961] 1 WLR 683; [1961] 2 All ER 145

The plaintiffs owned a house in Fulham, opposite which the defendants operated an oil depot. The plaintiff complained of the following: (i) acid smuts from a boiler in the depot which damaged the plaintiff's washing; (ii) the same acid smuts which damaged his car standing in the road outside; (iii) the smell of oil, which was unpleasant but caused no damage to health; (iv) noise from the boilers; (v) noise from lorries in the depot; (vi) noise from lorries on the road entering the depot. Held: the defendants were liable. Heads (i), (iii), (iv) and (v) were private nuisance, and heads (ii) and (vi) were public nuisance.

VEALE J: So far as the present case is concerned, liability for nuisance by harmful deposits could be established by proving damage by the deposits to the property in question, provided of course that the injury was not merely trivial. Negligence is not an ingredient of the cause of action, and the character of the neighbourhood is not a matter to be taken into consideration. On the other hand, nuisance by smell or noise is something to which no absolute standard can be applied. It is always a question of degree whether the interference with comfort or convenience is sufficiently serious to constitute a nuisance. The character of the neighbourhood is very relevant and all the relevant circumstances have to be taken into account. What might be a nuisance in one area is by no means necessarily so in another. In an urban area, everyone must put up with a certain amount of discomfort and annoyance from the activities of neighbours, and the law must strike a fair and reasonable balance between the right of the plaintiff on the one hand to the undisturbed enjoyment of his property, and the right of the defendant on the other hand to use his property for his own lawful enjoyment. That is how I approach this case.

It may be possible in some cases to prove that noise or smell have in fact diminished the value of the plaintiff's property in the market. That consideration does not arise in this case, and no evidence has been called in regard to it. The standard in respect of discomfort and inconvenience from noise and smell which I have to apply is that of the ordinary reasonable and responsible person who lives in this particular area of Fulham. This is not necessarily the same as the standard which the plaintiff chooses to set up for himself. It is the standard of the ordinary man, and the ordinary man, who may well like peace and quiet, will not complain, for instance, of the noise of traffic if he chooses to live on a main street in an urban centre, nor of the reasonable noises of industry, if he chooses to live alongside a factory.

Nuisance is commonly regarded as a tort in respect of land. In *Read* v *J. Lyons & Co. Ltd* [1947] AC 156, Lord Simonds said: 'he alone has a lawful claim who has suffered an invasion of some proprietary or other interest in land.' In this connection the allegation of damage to the plaintiff's motor-car calls for special consideration, since the allegation is that when the offending smuts from the defendants' chimney alighted upon it, the motor-car was not actually upon land in the plaintiff's occupation, but was on the public highway outside his door. In my judgment the plaintiff is also right in saying that if the motor-car was damaged in this way while on the public highway, it is a public nuisance in respect of which he has suffered special damage. . . .

I approach this question [of the smell] with caution, as Mr Gardiner asked me to do, since there has been no injury to health, but injury to health is not a necessary ingredient in the cause of action for nuisance by smell, and authority for that proposition is to be found in the judgment of Lord Romilly MR in *Crump* v *Lambert* (1867) 3 Eq 409, 412. I reject the contention that the evidence for the plaintiff has been exaggerated by people who feel strongly against the defendants on other grounds. I accept the evidence for the plaintiff, and it is right to add that the description by the witnesses of the nature of the smell was confirmed by my own experience on the night of February 10. On that night, at half past eleven, there was in Rainville Road and Wingrave Road, clearly emanating from the defendants' depôt, a nasty smell, which could properly be described, as the plaintiff has described it in his further and better particulars, namely, 'a pungent, rather nauseating smell of an oily character.' The defendants in my judgment are liable for nuisance by smell.

I turn now to the question of nuisance by noise. This question relates to two distinct matters: the noise of the plant and the noise of the vehicles, the latter complaint including the noise of the vehicles themselves and the attendant noises made by drivers shouting and slamming doors and banging pipes. It is in connection with noise that, in my judgment, the operations of the defendants at night are particularly important. After all, one of the main objects of living in a house or flat is to have a room with a bed in it where one can sleep at night. Night is the time when the ordinary man takes his rest. No real complaint is made by the plaintiff so far as the daytime is concerned; but he complains bitterly of the noise at night. . . .

I accept the evidence of the plaintiff as to noise and I hold it is a serious nuisance, going far beyond a triviality, and one in respect of which the plaintiff is entitled to complain. Because of the noise made by the boilers, I think that the plaintiff is not so much, certainly since the throbbing of the steam pumps ceased, troubled by the noise of the electric pumps. But that is because the noise of the pumps is largely drowned by the noise of the boilers, and even if the noise of the boilers stopped, it might be that the plaintiff could justifiably complain of the noise of the pumps.

. . . But bearing in mind, I hope, all the relevant considerations, in my judgment the defendants are liable in nuisance for the noise of their plant, though only at night. Applying and adapting the well-known words of Knight-Bruce V-C in *Walter* v *Selfe*, 64 ER 849, this inconvenience is, as I find to be the fact, more than fanciful, more than one of mere delicacy or fastidiousness. It is an inconvenience materially interfering with the ordinary comfort physically of human existence, not merely according to elegant or dainty modes of living, but according to plain and sober and simple notions among ordinary people living in this part of Fulham.

But the question of noise does not stop there. At intervals through the night tankers leave and come to the defendants' depôt. It has been urged upon me that the public highway is for the use of all, and that is true. But it must be borne in mind that these tankers are not ordinary motor-cars; they are not ordinary lorries which make more noise than a motor-car; they are enormous vehicles, some when laden weighing 24 tons, which, apart from the loud noise of the engine, may rattle as they go, particularly when empty and especially if they hit something in the road like a grating. They all enter the depot almost opposite the plaintiff's house, which involves a sharp turn in order to do so, often changing down into low gear at the same time. They leave by the exit gate which is also close to the plaintiff's house. The noise of a tanker was 83 decibels — in the 'very loud' category. . . .

It is said by the defendants that since the public highway is for the use of everyone, the plaintiff cannot complain if all the defendants do is to make use of their right to use the public highway. I agree, if that is all that the defendants have done. If a person makes an unreasonable use of the public highway, for instance, by parking stationary vehicles on it, a member of the public who suffers special damage has a cause of action against him for public nuisance. Similarly, in my view, if a person makes an unreasonable use of the public highway by concentrating in one small area of the highway vehicles in motion and a member of the public suffers special damage, he is equally entitled to complain, although in most cases concentration of moving as opposed to stationary vehicles will be more likely to be reasonable. . . .

In the particular circumstances of this case I do not think it matters very much whether one regards the alleged nuisance by vehicular noise as a private or a public nuisance. The history of the cause of action for private nuisance is set out by Lord Wright in *Sedleigh-Denfield* v *O'Callaghan* [1940] AC 880. The ground of responsibility is the possession and control of the land from which the nuisance proceeds, though Lord Wright refers to 'possibly certain anomalous exceptions.' Public nuisance on the other hand, as Denning LJ said in the Court of Appeal in *Southport Corporation* v *Esso Petroleum Co.* [1954] 2 QB 182 can cover a multitude of sins, great and small. In this latter case Devlin J, whose judgment is reported as part of the report of the proceedings in the House of Lords [1956] AC 218, said:

> It is clear that to give a cause of action for private nuisance the matter complained of must affect the property of the plaintiffs. But I know of no principle that it must emanate from land belonging to the defendant. Mr Nelson cited *Cunard* v *Antifyre Ltd* [1933] 1 KB 551, and I think that the statement of the principle is put there as clearly and concisely as it can be. Talbot J said; 'Private nuisances, at least in the vast majority of cases, are interferences for a substantial length of time by owners or occupiers of property with the use or enjoyment of neighbouring property; and it would manifestly be inconvenient and unreasonable if the right to complain of such interference extended beyond the occupier, or (in the case of injury to the reversion) the owner, of such neighbouring property.' It is clear from that statement of principle that the nuisance must affect the property of the plaintiff; and it is true that in the vast majority of cases it is likely to emanate from the neighbouring property of the defendant. But no statement of principle has been cited to me to show that the latter is a prerequisite to a cause of action; and I can see no reason why, if land or water belonging to the public, or waste land, is misused by the defendant, or if the defendant as a licensee or trespasser misuses someone else's land, he should not be liable for the creation of a nuisance in the same way as an adjoining occupier would be.

Note
Public nuisance.   An example of a person suffering damage over and above that suffered by the public at large is *Tate and Lyle* **v** *Greater London Council* [1983] 2 AC 509, where the plaintiffs operated a sugar refinery which had a jetty in the River Thames. The defendants' predecessors had built a terminal for the Woolwich Ferry which caused the channel to the plaintiffs' jetty to silt up. It was held that the plaintiffs did not have any *private* rights which enabled them to insist on a certain depth of water round their jetty, so there was no liability in *private* nuisance. However, in relation to *public* nuisance it was held the siltation caused by the ferry terminals was an interference with the public right of navigation, and that the plaintiffs had suffered particular damage over and above that caused to the public at large, and therefore the defendants were liable for public nuisance.

Section 2:   private nuisance: the interests protected

One of the issues which will has come to the fore recently is whether a plaintiff in private nuisance must have an interest in land to be able to sue. The traditional view was that the function of nuisance was to protect a person who has an interest in land in the enjoyment of his property. This included not only freeholders, but also lessees and even tenants at will, but it excluded those with no property interest. For example in *Malone* v *Laskey* [1907] 2 KB 141 it was said that a wife 'who had no interest in property, no right of occupation in the proper sense of the term' could not sue in nuisance for personal injuries arising out of a neighbour's activities. However, *Hunter v Canary Wharf* (below) has now extended the range of those who may sue in nuisance to include those who occupy property as a home, even though they have no actual property rights in the premises.

Nuisance will only protect certain interests of the plaintiff, and whether he has a protectable interest is a matter of law. Physical damage and interference with quiet enjoyment of land are covered, but it is not clear the extent to which the law protects recreational or aesthetic interests. Probably the tort does not protect the value of the property itself as opposed to an invasion of a protectable interest which causes a diminution in value, but *Thompson-Schwab v Costaki* (below) comes dangerously close to simply protecting property values. If the interest is not regarded as protectable, neither unreasonableness nor malice on the defendant's part can make it protectable.

Hunter v Canary Wharf
Court of Appeal [1996] 2 WLR 348; [1996] 1 All ER 482

The plaintiffs, of whom there were several hundred, claimed as either occupiers or persons with a legal estate in property that Canary Wharf Tower interfered with their television reception. This raised questions whether it was necessary to have an interest in property to sue in nuisance and whether television reception was a protectable interest. Held: the defendants were not liable.

PILL LJ: . . . The judge found that it was necessary to have a right of exclusive possession of the property to claim in private nuisance. In *Cambridge Water Co. v Eastern Counties Leather Plc* [1994] 2 AC 264, 297–298 Lord Goff of Chieveley referred to what he described as Professor Newark's seminal article on 'The Boundaries of Nuisance' (1949) 65 LQR 480 as much enhancing our modern understanding of the nature and scope of the law of nuisance. Professor Newark referred, at p. 482, to the origin of nuisance as 'a tort directed against the plaintiff's enjoyment of rights over land,' and, at p. 481, he stated that:

to trouble a man in the exercise of his rights over land without going so far as to dispossess him was a trespass or a nuisance according to whether the act was done on or off the plaintiff's land.

The link with the enjoyment of rights over land is undoubtedly preserved in the modern law. In *Read v J. Lyons & Co. Ltd* [1947] AC 156, 183 Lord Simonds stated that in nuisance 'he alone has a lawful claim who has suffered an invasion of some proprietary or other interest in land.'

For the defendants, Lord Irvine submits that in order to sue in private nuisance a plaintiff must establish a proprietary or possessory interest in land; mere occupation is insufficient. Nuisance is characterised by the protection of proprietary interests. Lord Irvine relies on the Court of Appeal decision in *Malone v Laskey* [1907] 2 KB 141. The plaintiff was injured when vibration caused by machinery upon adjoining premises of the defendants dislodged a bracket on premises where she lived with her husband whose occupation of the premises was a part of his remuneration as a company manager. Sir Gorell Barnes, P. stated, at p. 151:

no authority was cited, nor in my opinion can any principle of law be formulated, to the effect that a person who has no interest in property, no right of occupation in the proper sense of the term, can maintain an action for nuisance arising from the vibration by the working of an engine in an adjoining house.

Fletcher Moulton LJ stated, at p. 153, that 'a person in the position of the plaintiff, who was in the premises as a mere licensee, had no right' to sue. Kennedy LJ stated, at p. 155, that 'the mere existence of vibration amounting only to a private nuisance to the occupiers of the premises gave no cause of action to the plaintiff in respect of the alleged consequences of the vibration.'

In *Metropolitan Properties Ltd* v *Jones* [1939] 2 All ER 202, 205 Goddard LJ, sitting as an additional judge in the Queen's Bench Division, stated:

I am bound by *Malone* v *Laskey* [1907] 2 KB 141, in which the Court of Appeal appear to me to have laid down in terms that, unless the plaintiff in an action for nuisance had legal interest in the land which is alleged to be affected by the nuisance, he has no cause of action. . . .

For the plaintiffs, Mr Brennan distinguishes a claim in private nuisance for interference with the use and enjoyment in land from other forms of nuisance, namely, causing an encroachment on a neighbour's land and causing physical damage to that land. He submits that, in a claim based on interference, a plaintiff need prove only substantial occupation of the property, in the sense of an occupation of the property or lawful presence in property as his or her home, to be able to claim in private nuisance. He relies upon the decision of this court in *Khorasandjian* v *Bush* [1993] QB 727, Dillon and Rose LJJ, Peter Gibson J dissenting. It was held that harassment by unwanted telephone calls amounting to interference with the recipient's reasonable enjoyment of property where the recipient was lawfully present could be restrained quia timet as a private nuisance. Dillon LJ with whose judgment Rose LJ agreed, referred to the decision of the Appellate Division of the Alberta Supreme Court in *Motherwell* v *Motherwell* (1976) 73 DLR (3d) 62. In that case, notwithstanding *Malone* v *Laskey* [1907] 2 KB 141, the court held that the wife of the owner of property had the right to restrain harassing telephone calls to the matrimonial home, Clement JA stating, at p. 78:

Here we have a wife harassed in the matrimonial home. She has a status, a right to live here with her husband and children. I find it absurd to say that her occupancy of the matrimonial home is insufficient to found an action in nuisance.

Citing that judgment Dillon LJ stated, at p. 735:

I respectfully agree, and in my judgment this court is entitled to adopt the same approach. The court has at times to reconsider earlier decisions in the light of changed social conditions; . . . the wife of the owner is entitled to sue in respect of harassing telephone calls, then I do not see why that should not also apply to a child living at home with her parents.

Earlier in his judgment Dillon LJ referred to the defendant's acceptance, in relation to the telephone calls, that the plaintiff's mother could have claimed in private nuisance on the basis of persistent unwanted calls if she had a freehold or leasehold interest in the parental home. Dillon LJ stated, at p. 734:

To my mind, it is ridiculous if in this present age the law is that the making of deliberately harassing and pestering telephone calls to a person is only actionable in the civil courts if the recipient of the calls happens to have the freehold or a leasehold proprietary interest in the premises in which he or she has received the calls. . . .

It is conceded by the defendants that a spouse with an equitable interest in property under a resulting trust has the right to sue in nuisance. The acknowledgement by Parliament and the courts, it is submitted by the plaintiffs, of non-proprietorial rights in property requires the law to permit, as Dillon LJ did in *Khorasandjian* v *Bush* [1993] QB 727, a relaxation of the requirement for a legal possessory title in the property. Mr Brennan refers, with justification, to the complex inquiry often required to decide whether or not a spouse has an equitable interest in the matrimonial home. A spouse's right to protect the use and enjoyment of property should not depend on whether or not he or she can establish an interest in land, the enjoyment of one's home not varying in importance with whether or not, for example, one has contributed to the purchase price or can otherwise establish a resulting trust. Also, a difficulty is that the member of the family with title may be away from home when family members in occupation need to seek relief from a nuisance urgently.

If the plaintiffs are correct that a spouse without an interest in the property can sue, it is difficult to distinguish his or her position from that of a child residing in the family home. In *Devon Lumber Co. Ltd* v *MacNeill* (1987) 45 DLR (4th) 300 the New Brunswick Court of Appeal held, by a majority, that children lacking legal title were entitled to sue in nuisance. Stratton CJNB, having referred to Professor Fleming's opinion (*Fleming, The Law of Torts*, 6th ed. (1983), at pp. 393–394) that it would be 'senseless discrimination' to deprive a tenant's family of the right to sue, stated, at p. 303:

> I would accordingly conclude and hold that even though the children lacked any legal title to the property they had a right of occupation sufficient to support an action on their behalf for damages for any unreasonable and substantial interference with their lawful use or enjoyment of the family residence.

In other cases, the right to sue will, if the defendants are correct, depend upon prior resolution of the question whether a resident is a tenant or a licensee. That may be a complex question and its resolution does not depend upon the extent to which the land is occupied and enjoyed. Determining whether a person is in substantial occupation, in the sense for which the plaintiffs contend, may also be a difficult exercise in some cases but the test is at least directly related to the interest to be protected, that is the use and enjoyment.

I bear in mind that we are asked to decide the preliminary question without being under the discipline of having to decide a particular case and without even being provided with particulars of the nature of the occupancies which it is sought to protect. We are told that the main concern is with members of the owner's family but, upon the test advanced by the plaintiffs, the position of lodgers would also arise, as would, for example, people in residential homes for the sick or elderly and in institutions.

This part of the law of nuisance deals with interference with the use and enjoyment of land. In *Sedleigh-Denfield* v *O'Callaghan* [1940] AC 880, 902–903 Lord Wright identified the 'essential character' of the cause of action for damages for a private nuisance and how an action on the case for nuisance superseded the Assize of Nuisance. He stated:

> This action was less limited in its scope, because whereas the Assize was by a freeholder against a freeholder, the action lay also between possessors or occupiers of land. With possibly certain anomalous exceptions, not here material, possession or occupation is still the test.

In his *History and Sources of the Common Law* (1949) C. H. S. Fifoot stated, at p. 95:

The inheritance to which Case succeeded, though enlarged in scope, retained its original character. The plaintiff, if he need no longer be a freeholder, must still complain of an injury to land or its appurtenances.

A substantial link between the person enjoying the use and the land on which he or she is enjoying it is essential but, in my judgment, occupation of property, as a home, does confer upon the occupant a capacity to sue in private nuisance.

There has been a trend in the law to give additional protection to occupiers in some circumstances. Given that trend and the basis of the law of nuisance in this context, it is no longer tenable to limit the sufficiency of that link by reference to proprietary or possessory interests in land. I regard satisfying the test of occupation of property as a home provides a sufficient link with the property to enable the occupier to sue in private nuisance. It is an application in present-day conditions of the essential character of the test as contemplated by Lord Wright. It appears to me, as it did to Dillon LJ to be right in principle and to avoid inconsistencies, for example between members of a family, which in this context cannot now be justified. . . .

Is the interference with television reception capable of constituting an actionable private nuisance?
The judge answered this question in the affirmative. The presence of Canary Wharf made it impossible for the plaintiffs to watch television transmissions from Crystal Palace. As an interference with their enjoyment of their premises, it was an actionable nuisance.

In *Bridlington Relay Ltd* v *Yorkshire Electricity Board* [1965] Ch 436 the plaintiffs erected a mast in order to provide a relay system of sound and television broadcasts. The defendant erected an overhead power line the effect of which would be to interfere with the reception of radio and television transmission at the mast. Buckley J declined to grant an injunction. In the course of his judgment, Buckley J stated, at p. 447:

For myself, however, I do not think that it can at present be said that the ability to receive television free from occasional, even if recurrent and severe, electrical interference is so important a part of an ordinary householders' enjoyment of his property that such interference should be regarded as a legal nuisance, particularly, perhaps, if such interference affects only one of the available alternative programmes.

Buckley J accepted, at p. 446, that television had become a 'very common feature of domestic life,' that it was 'enjoyed almost entirely for what . . . must be regarded as recreational purposes' and held, at p. 448, that 'a user of an ordinary domestic aerial for domestic enjoyment could not succeed on a claim for nuisance.'

For the plaintiffs, Mr Brennan relies upon the judge's finding in this case that television reception now plays 'an important part of an ordinary householder's enjoyment of his property.' In *Nor-Video Services Ltd* v *Ontario* (1978) 84 DLR (3d) 221, 231 Robins J in the Ontario High Court stated:

Whatever may have been the situation in England at the time of *Bridlington*, in my opinion it is manifest that in Canada today television viewing is an important incident of ordinary enjoyment of property and should be protected as such. It is clearly a principal source of information, education and entertainment for a large part of the country's population; an inability to receive it or an unreasonable interference with its reception would to my mind undoubtedly detract from the beneficial use and ownership of property . . .

In the *Nor-Video* case, as in the *Bridlington* case [1965] Ch 436, what caused the interference with the television operation was an electrical power operation. In the present case, it is the presence of the building and not any activity in the building which interferes with the television signal. The tower is extremely tall but I am not prepared to assume that it is unique amongst buildings in interfering with television reception. Tall and bulky buildings have become a feature of urban landscapes. . . .

Lord Irvine submits that interference with television reception by reason of the presence of a building is properly to be regarded as analogous to loss of aspect. To obstruct the receipt of television signals by the erection of a building between the point of receipt and the source is not in law a nuisance.

In *Aldred's Case* (1610) 9 Co Rep 57b Wray CJ cited what he had said in *Bland* v *Moseley* (1587) 9 Co Rep 58a:

> for prospect, which is a matter only of delight, and not of necessity, no action lies for stopping thereof, and yet it is a great commendation of a house if it has a long and large prospect . . . But the law does not give an action for such things of delight (citing Ecclesias. 11.7.)

In *Attorney-General* v *Doughty* (1752) 2 Ves Sen 453 it was sought to prevent construction of buildings which would intercept the view from Gray's Inn gardens. Lord Hardwicke LC stated:

> I know no general rule of common law, which warrants that, or says, that building so as to stop another's prospect is a nuisance. Was that the case, there could be no great towns; and I must grant injunctions to all the new buildings in this town; . . .

. . . I accept the importance of television in the lives of very many people. However, in my judgment the erection or presence of a building in the line of sight between a television transmitter and other properties is not actionable as an interference with the use and enjoyment of land. The analogy with loss of prospect is compelling. The loss of a view, which may be of the greatest importance to many householders, is not actionable and neither is the mere presence of a building in the sight line to the television transmitter. While the authorities which established the limit of the tort of nuisance in this respect are old, the reasoning behind them is not only sound but is applicable to modern conditions. In circumstances such as the present, I would answer the question posed in the negative. Interference with television signals by, for example, the operation of machinery, is a different question which does not arise for determination in the present case. The Wireless Telegraphy Act 1949, as amended, provides sanctions in some circumstances.

Notes

1.   Lack of television reception probably reduces the value of a house but that is not by itself sufficient to create a protectable interest, although some cases such as *Thompson-Schwab* (below) came close to amounting to that.

2.   *Hunter* v *Canary Wharf* does not say that television reception can never be a protectable interest although *Bridlington Relay* (referred to in *Hunter*) did say that. Do you think that interference by electrical machinery ought to be a nuisance?

3.   As to extra-sensitive plaintiffs, the rule is that an extra-sensitive plaintiff can only sue if a person of ordinary sensitivity could have sued. In other words, a person cannot impose a higher burden of care upon his neighbour by engaging

in especially sensitive activities. In *Robinson* v *Kilvert* (1889) 41 ChD 88 the defendants manufactured paper boxes in the cellar of a building, and this required considerable heat which damaged the plaintiff's stock of brown paper on the floor above. It was found that the heat would not have injured normal paper, and therefore the defendant was not liable. If normal paper would have been harmed the plaintiff could have sued, even though his paper was actually more sensitive: see *Mackinnon Industries* v *Walker* [1951] 3 DLR 557.

Thompson-Schwab v *Costaki*
Court of Appeal [1956] 1 WLR 335; [1956] 1 All ER 652

The plaintiff owned 13 Chesterfield Street in London. The defendants, Blanche Marie Costaki and Carol Sullivan, were prostitutes who occupied 12 Chesterfield Street. The plaintiff complained of the existence of the brothel and of the fact that the prostitutes solicited in the street. He stated that Chesterfield Street was a good class residential street and that the existence of the brothel depreciated the value of his house and interfered with his comfortable enjoyment of it. Held: dismissing the appeal, that an interlocutory injunction would be granted on the grounds of nuisance.

LORD EVERSHED MR: The question raised by this appeal is a matter of some public interest and, I do not doubt, some public importance too. . . . Mr Lindner and Mr Stenham, for the defendants, have put the first plank in their case boldly, thus: they say that the law of nuisance, as it has been developed from the ancient assize, has never comprehended activities of this kind which, they say, though possibly shocking to the susceptibilities of ordinary people, does not in any material, that is physical, way interfere with the land of the plaintiffs or their use of it. That such is their case — whether entirely of their own motion or not I do not pause to inquire — is perhaps made plainer by the circumstance that the defence which they have, as we were told, put in makes it clear that, according to their submission, they should be free (that is, without impinging upon the civil rights of any other person) to use these premises for the purposes of prostitution to their heart's content and in any way they like. That certainly seems a bold plea. But Mr Lindner has pointed out with truth that no case has come before the courts in which this kind of activity has been held to constitute a common law nuisance.

In *Sedleigh-Denfield* v *O'Callaghan* [1940] AC 880, Lord Wright said: 'It is impossible to give any precise or universal formula, but it may broadly be said that a useful test is perhaps what is reasonable according to the ordinary usages of mankind living in society, or more correctly in a particular society. The forms which nuisance may take are protean.'

In the years 1955 and 1956 I daresay that the activities of prostitutes are less taboo in ordinary polite conversation than they were a hundred years ago; and it is true that so far as the evidence in this case goes there is nothing about the activities of the two defendants which is shown to be unlawful in the sense of being illegal or criminal. But it does not, to my mind, follow at all that their activities should, therefore, be regarded as free from the risk or possibility that they cause a nuisance in the proper sense of that term to a neighbour merely because they do not impinge upon the senses — for example, the nose or the ear — as would the emanation of smells or fumes or noises. In other words, the test as it seems to me (and I adopt it for the purposes of this appeal) is that which I have stated, namely, whether what is being done interferes with the plaintiffs in the comfortable and convenient enjoyment of their land, regard being had, to borrow Lord Wright's language, to the usages in this matter of civilized society, and regard being also had to the character, as proved, of the neighbourhood.

The plaintiffs have shown, in my opinion, a sufficient prima facie case to the effect that the activities being conducted at No. 12 Chesterfield Street are not only open, but they are notorious, and such as force themselves upon the sense of sight at least of the residents in No. 13. The perambulations of the prostitutes and of their customers is something which is obvious, which is blatant, and which, as I think, the first plaintiff has shown prima facie to constitute not a mere hurt of his sensibilities as a fastidious man, but so as to constitute a sensible interference with the comfortable and convenient enjoyment of his residence, where live with him his wife, his son and his servants. . . .

Let me say one other thing which might have been said earlier. It is, I should have thought, obvious, having regard to the proximity of other streets with a less savoury reputation, that if this kind of use of houses is allowed to creep into Chesterfield Street, the whole character of the street might very soon and very seriously change for the worse. That, I think, is a circumstance which it is proper to bear in mind in considering whether, pending the trial, an injunction should be granted to protect the plaintiffs in their use of their own residences. . . .

Question

What interest was being protected in this case? Would a centre for the re-habilitation of alcoholics or drug users be a nuisance? What about an AIDS hospice? Would a family of Eastenders be a nuisance in Belgravia?

Notes

1. *Thompson-Schwab* was followed in *Laws v Florinplace* [1981] 1 All ER 659, where an interlocutory injunction was granted on the grounds of nuisance, preventing the use of premises in Pimlico in London as a sex shop. Vinelott J said that there was at least a triable issue for the purposes of whether an interlocutory injunction should be granted as to whether a sex shop is in itself a nuisance. It was also said that, even though 80 per cent of the customers may be mature and normal men, the risk of the other 20 per cent being unbalanced and a danger to residents could not be brushed aside. Do you think that if the case had gone to full trial a permanent injunction should have been granted? If so, what interest was being protected? What if the defendants had been granted a licence by the local authority to operate a sex shop? (In fact they had not and were operating in breach of planning regulations.)

2. If the interest invaded is not regarded as a protected interest in law, not even an intentional or malicious interference will ground an action. In other words, malice cannot change an unprotected interest into a protected one. In *Mayor of Bradford v Pickles* [1985] AC 587 the defendant owned land through which water percolated which ultimately was collected in the Corporation reservoirs. The defendant wanted the Corporation to buy his land, or at least his rights to the water, and he deliberately obstructed the flow of water to the reservoir by sinking a shaft. It was held that as the plaintiffs had no right to receive percolating water, the fact that the defendant was acting maliciously could not convert into a nuisance what would otherwise not be a nuisance.

3. Malice can deprive a defendant of two arguments: first, that his use of land was reasonable, and, secondly, that the plaintiff's user was extra-sensitive. In *Hollywood Silver Fox Farm* v *Emmett* [1936] 2 KB 468 the defendant objected to the plaintiff's development of his land as a mink farm, and accordingly he fired shotguns near the plaintiff's mink pens. Firing shot guns does not make an unreasonable noise and is a reasonable use of land in the country. However mink are extra-sensitive, in that when subjected to loud noises they tend to devour their young. It was held that the defendant was liable. Intentionally causing harm is not a reasonable use of land, and if a person intends a consequence he cannot claim it is too remote or sensitive.

Section 3:   reasonable user

The standard required of an occupier is that of reasonable use of land. This is quite different from reasonableness in negligence for it relates to a balance between what it is reasonable for a person to do on his land and what it is reasonable for his neighbour to put up with. This relates not only to the kind of activity but also to its gravity and both will be subject to society's view at the time as to what is reasonable, as well as to the utility of the defendant's conduct. *Halsey* v *Esso Petroleum* (above, section 1) is a good example of this balancing process.

St Helens Smelting Co. v *Tipping*
House of Lords (1865) 11 ER 1483

The plaintiff owned property near the defendants' smelting works, and he complained that noxious gases, vapours and other matter caused damage to hedges and trees and interfered with the beneficial use of his land. Held: the defendants were liable.

LORD WESTBURY LC: My Lords, in matters of this description it appears to me that it is a very desirable thing to mark the difference between an action brought for a nuisance upon the ground that the alleged nuisance produces material injury to the property, and an action brought for a nuisance on the ground that the thing alleged to be a nuisance is productive of sensible personal discomfort. With regard to the latter, namely, the personal inconvenience and interference with one's enjoyment, one's quiet, one's personal freedom, anything that discomposes or injuriously affects the senses of the nerves, whether that may or may not be denominated a nuisance, must undoubtedly depend greatly on the circumstances of the place where the thing complained of actually occurs. If a man lives in a town, it is necessary that he should subject himself to the consequences of those operations of trade which may be carried on in his immediate locality, which are actually necessary for trade and commerce, and also for the enjoyment of property, and for the benefit of the inhabitants of the town and of the public at large. If a man lives in a street where there are numerous shops, and a shop is opened next door to him, which is carried on in a fair and reasonable way, he has no ground for complaint, because to himself individually there may arise much discomfort from the trade carried on in that shop. But when an occupation is carried on by one person in the neighbourhood of another, and the result of that trade, or occupation, or business, is a material injury to property, then there unquestionably arises a very different consideration. I think, my Lords, that in a case of that description, the submission which is required from persons living in society to that amount of discomfort which may be necessary for the legitimate and free exercise of the trade of their neighbours, would not apply to circumstances the immediate result of which is sensible injury to the value of the property.

Notes
1. In *Sturges* v *Bridgman* (1879) 11 ChD 852, at p. 865, Thesiger LJ said 'What would be a nuisance in Belgrave Square would not necessarily be so in Bermondsey'. Bermondsey was well known for its tanneries, which used urine and excreta in the tanning process.
2. With regard to interference with enjoyment, Knight-Bruce LJ said in *Walter* v *Selfe* (1851) 64 ER 849 that the question is:

> ought this inconvenience to be considered in fact as more than fanciful, more than one of mere delicacy or fastidiousness, as an inconvenience materially interfering with the ordinary comfort physically of human existence, not merely according to elegant or dainty modes and habits of living, but according to plain and sober and simple notions among the English people.

Section 4:   who is liable?

The creator of a nuisance is liable as is a person who is 'responsible' for its continuance. Thus an occupier can be liable for a nuisance created by a trespasser if he 'adopts' or 'continues' that nuisance (*Sedleigh Denfield*, below). Equally a person can be liable for a natural hazard which he ought to have removed and can be liable when he has authorised an act which in ordinary circumstances will amount to a nuisance, as in *Tetley* v *Chitty* [1986] 1 All ER 663, where a local authority authorised the use of its land in a residential area as a go-kart racing circuit.

Sedleigh-Denfield v *O'Callaghan*
House of Lords [1940] AC 880; [1940] 3 All ER 349; 164 LT 72

The Middlesex County Council had replaced a culvert with a pipe: the end of the pipe projected about two feet onto the defendant's land, and therefore the council were technically trespassing when they put the pipe there. The workmen placed a grating over the end of the pipe to prevent leaves blocking it, but this was done incorrectly, as the grating was placed directly onto the end of the pipe so the leaves would collect on the grating and block the pipe. The grating should have been placed a foot or two in front of the opening. After the pipe was in place the defendant's workmen regularly cleaned out the ditch and the end of the pipe. In 1937 a severe storm blocked the pipe and caused flooding on the plaintiff's neighbouring land. Held: allowing the appeal, the defendant was liable for the nuisance.

LORD ATKIN: In this state of the facts the legal position is not I think difficult to discover. For the purposes of ascertaining whether as here the plaintiff can establish a private nuisance I think that nuisance is sufficiently defined as a wrongful interference with another's enjoyment of his land or premises by the use of land or premises either occupied or in some cases owned by oneself. The occupier or owner is not an insurer; there must be something more than the mere harm done to the neighbour's property to make the party responsible. Deliberate act or negligence is not an essential ingredient but some degree of personal responsibility is required, which is connoted in my definition by the word 'use.' This conception is implicit in all the decisions which impose liability only where the defendant has 'caused or continued' the nuisance. We may eliminate in this case 'caused.' What is the meaning of 'continued'? In the context in which it is used 'continued' must indicate mere passive continuance. If a man uses on premises something which he found there, and which itself causes a nuisance by noise, vibration, smell or fumes, he is himself in continuing to bring into existence the noise, vibration, etc., causing a nuisance. Continuing in this sense and causing are the same thing. It seems to me clear that if a man permits an offensive thing on his premises to continue to offend, that is, if he knows that it is operating offensively, is able to prevent it, and omits to prevent it, he is permitting the nuisance to continue; in other words he is continuing it. The liability of an occupier has been carried so far that it appears to have been decided that, if he comes to occupy, say as tenant, premises upon which a cause of nuisance exists, caused by a previous occupier, he is responsible even though he does not know that either the cause or the result is in existence. . . .

In the present case, however, there is as I have said sufficient proof of the knowledge of the defendants both of the cause and its probable effect. What is the legal result of the original cause being due to the act of a trespasser? In my opinion the defendants clearly continued the nuisance for they come clearly within the terms I have mentioned above, they knew the danger, they were able to prevent it and they omitted to prevent it. In this respect at least there seems to me to be no difference between the case of a public nuisance and a private nuisance, and the case of *Attorney-General* v *Tod-Heatley* [1897] 1 Ch 560, is conclusive to show that where the occupier has knowledge of a public nuisance, has the means of remedying it and fails to do so, he may be enjoined from allowing it to continue. I cannot think that the obligation not to 'continue' can have a different meaning in 'public' and in 'private' nuisances. . . .

LORD WRIGHT: Though the rule has not been laid down by this House, it has I think been rightly established in the Court of Appeal that an occupier is not prima facie responsible for a nuisance created without his knowledge and consent. If he is to be liable a further condition is necessary, namely, that he had knowledge or means of knowledge, that he knew or should have known of the nuisance in time to correct it and obviate its mischievous effects. The liability for a nuisance is not, at least in modern law, a strict or absolute liability. If the defendant by himself or those for whom he is responsible has created what constitutes a nuisance and if it causes damage, the difficulty now being considered does not arise. But he may have taken over the nuisance, ready made as it were, when he acquired the property, or the nuisance may be due to a latent defect or to the act of a trespasser, or stranger. Then he is not liable unless he continued or adopted the nuisance, or, more accurately, did not without undue delay remedy it when he became aware if it, or with ordinary and reasonable care should have become aware of it. This rule seems to be in accordance with good sense and convenience. The responsibility which attaches to the occupier because he has possession and control of the property cannot logically be limited to the mere creation of the nuisance. It should extend to his conduct if, with knowledge, he leaves the nuisance on his land. The same is true if the nuisance was such that with ordinary care in the management of his property he should have realised the risk of its existence. . . .

Note
A person can be liable even for natural phenomena which cause a nuisance. In *Leakey* v *National Trust* [1980] QB 485 the plaintiffs owned houses next to a large mound in Somerset called the Burrow Mump which was owned by the defendants. Part of the mound subsided and encroached on the plaintiffs' houses. The defendants were held liable even though the mound was a natural one and the subsidence was caused by the forces of nature. It was said by the Court of Appeal that the defendant's obligation is what it is reasonable for him as an individual to do, taking account, for example, of his means, and the practicality of taking preventative measures.

Question
Would the defendant in *Sedleigh-Denfield* v *O'Callaghan* have been liable if, although knowing of the existence of the ditch and the pipe, he completely ignored them and was unaware of how the pipe and grating had been put together?

Section 5:   remoteness of damage

Substantive liability in nuisance does not depend on fault for as we have seen the controlling factor is reasonable use of land. In *Wagon Mound No. 2* [1967] 1 AC 617 Lord Reid said that 'negligence is not an essential element in nuisance' but nevertheless went on to say that foreseeability is relevant in relation to remoteness of damage. This has now been confirmed by the *Cambridge Water* case (below). Thus an occupier who creates a nuisance will be liable if his acts are an unreasonable use of land, but will only be liable in so far as the kind of damage which occurred was foreseeable. Hence 'fault' plays a different role in nuisance as it is only relevant at the remoteness stage and foreseeability for this purpose may be weaker than that required to establish a duty of care in negligence. Thus it may be premature to regard nuisance as being wholly subsumed under negligence.

Cambridge Water Co. v Eastern Counties Leather
House of Lords [1994] 1 All ER 53; [1994] 2 WLR 53

This case concerned contamination of the plaintiff's bore hole by a chemical which seeped into the ground water from the defendant's tannery. It was found that a reasonable supervisor at the tannery would not have foreseen that spillage of the chemical would cause contamination. For further facts see Chapter 23. During the course of discussing liability under the rule in *Rylands* v *Fletcher* Lord Goff made the following comments about the law of nuisance.

LORD GOFF:

Foreseeability of damage in nuisance
It is, of course, axiomatic that in this field we must be on our guard, when considering liability for damages in nuisance, not to draw inapposite conclusions from cases concerned only with a claim for an injunction. This is because, where an injunction is claimed, its purpose is to restrain further action by the defendant which may interfere with the plaintiff's enjoyment of his land, and ex hypothesi the defendant must be aware, if and when an injunction is granted, that such interference may be caused by the act which he is restrained from committing. It follows that these cases provide no guidance on the question whether foreseeability of harm of the relevant type is a prerequisite of the recovery of damages for causing such harm to the plaintiff. In the present case, we are not concerned with liability in damages in respect of a nuisance which has arisen through natural causes, or by the act of a person for whose actions the defendant is not responsible, in which cases the applicable principles in nuisance have become closely associated with those applicable in negligence: see *Sedleigh-Denfield* v *O'Callaghan* [1940] AC 880 and *Goldman* v *Hargrave* [1967] 1 AC 645. We are concerned with the liability of a person where a nuisance has been created by one for whose actions he is responsible. Here, as I have said, it is still the law that the fact that the defendant has taken all reasonable care will not of itself exonerate him from liability, the relevant control mechanism being found within the principle of reasonable user. But it by no means follows that the defendant should be held liable for damage of a type which he could not reasonably foresee; and the development of the law of negligence in the past 60 years points strongly towards a requirement that such foreseeability should be a prerequisite of liability in damages for nuisance, as it is of liability in negligence. For if a plaintiff is in ordinary circumstances only able to claim damages in respect of personal injuries where he can prove such foreseeability on the part of the defendant, it is difficult to see why, in common justice, he should be in a stronger position to claim damages for interference with the enjoyment of his land where the defendant was unable to foresee such damage. Moreover, this appears to have been the conclusion of the Privy Council in *Overseas Tankship (UK) Ltd* v *Miller Steamship Co. Pty (The Wagon Mound (No. 2))* [1967] 1 AC 617. The facts of the case are too well known to require repetition, but they gave rise to a claim for damages arising from a public nuisance caused by a spillage of oil in Sydney Harbour. Lord Reid, who delivered the advice of the Privy Council, considered that, in the class of nuisance which included the case before the Board, foreseeability is an essential element in determining liability. He then continued, at p. 640:

> It could not be right to discriminate between different cases of nuisance so as to make foreseeability a necessary element in determining damages in those cases where it is a necessary element in determining liability, but not in others. So the choice is between it being a necessary element in all cases of nuisance or in none. In their Lordships' judgment the similarities between nuisance and other forms of tort to which *The Wagon Mound (No. 1)* applies far outweigh any differences, and they must therefore hold that the judgment appealed from is wrong on this branch of the case. It is not sufficient that the injury suffered by the respondents' vessels was the direct result of the nuisance if that injury was in the relevant sense unforeseeable.

It is widely accepted that this conclusion, although not essential to the decision of the particular case, has nevertheless settled the law to the effect that foreseeability of harm is indeed a prerequisite of the recovery of damages in private nuisance, as in the case of public nuisance. I refer in particular to the opinion expressed by Professor Fleming in

Fleming on the Law of Torts, 8th ed. (1992), pp. 443–444. It is unnecessary in the present case to consider the precise nature of this principle; but it appears from Lord Reid's statement of the law that he regarded it essentially as one relating to remoteness of damage.

Notes

1. The passage in Fleming on Torts referred to by Lord Goff is as follows:

> The loss must, of course, not be too remote. Resolving all prior doubts, the Privy Council in *The Wagon Mound (No. 2)*, a case of public nuisance, held that this depended, as in negligence, on whether the injury was reasonably foreseeable rather than, as was once thought, on whether it was merely 'direct'. Admittedly, negligence in the narrow sense is not always essential to liability. It will be recalled that in *The Wagon Mound* the defendants had been found negligent with respect to the spillage of oil and it would have been Pickwickian to determine their liability for the subsequent fire by a different test in nuisance than in negligence. But the court went further and prescribed the same rule of remoteness for all cases of nuisance regardless of whether fault or negligence happened to be a necessary element of liability. Another important step was thus taken in consolidating the fault element in the modern law of nuisance and assimilating nuisance with the pervasive theory of negligence.

2. This principle will be important where a person knowingly does an unjustified act and can foresee some damage will follow but not damage of the kind that occurred. As Lord Goff pointed out, the control on 'substantive' liability is reasonable user and foreseeability only comes in as a matter of remoteness of damage. Thus in the *Wagon Mound (No. 2)* the defendants could foresee that the oil they discharged would foul neighbouring slipways but not that it would cause a fire. This may limit common law liability for pollution, for example where a person unjustifiably discharges waste which he has no reason to believe is toxic but which is later found to have caused damage. See further discussion of the *Cambridge Water* case in Chapter 23 and Cross, 'Does only the careless polluter pay?' (1994) 111 LQR 445.

Section 6:   statutory authority and planning permission

Statutory authority to engage in activities can be a defence to any tort, but it most commonly arises in relation to nuisance. If Parliament has authorised the commission of a nuisance there can be no liability, but statutes are rarely explicit on the issue, and the question will often be whether an authorised act will necessarily amount to a nuisance. If it will there is no liability, but where the interference with the plaintiff's interests is greater than or different from the necessary consequences of the authorised act, there will be no defence.

   Similar problems arise where the granting of planning permission might appear to authorise a nuisance. It appears that where 'zoning' issues are involved it may do so if the nuisance is an inevitable consequence of a change in character of the neighbourhood brought about by planning permission, but in other cases activities authorised by planning permission must be carried on in such a way as not to create a nuisance.

Allen v Gulf Oil Refining Ltd
House of Lords [1981] AC 1001; [1981] 2 WLR 188; [1981] 1 All ER 353

The plaintiffs sued for nuisances caused by the Gulf Oil refinery at Waterston in Wales. The Gulf Oil Refining Act 1965 authorised the company to compulsorily purchase land for the construction of a refinery, but said nothing about the use or operation of it. The House of Lords held (Lord Keith dissenting) that the power to purchase land for a refinery necessarily implied the operation of a refinery. Held: allowing the appeal, that the defence of statutory authority applied and the defendants were not liable.

LORD WILBERFORCE: We are here in the well charted field of statutory authority. It is now well settled that where Parliament by express direction or by necessary implication has authorised the construction and use of an undertaking or works, that carries with it an authority to do what is authorised with immunity from any action based on nuisance. The right of action is taken away: *Hammersmith and City Railway Co.* v *Brand* (1869) LR 4 HL 171, 215 *per* Lord Cairns. To this there is made the qualification, or condition, that the statutory powers are exercised without 'negligence' — that word here being used in a special sense so as to require the undertaker, as a condition of obtaining immunity from action, to carry out the work and conduct the operation with all reasonable regard and care for the interests of other persons: *Geddis* v *Proprietors of Bann Reservoir* (1878) 3 App Cas 430, 455 *per* Lord Blackburn. It is within the same principle that immunity from action is withheld where the terms of the statute are permissive only, in which case the powers conferred must be exercised in strict conformity with private rights: *Metropolitan Asylum District* v *Hill* (1881) 6 App Cas 193. . . .

My Lords, . . . Parliament considered it in the public interest that a *refinery*, not merely the works (jetties etc.), should be constructed, and constructed upon lands at Llandstadwell to be compulsorily acquired.

To show how this intention was to be carried out I need only quote section 5:

(1) Subject to the provisions of this Act, the company may enter upon, take and use such of the lands delineated on the deposited plans and described in the deposited book of reference as it may require for the purposes of the authorised works or *for the construction of a refinery* in the parish of Llandstadwell in the rural district of Haverfordwest in the county of Pembroke or for purposes ancillary thereto or connected therewith.   (2)   The powers of compulsory acquisition of land under this section shall cease after the expiration of three years from October 1, 1965.

. . .

I cannot but regard this as an authority — whether it should be called express or by necessary implication may be a matter of preference — but an authority to construct and operate *a refinery* upon the lands to be acquired — a refinery moreover which should be commensurate with the facilities for unloading offered by the jetties (for large tankers), with the size of the lands to be acquired, and with the discharging facilities to be provided by the railway lines. I emphasize the words *a refinery* by way of distinction from *the refinery* because no authority was given or sought except in the indefinite form. But that there was authority to construct and operate *a* refinery seems to me indisputable....

If I am right upon this point, the position as regards the action would be as follows. The respondent alleges a nuisance, by smell, noise, vibration, etc. The facts regarding these matters are for her to prove. It is then for the appellants to show, if they can, that it was impossible to construct and operate a refinery upon the site, conforming with Parliament's intention, without creating the nuisance alleged, or at least a nuisance. Involved in this issue would be the point discussed by Cumming-Bruce LJ in the Court of Appeal, that the establishment of an oil refinery, etc. was bound to involve some alteration of the environment and so of the standard of amenity and comfort which neighbouring occupiers might expect. To the extent that the environment has been changed from that of a peaceful unpolluted countryside to an industrial complex (as to which different standards apply — *Sturges* v *Bridgman* (1879) 11 ChD 852) Parliament must be taken to have authorised it. So far, I venture to think, the matter is not open to doubt. But in my opinion the statutory authority extends beyond merely authorising a change in the environment and an alteration of standard. It confers immunity against proceedings for any nuisance which can be shown (the burden of so showing being upon the appellants) to be the inevitable result of erecting a refinery upon the site — not, I repeat, the existing refinery, but any refinery — however carefully and with however great a regard for the interest of adjoining occupiers it is sited, constructed and operated. To the extent and only to the extent that the actual nuisance (if any) caused by the actual refinery and its operation exceeds that for which immunity is conferred, the plaintiff has a remedy....

LORD KEITH, *dissenting:* [The] issue is whether the Act of 1965 affords the appellants a good defence against the respondent's action for common law nuisance arising from the normal operation of a refinery upon the site in question, upon the assumption that the creation of a nuisance is a necessary incident of such operation, not avoidable by any reasonable measures which might be taken by the appellants. An undertaking has been given on behalf of the respondent that, if that issue is decided in her favour, she will not pursue the allegation contained in her pleadings that a nuisance has been created by negligence on the part of the appellants....

The defence upon which the appellants rely is commonly known as that of 'statutory authority.'...

Geddis v *Proprietors of the Bann Reservoir,* 3 App Cas 430 established that the authority of Parliament to construct and use certain works does not relieve the undertakers from the obligation to take due care that their operations do not cause injury to neighbouring proprietors. So the defence of statutory authority, the application of which has been extended to a wide field of industrial activities, does not avail against a claim that the creation of a nuisance has been brought about by negligence. In *Manchester Corporation* v *Farnworth* [1930] AC 171, 183 Lord Dunedin said:

When Parliament has authorised a certain thing to be made or done in a certain place, there can be no action for nuisance caused by the making or doing of that thing if the nuisance is the inevitable result of the making or doing so authorised. The onus of proving that the result is inevitable is on those who wish to escape liability for nuisance, but the criterion of inevitability is not what is theoretically possible but what is possible according to the state of scientific knowledge at the time, having also in view a certain common sense appreciation, which cannot be rigidly defined, of practical feasibility in view of situation and of expense.

For the purpose of disposing of the preliminary issue which I have described, it is to be assumed that the respondent's averments about the existence of a nuisance emanating from the appellants' refinery are true, and also that the nuisance would be the inevitable result, in the sense of Lord Dunedin's words, of operating, not the refinery which the appellants have actually built, but such a refinery as must reasonably be regarded as having been in the contemplation of Parliament when it passed the Gulf Oil Refining Act 1965.

The question whether upon these assumptions the defence of statutory authority is available to the appellants turns upon the ascertainment, upon a proper construction of the Act of 1965, of the extent of the authorisation thereby granted to the appellants by Parliament. . . .

. . . It is true that the burden of establishing that Parliament intended to take away the private right of individuals may be discharged by showing that such intention appears either from express words or by necessary implication: *Metropolitan Asylum District* v *Hill*, 6 AppCas 193, 208 *per* Lord Blackburn. I cannot, however find any necessary implication of such intention in a provision the operative purpose and effect of which merely is to confer powers of compulsory purchase. Any compulsory purchase powers, whether conferred by Parliament directly or under statutory delegated authority, must be conferred for a specific purpose. I do not consider that the mere mention of that purpose in the conferment of the powers is sufficient in itself to infer an intention to authorise any particular activity upon the acquired lands which might infringe the rights of others. The position would have been different if section 5(1) had specifically authorised the appellants to use a refinery upon the site in question. . . .

Note
An example of a case where a defendant did have statutory authority, but which did not provide a defence because the powers could have been exercised without causing a nuisance, is *Tate & Lyle* v *GLC* [1983] 2 AC 509, where the defendants built ferry terminals at Woolwich which caused siltation around the plaintiffs' jetty. The terminals were authorised by statute, but it was shown that the choice of design caused additional siltation, which need not have occurred if a different design had been adopted. The House of Lords held that the statute did not absolve the defendants from the need to 'have all reasonable regard and care for the interests of other persons' and that as the damage could have been avoided they were liable.

Wheeler v *Saunders*
Court of Appeal [1996] Ch 19; [1995] 3 WLR 466; [1995] 2 All ER 697

The plaintiff owned a house and holiday cottages adjacent to the defendants' pig farm. In 1989 and 1990 the defendants obtained planning permission for additional capacity by way of two 'Trowbridge' houses, each capable of holding 400 pigs. One of the houses was only 11 metres from the plaintiff's holiday cottage. The plaintiff sued for nuisance because of the smell and the defendant claimed that as he had planning permission he was not liable. Held: dismissing the appeal on this issue, that the defendants were liable.

STAUGHTON LJ: . . . What then was the effect of the planning permission for two Trowbridge houses? It was opposed by Dr and Mrs Wheeler, but nevertheless granted.

Does that mean that they have lost any right which they had previously enjoyed to live their lives free from the smell of pigs on their doorstep? Surprisingly, there appears to have been no direct authority on the point until recently. There have however been cases dealing with the question of whether statutory authority is a defence to a claim in nuisance. One such was *Allen v Gulf Oil Refining Ltd* [1981] AC 1001, where Mrs Allen complained of nuisance from an oil refinery built with statutory authority. Lord Wilberforce said, at p. 1011:

> It is now well settled that where Parliament by express direction or by necessary implication has authorised the construction and use of an undertaking or works, that carries with it an authority to do what is authorised with immunity from any action based on nuisance.

However, he added, at p. 1114, that the immunity was confined to harm which was the inevitable result of what Parliament had authorised. The Gulf company had to show that it was impossible to construct the refinery without creating the nuisance complained of.

I do not consider that planning permission necessarily has the same effect as statutory authority. Parliament is sovereign and can abolish or limit the civil rights of individuals. As Sir John May put it in the course of argument, Parliament cannot be irrational just as the Sovereign can do no wrong. The planning authority on the other hand has only the powers delegated to it by Parliament. It is not in my view self-evident that they include the power to abolish or limit civil rights in any or all circumstances. The process by which planning permission is obtained allows for objections by those who might be adversely affected, but they have no right of appeal if their objections are overruled. It is not for us to say whether the private bill procedure in Parliament is better or worse. It is enough that it is different.

In *Allen v Gulf Oil Refining Ltd* [1980] QB 156, before the Court of Appeal Cumming-Bruce LJ touched on the effect of planning permission on what would otherwise be a nuisance. He said, at p. 174: 'the planning authority has no jurisdiction to authorise a nuisance save (if at all) in so far as it has statutory power to permit the change of the character of a neighbourhood.'

One can readily appreciate that planning permission will, quite frequently, have unpleasant consequences for some people. The man with a view over open fields from his window may well be displeased if a housing estate is authorised by the planners and built in front of his house; the character of the neighbourhood is changed. But there may be nothing which would qualify as a nuisance and no infringement of his civil rights. What if the development does inevitably create what would otherwise be a nuisance? Instead of a housing estate the planners may authorise a factory which would emit noise and smoke to the detriment of neighbouring residents. Does that come within the first proposition of Cumming-Bruce LJ that a planning authority has no jurisdiction to authorise a nuisance? Or is it within the second, that the authority may change the character of a neighbourhood? The problem arose directly in *Gillingham Borough Council v Medway (Chatham) Dock Co. Ltd* [1993] QB 343. There planning permission had been granted for the development as a commercial port of part of the Bulmer Road dockyard in Chatham. This had the result that heavy goods vehicles in large numbers used roads in the neighbourhood for 24 hours a day, much to the harm of local residents. This was said to be an actionable public nuisance. Buckley J held that it was authorised by the grant of planning permission and so was not actionable. His reasoning closely followed the dictum of Cumming-Bruce LJ which I have quoted. He said, at p. 359:

> It has been said, no doubt correctly, that planning permission is not a licence to commit nuisance and that a planning authority has no jurisdiction to authorise

nuisance. However, a planning authority can, through its development plans and decisions, alter the character of a neighbourhood.

He concluded at p. 361:

In short, where planning consent is given for a development or change of use, the question of nuisance will thereafter fall to be decided by reference to a neighbourhood with that development or use and not as it was previously.

However, he did accept, at p. 360: 'it is only a nuisance inevitably resulting from the authorised works on which immunity is conferred.' . . .

What may matter is whether the subsequent nuisance flowed inevitably from the activity which was authorised by the two planning permissions. In my opinion it did. The Trowbridge houses were to contain 800 pigs based on slurry within 36 feet of the nearest holiday cottage. There was bound to be nuisance by smell. True the nuisance would be greater when the pigs were fed on whey, but there would inevitably be nuisance even if they were not. It follows that if this were a case where the buildings were authorised by statute, there would be immunity from any action based on nuisance. But, as I have already said, I consider that the case may be different where one is concerned with planning permission rather than statute.

Mr Stone submits that the decisions of the planning authority might have been challenged by way of judicial review had application been made in due time. He points out that the local government ombudsman was critical of the procedure adopted by the planning authority. He tempted us with the suggestion that a High Court judge might well have held the decisions to be wholly irrational. But, he says, the time for an application has long since expired. I see some force in that argument, although in my view it would be regrettable if the already crowded lists in the Crown Office must be filled with disappointed objectors to planning permission.

I accept what was said by Cumming-Bruce LJ: first, that a planning authority has in general no jurisdiction to authorise a nuisance, and secondly, if it can do so at all, that is only by the exercise of its power to permit a change in the character of a neighbourhood. To the extent that those two propositions feature in the judgment of Buckley J, I agree with his decision, but I would not for the present go any further than that.

It would in my opinion be a misuse of language to describe what has happened in the present case as a change in the character of a neighbourhood. It is a change of use of a very small piece of land, a little over 350 square metres according to the dimensions on the plan, for the benefit of the applicant and to the detriment of the objectors in the quiet enjoyment of their house. It is not a strategic planning decision affected by considerations of public interest. Unless one is prepared to accept that any planning decision authorises any nuisance which must inevitably come from it, the argument that the nuisance was authorised by planning permission in this case must fail. I am not prepared to accept that premise. It may be — I express no concluded opinion — that some planning decisions will authorise some nuisances. But that is as far as I am prepared to go. There is no immunity from liability for nuisance in the present case. I would dismiss the second part of this appeal.

Notes

1. As one of the other judges pointed out, the decision means that the defendants, having constructed the Trowbridge houses in accordance with planning permission, cannot now use them. But why should planning permission allow them to disregard other rules of law?

2. Sir John May said that apart from cases where the permission changes the character of the neighbourhood, even if the nuisance complained of was an inevitable consequence of the permission, that could not license the nuisance. Furthermore, he said that permission which inevitably resulted in a nuisance would be subject to judicial review on the ground of irrationality.

Section 7: remedies

Remedies for nuisance include abatement (self help), injunctions and damages. Interlocutory injunctions are commonly applied for in nuisance cases, and examples of the application of the principles in *American Cyanamid* v *Ethicon* [1975] AC 396 are *Hubbard* v *Pitt* [1975] ICR 308 and *Laws* v *Florinplace* [1981] 1 All ER 659. This section, however, will concentrate on whether a plaintiff should be awarded an injunction or be satisfied with damages. This is an area which has been subject to considerable economic analysis and raises wide questions of policy — for example, should a defendant be entitled to purchase a licence to commit an unlawful act by the payment of damages.

Kennaway v *Thompson*
Court of Appeal [1981] QB 88; [1980] 3 WLR 311; [1980] 3 All ER 329

In 1969 the plaintiff built a house near a man-made lake, which for a number of years had been used for motorboat racing. The defendants were held liable for the nuisance created by the noise, and at first instance the plaintiff was awarded damages of £16,000. Held: allowing the appeal, the plaintiff was entitled to an injunction limiting the use of the lake to certain days and to certain noise limits.

LAWTON LJ: Mr Kempster based his submissions primarily on the decision of this court in *Shelfer* v *City of London Electric Lighting Co.* [1895] 1 Ch 287. The opening paragraph of the headnote, which correctly summarises the judgment, is as follows:

Lord Cairns' Act 1858, in conferring upon courts of equity a jurisdiction to award damages instead of an injunction, has not altered the settled principles upon which those courts interfered by way of injunction; and in cases of continuing actionable nuisance the jurisdiction so conferred ought only to be exercised under very exceptional circumstances.

In a much-quoted passage, Lindley LJ said, at pp. 315-316:

... ever since Lord Cairns' Act was passed the Court of Chancery has repudiated the notion that the legislature intended to turn that court into a tribunal for legalising wrongful acts; or in other words, the court has always protested against the notion that it ought to allow a wrong to continue simply because the wrongdoer is able and willing to pay for the injury he may inflict. Neither has the circumstance that the wrongdoer is in some sense a public benefactor (e.g., a gas or water company or a sewer authority) ever been considered a sufficient reason for refusing to protect by injunction an individual whose rights are being persistently infringed.

A. L. Smith LJ, in his judgment, set out what he called a good working rule for the award of damages in substitution for an injunction. His working rule does not apply in this case. The injury to the plaintiff's legal rights is not small; it is not capable of being estimated in terms of money save in the way the judge tried to make an estimate, namely by fixing a figure for the diminution of the value of the plaintiff's house because of the prospect of a continuing nuisance — and the figure he fixed could not be described as small. The principles enunciated in *Shelfer's* case, which is binding on us, have been applied time and time again during the past 85 years. The only case which raises a doubt about the application of the *Shelfer* principles to all cases is *Miller* v *Jackson* [1977] QB 966, a decision of this court. The majority (Geoffrey Lane and Cumming-Bruce LJJ, Lord Denning MR dissenting) adjudged that the activities of an old-established cricket club which had been going for over 70 years, had been a nuisance to the plaintiffs by reason of cricket balls landing in their garden. The question then was whether the plaintiffs should be granted an injunction. Geoffrey Lane LJ was of the opinion that one should be granted. Lord Denning MR and Cumming-Bruce LJ thought otherwise. Lord Denning MR said that the public interest should prevail over the private interest. Cumming-Bruce LJ stated that a factor to be taken into account when exercising the judicial discretion whether to grant an injunction was that the plaintiffs had bought their house knowing that it was next to the cricket ground. He thought that there were special circumstances which should inhibit a court of equity from granting the injunction claimed. Lord Denning MR's statement that the public interest should prevail over the private interest runs counter to the principles enunciated in *Shelfer's* case and does not accord with Cumming-Bruce LJ's reason for refusing an injunction. We are of the opinion that there is nothing in *Miller* v *Jackson* [1977] QB 966 binding on us, which qualifies what was decided in *Shelfer's* case. Any decisions before *Shelfer's* case (and there were some at first instance, as Mr Gorman pointed out) which give support for the proposition that the public interest should prevail over the private interest must be read subject to the decision in *Shelfer's* case.

It follows that the plaintiff was entitled to an injunction and that the judge misdirected himself in law in adjudging that the approriate remedy for her was an award of damages under Lord Cairns's Act. But she was only entitled to an injunction restraining the club from activities which caused a nuisance, and not all of their activities did. As the judge pointed out, and the plaintiff, by her counsel, accepted in this court, an injunction in general terms would be unworkable.

Our task has been to decide on a form of order which will protect the plaintiff from the noise which the judge found to be intolerable but which will not stop the club from organising activities about which she cannot reasonably complain.

When she decided to build a house alongside Mallam Water she knew that some motor-boat racing and water skiing was done on the club's water and she thought that the noise which such activities created was tolerable. She cannot now complain about that kind of noise provided it does not increase in volume by reason of any increase in activities. The intolerable noise is mostly caused by the large boats; it is these which attract the public interest.

Now nearly all of us living in these islands have to put up with a certain amount of annoyance from our neighbours. Those living in towns may be irritated by their neighbours' noisy radios or incompetent playing of musical instruments; and they in turn may be inconvenienced by the noise caused by our guests slamming car doors and chattering after a late party. Even in the country the lowing of a sick cow or the early morning crowing of a farmyard cock may interfere with sleep and comfort. Intervention by injunction is only justified when the irritating noise causes inconvenience beyond what other occupiers in the neighbourhood can be expected to bear. The question is whether the neighbour is using his property reasonably, having regard to the fact that he has a neighbour. The neighbour who is complaining must remember, too, that the other man can use his property in a reasonable way and there must be a measure of give and take, live and let live.

Notes

1. For further discussion of this subject, see Ogus and Richardson, 'Economics of the Environment: a study of private nuisance' [1977] CLJ 2841; Tromans, 'Nuisance — prevention or payment?' [1982] CLJ 87; and Jolowicz, 'Damages in Equity — a study of Lord Cairns Act' [1975] CLJ 224.

2. This case also illustrates the principle that it is no defence that the plaintiff came to the nuisance, i.e. that the nuisance was already there and the plaintiff knew of it when she built the house. The rule was established in *Sturges* v *Bridgman* (1879) 11 Ch D 852, where a doctor built a consulting room near the premises of a confectioner which had been used for many years. The plaintiff succeeded in his claim for nuisance arising from noise and vibrations caused by the defendant. In *Miller* v *Jackson* [1977] QB 966 the plaintiff bought a house in 1972 near a cricket ground which had been used since 1905. The cricket club was liable for the nuisance created by balls being hit out of the ground and Geoffrey Lane LJ said he was bound by *Sturges* v *Bridgman,* but he also commented that 'it does not seem just that a long-established activity — in itself innocuous — should be brought to an end because someone chooses to build a house nearby and so turn an innocent pastime into an actionable nuisance'. The court in that case refused to grant an injunction, but that may not now be a possible way to resolve the problem after *Kennaway* v *Thompson.* How can such conflicts of interest be resolved?

22 LIABILITY FOR THE ESCAPE OF DANGEROUS THINGS

Many things are dangerous, more so today than in earlier times, but the approach of the law to such activities is haphazard. The general principle is that the more dangerous a thing is, the greater the obligation to take care to prevent it causing harm, and this is a matter for the law of negligence. In addition, there is statutory liability for injuries caused by some unsafe activities or things, as under the Health and Safety at Work Act 1974 or the Consumer Protection Act 1987. However, this chapter collects together those areas of the law where strict liability is imposed for escapes of dangerous things, and the subject is closely allied to nuisance.

The idea of strict liability is not new and has existed in the common law for centuries, and it was not until the rise and ultimate domination of the fault principle that strict liability was regarded as out of the ordinary. Today the fault principle is no longer seen as morally obvious, and the demands for strict liability for a range of activities is growing. This is usually achieved by statute and a few examples are given in section 3, but this is often done in response to a particular crisis or demand from a pressure group, and the liability for dangerous activities lacks coherence. The Pearson Commission was unable to formulate any satisfactory general principle and proposed an extension of strict liability by reference to particular activities, based on their propensity to create a high risk of injury or a risk of extensive injury.

As in the rest of the law of tort, the question whether strict liability should be imposed is a matter of how best to allocate the risk created by an activity. The move from liability for fault to strict liability is often based on the idea that it is unreasonable to expect a potential victim to bear the risk where the defendant has created an exceptional hazard, either by way of increased risk of injury or by way of risk of greater injury. This involves economic as well as social questions, and the extension of strict liability is a matter of considerable debate.

Section 1:   the rule in *Rylands* v *Fletcher*

In 1866 when Blackburn J formulated the rule in *Rylands* v *Fletcher*, he believed he was creating nothing new, but was merely formulating a general principle by gathering together existing examples of strict liability. This may have been rather ingenuous, since a general principle has capacity for a much wider application than individual instances, but in the event the principle has had very little effect. That it was *capable* of transforming the law cannot be doubted and we might have had a tort of strict liability for hazardous activities, but the rise of the fault principle hampered the growth of the doctrine. In the event the rule has been restricted by its origins in trespass and nuisance, and is probably now incapable of judicial development beyond the area of liability for escapes from land.

Rylands v *Fletcher*
House of Lords (1868) LR 3 HL 330; 37 LJ Ex 161; 19 LT 22

The defendant (Rylands) owned the Ainsworth Mill in Lancashire, and the plaintiff (Fletcher) owned the Red House Colliery nearby. In 1860 the defendant constructed a reservoir for his mill on land belonging to Lord Wilton and employed engineers and contractors to build it. During construction they found a number of old shafts, but it was not realised that these indirectly connected with the colliery. The contractors were negligent in not ensuring that the filled-in shafts could bear the weight of water, and on 11 December 1860 the partially filled reservoir burst through into the plaintiff's colliery. Held: dismissing the appeal, that the defendant was liable.

LORD CAIRNS LC: My Lords, the principles on which this case must be determined appear to me to be extremely simple. The defendants, treating them as the owners or occupiers of the close on which the reservoir was constructed, might lawfully have used that close for any purpose for which it might in the ordinary course of the enjoyment of land be used; and if, in what I may term the natural user of that land, there had been any accumulation of water, either on the surface or underground, and if, by the operation of the laws of nature, that accumulation of water had passed off into the close occupied by the plaintiff, the plaintiff could not have complained that that result had taken place. If he had desired to guard himself against it, it would have lain upon him to have done so, by leaving or by interposing, some barrier between his close and the close of the defendants in order to have prevented that operation of the laws of nature. . . .

On the other hand if the defendants, not stopping at the natural use of their close, had desired to use it for any purpose which I may term a non-natural use, for the purpose of introducing into the close that which in its natural condition was not in or upon it, for the purpose of introducing water either above or below ground in quantities and in a manner not the result of any work or operation on or under the land, — and if in consequence of their doing so, or in consequence of any imperfection in the mode of their doing so, the water came to escape and to pass off into the close of the plaintiff, then it appears to me that that which the defendants were doing they were doing at their own peril; and, if in the course of their doing it, the evil arose to which I have referred, the evil, namely, of the escape of the water and its passing away to the close of the plaintiff and injuring the plaintiff, then for the consequence of that, in my opinion, the defendants would be liable. . . .

My Lords, these simple principles, if they are well founded, as it appears to me they are, really dispose of this case.

The same result is arrived at on the principles referred to by Mr Justice Blackburn in his judgment, in the Court of Exchequer Chamber . . .

LORD CRANWORTH: My Lords, I concur with my noble and learned friend in thinking that the rule of law was correctly stated by Mr Justice Blackburn in delivering the opinion of the Exchequer Chamber. If a person brings, or accumulates, on his land anything which, if it should escape, may cause damage to his neighbour, he does so at his peril. If it does escape, and cause damage, he is responsible, however careful he may have been, and whatever precautions he may have taken to prevent the damage.

Court of Exchequer Chamber
(1866) LR 1 Ex 265

BLACKBURN J: We think that the true rule of law is, that the person who for his own purposes brings on his lands and collects and keeps there anything likely to do mischief if it escapes, must keep it in at his peril, and, if he does not do so, is prima facie answerable for all the damage which is the natural consequence of its escape. He can excuse himself by shewing that the escape was owing to the plaintiff's default; or perhaps that the escape was the consequence of vis major, or the act of God; but as nothing of this sort exists here, it is unnecessary to inquire what excuse would be sufficient. The general rule, as above stated, seems on principle just. The person whose grass or corn is eaten down by the escaping cattle of his neighbour, or whose mine is flooded by the water from his neighbour's reservoir, or whose cellar is invaded by the filth of his neighbour's privy, or whose habitation is made unhealthy by the fumes and noisome vapours of his neighbour's alkali works, is damnified without any fault of his own; and it seems but reasonable and just that the neighbour, who has brought something on his own property which was not naturally there, harmless to others so long as it is confined to his own property, but which he knows to be mischievous if it gets on his neighbour's, should be obliged to make good the damage which ensues if he does not succeed in confining it to his own property. But for his act in bringing it there no mischief could have accrued, and it seems but just that he should at his peril keep it there so that no mischief may accrue, or answer for the natural and anticipated consequences. And upon authority, this we think is established to be the law whether the things so brought be beasts, or water, or filth, or stenches. . . .

The view which we take of the first point renders it unnecessary to consider whether the defendants would or would not be responsible for the want of care and skill in the persons employed by them, under the circumstances stated in the case.

Notes

1. It may be that Lord Cairns in the House of Lords thought he was saying the same thing as Blackburn J, but the difference between 'which was not naturally there' in Blackburn's formulation and 'non-natural use' (Lord Cairns) is crucial and has enabled subsequent courts to limit the doctrine. It seems likely that the original point of the restriction was merely to exclude liability for natural lakes.

2. It is important to note that the plaintiff put forward two arguments for liability. The first was strict liability on the defendant for having constructed

the reservoir, and the second was vicarious liability for the negligence of his independent contractor. The decision was based solely upon the first ground. For the vicarious liability point, see now *Honeywill & Stein Ltd* v *Larkin* [1934] 1 KB 191.

3. The facts of this case and the reasons for it have attracted enormous attention. For a description of the present site (near the Bury to Bolton road), see A. W. B. Simpson *Leading Cases in the Common Law*, Chapter 8. For a discussion of the fact that only two Law Lords appear to have sat in the case (whereas the quorum is three), see (1970) 86 LQR 160 (Heuston) and 311 (Yale). For general studies see the judgment of Windeyer J in *Benning* v *Wong* (1969) 122 CLR 249, at p. 294; Linden, 'Whatever happened to *Rylands* v *Fletcher?*' in Klar, *Studies in Canadian Tort Law;* and Bohlen, 'The rule in *Rylands* v *Fletcher*' (1911) 59 U Pa L Rev 298 or his *Studies in the Law of Torts,* Chapter 7.

Cambridge Water Co. v *Eastern Counties Leather*
House of Lords [1994] 2 AC 264; [1994] 1 All ER 53; [1994] 2 WLR 53

Eastern Counties Leather operate a tannery at Shawston near Cambridge. As part of the tanning process the pelts need de-greasing and for some years the defendants used perchloroethene (PCE). Up to the end of 1976 this was delivered to their premises in drums and in transferring the chemical to machines there was a regular spillage of small quantities which over the years amounted to at least 1,000 gallons. The PCE soaked through the concrete and down through the strata and slowly dissolved into percolating ground water. The contaminated water affected the plaintiff's bore hole at Shawston Mill, some 1.3 miles from the tannery. It was found that a reasonable supervisor at the tannery would not have foreseen that such repeated spillage of small quantities of PCE would lead to any environmental hazard. (The spillage could have been expected to evaporate into the air and not seep through the concrete.) Even if he might have foreseen that the chemical would reach the aquifer he would not have expected it to affect the quality of the water as the minute quantities were not discoverable until the 1970's and a Department of the Environment circular did not declare such water unwholesome until 1982. The plaintiffs had to close the bore hole and drill a new one at a cost of £956,937. Held: allowing the appeal, that the defendants were not liable.

LORD GOFF: . . . In that passage [in *Rylands* v *Fletcher*] Blackburn J spoke of 'anything *likely* to do mischief if it escapes;' and later he spoke of something 'which he *knows* to be mischievous if it gets on his neighbour's [property],' and the liability to 'answer for the natural *and anticipated* consequences.' Furthermore, time and again he spoke of the strict liability imposed upon the defendant as being that he must keep the thing in at his peril; and, when referring to liability in actions for damage occasioned by animals, he referred, at p. 282, to the established principle that 'it is quite immaterial whether the escape is by negligence or not.' The general tenor of his statement of principle is therefore that knowledge, or at least foreseeability of the risk, is a prerequisite of the recovery of damages under the principle; but that the principle is one of strict liability in the sense that the defendant may be held liable notwithstanding that he has exercised all due care to prevent the escape from occurring . . .

The point is one on which academic opinion appears to be divided: cf *Salmond & Heuston on the Law of Torts*, 20th ed. (1992), pp. 324–325, which favours the prerequisite of foreseeability, and *Clerk & Lindsell on Torts*, 16th ed. (1989), p. 1429, para. 25.09, which takes a different view. However, quite apart from the indications to be derived from the judgment of Blackburn J in *Fletcher* v *Rylands*, LR 1 Ex 265 itself, to which I have already referred, the historical connection with the law of nuisance must now be regarded as pointing towards the conclusion that foreseeability of damage is a prerequisite of the recovery of damages under the rule. I have already referred to the fact that Blackburn J himself did not regard his statement of principle as having broken new ground; furthermore, Professor Newark has convincingly shown that the rule in *Rylands* v *Fletcher* was essentially concerned with an extension of the law of nuisance to cases of isolated escape. Accordingly since, following the observations of Lord Reid when delivering the advice of the Privy Council in *The Wagon Mound (No. 2)* [1967] 1 AC 617, 640, the recovery of damages in private nuisance depends on foreseeability by the defendant of the relevant type of damage, it would appear logical to extend the same requirement to liability under the rule in *Rylands* v *Fletcher*.

Even so, the question cannot be considered solely as a matter of history. It can be argued that the rule in *Rylands* v *Fletcher* should not be regarded simply as an extension of the law of nuisance, but should rather be treated as a developing principle of strict liability from which can be derived a general rule of strict liability for damage caused by ultra-hazardous operations, on the basis of which persons conducting such operations may properly be held strictly liable for the extraordinary risk to others involved in such operations. As is pointed out in *Fleming on the Law of Torts*, pp. 327–328, this would lead to the practical result that the cost of damage resulting from such operations would have to be absorbed as part of the overheads of the relevant business rather than be borne (where there is no negligence) by the injured person or his insurers, or even by the community at large. Such a development appears to have been taking place in the United States, as can be seen from paragraph 519 of the *Restatement of Torts* (2d) vol. 3 (1977). The extent to which it has done so is not altogether clear; and I infer from paragraph 519, and the Comment on that paragraph, that the abnormally dangerous activities there referred to are such that their ability to cause harm would be obvious to any reasonable person who carried them on.

I have to say, however, that there are serious obstacles in the way of the development of the rule in *Rylands* v *Fletcher* in this way. First of all, if it was so to develop, it should logically apply to liability to all persons suffering injury by reason of the ultra-hazardous operations; but the decision of this House in *Read* v *J. Lyons & Co. Ltd* [1947] AC 156, which establishes that there can be no liability under the rule except in circumstances where the injury has been caused by an escape from land under the control of the defendant, has effectively precluded any such development. Professor Fleming has observed that 'the most damaging effect of the decision in *Read* v *J. Lyons & Co. Ltd* is that it prematurely stunted the development of a general theory of strict liability for ultra-hazardous activities' (see *Fleming on Torts*, p. 341). Even so, there is much to be said for the view that the courts should not be proceeding down the path of developing such a general theory. In this connection, I refer in particular to the Report of the Law Commission on Civil Liability for Dangerous Things and Activities (1970) (Law Com No. 32). In paragraphs 14–16 of the Report, the Law Commission expressed serious misgivings about the adoption of any test for the application of strict liability involving a general concept of 'especially dangerous' or 'ultra-hazardous' activity, having regard to the uncertainties and practical difficulties of its application. If the Law Commission is unwilling to consider statutory reform on this basis, it must follow that judges should if anything be even more reluctant to proceed down that path.

Like the judge in the present case, I incline to the opinion that, as a general rule, it is more appropriate for strict liability in respect of operations of high risk to be imposed by Parliament, than by the courts. If such liability is imposed by statute, the relevant activities can be identified, and those concerned can know where they stand. Furthermore, statute can where appropriate lay down precise criteria establishing the incidence and scope of such liability.

It is of particular relevance that the present case is concerned with environmental pollution. The protection and preservation of the environment is now perceived as being of crucial importance to the future of mankind; and public bodies, both national and international, are taking significant steps towards the establishment of legislation which will promote the protection of the environment, and make the polluter pay for damage to the environment for which he is responsible — as can be seen from the WHO, EEC and national regulations to which I have previously referred. But it does not follow from these developments that a common law principle, such as the rule in *Rylands* v *Fletcher*, should be developed or rendered more strict to provide for liability in respect of such pollution. On the contrary, given that so much well-informed and carefully structured legislation is now being put in place for this purpose, there is less need for the courts to develop a common law principle to achieve the same end, and indeed it may well be undesirable that they should do so.

Having regard to these considerations, and in particular to the step which this House has already taken in *Read* v *J. Lyons & Co. Ltd* [1947] AC 156 to contain the scope of liability under the rule in *Rylands* v *Fletcher*, it appears to me to be appropriate now to take the view that foreseeability of damage of the relevant type should be regarded as a prerequisite of liability in damages under the rule. Such a conclusion can, as I have already stated, be derived from Blackburn J's original statement of the law; and I can see no good reason why this prerequisite should not be recognised under the rule, as it has been in the case of private nuisance. In particular, I do not regard the two authorities cited to your Lordships, *West* v *Bristol Tramways Co.* [1908] 2 KB 14 and *Rainham Chemical Works Ltd* v *Belvedere Fish Guano Co. Ltd* [1921] 2 AC 465, as providing any strong pointer towards a contrary conclusion. It would moreover lead to a more coherent body of common law principles if the rule were to be regarded essentially as an extension of the law of nuisance to cases of isolated escapes from land, even though the rule as established is not limited to escapes which are in fact isolated. I wish to point out, however, that in truth the escape of the PCE from ECL's land, in the form of trace elements carried in percolating water, has not been an isolated escape, but a continuing escape resulting from a state of affairs which has come into existence at the base of the chalk aquifer underneath ECL's premises. Classically, this would have been regarded as a case of nuisance; and it would seem strange if, by characterising the case as one falling under the rule in *Rylands* v *Fletcher*, the liability should thereby be rendered more strict in the circumstances of the present case.

The facts of the present case

Turning to the facts of the present case, it is plain that, at the time when the PCE was brought onto ECL's land, and indeed when it was used in the tanning process there, nobody at ECL could reasonably have foreseen the resultant damage which occurred at CWC's borehole at Sawston . . .

I wish to add that the present case may be regarded as one of what is nowadays called historic pollution, in the sense that the relevant occurrence (the seepage of PCE through the floor of ECL's premises) took place before the relevant legislation came into force; and it appears that, under the current philosophy, it is not envisaged that statutory liability should be imposed for historic pollution (see, e.g. the Council of Europe's Draft Convention on Civil Liability for Damage Resulting from Activities Dangerous to the Environment (Strasbourg 26 January 1993) article 5.1, and paragraph 48 of the Explanatory Report). If so, it would be strange if liability for such pollution were to arise under a principle of common law.

In the result, since those responsible at ECL could not at the relevant time reasonably have foreseen that the damage in question might occur, the claim of CWC for damages under the rule in *Rylands* v *Fletcher* must fail.

Natural use of land
I turn to the question whether the use by ECL of its land in the present case constituted a natural use, with the result that ECL cannot be held liable under the rule in *Rylands* v *Fletcher*. In view of my conclusion on the issue of foreseeability, I can deal with this point shortly.

The judge held that it was a natural use. He said:

In my judgment, in considering whether the storage of organochlorines as an adjunct to a manufacturing process is a non-natural use of land, I must consider whether that storage created special risks for adjacent occupiers and whether the activity was for the general benefit of the community. It seems to me inevitable that I must consider the magnitude of the storage and the geographical area in which it takes place in answering the question. Sawston is properly described as an industrial village, and the creation of employment is clearly for the benefit of that community. I do not believe that I can enter upon an assessment of the point on a scale of desirability that the manufacture of wash leathers comes, and I content myself with holding that this storage in this place is a natural use of land.

It is a commonplace that this particular exception to liability under the rule has developed and changed over the years. It seems clear that, in *Fletcher* v *Rylands*, LR 1 Ex 265 itself, Blackburn J's statement of the law was limited to things which are brought by the defendant onto his land, and so did not apply to things that were naturally upon the land. Furthermore, it is doubtful whether in the House of Lords in the same case Lord Cairns, to whom we owe the expression 'non-natural use' of the land, was intending to expand the concept of natural use beyond that envisaged by Blackburn J. Even so, the law has long since departed from any such simple idea, redolent of a different age; and, at least since the advice of the Privy Council delivered by Lord Moulton in *Rickards* v *Lothian* [1913] AC 263, 280, natural use has been extended to embrace the ordinary use of land. I ask to be forgiven if I again quote Lord Moulton's statement of the law, which has lain at the heart of the subsequent development of this exception:

It is not every use to which land is put that brings into play at that principle. It must be some special use bringing with it increased danger to others, and must not merely be the ordinary use of the land or such a use as is proper for the general benefit of the community.

Rickards v *Lothian* itself was concerned with a use of a domestic kind, viz. the overflow of water from a basin whose runaway had become blocked. But over the years the concept of natural use in the sense of ordinary use, has been extended to embrace a wide variety of uses, including not only domestic uses but also recreational uses and even some industrial uses.

It is obvious that the expression 'ordinary use of the land' in Lord Moulton's statement of the law is one which is lacking in precision. There are some writers who welcome the flexibility which has thus been introduced into this branch of the law, on the ground that it enables judges to mould and adapt the principle of strict liability to the changing needs of society; whereas others regret the perceived absence of principle in so vague a concept, and fear that the whole idea of strict liability may as a result be undermined. A particular doubt is introduced by Lord Moulton's alternative criterion — 'or such a use as is proper for the general benefit of the community.' If these words are understood to refer to a local community, they can be given some content as intended to refer to such matters as, for example, the provision of services; indeed the same idea can, without too much difficulty, be extended to, for example, the provision of services to industrial premises, as in a business park or an industrial estate. But if the words are extended to embrace the wider interests of the local community or the general benefit of the community at large, it is difficult to see how the exception can be kept within reasonable bounds. A notable extension was considered in your Lordships' House in *Read v J. Lyons & Co. Ltd* [1947] AC 156, 169–170, *per* Viscount Simon, and p. 174, *per* Lord Macmillan, where it was suggested that, in time of war, the manufacture of explosives might be held to constitute a natural use of land, apparently on the basis that, in a country in which the greater part of the population was involved in the war effort, many otherwise exceptional uses might become 'ordinary' for the duration of the war. It is however unnecessary to consider so wide an extension as that in a case such as the present. Even so, we can see the introduction of another extension in the present case, when the judge invoked the creation of employment as clearly for the benefit of the local community, viz. 'the industrial village' at Sawston. I myself, however, do not feel able to accept that the creation of employment as such, even in a small industrial complex, is sufficient of itself to establish a particular use as constituting a natural or ordinary use of land.

Fortunately, I do not think it is necessary for the purposes of the present case to attempt any redefinition of the concept of natural or ordinary use. This is because I am satisfied that the storage of chemicals in substantial quantities, and their use in the manner employed at ECL's premises, cannot fall within the exception. For the purpose of testing the point, let it be assumed the ECL was well aware of the possibility that PCE, if it escaped, could indeed cause damage, for example by contaminating any water with which it became mixed so as to render that water undrinkable by human beings. I cannot think that it would be right in such circumstances to exempt ECL from liability under the rule in *Rylands v Fletcher* on the ground that the use was natural or ordinary. The mere fact that the use is common in the tanning industry cannot, in my opinion, be enough to bring the use within the exception, nor the fact that Sawston contains a small industrial community which is worthy of encouragement or support. Indeed I feel bound to say that the storage of substantial quantities of chemicals on industrial premises should be regarded as an almost classic case of non-natural use; and I find it very difficult to think that it should be thought objectionable to impose strict liability for damage caused in the event of their escape. It may well be that, now that it is recognised that foreseeability of harm of the relevant type is a prerequisite of liability in damages under the rule, the courts may feel less pressure to extend the concept of natural use to circumstances such as those in the present case; and in due course it may become easier to control this exception, and to ensure that it has a more recognisable basis of principle. For these reasons, I would not hold that ECL should be exempt from liability on the basis of the exception of natural use.

However, for the reasons I have already given, I would allow ECL's appeal with costs before your Lordships' House and in the courts below.

Notes

1. This case does not 'abolish' strict liability, but careful attention needs to be paid to the role of foreseeability. The principal question is whether it must be shown both that the escape was foreseeable and that the kind of damage which occurred was foreseeable. The alternative and better view is that the escape need not be foreseeable: in other words the only question is *if* this thing escapes what kind of damage is foreseeable? Accordingly, there will be liability if there is a 'non-natural' use of land, the accumulation is likely to do mischief *if* it escapes and the damage which actually occurs is of the same 'kind' as that which was foreseeable if the thing escaped. For a discussion of this issue see Wilkinson (1994) 57 MLR 799; Weir (1994) 53 CLR 216.

2. This case is also important for the refusal to adopt a more general tort of strict liability for hazardous activities and for the restriction of the rule in *Rylands* v *Fletcher* to its historical origins, together with a strict interpretation of the elements of the tort. The Supreme Court of India took a very much wider view in **Mehta v Union of India** (1987) AIR (SC) 1086, where there was a discharge of toxic gas from a factory manufacturing chlorine gas in Delhi. The court rejected many of the traditional limitations of *Rylands* v *Fletcher,* adopting a more general tort of strict liability for engaging in hazardous activities. See Bergman (1988) 138 NLJ 420.

3. *Act of a stranger.* A defendant is not liable for the act of a stranger over whom he has no control. For another example, see **Perry v Kendrick's Transport** [1956] 1 WLR 85, where a child of about 10 threw a lighted match into the petrol tank of a bus. Parker LJ said that 'once [the defendants] prove that the escape was caused by the act of a stranger, whether an adult or a child, they escape liability, unless the plaintiff can go on to show that the act which caused the escape was an act of the kind which the occupier could reasonably have anticipated and guarded against'. Incidentally, was the petrol tank a 'non-natural' user, and did it 'escape' in the sense used in *Read* v *Lyons?*

4. *Non-natural user.* Perhaps the most bizarre example of non-natural user is *A-G* v *Corke* [1933] Ch 89, where the defendant allowed 200-300 caravan dwellers to place their caravans on his disused brickfield near Bromley in Kent, and some of them defecated on neighbouring land. The principle in *Rylands* v *Fletcher* was held to apply. Fortunately, however, children are not non-natural, as was decided in **Matheson v Northcote College** [1975] 2 NZLR 106, where children at the defendant's school 'escaped' and trespassed on the plaintiff's land and stole some grapes. The rule did not apply as children are not dangerous *per se,* but the school was nevertheless held to constitute a nuisance due to the lack of supervision. For general discussion of non-natural user see Newark, 'Non-natural user and the rule in *Rylands* v *Fletcher*' (1961) 24 MLR 557, and Williams 'Non-natural use of land' (1973) CLJ 310.

5. *Personal injuries.* In view of its origins in nuisance, it has often been questioned whether damages for personal injuries may be recovered. In *Read* v *Lyons* [1947] AC 156 it was doubted whether they could, but the matter was left open. In *Perry* v *Kendricks Transport* (above) it was assumed that personal injuries were covered, and an example of damages actually being awarded for

personal injuries is *Hale v Jennings Bros* [1938] 1 All ER 579, where a chair became detached from a 'chair-o-plane' in a fairground while it was revolving and struck the plaintiff, but the issue of damages for personal injuries was not discussed. There is, however, no definite authority against the recovery of damages for personal injuries.

6. *Escape.* In *Read v Lyons* [1947] AC 156 it was made clear that there must be an escape from the premises of the occupier to property not controlled by him. In that case there was an explosion in a munitions factory and it was held that there was no liability as the explosion was contained within the factory and the effects had not escaped beyond its boundaries.

7. In *Burnie Port Authority* v *General Jones Pty Ltd* (1992) 179 CLR 520 the High Court of Australia rejected *Rylands* v *Fletcher* altogether, saying that the situations envisaged by that doctrine can be dealt with by negligence. It was said that proximity would exist because of the special vulnerability and dependence of the plaintiff arising out of the hazardous activities of the defendant and that this would give rise to a non-delegable duty of care arising out of the defendant's control of the premises. It was also said that the standard of care would relate to the degree of danger and that it could even involve 'a degree of diligence so stringent as to amount practically to a guarantee of safety'.

Section 2: liability for fires

Fires are dangerous, and from earliest times there has been a special form of liabililty upon occupiers for damage caused by 'their' fires, although of course other torts such as negligence or nuisance also apply. The form of the law is complicated because the ancient common law action, together with negligence and nuisance (but not liability based on *Rylands* v *Fletcher*), is subject to a statutory defence which relieves an occupier of liability for fires which 'accidentally' begin. The position, therefore, is that an occupier is liable for damage done by a fire for which he, or his guest or his contractor, was responsible except where the fire began by mere chance. There is a debate about whether the common law action is based on occupation or control, but it seems likely that both are required: see Ogus, 'Vagaries in liability for the escape of fire' [1969] CLJ 104.

Balfour v Barty-King
Court of Appeal [1957] 1 QB 497; [1957] 2 WLR 84; [1957] 1 All ER 156

A large country house had been divided into separate houses, one of which was occupied by the defendants and another by the plaintiff. After a severe frost, pipes in the defendants' part were frozen, and two men were employed to unfreeze them. They used a blow lamp and in doing so they set fire to the lagging, and the fire spread to the plaintiff's house. Held: dismissing the appeal, that the defendants were liable.

LORD GODDARD CJ: The earliest case on the subject which the industry of counsel or our own researches have discovered is *Beaulieu v Finglam,* conveniently translated in

Mr Fifoot's History of Sources of the Common Law, 1st ed. (1949), p. 166. It will be noticed that the writ was founded upon a common custom of the realm and alleges that the defendant so negligently kept his fire (ignem suum) that the goods and chattels of the plaintiff were burnt. The court held that a man shall answer to his neighbour for each person who enters his house by his leave or knowledge or is a guest if he does any act with a candle or aught else whereby his neighbour's house is burnt. But, said the court, if a man from outside my house and against my will starts a fire in the thatch of my house or elsewhere whereby my house is burned and my neighbour's house is burned as well, for this I shall not be held bound, for this cannot be said to be done by wrong on my part, but is against my will. . . .

Sir William Holdsworth, in his History of English Law, Vol. XI, p. 607, thinks that by the time [*Turberville* v *Stamp* (1697) 91 ER 1072] was decided, 1698, lawyers were beginning to think it was anomalous that a man should be liable for fire damage not caused by negligence, and that this was one of the reasons for the Act of 1707, 6, Anne, c. 31, which provided that no action should lie against any person in whose house a fire should accidentally begin. This provision was re-enacted in the Fires Prevention (Metropolis) Act, 1774, s. 86, an Act which has been held to extend to the whole country. That it was necessary to give this measure of exemption to householders seems to show that by the common law there was an absolute duty to prevent the escape of fire, and this was the opinion of Blackstone, who says (Commentaries I, p. 431) that the common law was altered by the Statute of Anne. The two cases cited above, however, show that at common law the act of God and the act of a stranger were exceptions, and in *Musgrove* v *Pandelis* [1919] 2 KB 43, it was held that the statute which protects the householder in the case of an accidental fire leaves the other heads of liability at common law untouched. The citation in that case from the judgment of Lord Denman CJ in *Filliter* v *Phippard* (1847) 116 ER 506, shows that in his opinion the common law was that a person in whose house a fire originated and which afterwards spread to his neighbour's house was responsible for the damage, and it was to that liability that the statute was directed.

The precise meaning to be attached to 'accidentally' has not been determined, but it is clear from these last two cited cases that where the fire is caused by negligence it is not to be regarded as accidental. Although there is a difference of opinion among eminent text writers whether at common law the liability was absolute or depended on negligence, at the present day it can safely be said that a person in whose house a fire is caused by negligence is liable if it spreads to that of his neighbour, and this is true whether the negligence is his own or that of his servant or his guest, but he is not liable if the fire is caused by a stranger.

Who, then, is a stranger? Clearly a trespasser would be in that category, but if a man is liable for the negligent act of his guest, it is, indeed, difficult to see why he is not liable for the act of a contractor whom he has invited to his house to do work on it, and who does the work in a negligent manner. . . .

In the recent case of *Perry* v *Kendricks Transports Ltd* [1956] 1 All ER 154, Parker LJ referred to a stranger as a person over whom the defendant had no control. From one point of view it may be said that the test of an independent contractor is that he is left to carry out the work in his own way, but that is not, I think, the sense in which the Lord Justice is using the word 'control.' The defendants here had control over the contractor in that they chose him, they invited him to their premises to do work, and he could have been ordered to leave at any moment. It was left to the men who were sent how to do the work, and in our opinion the defendants are liable to the plaintiff for this lamentable occurrence, the more lamentable in that the persons ultimately responsible are insolvent.

Notes

1. In *Beaulieu* v *Finglam* (1401) YB 2 Hen IV, f. 18, pl. 6 (see Fifoot, *History and Sources of the Common Law*, p. 166), which is referred to above, it was argued that if liability were imposed the defendant would be 'undone and impoverished all his days'. Thirning CJ vigorously replied 'What is that to us? It is better that he should be utterly undone than that the law be changed for him.'

2. For another example of liability for the act of another, see *H. & N. Emmanuel Ltd* v *GLC* [1971] 2 All ER 835, where the defendants were liable for a fire started by demolition contractors on their land, even though they had been instructed not to light fires. Lord Denning said that a 'stranger' is 'anyone who in lighting a fire or allowing it to escape acts contrary to anything which an occupier could anticipate that he would do'.

3. The common law action does not apply to fires escaping from chattels. In *Mayfair* v *Pears* [1987] 1 NZLR 459 the defendant unlawfully parked his car on the plaintiff's property. The car caught fire and the fire spread to the plaintiff's buildings. The court held the defendant was not liable, as such liability would place a chattel owner under a stricter liability than a landowner, who could have the benefit of the statutory defence in the Act of 1774 (below).

FIRES PREVENTION (METROPOLIS) ACT 1774

Section 86
And no action suit or process whatever shall be had, maintained or prosecuted against any person in whose house, chamber, stable, barn or other building, or in whose estate any fire shall accidentally begin . . .

Notes

1. In *Filliter* v *Phippard* (1847) 11 QB 347; 116 ER 506 the defendant lit a fire on his land which spread to the plaintiff's fields. The defendant was held liable, the court pointing out that 'accidentally begin' means 'a fire produced by mere chance, or incapable of being traced to any cause, and so would stand opposed to the negligence of either servants or masters'. It was also pointed out that the Act extends to the whole of the country and not just to the metropolis. Note also that a fire which accidentally begins may be *continued* by carelessness, as in *Musgrove* v *Pandelis* [1919] 2 KB 43, where a fire 'accidentally began' in the carburettor of a car, but was carelessly continued because the chauffeur failed to turn off the petrol tap which was then fitted to all cars.

2. Negligence. Liability for damage caused by fires can also be imposed in other torts. An example of negligence is *Goldman* v *Hargrave* [1967] 1 AC 645, where lightning set fire to a redgum tree in Australia. The defendant cut the tree down but failed to put water on it. The smouldering fire revived and spread. The defendant was held liable.

3. Nuisance. An example is *Spicer* v *Smee* [1946] 1 All ER 489, where a fire was caused by defective electrical wiring which was probably carelessly installed by a contractor. It was held that the state of the wiring constituted a nuisance, and that the 1774 Act did not apply where a nuisance was created by an occupier or his contractor.

4. *Rylands* v *Fletcher.* In *Mason* v *Levy Autoparts* [1967] 2 QB 530 the defendants brought onto the land large quantities of combustible materials which inexplicably caught fire. MacKenna J, in holding the defendants liable, adopted a principle analogous to *Rylands* v *Fletcher* but slightly different from it, in that it was not the thing brought onto the land which escaped. He said there would be liability if '(1) he brought onto his land things likely to catch fire, and kept them there in such conditions that if they did ignite the fire would be likely to spread to the plaintiff's land; (2) he did so in the course of some non-natural use; and (3) the things ignited and the fire spread'.

Section 3: selected statutory liability

The motives for imposing strict liability by statute are often mixed. These include the inability of the common law to deal with the problem, as in the case of oil pollution, the need to protect the public from hazardous activities, and the need to limit liability. The latter two reasons are often combined, as in the case of nuclear escapes, where strict liability is imposed but with a limit of £20 million arising out of any one occurrence. The insurance industry will not undertake unlimited liability and a compromise of some kind is necessary. Alternatively, the excess liability could be borne by the taxpayer or, as in the case of oil pollution, by a levy on the industry.

NUCLEAR INSTALLATIONS ACT 1965

7. Duty of licensee of licensed site

(1) Subject to subsection (4) below where a nuclear site licence has been granted in respect of any site, it shall be the duty of the licensee to secure that —

(a) no such occurrence involving nuclear matter as is mentioned in subsection (2) of this section causes injury to any person or damage to any property of any person other than the licensee, being injury or damage arising out of or resulting from the radioactive properties, or a combination of those and any toxic, explosive or other hazardous properties, of that nuclear matter; and

(b) no ionising radiations emitted during the period of the licensee's responsibility—

(i) from anything caused or suffered by the licensee to be on the site which is not nuclear matter; or

(ii) from any waste discharged (in whatever form) on or from the site, cause injury to any person or damage to any property of any person other than the licensee.

(2) The occurrences referred to in subsection (1)(*a*) of this section are—

(a) any occurrence on the licensed site during the period of the licensee's responsibility, being an occurrence involving nuclear matter;

(b) any occurrence elsewhere than on the licensed site involving nuclear matter which is not excepted matter and which at the time of the occurrence—

(i) is in the course of carriage on behalf of the licensee as licensee of that site; or

(ii) is in the course of carriage to that site with the agreement of the licensee from a place outside the relevant territories; and

(iii)   in either case, is not on any other relevant site in the United Kingdom;
(c)   any occurrence elsewhere than on the licensed site involving nuclear matter which is not excepted matter and which—
(i)   having been on the licensed site at any time during the period of the licensee's responsibility; or
(ii)   having been in the course of carriage on behalf of the licensee as licensee of that site,
has not subsequently been on any relevant site, or in the course of any relevant carriage, or (except in the course of relevant carriage) within the territorial limits of a country which is not a relevant territory.

(3)   In determining the liability by virtue of subsection (1) of this section in respect of any occurrence of the licensee of a licensed site, any property which at the time of occurrence is on that site, being—
(a)   a nuclear installation; or
(b)   other property which is on that site—
(i)   for the purpose of use in connection with the operation, or the cessation of the operation, by the licensee of a nuclear installation which is or has been on that site; or
(ii)   for the purpose of the construction of a nuclear installation on that site,
shall, notwithstanding that it is the property of some other person, be deemed to be the property of the licensee.

(4)   Section 8 of this Act shall apply in relation to sites occupied by the Authority.

8.   Duty of Authority
[This section extends s. 7 to sites occupied by the United Kingdom Atomic Energy Authority.]

13.   Exclusion, extension or reduction of compensation in certain cases
(4)   The duty imposed by section 7, 8, 9, 10 or 11 of this Act—
(a)   shall not impose any liability on the person subject to that duty with respect to injury or damage caused by an occurrence which constitutes a breach of that duty if the occurrence or the causing thereby of the injury or damage, is attributable to hostile action in the course of any armed conflict, including any armed conflict within the United Kingdom; but
(b)   shall impose such a liability where the occurrence, or the causing thereby of the injury or damage, is attributable to a natural disaster, notwithstanding that the disaster is of such an exceptional character that it could not reasonably have been foreseen.

(6)   The amount of compensation payable to or in respect of any person under this Act in respect of any injury or damage caused in breach of a duty imposed by section 7, 8, 9 or 10 of this Act may be reduced by reason of the fault of that person if, but only if, and to the extent that, the causing of that injury or damage is attributable to any act of that person committed with the intention of causing harm to any person or property or with reckless disregard for the consequences of his act.

15.   Time for bringing claims under ss. 7 to 11
(1)   Subject to subsection (2) of this section and to section 16(3) of this Act, but notwithstanding anything in any other enactment, a claim by virtue of any of sections 7 to 11 of this Act may be made at any time before, but shall not be entertained if made at any time after, the expiration of thirty years from the relevant date, that is to say, the date of the occurrence which gave rise to the claim or, where that occurrence was a continuing one, or was one of a succession of occurrences all attributable to a particular happening on a particular relevant site or to the carrying out from time to time on a

particular relevant site of a particular operation, the date of the last event in the course of that occurrence or succession of occurrences to which the claim relates.

(2)   Notwithstanding anything in subsection (1) of this section, a claim in respect of injury or damage caused by an occurrence involving nuclear matter stolen from, or lost, jettisoned or abandoned by, the person whose breach of a duty imposed by section 7, 8, 9 or 10 of this Act gave rise to the claim shall not be entertained if the occurrence takes place after the expiration of the period of twenty years beginning with the day when the nuclear matter in question was so stolen, lost, jettisoned or abandoned.

16.   Satisfaction of claims by virtue of ss. 7 to 10

(1)   The liability of any person to pay compensation under this Act by virtue of a duty imposed on that person by section 7, 8 or 9 thereof shall not require him to make in respect of any one occurrence constituting a breach of that duty payments by way of such compensation exceeding in the aggregate, apart from payments in respect of interest or costs, £20 million or, in the case of the licensees of such sites as may be prescribed, £5 million.

Notes

1.   By further provisions in s. 16, if a claim is made after 10 years have elapsed from the date of the occurrence, it should be made to the appropriate government minister. A 'prescribed site' for the purposes of s. 16 is defined by the Nuclear Installations (Prescribed Site) Regulations 1983, SI 1983 No. 919 as, subject to other conditions, a small nuclear reactor with a thermal output not exceeding 600 kw. By s. 12 all other forms of liability are excluded.

Merlin v British Nuclear Fuels
High Court [1990] 2 QB 557; [1990] 3 WLR 383; [1990] 3 All ER 711

The plaintiffs owned a house called 'Mountain Ash' in Ravenglass, which is six miles south of the defendants' plant at Sellafield. Tests on dust from the house showed high levels of radioactive contamination which it was accepted originated from the defendants' plant. The plaintiffs put their house on the market for £65,000 but it was eventually sold at auction for £35,000. The Nuclear Installations Act 1965, s. 7 covers 'injury to any person' (which is defined in s. 26 as personal injury or loss of life) and 'damage to property' (which is not defined). The plaintiffs argued that 'damage' included economic loss, and that the high level of radioactivity itself amounted to personal injury and damage to property. The defendants argued that economic loss was not covered and that injury to the person did not include the risk of injury in the future. Held: the defendants were not liable.

GATEHOUSE J: 'Personal injury or damage to property' is a familiar enough phrase and in my judgment it means, as it does in other contexts, physical (or mental) injury or physical damage to tangible property. The word 'property' alone may well have a wider meaning in some contexts (e.g. in testamentary dispositions, or in the field of company law, where the expression 'all the company's property,' and so on, will extend to incorporeal property) but where used in the Vienna Convention and the Act of 1965, it does not in my judgment extend to incorporeal property or property rights. The plaintiffs' argument that 'property' included the air space within the walls, ceilings and floors of Mountain Ash; that this has been damaged by the presence of radionuclides and the house rendered less valuable as the family's home, seems to me to be too far fetched.

The Act of 1965 contains compromises. The principal compromises are these. It imposes absolute liability upon the licensee irrespective of negligence, and a greatly extended period for the bringing of claims — no doubt because, typically, the various types of cancer that can arise may take many years to manifest themselves. To balance this extended exposure of the licensee and his strict liability, there is introduced a maximum money liability in respect of any one occurrence (section 16) and, in my judgment, a restriction on the nature of the harm which qualifies for compensation, namely injury, including fatal injury, to the person or physical damage to tangible property.

It is true — and the evidence of Dr Phillips made this plain — that the dose required to produce any detectable damage to the molecular structure of inanimate objects such as building materials, furniture, etc., is enormous: infinitely greater than the level of radionuclides present in the plaintiffs' house. If 'damage to property' is restricted to physical damage to tangible property, it might be argued that in reality this is so unlikely to occur that there is really nothing to which the phrase would apply. But one obvious answer given by Mr Rokison for the defendants is that it would cover injury to livestock, which is probably just as likely to occur in the vicinity of a nuclear installation as injury to humans, and would clearly be an important head of compensation to local farmers.

I reject the argument that contamination of the plaintiffs' house per se amounts to damage to their property. All that such contamination as was admitted in this case amounts to is some increased risk to the health of its occupants. The Act of 1965 compensates for proved personal injury, not the risk of future personal injury. If the Act were concerned with risk a number of very difficult questions would arise. For instance risk to whom? Is it the plaintiffs' health risk that has to be evaluated, or, (and this was their concern) that of their children? Or is it that of potential purchasers of the house? The degree of risk depends, among other factors, on the length of time over which the individual is exposed to radioactivity. Is the court to attempt to forecast how many years each individual concerned is likely to live in the house?

Again, Mr Sedley conceded that there must be a cut-off line of contamination below which no compensation would be payable. How is the court to judge where this should be drawn? The Act provides no guidance. Is compensation to depend upon whether the plaintiffs' reaction to the advice they happened to receive was at least a reasonable response? Or is the test the reaction of a reasonable person in their position, which is not necessarily the same thing? Or is it a wholly objective test, based not on the particular advice given to the particular plaintiffs, but on the actual level of risk as assessed by the court as a result of expert evidence? . . .

A further argument in favour of the defendants' construction is this: I bear in mind the dangers of acceding to a 'floodgates' argument, nevertheless I incline away from a construction of the Act of 1965 which would result in the operator being in continual breach of the statutory duty to a possibly very large number of people. It is in the nature of nuclear installations that there will be some additional radionuclides present in the houses of the local population, over and above the naturally occurring radionuclides to which every one of us is continually exposed. If the mere presence of this additional source is enough to constitute damage under section 7, the result would inevitably be that the defendants were indeed in breach of their statutory duty every day to possibly thousands of citizens, each of whom would have a claim for compensation.

Whether there would in fact be an award in every case would then involve long and complex inquiry into the particular facts, such as has been carried out in this case, to ascertain objectively whether the resulting additional risk did or did not reach a level justifying a monetary award, and with no guidance as to what that level should be.

Another reason why in my view the Act of 1965 has no application here is the wording of section 7, which imports the element of causation. For there to be a breach of statutory duty, carrying with it a right to compensation, the plaintiff must establish that he has suffered injury or damage to his property *caused* — and I underline the word — caused by either an occurrence involving nuclear matter, section 7(1)(a), or an emission of ionising radiations on or from the site: section 7(1)(b).

Although there was some dispute as to whether the present facts fell within (a) as well as (b), I am satisfied that this is a paragraph (b)(ii) case, but it does not appear to matter; in either case there must be cause and effect. The mere presence of ionising radiations within the plaintiffs' property emitted from waste discharged from the site, is not enough to constitute a breach of statutory duty. There must be consequential damage. The radionuclides with which this case is concerned — plutonium isotopes and americium — are alpha emitters. These cannot do any significant damage to persons or property extenally, but when inhaled, ingested or otherwise enabled to enter the body they may induce cancers, but, of course, will not necessarily do so. The presence of alpha emitting radionuclides in the human airways or digestive tracts or even in the bloodstream merely increases the risk of cancer to which everyone is exposed from both natural and artificial radioactive sources. They do not per se amount to injury.

ENVIRONMENTAL PROTECTION ACT 1990

33. Prohibition on unauthorised or harmful deposit, treatment or disposal etc. of waste

(1) Subject to subsection (2) and (3) below, a person shall not—

(a) deposit controlled waste, or knowingly cause or knowingly permit controlled waste to be deposited in or on any land unless a waste management licence authorising the deposit is in force and the deposit is in accordance with the licence;

(b) treat, keep or dispose of controlled waste, or knowingly cause or knowingly permit controlled waste to be treated, kept or disposed of—

(i) in or on any land, or

(ii) by means of any mobile plant,

except under and in accordance with a waste management licence;

(c) treat, keep or dispose of controlled waste in a manner likely to cause pollution of the environment or harm to human health.

(2) Subsection (1) above does not apply in relation to household waste from a domestic property which is treated, kept or disposed of within the curtilage of the dwelling by or with the permission of the occupier of the dwelling.

(7) It shall be a defence for a person charged with an offence under this section to prove—

(a) that he took all reasonable precautions and exercised all due diligence to avoid the commission of the offence; or

(b) that he acted under instructions from his employer and neither knew nor had reason to suppose that the acts done by him constituted a contravention of subsection (1) above; or

(c) that the acts alleged to constitute the contravention were done in an emergency in order to avoid danger to human health in a case where—

(i) he took all such steps as were reasonably practicable in the circumstances for minimising pollution of the environment and harm to human health; and

(ii)   particulars of the acts were furnished to the waste regulation authority as soon as reasonably practicable after they were done.

63.   Waste other than controlled waste

(2)   A person who deposits, or knowingly causes or knowingly permits the deposit of, any waste—

(a)   which is not controlled waste, but

(b)   which, if it were controlled waste, would be special waste,

in a case where he would be guilty of an offence under section 33 above if the waste were special waste and any waste management licence were not in force, shall, subject to subsection (3) below, be guilty of that offence and punishable as if the waste were special waste.

[**Note:** by s. 75(4) 'controlled waste' means household, industrial and commercial waste. By 75(9) 'special waste' means waste which is so difficult to treat, keep or dispose of that special provision is required for dealing with it and regulations have been made in relation to it.]

73.   Appeals and other provisions relating to legal proceedings and civil liability.

(6)   Where any damage is caused by waste which has been deposited in or on land, any person who deposited it, or knowingly caused or knowingly permitted it to be deposited, in either case so as to commit an offence under section 33(1) or 63(2) above, is liable for the damage except where the damage—

(a)   was due wholly to the fault of the person who suffered it; or

(b)   was suffered by a person who voluntarily accepted the risk of the damage being caused;

but without prejudice to any liability arising otherwise than under this subsection.

(7)   The matters which may be proved by way of defence under section 33(7) above may be proved also by way of defence to an action brought under subsection (6) above.

(8)   In subsection (6) above—

'damage' includes the death of, or injury to, any person (including any disease and any impairment of physical or mental condition); and

'fault' has the same meaning as in the Law Reform (Contributory Negligence) Act 1945.

23 ANIMALS

The modern statutory liability for animals replaces the ancient rules of the common law, but to a large extent follows its structure. While some aspects of the law may seem primitive in these days of the dominance of negligence, this is not so, for the law provides relatively simple and straightforward rules for what is often minor damage or injury (the Pearson Commission (1978) thought there were about 50,000 injuries caused by animals a year). However, some animals cause very serious injury, and the modern tendency to keep ferocious breeds of dog has led to the demand for more stringent laws, and this control has so far been effected by use of the criminal law. However, it may be argued that there should be strict liability for injury caused by dogs, for not only do they cause a large number of injuries but also it seems strange that if a human being is attacked by a dog he must prove knowledge of this propensity on the part of the keeper, but if a sheep is attacked liability is strict. Why are sheep better protected than humans?

It is not only the statutory liability that can apply to animals, for other torts can also be relevant. For example, in *Draper v Hodder* [1972] 2 QB 556 the plaintiff, who was three years old, was savaged by a pack of Jack Russell terriers and he suffered over 100 bites, losing a large part of his scalp. The defendant was held liable in negligence because he ought to have realised that the dogs were liable to attack when they are in a pack. A further example of liability in negligence is the potential liability of a keeper or occupier of premises for damage done when an animal escapes onto the highway because of inadequate fencing (*Davies v Davies* [1975] QB 172, which discusses the exemption for common land in s. 8 of the 1971 Act).

The law of nuisance can also be relevant to liability for animals, for example for inconvenience caused by the crowing of cockerels (*Leeman v Montague* [1936] 2 All ER 1677) or the barking of dogs.

For a full study of the law on liability for animals, see North, *The Modern Law of Animals* (1972).

ANIMALS ACT 1971

2. Liability for damage done by dangerous animals

(1) Where any damage is caused by an animal which belongs to a dangerous species, any person who is a keeper of the animal is liable for the damage, except as otherwise provided by this Act.

(2) Where damage is caused by an animal which does not belong to a dangerous species, a keeper of the animal is liable for the damage, except as otherwise provided by this Act, if—

(a) the damage is of a kind which the animal, unless restrained, was likely to cause or which, if caused by the animal, was likely to be severe; and

(b) the likelihood of the damage or of its being severe was due to characteristics of the animal which are not normally found in animals of the same species or are not normally so found except at particular times or in particular circumstances; and

(c) those characteristics were known to that keeper or were at any time known to a person who at that time had charge of the animal as that keeper's servant or, where that keeper is the head of a household, were known to another keeper of the animal who is a member of that household and under the age of sixteen.

3. Liability for injury done by dogs to livestock

Where a dog causes damage by killing or injuring livestock, any person who is a keeper of the dog is liable for the damage, except as otherwise provided by this Act.

4. Liability for damage and expenses due to trespassing livestock

(1) Where livestock belonging to any person strays on to land in the ownership or occupation of another and—

(a) damage is done by the livestock to the land or to any property on it which is in the ownership or possession of the other person; or

(b) any expenses are reasonably incurred by that other person in keeping the livestock while it cannot be restored to the person to whom it belongs or while it is detained in pursuance of section 7 of this Act, or in ascertaining to whom it belongs; the person to whom the livestock belongs is liable for the damage or expenses, except as otherwise provided by this Act.

(2) For the purposes of this section any livestock belongs to the person in whose possession it is.

5. Exceptions from liability under sections 2 to 4

(1) A person is not liable under sections 2 to 4 of this Act for any damage which is due wholly to the fault of the person suffering it.

(2) A person is not liable under section 2 of this Act for any damage suffered by a person who has voluntarily accepted the risk thereof.

(3) A person is not liable under section 2 of this Act for any damage caused by an animal kept on any premises or structure to a person trespassing there, if it is proved either—

(a) that the animal was not kept there for the protection of persons or property; or

(b) (if the animal was kept there for the protection of persons or property) that keeping it there for that purpose was not unreasonable.

(4) A person is not liable under section 3 of this Act if the livestock was killed or injured on land on to which it had strayed and either the dog belonged to the occupier or its presence on the land was authorised by the occupier.

(5) A person is not liable under section 4 of this Act where the livestock strayed from a highway and its presence there was a lawful use of the highway.

(6)   In determining whether any liability for damage under section 4 of this Act is excluded by subsection (1) of this section the damage shall not be treated as due to the fault of the person suffering it by reason only that he could have prevented it by fencing; but a person is not liable under that section where it is proved that the straying of the livestock on to the land would not have occurred but for a breach by any other person, being a person having an interest in the land, of a duty to fence.

6.   Interpretation of certain expressions used in sections 2 to 5
(1)   The following provisions apply to the interpretation of sections 2 to 5 of this Act.
(2)   A dangerous species is a species—
   (a)   which is not commonly domesticated in the British Islands; and
   (b)   whose fully grown animals normally have such characteristics that they are likely, unless restrained, to cause severe damage or that any damage they may cause is likely to be severe.
(3)   Subject to subsection (4) of this section, a person is a keeper of an animal if—
   (a)   he owns the animal or has it in his possession; or
   (b)   he is the head of a household of which a member under the age of sixteen owns the animal or has it in his possession;
and if at any time an animal ceases to be owned by or to be in the possession of a person, any person who immediately before that time was a keeper thereof by virtue of the preceding provisions of this subsection continues to be a keeper of the animal until another person becomes a keeper thereof by virtue of those provisions.
(4)   Where an animal is taken into and kept in possession for the purpose of preventing it from causing damage or of restoring it to its owner, a person is not a keeper of it by virtue only of that possession.
(5)   Where a person employed as a servant by a keeper of an animal incurs a risk incidental to his employment he shall not be treated as accepting it voluntarily.

8.   Duty to take care to prevent damage from animals straying on to the highway
(1)   So much of the rules of the common law relating to liability for negligence as excludes or restricts the duty which a person might owe to others to take such care as is reasonable to see that damage is not caused by animals straying on to a highway is hereby abolished.
(2)   Where damage is caused by animals straying from unfenced land to a highway a person who placed them on the land shall not be regarded as having committed a breach of the duty to take care by reason only of placing them there if—
   (a)   the land is common land, or is land situated in an area where fencing is not customary, or is a town or village green; and
   (b)   he had a right to place the animals on that land.

10.   Application of certain enactments to liability under sections 2 to 4
For the purposes of the Fatal Accidents Act 1846 to 1959, the Law Reform (Countributory Negligence) Act 1945 and the Limitation Act 1980 any damage for which a person is liable under sections 2 to 4 of this Act shall be treated as due to his fault.

11.   General interpretation
In this Act—
   'common land', and 'town or village green' have the same meanings as in the Commons Registration Act 1965;
   'damage' includes the death of, or injury to, any person (including any disease and any impairment of physical or mental condition);

'fault' has the same meaning as in the Law Reform (Contributory Negligence) Act 1945;

'fencing' includes the construction of any obstacle designed to prevent animals from straying;

'livestock' means cattle, horses, asses, mules, hinnies, sheep, pigs, goats and poultry, and also deer not in the wild state and, in sections 3 and 9, also, while in captivity, pheasant, partridges and grouse;

'poultry' means the domestic varieties of the following, that is to say, fowls, turkeys, geese, ducks, guinea-fowls, pigeons, peacocks and quails; and

'species' includes sub-species and variety.

Question

What is an animal? Presumably it must be able to move independently, but must it also be able to feel sensations? Are bacteria animals? The Animals (Scotland) Act 1987 states that 'animal' does not include viruses, bacteria, algae, fungi or protozoa.

Section 1: statutory liability for dangerous species

See the Animals Act 1971, ss. 2(1) and 6(2) above. This form of liability derives from the common law rules relating to animals *ferae naturae* and is of ancient origin. Whether liability is strict depends not on the characteristics of the individual animal, but of the adults of that species. Thus, liability is strict whether the animals are young or tame. In *Behrens v Bertram Mills Circus* [1957] 2 QB 1 the plaintiffs, husband and wife, were dwarfs who made a living by exhibiting themselves at fairs, and they had a booth at Olympia while the defendant's circus was on. Their manager was looking after a dog, called Simba, which escaped as some Burmese elephants, including one called Bullu, were near. The dog snapped and barked: Bullu took fright and chased and killed it, but in doing so knocked over the plaintiffs' booth and injured them. It was held that the fact that the elephant was actually tame was irrelevant, as in law it was classified as a dangerous species. Devlin J also pointed out that the manner of the injury is irrelevant since liability is strict. He said (at p. 17) 'If a person wakes up in the middle of the night and finds an escaping tiger on top of his bed, and suffers a heart attack, it would be nothing to the point that the intentions of the tiger were entirely amiable . . . . It is not in my judgment practicable to introduce conceptions of mens rea and malevolence in the case of animals.'

Another example is *Tutin v Chipperfield* (1980) NLJ 807, where the actress Dorothy Tutin was taking part in a camel race for charity, when she fell off, injuring her back. The defendant was strictly liable under the Animals Act because, as camels are not domesticated in the British Isles, they are capable of being classed as a dangerous species. Are there any wild camels anywhere?

For criminal provisions relating to dangerous animals see the Dangerous Wild Animals Act 1976, which requires keepers of certain animals to obtain a licence from the local authority which can only be granted if the keeper has insurance against liability for any damage caused by the animal. The relevant animals are listed in the Dangerous Wild Animals (Modification) Order 1981 (SI 1981 No. 1173), and they include camels, wolves, alligators, emus, cobras, adders and other snakes, tigers, gibbons, and ostriches.

For legislation controlling dangerous dogs, see the Dogs Acts 1871 and 1906, the Dogs Amendment Act 1928, the Dogs (Protection of Livestock) Act 1953, the Guard Dogs Act 1975 and the Dangerous Dogs Acts 1989 and 1991.

Section 2:   statutory liability for non-dangerous species

See the Animals Act 1971, s. 2(2). This applies to any animal which is not defined as dangerous under s. 6 of the Act, and derives from the old *scienter* action, i.e. one based on the knowledge of the keeper as to the dangerous characteristics of the individual animal. The most difficult problem is to determine whether the likelihood of damage was due to characteristics of the animal which are not normally found in animals of the same species.

Curtis v *Betts*
Court of Appeal [1990] 1 WLR 459; [1990] 1 All ER 769

The defendants owned a bull mastiff called Max which weighed about 10 stone. It was their custom to put the dog into the back of a Land Rover to take it for a walk in a nearby park. One day the plaintiff, aged 10, who knew the defendants and their dog, approached while the dog was being led out to the Land Rover. For no apparent reason the dog jumped up at the plaintiff and bit him on the right side of the face in three places. Evidence was given (a) that such dogs 'tended to defend their own territory' and (b) that the defendants were aware of such behaviour. Held: dismissing the appeal, that the defendants were liable under the Animals Act 1971, s. 2(2).

SLADE LJ: . . . The keeper of an animal not belonging to a dangerous species will be liable for damage caused by it, provided that the plaintiff can show that each of the three requirements (which I will call respectively 'requirements (a), (b) and (c)') is satisfied. Lord Denning MR in *Cummings* v *Granger* [1977] QB 397, 404, described section 2(2) as 'very cumbrously worded,' and giving rise to 'severe difficulties.' I agree. Particularly in view of the somewhat tortuous wording of the subsection, I think it desirable to consider each of the three requirements separately and in turn.

As to requirement (a)
[Note: for requirements (a), (b) and (c) see the text of the Animals Act, s. 2(2) above.] The kind of damage in the present case was personal injury. The judge, rightly, did not find that this damage was 'of a kind which [Max], unless restrained, was likely to cause.' Indeed, he made it plain that in general Max was a docile and lazy dog. However, he found that Max's action 'in jumping up and biting a child on the side of the face was likely to cause severe damage.' By this route he found that the personal injury caused to Lee was of a kind 'which, if caused by the animal, was likely to be severe,' so that the second head of requirement (a) was satisfied.

. . . The broad purpose of requirement (a), as I read it, is to subject the keeper of a non-dangerous animal to liability for the damage caused by it in any circumstances where the damage is of a kind which the particular animal in question, unless restrained, was likely to cause or which, if caused by that animal, was likely to be severe, provided that the plaintiff can also satisfy the additional requirements (b) and (c). While conceivably the reference to the likelihood of severity of damage may give rise to questions of degree on particular facts, I would not, for my part, ordinarily anticipate difficulty in applying requirement (a) in practice.

. . . Max was a dog of the bull mastiff breed. If he did bite anyone, the damage was likely to be severe. For this simple reason, the judge was, in my judgment, right to hold that requirement (a) was satisfied.

As to requirement (b)

The construction and application of requirement (b) give rise to rather greater difficulties. In particular, on a first reading I was puzzled by the legislature's use of the phrase 'the likelihood of the damage or of its being severe,' instead of the simple phrase 'the damage,' especially since the subsequent phrase 'due to' at first sight appeared to me to bear the simple meaning 'caused by.' However another, broader, meaning is also given to the word 'due' by the *Shorter Oxford English Dictionary*, 3rd ed. (1944), namely 'to be ascribed or attributed.' If one reads the phrase 'due to' as bearing the broader sense of 'attributable to,' I think that this particular difficulty disappears.

Just as, in my view, requirement (a) in any given case falls to be considered having regard to the particular facts of that case, so too, in my view, in the consideration of requirement (b), the existence or non-existence of the relevant likelihood has to be determined having regard to the particular facts. If, therefore, the plaintiff is relying on the second limb of requirement (b), he will have to show that *on the particular facts* the likelihood of the damage or of its being severe was attributable to characteristics of the animal not normally found except at particular times or in particular circumstances corresponding with the particular facts of the case.

The broad purpose of requirement (b), as I read it, is to ensure that, even in a case falling within requirement (a), the defendant, subject to one exception, will still escape liability if, on the particular facts, the likelihood of damage was attributable to potentially dangerous characteristics of the animal which are normally found in animals of the same species. The one exception is this. The mere fact that a particular animal shared its potentially dangerous characteristics with other animals of the same species will not preclude the satisfaction of requirement (b) if on the particular facts the likelihood of damage was attributable to characteristics normally found in animals of the same species at times or in circumstances corresponding with those in which the damage actually occurred. In *Cummings* v *Granger* [1977] QB 397, 407 Ormrod LJ gave the examples of 'a bitch with pups or an Alsatian dog running loose in a yard which it regards as its territory when a stranger enters into it.' If in his example the damage is caused by a bitch accompanying her pups or an Alsatian dog defending its territory, requirement (b) will be satisfied.

It was, I think, common ground before us that, in concluding that requirement (b) was satisfied, the judge based his conclusion exclusively on the second limb of that requirement, i.e. he found that the likelihood of the severe damage being caused by Max was 'due to characteristics of the animal which are not normally found in animals of the same species . . . except at particular times or in particular circumstances.' That conclusion gives rise to two questions. (1) What were the relevant characteristics of Max? (2) In the particular circumstances, was the likelihood of the damage due, i.e. attributable, to those characteristics?

As to (1), the judge concluded that bull mastiffs have a tendency to react fiercely at particular times and in particular circumstances, namely when defending the boundaries of what they regard as their own territory. In my judgment, there was evidence before him amply sufficient to entitle him to make that finding. The defendants' expert

Animals 391

witness, Mrs Hand, in her written report described mastiffs as tending to be 'a natural protector of their own environment,' though she added that 'they are not looking for trouble.' Another witness called by the defendants, Mr Athol Hill, gave evidence that he was interested in dogs, particularly bull mastiffs, and that he had sold Max, who was one of a litter of 10, when he was a little over eight weeks old. He accepted in cross-examination that it is fair comment to suggest that they are territorial animals. When questioned by the court he said that they 'tended to defend their own territory.' ...

In my judgment, in the light of all the evidence and of his own common knowledge and experience, it was open to the judge, albeit without expert evidence to support his conclusion, to infer that Max regarded his territory as including the rear of the Land Rover. I do not think that he was obliged to accept as conclusive the evidence of Mrs Hand apparently dismissing as irrelevant the aggressive behaviour of the dog when inside the playground at the school gates. Though I do not attach too much weight to this point, I observe that Mrs Hand herself in her report had referred to mastiffs being natural protectors of 'their own environment.' It must be a question of fact and degree what their environment includes.

It follows that, in my judgment, there are no sufficient grounds for interfering with the judge's conclusion that the likelihood of the damage being severe was on the facts due to the relevant characteristics of the dog. Requirement (b) is thus satisfied. But were those characteristics known to the defendants?

Requirement (c)
I can deal with this point quite shortly. . . .

In this court Mr Gash accepted that, in the light of the judge's findings, this court must proceed on the basis that, contrary to their own evidence, the defendants knew at least that the two dogs had the habit of jumping up at the school gate in the playground and growling and snarling at passers-by. This concession was, in my opinion, a realistic one, having regard to all the evidence. In my judgment, it follows that the defendants must be taken to have known of Max's relevant characteristic, namely his tendency to react fiercely when defending what he regarded as his own territory. In my judgment, therefore, the remaining requirement, requirement (c), is satisfied and liability on the part of the defendants is established.

Notes
1. In *Smith* v *Ainger*, *The Times*, 5 June 1990, it was shown that the defendant's dog had a propensity to attack other dogs, and in an attack on the plaintiff's dog the plaintiff was knocked over. It was held that it must be shown that the dog was likely to cause personal injury to a human being, but that it was likely that if one dog attacked another the owner would intervene and might be bitten or knocked over. Accordingly, the defendant was liable.
2. In the same case it was said that 'likely' in s. 2(2)(a) (damage of a kind which the animal, unless restrained, is likely to cause) means an event 'such as might happen', or 'such as might well happen' or 'where there is a material risk that it will happen'. In other words, the risk does not have to be more than 50 per cent.

Section 3: defences

See the Animals Act 1971, s. 5. The provisions of s. 5(3) and the decision in *Cummings* v *Granger* (below) must be read in the light of the Guard Dogs Act 1975, which is discussed in note 2 below.

Cummings v Granger
Court of Appeal [1977] 1 QB 397; [1976] 3 WLR 842; [1977] 1 All ER 104

The defendant was the keeper of an Alsatian which was used to guard a scrap-yard in East London. One evening the plaintiff, who was a barmaid at a nearby pub, went into the yard with her friend, Mr Hobson, who wanted to collect some tools from his car. Mr Hobson had permission to enter the yard, but the plaintiff was a trespasser. She was attacked by the dog and her cheek was torn open. At the entrance to the yard was a notice saying 'Beware of the dog'. The dog was allowed to roam free in the yard at night. Held: allowing the appeal, that the defendant was prima facie liable under s. 2(2) of the 1971 Act, but that ss. 5(2) and 5(3) both provided defences. He was thus not liable to the plaintiff.

LORD DENNING MR: The statutory liability for a tame animal, like a dog, is defined in section 2(2) of the Act, subject to exceptions contained in section 5. Now it seems to me that this is a case where the keeper of the dog is strictly liable unless he can bring himself within one of the exceptions. I say this because the three requirements for strict liability are satisfied. The section is very cumbrously worded and will give rise to several difficulties in future. But in this case the judge held that the three requirements were satisfied and I agree with him for the following reasons. Section 2(2)(a): this animal was a dog of the Alsatian breed; if it did bite anyone, the damage was 'likely to be severe.' Section 2(2)(b): this animal was a guard dog kept so as to scare intruders and frighten them off. On the defendant's own evidence, it used to bark and run round in circles, espcially when coloured people approached. Those characterstics — barking and running around to guard its territory — are not normally found in Alsatian dogs except in circumstances where they are used as guard dogs. Those circumstances are 'particular circumstances' within section 2(2)(b). It was due to those circumstances that the damage was likely to be severe if an intruder did enter on its territory. Section 2(2)(c): those characteristics were known to the defendant. It follows that the defendant is strictly liable unless he can bring himself within one of the exceptions in section 5. Obviously section 5(1) does not avail. The bite was not *wholly* due to the fault of the plaintiff, but only *partly* so.

Section 5(3) may, however, avail the keeper. It says that if someone trespasses on property and is bitten or injured by a guard dog, the keeper of the guard dog is exempt from liability if it is proved 'that keeping it there for that purpose was not unreasonable.' The judge held that the defendant was unreasonable in keeping it in this yard. He said [1975] 1 WLR 1330, 1336-1337: 'It seems to me that it was unreasonable to keep an untrained dog, known to be ferocious and known to be likely to attack at least coloured people, if they came near the place, to protect a lot of old broken-down scrap motor cars in this yard, by night.'

I take a different view. This was a yard in the East End of London where persons of the roughest type come and go. It was a scrap-yard, true, but scrap-yards, like building sites, often contain much valuable property. It was deserted at night and at weekends. If there was no protection, thieves would drive up in a lorry and remove the scrap with no one to see them or to stop them. The only reasonable way of protecting the place was to have a guard dog. True it was a fierce dog. But why not? A gentle dog would be no good. The thieves would soon make friends with him. It seems to me that it was very reasonable — or, at any rate, not unreasonable — for the defendant to keep this dog there. Long ago in 1794 Lord Kenyon said in *Brock* v *Copeland* (1794) 1 Esp 203 that 'every man had a right to keep a dog for the protection of his yard or house.'

Alternatively there is another defence provided by section 5(2). It says that a person is not liable 'for any damage suffered by a person who has voluntarily accepted the risk thereof.' This seems to me to warrant a reference back to the common law. . . . The plaintiff certainly knew the animal was there. She worked next door. She knew all about it. She must have seen this huge notice on the door 'Beware of the Dog.' Nevertheless she went in, following her man friend. In the circumstances she must be taken voluntarily to have incurred this risk. So with any burglar or thief who goes on to premises knowing that there is a guard dog there. If he is bitten or injured, he cannot recover. He voluntarily takes the risk of it. Even if he does not know a guard dog is there, he might be defeated by the plea 'ex turpi causa non oritur actio.'

There is only one further point I would mention. This accident took place in November 1971 very shortly after the Animals Act 1971 was passed. In 1975 the Guard Dogs Act 1975 was passed. It does not apply to this case. But it makes it quite clear that in future a person is not allowed to have a guard dog to roam about on his premises unless the dog is under the control of a handler. If he has no handler, the dog must be chained up so that it is not at liberty to roam around. If a person contravenes the Act, he can be brought before a magistrate and fined up to £400. But it is only criminal liability. It does not confer a right of action in any civil proceedings. It may however have the effect in civil proceedings of making it unreasonable for the defendant to let a dog free in the yard at night (as this defendant did) and it may thus deprive the defendant of a defence under section 5(3)(b). But he might still be able to rely on the defence under section 5(2) of volenti non fit injuria.

Coming back to the present case, I think the defendant is not under any strict liability to the plaintiff because she was a trespasser and also because she voluntarily took the risk. . . .

Notes

1. This case has been much discussed: see, for example, Ingman (1977) 127 NLJ 895; Jackson (1977) 40 MLR 590; Spencer [1977] CLJ 39.

2. It is important to note that the question of liability under s. 2 was determined not by the characteristics of dogs in general but by the characteristics of Alsatians, since species in s. 2 is defined as including sub-species or variety by s. 11. Secondly, prima facie liability existed not because this Alsatian was ferocious and most are not, but because in the circumstances of roaming loose in what it regarded as its territory it was ferocious, whereas Alsatians in general are not.

3. The Guard Dogs Act 1975 was passed after public concern about guard dogs, especially Alsatians, attacking people and there had been considerable outrage about attacks on young childlren. The Act provides that it is a criminal offence to have a dog guarding premises unless it is under the control of a handler at all times or it is not at liberty to go freely about the premises. Although the Act creates only criminal and not civil liability, it surely could not be 'reasonable' to keep a guard dog for the purposes of s. 5(3) if it is unlawful to do so. Accordingly, the main ground for decision in *Cummings* v *Granger* would now be different. But suppose the existence of the dog was not unlawful because it was on a long lead, and the trespasser was a five year old who was unable to run away from the dog in time?

24 DEFAMATION

The law of defamation is at last undergoing change. For many years it was subjected to considerable criticism, especially in relation to the size of damages awards. The law was considered by the Faulks Committee in 1975 (Cmnd 5709) but nothing was done to reform it. However, in 1991 the courts themselves took steps to deal with the damages problem and the Defamation Bill 1996 proposes a number of significant reforms. None of the reforms address fundamental issues and it may be that questions need to be asked about the extent to which the law should protect reputation itself in the absence of any provable economic loss flowing from the tort, and about the extent to which the law inhibits the exposure of wrongdoing.

A further criticism of defamation is its highly technical nature, and especially the great importance and complexity of the pleadings, which often look as if the nineteenth century reforms of procedure never happened. For this reason it is sometimes difficult to select suitable cases to illustrate the law, for so often the judgments concentrate on procedure. This chapter omits statutes and cases on the distinction between libel and slander and on absolute privilege, in order to keep its length within reasonable bounds.

EUROPEAN CONVENTION FOR THE PROTECTION OF HUMAN RIGHTS AND FUNDAMENTAL FREEDOMS

Article 10

(1) Everyone has the right to freedom of expression. This right shall include freedom to hold opinions and to receive and impart information and ideas without interference by public authority and regardless of frontiers. This Article shall not prevent States from requiring the licensing of broadcasting, television or cinema enterprises.

(2) The exercise of these freedoms, since it carries with it duties and responsibilities, may be subject to such formalities, conditions, restrictions or penalties as are prescribed by law and are necessary in a democratic society, in the interests of national

security, territorial integrity or public safety, for the prevention of disorder or crime, for the protection of health or morals, for the protection of the reputation or rights of others, for preventing the disclosure of information received in confidence, or for maintaining the authority and impartiality of the judiciary.

Notes
1. Although this Convention is not part of English law it has been used to help to define the scope of the law of defamation: see for example *Derbyshire C.C.* v *Times Newspapers* [1992] 3 All ER 65 (CA) and [1993] 1 All ER 1011 (HL) and *Rantzen* v *Mirror Group Newspapers* [1993] 4 All ER 975 (CA). In the *Derbyshire* case (where the House of Lords held that in the public interest a local authority could not sue for libel), Lord Keith said that in relation to freedom of speech there was no difference between the common law and the Convention. He pointed out that 'necessity' in the Convention meant the existence of a pressing social need and that restrictions should be no more than is proportionate to the legitimate aim pursued. Accordingly, the law of defamation should now incorporate the public interest in freedom of speech, but it is likely that this principle will have limited effect beyond the existing limits of the defence of privilege.
2. In *Tolstoy Miloslavsky* v *United Kingdom* (1995) 20 EHRR 442 the applicant had been ordered to pay damages of £1,500,000 to Lord Aldington for a libel concerning the repatriation of Yugoslavs at the end of the Second World War. The European Court of Human Rights held this to be contrary to art. 10 as not being 'necessary in a democratic society'; and said that the law provided no adequate safeguards against a disproportionately large award.

Section 1:   who can be liable?

At common law any person who distributes a defamatory statement could be liable and this includes not only the author but also the printer, the publisher, the wholesaler and the retailer, even if they were unaware that the statement was defamatory. To some extent this extreme position was ameliorated by the Defamation Act 1952, s. 4 (innocent dissemination) but the provision was limited, complicated and generally regarded as unsatisfactory. This was especially so in the light of new technology both in printing (direct input) and electronic forms of communication. Accordingly, the Defamation Bill 1996 provides a defence for those other than authors, editors or publishers who are only involved in distribution of material so long as they have shown reasonable care. It is also very significant for providers of access to electronic systems of communication.

Even if a person is 'responsible' for the defamatory statement he can make an 'offer of amends'. This involves an offer to publish an apology, to bring the apology to the notice of those who received the defamatory statement, and to pay compensation. If the offer is refused the plaintiff cannot sue for defamation unless he can show that the defendant knew or had reason to know that the statement referred to the plaintiff and was defamatory.

DEFAMATION BILL 1996

1.—(1) In defamation proceedings a person has a defence if he shows that—
(a) he was not the author, editor or publisher of the statement complained of,
(b) he took reasonable care in relation to its publication, and
(c) he did not know, and had no reason to believe, that what he did caused or contributed to the publication of a defamatory statement.

(2) For this purpose 'author', 'editor' and 'publisher' have the following meanings, which are further explained in subsection (3)—

'author' means the originator of the statement, but does not include a person who did not intend that his statement be published at all;

'editor' means a person having editorial or equivalent responsibility for the content of the statement or the decision to publish it; and

'publisher' means a commercial publisher, that is, a person whose business is issuing material to the public, or a section of the public, who issues material containing the statement in the course of that business.

(3) A person shall not be considered the author, editor or publisher of a statement if he is only involved—

(a) in printing, producing, distributing or selling printed material containing the statement;

(b) in processing, making copies of, distributing, exhibiting or selling a film or sound recording (as defined in Part I of the Copyright, Designs and Patents Act 1988) containing the statement;

(c) in processing, making copies of, distributing or selling any electronic medium in or on which the statement is recorded, or in operating or providing any equipment system or service by means of which the statement is retrieved, copied, distributed or made available in electronic form;

(d) as the broadcaster of a live programme containing the statement in circumstances in which he has no effective control over the maker of the statement;

(e) as the operator of or provider of access to a communications system by means of which the statement is transmitted, or made available, by a person over whom he has no effective control.

In a case not within paragraphs (a) to (e) the court may have regard to those provisions by way of analogy in deciding whether a person is to be considered the author, editor or publisher of a statement.

(4) Employees or agents of an author, editor or publisher are in the same position as their employer or principal to the extent that they are responsible for the content of the statement or the decision to publish it.

(5) In determining for the purposes of this section whether a person took reasonable care, or had reason to believe that what he did caused or contributed to the publication of a defamatory statement, regard shall be had to—

(a) the extent of his responsibility for the content of the statement or the decision to publish it,

(b) the nature or circumstances of the publication, and

(c) the previous conduct or character of the author, editor or publisher.

(6) This section does not apply to any cause of action which arose before the section came into force.

2.—(1) A person who has published a statement alleged to be defamatory of another may offer to make amends under this section.

(2) The offer may be in relation to the statement generally or in relation to a specific

defamatory meaning which the person making the offer accepts that the statement conveys ('a qualified offer').

(3) An offer to make amends—

(a) must be in writing,

(b) must be expressed to be an offer to make amends under section 2 of the Defamation Act 1996, and

(c) must state whether it is a qualified offer and, if so, set out the defamatory meaning in relation to which it is made.

(4) An offer to make amends under this section is an offer—

(a) to make a suitable correction of the statement complained of and a sufficient apology to the aggrieved party,

(b) to publish the correction and apology in a manner that is reasonable and practicable in the circumstances, and

(c) to pay to the aggrieved party such compensation (if any), and such costs, as may be agreed or determined to be payable.

The fact that the offer is accompanied by an offer to take specific steps does not affect the fact that an offer to make amends under this section is an offer to do all the things mentioned in paragraphs (a) to (c).

(5) An offer to make amends under this section may not be made by a person after serving a defence in defamation proceedings brought against him by the aggrieved party in respect of the publication in question.

(6) An offer to make amends under this section may be withdrawn before it is accepted; and a renewal of an offer which has been withdrawn shall be treated as a new offer.

3.—(1) If an offer to make amends under section 2 is accepted by the aggrieved party, the following provisions apply.

(2) The party accepting the offer may not bring or continue defamation proceedings in respect of the publication concerned against the person making the offer, but he is entitled to enforce the offer to make amends as follows.

(3) If the parties agree on the steps to be taken in fulfilment of the offer, the aggrieved party may apply to the court for an order that the other party fulfil his offer by taking the steps agreed.

(4) If the parties do not agree on the steps to be taken by way of correction, apology and publication, the party who made the offer may take such steps as he thinks appropriate, and may in particular—

(a) make the correction and apology by a statement in open court in terms approved by the court, and

(b) give an undertaking to the court as to the manner of their publication.

(5) If the parties do not agree on the amount to be paid by way of compensation, it shall be determined by the court on the same principles as damages in defamation proceedings.

The court shall take account of any steps taken in fulfilment of the offer and (so far as not agreed between the parties) of the suitability of the correction, the sufficiency of the apology and whether the manner of their publication was reasonable in the circumstances, and may reduce or increase the amount of compensation accordingly.

(6) If the parties do not agree on the amount to be paid by way of costs, it shall be determined by the court on the same principles as costs awarded in court proceedings.

(7) The acceptance of an offer by one person to make amends does not affect any cause of action against another person in respect of the same publication, subject as follows.

(8)   In England and Wales or Northern Ireland, for the purposes of the Civil Liability (Contribution) Act 1978—

(a)   the amount of compensation paid under the offer shall be treated as paid in bona fide settlement or compromise of the claim; and

(b)   where another person is liable in respect of the same damage (whether jointly or otherwise), the person whose offer to make amends was accepted is not required to pay by virtue of any contribution under section 1 of that Act a greater amount than the amount of the compensation payable in pursuance of the offer.

(9)   [omitted]

(10)   Proceedings under this section shall be heard and determined without a jury.

4.—(1)   If an offer to make amends under section 2, duly made and not withdrawn, is not accepted by the aggrieved party, the following provisions apply;

(2)   The fact that the offer was made is a defence (subject to subsection (3)) to defamation proceedings in respect of the publication in question by that party against the person making the offer.

A qualified offer is only a defence in respect of the meaning to which the offer related.

(3)   There is no such defence if the person by whom the offer was made knew or had reason to believe that the statement complained of—

(a)   referred to the aggrieved party or was likely to be understood as referring to him, and

(b)   was both false and defamatory of that party;

but it shall be presumed until the contrary is shown that he did not know and had no reason to believe that was the case.

(4)   The person who made the offer need not rely on it by way of defence, but if he does he may not rely on any other defence.

If the offer was a qualified offer, this applies only in respect of the meaning to which the offer related.

(5)   The offer may be relied on in mitigation of damages whether or not it was relied on as a defence.

Section 2:   the meaning of 'defamatory'

It has never been easy to define what is meant by 'defamatory', and each attempt has met with criticism, although the suggestion of Lord Atkin in *Sim* v *Stretch* (below) is the most commonly accepted.

Sim v *Stretch*
House of Lords [1936] 2 All ER 1237; 52 TLR 669

Edith Saville was a maid employed by the plaintiff, Herbert Stretch, who then went to work for the defendant, Alexander Sim. The defendant sent a telegram to the plaintiff saying 'Edith has resumed service with us today. Please send her possessions and the money you borrowed also her wages to Old Barton. Sim.' It appeared that when Mrs Stretch had been away she had left money with the maid to pay the bills and had arranged that anything over she should pay out of her own money. She in fact paid out 14 shillings, which was later repaid to her. The plaintiff alleged that the telegram meant that he was in pecuniary difficulties and had to borrow from his servant. Held: allowing the appeal, that the words were incapable of a defamatory meaning.

LORD ATKIN: The question, then, is whether the words in their ordinary signification are capable of being defamatory. Judges and textbook writers alike have found difficulty in defining with precision the word 'defamatory.' The conventional phrase exposing the plaintiff to hatred, ridicule and contempt is probably too narrow. The question is complicated by having to consider the person or class of persons whose reaction to the publication is the test of the wrongful character of the words used. I do not intend to ask your Lordships to lay down a formal definition, but after collating the opinions of many authorities I propose in the present case the test: would the words tend to lower the plaintiff in the estimation of right-thinking members of society generally? Assuming such to be the test of whether words are defamatory or not there is no dispute as to the relative functions of judge and jury, of law and fact. It is well settled that the judge must decide whether the words are capable of a defamatory meaning. That is a question of law: is there evidence of a tort? If they are capable, then the jury is to decide whether they are in fact defamatory. Now, in the present case it is material to notice that there is no evidence that the words were published to anyone who had any knowledge at all of any of the facts that I have narrated above. There is no direct evidence that they were published to anyone who had ever heard of the plaintiff. The post office officials at Maidenhead would not be presumed to know him, and we are left without any information as to the officials at Cookham Dean. The plaintiff and his wife dealt at the shop at which was the sub-post office, but there is no evidence that the shopkeeper was the telegraph clerk the probability is that he was not. It might, however, be inferred that the publication of the telegram at Cookham Dean was to someone who knew the plaintiff. What would he or she learn by reading the telegram? That Edith Saville had been in the plaintiff's employment; that she had that day entered the defendant's employment; and that the former employer was requested to send on to the new place of employment the servant's possessions together with the money due to her for money borrowed and for wages. How could perusal of that communication tend to lower the plaintiff in the estimation of the right-thinking peruser who knows nothing of the circumstances but what he or she derives from the telegram itself. The defamatory imputation is said to be in the words 'the money you borrowed,' coupled with the request for the return of it sent in a telegram. It was said by the learned judge at the trial and accepted by the two members of the Court of Appeal who affirmed the judgment that the words were capable of conveying to anybody that the plaintiff had acted in a mean way borrowing money from his own maid and not paying her as he was required to and required to by telegram and also withholding her wages. With the greatest respect, that is imputing to the words a suggestion of meanness both in borrowing and in not repaying which I find it impossible to extract from their ordinary meaning. The sting is said to be in the borrowing. It happens that the phrase is substantially true. I myself have no doubt that if we were merely regarding legal technicalities the transaction which I have described as to the 14s. which was still unpaid could be covered by an indebitatus count for money lent as well as for money paid. In substance and in fact a justification of money borrowed would have been made out. But I am at a loss to understand why a person's character should be lowered in anyone's estimation if he or she has borrowed from a domestic servant. I should have thought it such a usual domestic occurrence for small sums to be advanced in such circumstances as the present, and with the assent of everyone concerned to be left outstanding for some days that the mere fact of borrowing from a servant bears not the slightest tinge of 'meanness.' Of course there may be special circumstances, and so large an amount may be borrowed or left so long unpaid that the facts when known would reflect on the character of the master. But to make an imputation which is based upon the existence of facts unknown and not to be inferred from the words attacked is surely exactly to come under the ban of Lord Esher [then Brett, LJ] cited in *Nevill* v *Fine Art & General Insurance*

Co. at p. 73: 'It seems to me unreasonable that, when there are a number of good interpretations, the only bad one should be seized upon to give a defamatory sense to the document.' It is not a case where there is only the choice between two reasonable meanings, one harmless and one defamatory. It is a case where there is only one reasonable meaning which is harmless, and where the defamatory meaning can only be given by inventing a state of facts which are not disclosed, and are in fact non-existent. I do not find much value in other cases where words are held to be incapable of being defamatory. Like cases on construction in other branches of law they often darken counsel rather than give light.

Notes

1. The Porter Committee in 1948 recommended that there should be no statutory definition, but the Faulks Committee in 1975 recommended the following, although it was never enacted: 'Defamation shall consist of the publication to a third party of matter which in all the circumstances would be likely to affect a person adversely in the estimation of reasonable people generally.'

2. Other definitions which had been suggested in the past include the following, of which perhaps the most famous is that of Parke B in *Parmiter* v *Coupland* (1840) 151 ER 340, where he said 'A publication, without justification or lawful excuse, which is calculated to injure the reputation of another, by exposing him to hatred, contempt or ridicule, is a libel.' In *Youssoupoff* v *Metro Goldwyn Mayer* (1934) 50 TLR 581 (where the plaintiff alleged that a film called 'Rasputin, the Mad Monk', suggested that she had been seduced by Rasputin), Slesser LJ added to that dictum the view that it would also be a libel if the statement 'tends to make the plaintiff be shunned and avoided and that without any moral discredit on her part'. This, he said, explains why it is defamatory to allege a person to be insane or suffer from a contagious disease. In the same case Scrutton LJ said that he preferred the definition of Cave J in *Scott* v *Sampson* (1881) 8 QBD 491, that a libel was a false statement about a person to his discredit.

3. In *Byrne* v *Deane* [1937] 1 KB 818 a golf club had some 'fruit machines' in the club house, and someone informed the police of the existence of these gaming machines and they required them to be removed. Someone then posted a notice in verse saying 'But he who gave the game away, may he byrne in hell and rue the day.' The plaintiff claimed that this accused him of disloyalty to the club, but the court held that it could not be defamatory to say of a person that he put in motion machinery for the suppression of a crime.

4. Opinion in society generally may be sharply divided on whether a person would be regarded as having acted reprehensibly. For example, is it defamatory to say of a trade union member that he has refused to support an official strike? Other trade unionists would regard that as disloyalty, but other people might applaud his action. In *Myroft* v *Sleight* (1921) 37 TLR 646 McCardie J thought it would not be defamatory, for it would merely be alleging 'independence of thought or courage of opinion or speech or manliness of action', although he did decide that it would be defamatory to say that a person who had voted for the strike had refused to leave work, for that would be to allege hypocrisy or underhand disloyalty.

Section 3:   what do the words used mean?

Words should be construed in their ordinary and natural meaning, but they may also have a hidden meaning — the innuendo. There are two kinds of innuendo, rather confusingly called a 'true' (or legal) innuendo and a 'false' (or popular) innuendo. A true innuendo occurs where there are facts known to the recipient of the information which gives the apparently innocuous statement a different meaning (e.g. to say (before the game became professional) 'X is paid for playing rugby', when the hearer knows that X is an amateur). A false innuendo is where the statement itself carries with it an implied meaning.

Lewis v *Daily Telegraph*
House of Lords [1964] AC 234; [1963] 2 WLR 1063; [1963] 2 All ER 151

The defendants published a story headed 'Inquiry on firm by City Police' which stated that the City of London Fraud Squad were inquiring into the affairs of Rubber Improvement Ltd, of which the plaintiff, John Lewis, was chairman. It was claimed that the story meant that the affairs of the company were conducted fraudulently or dishonestly, or in such a way that the police suspected that their affairs were so conducted. Held: dismissing the appeal, that the words could not mean that the plaintiff was actually guilty of fraud, and a new trial was ordered on the basis that the words were only capable of meaning that the police suspected fraud.

LORD REID: The essence of the controversy between the parties is that the appellants maintain that these passages are capable of meaning that they were guilty of fraud. The respondents deny this: they admit that the paragraphs are libellous but maintain that the juries ought to have been directed that they are not capable of the meaning which the appellants attribute to them. The learned judge directed the juries in such a way as to leave it open to them to accept the appellants' contention, and it is obvious from the amounts of the damages awarded that the juries must have done this.

The gist of the two paragraphs is that the police, the City Fraud Squad, were inquiring into the appellants' affairs. There is no doubt that in actions for libel the question is what the words would convey to the ordinary man: it is not one of construction in the legal sense. The ordinary man does not live in an ivory tower and he is not inhibited by a knowledge of the rules of construction. So he can and does read between the lines in the light of his general knowledge and experience of worldly affairs. . . .

What the ordinary man would infer without special knowledge has generally been called the natural and ordinary meaning of the words. But that expression is rather misleading in that it conceals the fact that there are two elements in it. Sometimes it is not necessary to go beyond the words themselves, as where the plaintiff has been called a thief or a murderer. But more often the sting is not so much in the words themselves as in what the ordinary man will infer from them, and that is also regarded as part of their natural and ordinary meaning. Here there would be nothing libellous in saying that an inquiry into the appellants' affairs was proceeding: the inquiry might be by a statistician or other expert. The sting is in inferences drawn from the fact that it is the fraud squad which is making the inquiry. What those inferences should be is ultimately a question for the jury, but the trial judge has an important duty to perform.

Generally the controversy is whether the words are capable of having a libellous meaning at all, and undoubtedly it is the judge's duty to rule on that. I shall have to deal later with the test which he must apply. Here the controversy is in a different form. The respondents admit that their words were libellous, although I am still in some doubt as to what is the admitted libellous meaning. But they sought and seek a ruling that these words are not capable of having the particular meaning which the appellants attribute to them. I think that they are entitled to such a ruling and that the test must be the same as that applied in deciding whether the words are capable of having any libellous meaning. I say that because it appears that when a particular meaning has been pleaded, either as a 'true' or a 'false' innuendo, it has not been doubted that the judge must rule on the innuendo. And the case surely cannot be different where a part of the natural and ordinary meaning is, and where it is not, expressly pleaded.

The leading case is *Capital and Counties Bank Ltd* v *Henty & Sons* (1882) 7 App Cas 741. In that case Lord Selborne LC said: 'The test, according to the authorities, is, whether under the circumstances in which the writing was published, reasonable men, to whom the publication was made, would be likely to understand it in a libellous sense.' Each of the four noble Lords who formed the majority stated the test in a different way, and the speeches of Lord Blackburn and Lord Watson could be read as imposing a heavier burden on the plaintiff. But I do not think that they should now be so read. In *Nevill* v *Fine Art & General Insurance Co. Ltd* [1897] AC 68 Lord Halsbury said: ' . . . what is the sense in which any ordinary reasonable man would understand the words of the communication so as to expose the plaintiff to hatred, or contempt or ridicule . . . it is not enough to say that by some person or another the words *might* be understood in a defamatory sense.' These statements of the law appear to have been generally accepted and I would not attempt to restate the general principle.

In this case it is, I think, sufficient to put the test in this way. Ordinary men and women have different temperaments and outlooks. Some are unusually suspicious and some are unusually naïve. One must try to envisage people between these two extremes and see what is the most damaging meaning they would put on the words in question. So let me suppose a number of ordinary people discussing one of these paragraphs which they had read in the newspaper. No doubt one of them might say — 'Oh, if the fraud squad are after these people you can take it they are guilty.' But I would expect the others to turn on him, if he did say that, with such remarks as — 'Be fair. This is not a police state. No doubt their affairs are in a mess or the police would not be interested. But that could be because Lewis or the cashier has been very stupid or careless. We really must not jump to conclusions. The police are fair and know their job and we shall know soon enough if there is anything in it. Wait till we see if they charge him. I wouldn't trust him until this is cleared up, but it is another thing to condemn him unheard.'

What the ordinary man, not avid for scandal, would read into the words complained of must be a matter of impression. I can only say that I do not think that he would infer guilt of fraud merely because an inquiry is on foot.

LORD DEVLIN: My Lords, the natural and ordinary meaning of words ought in theory to be the same for the lawyer as for the layman, because the lawyer's first rule of construction is that words are to be given their natural and ordinary meaning as popularly understood. The proposition that ordinary words are the same for the lawyer as for the layman is as a matter of pure construction undoubtedly true. But it is very difficult to draw the line between pure construction and implication, and the layman's capacity for implication is much greater than the lawyer's. The lawyer's rule is that the implication must be necessary as well as reasonable. The layman reads in an implication much more freely; and unfortunately, as the law of defamation has to take into account, is especially prone to do so when it is derogatory.

In the law of defamation these wider sorts of implication are called innuendoes. The word explains itself and is very apt for the purpose. . . .

An innuendo had to be pleaded and the line between an ordinary meaning and an innuendo might not always be easy to draw. A derogatory implication may be so near the surface that it is hardly hidden at all or it may be more difficult to detect. If it is said of a man that he is a fornicator the statement cannot be enlarged by innuendo. If it is said of him that he was seen going into a brothel, the same meaning would probably be conveyed to nine men out of ten. But the lawyer might say that in the latter case a derogatory meaning was not a necessary one because a man might go to a brothel for an innocent purpose. An innuendo pleading that the words were understood to mean that he went there for an immoral purpose would not, therefore, be ridiculous. . . .

I have said that a derogatory implication might be easy or difficult to detect; and, of course, it might not be detected at all, except by a person who was already in possession of some specific information. Thus, to say of a man that he was seen to enter a named house would contain a derogatory implication for anyone who knew that that house was a brothel but not for anyone who did not. . . . De Grey CJ [in *Rex* v *Horne* 2 Cowp 672] distinguished between this sort of implication and the implication that is to be derived from the words themselves without extrinsic aid, and he treats the term 'innuendo' as descriptive only of the latter. Since then the term has come to be used for both sorts of implication. . . .

. . . [Ord. 19, r. 6(2)] reads: '(2) In an action for libel or slander if the plaintiff alleges that the words or matter complained of were used in a defamatory sense other than their ordinary meaning, he shall give particulars of the facts and matters on which he relies in support of such sense.'

The word 'innuendo' is not used. But the effect of the language is that any meaning that does not require the support of extrinsic fact is assumed to be part of the ordinary meaning of the words. Accordingly, an innuendo, however well concealed, that is capable of being detected in the language used is deemed to be part of the ordinary meaning.

This might be an academic matter if it were not for the principle that the ordinary meaning of words and the meaning enlarged by innuendo give rise to separate causes of action. This principle, which originated out of the old forms of pleading, seems to me in modern times to be of dubious value. But it is now firmly settled on the authority of *Sim* v *Stretch* 52 TLR 669 and the House was not asked to qualify it. How is this principle affected by the new rule? Are there now three causes of action? If there are only two, to which of them does the innuendo that is inherent in the words belong? In *Grubb* v *Bristol United Press Ltd* [1963] 1 QB 309 the Court of Appeal, disagreeing with some observations made by Diplock LJ in *Loughans* v *Odhams Press Ltd* [1963] 1 QB 299, decided in effect that there were only two causes of action and that the innuendo cause of action comprised only the innuendo that was supported by extrinsic facts.

My Lords, I think, on the whole, that this is the better solution, though it brings with it a consequence that I dislike, namely, that at two points there is a divergence between the popular and the legal meaning of words. Just as the popular and legal meanings of 'malice' have drifted apart, so the popular and legal meanings of 'innuendo' must now be separated. I shall in the rest of my speech describe as a legal innuendo the innuendo that is the subject-matter of a separate cause of action. I suppose that it does not matter what terminology is used so long as it is agreed. But I do not care for the description of the popular innuendo as a false innuendo; it is the law and not popular usage that gives a false and restricted meaning to the word. The other respect is that the natural and ordinary meaning of words for the purposes of defamation is not their natural and ordinary meaning for other purposes of the law. There must be added to the implications which a court is prepared to make as a matter of construction all such insinuations and innuendoes as could reasonably be read into them by the ordinary man.

The consequence of all this is, I think, that there will have to be three paragraphs in a statement of claim where previously two have served. In the first paragraph the defamatory words will be set out as hitherto. It may be that they will speak for themselves. If not, a second paragraph will set out those innuendoes or indirect meanings which go beyond the literal meaning of the words but which the pleader claims to be inherent in them. Thirdly, if the pleader has the necessary material, he can plead a secondary meaning or legal innuendo supported by particulars under Ord. 19, r. 6(2). Hitherto it has been customary to put the whole innuendo into one paragraph, but now this may easily result in the confusion of two causes of action and in consequent embarrassment. The essential distinction between the second and third paragraph will lie in the fact that particulars under the rule must be appended to the third. That is, so to speak, the hallmark of the legal innuendo. . . .

Notes

1. In *Gillick* v *BBC, The Times,* 20 October 1995, Neill LJ said that the court should give to the material the natural and ordinary meaning which it would have conveyed to the ordinary reasonable reader or viewer, and that the reasonable reader was not naive but nor was he unduly suspicious, and he could read between the lines. He could read in an implication more readily than a lawyer and might indulge in a certain amount of loose thinking. But he must be treated as a man who was not avid for scandal and someone who did not select one bad meaning where other non-defamatory meanings were available. The court should be cautious of over-elaborate analysis of the material in issue and should not be too literal in its approach. Finally, a statement should be taken to be defamatory if it would tend to lower the plaintiff in the estimation of right thinking members of society generally, or be likely to affect a person adversely in the estimation of reasonable people generally.

2. An example of a true or legal innuendo is *Tolley* v *Fry* [1931] AC 333, where the defendants advertised their chocolate by a caricature of the plaintiff with a packet of their chocolate in his pocket, together with a doggerel verse which named him. This seems innocent enough, but the plaintiff was a well known amateur golfer, and it was claimed that people would think he had prostituted his amateur status and it was said that such a person would be asked to resign from any respectable club. The plaintiff won.

3. If a true innuendo is pleaded it is not necessary to show that the people who knew the special facts which rendered the statement defamatory actually believed the story. In *Hough* v *London Express Newspaper* [1940] 2 KB 507 it was said of Frank Hough, a boxer, that his 'curly headed wife sees every fight'. The curly headed woman was not Frank Hough's wife, and the true wife said that the statement meant that she had been falsely claiming to be his wife and that she had had his children without being married to him. This was a libel, even though the people called to give evidence as to the special facts pleaded to support the innuendo did not believe that the plaintiff was not Mrs Hough. Other people might have thought differently. What if *all* the people who knew of the special facts did not believe the story?

Charleston v News Group Newspapers
[1995] 2 AC 65; [1995] 2 WLR 450; [1995] 2 All ER 313

The plaintiffs played Harold and Madge Bishop in 'Neighbours'. The defendants published an article with the headline 'Strewth! What's Harold up to with our Madge?', below which was a picture of a man and a woman nearly naked in a pornographic pose with the faces of the plaintiffs superimposed on the figures. The article below made it clear that the photographs had been produced by a computer game company without the knowledge of the plaintiffs and went on to castigate the makers of the game. The plaintiffs claimed on the basis that the article conveyed that they had been willing participants in the production of the photographs. However, it was conceded that the article as a whole was not defamatory and the question was whether the headline and the photographs could be considered in isolation. Held: dismissing the appeal, that the defendants were not liable.

LORD BRIDGE: . . . The theme of Mr Craig's argument runs on the following lines. All the earlier authorities, he submits, are explicable on the basis that the allegedly defamatory matter with which they were concerned was located somewhere in a document in which there was no likelihood that it would be read in isolation. In such a situation it is natural and proper to look for the meaning conveyed to the reader by considering the publication as a whole. The techniques of modern tabloid journalism, however, confront the courts with a novel situation with which the law has not hitherto had to grapple. It is plain that the eye-catching headline and the eye-catching photograph will first attract the reader's attention, precisely as they were intended to do, and equally plain that a significant number of readers will not trouble to read any further. This phenomenon must be well known to newspaper editors and publishers, who cannot, therefore, complain if they are held liable in damages for any libel thus published to the category of limited readers.

At first blush this argument has considerable attractions, but I believe that it falls foul of two principles which are basic to the law of libel. The first is that, where no legal innuendo is alleged to arise from extrinsic circumstances known to some readers, the 'natural and ordinary meaning' to be ascribed to the words of an allegedly defamatory publication is the meaning, including any inferential meaning, which the words would convey to the mind of the ordinary, reasonable, fair-minded reader. This proposition is too well established to require citation of authority. The second principle, which is perhaps a corollary of the first, is that, although a combination of words may in fact convey different meanings to the minds of different readers, the jury in a libel action, applying the criterion which the first principle dictates, is required to determine the single meaning which the publication conveyed to the notional reasonable reader and to base its verdict and any award of damages on the assumption that this was the one sense in which all readers would have understood it. The origins and the implications of this second principle are the subject of a characteristically penetrating analysis in the judgment of Diplock LJ in *Slim v Telegraph Ltd* [1968] 2 QB 157, 171–172, 173, 174, from which it will, I think, be sufficient to cite the following passages:

Everyone outside a court of law recognises that words are imprecise instruments for communicating the thoughts of one man to another. The same words may be understood by one man in a different meaning from that in which they are understood by another and both meanings may be different from that which the author of the words intended to convey. But the notion that the same words should bear different meanings to different men and that more than one meaning should be 'right' conflicts with the whole training of a lawyer. Words are the tools of his trade. He uses them to define legal rights and duties. They do not achieve that purpose unless there can be attributed to them a single meaning as the 'right' meaning. And so the argument between lawyers as to the meaning of words starts with the unexpressed major premise that any particular combination of words has one meaning which is not necessarily the same as that intended by him who published them or understood by any of those who read them but is capable of ascertainment as being the 'right' meaning by the adjudicator to whom the law confides the responsibility of determining it. . . .

Where, as in the present case, words are published to the millions of readers of a popular newspaper, the chances are that if the words are reasonably capable of being understood as bearing more than one meaning, some readers will have understood them as bearing one of those meanings and some will have understood them as bearing others of those meanings. But none of this matters. What does matter is what the adjudicator at the trial thinks is the one and only meaning that the readers as reasonable men should have collectively understood the words to bear. That is 'the natural and ordinary meaning' of words in an action for libel. . . .

Juries, in theory, must be unanimous upon every issue on which they have to adjudicate; and since the damages that they award must depend upon the defamatory meaning that they attribute to the words, they must all agree upon a single meaning as being the 'right' meaning. And so the unexpressed major premise, that any particular combination of words can bear but a single 'natural and ordinary meaning' which is 'right,' survived the transfer from judge to jury of the function of adjudicating upon the meaning of words in civil actions for libel.

It is precisely the application of the principle so clearly expounded in these passages which, in a libel action where no legal innuendo is alleged, prevents either side from calling witnesses to say what they understood the allegedly defamatory publication to mean. But it would surely be even more destructive of the principle that a publication has 'the one and only meaning that the readers as reasonable men should have collectively understood the words to bear' to allow the plaintiff, without evidence, to invite the jury to infer that different groups of readers read different parts of the entire publication and for that reason understood it to mean different things, some defamatory, some not.

Whether the text of a newspaper article will, in any particular case, be sufficient to neutralise the defamatory implication of a prominent headline will sometimes be a nicely balanced question for the jury to decide and will depend not only on the nature of the libel which the headline conveys and the language of the text which is relied on to neutralise it but also on the manner in which the whole of the relevant material is set out and presented. But the proposition that the prominent headline, or as here the headlines plus photographs, may found a claim in libel in isolation from its related text, because some readers only read headlines, is to my mind quite unacceptable in the light of the principles discussed above.

I have no doubt that Mr Craig is right in his assertion that many 'News of the World' readers who saw the offending publication would have looked at the headlines and photographs and nothing more. But if these readers, without taking the trouble to discover what the article was all about, carried away the impression that two well known actors in legitimate television were also involved in making pornographic films, they could hardly be described as ordinary, reasonable, fair-minded readers.

Notes

1. Compare the rule in the tort of passing off that 'it is not sufficient that the only confusion would be to a very small unobservant section of the public, or, as Foster J put it recently (1979 FSR 117) if the only person who would be misled would be a 'moron in a hurry' (*BBC* v *Newsweek* [1979] RPC 441).
2. Is it right to say that words can only have one reasonable meaning or rather that there is a single meaning which would be conveyed to the reasonable reader?

Section 4:   do the words refer to the plaintiff?

The defamatory statement must be reasonably capable of applying to the plaintiff, although it is not necessary for him to be specifically referred to. It is sufficient if reasonable people who are aware of the special facts (which must be proved by the plaintiff) would believe that he was the person being referred to.

One of the most controversial aspects of this area of the law is the principle in *Hulton & Co.* v *Jones* [1910] AC 20, where the defendants published a humorous article about the behaviour in Dieppe of a fictitious character named Artemus Jones, referring to his being accompanied by a woman who was not his wife. A barrister named Artemus Jones successfully sued, even though the defendants had not intended to refer to him. *Newstead* v *London Express* (below) goes further, holding a statement to be defamatory of A even though it is true of B. The Faulks Committee considered this principle, but ultimately decided that it should be retained.

Newstead v *London Express Newspapers*
Court of Appeal [1940] 1 KB 377; [1939] 4 All ER 319; 1621 LT 17

Under the heading 'Why do people commit bigamy' the defendants published a story stating that 'Harold Newstead, a 30-year-old Camberwell man, who was jailed for nine months liked having two wives at once.' The allegation was true of a 30-year-old Camberwell barman, but not true of the plaintiff of the same name, who was a hairdresser in Camberwell and of about the same age. At first instance the plaintiff won, and was awarded one farthing in damages. Held: dismissing the appeal, that the defendants were liable.

SIR WILFRED GREENE MR: If the words used when read in the light of the relevant circumstances are understood by reasonable persons to refer to the plaintiff, refer to him they do for all relevant purposes. Their meaning cannot be affected by the recklessness or honesty of the writer.

I do not propose to refer to the authorities which establish this proposition, except to quote the words of Lord Loreburn LC in *E. Hulton & Co.* v *Jones* [1910] AC 20, where he said: 'What does the tort consist in? It consists in using language which others knowing the circumstances would reasonably think to be defamatory of the person complaining of and injured by it.' In the case of libel, once it is held that the words are capable of referring to the plaintiff, it is, of course, for the jury to say whether or not they do so refer. Subject to this, the principle is in truth an illustration of the rule that the author of a written document is to be taken as having intended his words to have the meaning which they convey when understood in the light of the relevant surrounding circumstances. In the case of libel, the same words may reasonably convey different meanings to a number of different persons or groups of persons, and so be held to be defamatory of more persons than one.

After giving careful consideration to the matter, I am unable to hold that the fact that defamatory words are true of A, makes it as a matter of law impossible for them to be defamatory of B, which was in substance the main argument on behalf of the appellants. At first sight this looks as though it would lead to great hardship. But the hardships are in practice not so serious as might appear, at any rate in the case of statements which are ex facie defamatory. Persons who make statements of this character may not unreasonably be expected, when describing the person of whom they are made, to identify that person so closely as to make it very unlikely that a judge would hold them to be reasonably capable of referring to someone else, or that a jury would hold that they did so refer. This is particularly so in the case of statements which purport to deal with actual facts. If there is a risk of coincidence it ought, I think, in reason to be borne not by the innocent party to whom the words are held to refer, but by the party who puts them into circulation. In matters of fiction, there is no doubt more room for hardship. Even in the case of matters of fact it is no doubt possible to construct imaginary facts which would lead to hardship. There may also be hardship if words, not on their faces defamatory, are true of A, but are reasonably understood by some as referring to B, and as applied to B are defamatory. But such cases must be rare. The law as I understand it is well settled, and can only be altered by legislation. . . .

MACKINNON LJ: If A publishes to another person, or persons, words which upon their reasonable meaning refer to B, if those words are defamatory as holding B up to hatred, ridicule, or contempt, and if the words so referring to B cannot be justified as true, A may be liable for damages to B.

Secondly, the reasonable meaning of the words, upon the question whether they refer to B must be tested objectively and not subjectively. The question is what do the words mean as words, not what do A in his own mind mean by them or intend them to mean.

Thirdly, A cannot plead as a defence that he was unaware of B's existence.

Fourthly, A cannot plead as a defence that the words are, in their reasonable meaning, equally capable of referring to C, and that when referring to C they are true.

Fifthly, there has been in some of the cases (notably by Farwell LJ in *Jones* v *Hulton & Co.*, [1909] 2 KB 444, reference to negligence or recklessness on the part of A in making the publication. If the words, on their reasonable meaning, do refer to B, I think it is immaterial whether A was either negligent or reckless in not ascertaining the existence of B, or guarding against the applicability to him of the words. If B establishes his claim, the jury in assessing his damages may take into account all the circumstances of the publication. The negligence or recklessness of A may well be among such circumstances. Further or otherwise negligence or recklessness on the part of A is immaterial.

It is hardly necessary to add, sixthly, the rule which is elementary, namely, that it is the primary duty of the judge to decide whether the words complained of are capable of a meaning that is defamatory of B, and only if he answers that question in the affirmative to leave to the jury the questions whether they are in fact defamatory of B, and, if so, what damages he shall be awarded.

In a case in which there is no question that the words are defamatory of him, if they refer to B, and the contest is only whether they do so refer, this preliminary question for the judge must be: 'Are these words on their reasonable meaning capable of referring to the plaintiff?' And if he answers that affirmatively I think that, properly, the first question to be left to the jury should be: 'Could the words used by the defendant be reasonably interpreted by those to whom they were published as referring to the plaintiff?

Note
The principle does not mean that any person with the same name as the person mentioned can sue, for the rule is that reasonable people must believe the story in fact refers to the plaintiff. Thus, in *Blennerhasset* v *Novelty Sales Service* (1933) 175 LTJo 393 the defendants advertised their Yo-Yo by saying that a Mr Blennerhasset had become obsessed by it and was under 'sympathetic surveillance' in the country. A stockbroker of the same name failed in his action for defamation because no reasonable person would think it applied to him.

Section 5: justification

It is a defence to show that the words are true 'in substance and in fact'. The main problem with this area of the law is that it is for the defendant to prove that the words are true: the plaintiff merely has to establish that the words are defamatory and have been published. However, the Faulks Committee recommended that the burden of proving truth should remain with the defendant.

Sutherland v *Stopes*
House of Lords [1925] AC 47; 132 LJ 550; 94 LJKB 166

Marie Stopes advocated the use of birth control and had established a clinic in London. The defendant wrote a book in which he alleged that the plaintiff was taking advantage of the poor, and he referred to her 'monstrous' campaign. The jury found the statements true in fact, but added that they were not fair comment. Held: that there was no evidence to support the finding that the comments were unfair, and Lord Shaw made the following comments about justification.

LORD SHAW: It remains to be considered what are the conditions and breadth of a plea of justification on the ground of truth. The plea must not be considered in a meticulous sense. It is that the words employed were true in substance and in fact. I view with great satisfaction the charge of the Lord Chief Justice when he made this point perfectly clear to the jury, that all that was required to affirm that plea was that the jury should be satisfied that the sting of the libel or, if there were more than one, the stings of the libel should be made out. To which I may add that there may be mistakes here and there in what has been said which would make no substantial difference to the quality of the alleged libel or in the justification pleaded for it. If I write that the defendant on March 6 took a saddle from my stable and sold it the next day and pocketed the money all without notice to me, and that in my opinion he stole the saddle, and if the facts truly are found to be that the defendant did not take the saddle from the stable but from the harness room, and that he did not sell it the next day but a week afterwards, but nevertheless he did, without my knowledge or consent, sell my saddle so taken and pocketed the proceeds, then the whole sting of the libel may be justifiably affirmed by a jury notwithstanding these errors in detail.

In the second place, however, the allegation of fact must tell the whole story. If, for instance, in the illustration given, the facts as elicited show what my writing had not disclosed — namely, that the defendant had a saddle of his own lying in my harness room, and that he took by mistake mine away instead of his own and, still labouring under that mistake, sold it — then the jury would properly declare that the libel was not justified on the double ground that there were facts completely explaining in a non-criminal sense anything that was done, and the jury would disaffirm the truth of the libel because, although meticulously true in fact, it was false in substance.

Then, as to the breadth of the justification. When a plea of truth in substance and in fact is made it affirms not only in the sense I have mentioned the facts, but it affirms all that attaches to them as their natural and reasonable meaning.

DEFAMATION ACT 1952

5. Justification

In an action for libel or slander in respect of words containing two or more distinct charges against the plaintiff, a defence of justification shall not fail by reason only that the truth of every charge is not proved if the words not proved to be true do not materially injure the plaintiff's reputation having regard to the truth of the remaining charges.

Notes

1. *Wakley* v *Cooke* (1849) 154 ER 1316 is an example of defining the meaning of the defamatory words and then deciding whether that meaning is true. The plaintiff was a coroner, and the defendants wrote that 'there can be no court of justice unpolluted which this libellous journalist, this violent agitator and sham humanitarian is allowed to disgrace with his presidentship'. The defendants attempted to justify 'libellous journalist' by saying that as proprietor of *The Lancet* he had in fact published one libel. It was held that justification was not made out: Rolfe B said that the words either meant that the plaintiff was habitually publishing libels in his paper, or that he had published them from sordid motives. Neither was made out.

2. In *Bookbinder* v *Tebbit* [1989] 1 All ER 1169 the Derbyshire C.C. overprinted all school stationery with the words 'Support Nuclear Free Zones'. The plaintiff, who was leader of the council, sued Norman Tebbit, then chairman of the Conservative Party over a statement which he claimed meant that he had acted irresponsibly in squandering money on the overprinting. The defendant sought to justify on the grounds that there were a number of occasions when the council had squandered money. It was held that the defence of general squandering of public money should be struck out. In other words, the defendant must justify the specific charge.

Section 6:   fair comment

'Fair comment' is probably a misnomer, as it is not necessary that the comment be reasonable or 'fair' in the usual sense, but rather the question is whether the opinion is honestly held. The Faulks Committee defined the defence as one where the defendant must show:

(a) that the facts alleged are true (subject to the Defamation Act 1952, s. 6 below);

(b) the expression of opinion is such that an honest man holding strong, exaggerated or even prejudiced views could have made;

(c) the subject matter of the comment is of public interest; and

(d) the facts relied on as founding the comment were in the defendant's mind when he made it.

Merivale v Carson
Court of Appeal (1887) 20 QBD 275; 58 LT 331; 4 TLR 125

The plaintiff and his wife were authors of a play called 'The Whip Hand'. The defendant was editor of 'The Stage', which published a critical review of which the innuendo was said to be that the play was of an immoral tendency. The defendants claimed the review was honest and there was no attack on the character of the authors. The jury awarded the plaintiffs one shilling damages. Held: that the appeal was dismissed.

LORD ESHER MR: What is the meaning of a 'fair comment'? I think the meaning is this: is the article in the opinion of the jury beyond that which any fair man, however prejudiced or however strong his opinion may be, would say of the work in question? Every latitude must be given to opinion and to prejudice, and then an ordinary set of men with ordinary judgment must say whether any fair man would have made such a comment on the work. It is very easy to say what would be clearly beyond that limit; if, for instance, the writer attacked the private character of the author. But it is much more difficult to say what is within the limit. That must depend upon the circumstances of the particular case. I think the right question was really left by Field J, to the jury in the present case. No doubt you can find in the course of his summing-up some phrases which, if taken alone, may seem to limit too much the question put to the jury. But, when you look at the summing-up as a whole, I think it comes in substance to the final question which was put by the judge to the jury: 'If it is no more than fair, honest, independent, bold, even exaggerated, criticism, then your verdict will be for the defendants.' He gives a very wide limit, and, I think, rightly. Mere exaggeration, or even gross exaggeration, would not make the comment unfair. However wrong the opinion expressed may be in point of truth, or however prejudiced the writer, it may still be within the prescribed limit. The question which the jury must consider is this — would any fair man, however prejudiced he may be, however exaggerated or obstinate his views, have said that which this criticism has said of the work which is criticised? If it goes beyond that, then you must find for the plaintiff; if you are not satisfied that it does, then it falls within the allowed limit, and there is no libel at all. I cannot doubt that the jury were justified in coming to the conclusion to which they did come, when once they had made up their minds as to the meaning of the words used in the article, viz. that the plaintiffs had written an obscene play, and no fair man could have said that. There was therefore a complete misdescription of the plaintiffs' work, and the inevitable conclusion was that an imputation was cast upon the characters of the authors. Even if I had thought that the right direction had not been given to the jury, I should have declined to grant a new trial, for the same verdict must inevitably have been found if the jury had been rightly directed.

Another point which has been discussed is this. It is said that if in some other case the alleged libel would not be beyond the limits of fair criticism, and it could be shewn that the defendant was not really criticising the work, but was writing with an indirect and dishonest intention to injure the plaintiffs, still the motive would not make the criticism a libel. I am inclined to think that it would, and for this reason, that the comment would not then really be a criticism of the work. The mind of the writer would not be that of a critic, but he would be actuated by an intention to injure the author.

Notes
1.   In *Turner* v *MGM Pictures* [1950] 1 All ER 449 at p. 461, Lord Parker approved the dictum of Lord Esher, but saying that he would 'substitute "honest" for "fair" lest some suggestion of reasonableness instead of honesty should be read in'.
2.   The relationship between malice and fair comment was discussed by the House of Lords in *Telnikoff* v *Matusevitch* [1991] 4 All ER 817, where it was said that if the defendant can show as an objective matter that the opinion was one which could be honestly held, he does not have to prove that he in fact held it. Rather it is then for the plaintiff to prove as part of his allegation of malice that the defendant did not in fact honestly hold that view. Hence the test of 'fair comment' is wholly objective, and the issue of the subjective state of the defendant's mind is a matter for the test of malice.
3.   Malice will destroy the privilege of fair comment, and this is so even where the comment might have been made honestly and fairly, but was in fact activated by malice. In ***Thomas* v *Bradbury Agnew Ltd*** [1906] 2 KB 627 the defendants had published a critical review in *Punch* to which they pleaded fair comment. There was extrinsic evidence of ill will between the reviewer and the author. This evidence was admitted, and the jury found for the plaintiffs. On appeal the defendants contended that the article itself did not go beyond the bounds of fair comment, and therefore extrinsic evidence of malice was irrelevant. Lord Collins MR said that this amounted to saying that fair comment was an absolute and not a relative standard, and he rejected that view, saying that it was quite immaterial that somebody else might without malice have written an equally damnatory criticism.

DEFAMATION ACT 1952

6.   Fair comment
In an action for libel or slander in respect of words consisting partly of allegations of fact and partly of expression of opinion, a defence of fair comment shall not fail by reason only that the truth of every allegation of fact is not proved if the expression of opinion is fair comment having regard to such of the facts alleged or referred to in the words complained of as are proved.

Section 7:   qualified privilege

The defence of qualified privilege is not as wide as is sometimes imagined, and in particular it is no defence for a newspaper to publish information which it believes to be in the public interest and which it believes to be true, and the Faulks Committee recommended that no change be made in this rule. The rule contributes to secrecy and the difficulty of exposing wrongdoing, whether of public bodies, companies, or individuals. The breadth of the defence of privilege is an important element in the extent of free speech.

Watt v Longsdon
Court of Appeal [1930] 1 KB 130; 142 LT 4; 45 TLR 619

Longsdon was the liquidator of the Scottish Petroleum Company which carried on business in Morocco and elsewhere. Watt, a managing director, and Browne, a manager, were in Casablanca. Browne wrote a letter to Longsdon, the liquidator, stating that Watt had left Casablanca, leaving behind an unpaid bill for £88 for whisky, and that he had been 'in immoral relations' with his housemaid, who was described as an old woman, stone deaf, almost blind and with dyed hair. Longsdon gave a copy of the letter to Mr Singer, the chairman of the board of directors, and to Mrs Watt. Longsdon also wrote a letter defamatory of Watt to Browne. The defendants claimed qualified privilege. Held: that there was evidence of malice which ought to be left to a jury and a new trial was ordered. It was also stated that the publication by Longsdon to Singer and Browne was privileged, but not the publication to Mrs Watt.

SCRUTTON LJ: Lord Esher MR says in *Pullman* v *Hill & Co.* [1891] 1 QB 524: 'An occasion is privileged when the person who makes the communication has a moral duty to make it to the person to whom he does make it, and the person who receives it has an interest in hearing it. Both these conditions must exist in order that the occasion may be privileged.' Lord Atkinson in *Adam* v *Ward* [1917] AC 309 expresses it thus: 'It was not disputed, in this case on either side, that a privileged occasion is, in reference to qualified privilege, an occasion where the person who makes a communication has an interest or a duty, legal, social, or moral, to make it to the person to whom it is made, and the person to whom it is so made has a corresponding interest or duty to receive it. This reciprocity is essential.' With slight modifications in particular circumstances, this appears to me to be well established law, but, except in the case of communications based on common interest, the principle is that either there must be interest in the recipient and a duty to communicate in the speaker, or an interest to be protected in the speaker and a duty to protect it in the recipient. Except in the case of common interest justifying intercommunication, the correspondence must be between duty and interest. There may, in the common interest cases, be also a common or reciprocal duty. It is not every interest which will create a duty in a stranger or volunteer. This appears to fit in with the two statements of Parke B already referred to . . . that the communication was made in the discharge of some social or moral duty, or on the ground of an interest in the party making or receiving it. This is approved by Lindley LJ in *Stuart* v *Bell* [1891] 2 QB 341, but I think should be expanded into

either (1) a duty to communicate information believed to be true to a person who has a material interest in receiving the information, or (2) an interest in the speaker to be protected by communicating information, if true, relevant to that interest, to a person honestly believed to have a duty to protect that interest, or (3) a common interest in and reciprocal duty in respect of the subject matter of the communication between speaker and recipient.

. . . In my opinion Horridge J went too far in holding that there could be privileged occasion on the ground of interest in the recipient without any duty to communicate on the part of the person making the communication. But that does not settle the question, for it is necessary to consider, in the present case, whether there was, as to each communication, a duty to communicate, and an interest in the recipient.

First as to the communication between Longsdon and Singer, I think the case must proceed on the admission that at all material times Watt, Longsdon and Browne were in the employment of the same company, and the evidence afforded by the answer to the interrogatory put in by the plaintiff that Longsdon believed the statements in Browne's letter. In my view on these facts there was a duty, both from a moral and a material point of view, on Longsdon to communicate the letter to Singer, the chairman of his company, who, apart from questions of present employment, might be asked by Watt for a testimonial to a future employer. Equally, I think Longsdon receiving the letter from Browne, might discuss the matter with him, and ask for further information, on the ground of a common interest in the affairs of the company, and to obtain further information for the chairman. . . .

The communication to Mrs Watt stands on a different footing. I have no intention of writing an exhaustive treatise on the circumstances when a stranger or a friend should communicate to husband or wife information he receives as to the conduct of the other party to the marriage. I am clear that it is impossible to say he is always under a moral or social duty to do so; it is equally impossible to say he is never under such a duty. It must depend on the circumstances of each case, the nature of the information, and the relation of speaker and recipient. . . . Using the best judgment I can in this difficult matter, I have come to the conclusion that there was not a moral or social duty in Longsdon to make this communication to Mrs Watt such as to make the occasion privileged, and that there must be a new trial so far as it relates to the claim for publication of a libel to Mrs Watt. . . .

Notes

1.   The general principles adopted by Scrutton LJ in this case were applied in *Beach v Freeson* [1971] 2 All ER 860 in the area of communication to public bodies. The MP Reg Freeson received a complaint from one of his constituents about the plaintiff solicitors, and the constituent asked him to write to the Law Society believing that the involvement of an MP would add weight to his complaint. The defendant did so, and added that he had received other complaints about the plaintiffs in the past. He sent the letter to the Law Society, and also a copy to the Lord Chancellor. On the question of privilege, the Court of Appeal said that the MP had a duty to pass on the complaint to the Law Society and a duty to make additional comments which he thought should be investigated. The Law Society, as the relevant disciplinary body, had a reciprocal interest in receiving the complaint. That letter was therefore privileged. The same was true of the letter to the Lord Chancellor, who had an interest in the proper administration of justice, but the court pointed out that the recipient must, as the Lord Chancellor did, have an actual interest in receiving the information, and it would not be enough merely for the sender mistakenly to believe that such an interest existed.

2. In *Watts* v *Times Newspapers* [1996] 1 All ER 152 the defendants had published an article libellous of a property developer. They later published an apology drafted by the developer which turned out to be libellous of the plaintiff. It was held that the developer could claim qualified privilege as he was allowed 'considerable latitude' to rebut the accusation against him, but Times Newspapers could not claim qualified privilege as it would have been possible to apologise without the libel, even though the developer had insisted on the defamatory words. Does this make sense? (Note: Times Newspapers could also have protected themselves by making the apology in open court.)

3. In the United States it is a defence to show that the plaintiff is a 'public figure', in which case there will only be liability if the defendant is actuated by malice: *New York Times* v *Sullivan* (1964) 376 US 254. The reasoning is based on freedom of speech in relation to matters of public interest. That defence has been rejected in this country: see *Bennett* v *Guardian Newspapers, The Times*, 28 December 1996, and the report by Neill LJ on Practice and Procedure in Defamation (1991), p. 164. Note also the Australian case of *Theophanous* v *The Herald and Weekly Times* (1994) 182 CLR 104 which establishes a privilege to publish material discussing political matters or concerning politicians, or the suitability of a person for public office.

Blackshaw v *Lord*
Court of Appeal [1984] 1 QB 1; [1983] 2 All ER 311; [1983] 3 WLR 283

The defendant (Lord) was a journalist on the *Daily Telegraph* and he was given a story by the press officer (Mr Smith) of the Department of Energy which related to alleged maladministration at the Ministry in making grants which had cost £52 million. The plaintiff's name was not given at that time. The defendant published an article under the heading 'Incompetence at the Ministry cost £52m', saying that 'Mr Alan Blackshaw, the official in charge . . . when the payments were being made, resigned from the civil service last month.' This was not true. The defendants claimed statutory and common law privilege. The jury awarded the plaintiff £45,000 damages. On appeal it was held: dismissing the appeal, that as to statutory privilege the article was not a fair report of what the press officer had said, and that common law privilege did not apply as there was no duty to make the plaintiff's name known to the public.

STEPHENSON LJ: The question here is, assuming Mr Lord recorded Mr Smith's conversation with him fairly and accurately, did Mr Lord (and his newspaper) publish his report of that conversation in pursuance of a duty, legal, social or moral, to persons who had a corresponding duty or interest to receive it? That, in my respectful opinion, correct summary of the relevant authorities is taken from the Report of the Committee on Defamation, para. 184 (a), repeated in *Duncan & Neill, Defamation*, para. 14.01.

I cannot extract from any of those authorities any relaxation of the requirements incorporated in that question. No privilege attaches yet to a statement on a matter of public interest believed by the publisher to be true in relation to which he has exercised reasonable care. That needed statutory enactment which the Committee on Defamation refused to recommend: see paragraphs 211-215. 'Fair information on a matter of public interest' is not enough without a duty to publish it and I do not understand Pearson J's ruling in *Webb* v *Times Publishing Co.* [1960] 2 QB 535 that a plea of a fair and accurate report of foreign judicial proceedings was not demurrable, was intended to convey that it was enough. Public interest and public benefit are necessary (*cf.* section 7(3) of the Defamation Act 1952), but not enough without more. There must be a duty to publish to the public at large and an interest in the public at large to receive the publication; and a section of the public is not enough.

The subject matter must be of public interest; its publication must be in the public interest. That nature of the matter published and its source and the position or status of the publisher distributing the information must be such as to create the duty to publish the information to the intended recipients, in this case the readers of the 'Daily Telegraph.' Where damaging acts have been ascertained to be true, or been made the subject of a report, there may be a duty to report them . . . provided the public interest is wide enough: *Chapman* v *Ellesmere* [1932] 2 KB 431. But where damaging allegations or charges have been made and are still under investigation (*Purcell* v *Sowler*, 2 CPD 215), or have been authoritatively refuted (*Adam* v *Ward* [1917] AC 309), there can be no duty to report them to the public.

. . . The general topic of the waste of taxpayers' money was, Mr Eady concedes, a matter in which the public, including the readers of the 'Daily Telegraph's' first edition, had a legitimate interest and which the press were under a duty to publish; but they had no legitimate interest in Mr Lord's particular inferences and guesses, or even in Mr Smith's, and the defendants had certainly no duty to publish what Mr Eady unkindly called 'half-baked' rumours about the plaintiff at that stage of Mr Lord's investigations.

There may be extreme cases where the urgency of communicating a warning is so great, or the source of the information so reliable, that publication of suspicion or speculation is justified; for example, where there is danger to the public from a suspected terrorist or the distribution of contaminated food or drugs; but there is nothing of that sort here.

Note
This case severely limits the freedom of the press, for not only is common law privilege very narrowly defined, but also it was said that that statutory privilege under s. 7 of the Defamation Act 1952 would only apply to 'official' information issued to the public and not to information for which the government does not accept responsibility. Now that the government often chooses whether to release information officially or unofficially this creates serious risks for the press, as does the absence of privilege for information believed to be in the public interest. An example of common law privilege of the kind referred to in *Blackshaw* is *Camporese* v *Parton* (1983) 150 DLR (3d) 208, where the defendant published an article claiming that the plaintiff was importing and selling canning lids which were defective and which could cause food in tins to become poisonous. It was held that this was privileged because the defendant honestly believed the story to be true and it was a matter of vital concern to the public.

DEFAMATION BILL 1996

14.—(1) A fair and accurate report of proceedings in public before a court to which this section applies, if published contemporaneously with the proceedings, is absolutely privileged.

(2)   A report of proceedings which by an order of the court, or as a consequence of any statutory provision, is required to be postponed shall be treated as published contemporaneously if it is published as soon as practicable after publication is permitted.

(3)   This section applies to—
   (a)   any court in the United Kingdom;
   (b)   the European Court of Justice or any court attached to that court;
   (c)   the European Court of Human Rights, and
   (d)   any international criminal tribunal established by the Security Council of the United Nations or by an international agreement to which the United Kingdom is a party.

In paragraph (a) 'court' includes any tribunal or body exercising the judicial power of the state.

(4)   [omitted]

15.—(1)   The publication of any report or other statement mentioned in Schedule 1 to this Act is privileged unless the publication is shown to be made with malice, subject as follows.

(2)   In defamation proceedings in respect of the publication of a report or other statement mentioned in Part II of that Schedule, there is no defence under this section if the plaintiff shows that the defendant—
   (a)   was requested by him to publish in a suitable manner a reasonable letter or statement by way of explanation or contradiction, and
   (b)   refused or neglected to do so.

For this purpose 'in a suitable manner' means in the same manner as the publication complained of or in a manner that is adequate and reasonable in the circumstances.

(3)   This section does not apply to the publication to the public, or a section of the public, of matter which is not of public concern and the publication of which is not for the public benefit.

(4)   Nothing in this section shall be construed—
   (a)   as protecting the publication of matter the publication of which is prohibited by law, or
   (b)   as limiting or abridging any privilege subsisting apart from this section.

SCHEDULE 1

QUALIFIED PRIVILEGE

PART I
STATEMENTS HAVING QUALIFIED PRIVILEGE WITHOUT EXPLANATION OR CONTRADICTION

1.   A fair and accurate report of proceedings in public of a legislature anywhere in the world.

2.   A fair and accurate report of proceedings in public before a court anywhere in the world.

3.   A fair and accurate report of proceedings in public of a person appointed to hold a public inquiry by a government or legislature anywhere in the world.

4.   A fair and accurate report of proceedings in public anywhere in the world of an international organisation or an international conference.

5.   A fair and accurate copy of or extract from any register or other document required by law to be open to public inspection.

6.   A notice or advertisement published by or on the authority of a court, or of a judge or officer of a court, anywhere in the world.

7.   A fair and accurate copy of or extract from matter published by or on the authority of a government or legislature anywhere in the world.

8.   A fair and accurate copy of or extract from matter published anywhere in the world by an international organisation or an international conference.

PART II
STATEMENTS PRIVILEGED SUBJECT TO EXPLANATION OR CONTRADICTION

9.—(1)   A fair and accurate copy of or extract from a notice or other matter issued for the information of the public by or on behalf of—

(a)   a legislature in any member State or the European Parliament;

(b)   the government of any member State, or any authority performing governmental functions in any member State or part of a member State, or the European Commission;

(c)   an international organisation or international conference.

(2)   In this paragraph 'governmental functions' includes police functions.

10.   A fair and accurate copy of or extract from a document made available by a court in any member State or the European Court of Justice, or any court attached to that court, or by a judge or officer of any such court.

11.—(1)   A fair and accurate report of proceedings at any public meeting or sitting in the United Kingdom of—

(a)   a local authority or local authority committee;

(b)   a justice or justices of the peace acting otherwise than as a court exercising judicial authority;

(c)   a commission, tribunal, committee or person appointed for the purposes of any inquiry by any statutory provision, by Her Majesty or by a Minister of the Crown or a Northern Ireland Department;

(d)   a person appointed by a local authority to hold a local inquiry in pursuance of any statutory provision;

(e)   any other tribunal, board, committee or body constituted by or under, and exercising functions under, any statutory provision.

(2)   In sub-paragraph (1)(a)—

'local authority' means—

(a)   in relation to England and Wales, a principal council within the meaning of the Local Government Act 1972, any body falling within any paragraph of section 100J(1) of that Act or an authority or body to which the Public Bodies (Admission to Meetings) Act 1960 applies,

(b)   in relation to Scotland, a council constituted under section 2 of the Local Government etc. (Scotland) Act 1994 or an authority or body to which the Public Bodies (Admission to Meetings) Act 1960 applies,

(c)   in relation to Northern Ireland, any authority or body to which sections 23 to 27 of the Local Government Act (Northern Ireland) 1972 apply; and

'local authority committee' means any committee of a local authority or of local authorities, and includes—

(a)   any committee or sub-committee in relation to which sections 100A to 100D of the Local Government Act 1972 apply by virtue of section 100E of that Act (whether or not also by virtue of section 100J of that Act), and

(b)   any committee or sub-committee in relation to which sections 50A to 50D of the Local Government (Scotland) Act 1973 apply by virtue of section 50E of that Act.

(3)   A fair and accurate report of any corresponding proceedings in any of the Channel Islands or the Isle of Man or in another member State.

12.—(1)   A fair and accurate report of proceedings at any public meeting held in a member State.

(2)   In this paragraph a 'public meeting' means a meeting bona fide and lawfully held for a lawful purpose and for the furtherance or discussion of a matter of public concern, whether admission to the meeting is general or restricted.

13.—(1)   A fair and accurate report of proceedings at a general meeting of a UK public company.

(2)   A fair and accurate copy of or extract from any document circulated to members of a UK public company—

(a)   by or with the authority of the board of directors of the company,

(b)   by the auditors of the company, or

(c)   by any member of the company in pursuance of a right conferred by any statutory provision.

(3)   A fair and accurate copy of or extract from any document circulated to members of a UK public company which relates to the appointment, resignation, retirement or dismissal of directors of the company.

(4)   In this paragraph 'UK public company' means—

(a)   a public company within the meaning of section 1(3) of the Companies Act 1985 or Article 12(3) of the Companies (Northern Ireland) Order 1986, or

(b)   a body corporate incorporated by or registered under any other statutory provision, or by Royal Charter, or formed in pursuance of letters patent.

(5)   A fair and accurate report of proceedings at any corresponding meeting of, or copy of or extract from any corresponding document circulated to members of, a public company formed under the law of any of the Channel Islands or the Isle of Man or another member State.

14.   A fair and accurate report of any finding or decision of any of the following descriptions of association, formed in the United Kingdom or another member State, or of any committee or governing body of such an association—

(a)   an association formed for the purpose of promoting or encouraging the exercise of or interest in any art, science, religion or learning, and empowered by its constitution to exercise control over or adjudicate on matters of interest or concern to the association, or the actions or conduct of any person subject to such control or adjudication;

(b)   an association formed for the purpose of promoting or safeguarding the interests of any trade, business, industry or profession, or of the persons carrying on or engaged in any trade, business, industry or profession, and empowered by its constitution to exercise control over or adjudicate upon matters connected with that trade, business, industry or profession, or the actions or conduct of those persons;

(c)   an association formed for the purpose of promoting or safeguarding the interests of a game, sport or pastime to the playing or exercise of which members of the public are invited or admitted, and empowered by its constitution to exercise control over or adjudicate upon persons connected with or taking part in the game, sport or pastime;

(d)   an association formed for the purpose of promoting charitable objects or other objects beneficial to the community and empowered by its constitution to exercise control over or to adjudicate on matters of interest or concern to the association, or the actions or conduct of any person subject to such control or adjudication.

15.—(1)   A fair and accurate report of, or copy of or extract from, any adjudication, report, statement or notice issued by a body, officer or other person designated for the purposes of this paragraph—

(a)   for England and Wales or Northern Ireland, by order of the Lord Chancellor, and

(b)   for Scotland, by order of the Secretary of State.

(2)   An order under this paragraph shall be made by statutory instrument which shall be subject to annulment in pursuance of a resolution of either House of Parliament.

PART III
SUPPLEMENTARY PROVISIONS

16.—(1) In this Schedule—

'court' includes any tribunal or body exercising the judicial power of the State;

'international conference' means a conference attended by representatives of two or more governments;

'international organisation' means an organisation of which two or more governments are members, and includes any committee or other subordinate body of such an organisation; and

'legislature' includes a local legislature.

(2)   References in this Schedule to a member State include any European dependent territory of a member State.

(3)   In paragraphs 2 and 6 'court' includes—

(a)   the European Court of Justice or any court attached to that court and the Court of Auditors of the European Communities,

(b)   the European Court of Human Rights;

(c)   any international criminal tribunal established by the Security Council of the United Nations or by an international agreement to which the United Kingdom is a party, and

(d)   the International Court of Justice and any other judicial or arbitral tribunal deciding matters in dispute between States.

(4)   In paragraphs 1, 3 and 7 'legislature' includes the European Parliament.

Section 8:   damages

Damages for defamation are 'at large', and there has been considerable concern recently at the high level of awards in some cases. The record award so far is £1,500,000 in favour of Lord Aldington, awarded against Count Tolstoy and Mr Watts for allegations concerning the repatriation of Yugoslavs at the end of the war, but in view of its size this award was held to be contrary to art. 10 of the European Convention on Human Rights (see above).

Damages, with the exception of exemplary damages which are discussed below, are intended to be compensatory, but in the words of Windeyer J in *Uren v John Fairfax* (1967) 117 CLR 118:

a man defamed does not get damages *for* his damaged reputation. He gets damages *because* he was injured in his reputation, that is simply because he was publicly defamed. For this reason, compensation by damages operates in two ways — as a vindication of the plaintiff to the public and as a consolation to him for a wrong done. Compensation is here a solatium rather than a monetary recompense for a harm measurable in money.

In the Defamation Bill 1996 it was proposed that damages would be based on what the plaintiff's reputation would be if all the facts about him were known.

Accordingly, the defence would have had to show that because of certain facts the plaintiff would not deserve his present reputation (subject to exclusion regarding lapse of time and of relative unimportance). This would have had interesting results and would no doubt have provided considerable business for inquiry agents. However this clause was withdrawn in committee.

Damages can include compensation for injury to feelings, and 'aggravated' damages can be awarded for the subsequent conduct of the defendant, including a failure to make a sufficient apology; a repetition of the libel; conduct calculated to deter the plaintiff from proceeding; persistence in a plea of justification which is bound to fail; and persecution of the plaintiff by other means. However, awards in this area are not split up into their component parts, but rather the jury will name a global sum, and it is the overall level of these sums which has caused concern.

Exemplary damages are awarded to 'punish' the defendant where he knew that he was committing a tort (or was reckless) but went ahead anyway because he expected to profit from the tort. For an example see *Cassell v Broome* [1972] AC 1027 where the defendants had published a book called *The Destruction of Convoy PQ 17* which wrongly blamed Commander Broome for the disaster. He was awarded £25,000 exemplary damages. See also *John v MGN* below.

John v MGN Ltd
[1996] 2 All ER 35

In 1992 the *Sunday Mirror* published a story that 'rock superstar Elton John is hooked on a bizarre new diet which doctors have warned could kill him'. It stated that Elton John had been observed at a party in California chewing snacks and then disposing of them in his napkin. The story was completely false and at first instance the plaintiff was awarded compensatory damages of £75,000 and exemplary damages of £275,000. Held: allowing the appeal, that compensatory damages should be £25,000 and exemplary damages £50,000.

SIR THOMAS BINGHAM MR: . . .

Compensatory damages
The successful plaintiff in a defamation action is entitled to recover, as general compensatory damages, such sum as will compensate him for the wrong he has suffered. That sum must compensate him for the damage to his reputation; vindicate his good name; and take account of the distress, hurt and humiliation which the defamatory publication has caused. In assessing the appropriate damages for injury to reputation the most important factor is the gravity of the libel; the more closely it touches the plaintiff's personal integrity, professional reputation, honour, courage, loyalty and the core attributes of his personality, the more serious it is likely to be. The extent of publication is also very relevant: a libel published to millions has a greater potential to cause damage than a libel published to a handful of people. A successful plaintiff may properly look to an award of damages to vindicate his reputation: but the significance of this is much greater in a case where the defendant asserts the truth of the libel and refuses any retraction or apology than in a case where the defendant acknowledges the falsity of

what was published and publicly expresses regret that the libellous publication took place. It is well established that compensatory damages may and should compensate for additional injury caused to the plaintiff's feelings by the defendant's conduct of the action, as when he persists in an unfounded assertion that the publication was true, or refuses to apologise, or cross-examines the plaintiff in a wounding or insulting way. Although the plaintiff has been referred to as 'he', all this of course applies to women just as much as men.

There could never be any precise, arithmetical formula to govern the assessment of general damages in defamation, but if such cases were routinely tried by judges sitting alone there would no doubt emerge a more or less coherent framework of awards which would, while recognising the particular features of particular cases, ensure that broadly comparable cases led to broadly comparable awards. This is what has happened in the field of personal injuries since these ceased to be the subject of trial by jury and became, in practice, the exclusive preserve of judges. There may be even greater factual diversity in defamation than in personal injury cases, but this is something of which the framework would take account.

The survival of jury trial in defamation actions has inhibited a similar development in this field. Respect for the constitutional role of the jury in such actions, and judicial reluctance to intrude into the area of decision-making reserved to the jury, have traditionally led judges presiding over defamation trials with juries to confine their jury directions to a statement of general principles, eschewing any specific guidance on the appropriate level of general damages in the particular case. While some distinguished judges (e.g. Diplock LJ in *McCarey* v *Associated Newspapers Ltd (No. 2)* [1964] 3 All ER 947 at 960, [1965] 2 QB 86 at 109) have considered that juries should be informed in broad terms of the conventional level of awards for personal injuries, not by way of analogy but as a check on the reasonableness of an award which the jury are considering, this has not been an authoritative view (see *Cassell & Co Ltd* v *Broome* [1972] 1 All ER 801 at 824, [1972] AC 1027 at 1071). Even in the rare case when a personal injury claim was to be tried by a jury it was thought inappropriate that a jury should be informed of the conventional level of awards (*Ward* v *James* [1965] 1 All ER 563 at 575–576, [1966] 1 QB 273 at 302), a striking departure from the modern practice when judges are sitting alone.

Whatever the theoretical attractions of this approach, its practical disadvantages have become ever more manifest. A series of jury awards in sums wildly disproportionate to any damage conceivably suffered by the plaintiff has given rise to serious and justified criticism of the procedures leading to such awards. This has not been the fault of the juries. Judges, as they were bound to do, confined themselves to broad directions of general principle, coupled with injunctions to the jury to be reasonable. But they gave no guidance on what might be thought reasonable or unreasonable, and it is not altogether surprising that juries lacked an instinctive sense of where to pitch their awards. They were in the position of sheep loosed on an unfenced common, with no shepherd.

While the Court of Appeal reaffirmed the fundamental soundness of the traditional approach in *Sutcliffe* v *Pressdram Ltd* [1990] 1 All ER 269, [1991] 1 QB 153, the court did in that case recommend trial judges to draw the attention of juries to the purchasing power of the award they were minded to make, and of the income it would produce (see [1990] 1 All ER 269 at 283–284, 289, 293, [1991] 1 QB 153 at 178–179, 185–186, 190). This was thereafter done, and juries were reminded of the cost of buying a motor car, or a holiday, or a house. But judges were still constrained by authority from steering the jury towards any particular level of award.

Following the enactment of s. 8(2) of the Courts and Legal Services Act 1990 and the introduction of RSC Ord 59, r. 11(4) in its present form, the Court of Appeal was for the first time empowered, on allowing an appeal against a jury's award of damages, to substitute for the sum awarded by the jury such sum as might appear to the court to be proper. . . .

In *Rantzen v Mirror Group Newspapers (1986) Ltd* [1993] 4 All ER 975, [1994] QB 670 the newspaper appealed against a jury's award of £250,000, contending that the size of the award was wholly disproportionate to the damage done to the plaintiff's reputation. The court concluded that at that time it would not be right to allow reference to be made to awards by juries in previous cases. But it took the view that awards made by the Court of Appeal stood on a different footing: over a period of time awards made by the Court of Appeal would provide a corpus to which reference could be made in subsequent cases (see [1993] 4 All ER 975 at 995, [1994] QB 670 at 694) . . .

For the newspaper in the present case Mr Gray QC repeats the argument which he advanced, and which was rejected, in *Rantzen* on the permissibility of referring to levels of awards in personal injury cases. He recognises the difficulty of seeking to persuade the court now to accept an argument which it so recently rejected, but contends that a number of factors justify reconsideration of that ruling and a different result.

First, Mr Gray points out that the corpus of experience which the court in *Rantzen* envisaged as a source of guidance has in practice scarcely developed, with the result that juries still receive little assistance from that source.

Secondly, Mr Gray points to the continuance of what appear to be grossly excessive awards. He instances the award of £750,000 to Mr Graham Souness, settled (after the newspaper appealed) for £100,000; and the award of £1.5m to the plaintiffs in *Walker v Shehan* [1995] CA Transcript 1092, again settled on appeal.

Thirdly, he draws attention to the changing views of a majority in the High Court of Australia. In *Coyne v Citizen Finance Ltd* (1991) 172 CLR 211 a minority favoured permitting reference to personal injury awards in directing libel juries. In *Carson v John Fairfax & Sons Ltd* (1993) 178 CLR 44 the balance of opinion had swung. It was now a majority, led by Mason CJ, who favoured permitting such reference.

Fourthly, Mr Gray relies on art. 10 of the European Convention on Human Rights, coinciding (as this article has been authoritatively held to do: see *A-G v Guardian Newspapers Ltd (No. 2)* [1988] 3 All ER 545 at 580–582, 597, 615, 627, 652, 660, [1990] 1 AC 109 at 156–159, 178, 203, 218, 273, 283 and *Derbyshire C.C v Times Newspapers Ltd* [1993] 1 All ER 1011 at 1020, [1993] AC 534 at 550) with the provisions of the English common law. This was an argument also advanced in *Rantzen*, but since then the European Court of Human Rights has decided *Tolstoy Miloslavsky v UK* (1995) 20 EHRR 442. In that case an award was made of £1.5m compensatory damages, and the court held that the size of the award, in conjunction with the lack of adequate and effective safeguards at the relevant time (before *Rantzen*) against a disproportionately large award, amounted to a violation of the defendant's rights under art. 10 of the convention.

We are persuaded by Mr Gray's argument that this subject deserves reconsideration, despite the short period since the *Rantzen* ruling was given. Any legal process should yield a successful plaintiff appropriate compensation, that is, compensation which is neither too much nor too little. That is so whether the award is made by judge or jury. No other result can be accepted as just. But there is continuing evidence of libel awards in sums which appear so large as to bear no relation to the ordinary values of life. This is most obviously unjust to defendants. But it serves no public purpose to encourage plaintiffs to regard a successful libel action, risky though the process undoubtedly is, as a road to untaxed riches. Nor is it healthy if any legal process fails to command the respect of lawyer and layman alike, as is regrettably true of the assessment of damages by libel juries. We are persuaded by the arguments we have heard that the subject should be reconsidered. This is not a field in which we are bound by previous authority (*Sutcliffe v Pressdram Ltd* [1990] 1 All ER 269 at 283, [1991] 1 QB 153 at 178) but it is necessary for us to review the arguments which have found favour in the past.

In considering the criticisms of the present lack of guidance which is given to juries on the issue of compensatory damages we have examined four possible changes in the present practice: (a) reference to awards by other juries in comparable actions for defamation; (b) reference to awards approved by the Court of Appeal or substituted by the Court of Appeal in accordance with Ord 59, r. 11(4); (c) reference to the scale of damages awarded in actions for personal injuries; and (d) submissions by counsel as to the appropriate award, coupled with some guidance by the judge as to the appropriate bracket.

Other awards in actions for defamation

We wholly agree with the ruling in *Rantzen* that juries should not at present be reminded of previous libel awards by juries. Those awards will have been made in the absence of specific guidance by the judge and may themselves be very unreliable markers.

The position may change in the future if the additional guidance which we propose later in this judgment is given and proves to be successful. As was pointed out in the course of argument, however, comparison with other awards is very difficult because the circumstances of each libel are almost bound to be unique. Furthermore, the corpus of such awards will be likely to become unwieldy and time would be expended on the respective parties pointing to features which were either similar or dissimilar in the other cases.

Awards approved or substituted by the Court of Appeal.

We agree with the ruling in *Rantzen* that reference may be made to awards approved or made by the Court of Appeal. As and when a framework of awards is established this will provide a valuable pointer to the appropriate level of award in the particular case. But it is plain that such a framework will not be established quickly: it is now five years since s. 8(2) of the 1990 Act and Ord 59, r. 11(4) came into force, and there is no case other than *Gorman, Rantzen* and *Houston* in which the court has itself fixed the appropriate level of award.

It is true that awards in this category are subject to the same objection that time can be spent by the parties on pointing to similarities and differences. But, if used with discretion, awards which have been subjected to scrutiny in the Court of Appeal should be able to provide *some* guidance to a jury called upon to fix an award in a later case.

Reference to damages in actions for personal injuries

. . .

It has often, and rightly, been said that there can be no precise correlation between a personal injury and a sum of money. The same is true, perhaps even more true, of injury to reputation. There is force in the argument that to permit reference in libel cases to conventional levels of award in personal injury cases is simply to admit yet another incommensurable into the field of consideration. There is also weight in the argument, often heard, that conventional levels of award in personal injury cases are too low and therefore provide an uncertain guide. But these awards would not be relied on as any exact guide, and of course there can be no precise correlation between loss of a limb, or of sight, or quadriplegia, and damage to reputation. But if these personal injuries respectively command conventional awards of, at most, about £52,000, £90,000 and £125,000 for pain and suffering and loss of amenity (of course excluding claims based on loss of earnings, the cost of care and other specific financial claims), juries may properly be asked to consider whether the injury to his reputation of which the plaintiff complains should fairly justify any greater compensation. The conventional compensatory scales in personal injury cases must be taken to represent fair compensation in such cases unless and until those scales are amended by the courts or by Parliament. It is in our view offensive to public opinion, and rightly so, that a defamation plaintiff should recover damages for injury to reputation greater, perhaps by a significant factor, than if that same plaintiff had been rendered a helpless cripple or an insensate vegetable. The time has in our view come when judges, and counsel, should be free to draw the attention of juries to these comparisons.

Reference to an appropriate award and an appropriate bracket

It has been the invariable practice in the past that neither counsel nor the judge may make any suggestion to the jury as what would be an appropriate award. This practice was in line with the practice followed in actions for personal injuries when such actions were tried with a jury. In *Ward* v *James* [1965] 1 All ER 563 at 576, [1966] 1 QB 273 at 302 the Court of Appeal gave reasons as to why no figures should be mentioned. It was said:

If the judge can mention figures to the jury, then counsel must be able to mention figures to them. Once that happened, we get into the same trouble again. Each counsel would, in duty bound, pitch the figures as high or as low as he dared. Then the judge would give his views on the rival figures. The proceedings would be in danger of developing into an auction.

...

We have come to the conclusion, however, that the reasons which have been given for prohibiting any reference to figures are unconvincing. Indeed, far from developing into an auction (and we do not see how it could), the process of mentioning figures would, in our view, induce a mood of realism on both sides.

In personal injury actions it is now commonplace for the advocates on both sides to address the judge in some detail on the quantum of the appropriate award. Any apprehension that the judge might receive a coded message as to the amount of any payment into court has not to our knowledge been realised. The judge is not in any way bound by the bracket suggested, but he finds it helpful as a check on his own provisional assessment. We can for our part see no reason why the parties' respective counsel in a libel action should not indicate to the jury the level of award which they respectively contend to be appropriate, nor why the judge in directing the jury should not give a similar indication. The plaintiff will not wish the jury to think that his main object is to make money rather than clear his name. The defendant will not wish to add insult to injury by underrating the seriousness of the libel. So we think the figures suggested by responsible counsel are likely to reflect the upper and lower bounds of a realistic bracket. The jury must, of course, make up their own mind and must be directed to do so. They will not be bound by the submission of counsel or the indication of the judge. If the jury make an award outside the upper or lower bounds of any bracket indicated and such award is the subject of appeal, real weight must be given to the possibility that their judgment is to be preferred to that of the judge.

The modest but important changes of practice described above would not in our view undermine the enduring constitutional position of the libel jury. Historically, the significance of the libel jury has lain not in their role of assessing damages, but in their role of deciding whether the publication complained of is a libel or no. The changes which we favour will, in our opinion, buttress the constitutional role of the libel jury by rendering their proceedings more rational and so more acceptable to public opinion.

Exemplary damages

A summary of the existing English law on exemplary damages in actions for defamation, accepted by the Court of Appeal in *Riches* v *News Group Newspapers Ltd* [1985] 2 All ER 845 at 850, [1986] QB 256 at 269 as concise, correct and comprehensive, appears in *Duncan and Neill on Defamation* (2nd edn., 1983) para. 18.27. The passage remains a correct summary of the relevant law. So far as relevant to this case, and omitting footnotes and references, the passage reads:

(a) Exemplary damages can only be awarded if the plaintiff proves that the defendant when he made the publication knew that he was committing a tort or was reckless whether his action was tortious or not, and decided to publish because the prospects of material advantage outweighed the prospects of material loss. 'What is necessary is that the tortious act must be done with guilty knowledge for the motive that the chances of economic advantage outweigh the chances of economic, or perhaps physical, penalty'. (b) The mere fact that a libel is committed in the course of a business carried on for profit, for example the business of a newspaper publisher, is not by itself sufficient to justify an award of exemplary damages. (c) If the case is one where exemplary damages *can* be awarded the court or jury should consider whether the sum which it proposes to award by way of compensatory damages is sufficient not only for the purpose of compensating the plaintiff but also for the purpose of punishing the defendant. It is only if the sum proposed by way of compensatory damages (which may include an element of aggravated damages) is insufficient that the court or jury should add to it enough 'to bring it up to a sum sufficient as punishment'. (d) The sum awarded as damages should be a single sum which will include, where appropriate, any elements of aggravated or exemplary damages . . . (f) A jury should be warned of the danger of an excessive award. (g) The means of the parties, though irrelevant to the issue of compensatory damages, can be taken into account in awarding exemplary damages . . .

This summary of the law was not challenged in argument before us, and it was not seriously argued that we could rule (even if we wished) that exemplary damages are not recoverable in defamation if the conditions required by authority for making such an award are established to the proper satisfaction of a jury. We were, however, reminded by the newspaper that in English law the award of exemplary damages is regarded as exceptional and in some ways anomalous. Authority, it was said, does not encourage any broadening of the categories of case in which such awards may be made nor any relaxation of the conditions for making them. Since art. 10 of the European Convention on Human Rights requires any restriction on freedom of expression to be prescribed by law and necessary in a democratic society for the protection of reputation, it was argued that the conditions for making an exemplary award should be closely scrutinised and rigorously applied. Our attention was accordingly drawn to certain aspects of the conditions established by authority.

First, the state of mind of the defendant publisher. Little difficulty arises in the straightforward but relatively rare case in which it can be shown that the defendant actually knew that he was committing a tort when he published. The alternative state of mind — recklessness — is not so easy. . . .

Lord Kilbrandon referred to a publisher knowing or not caring whether his material is libellous and to a publisher knowing or having reason to believe that publication would subject him to compensatory damages (see [1972] 1 All ER 801 at 876, [1972] AC 1027 at 1133).

Where actual knowledge of unlawfulness is not in issue, a jury direction based on reference to 'reckless, not caring whether the publication be true or false' is sanctioned by long usage and is not incorrect. The crucial ingredient of this state of mind is, however, a lack of honest or genuine belief in the truth of what is published. That is what makes the publisher's conduct so reprehensible (or 'wicked') as to be deserving of punishment. Carelessness alone, however extreme, is not enough unless it properly justifies an inference that the publisher had no honest belief in the truth of what he published.

It seems to us therefore that the phrase 'not caring whether the publication be true or false', though an accurate formulation of the test of recklessness, is capable of leading to confusion because the words 'not caring' may be equated in the jury's minds with 'mere carelessness'. We therefore consider that where exemplary damages are claimed the jury should in future receive some additional guidance to make it clear that before such damages can be awarded the jury must be satisfied that the publisher had no genuine belief in the truth of what he published. The publisher must have suspected that the words were untrue and have deliberately refrained from taking obvious steps which, if taken, would have turned suspicion into certainty.

Secondly, the publisher must have acted in the hope or expectation of material gain. It is well established that a publisher need not be shown to have made any precise or arithmetical calculation. But his unlawful conduct must have been motivated by mercenary considerations: the belief that he would be better off financially if he violated the plaintiff's rights than if he did not. Mere publication of a newspaper for profit is not enough.

We do not accept, as was argued, that in seeking to establish that the conditions for awarding exemplary damages have been met the plaintiff must satisfy the criminal, rather than the civil, standard of proof. But a jury should in our judgment be told that as the charge is grave, so should the proof be clear. An inference of reprehensible conduct and cynical calculation of mercenary advantage should not be lightly drawn. In *Manson* [1965] 2 All ER 954 at 959, [1965] 1 WLR 1038 at 1044 Widgery J directed the jury that they could draw inferences from proved facts if those inferences were 'quite inescapable', and he repeatedly directed that they should not draw an inference adverse to the publisher unless they were sure that it was the only inference to be drawn (see [1965] 2 All ER 954 at 959, 960, [1965] 1 WLR 1038 at 1045).

It is plain on the authorities that it is only where the conditions for making an exemplary award are satisfied, and only when the sum awarded to the plaintiff as compensatory damages is not itself sufficient to punish the defendant, show that tort does not pay and deter others from acting similarly, that an award of exemplary damages should be added to the award of compensatory damages. Since the jury will not know, when making their decision, what costs order will be made, it would seem that no account can be taken of the costs burden which the unsuccessful defendant will have to bear, although this could in itself have a punitive and deterrent effect. It is clear that the means of the defendant are relevant to the assessment of damages. Also relevant are his degree of fault and the amount of any profit he may be shown actually to have made from his unlawful conduct.

The authorities give judges no help in directing juries on the quantum of exemplary damages. Since, however, such damages are analogous to a criminal penalty, and although paid to the plaintiff play no part in compensating him, principle requires that an award of exemplary damages should never exceed the minimum sum necessary to meet the public purpose underlying such damages, that of punishing the defendant, showing that tort does not pay and deterring others. The same result is achieved by the application of art. 10. Freedom of speech should not be restricted by awards of exemplary damages save to the extent shown to be strictly necessary for the protection of reputations.

The European Convention on Human Rights
The European Convention on Human Rights is not a free-standing source of law in the United Kingdom. But there is, as already pointed out, no conflict or discrepancy between art. 10 and the common law. We regard art. 10 as reinforcing and buttressing the conclusions we have reached and set out above. We reach those conclusions independently of the convention, however, and would reach them even if the convention did not exist.

Notes
1. In *Rantzen v Mirror Group Newspapers* [1993] 4 All ER 975, the defendants falsely stated that Esther Rantzen had knowingly protected a teacher who had sexually abused children. The jury awarded her £250,000 and this was reduced on appeal to £110,000. In *Hunt v Severs* [1994] AC 350, the plaintiff suffered from paraplegia below the seventh vertebra; spinal fusion; pulmonary embolus; paralysis of bowel; perforation of bowel and muscle spasm. She was awarded general damages of £90,000. If personal injury awards are to be referred to in defamation actions, could the award in *Rantzen* stand?
2. Defamation trials are usually held before juries: the Supreme Court Act 1981, s. 69 states that in respect of libel or slander 'the action shall be tried with a jury unless the court is of the opinion that the trial requires any prolonged examination of documents or accounts or any scientific or local investigation which cannot be conveniently be made with a jury'. For the meaning of this section, see *Beta Construction v Channel 4 TV*, [1990] 1 WLR 1042.

INDEX